Soviet Risk-Taking and Crisis Behavior

Studies of the Russian Institute **RI** *Columbia University*

The Russian Institute of Columbia University sponsors the
Studies of the Russian Institute in the belief that their publication
contributes to scholarly research and public understanding.
In this way the Institute, while not necessarily endorsing their
conclusions, is pleased to make available the results of some of
the research conducted under its auspices. A list of the
Studies of the Russian Institute appears at the back of the book.

Soviet Risk-Taking and Crisis Behavior

A theoretical and empirical analysis

HANNES ADOMEIT

London
GEORGE ALLEN & UNWIN
Boston   Sydney

George Allen & Unwin (Publishers) Ltd,
40 Museum Street, London WC1A 1LU, UK

George Allen & Unwin (Publishers) Ltd,
Park Lane, Hemel Hempstead, Herts HP2 4TE, UK

Allen & Unwin Inc.,
9 Winchester Terrace, Winchester, Mass. 01890, USA

George Allen & Unwin Australia Pty Ltd,
8 Napier Street, North Sydney, NSW 2060, Australia

First published in 1982

British Library Cataloguing in Publication Data

Adomeit, Hannes
    Soviet risk-taking and crisis behaviour.
1.   Soviet Union – Foreign relations – 1945-
I.   Title
327.47   DK274
ISBN 0-04-335043-7

Library of Congress Cataloging in Publication Data

Adomeit, Hannes.
    Soviet risk-taking and crisis behavior.
Bibliography: p.
Includes index.
1.   Soviet Union – Foreign Relations – 1917-
I.   Title.
DK266.A48   327.47   81-19117
ISBN 0-04-335043-7 (pbk.)   AACR2

Set in 10 on 11 point Times by Red Lion Setters, London
and printed in Great Britain
by Mackays of Chatham

Contents

DK
266
A 48
1982

Acknowledgements

Many sincere thanks are due to a number of colleagues for their help and criticism but I am grateful most of all to Marshall Shulman, Seweryn Bialer and Zbigniew Brzezinski for guiding me along the arduous path from the initial discussion of the project as a PhD thesis in 1972 to its completion as a book in 1982. Without their encouragement and suggestions for improvement in content, structure and style no publishable manuscript would ever have been produced. Others who read the manuscript or large parts thereof and told me where I was wrong or unclear, and who added ideas, were Herbert Dinerstein, Alexander Erlich, Peter Juviler and Donald Puchala. Staff members of the International Institute of Strategic Studies in London, especially its former director, François Duchêne, and Ian Smart, one of its former assistant directors, discussed parts of the project with me, and I am indebted to them and the IISS for publishing, in 1973, some of my first ideas on the subject as an Adelphi Paper. Malcolm Mackintosh and John Erickson were very kind in helping me to clarify many matters concerning Soviet military power and strategy, and the role of the military in Soviet foreign policy.

Thanks are due also to my colleagues at the Institute of Soviet and East European Studies and the editorial board of *Soviet Studies*, both at the University of Glasgow. It would be difficult to conceive of any aspect of Soviet politics about which I did not benefit from their advice; and I am grateful to them for frequently taking on some of my administrative and editorial duties so as to give me more time for writing.

Concerning the financial aspects of the book, I wish to express gratitude to the Friedrich-Ebert-Stiftung, Columbia University, and the Woodrow Wilson National Fellowship Foundation for providing the support needed for postgraduate and doctoral studies and hence for helping me to get the project well on its way.

My final thanks go to my fellow members and friends at the Scottish Wildlife Trust, the Royal Society for the Protection of Birds and the Scottish Ornithologists' Club, who constantly reminded me that mere ruffling of feathers for display is not enough to produce a good book but also that there is much more to life than Soviet hawks and doves.

Foreword

When I first began teaching, several centuries ago, my mentor said to me: 'You may not be ready to believe this, but you will find that your greatest pleasure will come when your best students stand on your shoulders and push past you.'

I was reminded of this conversation when I read the manuscript for this book. As a graduate student, Hannes Adomeit had been sent to me by a valued colleague and friend, Richard Löwenthal, with a note alerting me to Adomeit's potentialities. Thoughtfully and critically, Adomeit took whatever I had to give, and built upon it. Now it is my turn to learn from him.

Adomeit's book is an important contribution to the study of international politics, and of Soviet behavior in particular.

First of all, Adomeit illustrates strikingly how far we have come from Churchill's aphorism about Soviet behavior as a riddle, enigma, etc. He helps to bring intellectual order to a subject that is too often governed by subjectively determined stereotypes, by the pictures in our heads, and he does this by thorough and painstaking case studies of two important episodes in the Soviet effort to strengthen its influence in Central Europe. By his workmanlike reconstruction of the Berlin crises of 1948 and 1961, Adomeit has contributed substantially to our understanding of the steps by which the most critical territorial issue in post-war relations between the Soviet Union and the West was probed and – if not resolved – at least was transformed into a provisionally stabilized definition of the outer limits of Soviet power.

In so doing, Adomeit's study also examines the regularities to be found in Soviet behavior, and tests them against recent theoretical literature on risk-taking and decision-making in international politics. It is by no means the least of his accomplishments that he distinguishes forcefully and vividly between the game-theorist and the real-life decision-makers, both Soviet and Western. His equally competent familiarity with both Soviet and Western sources marks this work as an advance over previous scholarship which has generally been limited to one or the other side of this interacting relationship. It is also worth mentioning that Adomeit's sophisticated and sensible discussion of the functions of ideology in Soviet policy-making is a notable contribution to this often misunderstood subject.

Whether one agrees completely with Adomeit's conclusions or not – and I find myself with judgment reserved on several points – it will not be possible to discuss these complex and critical matters in the future without reference to Adomeit's rigorous examination of the detailed evidence he has marshalled.

By the clarity of his intelligence and the breadth of his scholarship, Adomeit has advanced our knowledge and understanding of a critical period in our history, and has refined our methodology for the study of Soviet foreign policy. This is therefore an achievement deserving of widespread recognition.

Marshall D. Shulman
January 1982

Introduction

For what purposes and under what conditions are the Soviet leaders prepared to take risks in international relations? This is the central question of this book. The topic is obviously not merely of historical interest. Whereas it may be correct that politically and economically the global distribution of power has become more ambiguous and diffuse, the basic pattern of bipolarity nevertheless has remained unaltered in the military-strategic and security spheres. If anything, it has even deepened, given the huge costs of modern strategic weapons and their delivery systems and the rapid advances in military technology. Unchanged are also the basic adversary relationship between the two superpowers, notwithstanding the necessary epithet of 'limited', the obvious mixture of elements of cooperation and confrontation, and the erratic shifts in the geographical center of conflict – Cuba, Berlin, the Middle East, Vietnam, Angola, the Horn of Africa, Afghanistan, or the Persian Gulf.

To this have to be added substantial improvements in the Soviet military potential which have taken place over the past fifteen years, both quantitatively and qualitatively, at four different levels. At a first level, that of strategic nuclear forces, the Soviet Union has achieved parity with the United States and, by the mid-1980s, is expected to have a 'first strike' capability against US land-based intercontinental ballistic missiles. Even without that possibility, the fact itself of loss of US strategic superiority is considered to have significantly changed the political context of superpower relations.

At a second level, that of medium and intermediate-range nuclear systems, the Soviet Union has carried out a variety of programs, of which the deployment of the SS-20 missiles and Backfire supersonic bombers are only the most widely noted. With the help of programs such as these the Soviet High Command has provided its nuclear forces aimed at Western Europe with greater accuracy, striking power, range and mobility. This, in the opinion of many West European and American observers, is of considerable military and political importance, as early recourse to nuclear weapons by NATO at the central front has long been regarded as essential to offset severe imbalances in favor of the Warsaw Pact in conventional power.

In fact at that level, the third in this enumeration, the asymmetries since the mid-1960s have become more acute. This is so because of the Soviet Union's incessant modernization efforts, addition of more firepower to its divisions and expansion of manpower in Central Europe by about 150,000 men since 1967. As a result the forces and armaments deployed by the Warsaw Pact against NATO at the central front, in terms of divisions and manpower, artillery, tanks and aircraft, are widely regarded as 'excessive' and 'well beyond defensive needs'. Concern has also been expressed about the possibility that owing to the dramatic increase in the number, quality and range of attack aircraft, the Soviet Union may for the first time in post-World War II history be capable of eliminating, even in a purely *conventional* strike, most of NATO's forward-based systems.

Taken in conjunction, the changes in the US-Soviet military-strategic, continental and conventional power balances undoubtedly add up to a reduction in the flexibility of wartime options for the United States and its European allies. They may well provide conditions contributing, on the one hand, to Western psychological vulnerabilities and, on the other, to increased Soviet confidence in international crises.

Whereas the military developments at the three levels mentioned are held to affect the respective degrees of *commitment* in crises, significant increases in Soviet capabilities at a fourth level, that of medium- and long-range air and naval power, can be said to widen the *geographical scope* of possible crises and confrontations. Not only did the Soviet Union demonstrate its ability to intervene in its own sphere of influence (for example, in Hungary in 1956 and Czechoslovakia in 1968) and in areas contiguous to the USSR (for example, in Afghanistan in 1979) but it did so also in areas remote from Soviet territory: first, with its supply operations and the alert status of its seven airborne divisions during the October 1973 war in the Middle East; then in 1975–6 in supporting the Cuban intervention in Angola; and, finally, on a more massive scale, by supporting the Cuban-Soviet military intervention in 1977–8 in Ethiopia.

This picture of evolving military capabilities tendentially deepening Soviet commitments and broadening the geographical scope of conflict can be supplemented by Soviet declarations of intent. Such declarations range from Admiral Gorshkov's assertions, from 1967 onwards, of the need for the USSR – and especially its Navy – to 'protect far-flung state interests' and Brezhnev's claim at the Twenty-Fifth CPSU Congress in 1976 that the Soviet Union now has to take into account the state of affairs in 'virtually every corner of the globe', to repeated clarifications by the Soviet leaders in the 1970s that Soviet aid – including military aid – to 'national liberation movements' is consistent with détente and in conformity with 'peaceful coexistence'.

If the potential new sources of conflict can therefore be interpreted as having multiplied this does not mean that the old ones have disappeared. Fundamentally the dilemma over Berlin has remained unsolved. Despite the Quadripartite Agreement of 3 September 1971 the city's situation is still abnormal by any standard of international comparison. West Berlin still exists as a militarily indefensible enclave in (within?, on?) the territory of the GDR, still giving rise to international complications in various combinations between and among the Western allies, West Germany, the Soviet Union, the GDR and the other countries of the Warsaw Pact. With some variation the issues are still the same as before, including the quadripartite status, the Federal German presence in West Berlin, misuse or abuse of access ('rights'?) and the controversial extent of social, economic and political links with the outside world.

In more detail, the unresolved nature of the Berlin problem surfaces in plans for the establishment of EEC institutions and the holding of elections for the European Parliament in West Berlin; it is evident in the Soviet cancellation of the agreement in principle to supply electricity to West Berlin via GDR territory from a nuclear power plant to be built near Kaliningrad (Königsberg) by West Germany; it makes itself felt in the fact that several agreements in various fields, ready for signature by the USSR and West

Germany for a number of years, have not been finalized; and it is reflected in several joint statements issued by the three Western allies in the past few years protesting against restrictions on freedom of movement in the city and East German challenges of the four-power agreement. Who is to say with certainty whether these instances are merely distant rumblings of a bygone era or already the harbingers of renewed East–West confrontation over Berlin?

In the final analysis risk acceptance and rejection – in Berlin and elsewhere – depend not only on objective conditions but to a large extent on perceptions of the adversary's risk-taking propensities, his priorities and commitments and on mutual expectations and beliefs about probable responses and counteractions. In this way generally accepted results of scholarship about crisis behavior of the superpowers influence the policy-making process not only in Western countries but also in the Soviet Union. In short, it matters a great deal what 'we' think about 'them'.

When thinking about such a phenomenon as Soviet risk-taking, two major approaches can be used: process analysis, and analysis of possible determinants or factors of behavior. Concerning the first approach, the questions which can be asked – and will be asked throughout this book – are connected with recurrent patterns of action, and some of them can be stated as follows.

(1) To what degree has the Soviet Union relied on persuasion, dissuasion, deterrence, coercion, threats and ultimatums, either of a verbal or non-verbal variety, to achieve stated objectives in crises?

(2) What inferences can be drawn from Soviet verbal communications and actual Soviet behavior for the Soviet leaders' awareness of risks and their confidence to control the force of events?

(3) Are there specific risk thresholds beyond which the USSR simply refuses to continue in a competition in risk-taking?

(4) Does Soviet crisis behavior warrant the assumption that the USSR tacitly observes commonly accepted rules and conventions of crisis management?

As regards the second approach, that of identifying possible determinants or factors of Soviet risk-taking, some of the questions of importance examined in this study include the following.

(1) Has Soviet ideology been eroded to such an extent that it has ceased to be a factor of any consequence? Or have objective requirements of crisis behavior consistently relegated ideological considerations to a place of lesser importance?

(2) To what extent have Soviet leaders been guided by security interests in their decisions to accept or reject risks? And how are these interests to be defined in concrete international conditions?

(3) How does the balance of interests compare in its influence on Soviet behavior with the balance of power? Are there clear-cut correlations between various states of the military-strategic balance (inferiority, parity, superiority) and Soviet risk-taking propensities?

(4) To what extent does the personality of the dominant leader, power

struggle in the leadership and institutional conflict matter for Soviet behavior? Is it possible to apply Western models of decision-making?

Answers to these questions, or to some of them, are widely scattered in the Western literature. More important, these answers usually do not represent the end result of analysis of one or more case studies of Soviet crisis behavior but they are generalizations *per se*. In this field there is a curious lack of concern for the principle of cumulativeness in the social sciences – the need to arrive at conclusions on the basis of a series of in-depth studies and comparisons.

For understandable reasons authors of new books would be expected to give a peppy sales talk of this kind and their assertions as to the burning need for filling a major gap in the field are somewhat suspect. It may be permitted, therefore, to quote at length a perhaps more unbiased critic who makes the very same point, and who makes it as eloquent and strong as this writer would have wished to make it.

> In contrast to the rich accumulation of US foreign policy case studies, the Soviet foreign policy case study literature is small, fragmented, and generally underdeveloped. This applies not only to theory-oriented works that employ case studies as vehicles for generating or testing hypotheses about crisis or foreign policy decisionmaking, but also to traditional historical-narrative case studies designed primarily to advance knowledge about a particular international crisis or foreign policy decision.
>
> As the primary external actor in most major US crisis decision-making situations since World War II, the Soviet Union has figured prominently in most US foreign policy decisionmaking case studies. However, Soviet behavior has been treated in such studies not as an object of inquiry *per se*, but as an input to US decisionmaking, part of the external setting in which US decisionmakers have operated. The object of empirical research has been American decision-makers' perceptions of Soviet behavior, not that behavior itself. Rarely have any new insights about Soviet foreign policy behavior or the Soviet decisionmaking process emerged from such work; few students of American foreign policy have either been equipped or found it necessary for their purposes to engage in original research on Soviet behavior.
>
> The small case study component of the academic literature on Soviet foreign policy is disproportionate both to the size of the general literature and to the intrinsic importance of Soviet crisis behavior for the broad field of international relations.[1]

To confirm this point with regard to the two crises at issue, it proved impossible to find one single book, or even one single article, concerned specifically with Soviet policy in the Berlin crisis of 1948. As regards Soviet crisis behavior in 1961, matters were the same – until they were made worse; midstream in the research for this study there appeared a voluminous book which, in this writer's view, amounts to a very serious distortion of basic features of Soviet crisis behavior and set back the effort to generalize about such behavior.[2] It is hoped that the present endeavor will prove to be a more useful step in the right direction.

In order to approach the problem in a more satisfactory manner the following procedure has been adopted. The first part of the book sets out to define the concept of risk and to examine its analytical relevance for foreign policy, its measurement and its relation to the dynamics of crisis. In the process two major analogies will be used. Their presentation proceeds from the simple to the complex, and they will be employed in the formulation of a set of factors shaping risk-taking and crisis behavior. A transition between theory and practice will be provided by a discussion of generalizations about *Soviet* risk-taking and crisis behavior as found in the Western literature.

The second part of the book consists of in-depth analysis of Soviet behavior in the Berlin crises of 1948 and 1961. An identical organizational structure is applied to both case studies. Each first chapter features various interpretations of Soviet behavior in the crisis and attempts to identify the major research problems posed. The second chapter in each case summarizes the main events prior to and during the crisis and endeavors to identify 'objective' risks and 'subjective' perceptions. The third chapter deals with possible factors of Soviet risk-taking in the following sequence: (1) ideology; (2) security and state interests, including economic and political interests, as defined by specific international, intra-bloc and domestic requirements; (3) military power, at the conventional and the military-strategic level; and (4) domestic influences on three levels – individual, group and systemic. The fourth chapter takes into account that policy is not static and shaped only by immovable factors but that it is influenced considerably by the actual course of events. This chapter, therefore, looks at the processes unleashed by the crisis and examines whether and, if so, how the USSR responded to them. Finally, the fifth chapter in each case study attempts to identify the lessons drawn by the various actors, the consequences produced by the crisis and the likely degree of success or failure as perceived by the Soviet leaders.

What remains for the third and last part of the book is to compare Soviet policy in the two crises in one specific area (East Central Europe) and of two different leaderships (Stalin and Khrushchev) with each other, and to relate it to Soviet behavior in other geographical areas and another (Brezhnev's) leadership. This procedure should reveal whether general patterns of Soviet crisis behavior do exist and, if so, why.

Notes: Introduction

1 Arnold L. Horelic, A. Ross Johnson and John D. Steinbruner, *The Study of Soviet Foreign Policy: A Review of Decision-Theory-Related Approaches*, R-13334 (Santa Monica, Calif.: Rand Corporation, December 1973), p. 41. A footnote at the end of the second paragraph states 'A partial exception is Allison (1971), treated below', the reference being to Graham T. Allison, *Essence of Decision: Explaining the Cuban Missile Crisis* (Boston, Mass.: Little, Brown, 1971).
2 The book in question is by Robert M. Slusser, *The Berlin Crisis of 1961: Soviet-American Relations and the Struggle for Power in the Kremlin, June–November 1961* (Baltimore, Md, and London: Johns Hopkins University Press, 1973).

PART ONE
Theory

1
Risk and Risk-Taking

What does it mean when the political theorist Raymond Aron writes that the 'theory of international relations starts from the plurality of autonomous centers of decision, hence from the risk of war';[1] when General Lucius D. Clay thought during the Berlin crisis of 1948 that the risks of war were 'about one in four';[2] when Colonel Penkovsky stated that Soviet military leaders were concerned about the 'big risk' Khrushchev took in August 1961 in building the Berlin Wall;[3] or when Kennedy is reported as saying that the risks of nuclear war during the Cuban missile crisis were 'between one out of three and even'?[4] Surely the concepts of probability used there have nothing to do with observed frequencies of outcomes, because nuclear war has not occurred at the time of this writing and, as Anatol Rapoport once wrote ironically, 'in all likelihood, no more than a very few can occur'.[5]

It may be useful, therefore, briefly to clarify the concept of risk in international relations and to do so by pondering the implications of the sad fate of a certain Karl Kretschmer who, as far as is known, until his death had been unconnected with the theoretical study of risk.

I OBJECTIVE AND SUBJECTIVE RISKS

On Sunday 1 August 1976, early in the morning, 22-year-old Karl Krestchmer drove on to the Reichsbrücke in Vienna. Seconds later he died as the bridge collapsed into the River Danube. It is unlikely that he would have been much concerned about imminent danger. Not only was this bridge, like any other major city bridge in Vienna, considered to be perfectly safe, but in the early morning hours of that day the bridge carried only four vehicles, whereas it would carry several hundreds during a normal weekday rush hour. If anything it was less of a risk to cross the bridge at that time than at almost any other.[6]

Risk in this example refers to a *probability* residing in events. On the basis of adequate information about the weight of the vehicle, the condition and the maximum weight load of the bridge, an independent observer could have established an approximate probability range for the collapse of the bridge. The laws of physics would have established the chances of death or survival somewhere on a continuum ranging from zero to one. (A probability of 0·1 means that the risk is marginal, a probability of 0·9 makes the action of the driver appear as very risky, and the 'probability' of 1 makes the occurrence of the event certain.) The riskiness of an action in these terms, then, is entirely unaffected by the information level and the perceptions of the actor. Regardless of whether the actor knows, believes, thinks, or feels that the action may involve risk (the probability of collapse), his enterprise is *objectively* risky.

Similarly, a gambler usually knows that a 1 on die has the same chance to come up as any of the other five faces, that is, the statistical probability of the 1 to come up is 0·166. 'Probability' in this case refers to an objectified statement about an observed frequency of outcomes. In the bridge example, too, measurements and experimental tests could have established the range of probability in which it would have been safe or unsafe to cross the bridge.[7] Although the concept of probability in this case does not fulfill the requirements for a mathematical definition, procedures and results of the measurement are nevertheless verifiable and objective.[8]

But there is also a *subjective* dimension to risk implying a different concept of probability. If the driver has no or only insufficient information about the objective situation in which his action must take place, he may still (presumably without expressing it in numerical terms) assign a certain level of risk to his action. The same would be true for a prospective resident of, say, New York, who makes his decision of whether or not to live in the city dependent on his likely chances of survival. The probability concept in such cases is obviously different from the one discussed above. It conforms to the statistical notion of 'degree of belief', and it applies wherever the factors responsible for outcomes are too complex by their very nature to be measured accurately and expressed in statistical relationships, or when reference is made 'to events which by their nature can occur only once'.[9]

It is precisely this concept of probability which is relevant in international relations. There are always objective risks which need to be recognized and in the process of which the political scientist can be of some help. But under conditions of complex relationships and limited information, decision-making is of necessity a subjective process. Objective risks may be present but a corresponding appreciation – risk awareness – may be lacking. It is the subjective dimension of risk-taking, and the numerous influences and differing degrees of belief affecting a decision, which shall now be analyzed in a more systematic fashion. This shift in attention involves the possible motivations, rationalizations and reasons determining political action. Although mixed motives may be present, for analytical purposes two basic types, or categories, of behavior can be discerned: irrational and calculated risk-taking.

II   IRRATIONAL RISK-TAKING

Irrational behavior here is taken to be activity determined or distorted by psychic factors. If it is *determined* exclusively by psychic influences or pressures, reason as an organ for control, direction, or guidance does not intervene at all; if human behavior is only influenced or *distorted* by irrational influences, reasoning may be present but the resulting action will show the impact of stimuli unconnected with the objective requirements of a given situation.

Irrational behavior does not presuppose the operation of influences on the actor 'of which he is unaware and which he would not consider a legitimate influence upon his decision if he were aware of it'.[10] The schizophrenic personality may painfully realize the logical requirements of a given context, yet he may feel compelled to act contrary to them; the neurotic personality may feel that a situation requires self-control, yet he may be unable to exert it. Irrational behavior does not preclude a broad range of risk awareness. A truck driver who approaches a bridge may realize that it is unsafe. Yet he may be psychologically compelled to cross it; this would be a clear case of psychopathological behavior of which a schizophrenic is capable. He may have the delusion of fighting a quixotic game against nature, he could want to invite the judgment of fate, or prove some point which he artificially constructed in his mind. There is hardly any limit to the rationalizations of which the pathological mind is capable.

Admittedly, pathological behavior of this nature in real life may not be very widespread. This is different with neurotic behavior. A neurotic person who is unable to challenge authority and circumvent orders may reluctantly and hesitatingly follow the orders of the company or the army superiors because he is afraid to tell them that the bridge is (or might be) unsafe. He may fear that his 'cowardice' may be derided. This, it appears, is a more typical example of fatal actions based on internal psychological pressures against better judgment.

Lastly, a generally rational person may suffer from a temporary distortion or reduction of his conscious qualities. Factors of this nature may include the influence of drugs or alcohol. Temporary emotional states such as panic may intervene. Even a generally very cautious or 'safe' driver can be absentminded, react emotionally, be preoccupied with personal problems, or simply be tired. All these irrational influences may be at work at a crucial, possibly fatal, moment.

It would be very reassuring if no link could be established between irrational behavior and decision-making in international politics. Such links, however, have been established. They are expressed in very general terms by Almond, Pye and Shils, who consider radicalism and communism as manifestations of psychologically deviant, abnormal behavior. As there are a good many 'radical' regimes in the world, ranging from Gaddafi to Khomeini, and as there is no shortage of 'communist' or 'socialist' countries, the scope for irrational risk-taking should be quite broad – provided, of course, the theories are valid.

On a less general level the 'diabolic' and 'insane' nature of Hitler, Stalin's 'paranoia' and Khrushchev's 'impulsiveness' have been used as explanations of risk-taking. Even the use of drugs has been held responsible for decisions which might not have been taken in a more sober frame of mind. Anthony Eden, for instance, is said to have been under the influence of drugs during the Suez crisis, and some American observers have drawn a connection between drugs and Kennedy's 'somber' mood after the summit meeting with Khrushchev in June 1961.

Psychology establishes other links between irrational behavior and decision-making in international relations. Risk-taking is present in what the psychologist Harry Stack Sullivan calls 'selective inattention'. Selective inattention is a 'psychological mechanism that', according to Ralph K. White, another psychologist, seems 'to be present whenever nations stumble toward war'.[11]

Some person might call it resistance or repression, though Freudians give a more restrictive meaning to each of these terms. Others might call it ignoring, forgetting, inhibition of curiosity, perceptual defense, or just plain not paying attention. Whatever the name we give it, it is an unrealistic [that is, irrational] way of dealing with inconvenient or embarrassing facts.[12]

Another social scientist, Leon Festinger, speaks of avoidance of 'cognitive dissonance' whereby decision-makers tend to retain thoughts that are in harmony with an activity that is well launched.[13] Hence, although rational or calculated risk-taking may be the 'normal' type of risk-taking, it is necessary to bear in mind that the operation of irrational factors in the making of decisions can by no means be excluded.

III CALCULATED RISK-TAKING

Calculated risk-taking is defined here as a conscious process. It is behavior which weighs means for the achievement of ends. In order to meet criteria of rational behavior it is not necessary to have a clearly developed set of priorities or hierarchy of values. Only that personal, group, national or other values must be part of the decision-making process. Rational behavior, including calculated risk-taking, is also not to be confused with 'unemotional' behavior. Indeed, it is not evident why reasoning would have to be 'cold' and cannot, for example, be passionate and deeply committed. What is necessary, however, for rational behavior to be present is the capacity to divorce emotion from the logical requirements of a problem.

To return to the example of a truck driver about to cross a bridge. Assuming that he is aware of 'some' risk and that he knows the penalties for not crossing (delay, violation of the company's instructions, becoming the laughing stock of his colleagues, getting fired from his job, and so on) and the rewards for safely crossing (being on time, faithfully carrying out the instructions of the company, being respected by his colleagues, getting a salary raise, and so on), what would be the influences emanating from the structure of the situation which will affect his decision?

First, it is evident that the actor's decision will depend on the perceived risk itself. If the probability of collapse of the bridge is too high (approaches 1) the driver will tend to refuse to cross. If the risk is low (approaches 0) the driver will tend to go ahead. Secondly – and on this point economic theory has paved the way considerably for analysis – it will depend on the relative payoffs connected with the different outcomes. Prior to James Bernouilli's St Petersburg Paradox,[14] it was generally agreed that the *absolute* payoff, that is, the maximum expected gain, decided the choice for one strategy over the other. Today, however, it is widely and more accurately postulated that it is not the expected absolute payoff but the *utility function* of the actor which determines the choice among alternatives. Put differently, the actor decides for himself what the different utilities connected with individual outcomes are to him.

In the present example, assuming that the driver is a member of the armed forces, and that a refusal to cross the bridge would amount to a violation of an official order and could entail court martialing and jail, it is difficult to say what his decision will be unless one knows the personality of the actor. The penalty of jail will appear different to different actors. Similar problems are posed if there are monetary rewards for crossing the bridge. An actor who values safety over money will not easily be enticed to cross an unsafe bridge even if the reward is substantially increased. An important point to remember in all this is that what appears foolish, nonrational or irrational to an outside observer may be entirely rational behavior from the point of view of the values and priorities of the actor.

There is another factor which may shape calculated risk-taking. An actor may realize that it is necessary, or even absolutely necessary, to cross the bridge, no matter how high the risks. This would be the case if he were standing with his truck in the middle of a burning ammunition dump with the bridge as the only way out. [15] A calculation of a probability of staying and dying as 0·9 and a risk of 0·5 for crossing the bridge also leaves no reasonable choice other than crossing (provided there are no other positive payoffs attached to staying). Should the probability of death by staying decrease further, the decision of what to do will again depend on the mixture of risks, penalties and rewards.

On the basis of the above considerations, calculated risk-taking in international relations can be taken to represent a conscious choice by national actors, or their component parts (individuals, groups, institutions, and so on), among several alternatives and that this choice depends, first of all, on the perceived risk of disaster. The bridge analogy also suggests that rational decision-making takes into account objectives and values – the 'utility function' – of the actor. Nations, like individuals, differ from each other; they have different goals, interests, traditions, cultures, geopolitical conditions, different levels of industrialization and unequal amounts of power. A combination of these factors leads to different foreign policy commitments and, consequently, to different answers to the question: 'for what purposes is it worth taking risks?'

During the decision-making process in the Cuban missile crisis some members of the Executive Committee at first thought that it was 'unnecessary' for the United States to run the risks connected with an air strike against the missile sites or a blockade of Cuba. Western arguments and Dubček's convictions in the Czechoslovak crisis of 1968 held that the security interests of the USSR were not really threatened and that it would be nonsensical for the Soviet Union to accept the risks of intervention. And at the time of the 1961 Berlin crisis most of the Western political leaders thought that it was 'not worth it' to take higher risks to challenge the construction of the Wall. But if these actors decided on the basis of calculations, taking into consideration their own values or interests (utility functions), the taking of risks in these instances, as in the bridge analogy, cannot be called irrational, nonrational or the like.

Nations, like the driver in the bridge analogy, may be faced with choices between two evils where failure to accept risks of one kind may entail risks of another. 'We have accepted the risk of war', stated an Indian government official shortly before the outbreak of hostilities with Pakistan at the end of 1971, 'because we believe the risks to India of letting things go on as they have been are far greater than the risks of war'. [16]

IV   RISK-TAKING AS AN OUTCOME

The taking of risks has so far been portrayed merely as the irrational or rational taking of decisions but it is possible to see it also as the outcome of processes over which the actor has no or only limited control. This is the case, for instance, when the driver of the vehicle acts in discharge of specific functions for a company or the armed forces. His action then forms part of an environment which transcends the simple situation of crossing or not crossing. The organization, by means of instructions, routines and operating procedures, is channeling his behavior in rather narrowly circumscribed directions. Risk-taking as an outcome now occurs when the company or armed forces instruct the driver to cross the bridge, having provided him with the false information that the bridge is safe. It manifests itself also if the organization has accurate information in its file to the effect that the bridge is unsafe but by some bureaucratic mistake fails to convey this vital information to the driver. Finally, it applies when the driver approaches the bridge and decides to stop, but his brakes fail. Quite clearly his *decision* was to stop but the *outcome* did not correspond to his intentions.

Although all this is simple enough the lessons to be derived from it are not always properly recognized.[17] First, the outcome of a decision is fundamentally different from the decision itself. Secondly, risks are taken on the basis of information and this information may be wrong, misleading, inaccurate, scanty, biased or simply lacking – and woe to the decision-maker who fails to take this into account. Thirdly, implementation of a decision may be inadequate, late, excessive, contrary to expectation, or simply lacking – and failure to take this into account, too, may have disastrous consequences. Information and implementation therefore are but part and parcel of the structure in which risk-taking proceeds; they are not decisions in their own right.

The discussion in the bridge analogy of risk-taking as an outcome of processes which are not, or not entirely, under the control of the decision-maker also has illustrative value for international relations theory. Domestic and alliance systems can be regarded as the equivalents of the company or army which set the framework for risky actions. Inaccurate intelligence and information processes, breakdown of communications, inadequate evaluation and the following of established routines and false precedents, in international relations, too, may influence or determine risk-taking. All of this will be referred to later at greater length. The reason why brevity is advisable at this stage is because the heuristic value of the analogy is still quite limited. Its main deficiency is the absence of *shared risk*. There is no process of interaction. The bridge does not perceive, act, communicate or respond to challenges. It has no values. It is indifferent to initiatives of intimidation and to threats and it is impervious to the likelihood of collapse. But international politics includes all these elements; it is to a great degree a process of interaction of governmental and nongovernmental units, and not only the sum total of foreign policy actions of the individual national components. In order to illuminate processes under conditions of risk in international politics it is necessary to construct a more complex analogy or model of risk-taking.

Notes: Part One, Chapter 1

1 Raymond Aron, *Peace and War: A Theory of International Relations* (New York: Knopf, 1966), p. 16.
2 Lucius D. Clay, *Decision in Germany* (Garden City, NY: Doubleday, 1950), p. 367.
3 Oleg Penkovsky, *The Penkovsky Papers*, Trans. P. Deriabin with an introduction and commentary by Frank Gibney and a foreword by Edward Crankshaw (London: Collins, 1965), pp. 131–2, 136–8, 142 and 161.
4 Theodore Sorensen, *Kennedy* (New York: Harper & Row, 1965), p. 705.
5 Anatol Rapoport, *Strategy and Conscience* (New York: Harper & Row, 1964), p. 25. The following brief discussion of statistical concepts of probability draws on Rapoport's more detailed study.
6 This account is based on the report of the incident in the *International Herald Tribune*, 3 August 1976.
7 Thus in the case of the Reichsbrücke experts preliminarily established rust, metal fatigue and a defective pier as the probable causes for the collapse. After further measurements it would ultimately have been possible to assign an approximate probability range (riskiness) to the driver's action in crossing the bridge on 1 August 1976.
8 Based on De Finetti, 'Recent suggestions for the reconciliation of theories of probability', in J. Neyman, *Proceedings of the Second Berkeley Symposium on Mathematical Statistics and Probability* (Berkeley, Calif.: University of California Press, 1951); Rapoport, *Strategy and Conscience*, p. 25.
9 ibid.
10 Sidney Verba, 'Assumptions of rationality and non-rationality in models of the international system', in James E. Rosenau (ed.), *International Politics and Foreign Policy* (New York: The Free Press, 1969), p. 218.
11 Ralph H. White, 'Selective inattention', *Psychology Today*, vol. 5, no. 5 (November 1971), p. 47.
12 ibid.
13 Leon Festinger, *Cognitive Dissonance* (San Francisco: W. H. Freeman, 1962).
14 Bernouilli, a mathematician, 'analyzed a game in which the player tosses a coin until it falls "tails" and collects doubling amounts with each successive "heads". Thus if the first toss is tails, he collects nothing; if the first tail is preceded by one "heads", he collects 1 unit; if the first tail is preceded by two consecutive heads, he collects $1 + 2 = 3$ units; for three successive heads he collects $1 + 2 + 4 = 7$ units; etc. In general, if the first tail is preceded by k heads, the tosser collects $2^k - 1$ units. The game is now known as the St Petersburg Game' (Rapoport, *Strategy and Conscience*, p. 13). Bernouilli's original discussion, 'Exposition of a new theory on the measurement of risk', was published in *Econometrica*, no. 22 (1954), pp. 23–6.
15 This example was used by Jan F. Triska, 'The Soviet Union: reckless or cautious?', in Jan F. Triska and David D. Finley, *Soviet Foreign Policy* (New York: Macmillan, 1968), p. 319.
16 'Why India won't risk peace', *Newsweek*, 6 December 1971, p. 38.
17 See discussion of Graham T. Allison's organizational process model, pp. 34–6, below.

2
A Chess Game Named Disaster

International relations analysts, who tend to view relations among states as a rational process, have often compared its structure with a game of chess. The employment of forces for specific long-term or short-range objectives, the difference between strategy and tactics, the relationship of strategy to means and goals, processes of interaction, strategy preferences for offensive and defensive plays and the comforting notion that it is always the better, more skillful player who wins demonstrate the heuristic value of a comparison of chess and international relations. This is so despite the apparent short-comings such as the conflict nature of the game, the clear definition of rules, the simple object of winning and the limitation of the number of outcomes (win, lose and draw).

For the demonstration of problems connected with risk another outcome must be added to the game which can appropriately be called 'disaster'. This outcome must be *equally* disadvantageous to *both* players; and the negative payoff connected with this outcome must be higher than just losing the game. According to the rules of this modified chess game named disaster, as developed by Thomas C. Schelling,[1] disaster occurs if one player has moved a knight (or his queen) across the center line and when the other player also moves his queen (or a knight) across the center line into the opponent's half of the board. The game is then terminated and a heavy fine is levied on both players.

A new dynamics enters into the game because of this modification. The player who moves his knight across the center line and protects it well with other pieces severely restricts the field of operation of the opponent's queen. But his move is risky because it represents the first of a binary set of moves that may lead to disaster. The same is true when a player moves his queen across the center line and both of the opponent's knights are confined to his side of the board. The essence of the game, therefore, is the acceptance of risk in exchange for restrictions in the opponent's freedom of maneuver.

But what is the likelihood of disaster occurring? It is, as Schelling argues, rather small. This is so because of the high costs attached to the outcome and because the players know that the completion of the binary set of moves will certainly and automatically lead to disaster.

So why not transfer the lessons of this game to international politics and construct a 'doomsday machine' which would launch all strategic nuclear missiles and bombers against the opponent as soon as specific, previously announced contingencies are met? This is inadmissible if it is agreed that responsible political leadership consists in retaining as much flexibility as possible to meet contingencies as they arise. On the strength of this logic it is unacceptable to maneuver oneself *or* the opponent into a position where the choice is all or nothing, humiliation or defeat. While defending their own vital interests, President Kennedy was to say in reference to the Cuban missile crisis, 'nuclear powers must avert those confrontations which bring an adversary to the choice of either a humiliating defeat or a nuclear war'.[2]

The unrealistic narrowing of choice (capitulation or defeat) is not the only limitation of the game analogy. In the game as constructed, 'there is always some moment, or some final step, in which one side or the other has the last clear chance to turn the course of events away from disaster'.[3] In the real world, however, the problems of political and technical control, implementation of contingency plans, ambiguities connected with perception and interpretation of events, and uncertainties about the possible reactions of the opponent do not allow the construction of such a clear borderline.

Finally, although disaster threatens both players once a knight or a queen has crossed the center line, the respondent to the risk-initiation move is confronted with a choice that is *not risky*. Risk implies uncertainty. There is no *probability* of disaster – in the present case disaster is *certain* once the crucial move is made by the respondent to the challenge. He cannot ask for any extenuating circumstances, nor is it admissible for the analyst to say that there was any miscalculation. A model of risk-taking more closely approaching reality is called for.

Disaster May Occur because It Is Probable, not Certain

A closer approximation of the model to reality must include risky choices for both players; that is to say, the outcomes must be probabilistic. Disaster shall not occur automatically when queen and knight of opposite color have crossed the center line.

> Instead, when that occurs, the referee rolls a die. If an ace [number 1] comes up the game is over and both players are scored with disaster, but if any other number appears the play goes on. If after the next move the queen and knight are still across the center line the dice are rolled again, and so on.[4]

The first set of problems associated with this modification are definitional and conceptual. Two clarifications are needed – explanation of the concepts of 'risk' and 'uncertainty'. When political scientists talk of risks they have something in mind which is puzzling to an economic theorist: a degree of belief about the likelihood of a catastrophe in the relations among states. Risks, in the mind of the political scientist, refer to conditions which are more or less likely to result in war. This is not at all what the economic theorist has in mind. For him, risk does not refer to situations involving probable bankruptcy of the firm; the term assumes only that each outcome of a given set of strategies is probabilistic, and that the probabilities are known to the decision-maker.

The political scientist must also pay attention to the specific meaning of the term 'uncertainty'. Schelling writes that we must 'add uncertainty to this artificial chess game',[5] and then introduces the die. However, according to the economic theorist he did not add uncertainty to the game at all because this condition refers to games 'against nature' where the probabilities of the states of nature are either unknown or (and this would amount to the same) where outcomes are entirely random.[6] However, in the chess game named disaster forecast information is exact, although probabilistic. It is therefore a game under conditions of risk, not uncertainty.

The next step in the procedure is to ask: '*What will determine the behavior of the players after the introduction of probabilistic elements?*' Six factors need to be considered. They are: (1) the known probability of disaster; (2) the state of the game; (3) the utility functions of the players; (4) the difference between defeat and disaster; (5) personality traits; and (6) perceptions. All factors operate simultaneously and at any given time in the game.

I THE RELEVANCE OF PROBABILITIES

The first and most basic observation to make is as follows. *The higher the risk of disaster, the lower the risk-taking propensity of the players; the lower the risk of disaster, the higher the tendency of the players to accept risks.* The same reasoning applies here as in the case of the vehicle driver who takes a calculated risk: the less safe he considers the bridge to be, the more reluctant he will be to cross the bridge.

In the present chess game, the probability of an ace turning up is $\frac{1}{6}$ or 0·166. This allows each player to calculate the *expected occurrence of disaster as being:*

$$\tfrac{1}{6} + \tfrac{5}{6} \times \tfrac{1}{6} \times 2 + (\tfrac{5}{6})^2 \times \tfrac{1}{6} \times 3 \ldots (\tfrac{5}{6})^k \times \tfrac{1}{6} \times (k+1) + \ldots$$

That is to say, disaster must be expected to occur at the sixth throw. The fact that this probability would generally be considered too high for the acceptance of the disaster position does by no means rule out risk-taking. Whether or not it occurs depends largely on the state of the game.

II RISKS AND THE STATE OF THE GAME

Concerning this factor influencing the risk-taking propensities of the players, two main propositions can be advanced. First, *the player with the stronger position on the chessboard will tend to avoid the taking of risks; the player with the weaker position will tend to accept them.* Secondly, *risk-taking by a player with the stronger position on the board can be explained as an attempt to create a* fait accompli.

The rationale of the first proposition is that the strong player really does not need to engage in risk-taking because the trends point to his victory. Both sides started out with equal amounts of 'power'. The construction of a strong position amounts to a change in the status quo which threatens the outcome 'defeat' to the weaker player. In turn, the weak side can now threaten with 'disaster'. What has happened is that an asymmetry of interests has been created. The weak side may no longer be so intensely interested in avoiding risks, because risk-taking gives him a chance to force the stronger player to give up his advantage. The status quo could be reestablished if the stronger player were forced to retreat with his queen (knight) to his side of the board.

This permits characterization of the game as a bargaining game, and the shared risk of disaster may now lead to what Schelling has called 'competition in risk taking'. To see the behavior of the weaker player on the board as blackmail would be to superimpose moral categories; but the fact is that the willingness to threaten the opponent and himself with disaster is both a game-rational and credible strategy of persuasion, flowing from the disparity in positions. It is reasonable for him to expect that the stronger opponent can be persuaded to accept temporary disadvantages rather than expose a probable victory to the risk of disaster.

These considerations about the state of the game suggest a serious challenge to accepted postulates of *deterrence theory*. What deters the taking of risks, according to classical formulations, are primarily the fears of punishment. Logically this leads to the proposition advanced in the literature of deterrence that the greater the punitive means available to an opponent, the lower the readiness of an actor to engage in risky actions; consequently a weaker power is said to have a built-in tendency to *avoid* challenging a stronger power. In contrast to that the above discussion implies the possibility that a weak player will exploit his own relative weakness to force concessions of the opponent. He may view the taking of risks as the only possible recourse for changing adverse trends on the board.

Examples of this in international relations come readily to mind. They can be said to include the whole theory and practice of guerrilla warfare, the Vietnam War, the Pueblo incident, the Prague Spring, Romanian opposition in the Warsaw Pact and Chinese intransigence towards the Soviet Union. In all of these cases, deterrence and intimidation failed, within certain limits, to deter risk-taking. In fact it is a deplorable observation to be made in international politics that there is often no other way out for a weak power than to engage in risk-taking if independence and survival are to be safeguarded in a hostile environment. This can be shown by the fate of Germany through the centuries, whose position in the middle of Europe made it a frequent target of foreign intervention when it was weak but which, perhaps as a consequence, tended to give an excessive interpretation to its security interests when it was strong. Similarly the foreign policies of Poland, because of its weakness *vis-à-vis* Austria-Hungary, Prussia and Russia in the nineteenth century and its continued precarious situation between Nazi Germany and Stalinist Russia in the 1930s, were made risky from the very outset. The situation of Lithuania, Latvia and Estonia between Germany and Russia demonstrates the same point.

Even Soviet-American relations in the post-World War II era can be interpreted as revealing the tendency for a relatively weak power to change adverse trends on the international chessboard. This would be true, most of all, of Khrushchev's attempted shortcut to military-strategic parity by emplacing missiles in Cuba but it was also, as will be shown, a major force behind the dynamics of the Berlin crisis of 1948 and 1961. Whether or not it would be correct to draw the obverse conclusion and take it for granted that the proverbial 'shift in the correlation of forces in favor of socialism' is holding out the promise of a status quo-oriented Soviet Union adverse to taking risks, is quite another matter.

Briefly to ponder this question for a moment, what actually – limiting oneself to the state of the game on the board – is it that may persuade a relatively stronger player to take risks? The answer lies in the difference between the expected number of moves until defeat of the opponent and the expected occurrence of disaster. If there remains only one move for the stronger player until the *fait accompli* of defeat, while disaster must be expected at the sixth throw of the dice, the costs for avoiding the disaster position may determine his strategy. This is illustrated in Figure 2.1.[7]

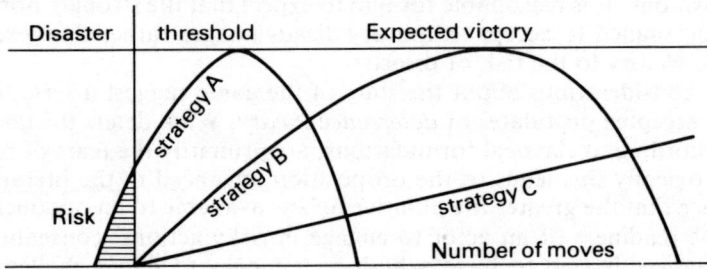

Figure 2.1   *Strategies of risk as a function of expected number of moves until defeat of the opponent.*

Strategy B is meant to show that the strong player can expect victory soon. He will therefore decide to avoid the risk strategy A. But if only strategies C and A are available he faces a dilemma. Now he may decide to accept the risk challenge of the opponent and shun the ambiguity of very remote, uncertain victory. He should now prefer A over C. In contrast, the unreasonable choice of strategy C over A amounts to overprotectionism; it could be compared to putting dangerously little air pressure into tires for fear of overpressure.[8]

The refusal to accept reasonable risks is not unknown in international relations. In 1935 and 1936 Nazi Germany was still so vulnerable that any serious competition in risk-taking would have ended in favor of France and Britain. The continued avoidance of reasonable risks on the part of the latter progressively increased the likely costs to the West as well as the scope of possible disaster. But barring idiosyncratic or subjectivist influences, and assuming conflict as the main structural principle of a relationship, there is great temptation to shun overprotectionism and decide upon the risky strategy – strategy C – before opportunities for victory vanish in thin air.

This has implications for the analysis of Soviet foreign policy. Considering on the one hand the enormous build-up of Soviet military power and the relative advantages it has achieved over the West in a number of military spheres and on the other hand – not unconnected with it – the decline in the economic growth rates (which are now assumed to have fallen below the growth rates of military expenditures), the undiminished strength of the Sino-Soviet rift, the continuing problem of legitimacy of Soviet rule in Eastern Europe, the declining attractiveness of Soviet ideology in Western Europe, the doubts about the merits of the Soviet model in the Third World, and the military programs in the West designed to compensate for Soviet advantages, there may well be some temptation for the Soviet leadership to exploit its strength before it is too late. Whether or not this temptation will be resisted depends on still other variables, not simply on the state of the game.

III   THE UTILITY OF UTILITY FUNCTIONS

The formulation of the main proposition must of necessity be very general: *the utility functions of the players will influence risk-taking propensities.* This statement needs further explanation. As alluded to briefly in the bridge analogy, the utility function in economic and game theory is the value system of a player which determines the utility he associates with each outcome. Allowance must therefore be made for the possibility that the negative or positive utility associated with a known outcome is different for different players. But do these differences in values (or utilities) make a difference if behavior is postulated to be rational?

Supposing a player backed financially by the General Motors Corporation faces a player on a Columbia University fellowship. Evidently the utility 10 dollars have for the General Motors player is not the same as for the student. Since the threat of disaster is nearly meaningless for the former, only the latter must be expected to be preoccupied with risk. For the student risk avoidance will most likely become a matter of principle.

The difference in utilities in that case is the result of disparities in monetary power. The significance of utility functions, however, does not disappear even if equal monetary power is assumed, for instance, when two graduate students play against each other. The players may now still assign different values to money. One player may regard the spending of money liberally, carelessly and generously; the other may be a chronic saver and miser. Again, risk-taking propensities will vary accordingly.

In international relations too, as touched upon earlier, different values, goals, interests and traditions of the political leadership influence the course of the game. If war and loss of human life appear less repulsive to one leadership in power than to another, or less incompatible with the priorities of the domestic system, deterrent or compellent threats by an adversary may be ineffective. Projections of one's own values, then, are highly dangerous. The image of the liberal decision-maker in Western democracies has often been that the employment of force is equally painful to any opponent because it would be painful to himself, his own political leadership and his own society. This may not be the case. The evidence of the Vietnam War with regard to the Vietcong and the North Vietnamese leadership shows perhaps most clearly that the willingness to expose human life to risk is different in different societies.

The utility functions of players matter not only in crises but also in war, which can be imagined as a succession of decisions involving progressing degrees of disaster, ranging from lost skirmishes, lost battles, defeat of armies, defeat on various fronts, defeat in war and occupation of the country to total annihilation. This can be illustrated by two examples, the decision by the German emperor and the military to resume unrestricted U-boat warfare on 9 January 1917, and the decision of the Count Lvov government in June 1917 to renew large-scale offensives at the western front under the command of General Brussilov. These decisions were taken in disregard for the vastly increased scope of disaster. They would not have been taken if other groups with different values and goals had been responsible. Chancellor Bethman Hollweg, the Social Democrats and the Left Liberals opposed the decision in Germany; and the Bolsheviks were against the war effort of the Russian provisional government as a whole. Different groups may have different values and therefore different risk-taking propensities.

IV THE DIFFERENCE BETWEEN DEFEAT AND DISASTER MAKES A DIFFERENCE

In the previous discussion of utility functions disaster was treated as absolute while the players attached different significance or values to this outcome (negative payoff). The same problem can be stated as a relative difference between defeat and disaster for each player. This leads to the following proposition. *The lower the difference between defeat and disaster, the higher the risk-taking propensity of the player; the higher the difference between defeat and disaster for the player, the lower his risk-taking propensity.*

To explain, if the fine levied on the two players is 10 dollars for disaster and 9·95 dollars for defeat, it must be expected that both players will engage in risk-taking because 'it doesn't make much difference' whether one is fined for defeat or disaster. It was this difference in the relative negative payoffs which exerted an analogous influence on the truck driver of the previous example: if the driver is faced with execution for not obeying orders, or if he faces the prospect of burning alive in the ammunition dump, 'it doesn't make much difference' to him whether or not he crosses the bridge.

In international relations this structure of risk-taking appears to be similar. Nations have frequently gone to war reasoning that costs attached to defeat without war would be equivalent to the costs of war itself. This is the rationale underlying preemptive strikes or preventive war. It is the adoption of a position that 'it is better now than later' to face up to a threat. In fact risk-taking becomes more advisable if the costs of defeat are certain and immediate, while disaster is only probable. Israel's surprise attack of 6 June 1967 is a case in point. The blockade of the Gulf of Aqaba and the introduction of Egyptian troops in the Sinai Peninsula constituted a serious defeat. From Israel's point of view it was clearly preferable to accept the risks of only potential disaster rather than the serious and immediate costs of the Egyptian moves. Similarly it took Hitler's occupation of Bohemia and Moravia in the spring of 1939 for the French and British leaders to wake up to the fact that one serious defeat after another had been inflicted on them, making the risk of disaster (war with Germany) appear less unacceptable than previously.

V THE PSYCHOLOGY OF RISK

Thus far the discussion of the various factors shaping risk-taking has been concerned exclusively with differences in conscious choices and value prefer-ences. But this is not enough. People making decisions are not merely guided by conscious choices but influenced also by psychological motivations. The next proposition to be examined, therefore, could be stated as follows. *A player with high risk-taking propensities will tend to take high risks; a player with low risk-taking propensities will tend to take low risks.* This does read very much like a truism. But unfortunately truisms need to be stated and explained, particularly when there is doubt as to their very existence. In the world of gaming and game theory, for instance, it is still possible to come across idealized actors who have neither values nor psychological motiva-tions, and are therefore interchangeable.

Values and motivations, however, do matter and very often they are inter-related. Writing about Larrissa Amalrik and Pavel Litvinov, who on 25 August 1968 were demonstrating in Red Square against the Warsaw Pact intervention in Czechoslovakia, a Western journalist reported that the two protesters 'were equally aware of the personal risk' they were taking. How-ever, they and other fellow dissidents accepted these risks because

> By setting examples of personal courage as well as integrity, the new revolutionaries expect, as did their forebears a century ago, to inspire or to shame others into stepping forward – and they have.[9]

This example shows a merger of personal commitment (values) and courage (psychological motivation). Both factors coincide also in a more negative stereotype, that of the compulsive gambler who, of course, is gambling for money but who nevertheless differs from the more 'normal' player by (innate?) psychological proclivities. To quote from the confession of Dostoyevsky's gambler:

> I remember that – oh, strange sensation – I suddenly, and without any challenge from my own presumption, became obsessed with a *desire* to take risks. If the spirit has passed through a great many sensations, possibly it can no longer be sated with them, but grows more excited, and demands more sensations, and stronger and stronger ones, until at length it falls exhausted. Certainly, if the rules of the game had permit-ted even of my staking fifty thousand florins at a time, I should have staked them.[10]

Gamblers, gold diggers, test pilots, explorers, construction workers on the top of skyscrapers, army experts defusing explosive devices and astronauts in search of scientific information have at least one trait in common: they are willing to expose themselves to higher risks than their fellow men.

That there are wide differences in risk-taking propensities is suggested not only by large national statistics[11] but also by smaller samples, such as results of experiments conducted by John Cohen, a social scientist.[12] His observa-tions of pedestrians crossing the street at a dangerous corner despite heavy car traffic showed that persons in the age range from 16 to 30 took greater risks than older persons, and that men took greater risks than women. This study, however, is inconclusive because the pedestrians were not asked *why* they took high risks – perhaps they had very good reasons for doing so.

More interesting as regards motivational factors of risk-taking are studies reported by John Atkinson,[13] Ward Edwards[14] and Scodel *et al.*[15] In these laboratory experiments ambition and achievement orientation were correlated with risk-taking behavior, showing that *on average* 'persons with high need of achievement *tend* to prefer moderate risks to either large or small risks'.[16] Thus while the distinction between value-oriented and motivational (psychological) risk-taking is a valid one to make for analytical purposes, it is doubtful whether modern psychology has advanced far enough to make such a distinction operationable. To quote a psychologist interested in international politics:

> Because healthy individuals do take risks in accordance with their individual aims and perception of the situation, and because personality tests and laboratory risk-taking experiments work on the basis of *averages*, we are ill-prepared to predict the behavior of a normal individual in *a* situation in real life.[17]

It may be added that not only prediction but mere explanation of risk-taking behavior is a difficult task – and perhaps irrelevant if such an analysis were based entirely on psychological grounds, correlating risk-taking to a few selected variables. What may help, though, is general knowledge of the character and personality of the actor. The behavior of the truck driver or the chess player in the present examples is more predictable if we know more about him and his behavior in the past. In the chess game named disaster and in international relations 'knowing your opponent' becomes an important asset.

VI PERCEPTIONS OF RISK

To 'know your opponent' is another way of saying 'perceptions matter'. A player must ask himself: 'What are my opponent's risk-taking propensities? How does he see the state of the game? What is the likely difference between defeat and disaster for him? How much utility does money [or whatever the penalty for disaster] have for him?' And, finally: 'What kind of an image does he have about me?' The behavior of the player will depend on the answers he himself gives. Rationality of the game-theoretical type is thereby diluted, because rational behavior now depends on answers which are not verifiable at all, or not in exact terms.

Whereas perceptions in this case were connected with *personalities*, they are of importance also in the analysis of *events*. Because of the complexity of chess different results may obtain from the assessments of the course and state of the game. For instance, two equally strong players will hesitate to make any prediction of the outcome of the game after the first three or four moves. But as they pursue their own strategies, controversies may arise as to who has the relatively stronger or weaker position on the board. It is entirely possible that a player perceives his position to be weak, not realizing that there is an excellent move out of a dilemma and that he therefore unnecessarily chooses a risky strategy to try to turn the course of the game in his favor.

These considerations serve to support John F. Kennedy's comment to the effect that for the taking of decisions 'perceptions are more important than reality'. All too often there is a substantial gap between the two. This is quite understandable. Phenomena in the real world are almost boundless; hence a *selection* has to be made. But unfortunately for the decision-maker (and the rest of us), information passes through various stages of preselection by newspapers, advisers and intelligence organizations, so that images of reality are built on an inevitably biased and – despite the welter of 'data bits' – relatively narrow foundation.

It is not surprising therefore that people who are faced with such a problem consciously or subconsciously have recourse to a *framework of reference*. Clarity and order are then brought to bear on the confusion. The effect can be quite salutary and immediate, as, for instance, for an observer of chess for whom the hitherto senseless movement of various pieces of carved wood on a chequered board changes into threats, traps and offensive and defensive strategies after he has learned the rules of the game. The mind has to be properly structured to recognize the significance of a specific event. Precisely because frames of reference have such salutary and comforting effects is it possible to explain why they tend to be retained even when they are wrong, the best example of this in the natural sciences probably being the stubborn defense for centuries of the Ptolemaic view of the universe. Even exposure to information at variance with the model one has constructed may be of little effect because of the 'tendency to interpret the very data which would lead one to change one's model in such a way as to preserve that model'.[18]

This phenomenon is not uncommon in international politics. For decades the model of aggressive (because totalitarian) and monolithic world communism was stubbornly defended. Its logic seemed to necessitate incessant intervention – in Guatemala, Iran, Lebanon, Laos, Cuba and the Dominican Republic. A more sophisticated view of the relationship between ideology and nationalism, and the role of anticolonial and national liberation movements, however, would have justified the taking of lesser risks. But as with the Ptolemaic model, if the gap between reality and perception, and between fact and theory, becomes too wide, change will ultimately take place. Today US diplomacy is actively trying to exploit the Sino-Soviet rift; and whereas in 1965 President Johnson intervened in the Dominican Republic to put a stop to international 'communist subversion' in the western hemisphere, in 1979 President Carter accepted the victory of the Sandinistas in Nicaragua as a more or less autonomous process and a more or less internal affair.

Interim Summary and Persisting Inadequacies of the Model

This brief discussion has served its purpose if it has begun to show the complexity of the problem and contributed to a decent burial of 'game theory man'. This strange creature in the scientific zoo of gaming and game theory in the world of Martin Shubik, a management scientist, has no personality; he really does not learn anything or change his opinion in the course of play. He invariably knows all the rules of the game; he usually is able to compute and calculate accurately at great speed. He is assumed to always know what he wants and to know what the others want.[19]

Indeed the kind of actor required for game theory and other formal theories of rational decision bears little resemblance to the actor crossing a bridge, playing the disaster chess game or conducting policy in international relations. Any theory of decision under risk, therefore, cannot be meaningful unless it is based on descriptive (rather than formal) criteria of analysis, and unless it relies on behavioral data. Such a theory would also have to take into account the result of the exercise as conducted thus far: no matter how rational the structure of the game, and no matter how rational human behavior is assumed to be, it is still inadmissible to regard the players as interchangeable.

Although game-theory man has by now been transformed into a more credible human being, severe limitations of the game itself still persist. The *environment of risk* in which decision-making takes place needs further modification so that it can approach reality to a higher degree. At least five deficiencies can be listed: (1) the probabilities of outcomes were known exactly and could meaningfully be stated in numerical terms; (2) the level of risk was unaffected by the actions of the players; (3) the players did not communicate with each other; (4) only two players were playing the game; (5) there were no time constraints. These deficiencies can still be remedied.

Notes: Part One, Chapter 2

1   Thomas C. Schelling, *Arms and Influence* (New Haven, Conn. and London: Yale University Press, 1966), p. 100.
2   Robert F. Kennedy, *Thirteen Days: The Cuban Missile Crisis* (London: Macmillan and Pan, 1969), p. 124.
3   Schelling, *Arms and Influence*, p. 101.
4   ibid., p. 102.
5   ibid.
6   As one economic theorist writes, in decision-making under uncertainty 'we know the environments but *nothing whatever* about the probabilities associated with those environments. This condition represents one extreme of the partial-uncertainty dimension. Forecast information has reached the zero limit, and, as a result, many decision options are available' (Martin K. Starr, *Management: A Modern Approach*, (New York: Harcourt Brace Jovanovich, 1971, pp. 151−2).
7   Figure 2.1 represents a modification of a planning model constrained by ruin thresholds as developed by Starr, *Management*, p. 405.
8   See the discussion by Starr, ibid., pp. 404−5. When conditions of a similar nature arise in business the 'objective function of the manager may be changed from maximization of profit to minimization of penalties, or even avoidance of ruin'. Faced with a choice between strategy A and strategy C, the unreasonable refusal to take risks resembles that of many organizations which, 'because of a conservative ruin criterion or overprotective action limits, forgo unusually promising opportunities'.
9   Anatole Shub, *The New Russian Tragedy* (New York: Norton, 1969), pp. 54−5.
10 Fyodor Mikhailovich Dostoyevsky, *The Gambler*, trans. C. J. Hogarth (London: Dent, 1948), pp. 272−3.
11 According to Gamblers Anonymous, an organization which helps compulsive gamblers,

there are '10 million compulsive gamblers [in the United States] who need help' (*Newsweek*, 10 April 1972, p. 50).

12 John Cohen, *Chance, Skill and Luck* (Baltimore, Md.: Penguin, 1960).

13 John W. Atkinson, 'Motivational determinants of risk-taking behavior', *Psychological Review*, vol. 54 (1957), pp. 359–72.

14 Ward Edwards, 'Probability preferences among bets with differing expected values', *American Journal of Psychology*, vol. 67 (1954), pp. 56–7.

15 Alvin Scodel, Philburn Rotoosh and J. Sayer Minas, 'Some personality correlates of decision making under conditions of risk', in Dorothy Willner (ed.), *Decisions, Values and Groups*, vol. I (New York: Pergamon, 1960).

16 Joseph de Rivera, *The Psychological Dimension of Foreign Policy* (Columbus, Ohio: Charles E. Merrill, 1968), p. 175. The present discussion relies on de Rivera's presentation of the literature and the findings.

17 De Rivera, *The Psychological Dimension of Foreign Policy*, p. 175; see also the article by Harry B. Williams, 'Some functions of communication in crisis behavior', *Human Organization*, vol. 16, no. 2 (Summer 1957), pp. 15–19.

18 Raymond A. Bauer, 'Problems of perception and the relations between the United States and the Soviet Union', *Journal of Conflict Resolution*, vol. 5 (1961), p. 227.

19 Martin Shubik, 'On gaming and game theory', *Management Science*, vol. 18, no. 5 (January 1972), p. P-52. It is theoretically possible for a chess player to put the next or next two moves into a formal game-theoretical matrix. However, the *possible* combinations are so vast that such an endeavor would be agonizingly complicated. Since there is no rational solution to chess, the present disaster chess game under conditions of risk is to be understood as an effort at gaming.

3
Pandora's Marble Pot

The disaster chess game will now be modified in the following way. The referee, instead of throwing a die, is appointed keeper of a marble pot containing marbles of six different sizes. Each one of the marbles carries a letter, a D (for disaster) on the smallest type, and an S (for survival) on the bigger types of marble. Once the players move into the risk position on the chessboard the referee, instead of throwing the die, reaches in the pot and draws a marble. Disaster occurs when he draws a D marble.

It is also explained to the players that the difference in the size of the marbles varies only slightly, and that their distribution may be unequal, that is, that there may be more small (disaster) marbles in the pot than larger (survival) marbles, or the opposite. At the beginning of the game the players may examine the approximate distribution of marbles by reaching into the pot, but do so only briefly and blindfolded.

The players are also given an equal number of marbles, half of which are of the small, the other of the larger variety. At any time in the game, the players are told, they may dilute the disaster probability by throwing survival marbles into the pot – openly or concealed from the other players – or they may do the very opposite, that is, use the disaster type of marble and thereby increase the risk of disaster.

In addition teams may be formed on both sides. The team members may talk to each other and to members on the other side and they may strike bargains with them and explain their moves. Finally, the referee or the teams themselves may impose time limits on the game. Processes of risk-taking can now be discussed much more accurately and realistically.

The Degree of Belief under Conditions of Partial Uncertainty

The modification of the game now creates a much more ambiguous framework of risk-taking. Of course there still remains an objective dimension to risk in as much as the proportion of disaster to survival marbles is fixed. But a significant change occurs in the subjective dimension: the players can no longer calculate the probability of disaster. They are not sure about the exact condition of the environment. The threads from the bridge analogy can now be picked up. Probability now corresponds to the concept of *degree of belief*. The player who briefly assesses the risk distribution resembles the driver in the previous analogy who, on the basis of incomplete and insufficient information, stops and thinks about the probable risks of crossing the bridge. In economic theory this is a clear case of decision-making under *partial uncertainty*. This theory assumes that the shape of the distribution of probabilities (such as normal, Poisson, or binominal) is not known but some information is available about the parameters and/or character of the distribution (such as averages, modes, medians, or various measures of symmetry, skewness, and dispersion).[1]

I PERCEPTIONS AND THE PSYCHOLOGY OF RISK AT A HIGHER LEVEL OF COMPLEXITY

For the players the new conditions of partial uncertainty present complex tasks of judgment of an entirely subjective dimension. Risk-taking by the players will now vary according to a new set of perceptions — about the probable distribution of marbles; the intended meaning of the opposing team's use of D- and S-type marbles; the purpose behind the other side's messages; the significance of interaction among team members on the other side; the influence of time constraints on their behavior; and the view the opposing team may have formed about one's own messages, moves and risk-taking propensities. The players are now called upon to grasp complex conditions intuitively. Literally 'gaining a feel for the system' becomes an important asset in risk-taking and an important part of the behavior of the players.

As for the psychology of risk in the new conditions, what matters now in addition to the factors mentioned previously is the degree of confidence of the players and the faith they have in their own judgments about events and personalities. Risk-taking will be affected in ways depending on what the player is confident about. Results of formal experimental gaming concerned with decision-making processes under conditions of risk and ambiguity provide some insight into these psychological processes.

> What these decision makers share is that differences in relative 'vagueness' of opinion seem relevant to their choices. For their behavior in situations presenting such differences, the 'neo-Bernouillan' theory gives wrong predictions and, by their lights, bad advice. Indeed, it sometimes seems to them, intolerantly, that the advice of the latter approach to *ignore* their own perceptions of ambiguity, their occasional unease with their best judgments of probability, could lead to *wildly irrational* decision making; for they suspect that scarcely any faculty of discrimination is more closely related to survival than an ability to tell the difference between knowing a great deal about the consequence of their actions and knowing very little.[2]

That is to say, the gaming results reveal a correlation between risk aversion and decreases in information about the environment in which risk-taking is to proceed. This would be the general rule. But it is also a matter of common sense that different people cope differently with ambiguity, vagueness and complexity. In the unmodified chess game named disaster, where the risks were *known*, there was no scope for wishful thinking. Now, however, excuses and rationalizations can freely be constructed.

II   NONVERBAL COMMUNICATIONS

Another whole new range of factors affecting risk-taking is connected with communications, signalling and the credibility of commitments. The D and S marbles in the hands of the players represent a certain amount of power, which can be used to increase or decrease the level of risk. Such use of marbles of any type represents a form of nonverbal communication to the opponent.

On the surface some of these communications could be interpreted as being quite unambiguous and effective. For instance, when a player commits all his D marbles to the pot right at the beginning of the game there appears to be no other reasonable interpretation than that the intent is one of deterrence. Deterrence is based on what might be called 'massive retaliation', the warning that the fulfillment of a certain contingency will pose extreme risks for the adversary. Depending on the availability of a very high proportion of disaster marbles relative to the distribution in the marble pot, the fulfillment of the contingency (moving into the disaster position by the opponent) may make the objective risks very high. But risks will be incurred by *both*. The effectiveness of the threat, therefore, is reduced considerably in its credibility.

Hence as far as any such doctrine of massive retaliation is concerned it was as correct to say in the 1950s as it is today that

> the leaders of the Soviet Union . . . will hardly endow the doctrine with much credibility. They will see that we have the capability to implement our threat, but they will also observe that, with their own nuclear capability on the rise, our decision to use the weapons of mass destruction will necessarily come only after an agonizing appraisal of costs and risks, as well as of advantages. Our record of performance after World War II is unlikely to increase their apprehension . . . Finally, the state of domestic [American] and [Western] allied opinion will provide them with ample reason that the doctrine is, if not a case of outright bluff, at the very most a proposal that will still have to undergo searching and prolonged debate before becoming accepted policy.[3]

But if massive retaliation is not a very effective strategy to deter risk-taking, what about 'graduated deterrence'? There are problems with this strategy too. Both in the present game and in international relations an agonizing appraisal needs to be made as to *how high* the level of risk has to be in order to force the opponent to withdraw from the crisis position. Let us consider the dilemma from the point of view of player A who adopts a strategy of graduated deterrence.

First sequence

Player A moves and adds a few disaster marbles. (Rationale: to deter risk-taking of B.)

Player B is unimpressed and moves into crisis position, but adds survival marbles. (Interpretation by A: B is willing to accept risks, but only of a small magnitude.)

Second sequence

Player A adds some more disaster marbles. (Rationale: to coerce B to withdraw because of the higher degree of risk.)

Player B remains in disaster position but does not add any more survival marbles. (Interpretation by A: B is worried, but the level of risk is not high enough to make him withdraw from the crisis.)

Of course, in the third sequence of moves and thereafter player A can add a progressively higher quantity of disaster marbles, hoping each time that the display of consistency and determination will compel the opponent to withdraw, but such a strategy is not gratuitous. Player A increases the risk of disaster not only for the opponent but also for himself.

Processes of this kind resulting from a strategy of graduated deterrence have been visualized in international relations. Again under the conceptual assumption that war can be taken to mean a progressive increase in risk of annihilation,[4] the United States could react as follows to a limited Soviet attack upon Western Europe.

> [It] might feel that its first blow against a Soviet city would so convince the Soviets of the West's determination to carry out the 'city-a-day' threat that the war would end at that point. The Soviets might believe that their first counterreprisal would be sufficient to discourage the West from continuing the exchange. Clearly, if each side persisted for some time in the expectation that the opponent would capitulate after the next exchange, or the next few exchanges, an amount of city destruction approaching the dimension of all-out war might result. In this event, of course, both sides would have 'miscalculated' – they would have failed to appraise correctly the other side's determination and expectations.[5]

Although, as can be seen from this example, there are as many problems attached to the strategy of massive retaliation as to that of graduated deterrence (or 'flexible response'), the latter appears preferable in crisis situations, if only for the reason mentioned above: the manipulation of small amounts of power with gradual increases in risk preserves some freedom of action – not only for the actor himself but also for the opponent.

III VERBAL COMMUNICATIONS: PRISONERS ESCAPING FROM THEIR ARTIFICIAL DILEMMA

According to conventional wisdom, 'actions speak louder than words'. However, actions as a form of nonverbal communication, though loud, may be so ambiguous in their communication content that they may fail to achieve the purposes for which they were designed.

To consider a case from recent military history, in World War II Japanese balloons drifted across the Pacific causing heavy forest fires in California and Oregon. American military and political leaders perceived this to be a rather ineffective effort of war-fighting. The intended message, however, was not one of war-fighting but deterrence, an attempt to warn the United

States that Japan had the capability to engage in bacteriological warfare, and that any use of bacteriological weapons against Japan would be met with an equivalent response.[6] It is useful and often necessary, therefore, for nonverbal moves to be accompanied by verbal communications: by messages, letters, notes, exchanges, executive speeches, declarations or planned leaks.[7]

In the present game, agreements can now be concluded not to play a risky game (that is, by agreeing not to move into the crisis position), or only to play a game of limited risk (for instance, not to use D marbles for several moves). With the increase in the players' freedom of action, what will be the impact on the course of the game?

Again, there is no single answer. The increased complexity of the game structure allows no general solution to rational behavior. In general, verbal communications can have multiple functions. They can be used in order to explain, to justify, to assure, to warn, to threaten and to bluff, but for the most part words belong to one of two categories: genuine explanation or deception. It therefore depends entirely on how well one knows the opponent whether he can be trusted or whether his pronouncements must be viewed with suspicion. Needless to say, if there is a persistent credibility gap in the relations between the two players, words will tend to become nearly meaningless and be disregarded. This, however, will rarely be the case in a game or in international relations. There will always be some kind of mixture of suspicion and trust. There will always be degrees of doubt as to the genuine or bluff content of messages.

Conceivably it could be argued the following way: honesty, trust, and cooperation in this game simply do not pay. To be honest would be the same as being the only person in a game of poker to play with open cards. As in the Prisoner's Dilemma[8] it is of course of foremost interest to both players to avoid risks. Neither player wants disaster to occur. Cooperation, indeed, would be more advantageous than defection – provided that *both* players cooperate. But what will guarantee that this will happen? When the opponent feels that he is on the verge of defeat, will he not resort to threatening disaster? Precisely because the other player cannot be trusted, it just does not pay to be honest and to cooperate.

This line of reasoning shows the serious limitations of arguing with the Prisoner's Dilemma as an intellectual frame of reference. In the Prisoner's Dilemma the worst outcome for cooperation by one prisoner and defection by the other is 'hanging' for the trusting and therefore allegedly non-rational actor. In contrast, according to the present model, the worst penalty for cooperation by one side and defection by the other is at most only *possible defeat, not certain disaster*. In the present game the defector, too, by breaking an agreement, exposes himself to risks of disaster; he may suffer a loss of prestige and credibility; and in the long run he may still be defeated.

Processes of the kind do occur in international politics. During the summer and fall of 1962 Khrushchev assured Kennedy through intermediaries that 'Nothing will be undertaken before the American Congressional elections that could complicate the international situation or aggravate the tension'; that: 'No missile capable of reaching the United

States [will] be placed in Cuba.'[9] The breach of trust discovered before the completion of a *fait accompli* confronted Khrushchev with risks; these risks were increased by countermoves of the Kennedy administration; as well as suffering a loss of credibility, Khrushchev had to retreat and lost this specific gamble.

The primary example for the reference to the Prisoner's Dilemma is the analogy to the arms race. Again, unrealistically, the worst possible outcome is catastrophe for the party who is nonrational enough to trust, while the other defects and wins. But even in the example of the arms race abandonment of honesty and the recourse to bluff and deception may result even in a short time in the loss of prestige and credibility, and in an inferior military-strategic position. As regards the Soviet Union, the deliberately fostered bomber gap in the mid-1950s and the fueling of Western fears of a missile gap in 1958–61, with all the negative consequences for the Soviet position in the arms race, are widely known; both examples disprove the point that deception and bluff always pays.

In fact from a historical perspective it appears almost as if disaster struck the defector as often as, or more often than, the trusting player. Beginning from March 1935 Hitler claimed parity between the *Luftwaffe* and the Royal Air Force, and later on superiority for the German air force. While these claims did play an important role during the pre-World War II crises, and worked to the short-term advantage of Nazi Germany, the unjustified claims led to a 'sudden and abrupt decision to push all-out for a large bomber capacity' in the United States and to a vast expansion of air defense and air force capabilities in Britain.[10] While the decision in the United States had strategic implications which in the long run contributed to the defeat of Germany, the British decision was more immediately effective and helped to assure victory in the Battle of Britain.

Even a comparatively minor defection such as the movement of surface-to-air (SAM-2 and SAM-3) missiles by the Soviet Union after the ceasefire of 7 August 1970 in the Middle East could be interpreted neither as an advantage without cost to Egypt or the USSR, nor as a disaster for Israel. Politically, it immediately undermined the shaky credibility of the Soviet Union as an eventual guarantor of any Middle-East settlement – as a direct participant, or indirectly within a United Nations context – and thereby limited its options. At the same time the Soviet move strengthened Israel's plea for increased United States military and political assistance, thereby worsening Egypt's security problem.

To sum up, reasoning on the basis of the Prisoner's Dilemma amounts to the voluntary imprisonment of the intellect. International relations cannot be represented as a situation in which one single dilemma is being played out. It is rather a long-term dynamic process of many successive games that permit learning.[11] The assumption that there is a referee, governor or hangman who enforces a penalty is unrealistic in international relations. Equally unrealistic are the game's constraints of the players' complete ignorance of each other's personalities, the lack of a shared risk of disaster and the absence of communication of both the nonverbal and verbal variety. As communications are an important means of establishing credibility and trust, defection means to lose both and pay a heavy price.

IV   DOMESTIC FACTORS OF RISK-TAKING

Thus far the idea has been preserved that decisions must be seen as made by a unified actor who has '*one* set of perceived options, and a *single* estimate of the consequences that follow from each alternative'.[12] This was the idea embodied in Allison's rational actor model (model I). But what will be the differences introduced for the course of the game if attention is paid to the modification that several players with specific values, interests and goals and semi-independent organizations with differing standard operating procedures are facing each other across the board? In other words, what is the relevance of what used to be called the organizational process model (model II) and governmental (bureaucratic) politics model (model III)?[13]

Organizational Process: Model or Muddle?

No one can deny the importance of organizational processes for political outcomes. However, it is not very useful to see organizations as actors in their own right, making decisions on the same level as the other two model actors.

To begin with there are serious problems with the theoretical and illustrative exposition of the organizational process model. This can be shown by reference to Allison's introduction of a chess game modification, which provides that

> the chess player might not be a single individual but rather a loose alliance of semi-independent organizations, each of which moved its set of pieces according to standard operation procedures. For example, movement of separate sets or pieces might proceed in turn, each according to a routine, the king's rook, bishop, and their pawns repeatedly attacking the opponent according to a fixed plan.[14]

Such a view of the game is absurd. Chess by its very nature depends on a *unified* approach to the game and *single* coordination and control of all the pieces on the board. The picture of organizations operating separately, taking turns and moving their own pieces according to a 'fixed plan' cannot be applied to a game that, as noted, has no rational solution.

There are problems also at the empirical level. One hidden assumption seemingly making the model work is the condition that there is somewhere a breakdown, or an absence of coordination, control and supervision. The President had decided that the missiles should be withdrawn from Turkey, but it had not happened. The blockade ring around Cuba was decided upon, but the navy did not implement the decision according to the presidential orders. Khrushchev had decided to install missiles in Cuba, but organizations failed to camouflage the project sufficiently and failed to provide for adequate protection. The Executive Committee needed an estimate of the effectiveness of an air strike against the missile sites and the commander of the tactical air force estimated that it was impossible to guarantee 100 percent effectiveness; but this estimate was probably incorrect. All this empirical evidence is evidence only of the fact that decisions depend on information; that decisions are often made without sufficient consideration of problems of coordination; and that decisions are sometimes not, or not properly and efficiently, implemented.

If the organizational process model is to be considered as a model in its own right it must be assumed that the decision level is equal to that of a model I and model III actor. This, however, is not the case. Model I and model III actors are decision-makers of a higher order who involve organizations in processes of *intelligence, deliberation* and *implementation*. Their decisions are made on the basis of organizational inputs, but the delivery of an accurate or inaccurate piece of information is not the equivalent of a decision itself. Allison does not make this clear.

> For example, Chinese entry into the Korean War – that is, the fact that Chinese soldiers were firing at UN soldiers south of the Yalu in 1950 – is an organizational action: the action of soldiers in platoons, which form companies, which in turn comprise armies, responding as privates to lieutenants who are responsible to captains and so on to the commander, moving into Korea, advancing against enemy troops, and firing according to fixed routines of the Chinese army.[15]

What tends to get lost in this vivid account is the fact that the Chinese private soldiers knew all along how to shoot at Americans according to their manuals. What needs to be mentioned is a missing link: initially someone had to give the orders. A *decision* had to be made first whether to intervene or not to intervene. If fixed routines of the Chinese army had anything to do with this, they only figured as a factor in the calculations of the political leadership, posing the question whether the Chinese People's Army could or could not be considered an effective instrument of intervention. Once this question was answered, the Chinese private in the bush still had to decide whether or not to fire at Americans; the commander of a battalion still had to decide whether to attack a certain point – but these decisions are decisions of a lower order.

It is useful at this stage to refer to the bridge analogy and to the three points which are as valid there as they are in the present context, namely, that the outcome of a decision is fundamentally different from the decision itself, that decision-making depends on information and that the implementation of a decision may be inadequate or lacking entirely.[16] It would be odd indeed in the example of the failing brakes to label the vehicle a 'decision-maker' – it was the driver who had rejected the risk of crossing, only the outcome did not respond to his decision.

In the chess game too, someone, or some group, has to make basic decisions – where to move, which piece to move, whether to accept or reject the crisis position, and whether to add or withdraw disaster or survival marbles. These are basic decisions. Of course there is no guarantee that the information as to the intentions and discussions of the opponents is correct; the intelligence organization of the team may have blundered. There is the grave possibility that a decision was taken to add survival marbles, but that disaster marbles were thrown into the pot instead; the organization responsible for carrying out the decision may have committed this grave error. It serves the decision-makers right if they trust all incoming information and if they neglect to verify implementation of decision. However, it appears neither legitimate nor accurate to endow failures, mistakes and neglect with the characteristics of a decision in its own right.

It is perhaps due to these considerations that Allison and Halperin – without explicitly repudiating it – have made short shrift of the organizational process model, integrating it in one single 'paradigm' and 'treating the factors emphasized [previously] as *constraints*'.[17]

Bureaucratic Politics

For the purpose of analyzing the relevance of a bureaucratic politics model it is convenient to start again by quoting Allison and his illustration from a chess game. He writes:

> It is conceivable, furthermore, that the pattern of play might suggest to an observer a Model III assumption: a number of distinct players, with distinct objectives but shared power over the pieces, could be determining the moves as the resultant of collegial bargaining. For example, the black rook's move might contribute to the loss of a black knight with no comparable gains for the black team, but with the black rook becoming the principal guardian of the palace on that side of the board.[18]

Again the illustration, unfortunately, is absurd. There is no conceivable gain for any individual player or any faction on the black team if the black rook becomes the 'principal guardian of the palace'. However, the main point of substance is well taken and remains valid: to introduce into the game a number of players with distinct objectives and shared power over the pieces may lead to changes in the way in which the game is played. What are some of these changes?

First, the difficulty of accurate perception climbs up yet another rung in the ladder of complexity. Allowance must now be made by the members of the other team for the possibility that both verbal and nonverbal communications are not messages for opponents, but performances for the benefit of selected domestic audiences. In foreign policy, these domestic audiences may also be important allies – East Germany, for instance, in relation to the Soviet Union, or Western Europe in relation to the United States.

Secondly, communications and negotiations may be conducted with the purpose of awaiting or influencing domestic policy changes on the other team. Should one team perceive a split in the opponent's team into risk-accepting hawks and risk-avoiding doves it may be well advised to devise appropriate tactics to strengthen the domestic position of the doves. Also risk-taking may be postponed (as in the case of Khrushchev awaiting the outcome of the American presidential elections in 1960) when a change in principal players seems imminent.

Thirdly, the content of bargaining itself may be affected. A frequently used bargaining asset in international relations has been the claim by chief negotiators that the opponent should make concessions because of pressures exerted by domestic and alliance politics. The merit of such a claim is quite

evident in governmental systems where political dissent is highly institution-
alized (as in Western democracies) or where the alliance structure is plural-
istic (as in NATO). There is more doubt as to the merit of such a claim if it is
made by more centralized regimes with a tightly controlled alliance system –
as, for instance, when Stalin during the Yalta and Potsdam conferences not
only referred to expectations of the Soviet and Polish peoples (that is, Polish
communists), but also to the demands of his fellow Politburo members.

Finally, and most important, the decision itself may be affected. Supposing two factions of nearly equal strength are arguing over the optimal strategy to be pursued and whether to take risks or not. The stronger faction will
carry the day with its preferred solution. But a few players may change their
minds. The other faction may thereby become the stronger of the two and
proceed with *its* preferred solution. What results from this dynamic of the
game – particularly if the changes in alignment are frequent – is erratic
playing by the team in question.

Bargains may even be struck which are unconnected with the game but
which nevertheless may find their result on the board. Let us take two recent
examples from international relations – the opposition of the Christian
Democrats and Christian Socialists in West Germany to the ratification of
the treaties with the USSR and Poland within the context of the
government's *Ostpolitik*, and the decision by the Labour government in
Britain to submit the question of Britain's membership of the EEC to a referendum. Both must be explained primarily in terms of intra-party and electoral politics. If the outcome of domestic politics had been rejection of the
Ostverträge and withdrawal of Britain from the common market it would be
valid to say that the decisions were nonrational to the extent that party and
electoral politics had prevailed over the rational requirements at issue.

To add some illustrative examples from the American context, where such
phenomena seem to be particularly rampant: the origins of the Jackson–
Vanik Amendment, the Congressional policies favoring Greece over Turkey
and Israel over the Arabs and the attitudes taken – and votes cast – on the
Panama Canal Treaty and SALT look very much like deference to various
domestic lobbies and electoral posturing rather than a response to international political and strategic requirements.

But these very examples from the West German, British and American
contexts show the serious limitations of the bureaucratic politics model as
discussed by American political scientists, notably by the two perhaps most
influential proponents of that model, Allison and Halperin. As demonstrated convincingly by a British critic, they base their model not only on a false
dichotomy of logic versus politics, but also – as a precondition of this dichotomy – on a narrow view of politics.[19] The domestic political dimension of
foreign policy, however, is something more substantive than 'the parochial
preoccupations of ambitious bureaucrats, suspicious military men and elec-
tioneering Presidents, and something broader than the attempts within the
establishment to strike bargains that satisfy these divergent preoccupations'.[20] The superficialities of the moment are not the same as the essence of
a process. In order to understand the relationship between domestic politics
and foreign policy, to continue this criticism, it is necessary to stand back
'from the immediate battles with a long-term rather than a short-term

perspective, examining the shared images, assumptions and beliefs and the "rules of the game".[21]

Thus the bureaucratic politics model may be useful for analyzing some categories of decision, for instance, those concerning weapons procurement.[22] However, it appears much less helpful in the examination of foreign policy, *and least of all international crises*. Indeed it would be a sad reflection on any political system if it were true that: 'Threats to interests from rival organizations, or competing political groups, are far more real than threats from abroad.'[23] Surely, in conditions of international crisis, individuals, groups and organizations are severely limited in their support for parochial solutions. Typically a rallying around the flag occurs in times of crisis. National interests, values and consensus then tend to become the primary domestic determinants of foreign policy. Political leaders of all ages have shown an awareness of these processes by exaggerating external threats or even artificially manufacturing a crisis.[24]

To sum up, the most appropriate research procedure for the analysis of risk-taking in international politics appears to be the consideration of a nation's behavior in terms of a rational actor model. Organizational processes should of course not be deleted; where relevant, they should enter into the analysis as factors affecting information, deliberation and implementation of decisions. Processes of bureaucratic or governmental politics too, where relevant, should be taken into account – not, however, in the form of a separate model, let alone paradigm, but as a modifying and supplementary aspect of the main approach.

These observations do not only apply to Western pluralist systems but – as the further development of the argument in this book is trying to show – even more so to centralized political systems, notably that of the Soviet Union.

V   TIME CONSTRAINTS

The final addition to the chess game named disaster, the imposition of time constraints, also makes for a difference in the course of the game. Actions, if not immediately challenged, can quickly be transformed into *faits accomplis* which may be irreversible, or reversible only by accepting increased risks and costs.

To take some examples from international politics, it is clear that during the Cuban missile crisis the adoption of a 'wait and see' attitude by the United States would have meant combat readiness of Soviet missiles, increased surface-to-air protection of the Soviet installations and the difficulty of asking the Soviet Union 'to undo what had been accomplished', instead of 'to stop doing what is being done'.[25] In the case of Soviet intervention in East Central Europe any form of Western military assistance to anti-Soviet revolts would only have been technically feasible within a brief span of time *before* the Soviet Union managed to get things under control.

Scarcity of time means less time for the consideration of the state of the game. This increases the danger that moves will be taken which are not in the best interests of the actor. (Everyone who has played an instant-move chess game, recorded and replayed it at leisure realizes how many opportunities were neglected and how many threats overlooked.) The sword of Damocles hanging over the team makes deliberations hectic. It is virtually impossible now to let everyone speak up. Established routines and ingrained personality traits will claim a greater share of the action.

Relations with the adversary will tend to be affected in much the same way. Exchanges will tend to be curtailed and negotiations and discussions abbreviated. The image of the adversary is now likely to become a constant variable with little or no opportunities left for discerning possible changes in the composition of the other team and its behavior. Verbal and nonverbal communications, ambiguous by nature, are subject to even more misinterpretation and miscalculation. The reduced time available for calculations will also tend to intensify the reliance on innate, spontaneous behavioral attributes and intuition. This does not necessarily lead to greater risk-taking. The resentment of a player against playing under time constraints may outweigh his general proclivities for the acceptance of risk and ambiguity. Actions may then be taken with a view to removing time pressures and increasing the room for maneuver.

On 23 October 1962, for instance, the Executive Committee had decided that if a U-2 plane were shot down the United States would retaliate with a strike against a single SAM site. On 27 October this contingency occurred. But now that the time had come to implement that decision the President reconsidered.[26] Despite the postponement of action it still remained true at that moment that 'what hope there was [of avoiding a direct military clash between the superpowers] now rested with Khrushchev's revising his course within the next few hours'.[27]

Finally, time pressures work in the direction of *unification and centralization of decision-making*. They thereby reinforce what was said above about the primary domestic determinants in international crises and the restoration of rational actor qualities to decision-making. This reinforcement tends to occur because now the principal players in the team will confer only with the most skillful, most trusted and most powerful co-players.[28] Criticism, dissent and mutual recrimination literally must wait until the crisis is over. Only then is it reasonable to expect power realignment in the domestic national system or the alliance – as evident, for instance, in the weakening of Khrushchev's power and the worsening of Sino-Soviet relations after the Cuban missile crisis.

All the previous chapters in this theoretical part have illustrated the processes and dynamics of risk-taking by means of two analogies (crossing a bridge and a disaster chess game) under increasingly complex conditions. Where appropriate, parallels to international relations have been provided. What is still lacking, however, is the integration of the lessons derived into a concept of crisis in international relations and in superpower relations in particular.

Notes: Part One, Chapter 3

1 Starr, *Management*, pp. 150–1.

2   Daniel Ellsberg, 'Risk, ambiguity, and decision', PhD dissertation, Harvard University, 1963, pp. 294–5. For Bernouilli's theory see above, p. 13, note 14.

3   William W. Kaufmann, *The Requirements of Deterrence* (Princeton, NJ: Center of International Studies, 1954), p. 11.

4   It may be useful to refer to Figure 4.1 on p. 43 for an illustration of these conceptual interrelationships. Concerning the idea of war as involving a series of decisions with increasing risks of disaster, see also p. 21.

5   Glenn H. Snyder, *Deterrence and Defense: Toward a Theory of National Security* (Princeton, NJ: Princeton University Press, 1961), p. 203.

6   This example of misperception was reliably reported to Warner S. Schilling by Japanese researchers.

7   The complex problem of communication and perception cannot be treated in as much detail here as would be desirable. Much of the ground has been covered by Robert Jervis, *Perception and Misperception in International Politics* (Princeton, NJ: Princeton University Press, 1976).

8   The Prisoner's Dilemma was, as far as I am aware, first used by Robert C. Tucker of Princeton University to explain problems of decision-making. It involves two prisoners who are being told by a judge that the prisoner who confesses to the jointly committed crime – who 'squeals' or 'defects' – will go free whereas the other prisoner will be hanged. If both prisoners confess they will both receive a lenient sentence. And if both of them refuse to confess they will go free. The decisions taken or the 'strategies' adopted are either 'cooperative' (refusal to confess) or 'noncooperative' ('squealing' or 'defection').

9   Both of Khrushchev's messages, as well as more Soviet assurances of the same nature, are quoted by Allison, *Essence of Decision*, pp. 40–1.

10 George H. Quester, *Deterrence before Hiroshima: The Airpower Background of Modern Strategy* (New York: Wiley, 1966), pp. 129–30.

11 This is demonstrated also by deviation from the 'rational' solution of the Prisoner's Dilemma in experiments where a *series* of games is played; see Anatol Rapoport and Albert McSchammah, *Prisoner's Dilemma: A Study in Conflict and Cooperation* (Ann Arbor, Mich.: University of Michigan Press, 1965), pp. 198–227.

12 Allison, *Essence of Decision*, pp. 32–3.

13 In his article, 'Conceptual models and the Cuban missile crisis', *American Political Science Review*, vol. 62, no. 3 (September 1969), pp. 689–718, Allison called models II and III 'bureaucratic politics' and 'organizational process' models. In his *Essence of Decision* model III figures as 'governmental (Bureaucratic) politics' model. However, in his article with Morton H. Halperin, 'Bureaucratic politics: a paradigm and some policy implications', in Raymond Tanter and Richard H. Ullman, *Theory and Practice in International Relations* (Princeton, NJ: Princeton University Press, 1972), pp. 40–79, his original models II and III are merged to form one single 'bureaucratic politics' model. For the possible reason of this change see below, pp. 34–6.

14 Allison, *Essence of Decision*, p. 7.

15 ibid., p. 78.

16 See above, p. 14.

17 Allison and Halperin, 'Bureaucratic politics', p. 40, fn. (my italics). In this context it is interesting to note that in *Essence of Decision* Allison is able to rely on a great number of political scientists who adhere predominantly to models I and III but unable to cite political scientists who support his second model. Support for his organizational process model seems to be derived entirely from economic theory.

18 Allison, *Essence of Decision*, p. 7.

19 Lawrence Freedman, 'Logic, politics and foreign policy process: a critique of the bureaucratic politics model', *International Affairs* (London), vol. 52, no. 3 (July 1976), pp. 436–7. There are other critiques of the bureaucratic politics model, for instance, Stephen D. Krasner, 'Are bureaucracies important? (or Allison Wonderland)', *Foreign Policy*, no. 7 (Summer 1972). However, Freedman's criticism is by far the more serious as it challenges the basic premises and assumptions of the model.

20 Freedman, 'Logic, politics and foreign policy process', p. 448.

21 ibid., p. 449.

22 Not surprisingly, perhaps, Morton H. Halperin's *Bureaucratic Politics and Foreign Policy* (Washington, DC: Brookings Institution, 1974), is primarily about a topic accurately described in the title of his previous study, *The Decision to Deploy the ABM: Bureaucratic*

and Domestic Politics in the Johnson Administration (Washington, DC: Brookings Institution, 1973). Among the more recent follow-ups to the pattern are Edmund Beard, *Developing the ICBM: A Study in Bureaucratic Politics* (New York: Columbia University Press, 1976), and Ted Greenwood, *Making the MIRV: A Study of Defense Decision-Making* (Cambridge, Mass.: Ballinger, 1975).

23 Allison and Halperin, 'Bureaucratic politics', p. 58. Similarly, according to Halperin, *Bureaucratic Politics and Foreign Policy*, p. 23, individuals at the top of organizations often 'see national security in terms of organizational interests'.

24 After an article and a book on the Cuban missile crisis, where Allison applied two elaborate models in addition to the rational actor model, it does come as something of a surprise to read that 'In general, Model I [the rational actor model] is more useful for explaining actions where national security interests dominate' (Allison and Halperin, 'Bureaucratic politics', p. 58). Did Allison choose the wrong subject (decision-making in an international crisis) to make his case?

25 The phrases are used by Alexander L. George, David K. Hall and William R. Simons, *The Limits of Coercive Diplomacy: Laos, Cuba, Vietnam* (Boston: Little, Brown 1971), pp. 22–3.

26 Theodore Sorensen, *Kennedy*, pp. 798 and 713.

27 Robert F. Kennedy, *Thirteen Days: The Cuban Missile Crisis* (London: Macmillan and Pan, 1969), p. 107.

28 For corroboration of this proposition for United States decision-making see, for example, the case study by Glenn D. Paige, *The Korean Decision* (New York: The Free Press, 1968).

4
Crisis and Risk in International Relations

When one talks about a crisis – a personality or identity crisis, a pulmonary or coronary crisis, a financial or economic crisis, or a domestic or national crisis – the meaning of this is usually clear. There is a probability of a breakdown, collapse or destruction of the psychological, physiological, economic or political system. In the chess game named disaster, too, a crisis had a relatively well-defined meaning: whenever the queen (or a knight) moved across the center line the players found themselves locked in a crisis; varying probabilities of disaster then obtained.

But what is a crisis in international politics? Evidently it too must have something to do with the possibility or probability of a breakdown, collapse or disaster. And quite clearly such breakdown or collapse must refer to relationships among states. When it occurs the new state of affairs is called war – or, rather, *should be*, because contrary to this understanding the concept of crisis has been applied to alliance relations, where the notion of risk (possibility or probability) of war is absent, for instance, in Anglo-American relations during the Suez and Skybolt crises.[1] Richard E. Neustadt is quite explicit about this when he writes that the 'classic question' asked of adversaries, '[I]f we do harm to others in their terms what could they do to us in ours?', was absent from the two crises.[2] The analytical focus of his book, however, is on crises in *adversary* relations and although it may be true that alliance relations and crises between allies are 'not altogether different' from relations among adversaries,[3] there is a difference, and this difference matters: in adversary relations there is a risk of war.

One important example of writing pertaining to adversary crises involving the risk of war is Herman Kahn's *On Escalation*.[4] As this book 'provided a form of intellectual order for all dimensions of contemporary conflict with the notion of escalation'[5] and has been quite influential in scholarly debate and perhaps policy-making it cannot be ignored here.

It is doubtful, however, whether one can build on to Kahn's concepts and approaches. In the first place, there is a strong flavor of artificiality in his 'escalation ladder'. This ladder consists of forty-four rungs, all of which above rung twenty – that is, the greater number of rungs – involving some kind of nuclear exchange.[6] Skepticism as to whether such elaborate differentiation is meaningful analytically is advisable. Similarly the study provides no explanation of why such escalation thresholds exist and, assuming their existence, how they influence political behavior. As one critic has argued, it would be hazardous for the policy-maker to put much faith in the existence of escalation ladders because they 'may offer an illusion of control or a margin of safety that is likely to be negated by the systemic nature of con-flict'.[7] It would also be dangerous to assume symmetry of perceptions because 'In the mind of the adversary, some of the rungs may be missing'.[8]

Also Kahn's crisis concepts are quite complex. There is 'subcrisis maneuv-ering', and there are 'ostensible crises', 'traditional crises', 'intense crises' and (rungs twenty-one to twenty-five) 'bizarre crises'.[9] In all this academic quest for differentiation one basic point seems to have been overlooked: when a crisis has ended it has ended. For most people this would appear to be the case when 'large conventional war' (rung twelve of the ladder) has begun. To reintroduce the term thereafter is bound to lead to confusion.

Empirically and theoretically Oran Young's study of bargaining in four international crises appears to be more satisfactory than most of the studies on this topic.[10] Conceptually it steers the necessary middle course between crises without risk (Neustadt) and risks without crises (Kahn). Young intro-duces a threefold differentiation of international relations on a continuum ranging from full cooperation to total war, the differentiations being 'normal interaction', 'crisis' and 'war'.[11] Correspondingly there are 'risks of crisis', 'risks of war' and 'risks of mutual annihilation'. These concepts are shown in Figure 4.1.[12]

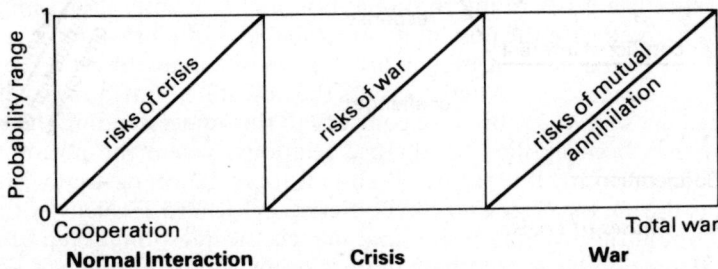

Figure 4.1   *The concepts of risk and crisis.*

In detail, relations among states will always contain elements of cooperation and political conflict; coercion by diplomatic, economic and military-political means short of the overt use of force may form part of their 'normal inter-action'. However, while there is always *some* risk of crisis in relations among adversaries, any increase in coercive and conflict elements will increase the probability that a crisis will occur. Risks of crisis then turn into risks of war and a qualitatively new situation now prevails. The crisis ends with the outbreak of war, and new risk calculations concerned with the probable costs of war-fighting now that deterrence has failed apply from this point onwards.

All this does not yet provide an important missing link, that is, there is as yet no answer to the question of what it is that accounts for a transformation of risks of crisis into risks of war. Such transformation can be said to occur only if two actions are taken and two conditions met. The first action is that of a *challenge* posed by one power, the second a *response in kind* by the adversary.[13] The first condition is that of commitment, resolve or determina-tion by both sides to engage in a competition in risk-taking; the second requires dangers of escalation, imperfect control over local actors and the 'force of events', that is, the existence of what has been called in Soviet scholarly literature the *nekontroliruemyi element*, or 'uncontrollable element', in crises.[14] Where challenge and response collide they eventually produce a *confrontation* – the most acute phase or 'core' of a crisis. These distinctions are aptly described by Snyder and Diesing.[15] Figure 4.2 combines their and Oran Young's discussion of the dynamics, processes and phases of crisis with the concepts used here.

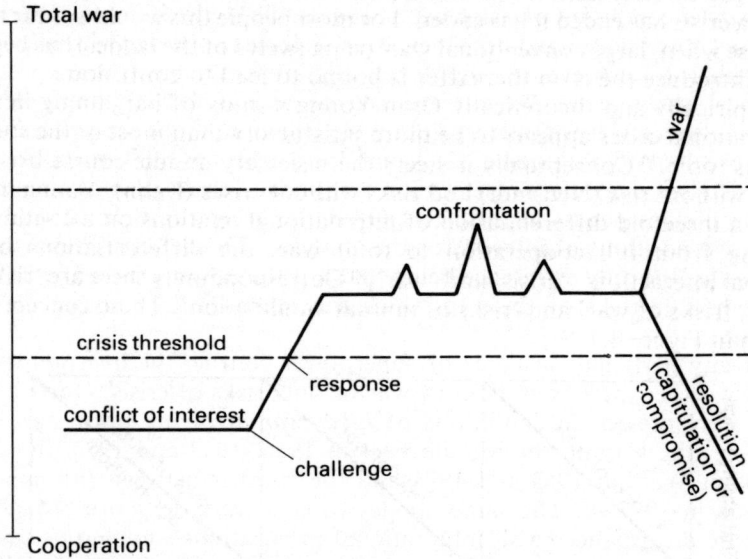

Figure 4.2   *Phases of crisis.*

It is less useful to go over the ground which has been covered by the extensive literature on crisis theory than to build upon it. One final comment may therefore be permitted concerning one of Young's propositions. Young writes that: 'By definition, a crisis constitutes a break in the pattern of interactions characteristic of the preceding flow of international politics.'[16] In reality it would be difficult to find an example where the basic political attitudes, perceptions and interests had significantly changed. It is far more typical that 'a crisis tends to *highlight or force to the surface* a wide range of factors and processes which are central to international politics in general',[17] and that – as regards adversary crisis – elements of conflict in their relations are intensified, not broken or reversed. This pattern is underlined by the fact that crises in particular geographical areas, involving a particular set of participants, have flared up time and again, for instance, in Berlin, East Central Europe, in Southeast Asia, on the Indian subcontinent and in the Middle East.

It is for these reasons that it is possible to follow the conceptual distinction made in Soviet scholarly literature between *konfliktnost'* and *konflikt*, the former referring to the 'fundamental contradiction between socialism and imperialism' (that is, in Western terms the basic adversary relationship), the latter defined as an 'entirely concrete international political process having predetermined origins, content and form, system and structure and phases of development' (that is, a crisis).[18]

A Classification of Cases[19]

If the adversary relationship between the superpowers is considered as a game under conditions of risk played between the Soviet Union and her allies and the United States and her allies, four different positions with important consequences for preventive diplomacy and crisis management are possible. (1) Local actors or the West create risks of crisis (step one: the challenge); however, the Soviet Union does not respond in kind, and a superpower crisis therefore does not take place. (2) Again, local actors or the West create risks of crisis (step one), the Soviet Union responds to the challenge (step two), and both sides persist in their commitments, accepting risks of war. The other two positions of interest for the analysis of Soviet crisis behavior are analogous, the only difference being that it is the Soviet Union and its allies which initiate risks of crisis to which the West (3) does not or (4) does respond.

For any particular instance of superpower conflict the question can be asked whether there were risks of war or only risks of crisis. Only risks of crisis were present in conditions of *local war* involving third states, for example, the wars in the Middle East in 1956, 1967 and 1973, the Indo-Pakistani Wars in 1965 and 1971 and the conflict between Ethiopia and Somalia in 1977–8. The same applies to *civil wars* or, more broadly, to domestic disturbances with international implications – numerous cases in Africa, for instance (Congo, Biafra and Angola), the Dominican Republic in 1965 and the Middle East in 1957 and 1958. Risks of crisis also obtained in cases of *limited war* where one superpower was engaged in actual war fighting against a country not formally protected by the adversary superpower in a treaty of mutual assistance; primary examples of this category include the Korean and Vietnam Wars.

The frequently used distinctions between local war, civil war and limited war are somewhat artificial because transitions are fluid and elements of all three categories are often mixed. There were civil war aspects as well as local and limited war elements in the Taiwan Straits confrontation of 1958 and in the Korean and Vietnam Wars. However, viewed from the perspective of superpower relations, all these cases of local crisis and conflict share the basic feature of low-risk situations.

The same is true for Soviet intervention in its sphere of influence in Eastern Europe (East Germany, 1953, Hungary, 1956 and Czechoslovakia, 1968) and also for the first example in the post-World War II period of the massive use of force by the USSR in a country of the Third World: the Soviet occupation of Afghanistan in 1979–80.

If these stringent criteria are applied to international crises and conflicts in the post-World War II period, three cases stand out as qualitatively different situations in which genuine risks of war could be thought to be present in superpower relations: the Cuban missile crisis of 1962 and the Berlin crises of 1948 and 1961. The challenge to the status quo by the Soviet Union, utilizing

Table 4.1 *Risk and Crises in Superpower Relations*

Initiatives by local actors or the West		Initiatives by the Soviet Union or Soviet 'proxies'	
Risks of crisis	*Risks of war*	*Risks of crisis*	*Risks of war*
1947 Greek Civil War	no examples	1946 Iranian crisis	1948 Berlin blockade
1954 Indochina conflict		1948 Czechoslovak coup	1961 Berlin Wall
1956 Suez crisis		1950–2 Korean War	1962 Cuban missile crisis
1957 Syrian crisis		1953 Soviet intervention in East Germany	
1958 Middle East crisis		1956 Soviet intervention in Hungary	
1958 Taiwan Straits (Quemoy) crisis		1968 Soviet intervention in Czechoslovakia	
1960 Congo crisis		1965–76 Vietnam War	
1960–1 Laos crisis		1970 Egypt: expansion of Soviet military commitment	
1967 Arab-Israeli War		1970 Cuba: Soviet attempt to construct naval facilities for nuclear submarines	
1969 Nigerian Civil War		1975–6 Cuban-Soviet intervention in Angola	
1970 Jordanian Civil War		1977–8 Cuban-Soviet intervention in Ethiopia	
1972 US blockade of North Vietnamese harbors		1979 Vietnamese intervention in Kampuchea	
1973 Arab-Israeli War		1979 Soviet intervention in Afghanistan	
1979 Chinese 'punishment' of Vietnam			

military-political pressures, was met by a response in kind on the American side. The lineup of opposing military forces in a direct confrontation, the high degree of political commitment on both sides and the reduced ability to control events combined to create real dangers of a military clash.[20]

Table 4.1 applies these distinctions and orders the various conflicts and crises in superpower relations according to (1) who was responsible for initiating them and (2) the type of risk which obtained in each case.

Before turning to wisdoms and conventional wisdoms about *Soviet* behavior a brief summary of the main points made thus far about the concept of crisis and processes of risk-taking is provided.

Crises, Risks and Risk-Taking: a Summary

(1) A crisis in international relations can be understood as a process of interaction between adversaries occurring at higher levels of intensity than the ordinary flow of events.[21] Crises *reinforce, aggravate and heighten previously existing conflict patterns*. Crisis characteristics include an accelerated pace of events, difficulties of coordination and control, dangers of misperception and miscalculation and inaccurate communications, often under conditions of psychological stress and time constraints. Crisis perceptions are: an important turning point in history is imminent, vital interests are at stake, and there is an increased danger of war.

(2) The essence of crisis is the *unpredictable, indeterminate*, or *uncertain* nature of outcomes. Because of the presence of such probabilistic elements, and because of the likelihood of war, the concept of risk is inherent in the definition of crisis. The intensity of a crisis, therefore, is a function of the level of risk.

(3) A crisis in international relations can be pictured as lying on a continuum ranging from cooperation to total war. In *normal interaction* elements of cooperation and conflict will be mixed, which is expressed in such terms as 'limited adversary relationship', 'agreement to disagree', 'partial cooperation' and 'peaceful coexistence as a form of class struggle'. Diplomatic, economic and military-political pressures short of the overt use of force may be part of normal interaction between the adversaries. An increase in coercive and conflict elements, however, may result in a *crisis* and create risks of war. The probability of war rises as the crisis moves into *confrontation* as its most acute phase. The crisis ends either by capitulation or compromise, or with the outbreak of *war* – the occurrence of disaster in the modified chess game. Beyond that lie the costs of war-fighting and varying degrees of disaster.

(4) Transitions from the normal flow of international relations to crisis may be abrupt or fluid. Crises may arise suddenly or summate a gradual, escalatory process. This suggests that the transitions in the middle of the continuum, from crises to armed conflict, may be equally abrupt or equally gradualistic. There is *no consistent rung-by-rung escalation or de-escalation ladder*.

(5)   Although there are *objective* dimensions to risk, risk calculations in international relations by analysts and actors alike are *subjective*, conforming to the notion of 'degree of belief'.

(6)   Risk-taking basically can be classified in two types – *irrational* and *calculated* risk-taking. The first type involves psychological processes and motivations, the second values and interests. In real-life decisions both dimensions tend to be mixed.

(7)   The *outcome* of a decision does not necessarily conform to the decision itself. The reason for this is the fact that implementation may be difficult or impossible to control, inefficient, inaccurate, or simply lacking.

Turning to some of the most important characteristics which act on a typical decision-maker in an international crisis, the following summary of propositions may help serve as a guideline.[22]

Irrational Elements Affecting Crisis Decision-Making
The greater the crisis intensity,

● the greater the degree of tension and stress affecting decision-makers;
● the greater the degree to which the adversary is stereotyped;
● the more often decisions will be made on the basis of affect rather than calculation;
● the greater the impact of inadequate perception and selective inattention;
● the greater the tendency to rely on personality preferences, cultural conditioning and intuition.

Other Elements Affecting Crisis Decision-Making
The greater the crisis intensity,

● the less the ability to consider more than a very few alternatives;
● the greater the tendency to cut off discussion and communication in the domestic context;
● the less the ability to control, perceive and evaluate events and organizational processes;
● the greater the tendency to rely on traditional patterns of political behavior and precedents;
● the greater the pressures to reach decisions fast.

Elements Restoring Characteristics of the Rational Actor Model
Although governments are composed of groups, bureaucracies and organizations and hence give rise to the possibility of nonrational decision-making in foreign policy, elements of rational decision-making will tend to be restored *in crises*. This is due to

● a tendency for the *centralization of decision-making* in the hands of a narrow circle of the leadership (a tendency which in turn is caused by time pressures and the necessity to curtail discussion);
● a tendency for *shared values* and *common interests* of national survival to

take precedence over bureaucratic, organizational and other parochial, domestic political, economic or ideological interests.

The question of what it is that makes a player, an international actor, take risks can only be answered by taking into account a combination of objective conditions and subjective assessments and the unique personality of the actor. The answer to this question is therefore of necessity complex. It could be expressed as follows.
An actor will take risks if

- he perceives the risks to be low;
- the status quo is being changed to his disadvantage;
- he can hope to create a *fait accompli* before the increase in risk threatens to become prohibitive;
- he feels that vital interests are at stake;
- the difference between defeat and disaster is marginal, that is, if the costs for risk avoidance are high;
- he was successful in previous crises with the adversary or with other adversaries;
- his confidence about the effectiveness of coordination and control over events is high;
- his confidence about the effectiveness of minimizing irrational and nonrational influences on his side is high;
- calculated, as opposed to irrational and nonrational, elements of decision-making have prevailed on the other side;
- the personality of the adversary (that is, his traditions, culture and national character and his ideological, social and political background) makes it appear unlikely that he (the adversary) will persist in a competition in risk-taking.

What is it that has been said about the risk-taking propensities of one specific actor in international crises: the Soviet Union?

Notes: Part One, Chapter 4

1 Richard E. Neustadt, *Alliance Politics* (New York and London: Columbia University Press, 1970).
2 ibid., p. 73.
3 ibid., p. 2. This proposition appears acceptable. But less so is the view that 'one of the more successful techniques of crisis management has been to turn it [an adversary crisis] into [an] intramural [that is, alliance] crisis'. This is the view expressed by Coral Bell, *The Conventions of Crisis: A Study in Diplomatic Management* (London: Oxford University Press for the Royal Institute for International Affairs, 1971), p. 8. The advice to be derived from this for the policy-maker is apparently as follows: 'When threatened by an adversary crisis, work towards wrecking your own alliance system. You will then manage the crisis successfully.' It is doubtful whether policy-makers have ever acted in accordance with such advice.
4 Herman Kahn, *On Escalation: Metaphors and Scenarios* (New York: Praeger, 1965).
5 Colin S. Gray, 'What RAND hath wrought', *Foreign Policy*, no. 4 (Fall 1971), pp. 117–18.
6 Kahn, *On Escalation*, p. 39.
7 Gray, 'What RAND hath wrought', p. 118.
8 loc. cit. For similar criticism see Larry Temple Caldwell, 'Toward a theory on the political

uses of strategic military power by the United States and the Soviet Union', PhD dissertation, Tufts-Fletcher School of Law and Diplomacy, 1968.

9   Similarly inventive is Coral Bell with her distinctions of (1) 'adversary crises of the central balance', (2) 'intramural crises of the power spheres or alliances systems of the dominant powers', (3) 'adversary crises of local balances', (4) 'intramural crises of regional alliances or organizations', as well as 'pseudocrises' and 'subcrises'; Bell, *The Conventions of Crisis*, pp. 8–9.

10   Oran R. Young, *The Politics of Force: Bargaining during International Crises* (Princeton, NJ: Princeton University Press, 1968).

11   Similarly, Glenn H. Snyder and Paul Diesing, *Conflict among Nations: Bargaining, Decision Making and System Structure in International Crises* (Princeton, NJ: Princeton University Press, 1977), p. 10, conceive of crisis as 'an intermediate zone between peace and war'.

12   The attentive reader of my Adelphi Paper (see note 19, below) will have noticed that the increase in risk is depicted in this figure as a *linear* rather than an *exponential* progression. The reason for this is an acknowledgment of the criticism that there is no particular reason why, for example, risks of war should grow more rapidly at the end of the crisis spectrum than at the beginning. But whatever the mode of graphic illustration, one should not assume a gradual and consistent increase or decrease in risk for any part of the spectrum.

13   For example, no crisis in the sense of the word as used here occurred in May 1972 when the Soviet Union failed to respond in kind to what has to be regarded as a challenge by the United States: the blockade of North Vietnamese harbors.

14   V. V. Zhurkin and E. M. Primakov (eds), *Mezhdunarodnye konflikty* (Moscow: Izdatel'stvo 'Mezhdunarodnye otnosheniia', 1972), p. 21.

15   Snyder and Diesing, *Conflict among Nations*, pp. 11–15. The basic outline of Figure 4.2 is taken from p. 15.

16   Young, *Politics of Force*, p. 61.

17   Glenn Snyder, 'Crisis bargaining', in Charles F. Hermann (ed.), *International Crises: Insights from Behavioral Research* (London: Collier Macmillan, 1972), p. 127 (my italics).

18   Zhurkin and Primakov (eds), *Mezhdunarodnye konflikty*, p. 29.

19   This follows my study, *Soviet Risk-Taking and Crisis Behaviour: From Confrontation to Coexistence?*, Adelphi Paper No. 101 (London: International Institute for Strategic Studies, 1973), pp. 4–5.

20   It may be objected that the Arab-Israeli War of October 1973 should have been included in this special category because it, too, produced a direct confrontation between the superpowers. There is, however, sufficient reason not to do so. For military clashes to have taken place between the superpowers it would have been necessary for the Soviet Union to intervene first (which would have been, as this writer is convinced, only in the form of a symbolic presence of troops in Cairo to dissuade *Israel* from further violation of the cease-fire agreement; see below, p. 254, and William B. Quandt, *Soviet Policy in the October 1973 War*, R-1864-ISA, Santa Monica, Calif.: Rand Corporation, May 1976, especially pp. 33–4). If Israel could still not have been dissuaded from further violation of the cease-fire agreement, Soviet forces would have had to be committed to joint military operations with Egypt. Next, US forces would have had to be dispatched to Israel and committed to military operations with Israel despite the fact that the US had already put Israel under pressure *to cease her military operations*. All these considerations show that – contrary to the impression conveyed by the Stage Three worldwide alert of US forces – it would be overstating the case to speak of a direct confrontation of the superpowers in the same sense as in the two Berlin crises and Cuba.

21   Young, *Politics of Force*, p. 15.

22   The summary of propositions under the first two headings draws on Robert Jervis, 'The costs of quantitative study of international relations', in Klaus Knorr and James N. Rosenau (eds), *Contending Approaches to International Politics* (Princeton, NJ: Princeton University Press, 1969), pp. 182–4.

5
Soviet Risk-Taking and Crisis Behavior: Wisdoms and Conventional Wisdoms

I DYNAMIC ELEMENTS OF SOVIET RISK-TAKING

The only study of Soviet risk-taking and crisis behavior of which this writer is aware is the essay by Triska and Finley entitled 'The Soviet Union: reckless or cautious'.[1] Although the study conveys the impression of objectivity, not least because of numerous tables and elaborate symbolism (for example, the symbols $R_1 R_{A1} = E_{gA} R_{A1}$ refer to an 'initial action (input, initial risk) taken by A to gain benefit (proportionate to expected gain)'), it turns out nevertheless that the subjective element looms large. Rankings of the intensity or 'seriousness' of a crisis, as well as rankings concerning the 'bidding' of participants in crises, were determined 'independently by five expert judges'.[2] However, either the expertise of these experts leaves something to be desired, or something is wrong with the complex cumulative index of several 'independent variables' which lie at the basis of the ranking order.

For instance, which crisis should be considered as more risky – the Berlin ultimatum of 1958 or the Berlin crisis of 1961? Surely, as the Berlin ultimatum of 1958 involved only the announcement of an intention to do something which was never done, and as contrary to that the construction of the Berlin Wall involved physical measures and the mobilization of military forces and hence posed the risk of Western counteraction or riots of the German population, it would seem to be a matter of common sense to allocate a higher level of riskiness to the latter crisis. Not so, say the independent experts. The 'Proposal on Berlin' of 1958 scores higher points on the risk scale than the 'Berlin Wall' of 1961.[3]

Similar doubts as to the soundness of the experts, or the usefulness of the categorizations with which they were faced, apply to the view that the Bay of Pigs invasion of 1961 was more risky than either the Berlin ultimatum of 1958 or the Berlin crisis of 1961. It is of course true that *if* in the spring of 1961 the United States had intervened in Cuba with troops of its own, and *if* the Soviet Union had then responded in turn with the dispatch of troops or direct missile threats against the United States, such a situation would have been risky indeed. However, none of this happened and none of this was intended.

Thus there is a suspicion to be derived from this example that if the independent experts had been asked directly, 'do you consider the Bay of Pigs invasion more risky than the Berlin crisis of 1961?', they might have given a different answer than the one expressed in the table. Why, then, an answer that is contrary to common sense? An explanation can probably be found in the fact that contiguity to the United States receives a very high score on the scale of riskiness – no doubt with a view to the Cuban missile crisis. The same high score is mechanistically applied to the Bay of Pigs invasion. But inherently – unless one already has the Cuban missile crisis in mind as one concrete example – there is no reason why contiguity to the United States should create a riskier situation for the USSR than contiguity of an area to the Soviet Union. In fact it would seem to be more valid to argue exactly the opposite.

But what about some of the main propositions derived from the endeavor? One of such propositions reads: 'The riskier (the more serious) the crisis, the more cautious the USSR.'[4] This is a statement that sounds quite reasonable. It can be stated with equal confidence that one of the ways in which such caution would be expressed, or could be measured, would be the degree to which the Soviet Union refrains from the use of force. According to the study in question, however, this is not the case as a second proposition asserts: 'The more risky (serious) the crisis, the *more force* the USSR tends to use (in all crises).'[5] It would be very difficult to provide any example of Soviet foreign policy where this ever applied.

But the problem does not end here. A third proposition holds that 'the more force the USSR uses, the less the Soviet *perception* of the crisis as being risky for the USSR (e.g., Hungary)'.[6] In other words when the USSR uses force the crisis – as asserted in the second proposition – is objectively risky, but at the same time – as stated in the third proposition – the USSR does not perceive the crisis as being so. What this amounts to is the claim that there is a general divergence of objective conditions of risk and Soviet perceptions. This is hard to believe.

Looking at the third proposition in isolation, there is much to be said for the validity of the example used. Indeed, when the Soviet Union intervened in Hungary in 1956 it did not (not least because of the concurrent Suez crisis) perceive its action as being risky. But the same could not be said for the Soviet use of force against the Japanese in the summers of 1938 and 1939. In these instances Stalin must have been aware of the tremendous risks involved in standing up to a formidable threat to Soviet security. Caution is advised, therefore, when Soviet behavior in Eastern Europe in the post-World War II era is extended to cover Soviet behavior 'in all crises'.

To abandon the study by Triska and Finley at this stage (some more propositions contained in it will be featured later) and turning to another collection of propositions about Soviet risk-taking, there emerges a much more complex, much more differentiated and much more satisfactory picture. In a relatively brief reconsideration and updating of Leites's 'operational code' of the Politburo,[7] Alexander George proceeds from the assumption that there are important limits on the possibility of decision-making in politics according to models of 'pure' rationality.[8] Among such limits, according to George, are the following: (1) the political actor's information about situations with which he must deal is usually incomplete; (2) his knowledge of ends–means relationships is generally inadequate to predict reliably the consequences of choosing one or another course of action; and (3) it is often difficult for him to formulate a single criterion by means of which to choose the 'best' alternative course of action. Because of these constraints on decision-making, *beliefs* of the political leadership are of importance. In order to explain or predict decisions it is necessary to focus on the decision-makers' *Weltanschauung*, 'cognitive map', 'political culture', 'operational code', or whatever term may be preferred.[9]

An important part of the traditional 'instrumental beliefs' of Bolshevik (and, later, Soviet) leaders with regard to the question, 'how are goals of action to be pursued most effectively?' – according to Leites and George – was the following answer in three maxims: 'push to the limit', 'engage in pursuit' of an opponent who begins to retreat or make concessions, *but* 'know when to stop'.[10] Conversely, in conditions where Bolshevik (and, later, Soviet) leaders felt themselves put on the defensive by actions of the opponent, the maxims summarizing traditional forms of behavior were: 'resist from the start' any encroachment by the opponent, no matter how slight it appears to be; *but* 'don't yield to enemy provocations' and 'retreat before superior force'.[11]

As regards the Soviet leaders' beliefs about the control of the force of events and the acceptance of risks the following propositions can be made on the basis of George's and Leites's approach.[12]

(1) It is imperative not to embark on forward operations against an opponent which are not carefully calculated in advance. Move forward only after careful preparation.

(2) It is necessary not to undertake any action that has an uncertain chance of yielding any payoff but is coupled, at the same time, with a large risk of severe loss if it fails.

(3) It is wise not to permit one's calculations and choice of action to be dominated by prospects of immediate or short-term gains while ignoring the possibility of the longer-range costs and risks attached to the same action.

(4) It is possible to make advances at the expense even of a stronger opponent. The opponent can be deterred by various constraints from translating his basic and always present hostility into an operational plan for all-out attack.

(5) It is feasible to control the force of events and scale down the level of risk by limiting the means employed for objectives which in themselves may be quite ambitious.

(6) It is advisable not to settle for a single probability estimate of unwanted risks that may develop in the future; rather such estimates of probability are to be subjected to sequential analysis.

While making allowance for the possibility that these elements, or at least some of them, have undergone change in the course of the evolution of Soviet foreign policy, both Leites and George are uncertain about the degree to which such change has taken place. Certainly some of these points are still seen as being valid and some of them are made even more strongly by other analysts.

Richard Pipes, for example, proceeds from the assumption that Soviet foreign policy conforms to principles inherent in the Soviet military concept of 'the art of operations' (*operativnoe iskusstvo)* [13] in 'an innovative linking of politics with warfare – in other words, . . . the militarization of politics, which Lenin was the first statesman to accomplish', [14] and in 'an interminable succession of probings, which like military reconnaissance are meant to draw enemy fire and reveal his capabilities, dispositions, and intentions'. [15] On the basis of these assumptions about operational principles Pipes puts forward the following propositions, which closely resemble those of Leites and George:

(1)   Soviet leaders act according to the proverb, 'If you don't know the ford, don't step into the river.' They do not plunge into contests blindly; they rarely gamble, unless they feel the odds are overwhelmingly in their favor. [16]

(2)   Soviet leaders are quite prepared to pull back when resistance on any one sector of the enemy front turns out to be stronger than anticipated: there are always other sectors which are less staunchly defended and where one's force can be applied to better advantage. [17]

Pipes is in agreement with yet another of Leites's axioms as revised by George – the taking of risks by proceeding in sequential analyses and by adjusting the next move to the adversary's response. 'Much attention', he writes, 'is paid in Moscow to these responses.' [18]

At the root of all these generalizations lies a perception of fundamental differences in the Soviet as compared to the American approach to politics. Such differences were first explored systematically by Brzezinski and Huntington and summarized pointedly in the aphorism: 'To the Bolshevik, politics is the craft of conflict; to the American, it is the art of compromise'. [19] In Pipes's view, too, a country like the United States whose preoccupation is commercial, 'is inherently predisposed toward compromise' and inclined to make 'concessions in advance of actual negotiations'; but for a country like the Soviet Union, 'without a great commercial tradition and furthermore impelled by ideology toward intransigence, this assumption does not hold'. [20]

It is obvious that these views have normative implications with respect to Western behavior not only *in* international crises, but also in conditions where there is only a *risk* of crisis. One such piece of advice with regard to Soviet probing would be the following maxim: 'be on guard from the start' and 'negotiate only if tangible concessions are made' by the Soviet Union. This is probably meant by Pipes when he writes:

Militancy is so entrenched in the mentality of the Soviet elite, it follows so naturally from the character of its personnel and its relationship to the population at large, that it is doubtful whether the best way to ease East – West tensions is by attempting a piecemeal resolution of specific disagreements. Those who urge so in the name of pragmatism are in fact motivated by impatience. [21]

or when he claims that: 'In principle, it does not pay to be too clever with Russian politicians: they are inclined to interpret ambiguity as equivocation, equivocation as weakness, and weakness as a signal to act.' [22]

It would be a complete misreading of American scholarship on the Soviet Union to assume that such views are held unanimously or even shared widely. This is (was?) particularly true in an era of détente in which the basic motivations of Soviet foreign policy were often held to be primarily economic and the Soviet Union was seen as becoming a 'mostly conservative force in world affairs . . . burdened with the defense of far-flung political and economic interests'.[23] In this vein two authors analysing the 'Soviet diplomacy of force in the Third World' come to the conclusion of a Soviet (and American) 'bias in favor of the *status quo*'.[24] Nowadays, 'the realistic aim of the forward positioning of forces seems to be not to maximize gains, but to minimize losses'. The authors continue:

> Surely it is a positive step when the USSR is transformed from a power totally confronting the international system from outside into a power 'on the make' within the system, subject to the conditioning effect of its rules and checks and balances.[25]

Perceptions of this kind are a clear challenge to the view that there is something fundamentally different about the USSR and Soviet foreign policy. This is in fact made quite explicit by Jerry Hough who writes: 'the Brezhnev era would be best understood if we ascribed to the General Secretary the type of motivations that we attribute to most politicians in the West.' If, Hough argues,

> Brezhnev's actions and policies are examined in the light of the hypothetical requirements of 'electoral' policies *vis-à-vis* the Central Committee, it is striking how many [of these actions and policies] can be explained in those terms.[26]

II FACTORS OF SOVIET RISK-TAKING

Leites's and George's 'operational code', and 'instrumental belief system', Brzezinski and Huntington's 'craft of conflict' and Pipes's 'deep entrenchment of militancy in the mentality of the Soviet elite' are all based on the view that ideology, and the way in which ideology influences perceptions and behavior, continues to matter for Soviet foreign policy. It is only a step from this platform of argument to the next one up, namely, that ideology provides for a coherent set of principles, shaping not only reflexes and responses in crises but also the basic starting position and interests of the USSR in international crises. It is probably this idea of coherence and congruence of ideology and policy which lies at the heart of statements like the following:

> The Soviet government conducts a 'total' foreign policy which draws no distinction between diplomatic, economic, psychological, or military means of operation. It also does not differentiate in any fundamental respect between domestic and foreign relations.[27]

and which finds its expression in the view that policy (including foreign policy) in the Soviet Union is shaped to a large extent by

(1) the psychological-ideological compulsion of totalism – especially pronounced in Leninism; that is, the need to provide a homogeneous analytical framework to the entire domain of public policy; and (2) the structural connexity of seemingly discrete dimensions of policy in a system of total central control but limited resources.[28]

The view of close interrelationships between Soviet domestic politics, foreign policy and policies toward the world communist movement, and of a unified approach to military strategy, economics, trade and aid, held together by the binding glue of ideology, leads to an important line of argument with regard to the explanation and prediction of Soviet risk-taking. It could be said that risk-taking is correlated with a leftist period in ideological commitments and priorities and risk avoidance with a rightist period. Characteristics of such a leftist swing would include, in domestic politics, emphasis on mobilization, transformation, heavy industry and centralization; in international relations, revolutionary expectations, militancy, violence and perceptions such as the triumph of the 'madmen' over the 'men of reason' in Western leadership, and the inevitability of conflict. In contrast those of a rightist period can be said to include priority for stability, rationality and pragmatism; emphasis on consumer goods production in economics; and decentralization in domestic politics. In international politics equivalent priorities would be the emphasis on peaceful coexistence, perceptions of the capitalist leaders as being 'reasonable', and the view that conflict is limited primarily to the realm of ideology, whereas broad possibilities exist for cooperation in the economic and political spheres at the state level.

According to Alexander Dallin, who neatly categorized these different elements, all this constitutes an important framework of analysis.[29] He sees

an inner logic that links a 'revisionist' attitude in foreign affairs to 'revisionism' at home and in doctrine, and similarly translates 'sectarianism', or Stalinism, or conservatism into a totality of interlocking views on both internal and external affairs.[30]

The case studies will show to what extent such a congruence of views, attitudes and policies can indeed be postulated. But even at this stage it may be useful to point out that there is a potential contradiction in Dallin's own line of reasoning when he states – his view of 'totality' and 'fundamental congruence' notwithstanding – that 'Creeping pluralism invades totalitarian life as it must invade all developing politics', that 'Soviet society becomes increasingly permeated by an awareness of multiple truths, multiple interests, and multiple forces at work both at home and abroad',[31] and that the Sino-Soviet conflict had struck a 'fatal blow' to dominant and time-honored ideological perceptions and had led to 'substantial disorientation and cognitive dissonance'.[32]

The last argument is much more in line with the dominant trend (at least in the United States) of proclaiming the 'waning of ideology' or, even more strongly, the 'end of ideology' in Soviet foreign policy. In the apt words of William Zimmerman, many Western analysts (including himself) had formed a 'well-founded judgment' that ideology 'explained very little of Soviet behavior in the post-war period'; with the exception of Eastern

Europe, the USSR had 'very seldom followed the course which the postulated role of ideology would seem to imply'.[33] In short, ideology was being relegated in the Soviet Union to being merely the 'language of politics' and the 'language of analysis'; 'Western and Soviet perspectives on the basic structure of the modern international system are essentially similar'; and for all these reasons: 'It seems evident that much of the importance attached to ideology in explaining Soviet foreign policy has been misplaced'. [34]

As regards studies with a claim to scientific and objective methodological procedure there appears little that can be gained on this problem of ideology so notoriously difficult to measure in its importance. Triska and Finley subjected the materials of the Twenty-Second Party Congress (1961) to content analysis, and this is one of their major findings:

> We have found Marxism-Leninism strikingly correlated with the time span under consideration by the decision-maker. In the context of analysis of long-range planning and expectations, the evidence of doctrinal impact is far higher than in the context of relatively short-range analysis and expectations. In the latter context, the impact of doctrine has been found very small indeed, and no significant variation has been observed for crisis behavior, although this remains an open question in some respects.[35]

As in the case of the authors' study of Soviet risk-taking it is doubtful whether the findings are useful. It is hazardous to generalize from the analysis of materials from one particular CPSU Congress about the relevance of ideology to Soviet foreign policy in general, and to Soviet crisis behavior in particular.

The theme of the waning of ideology is closely related to a second possible factor of Soviet risk-taking – the Soviet national interest. Under the continued assumption of a dichotomy of ideology and national interest the authors of a study of the Indo-Pakistani crisis of 1971 and superpower relations concluded that the crisis revealed the 'high value now placed by Moscow on coercive naval diplomacy' and generalized from that as follows: 'In retrospect, this appears a normal, almost predictable evolution, a manifestation of the gradual erosion of ideology and the ascendancy of "state interests" in the Soviet calculation.' [36] This framework of analysis frequently leads to the view of a 'gap between the theory and practice of Soviet foreign policy', the Soviet leadership in essence paying lip-service to Marxist-Leninist ideology while pursuing Soviet national interests. [37]

The analytical dilemma into which such a juxtaposition of Marxist-Leninist ideology and the Soviet national interest leads can be shown by reference to a book by W. W. Kulski. [38] The author writes that he wanted to devote special attention to the 'relationship between official Marxist-Leninist ideology and the national interests of the Soviet Union'. He then announces unambiguously: 'This book helps to clarify the issue, showing that the Soviet leaders overlook ideological considerations in favor of protecting Soviet national interests.' [39] The priority of national interests is being 'affirmed by all Soviet sources'. [40] As far as Soviet-American relations were concerned, 'ideology plays a minor role in this relationship' [41] and 'the pragmatic nature of Soviet foreign policy stands out from even a brief review of Soviet attitudes on all sorts of governments in the developing countries'.[42] In essence, 'the USSR is only a new name for old Russia'.[43]

Is it therefore quite all right to discard ideology as a factor of Soviet foreign policy? Apparently not, for Kulski also argues that 'one can assume that they [the Soviet leaders] believe in Marxism-Leninism and that it would be unpleasant for them to sacrifice their beliefs on the altar of national interests'. Secondly, unconcealed deviations from Marxism-Leninism in foreign policy 'could undermine a fundamental tenet of the Soviet state system'. Thirdly, 'Soviet influence within the Communist movement . . . would be even more eroded if the USSR were publicly to adopt a nonchalant attitude toward the ideology shared with foreign Communists'.[44]

In a way then – but contrary to the author's original declarations – the book helps to clarify the fact that it is unwise to offer simple clarifications. It would seem that the problems with the dichotomy of Soviet ideology and the Soviet national interest can be alleviated provided the two elements are seen not as contradictory, but as *complementary* aspects of Soviet policy,[45] that ideology is regarded as being differentiated according to various *functions* which may play a greater or lesser role according to particular issues in question, and that the national interest is considered not as one single entity, but as a complex of *interests* (with the emphasis on the plural) which themselves may have ideological dimensions to a greater or lesser extent.

Another reasonable working hypothesis for the analysis of Soviet crisis behavior is the view that what matters is not only the 'balance of interests' but also the 'balance of forces'.[46] To that extent military power constitutes a third important factor shaping Soviet risk-taking. The question is only: in what way? Different answers to this question are possible and different answers have been given.

One set of propositions is connected with increase in conventional capabilities, particularly of the Soviet navy and air force. If it is true (as Western analysts put it) that the Soviet Union 'is now pressing outward for a role commensurate with its status as one of the two superpowers in the world',[47] that it has come to act increasingly on the basis of self-proclaimed global interests and (as Brezhnev put it) that it is now 'taking into account, in one way or another, the state of affairs in virtually every corner of the globe',[48] the USSR may be prone to the same or similar mistakes of risky overextension and overcommitment as occurred in American foreign policy in the 1950s and 1960s.

Assumptions of this kind probably lie at the root of many Western apprehensions. For instance, in 1969 Walter Laqueur predicted that 'Soviet military power is likely to grow and lead to a higher risk policy'.[49] In 1971 Andrew Pierre feared that a 'more assertive self-confidence based on world recognition of Soviet-American parity – possibly codified in a SALT agreement – could induce a greater propensity for Soviet risk taking'.[50] And in the same year Alexander Dallin stated that whereas the possession and awareness of nuclear power have engendered a commitment to avoid confrontations that could lead to the use of the ultimate weapon, 'there is also likely to be an instinctive tendency – now that gross strategic parity with the United States seems to have been attained – to take somewhat greater gambles in the pursuit of Soviet objectives'.[51]

Whereas views of this kind can be summarized in the axiom of 'capabilities induce intentions', another axiom connected with military power is the assumption that advantages in the distribution of power strengthen determination and resolve in international crises. For instance, although – as mentioned – Triska and Finley do not indicate how Soviet perceptions were measured in their study, they propose as one of their findings the following: 'The greater the Soviet weapons-military parity with the West, the lower the Soviet perception of risk in actual East–West conflicts.' [52] In other words, parity induces confidence.

The problem recurs in the analysis of the role of military power for shaping Soviet (and American) behavior in specific crises. Zbigniew Brzezinski has argued with regard to the Cuban missile crisis and Berlin that

> Had strategic symmetry prevailed it might have proven much more difficult for the United States to achieve its principle objective in Cuba (the removal of hostile missiles) through the exercise of its own conventional superiority (naval blockade) while simultaneously offsetting its own conventional inferiority in a politically sensitive and vital area (West Berlin) by the inhibiting threat of American strategic superiority. [53]

However, the view that Soviet risk-taking propensity can be considered a direct function of the military-strategic balance, and the assumption that capabilities induce intentions, has been challenged by other analysts. Phil Williams, a British scholar, argues that

> Nuclear holocaust will hardly be an attractive option even to the side that has the capacity to 'win'. So long as neither superpower regards nuclear war with equanimity, therefore, the strategic balance is unlikely to be the major determinant of either side's resolve. [54]

Marshall Shulman expresses much the same view when he writes:

> The argument that parity would increase the Soviet propensity to take additional risks, or diminish the American resolution in responding, ignores the fundamental inhibitions of mutual deterrence, which are not substantially changed by disparities in the respective arsenals. [55]

Turning to yet another factor shaping Soviet risk-taking and crisis behavior – domestic politics – it is almost a truism to say that 'foreign policy begins at home'. However, it is not altogether clear how domestic political processes affect foreign policy in general and how they shape crisis behavior in particular. It is also difficult to select the appropriate level of analysis. Is it the personality and idiosyncracies of the *individual* leader, the processes engendered by a more or less collective *leadership*, or the priorities and commitments of the Soviet *system* as a whole that accounts for risk-taking propensities in a given situation?

One of the at first sight surprising propositions is the view that despite considerable differences in personality and style of leaders as diverse as Stalin and Khrushchev, their risk-taking propensities in essence did not really differ very much. This is expressed by Triska and Finley in one of their findings as follows.

The difference between Stalin and Khrushchev as Soviet risk-takers had been minimal. True, in low-tension cases, Khrushchev was more active, flamboyant, ribald, imaginative, and inventive; however, in high-tension crises, he was as cautious, conservative, and circumspect as Stalin.[56]

Thomas Wolfe agrees with this view to the extent that he thinks that 'Khrushchev's actual performance during the various crises in which he was an actor does not bear out the allegation of his propensity to take large risks'.[57] And in Aspaturian's opinion, too, the characterization of Khrushchev 'as being a higher risk taker than Stalin, whose foreign policies, in retrospect, appear cautious by comparison' is confusing and could be explained by the 'unprecedented technological revolution in weaponry after Stalin's death. Under these conditions, any . . . confrontation between the US and the USSR risks a high level of harm.'[58] Would it be true to say, then, that the personality of the leader in the Soviet context does not matter very much because the Soviet system sets stringent limits to the freedom of action of any particular occupant of high office?

The second level of analysis is usually considered to be the most important of the three levels, because it is there that processes of decision-making, the power struggle, interest groups or *ad hoc* groupings and their influence on foreign policy are being considered. This is probably what is meant by Gallagher and Spielmann when they write that 'the character of the leadership is the dominant factor that determines how the whole system operates'.[59]

Although the problem of Soviet decision-making and foreign policy is a subject that in itself deserves book-length treatment, the most important points for this study can be made very briefly as follows. Analyses in the 1950s and the early 1960s were usually agreed that the monopoly of power wielded by the CPSU and its core, the Politburo, contributed to a high degree of centralization in decision-making and facilitated a careful subordination of means and foreign policy tactics to strategic objectives. However, without being aware of the conceptual difficulty involved, it was argued at the same time that Soviet domestic politics is a 'battlefield' of personal power struggles in which victors 'triumph', enemies are 'scattered' or 'crushed' and supporters of alternative policy courses 'doomed' from the very beginning.[60] As late as 1965 it was argued that: 'In a very important sense the subordination of Soviet interests abroad to the demands of domestic power struggle is only a special case of the more general practice of Soviet leaders of making policy a pawn in personal contests.'[61] Hence the possibility existed in the minds of many analysts (and still exists today, as will be shown by reference to the Berlin crisis of 1961) that 'an individual contestant in the power struggle may see his only hope for victory in taking a desperate step which would jeopardize the existence of the Soviet system, or even the peace of the world'.[62]

Whereas the first view implied that foreign policy is basically a process conforming to requirements of rationality in decision-making, the latter considered foreign policy as an outcome of irrational or nonrational processes. Only in the course of the 1960s was there a sharpening of awareness as to the fundamental difference of the concepts involved.

Nevertheless, on the basis of this sharpened awareness it is still being asserted that: 'The dominant feature of bureaucratic politics in the Soviet Union is the continuous "struggle for power".'[63] And in detail:

> An occupant's position in the central game is always uncertain ... Members of the Politburo and the Central Committee are aware of the historical tendency for one man to become preeminent. Thus while a central problem of life for the leader is managing to stay on top, a large part of the problem for Politburo members is how to keep the leadership collective. This fact yields a relevant proposition: policy issues are inextricably intertwined with power plays.[64]

Implied in this image, which in turn is influenced by Kremlinological analysis, is the axiom, 'where you stand depends on where you sit'. But this is precisely what Ploss is attacking when he writes that one of the pitfalls 'to be avoided is the foregone conclusion that a topmost leader's adherence to any one of the major apparatuses of Soviet rule presupposes his orientation as a "world revolutionist" or a "coexistence man"'.[65]

All this is closely related to a third level of analysis – the evolution of the Soviet system and its implications for Soviet risk-taking. Certainly one cannot go wrong with this proposition: 'The attitude towards risk depends upon the needs of the system making the decisions.'[66] This will undoubtedly remain a timeless truth. But what sort of a system is the Soviet system, what are its needs, how have they developed over time, and what is the result in terms of behavior? Liberal and 'liberal' Marxist opinion in the 1950s adhered to the optimistic assumption that industrialization 'tends to awaken the democratic aspiration of the masses'[67] and would lead to a more open system that, with increasing differentiation, increasing pragmatism and increasing rationality, would be inclined to become saturated and status quo-oriented. Whether or not these tendencies exist is doubtful. But even if *some* of the elements apply, they may work at cross-purposes. Dallin writes:

> If the tendency to make better use of specialists has made for greater competence and improved information – that is, has made for greater rationality – the contending pressures of narrower self-interest expressed in occupational groups tend to make politics, on the contrary, a more irrational [nonrational, according to the distinctions used in this book] product of these rival forces.[68]

The undoubtedly greater differentiation of the Soviet system today as compared, say, to the Stalinist system in the 1930s and 1940s has given much validity to analyses focusing on the influence of interest groups of sorts in the Soviet context and on processes of bureaucratic politics. However, to some analysts this tendency has gone far enough. Gallagher and Spielmann write:

> In the issue of centralization versus particularism, the latter has received much more attention by students of the Soviet Union since Stalin's death. In part this attraction for the pluralistic rather than the monistic features of Soviet society can be ascribed to the fashions of political science.[69]

What is evidently needed – as regards the analysis of Soviet foreign policy – is a sensible combination of decision-making theory with strategic analysis. This is one of the purposes underlying the research procedure in the empirical part that is to follow. Overall the two case studies look at all four of the above-mentioned factors shaping Soviet crisis behavior (ideology, political, economic and other interests, military power and domestic politics) and they try to identify the working of dynamic characteristics and operational principles of such behavior.

Notes: Part One, Chapter 5

1   Chapter IX of Jan F. Triska and David D. Finley, *Soviet Foreign Policy* (New York and London: Macmillan/Collier Macmillan, 1968), pp. 310–49.

2   ibid., p. 337. The authors do not state explicitly whether their table IX–4 concerning the bidding of participants in crises is based on the opinion of the expert judges. However, this is the impression conveyed as no other procedure for arriving at the table was explained.

3   Table IX–3, p. 340. It is not clear whether it was because of the embarrassment of such a result or whether it is due to a printing mistake that in the enumeration of the eleven most risky crises, number 7 (Berlin, 1958) is *not* followed by number 8 (Berlin, 1961), but by number 9 (Suez, 1956) (ibid., p. 339).

4   ibid., p. 347.

5   ibid. (my italics).

6   ibid. (my italics).

7   The reference is to the following studies by Nathan Leites: *The Operational Code of the Politburo* (New York: McGraw-Hill, 1951); *A Study of Bolshevism* (Glencoe, Ill.: The Free Press, 1953) and the later, revised, version, *Kremlin Moods*, RM-3535-ISA (Santa Monica, Calif.: Rand Corporation, 1964).

8   Alexander L. George, 'The "operational code": a neglected approach to the study of political leaders and decision-making', in Erik P. Hoffman and Frederic J. Fleron, Jr (eds), *The Conduct of Soviet Foreign Policy* (Chicago, Ill., and London: Aldine-Atherton/Butterworth, 1971), pp. 165–90.

9   ibid., pp. 171–2.

10   ibid., p. 181.

11   ibid., p. 182.

12   This is a condensed and slightly modified summary of a number of propositions presented by Alexander George in various contexts in 'The "operational code"', pp. 180–4.

13   Richard Pipes, 'Some operational principles of Soviet foreign policy', in Michael Confino and Shimon Shamir (eds), *The USSR and the Middle East* (Jerusalem: Israel University Press, 1973), p. 6. The points made in Pipes's article were submitted to the US Senate Subcommittee on National Security and International Operations, and they are restated in his 'Operational principles of Soviet foreign policy', *Survey*, vol. 19, no. 2 (Spring 1973), pp. 41–61.

14   Pipes, 'Some operational principles', p. 7.

15   ibid., p. 22.

16   ibid., p. 11.

17   loc. cit.

18   ibid., p. 22.

19   Zbigniew Brzezinski and Samuel P. Huntington, *Political Power: USA/USSR* (New York: Viking Press, 1965), p. 38.

20   Pipes, 'Some operational principles', pp. 20–1.

21   ibid., p. 12.

22   ibid., p. 23.

23   This is the opinion expressed by the *New York Times* in early 1979 in the context of Soviet reactions to the upheavals in Iran, as quoted by Francis Fukuyama, 'A new Soviet strategy', *Commentary* (October 1979), p. 52.

24   James M. McConnell and Bradford Dismukes, 'Soviet diplomacy of force in the Third World', *Problems of Communism*, vol. 28, no. 1 (January–February 1979), p. 26.

25 ibid.
26 Jerry F. Hough and Merle Fainsod, *How the Soviet Union is Governed* (Cambridge, Mass.: Harvard University Press, 1979), p. 263.
27 Pipes, 'Some operational principles', p. 9.
28 Alexander Dallin, 'Domestic factors influencing Soviet foreign policy', in Confino and Shamir (eds), *The USSR and the Middle East*, p. 41; this article is a restatement of his arguments in 'Soviet foreign policy and domestic politics: a framework for analysis', *Journal of International Affairs*, vol. 23, no. 2 (1969), pp. 250–65.
29 This is the rationale of the title of Dallin's article, 'Soviet foreign policy and domestic politics: a framework for analysis'.
30 Dallin, 'Domestic factors', p. 32.
31 Dallin, 'Soviet foreign policy', pp. 258 and 263. Despite the strong statements about pluralism (in 1969) his later views (in 1973) seem to represent a falling-back on that point when he merely acknowledges that: 'Though it is perhaps too soon to be sure, it is likely that the traditional Leninist compulsion to totalism is withering' (Dallin, 'Domestic factors', p. 41).
32 Dallin, 'Domestic factors', p. 32.
33 William Zimmerman, 'Soviet foreign policy in the 1970s', *Survey*, vol. 19, no. 2 (Spring 1973), pp. 193–4; this theme is also expressed in his article, 'Elite perspectives and the explanation of Soviet foreign policy', *Journal of International Affairs*, vol. 15, no. 1 (1970), pp. 84–98, and in his book, *Soviet Perspectives on International Relations: 1956–1967* (Princeton, NJ: Princeton University Press, 1969).
34 Zimmerman, 'Elite perspectives', p. 27.
35 'Doctrine and events in Soviet foreign policy', in Triska and Finley, *Soviet Foreign Policy*, p. 125.
36 James McConnell and Anne M. Kelly, 'Super-power naval diplomacy: lessons of the Indo-Pakistani crisis 1971', *Survival*, vol. 15, no. 6 (November/December 1973), pp. 293–4.
37 Robin Edmonds, *Soviet Foreign Policy 1962–1973: The Paradox of Super Power* (London: Oxford University Press, 1973), pp. 2, 6 and 153. See my review in *Soviet Studies*, vol. 28, no. 2 (April 1976), pp. 301–3.
38 W. W. Kulski, *The Soviet Union in World Affairs: A Documented Analysis, 1964–1972* (Syracuse, NY: Syracuse University Press, 1973), reviewed by me in *Survival*, vol. 16, no. 4 (July/August 1974), pp. 201–2.
39 Kulski, *The Soviet Union in World Affairs*, p. ix.
40 ibid., p. 24.
41 ibid., p. 80.
42 ibid., p. 212.
43 loc. cit.
44 ibid., p. 21.
45 Kulski writes: 'An ever increasing conflict exists between the ideology professed by the regime and the practical needs of the state – or national interests' (ibid., p. 20).
46 The term 'balance of interests' is used by Osgood in reference to the Cuban missile crisis, in Robert E. Osgood and Robert W. Tucker, *Force, Order and Justice* (Baltimore, Md: Johns Hopkins University Press, 1967), p. 156. For a good discussion of this point see Phil Williams, *Crisis Management: Confrontation and Diplomacy in the Nuclear Age* (London: Martin Robertson, 1976), pp. 155–64.
47 Marshall D. Shulman, 'What does security mean today?', *Foreign Affairs*, vol. 59, no. 4 (July 1971), p. 613.
48 Brezhnev in his report to the Twenty-Fifth Party Congress on 24 February 1976, *Pravda*, 25 February 1976.
49 Walter Z. Laqueur, *The Struggle for the Middle East: The Soviet Union in the Mediterranean, 1958–1968* (New York: Macmillan, 1969), p. 160.
50 Andrew J. Pierre, 'America down, Russia up: the changing political role of military power', *Foreign Policy*, vol. 4 (Fall 1971), p. 183.
51 Dallin, 'Domestic factors', pp. 51–2.
52 Triska and Finley, *Soviet Foreign Policy*, p. 347.
53 This was argued by Brzezinski in 'USA/USSR: the power relationship', *International Negotiation. The Changing Strategic Balance: Some Political Implications*, Memorandum for the Subcommittee on National Security and International Operations of the Committee on Government Operations, US Senate (Washington: Government Printing Office, 1972), p. 9, as quoted by Phil Williams, *Crisis Management*, p. 157.

54   Williams, *Crisis Management*, p. 158.
55   Shulman, 'What does security mean today?', p. 617.
56   Triska and Finley, 'The Soviet Union: reckless or cautious?', in *Soviet Foreign Policy*, p. 347. I find it difficult to understand what is meant by the sequel to this quotation: 'Khrushchev was simply more sophisticated, and more aware of and better skilled in employing a risk-reducing emergency strategy mechanism coupled with the initial risk action.'
57   Wolfe, *Soviet Power and Europe*, p. 95, fn. 99.
58   Vernon V. Aspaturian, *Process and Power in Soviet Foreign Policy* (Boston, Mass.: Little, Brown, 1971), pp. 74–5.
59   Matthew P. Gallagher and Karl F. Spielmann, Jr, *Soviet Decision-Making for Defense: A Critique of US Perspectives of the Arms Race* (New York: Praeger, 1972), p. 27.
60   Edward Crankshaw, *Khrushchev: A Career* (New York: Viking Press 1967), pp. 207, 239 and 245.
61   John A. Armstrong, 'The domestic roots of Soviet foreign policy', in Hoffmann and Fleron (eds), *The Conduct of Soviet Foreign Policy*, p. 55 (reprinted from an article written in 1965).
62   ibid., p. 58.
63   Allison, *Essence of Decision*, p. 182.
64   ibid.
65   Sidney I. Ploss, 'Studying the domestic determinants of Soviet foreign policy', in Hoffmann and Fleron (eds), *The Conduct of Soviet Foreign Policy*, p. 89.
66   Morton A. Kaplan, *System and Process in International Relations* (New York: Wiley, 1957), p. 208.
67   Isaac Deutscher, as quoted in Daniel Bell, 'Ten theories in search of reality: the prediction of Soviet behavior'. Bell's article was published in 1958; quoted here from Aspaturian, *Process and Power*, p. 296.
68   Dallin, 'Domestic factors', pp. 52–3.
69   Gallagher and Spielmann, *Soviet Decision-Making for Defense*, p. 23.

PART TWO
Case Studies

6

Interpretations, Ambiguities and Questions

Vision and perhaps even planning is implied in Stalin's dictum of April 1945, 'This war is not as in the past; whoever occupies a territory imposes his own social system'.[1] However, to accept this view would be giving too much credit to Stalin's foresight as well as endowing events with a false sense of historic inevitability. In particular, close examination of Soviet policy in 1948 produces little evidence indeed to show that Stalin was aware of the dynamism which the first major East–West crisis would unleash, or that he had a clearly mapped-out plan for the future of Germany, or that he could have foreseen, or even desired, the preservation of a complex state of affairs later rightfully to be called abnormal. Berlin in 1948, as well as Germany as a whole, represented one of the many gray international areas of undetermined status and allegiance, thus providing the potential to change normal adversary relations into a crisis with unpredictable consequences.

The Berlin Blockade: a Defensive Measure?

If one could rely on Soviet interpretations of the origin and dynamics of the 'so-called Berlin crisis' matters would be quite straightforward and simple. 'International complications' arose solely because of a provocative overreaction by the United States and its allies. This view of the course of events is based on the euphemistic form in which the blockade was announced – if indeed it is legitimate to speak of any announcement at all. On 12 June, five days after the Western powers had made public their plan to create a West German state (London recommendations), the Elbe autobahn bridge was merely said to be 'closed for repairs'.[2] On 23 June, the day when the Western currency reform was extended to the Western sectors of Berlin, traffic along the rail lines between the three Western zones and Berlin was stopped and the same innocuous rationale was invoked.[3] The official paper of the Soviet military administration in Germany, *Tägliche Rundschau*, did not even hint at the *fait accompli* of a blockade but explained:

> According to informed sources, the technical difficulties on the Berlin –Helmstedt railroad line, which have already been announced, are much more serious than originally believed.

Therefore, it is difficult to say at the present time when the passenger and freight service, which has been suspended in both directions, can be resumed.[4]

The statement of the problems in technical terms implied that the 'traffic restrictions', although clearly inconvenient to the West, were 'only of a temporary nature' – a theme repeatedly advanced by Soviet officials.[5] In his letter to General Robertson therefore, the head of the SMA, Marshal V. D. Sokolovsky, estimated that the duration of the restrictions would only be 'several weeks'.[6] Hence the Soviet rationale of 'much ado about nothing'.

The second major line of interpretation and justification is economic. The Khrushchev-era version of *A Short History of the USSR* sums up these arguments as follows:

On June 20, 1948 [18 June is the correct date] a secretly prepared money reform was suddenly announced in the three Western Zones. The devalued old German marks instantly flooded Eastern Germany, creating a danger to its economy.
The Soviet occupation authorities were compelled to take urgent measures. To block off currency profiteers all vehicles and passengers arriving from Western Germany were thoroughly checked.[7]

This account merely echoes the statements of Marshal Sokolovsky as formulated in his letter to General Robertson. Sokolovsky wrote on 29 June, 'I would like to assure you that your opinion regarding the restrictions of movements of the German population is correct', that they are of a 'temporary nature and taken *for the protection of the currency* of the Soviet zone'.[8]

It is consistent with both explanations that the notion of a blockade continues to be strictly denied by Soviet political leaders, commentators and historians. Even Khrushchev, when he assured the West some weeks before the August 1961 crisis that 'there will be no blockade of West Berlin',[9] still did not acknowledge officially that there had ever been one. The closest Soviet bloc commentators have ever come to the idea of a blockade is that of a 'self-blockade'. In the later view of two East German authors, the 'imperialist forces' in 1948

de facto organized a self-blockade by not only rejecting all offers by the SMA and the DWK [German Economic Commission in East Berlin] to take over the supply system for all of Berlin, but also by trying to prevent the population from buying goods in the Eastern part of the city.[10]

This idea, that there was no blockade because the SMA 'offered to supply food to West Berlin' while the 'Western occupation authorities rejected the offer' and chose to 'manufacture' a crisis, is supplied elsewhere and frequently.[11]

Beyond (or behind) the rationale of technical difficulties and currency problems, there is a third, much more comprehensive theme advanced by Soviet spokesmen. This theme is political and speaks of 'self-defense' and the 'safeguarding of Soviet security interests'. The communiqué of the Foreign Ministers' Conference of the Soviet Union, Albania, Bulgaria,

Czechoslovakia, Yugoslavia, Poland, Romania and Hungary, held in Warsaw from 23 to 24 June 1948, for instance, mentioned the currency issue only in passing. The main subject was the general line of the Western allies' policy toward Germany as expressed in the London agreement of 7 June. By their announced plans for the merger of the three Western zones and the projected creation of a separate West German state, the United States, Britain and France had 'complete[d] the division and dismemberment of Germany'; they had 'encourage[d] German revanchist elements' and 'subordinate[d] the economy of Western Germany to the aims of the USA and Britain'; they had acted in an 'anti-democratic spirit' and, last but not least, committed a 'gross violation of the Yalta and Potsdam agreements'.[12]

Broader political issues were also advanced by Stalin and Molotov in their discussions with the three Western ambassadors in Moscow in August. The Soviet leaders reemphasized the point made in an earlier Soviet note (14 July) that the conversations regarding Berlin were of 'no useful purpose except within the framework of conversations regarding all of Germany'.[13] According to the account by Walter Bedell Smith, US ambassador to the Soviet Union and a participant in the Moscow discussions, Stalin made it clear 'in no uncertain terms' that the Western powers had 'forfeited their right to occupy Berlin' by their introduction of a new currency in Berlin and by their 'decision to set up a Western German government at Frankfurt'. Stalin then developed the argument that the communications restrictions in Berlin were a measure of 'self-defense' by the Soviet government because of the actions of the Western powers to which he had referred.[14]

In Soviet interpretations, then, there is a threefold mixture of recognizable origins of the Berlin crisis: (1) technical difficulties; (2) the safeguarding of the financial and economic viability of the Soviet zone; (3) self-defense against 'the creation of a militaristic state' in Western Germany and 'its inclusion in the military alliance of the USA, England and France'.[15]

Revisionist historians in the West have accepted substantial elements of the Soviet version of the Berlin crisis. Joyce and Gabriel Kolko write: 'The United States would let nothing keep it from dividing Germany – and Europe – in two . . . In every meaningful sense, it was the United States that destroyed the Control Council.'[16] The United States, they argue, invented the crisis over Berlin to frighten Congress into accepting the Truman administration's warlike views. 'The blockade had proved an always available but manageable crisis for recalcitrant domestic and foreign politicians alike; it conjured up a sufficiently ominous Soviet presence.'[17]

While these interpretations of the Berlin crisis as manufactured artificially by the West for its own convenient purposes are shared only by few Western analysts, the argument of 'defensive measures' has received more widespread support. George F. Kennan, for example, writes in his memoirs that the two events that 'threw official Washington into such a dither' – the 'consolidation [sic] of Communist power in Czechoslovakia' and the 'attempt by the Russians to force the Western Allies out of Berlin' – were 'defensive reactions' on the Soviet side to the initial success of the Marshall Plan and to the preparations to set up a separate German government in Western Germany.[18] Like the communist-inspired strikes in France and Italy in 1947, they represented Moscow's attempt 'to play, before it was too late, the various political cards it still possessed on the European continent'.[19]

There is one important point which advocates of the theory of deliberate exaggeration of the Soviet threat and creation of an artificial crisis in Berlin may now quote in their support. In his edition of the several hundred cables and letters sent by General Lucius D. Clay, the US military governor in Germany, from Berlin to Washington, Jean Edward Smith writes that the primary purpose of Clay's often-quoted cable of 5 March 1948 to General Chamberlin, Director of Intelligence of the General Staff of the US Army, that war 'may come with dramatic suddenness', was to assist the military chiefs in their congressional testimony; Clay's cable, in Smith's view,

> stands in sharp contrast with his many other cables of that period, for in point of fact Clay was advising Washington of exactly the opposite. That Washington chose to publicize that one phrase . . . and to play down the dozens to the contrary, will have to be evaluated anew.[20]

Soviet 'Aggression' and 'Expansionism'

In sharp contrast to the main theme of Soviet and Western revisionist interpretations most Western analysts have put the Berlin crisis into the general context of what Thomas Wolfe has called an 'aggressive phase of Soviet policy in the Zhdanovist period'.[21] Malcolm Mackintosh, another Western specialist on Soviet affairs, agrees with this view and speaks of a Soviet political offensive in Europe in 1948.[22] In much the same vein Adam Ulam writes about a general 'pushfulness' of Stalin's foreign policy after the war, of an 'aggressive Soviet posture between 1945 and 1950'; the Soviet leaders, encouraged by their success in retaining control over the areas reached by their armies in Europe, were carrying on the momentum of expansion culminating in the Berlin crisis as an act of 'semi-aggression'.[23]

Western leaders, who had to make decisions on the basis of *ad hoc* interpretations of Soviet foreign policy, shared the concern about a general Soviet offensive and thin borderlines between Soviet risky political initiatives and actual military conflict. The British Foreign Minister, Ernest Bevin, saw as one of the root problems of the Berlin crisis the 'insistence on Soviet predominance in Germany'.[24] President Truman, Senator Vandenberg and other American officials and political leaders are on record with similar interpretations.[25]

Taking into account the broad divergencies of interpretation, encompassing the official Soviet views on one extreme and the views of American and British decision-makers on the other, it is difficult to arrive at a 'correct' explanation. But beyond this lie still other, more specific, problems of interpretation concerning the possible determinants of Soviet behavior in the Berlin crisis.

Contextual Factors of Soviet Behavior

In 1947 and 1948 agitated controversies took place in the Soviet Union concerning the nature of capitalism and imperialism, and the relationship between the two opposed social systems. These *ideological discussions* may have theoretical as well as practical significance for Soviet risk-taking in the Berlin crisis. It may make a difference for policy direction whether ideology proclaims 'fundamental changes in the correlation of forces between the two systems' in favor of socialism (as evident, for instance, in the 'growth of power authority and influence of the Soviet Union', the 'establishment of the People's Democracies', the 'evolution of the national liberation movement', the 'development of contradictions in the strongest capitalist country, the United States of America' and a sharpening of the 'general crisis of capitalism');[26] or whether the 'shift in the correlation of forces' is not as far-reaching, the assumed 'crisis of capitalism' not as deep and its 'collapse' not as imminent as so often predicted – a position advocated most forcefully by Eugene Varga, who in 1948 was still an important member of the Institute of Economics at the USSR Academy of Sciences. (He acknowledged, for instance, that 'the function of the state as an instrument for the enrichment of the finance oligarchy may in certain instances come in conflict with its function as an institution for national defense';[27] capitalism, in his view, is adaptable and the bourgeois state capable of planning and taking an active role in the economy.)[28]

What follows easily from the first set of ideological formulations (the relative weakness of the adversary) for policy is to seize the opportunities of the moment and attempt to tilt the correlation of forces even further in the direction of socialism. Conversely the second series of ideological assertions (appreciation of the relative strength of capitalism) requires a greater degree of caution.

Reconstruction of the predominant ideological line is important also because the nature of imperialist contradictions, in Leninist ideology, is closely linked with the probability of war of three types – 'war between two imperialist camps' (like World War I); 'war between two imperialist groups historically coinciding with a just war of a socialist state and the toiling masses of fascism, as was the case in World War II'; or, finally, 'war of the imperialists against a socialist state, or a group of such states'.[29]

What matters also is the degree of social, economic and political differentiation recognized by Soviet ideological perceptions. Whether or not it is possible to form alliances with noncommunist, progressive elements, cooperate with newly independent countries in Asia, utilize nationalism and neutralism in Europe, encourage local parties to pursue a parliamentary road to socialism and cooperate economically with developed capitalist countries – only the answers to all these questions give concrete meaning to the ambiguous term 'peaceful coexistence'. It is these concrete answers which also establish a general ideological framework for risk-taking, and it is fair to assume that local actors – like the Soviet military administration in Germany and the German communists in the case at issue – will act not only according to specific instructions from the center but also in conformity with the general ideological and political framework.

Risk-taking, at least that of the rational variety, is closely related to the pursuit of a variety of *interests*. But what were the interests of the Soviet Union which were affected in the Berlin crisis? Was the Berlin crisis a lever to achieve larger political objectives, was Berlin in itself the prize of risk-taking, or is it correct to say that 'From the Soviet point of view, Berlin was both a lever and a prize'? [30] Regarding the first view, that of Berlin as a lever, it is interesting to note that at the conference of the four military governors near Potsdam on 3 July Marshal Sokolovsky stated that the traffic restrictions would continue until the Western allies 'had abandoned [their] plans for a West German Government'. [31] For the theory that Berlin was used as a lever also speaks Stalin's and Molotov's position, adopted during the Moscow discussions in August 1948 (as mentioned above), that conversations regarding Berlin were not practical except within the framework of conversations regarding all of Germany; it is supported also by the conviction of Walter Bedell Smith, the chief American negotiator at the talks in Moscow, that 'we could have produced an agreement in fifteen minutes at any time by an offer to abandon the London decisions'. [32]

There is also an important economic aspect to the issue of leverage. In late 1947, as the former US Secretary of State, Byrnes, recalls, Molotov responded to a question about the 'real Soviet motives in Europe' that he (Molotov) 'was willing to give up practically anything else' in order to get a quadripartite arrangement on the Ruhr. [33] In its note of 14 July 1948 the Soviet government complained that 'such a very important center of German military industry as the Ruhr district has been taken out from under the control of the four powers'. [34] And again, during the Berlin discussions in Moscow in August, the Soviets mentioned the Ruhr repeatedly. [35] Both aspects, the political and the economic, may complement each other. They may be seen as parts of the manipulation of risk, using Berlin as an instrument to force Western concessions on the political and economic orientation of Germany as a whole.

However, there is also the interpretation of Soviet risk-taking for the purpose of gaining Berlin as a *prize*, which can be made equally persuasive. For instance, Alexander Werth – a former British correspondent in the Soviet Union – writes that: 'Having accepted the *fait accompli* of a separate Western Germany, the Russians tried to put an end to the Berlin "anomaly" with their 1948 blockade of the former Reich capital.' [36] The starting point for such a view would be Stalin's changes of policy and attitudes towards the dismemberment of Germany.

At Tehran, it could be argued, the Soviet government had supported dismemberment of Germany, but already at Yalta Soviet enthusiasm for the scheme had abated. At the time of the German capitulation in May 1945 and during the Potsdam conference the Soviet leaders, with the support of German communists, had posed as the champions of German unity. In what may be an accurate description of Stalin's hopes, Djilas reported that in the spring of 1946 Stalin and other Soviet leaders had asserted that 'all of Germany must be ours, that is Soviet, Communist'. [37] But in January 1948, only a few months before the Berlin crisis, both privately at a dinner and in a meeting with Yugoslav and Bulgarian communists, Stalin had reversed his position and stressed now that Germany would remain divided: 'The West will make Western Germany their own, and we shall turn Eastern Germany into our own state.' [38] If this is indeed a correct portrayal of the evolution of Stalin's views, all of Berlin in 1948 would have to be made 'part of the Soviet occupation zone'. And this is precisely what Moscow and the Soviet military administration in Germany contended during the Berlin crisis.

Concerning the influence of *military* factors on Soviet risk-taking during the Berlin crisis, it is well to remember that the use of military power for political ends is a striking characteristic of Stalin's foreign policy. In contrast to American political leaders, Stalin recognized at an early stage during World War II the potential political advantages that could be derived from advancing the Red Army as far as possible into Eastern Europe, Germany and Czechoslovakia in the West, and into northeast China, Manchuria, Korea and Sakhalin in the Far East. In the latter case, powerful Soviet offensives continued even *after* the announcement of Japanese capitulation. The overriding political steering of military campaigns is reflected also in criticisms made by Soviet generals. In recurring conflicts over saving lives and resources as against making speedy military advances, Soviet generals frequently urged to minimize losses, while Stalin pushed ahead in an attempt to secure as much territory as possible.[39] As a consequence, history received a tremendous kick forward with the help of Russian military boots. Almost everywhere, with the exception of the Soviet occupation zone in Austria, the Soviet military presence was ultimately translated into political control.

Yet during the war there were basically no complications. Stalin's military advances in the West and the Far East were operations without major risks of crisis as defined here. Only the breakup of the wartime alliance led to the emergence of more significant risks for Stalin. The military balance was thus bound to affect Soviet behavior in the Berlin crisis.

The first and foremost question which arises in that context is connected with nuclear diplomacy. Given the American monopoly of nuclear weapons in 1948 why did Stalin risk embarking on a challenge of the United States at all? Was it not to be expected (particularly under the theories expounded by revisionist historians in the West and by academic specialists in the Soviet Union that the atomic weapon was used as a diplomatic tool of pressure and even blackmail against the USSR as early as 1945) that the United States, invoking its nuclear monopoly, would serve an ultimatum to the USSR to reopen at once the communications between Berlin and the Western zones or face serious consequences?

The problem becomes even more puzzling if it is taken into account that among the set of leftist ideological propositions that triumphed in 1948 was also the traditional Leninist thesis of the inevitability of wars. It does not appear wise to communicate to an adversary that one acts under the assumption that war is inevitable, and even less prudent to do so when one happens to be at a significant strategic disadvantage – unless of course there is certainty that the adversary will not exploit his advantage. This in turn not only raises complex questions about the objective military conditions applying in 1948 but also poses a problem as to the likely Soviet perceptions of the political will and determination of the adversary to assert his interests, even if it meant using force.

There are other problems. As noted in the theoretical part, recent trends in political science about the influence of *domestic politics* on foreign policy-making emphasize that rational actor models alone are not adequate to explain decisions, and that attention has to be paid to nonrational factors of decision-making. In the present context, analytical problems are caused by Stalin's personality, by the possibility that Stalin's paranoia led to significant distortions of rationality in foreign policy. Robert Tucker has been an outspoken adherent of this view.[40] Similarly Nathan Leites in his writings notes the specific impact by Stalin and Stalin's personality on the operational code of the Bolsheviks.[41] Alexander George, reconsidering and updating Leites's approach, writes that

> Even before the accentuation of Stalin's paranoid tendencies in later years, idiosyncratic elements of his personality had probably rendered his adherence to the Bolshevik belief system relatively impervious to reality-testing.[42]

Given the appearance of more and more books on Stalin and his personality, is what Marshall Shulman wrote in 1963 still correct today, that 'there is a lingering uncertainty over the extent to which Stalin was paranoid rather than cynical'?[43] Beyond that, although the discussion about bureaucratic and governmental politics and decision-making had not begun in earnest in 1963, we find the view expressed even then that

> It is reasonable to suppose that, even in a dictatorial society, much of what is done in the name of a leader is necessarily the product of a bureaucracy, and may imply any degree of responsibility from his active guidance to his inattention.[44]

This raises the general problem of interrelationships between Stalin's personality and organizational processes in the Stalinist system. While there is little disagreement that Stalinism is characterized by a high degree of centralization in decision-making, controversies still persist as to the likely distortions in the gathering, screening and transmission of information and the implementation of policy.

The Dynamics of Crisis

It is useful to base the analysis of Soviet behavior in international crises on the view that such behavior is not only determined by constant variables, or 'factors' as they are called here, but that it is also a function of the degree of determination and resolve displayed by the opponent, and of Soviet control – or lack of it – over the force of events. Evidently such a protracted crisis as that in Berlin in 1948 cannot but have several phases of development and must make it appear likely that the same event (for example, the blockade, the airlift, or the proposal to send an armed convoy along the autobahn) is of different significance in different phases of the crisis. It will be necessary, therefore, to embark on a workable ordering of events according to stages of development.

It will also be necessary to look more closely at the likely Soviet perceptions and calculations in the crisis. We do know what many Western observers thought. For instance, the chief correspondent of the *New York Times* at the United Nations reported on 30 June that 'It is generally believed that the

Berlin dispute constitutes the most serious clash between the United States and the Soviet Union since the end of the war'.[45] 'I admit', said Frank Howley, the American representative at the allied Kommandatura in Berlin, 'the Russian military maneuvers just outside the city disturbed me as much as they did the Germans. The Russians might very well follow up the blockade by moving into Berlin.'[46] And on 21 July Clay said to Forrestal that he thought the risks ('chances of war') were 'about one in four'.[47] With the benefit of hindsight, we can now say that many of the Western apprehensions were exaggerated. But what were the most likely Soviet perceptions and calculations?

Answering this question is not made easier by curious contradictions in Soviet communications during the crisis and apparent inconsistencies in later Soviet interpretations. As will be shown in the next chapter, a great deal of the (at times very sparse) Soviet coverage of events in 1948 can be summarized by the phrase 'much ado about nothing', and even much later the dramatic aspects of the events are often denied by references to the 'Berlin crisis' or by the qualification of 'so-called'. Perhaps surprisingly in view of these subdued notes, the Institute of History in the 1965 edition of its *Short History of the USSR* states that it was only 'the restraint and skill of the Soviet diplomats that averted a breach of peace in those alarming months'.[48] Other publications speak of an 'adventurist course of unleashing a new world conflict' (with reference to the USA)[49] and admit that the world in 1948 was 'at the brink of war'.[50]

While all this may appear confusing there is more design, purpose and consistency in the verbal communications of 1948 and later interpretations than seems possible at first. However, before entering upon these more complex questions of interpretation it is important to provide a factual background, concentrating on the much neglected aspect of the Soviet role in the evolution of events.

Notes: Part Two, Chapter 6

1 Milovan Djilas, *Conversations with Stalin*, trans. Michael B. Petrovich (New York: Harcourt Brace & World, 1962), p. 114.

2 US Department of State, *The Berlin Crisis: A Report on the Moscow Discussions, 1948* (Washington, DC: Government Printing Office, 1948), p. 4.

3 ibid. The argument of 'technical difficulties' was advanced again when barge traffic was halted; see the TASS report of 10 July 1948, *Pravda*, 11 July 1948. There appears to be no earlier Soviet report of restrictions along the canals.

4 *Tägliche Rundschau*, 25 June 1948, based on a report by the East German news agency ADN of 24 June 1948.

5 Letter of Marshal V. D. Sokolovsky to the British military governor in Germany, General Robertson, of 29 June 1948, *Pravda*, 1 July 1948; see also TASS report of 10 July 1948, ibid., 11 July 1948.

6 ibid., 1 July 1948. SMA stands for Soviet military administration (in Germany).

7 Academy of Sciences of the USSR, Institute of History (ed.), *A Short History of the USSR, Part II* (Moscow: Progress Publishers, 1965), p. 274. For the economic justification of the blockade see also Marshal Sokolovsky's letters to the American military governor in Germany, General Lucius D. Clay, of 20 and 22 June 1948, *Pravda*, 22 and 23 June 1948, and V. G. Trukhanovskii (ed.), *Istoriia mezhdunarodnykh otnoshenii i vneshnei politiki SSSR, Vol. III: 1945–1963* (Moscow: Izdatel'stvo 'Mezhdunarodnye otnosheniia', 1964), p. 221.

 8   *Pravda*, 1 July 1948 (my italics).
 9   N. S. Khrushchev, speech at the Soviet-Vietnamese friendship meeting, 28 June 1961, as quoted in N. S. Khrushchev, *To Avert War: Our Primary Task* (Moscow: Foreign Languages Publishing House, 1963), p. 150; see also *Pravda*, 29 June 1961. Khrushchev made the same point on 8 September 1961, at a Soviet-Indian friendship meeting, ibid., 9 September 1961.
10   Gerhard Keiderling and Percy Stulz, *Berlin 1945–1968: Zur Geschichte der Hauptstadt der DDR und der selbständigen politischen Einheit Westberlin* (East Berlin: Dietz Verlag, 1970), p. 160.
11   *A Short History of the USSR*, p. 274. See also the tenor of *Pravda* articles in late June and early July 1948 and Trukhanovskii (ed.), *Istoriia mezhdunarodnykh otnoshenii*, p. 221.
12   Statement of the Foreign Ministers of the USSR, Albania, Bulgaria, Czechoslovakia, Yugoslavia, Poland, Romania and Hungary, *Pravda*, 25 June 1948.
13   Walter Bedell Smith, *My Three Years in Moscow* (Philadelphia, Pa: Lippincott, 1950), p. 241.
14   ibid., p. 244.
15   Trukhanovskii (ed.), *Istoriia mezhdunarodnykh otnoshenii*, p. 219.
16   Joyce and Gabriel Kolko, *The Limits of Power: The World and United States Foreign Policy, 1945–1954* (New York: Harper & Row, 1972), as quoted by Gaddis Smith, 'The Berlin blockade through the filter of history: visions and revisions of the cold war', the *New York Times Magazine*, 29 April 1973, p. 51.
17   ibid.
18   George F. Kennan, *Memoirs 1925–1950* (Boston, Mass. and Toronto: Little, Brown, 1957), p. 401.
19   ibid.
20   Jean Edward Smith (ed.), *The Papers of General Lucius D. Clay: Germany 1945–1949*, 2 vols (Bloomington, Ill., and London: Indiana University Press, 1974), p. xxviii, and the editorial note to document 340, p. 568.
21   Thomas W. Wolfe, *Soviet Power and Europe: 1945–1970* (Baltimore, Md, and London: Johns Hopkins University Press, 1970), p. 19.
22   Malcolm Mackintosh, *Strategy and Tactics of Soviet Foreign Policy* (New York and London: Oxford University Press, 1962), p. 25.
23   Adam B. Ulam, *Expansion and Coexistence: The History of Soviet Foreign Policy, 1917–67* (New York: Praeger, 1968), pp. 502, 438 and 497.
24   Bevin in the House of Commons, 30 June 1948, *Documents on Germany under Occupation: 1945–1954* (London and New York: Oxford University Press for the Royal Institute of International Affairs, 1955), p. 309.
25   Harry S. Truman, *Memoirs, Vol. II: Years of Trial and Hope* (Garden City, NY: Doubleday, 1956), pp. 120–4; Arthur H. Vandenberg, Jr. (ed), *The Private Papers of Senator Vandenberg* (Boston, Mass.: Houghton Mifflin, 1952), p. 455; John Foster Dulles, *War or Peace* (New York: Macmillan, 1950), pp. 2–3 and 130–1.
26   A. Shneerson, 'Obostrenie obshchego krizisa kapitalizma', *Planovoe khoziaistvo*, no. 4 (July–August 1948), p. 84.
27   In a discussion of an enlarged session of the Learned Council of the Institute of Economics at the Academy of Sciences of the USSR, held from 2 to 5 October 1948, in Moscow, *Voprosy ekonomiki*, no. 9, (1948), p. 57. For details about the Varga controversy and its implications see below, p. 115.
28   This is the argument put forward in Varga's *Izmeneniia v ekonomike kapitalizma v itoge vtoroi mirovoi voiny*, prepared under the auspices of the Academy of Sciences of the USSR (Moscow: OGIZ, 1946).
29   I. Lemin of the Institute of Economics in the discussion cited in note 27, above, *Voprosy ekonomiki*, no. 9 (1948), p. 60.
30   Walter Phillips Davison, *The Berlin Blockade: A Study in Cold War Politics* (Princeton, NJ: Princeton University Press, 1958), p. 144.
31   Lucius D. Clay, *Decision in Germany*, p. 367.
32   W. B. Smith, *My Three Years in Moscow*, p. 253.
33   Walter Millis (ed.), *The Forrestal Diaries* (New York: Viking Press, 1951), p. 347.
34   *Pravda*, 16 July 1948.
35   According to Charles E. Bohlen, State Department Counsellor at that time, as quoted in Millis (ed.), *The Forrestal Diaries*, p. 347.

36   Alexander Werth, *Russia, the Post-War Years* (London: Robert Hale, 1971), p. 248.
37   Djilas, *Conversations with Stalin*, p. 153.
38   ibid.
39   See the discussion by Ulam, *Expansion and Coexistence*, p. 387.
40   Robert C. Tucker, 'Stalinism and the world conflict', *Journal of International Affairs*, vol. 8, no. 1 (1954); 'The dictator and totalitarianism', *World Politics*, vol. 17 (July 1965), pp. 555–83; and *The Soviet Political Mind: Studies in Stalinism and Post-Stalin Change* (London: Pall Mall Press, 1963).
41   Nathan Leites, *The Operational Code of the Politburo, A Study of Bolshevism*, and *Kremlin Moods*.
42   Alexander L. George, 'The "operational code"', p. 187.
43   Marshall D. Shulman, *Stalin's Foreign Policy Reappraised* (New York: Atheneum, 1965), p. 261; first published by Harvard University Press in 1963.
44   ibid.
45   As quoted by Young, *Politics of Force*, p. 179.
46   Frank Howley, *Berlin Command* (New York: Putnam, 1950), p. 199.
47   Millis (ed.), *The Forrestal Diaries*, p. 460.
48   *A Short History of the USSR*, p. 274.
49   V. N. Vysotskii, *Zapadnyi Berlin i ego mesto v sisteme sovremennykh mezhdunarodnykh otnoshenii* (Moscow: Izdatel'stvo Mysl, 1971), p. 164.
50   Keiderling and Stulz, *Geschichte Berlins 1945–1968*, p. 150.

7

Evolution of the Crisis: Events, Perceptions, Risks and Stages of Development

It is difficult to find an exact starting point for the sequence of events that was to lead to the full imposition of the blockade of Berlin. Nevertheless the breakup of the Foreign Ministers' Conference, held in London from 25 November to 15 December 1947, was felt to be an important landmark of European history. In the view of contemporary observers the dissolution of the conference without any arrangement to meet again 'left the world anxiously conscious that forces were being arrayed on either side of a gulf which, if means to bridge it were not found in the immediate future, might contain the seeds of a world war'.[1]

The blame for the failure of the London Foreign Ministers' Conference was put squarely on the West by Soviet spokesmen. In a statement to the Soviet press Molotov stated that some progress had been made 'towards reconciling the positions of the four governments'; however, 'the American delegation hurriedly undertook to disrupt the entire work of the London Conference'.[2] Molotov only alluded to some of the major causes of disagreement: (1) reparations, which were presumably one of the unspecified 'various minor matters to which reference has sometimes been made in recent statements' and which called forth Molotov's charge that the United States 'utterly disregards' the interests of states which had suffered from German aggression; (2) the Western demand of free and unlimited movement of resources, commodities, information and people throughout the whole of Germany without regard to zonal barriers, which showed to Molotov that the 'concern [of the Western powers] was for the convenience of foreign export companies selling their goods in Germany rather than for the actual reestablishment of a German state'; and (3) the formation by 31 January 1948 of a provisional German government on a federal level, with two chambers, empowered to draft a constitution to be submitted to the German people for a referendum by 31 March 1949, a proposal that was not discussed publicly by Molotov but rejected in general terms by the allegation that 'The policy of disintegrating Germany finds expression in the Anglo-Franco-American proposal that "all power should be vested in the *Länder*" with the exception of certain minor functions which are to remain within the competence of the central German bodies', and in ambiguous references to the effect that the Western powers wanted to impose unity without the 'active participation of the German people themselves and their progressive democratic forces'.[3]

Reactions and directions for future policy on the Western side emerged in a meeting on 18 December 1947 between, among others, Secretary of State Marshall, Foreign Minister Bevin, General Clay, General Robertson and Robert Murphy of the State Department. The views expressed at this meeting were that the Russians had run up against a 'solid front' (Marshall) and that 'they must now, like us, be thinking hard' (Bevin). The most immediate problem, it was felt, was that of currency reform, and on this issue every effort should be made to secure Soviet cooperation and avoid a final break (Clay, Marshall). But if the Soviet Union did not agree to a central currency reform in Germany by the next session of the Allied Control Council ten days later, the Bizone should go ahead with a separate reform, and if possible the French zone should be included; money for that purpose was already in Germany (Clay). Concerning Berlin, the Western allies would 'obviously have difficulties there but their intention was to put up with minor annoyances and to hold out as long as possible'.[4]

The stalemate at the quadripartite conference in London also provided new impetus to developments which were to end in the creation of a separate West German state. Discussions on this topic took place from 7 to 8 January 1948 in Frankfurt between the British and American military governors on the one hand and the prime ministers of the German *Länder* on the other, resulting in measures such as the strengthening of the German *Wirtschaftsrat* (Economic Council, the forerunner of a West German government); the establishment of German administrative institutions at Bizonal level; and the transfer of British and American staff from remote Berlin to Western Germany to increase efficiency and cooperation in the Bizone. This charter for economic cooperation in the Bizone (the Frankfurt Charter) was begun to be applied on 15 February and to be in full operation by 1 April.[5]

The dilemma facing the United States and Britain was clearly outlined by Clay:

> Anything that we do to strengthen the Bizonal administration will create a hazard with respect to USSR in Berlin. On the other hand, appeasement of USSR will continue the present unsatisfactory administration of Bizonal Germany and make economic reconstruction difficult if not impossible.[6]

But on the side of the Anglo-Americans in early 1948 there was a clear desire to extricate themselves from the unpopular direct military rule in Germany. 'The resentment of the Germans against colonial administration is increasing daily', Clay wrote in late 1947,[7] and at the beginning of 1948 he thought that the internal situation in Germany was 'more tense than at any time since surrender.'[8] Strikes and demonstrations of industrial workers against low food rations took place in January in the Ruhr, later in Bavaria and then spread to the whole Bizone in February embracing several million clerical and other salaried employees.[9] Also in January and February negotiations were being conducted for a treaty of economic and political cooperation among Western European nations (Britain, France and the Benelux countries).

The decisions of the Frankfurt meeting of 7 to 8 January were strongly criticized in the Soviet press and by Soviet officials in Germany;[10] the most ominous statement, however, was published in the paper of the Soviet military administration, *Tägliche Rundschau*, which alleged that the Frankfurt decisions had violated the control system of Germany and that this violation could not persist without having an effect on the status of Berlin.[11] At the meeting of the Allied Control Council of 20 January Marshal Sokolovsky demanded abandonment of the Anglo-American plan for strengthening the economic administration of the Bizone, which he called a new step towards the division of Germany;[12] and in what may be regarded as a counterpart of sorts to the Frankfurt Charter Sokolovsky gave formal effect to a decision of the previous year, establishing a German Economic Commission (DWK) and apparently providing for a greater German role in deciding economic affairs in the Soviet zone.[13]

On the basis of the Frankfurt Charter preparations were made in the West for a conference of Western powers to discuss the formation of a West German government, scheduled to be opened in London on 19 February. In anticipation of this event the Soviet government sent brief formal notes to Britain, France and the United States on 13 February claiming that the holding of the conference would be a 'violation of the Potsdam agreements',[14] and a conference of three Slavic countries – Poland, Yugoslavia and Czechoslovakia – was convened in Prague from 17 to 18 February. The three foreign ministers demanded 'respect for the principles of quadripartite control of the whole of Germany' and 'consultation of Czechoslovakia, Poland, and Yugoslavia and other interested states in questions directly concerning them'.[15] Undoubtedly the conference hoped to influence the French attitude in the London conference.

When the London conference of Western countries began it coincided with the seizure of power by the communists in Czechoslovakia during a cabinet crisis from 17 to 25 February. Even in retrospect it is not possible to establish the precise role of the Soviet Union in the course of events. However, the methods used by the local Communist Party, such as display of armed force, mass demonstrations and action committees, President Beneš's fear that a state of civil war might induce Soviet troops to 'restore order', and the fact that the combination of more or less direct Soviet pressure in conjunction with local Communist Parties had been used successfully elsewhere in Eastern Europe since 1939 convinced many of a large share of Soviet responsibility.[16] No matter whether this was a fair opinion, the communist seizure of power in Czechoslovakia profoundly influenced Western perceptions in the Berlin crisis as the possibility existed that similar tactics, but backed more strongly and directed by Soviet military power, might be used to abolish the Western presence in that city.[17]

There is no doubt that the events in Prague also overshadowed and influenced the negotiations in London and Brussels. The first stage of the London conference, which began as a tripartite meeting between the United States, Britain and France on 23 February, and continued with participation of the Benelux countries from 25 February onwards, ended on 7 March in an agreement of principle concerning (1) the establishment of a federal system of government for Germany; (2) Germany's representation in the European Recovery Program; (3) international control of the Ruhr; (4) closer economic integration of France with the Anglo-American zone; and (5) association of the Benelux countries in policy relating to Germany.[18] The negotiations in Brussels of the same group of countries (except for the United States), which had begun officially on 4 March, were concluded with the formation of the Western European Union on 17 March. The treaty provided for economic and political cooperation of the countries concerned; article IV – clearly with a view to new dangers from the Soviet Union – provided for collective security of the signatory countries against 'armed attack in Europe'.[19]

On the next day (18 March) the Soviet Union completed a network of bilateral Treaties of Friendship, Cooperation and Mutual Assistance in Eastern Europe by signing such a treaty with Bulgaria.[20] Treaties of this type were already in existence with Yugoslavia (April 1945), Poland (April 1945) and Czechoslovakia (December 1945); on 4 February 1948 the first such treaty with a former enemy state was concluded with Romania; Hungary followed suit on 18 February; and after the treaty with Bulgaria had been concluded, pressure was put on Finland to sign also.[21] Thus the movement to organize the respective spheres of influence in Europe in military blocs and to strengthen their military potential gained momentum.

No new elements were contained in the note of the Soviet government dated 6 March 1948, concerning the London conference of Western powers on the German problem. In essence the note reminded the Western powers that the Soviet Union considered the holding of the conference a violation of the Potsdam Agreement and the decisions taken there (in London) invalid, and it repeated at length the Soviet version of how the West had set out to divide Germany as witnessed primarily in the last meetings of the Council of Foreign Ministers.[22] The note, however, completed a phase of gestures, charges and countercharges at the diplomatic level. At the end of March there began a phase of more direct measures specifically aimed at the status of Berlin and the Western presence there. It is a phase in which all the elements of the later blockade are present, though at a reduced level of risk.

Warning Signals of Crisis

The first intimation of the new phase, which was to last through increases and decreases in tension until the imposition of a full blockade, was the dramatic gesture of the walkout of the Soviet delegation from the Allied Control Council on 20 March. The head of the delegation, Marshal Sokolovsky, read a prepared statement to the effect that by refusing to give an account of their separate actions in the Western zones and by failing to disclose the content of the decisions adopted at the secret conference in London the Western powers had brought the agreement for the control machinery in Germany to a standstill. In his words, 'the Control Council for all practical purposes has ceased to exist as an organ of supreme power in Germany'.[23] The meetings of the Coordinating Commissions of the Control Council were suspended, and they too were never to resume.

For the time being, however, the fears that quadripartite control of Berlin through the Kommandatura would also cease to function proved to be premature. What is more, the Soviet commandant, Major General Kotikov, used his position there in an attempt to extend Soviet influence to the whole of the city. On 23 March he 'instructed' the chairman of the Berlin city assembly, Dr Suhr (a Social Democrat), to rule out in the assembly all 'anti-Soviet propaganda'.[24] The threat implied by this action was Soviet control of all political activity in Berlin.

A second, equally ominous, threat appeared on the horizon in the form of reports published in the East German and Soviet press claiming that thousands of hungry people were crossing from the Bizone into the Eastern zone endangering food supplies there; also reported were 'criminal activities of armed bandits' along the borders and the infiltration of spies and saboteurs interfering in the normal development of life in the Soviet zone.[25] The logic inherent in these reports, of course, was that stricter border measures were called for to put a stop to all this.

A third series of measures consisted in the spreading of a mixture of fact and rumor about Soviet preparations for war. Clay confirmed in response to an inquiry from Washington that it was correct that 'Soviet papers have published [a] statement that Soviet dependents are being evacuated from Berlin [on] 1 June', but he doubted whether they would in fact depart. 'It may be just a part of the "war of nerves".'[26] In reference to rumors of Soviet troop movements Clay said that '[Brigadier] General [Walter Wood] Hess [Jr] does report large concentration near Eisenach which commands approach to Dresden–Frankfurt *Autobahn* and what may have some significance first report of heavy pontoon bridge train southeast of Berlin'.[27] Later, the movement of troops, including tank forces and troop concentrations in the area of Berlin were also reported in the Western press.[28]

A fourth, more dramatic and tangible, series of measures concerned access to and egress from Berlin by road and rail. It is on this issue that Soviet pressures were applied most severely, and where the dangers of direct political confrontation, the taking of retaliatory measures and the use of armed force were all anxiously debated in urgent telegrams and emergency meetings in the West. Moreover the background and (shaky) legal basis of Western access to Berlin in 1948 was (and still is?) not widely known. Secretary Royall, for instance, felt obliged to ask Clay at the end of March 1948 whether *he* knew anything about access rights because 'The State Department has not yet located any such information'.[29] It is appropriate, therefore, to provide some detail on this issue.

The only agreement on access rights existing in 1948 was oral and informal. It dates back to a meeting held between, among others, General Clay, Lieutenant General Sir Ronald Weeks and Marshal Zhukov at Zhukov's military headquarters on 29 June 1945.[30] According to the only 'authoritative' record of the proceedings, a memorandum taken by a member of the American delegation, the participants concurred that the British and American forces – the French to be included later – should have the right to use *one road* (the Hanover–Braunschweig–Magdeburg–Berlin autobahn). 'General Clay defended requests for several roads', the memorandum continues, but this was not acceptable to the Russians. Concerning access to Berlin by rail, 'The British agreed not to make further demands for the Hamburg–Berlin railway', and as a consequence also only *one rail link* for use by the Western powers came to be accepted. Even these Soviet concessions were undermined by vague qualifications. The memorandum records:

[Marshal Zhukov stated that it] was apparent that all roads and lanes cut across [the] Russian zone of occupation and due to [the] necessity of protecting these roads and lanes an extremely difficult administrative problem arises.[31]

Discussion of the topic concluded with a comment by 'Marshal Zhukov [who] stated that possibly all points discussed at this conference may be changed'.[32] The Western representatives at the conference apparently did not ask for clarification of what was implied by 'difficult administrative problems' nor did they seem to have inquired about the conditions under which changes in the arrangement on access were to be made.

These changes occurred unilaterally on 31 March 1948, in a letter by General Dratvin, the deputy governor of the Soviet military administration, to the American, British and French chiefs of staff, giving twenty-four hours' notice of 'certain supplementary provisions'.[33]

Deleting some detail and ambiguity the new rules can be summarized as follows: (1) all military and civilian employees of the Western allies and their dependents proceeding by train or car through the Soviet zone of occupation had to present documents certifying that they belonged to agencies of the Western allied military administration in Germany; (2) freight to be carried by rail, belonging to the Western military authorities and intended for shipment *to* the Western zones of Germany, was to be loaded and was allowed to pass only with special authorization by the office of the Soviet commandant in Berlin or the foreign trade administration of the SMA. Apparently no change was contemplated for freight traffic by rail from the Western zones *into* the Soviet zone (which was to be cleared 'on the basis of accompanying documents'), nor did there seem to be, as far as could be gathered from General Dratvin's letter, any change with regard to the customary procedure whereby the papers of German civilians – drivers and passengers in cars and trains, including the separate railway carriage on allied military trains – were examined and at times their belongings searched.

The significance of these measures lay in the question whether the Soviet authorities had the right to determine what persons or goods were allowed to enter or leave Berlin. Once this right was accepted as it applied to passengers and cargo carried by rail, it could be extended to cover all means of transportation.[34]

The American and British response to these measures was to accept the new regime for identification of passengers proceeding by automobile, but to reject the provision of inspection of military passengers and cargo on trains. As a consequence, on 1 April two British trains which had entered the Soviet zone (stocked with rations for several days) were stopped; two American military trains backed out of the Soviet zone. The passenger service by rail to Berlin was suspended, and an airlift for passengers and some outward-bound cargo was instituted in its place.

The SMA had selected the form of pressure on access quite skillfully. As they were in control of the signal system they could, and did, shunt trains into sidings without any use of force. Hence General Clay was forced to summarize the changed situation as it presented itself on 2 April 1948, as follows.

Highway and air traffic conditions are normal today. Civil freight for
Germans moving normally. Military freight into Berlin appears to be
moving normally so far free from attempted search. Passenger trains
not moving in view of Soviet action. Also, no outward movement by
rail of military freight as no loadings can be made without Soviet
permission and this we will not ask.[35]

By 10 April acute problems were becoming clear. Clay explained that there
was 'No interference with German supplies coming into Berlin but basic
motive of Soviet action was to stop all German export from Berlin [by
rail]'.[36] Several weeks later Soviet authorities notified the Magistrat (city
government) of Berlin that new regulations covering German freight by railway for the West were being drawn up, and that until they were brought into
force no further movement of goods would be approved.[37] Thus, the
viability of Berlin (*West* Berlin) was being put into serious jeopardy if it
intended to rely on economic links with Western Germany.

Whereas the 'criminal activity of armed bandits' at the demarcation lines
and the 'mass movement of hungry people' had been used as arguments in
anticipation of the restrictive measures announced by General Dratvin, a
new theme was added after the fact – the large-scale 'pillage' of Berlin by the
removal of industrial equipment and financial assets to the Western zones.
This case was argued in the 2 April meeting of deputy commanders of the
allied Kommandatura by Colonel Yelizarov. He charged that the three Western powers were conniving in this and that they had already removed 300
entire firms.[38] When the Chief of Staff of the SMA, Lieutenant General
Luk'ianchenko, was asked about the reports of industrial removals, he used
the occasion to establish a link between the alleged pillage of Berlin and
access to the city, invoking a broad interpretation of Soviet rights. He argued
that the communications between Berlin and the Western zones of occupation cross the Soviet zone; the maintenance of these links and the regulation
of movements thereon had to be carried out by Soviet military authorities or
agencies empowered by them to act on their behalf; and it was this that
guaranteed 'order' and the 'safeguarding of legality'.[39]

In this way the attempt was being made to erode even further the weak
legal basis of the links between (West) Berlin and the Western zones. General
Hays, in response to General Dratvin's letter of 31 March, had asserted the
right of free and unrestricted utilization of the established corridors
pursuant to the 1945 agreement at Zhukov's headquarters. To this General
Dratvin replied that

I cannot help but consider as a misunderstanding and an error the
statement in your letter that there was some sort of agreement concerning free and unrestricted utilization of [access].[40]

The problems of access to and egress from Berlin, however, were not exhausted by all this.

A fifth indication of increasing pressure, which can be dealt with briefly,
concerned all inland water traffic into or through the Soviet zone. Skippers
were taken off barges and told to get new permits from Soviet authorities in
Berlin.[41]

Sixthly, air access was affected also. Starting on 31 March, Soviet fighter aircraft began making mock attacks on American planes in the air corridor between Western Germany and Berlin. [42] Only a few days after this practice of 'buzzing' or 'frolicking' Western aircraft had begun, a serious air accident occurred. On 5 April a passenger aircraft of British European Airways on the regular service to Berlin, while preparing to land at Gatow Airport, collided with a Soviet fighter aircraft and crashed in the Soviet zone. All persons on board the two aircraft were killed. [43] General Robertson protested against the interference with air traffic in a meeting with Marshal Sokolovsky, and although the latter appeared 'ill at ease and on the defensive' and stated that there was no intention of interfering with any aircraft using the corridor, [44] he did not admit that the presence of the fighter aircraft in the vicinity of the airport without warning was a violation of agreed safety regulations; in fact in a letter on the next day Sokolovsky went on the offensive and charged that the British attempt to represent the air accident as the result of a deliberate attempt on the part of the Soviet pilot 'can only be regarded by me as slander'. What is more, he hoped that in future British planes would obey flight regulations – 'That will release me from the necessity of taking measures to guard flight security over the Soviet zone of Germany, and particularly over Soviet airfields in the Berlin area'. [45]

Approximately one month after Sokolovsky's dramatic walkout from the Allied Control Council, General Kotikov's instruction to the chairman of the city assembly to rule out anti-Soviet propaganda, and the beginning of reports about 'armed bandits along the zonal borders' which had served as justification for the restrictions on access, new threats appeared on the horizon in the form of reports in the Soviet-licensed press in Germany about 'gangsterism' in the Western sectors of Berlin, 'persecution of democratic elements' and their 'deportation' to the Western zones, and the incorporation of former members of the Gestapo into the police force. [46] The alleged persecution of progressive elements was also raised by General Kotikov in the 23 April meeting of the allied Kommandatura where he charged that 40,000 persons had been arrested in the American and British sectors since 1945. [47] Arguments of this kind could, if the need arose, be used to justify measures for the 'restoration of order' in Berlin.

To conclude this account of Soviet pressures *in* Berlin, some more examples can be listed, including the establishment of a Soviet military post with a barrier at a crossroad just inside the British sector, [48] the failure of Soviet authorities to move large quantities of mail, [49] confiscation of industrial equipment of West German firms in the Soviet sector, with a total value of about $8·5 million, on grounds that these firms had been connected with Nazi organizations (which produced the effect of bankrupting several major firms), [50] and last but not least the vicious practice of kidnapping public figures living in the Western sectors. [51]

To conclude the enumeration of Soviet measures concerning *access to* Berlin, the situation as it presented itself on 7 May, and as summarized by Clay, included several more restrictions than the list which he had communicated to Washington about one month earlier.

Some German freight leaves Berlin cleared with Soviet authorities by

Germans. None of our military freight leaves as it requires Soviet permission which I will not request. There is no change in passenger situation except Soviets have also stopped the international train which mainly accommodated French. We have received no reply to our letter stating we were willing to discuss regulations except the right of entry to our passenger trains.

At the moment, we propose no further action and in fact there is little we can do.[52]

In sum, by 18 June – the day of the promulgation of a new currency law in the three Western zones of Germany – all outgoing rail traffic (except for the return of empty cars) and barge traffic and all passenger traffic by rail in and out of Berlin had been stopped; travel on the Autobahn and other roads was permitted only for those passengers who subjected themselves to Soviet check. Thus, 'on the day of the currency reform *there remained by land and water only the one-way movement of food and supplies for the civilian population of Berlin*'.[53] As Robert Murphy – assigned to work in Berlin as civilian adviser to the American military government – was to say in retrospect: 'The Russians certainly gave us plenty of warnings about the Berlin blockade.'[54]

Nevertheless the concentrated account of measures may convey a false sense of drama that for many did not exist. First, 'In a city of 3,250,000, only a small number are affected by the restrictive measures so far', wrote the Berlin correspondent of *The Times* in mid-May 1948; 'German morale, after a sharp fall early in April, has recovered and is probably as good as it ever has been.'[55] Secondly, and this was to be of crucial importance for the more severe measures which the Soviet Union was to adopt later, 'The restrictive measures taken have inconvenienced both the western allies and the Germans, but no vital spot has been touched either administratively or politically'.[56]

Soviet Diplomacy Prior to the Blockade

A similar note of caution is well in place when considering Soviet diplomatic moves immediately prior to the full imposition of the blockade. The fact is that far from accompanying the physical pressure at the local level with vitriolic propagandist barrages, Soviet diplomacy adopted a more conciliatory stance, or at least was sufficiently ambiguous to permit interpretation to that effect. The first such instance was the Soviet – Finnish Treaty of Friendship, Cooperation and Mutual Assistance signed on 6 April 1948. In February and March 1948, when the USSR had begun to bring pressure on Finland for the conclusion of such a treaty,[57] it was assumed that 'the form of [the] pact which the Soviets had in mind for Finland was similar to the pact signed with Hungary this week [in Moscow on 18 February 1948]', that 'such a pact would be a long stride towards the inclusion of Finland within the Soviet system',[58] and that unless the Finnish President went to Moscow there was the strong possibility of a *coup* similar to the one that had occurred in Czechoslovakia.[59] However, when the treaty was signed, it provided for a measure of independence which, in the wake of Finland's defeat and the always present shadow of Soviet power, appeared acceptable to many Finns.

Another indication of moderation appeared on 4 May in the meeting between the American ambassador to Moscow, Smith, and Foreign Minister Molotov. The background to this meeting lay in the significant losses of the Italian Communist Party in the Italian parliamentary elections of 18 April, in which the Christian Democrats won 47·9 percent of the votes against 30·5 percent for the parties of the Popular Front. The election result, attributed in the Soviet press to 'large-scale electoral fraud committed by the Catholic organizations and the Christian Democrats' and to interference by the United States by means of a 'special secret fund' set up to finance anti-communist activity in Italy and elsewhere,[60] in the view of the Acting Secretary of State, Lovett, confronted the Soviet Union with the 'necessity of making a very fundamental decision', either to accept the fact that 'Europe outside the iron curtain has in effect been denied to Communist power' or to 'undertake some spectacular further move designed to recoup the loss of prestige'. In order to discourage the Soviet Union from embarking on the second course of action, Lovett thought it wise to take some initiative, but he clarified: 'What we have in mind is merely a statement of US position and policy and in no sense an indirect bid for agreement or even negotiation at this time.'[61]

In the meeting of 4 May, where this statement of position was delivered, the American ambassador found Molotov 'serious, attentive and courteous. He [Molotov] showed no sign of hostility or antagonism and might even have been described as conciliatory'.[62] Significantly, in the subsequent discussion no reference was made to the German problem or Berlin. On 9 May Molotov called Smith to a meeting where he in turn delivered a similar statement of position from the Soviet point of view; and although Molotov's statement dealt with Soviet-American relations, American 'interference' in Greece and elsewhere, the European Recovery Program, the Brussels Treaty (WEU) and other topics, it too avoided the ongoing six-power conference in London, the German problem and Berlin. Also, in Smith's words, 'No proposal or feelers of a more definite nature were made during subsequent conversation'.[63]

Suspicions about the motives underlying the conciliatory Soviet gestures were fueled, however, when the Soviet Union suddenly, on 10 May, not only made public the very fact of a bilateral Soviet-American meeting, but rendered a distorted picture of the content of the exchanges;[64] published a series of reports from all over the world to the effect that there were 'eager responses' to the Soviet Union's readiness to engage in negotiation, especially among the American public;[65] and featured a letter by Henry Wallace (the candidate of the Progressive Party in the US presidential elections) to Stalin[66] and a response by Stalin suggesting that Wallace's 'program' could serve as a 'good and fruitful basis' for agreement on various aspects of Soviet-American relations.[67]

Nevertheless there are other elements of this Soviet 'peace offensive' of sorts prior to the blockade. In Greece – one of the four countries of most concern to the Anglo-American containment strategy after the communist coup in Czechoslovakia (the other countries being Iran, Turkey and Italy) – the leader of the guerrillas, Markos Vafiades, proposed on 4 June the termination of the civil war and emphatically termed his proposals 'honest', 'peaceful', 'serious' and 'very sincere'.[68] Although this move can be explained largely as the result of the political and military successes achieved by the Greek government forces in the spring of 1948, it can also be seen, as it was at that time, as being 'in line with current Soviet "peace" programs'.[69]

Other ingredients of the 'peace offensive' noted at that time were the easing of propagandist attacks by Communist Parties in the West; some minor concessions on the issue of obtaining a four-power treaty on Austria; and the halving of reparations obligations of Finland, Romania and Hungary, which was heralded by an editorial in *Pravda* as an 'important decision' with significance 'extending far beyond the confines of the relations of the Soviet Union with these states' in that it would 'promote the strengthening of friendly relations between the Soviet Union and other countries'.[70]

Possible Reasons for the Soviet 'Peace Offensive'

In order to provide a meaningful framework for the analysis of the objectives of Soviet policy in the Berlin crisis it is important to abandon the strict enumeration of selected facts at this stage and analyze the possible reasons for the Soviet attitude in April, May and early June 1948. Reviewing the evidence it does not appear that the Soviet Union in this period was planning to take an initiative towards the establishment of political or economic unity of Germany, or that it thought it feasible that the Western powers would agree to a single currency in Germany on the basis of the continued economic and political division of Germany.

In the concrete circumstances of the spring of 1948 the lack of a resourceful and credible initiative for the reestablishment of German unity meant that the Anglo-Americans were going to press ahead with their plans for the strengthening of the political and economic unity of the western parts of Germany. In fact, the London conference of six powers (The United States, Britain, France and the Benelux countries), was resumed on 20 April, ended on 1 June and produced a statement on 7 June, which, in accordance with the agreements in principle reached on 7 March, provided for (1) the rapid establishment of a functioning government in Western Germany comprising all three Western zones. For this purpose a Constituent Assembly was to draw up a constitution – 'a federal form of government which adequately protects the rights of the respective States' – which was to be submitted to the German people in a referendum. (The Constituent Assembly unofficially was projected to convene by 1 September.) (2) International control of the Ruhr to be exerted by the six powers jointly with the purpose of allocating coal, coke and steel as between German consumption and export. (3) Security to be safeguarded *vis-à-vis* renewed German aggression and – presumably with the Soviet Union as a new threat in mind – no general withdrawal of forces from Germany until the peace of 'Europe' was secured.

The problem from the Anglo-American point of view, and conversely the opportunity from the Soviet angle, was the certainty of a hostile reaction to these government recommendations by French parliament and French public opinion, and the ultimate possibility of an outright rejection of the provisions of the London scheme by France. Concretely, the opportunity for Soviet diplomacy was the effective prevention or delay of the planned merger of the Bizone with the French zone and, as it was unlikely that the Germans would go along with a *de facto* dismemberment of the western parts of Germany in addition to the East/West division, also the prevention or delay of a West German government. However, in the face of nationalist agitation by the Gaullists, outright hostility by the communists, and the enticing proposal by Leon Blum to delay the formation of a German government and reopen discussions with the Soviet Union, the Foreign Affairs Committee of the French National Assembly on 9 June supported government policy by 21 to 20 votes. The extremely narrow margin, rather than reassuring Washington and London, gave rise to new apprehensions about the attitude of the National Assembly as a whole. When the vote on the London recommendations was finally taken on 17 June the government of Prime Minister Schuman received the smallest majority it had ever had on a matter where its future was at stake (297 to 289 votes). The road to the formation of a West German government was now clear. Soviet expectations about the prevention or delay of the London scheme via France were defeated. On the next day (Friday, 18 June) a currency reform was announced in the three Western zones.[71]

The Currency Reform and the Blockade of Berlin

If the question were to be asked whether the Soviet Union would have imposed a blockade of Berlin in 1948 if the French National Assembly had rejected the London recommendations, the answer would have to be 'yes' – notwithstanding the importance of the French connection for Soviet policy on the German problem. The reason for this confident answer lies in the curious reversal of a decision by the SMA on the weekend preceding the actual proclamation of the currency reform. Clay reported to Washington that

> At approx[imately] 18.00 hours [Friday] 11 June Soviet auth[orities] advised British Transport Element that eff[ective] immediately no east-bound rail traffic (mil[itary] or civilian) would be accepted through the Helmsted gateway (our only entry point) for Berlin until further notice.[72]

However, only less than twenty-four hours later, on Saturday 12 June at 15.00 hours, Soviet authorities informed the British that all railway traffic, military and civilian, to Berlin would be accepted under normal documentation.[73] Clay's *ad hoc* judgment appears to have been valid when he reasoned: 'It is quite possible that [the] tightening of controls nearing the weekend resulted from Soviet apprehension that western zone currency reform might take place over the weekend.'[74]

While the sudden reversal concerning the stopping of rail traffic can be explained plausibly as having been caused by a false alarm in response to the anticipated currency reform, the SMA proceeded nevertheless with its preparations for a complete blockade by announcing on 13 June that the autobahn bridge over the River Elbe to Berlin would be closed 'for repairs'. The announcement did not mention a detour, but on 14 June the transport administration of the SMA declared that a vehicle ferry would be instituted. On 15 June such a service was indeed provided, but at the same time the closure of the bridge seriously impeded the large-scale transportation of goods by road.[75] The viability of the Western sectors of Berlin now appeared to depend almost entirely on rail transport and barge traffic.

It is appropriate again to abandon at this point the strict account of events and look more closely at the significance of the currency reform as a trigger of the blockade. To begin with, it was clearly recognized at the time that, although the London recommendations did not make explicit reference to currency reform, such a reform was 'not likely to be long delayed' and that 'It is when this step has been taken that a definite Russian reaction to the western programme can be expected'.[76] Clay thought that the move 'to force us from Berlin', if it was to come at all, 'will come when we install [a] separate currency reform'.[77] The reason why this was so is not only because a currency reform is a tangible, dramatic and virtually irrevocable measure of a different order than declarations of intent and 'recommendations' which, depending on the circumstances, may or may not be implemented. It is because of the fact that whichever power in Germany proclaimed a currency reform first immediately forced the other to adopt countermeasures in order to prevent the flooding of its zone by the old Reichsmarks, Rentenmarks and allied military marks, valid in one part of Germany but invalid in another. It is also because of the requirement to prevent the transfer of goods which could have been bought by the sudden inrush of old currency. It is, finally, because of the necessity to decide on the kind of currency to be issued in Berlin – a decision that would determine the question not only of who would control the city economically, but also who would rule it politically.

The problem of currency reform had been under discussion at the quadripartite level for more than two years when the issue was finally 'resolved' in June 1948. As early as May 1946 Clay reported to Washington that currency reform in Germany was 'essential and of immediate urgency'.[78] The reasons why this was so are numerous. They included the large-scale hoarding of stocks (both raw materials and finished products), the socially disruptive activities of the black market, the practice of trading by barter, the disincentives for labor to offer itself to the market and, most of all, rampant inflation and lack of confidence in the Reichsmark. Although the precise impact is difficult to estimate, one of the major contributory causes of inflation and the lack of confidence in the notes in circulation was the fact that in 1945 a duplicate set of plates for the printing of allied military marks had been given to the Russians. Although their printing presses issued currency which was valid in all of Germany, it was impossible to check how much money was printed because, as Clay deplored, 'Agreement to account quarterly for issue of Allied military marks has never been met by Soviet representatives'.[79] Strictly speaking, apart from being an important cause of inflation, the printing of money by the SMA amounted to involuntary economic assistance of the Soviet zone by the Western zones.

In these conditions it was virtually a foregone conclusion that the Western powers would reject the proposal, put forward time and again by Soviet representatives in negotiations about central currency *reform*, that the SMA be issued again a separate set of plates for the printing of currency in Leipzig. Although the USSR offered that such printing be checked by a quadripartite committee, Clay rightly pointed out that such a committee 'could not in fact check the printing of money'.[80] The USSR later changed its mind and agreed in principle to the central printing of new currency under quadripartite control in Berlin.[81] However, the practical details of the agreement were never worked out. This was due less to the technical complexities of the matter than to (1) the fundamental difficulty of arriving at any sort of common agreement about money supply and other issues of monetary policy as long as the veto principle was applied by a quadripartite finance committee; and (2) the basic problem of maintaining one currency in two or more geographical entities with radically different economic and social policies and without free movement of capital and labor.[82]

It is for these reasons that no one, least of all the SMA, could in any way have been surprised by the announcement of a separate currency reform in the Western zones. Nevertheless, Marshal Sokolovsky wrote to the three Western military governors on 22 June that the SMA, 'for political and ethical reasons, did not consider it possible to prepare for a separate currency reform in its zone' and that this was shown by the improvised measure of having to affix special stamps to the Reichsmark and Rentenmark.[83] This description of unpreparedness was later repeated by a Soviet official turned 'historian' at the embassy of the USSR in East Berlin.[84] However, in reference to the meeting of the Allied Control Council of 31 January 1948, a TASS correspondent even then had reported the correct information that the Americans 'already have printed notes for a separate monetary reform in the western zones of Germany'.[85] The expressions of surprise, then, were hardly credible, and the question was not really whether the SMA would follow suit with a currency reform of its own, but when and how and, foremost, whether it would attempt to make its currency valid in the whole of Berlin. There is no doubt that the Soviet Union was attempting to do just that.

The basis for this attempt was the Western decision to *exclude* the Western sectors of Berlin from the currency reform. The assumption was that 'Berlin and surrounding areas [are] so closely related economically,'[86] and that there would be such severe economic difficulties resulting from the simultaneous circulation of two different currencies in one city without a fixed rate of exchange, that it was necessary to have only one currency in Berlin. This was felt so strongly that the American military government was about to commit a fundamental error in the contest over Berlin. Clay sent a cable to Washington in which he stated:

[We] propose when [the] time comes to negotiate with [the] Soviets for monetary union of Berlin with [the] Soviet zone, provided that [the] issue of Soviet mark in Berlin is under Kommandatura agreement and control. This would provide for reaffirmation of existing four-power Kommandatura sovereignty in Berlin. As in [the] case of monetary union between Liechtenstein and Switzerland, sovereignty would not be questioned if such agreement can be obtained.[87]

Apart from the suspicion that the comparison of Switzerland with the Soviet Union leaves something to be desired, the proposal of issuing Soviet marks under four-power agreement is inconsistent with the rejection of a quadripartite committee to 'control' Soviet printing of currency in Leipzig. It is probably because of this and for the valid reason of an anticipated change of monetary control into political control that the State Department thought that the use of Soviet marks as legal tender in the Western sectors was not 'politically advisable'.[88]

To continue with the account of events, the contest for Berlin began in earnest on the weekend of 18 to 19 June, when Colonel Yelizarov declined an invitation to attend the scheduled session of the deputy commandants (which was the prelude to the officially declared end of the Kommandatura as an organ of four-power administration of the city);[89] when the road links to Berlin, including the autobahn, were closed by order of the SMA;[90] when Marshal Sokolovsky issued a 'Proclamation by the Soviet military administration in Germany to the German population' which forbade the introduction of old and new currency from the Western zones into the Soviet zone; and when he applied this measure not merely to the Soviet zone and the Soviet sector of Berlin, but also to the whole of Berlin with the justification that Berlin 'lies in the Soviet zone of Germany and economically forms part of the Soviet zone'.[91]

After an exchange of letters between the American and British military commanders in Germany and their Soviet counterpart,[92] agreement was reached to conduct four-power discussions on the currency problem in Berlin at the level of economic and monetary experts. In the course of these discussions, held on 22 June, the Soviet delegation insisted on *one* currency only for the Soviet zone and the area of Greater Berlin. Moreover the head of the Soviet finance administration in Germany, Maletin, issued a clear and unmistakable threat during these four-power discussions:

> We warn both you and the German population [Maletin said] that we will use economic and administrative sanctions which will enforce the transition to a single currency in Berlin and the currency of the Soviet zone.[93]

By Order No. 111 of the Soviet military administration of 23 June a currency reform was promulgated for the Soviet zone and the area of Greater Berlin to commence on 24 June,[94] and on the same day (23 June) a letter from the Soviet Chief of Staff of the SMA, Lieutenant General Luk'ianchenko, to the acting mayor of Berlin amplified the threat made by Maletin on the previous day. Luk'ianchenko bluntly asserted:

> These measures are necessary since Berlin lies in the Soviet zone, and economically forms a part of it. In future no other currency will circulate in Berlin except the currency of the Soviet occupation zone. Any breach of this order [*sic*] will entail suitable steps by the military authorities.[95]

Nevertheless the commandants of the three Western sectors promulgated an order at 1.30 p.m. on 23 June declaring the Soviet order null and void in the Western sectors. At 8.00 p.m. of the same day provision was made for the introduction of the Deutschmark to the Western sectors of Berlin, to be distinctly marked with a rubber stamp bearing the letter B; whereas non-essential goods were to be allowed to seek such price differential as might develop between the Deutschmark B and the Soviet zone mark, basic food-stuffs, rents and public utilities could be sold in either currency.[96]

Evidently there was still hope left among the Western powers that some degree of economic unity between West Berlin and the Soviet zone could be maintained. However, the time of decision for the Soviet Union had come precisely on that evening of 23 June. It presented itself in the form of two alternatives: (1) to accept that the attempt to incorporate the Western sectors of Berlin into the economic and monetary system of the Soviet zone had failed; or (2) to try to muster more pressure which might ultimately succeed in making the Western presence in Berlin untenable. The latter course of action was adopted. During the night of 23–4 June, by order of Major General Kvashin, chief of the transport department of the SMA, all rail traffic between Berlin and Helmstedt was 'suspended' because of a 'technical disturbance' on that stretch of line.[97] But in practice this meant that, apart from a trickle of motor traffic on minor roads and gradually diminishing barge traffic, all forms of ground communications between Berlin and the Anglo-American zone had been stopped. At the same time (24 June) all electric power flowing from East Berlin and the Soviet zone to the Western sectors of Berlin was cut. Finally, on the same day the SMA sent an order to the central food office of Berlin saying that henceforth no food would be delivered from the Soviet sector to the other sectors of Berlin.[98] The blockade had begun.

Stages and Phases of Crisis: the First Phase[99]

Ordering of the crisis according to phases is a somewhat arbitrary matter depending on subjective judgment. It is largely a matter of degree and blurred transitions rather than clearly recognizable incisions. With this reservation in mind it is appropriate to discern a first phase lasting from 24 June to 6 July, characterized by cautious assessments of the extent and scope of the adversary's determination, by an initial testing of the significance and impact of the blockade, by the formulation of basic positions and responses in the West and in the Soviet Union and by the attempt to resolve the issue locally.

On the Soviet side two platforms of crisis bargaining were produced on the very same day on which the blockade began, one pertaining primarily to the local level, the other to the international level. In Berlin the organ of the SMA in Germany published an article which repeated the by now familiar thesis that Greater Berlin 'lies in the Soviet zone of occupation' and 'economically forms a part of it', and added to this the uncontroversial observation that 'the whole mechanism of joint administration' of Germany and Berlin had collapsed;[100] but it went much beyond the usual invocation of the Soviet position when it added that 'with it [the collapse of four-power administration of Germany and Berlin] lapses any legitimate ground for the continued presence of the American, British and French authorities in Berlin', only to arrive at the *ultima ratio* of the argument namely, that 'the Soviet Military Administration is the only legitimate occupation authority [in Berlin]. As a consequence its orders have the force of law for the whole of Berlin'. [101]

At the international level 'on the initiative of the USSR and Poland', a Foreign Ministers' Conference of Soviet bloc countries was called to take place in Warsaw (23–4 June). A new device of crisis bargaining was thus ushered in in the East – a multilateral conference designed to enhance the legitimacy of risk-taking and to demonstrate the resolve of countries said to be united on common principles. (The transformation of the government in Prague had proceeded far enough to justify the inclusion of Czechoslovakia as a participant, while the open break with Yugoslavia was still four days away and admited of Yugoslavia's participation.) The statement of the eight foreign ministers dealt almost exclusively with the London recommendations (the latter referred to as *resheniia*, that is, decisions) and was directed primarily against the plans for the formation of a West German government with all its implications. No direct link was established between the general assessment of the German problem and the London recommendations on the one hand, and the physical measures already taken at the local level in Berlin on the other. [102] Evidently the Soviet Union did not want to commit the full weight of the Soviet government and that of the other seven countries to measures which, at least officially, were only of 'technical' and 'local' significance.

It is in this way – gradually, physically and at the diplomatic level – that the Soviet Union had constructed its starting position for crisis bargaining. At this stage of the game under conditions of risk it was clearly up to the Western powers to make the next move.

In the West there were no contingency plans to deal with the crisis – a surprising fact considering the persistence of clear warning signals during the months preceding the blockade. An adequate response to the blockade had to be improvised *ad hoc*. But then it was not altogether clear whether some of the technical difficulties would not disappear as suddenly as they had appeared, as had happened for instance on the weekend of 11–12 June. In a reference to one of Sokolovsky's statements even Clay found 'little lead to what their [the Russians'] next move will be'. [103] But at the same time Clay was convinced that firmness, including the dispatch of an armed convoy to Berlin, would be the correct remedy to adopt. 'It is our view here', he said as early as 27 June, 'that they [the Russians] are bluffing and that their hand can and should be called now.' [104] Robert Murphy of the State Department, acting as Clay's political adviser in Berlin, shared this opinion about calling the Soviet bluff. [105] However, this view did not prevail in Washington.

At a high-level meeting of the Departments of State and Defense and the Joint Chiefs of Staff on 28 June the options available to the United States were summarized as follows. (1) Decide now 'to withdraw from our position in Berlin'; (2) decide at this time 'to retain our position in Berlin by all possible means . . . accepting the possibility of war as a consequence if necessary' and (3) 'To maintain our unprovocative but firm stand in Berlin, utilizing first every local means, and subsequently every diplomatic means.' [106] The president on the same day decided on the third alternative saying that the United States was 'going to stay [in Berlin]. Period.' [107] But this decision meant very little in practice as no concrete steps were outlined as to how to cope successfully with the blockade if it continued. The preference for avoiding a provocative stand meant that no physical action was contemplated to break the blockade by force. It appears that there was an optimistic feeling that somehow things would take care of themselves. Surprisingly they did.

The *deus ex machina* was a decision taken at the local level on the very first day when the blockade began. In the morning of 24 June Clay asked Lieutenant General Curtis LeMay, commander of the United States Air Force in Europe, to place the entire fleet of C-47 aircraft at the disposal of an emergency service to Berlin and to make available as many other transport aircraft as possible. [108] Clay estimated that 500 tons of supplies daily were needed for the allied forces in Berlin, 2,000 tons a day for normal food supplies of the German population and 4,000 tons for the operation of the economy of the Western sectors of Berlin at a minimum level. [109] On 27 June he expected that 'With this airlift, we should be able to bring in 600 or 700 tons a day'. [110] This was no more than about one third of the daily food requirements of the German population. Hence the airlift was not conceived of as a solution, and no one seriously suggested it. The advantage seen initially was that such an airlift, though inadequate as a sustained operation, 'will substantially increase the morale of the German people and will unquestionably seriously disturb the Soviet blockade'. [111]

At the same time attempts were being made locally to achieve the reopening of communications between Berlin and the Western zones, first in a letter by General Robertson to Marshal Sokolovsky on 26 June, demanding the restoration of normal traffic. [112] To this Sokolovsky replied on 29 June with a letter which was conciliatory in tone, ambiguous as to the reasons for the imposition of the traffic 'restrictions' and vague as to when and how normal communications could be restored. [113] The three Western military governors discussed this letter and agreed that 'it offers no promise of compromise but is carefully worded not to entirely lock the gate'. [114] The final act of the attempt to resolve the issue locally was initiated by Robertson's letter of 2 July which again suggested the restoration of normal traffic 'at once' and proposed a meeting of the four military governors. [115] It was only the latter point to which Sokolovsky agreed.

Two aspects about this meeting are worth noting. First, it lasted only from 17.00 hours to 17.30 hours (3 July), and if allowance is made for the time lost in translations the actual proceedings must have been very brief indeed. Secondly, as reported by Clay to Washington, 'Marshal Sokolovsky made no special reference to the currency situation in speaking about the conditions at Berlin' and 'for the first time related the Berlin situation to the London conference as a whole'. [116] This was confirmed by the TASS reports about the meeting which quoted Sokolovsky to the effect that the participants of the London conference 'evidently had to think about the consequences of [their] decisions, to think also about the Berlin problem' and to think about 'all the difficulties to which they [the London decisions] would inevitably lead'. [117] Clay aptly summarized:

The three western Military Governors are agreed that Marshal Sokolovsky is under instructions which permit him no latitude in negotiating
the transport question alone or even in connection with other subjects
unless there is a complete discussion of the German problem . . . It is
clear that further action here by the three western Military Governors
would serve no useful purpose.[118]

In accordance with the third option adopted by President Truman on 28
June the next phase was to take place at a higher level.

The Second Phase (6 July to 2 August)

This phase of the crisis contains a series of fruitless diplomatic exchanges,
the tightening of the blockade,[119] the demonstration of the effectiveness of
the airlift to feed the population of the three Western sectors and even to
maintain some industrial activity, the strengthening of the morale of the
population in Berlin, but also more insistent reminders by the American
military government in Germany that the time had come to break the blockade by force.

Predictably, the Western notes of 6 July considered it 'intolerable that any
one of the occupying authorities should attempt to impose a blockade upon
the people of Berlin' and insisted that 'the arrangements for the movement
of freight and passenger traffic between the Western zones and Berlin be
fully restored'; but they also declared the readiness to negotiate 'in Berlin
among the four Allied Occupying Authorities' on questions *relating to the
City of Berlin* provided the traffic restrictions were lifted prior to negotiations.[120]

To this the Soviet Union replied on 14 July, charging the West – equally
predictably – with violation of the 'decisions adopted at Yalta and Potsdam',
particularly the decisions concerning the 'demilitarization and democratization of Germany', the 'removal of the base itself of German militarism',
and the 'obligation of Germany to pay reparations'.[121] Concerning the
blockade there was no change in the Soviet position. The note recognized the
'difficulties in supplying the Berlin population of the Western sectors',
expressed 'concern for the well-being of the Berlin population by assuring
them normal supplies in all essentials' and reiterated that the SMA was
'striving for the speediest elimination of the difficulties which have arisen
recently in this matter' – but apart from that no specific proposals on how to
terminate the blockade were made and the local conditions along the access
routes remained completely unchanged. In fact the note declared that the
USSR could not 'link the beginning of . . . negotiations with the fulfilment of
any preliminary conditions', nor could it agree to the idea that these negotiations should be limited to the problem of Berlin. For all practical purposes
the net result of the diplomatic exchanges was a deadlock as complete as that
existing on the ground.

There were, however, new developments in the supply of Berlin by air. As
early as 30 June, Secretary of State Marshall stated publicly in Washington:
'It has been found after study that the tonnage of foodstuffs which can be
lifted by air is greater than had at first been assumed.'[122] On 1 July Clay

announced in Frankfurt that an attempt would be made to deliver coal to Berlin by air.[123] The American commandant in Berlin, Frank Howley, wrote that 'The airlift was a reality by the first week in July',[124] and according to Forrestal, 'By mid-July there was a feeling in Washington that the airlift had begun to demonstrate its effectiveness'.[125] On 10 July Clay reported to Washington that the American airlift had reached a peak delivery of 1,000 tons. With additional planes, Clay estimated,

> we should come very close to 2,000 tons a day with [the] American [air]lift. I believe the British will reach at least 1,000 tons per day. Three thousand tons per day would provide us with food, essential coal, and even some raw materials to maintain some industrial activity in the western sectors.[126]

On 23 July Clay stated in Washington that the airlift had reached a capacity of 2,000 tons a day and that it was hoped to increase this to 4,500 tons.[127]

But although the airlift proved much more effective than had originally been assumed, hardships made themselves felt in the city as early as July. On 8 July the Western commandants had to order drastic cuts in the use of electricity; some days later this was extended to the use of gas; restrictions on traffic in the Western sectors became necessary in order to save electricity and the food rations had to be cut.[128] Despite this, and undoubtedly because of the impressive efforts of the supply operation by air and the clear indications that the Western allies were determined to stay, the morale of the population in Berlin improved. This became evident on numerous occasions, but most vividly on 11 July at a rally of about 30,000 people where Ernst Reuter (a prominent member of the Social Democratic Party and later a mayor of Berlin) defiantly said that the whole technological strength of Western civilization would be concentrated on Berlin, and this language would be understood even in Moscow. 'We will', he added, 'put a brake on the Russian pretensions to power in Berlin.'[129]

Taking into account the hardships that would be caused to the population of Berlin during the winter if the blockade continued, the unlikelihood of the lifting of the blockade prior to negotiations, the delay that would be caused by protracted negotiations in the United Nations or elsewhere, the huge and increasing expense of the airlift and the possible encouragement of further Soviet moves if Western countermeasures failed to be taken, Clay became increasingly determined to force the issue.

> I am strongly of the view [he wrote to General Omar Bradley on 10 July] that if the blockade is not lifted with technical difficulties still alleged as the reason, we should advise the Soviet Government that we are prepared to overcome these technical difficulties and that we propose on a specific date to send in a convoy accompanied by the requisite bridge equipment to make our right of way into Berlin usable.[130]

This was spelled out in more detail in a telephone conference two days later. The Soviet government was to be notified that the three Western allies regretted not being able to wait any longer for the lifting of the blockade and that they would be moving troops with equipment to reestablish the road links. The forces envisaged for this operation on the American side were to be the equivalent of a constabulary regiment reinforced with various special units, an infantry battalion to be provided by Britain and a detachment of tank destroyers by France.[131] Clay became more insistent after the deadlock resulting on 14 July following the fruitless exchange of notes between the Western powers and the Soviet Union. On 15 July he wrote:

> The intransigent Soviet position as indicated in the [Soviet] note [of July 14] should be tested and I see no way in which it can be tested except by proceeding promptly with the movement of the armed convoy as I have recommended previously. I would, therefore, like to recommend that we be given authority to proceed with this convoy movement as quickly as it can be arranged here.[132]

There is no precise record of how this request for authorization to proceed promptly with the armed convoy was received. Suffice it to say that on 19 July General Clay and Ambassador Murphy were summoned to Washington for consultations and to report to the National Security Council and the President on the situation in Berlin.[133] Thereafter the proposals to reopen communications by force disappear from Clay's personal papers. Approximately at the same time Forrestal was reporting to Marshall: 'for your information only, the Joint Chiefs of Staff do not recommend supply to Berlin by armed convoy in view of the risk of war involved and the inadequacy of United States preparation for global conflict.'[134]

The Western notes of 6 July had contained the refusal to conduct negotiations prior to the lifting of the blockade. This was evidently an untenable position if the use of force to open communications was ruled out. The West, therefore, reconsidered. As Marshall was to cable to the various US embassies, 'an effort should be made to approach Stalin directly' and to discuss with him 'some practical arrangement which would provide a resolution of the Berlin situation without loss of prestige to either side'.[135]

The Third Phase (2 to 30 August)

This phase is characterized by, in all but name, negotiations in Moscow and attempts to find a 'compromise solution' in which Western concessions on Germany or Berlin would be traded off for the lifting of the blockade. Meetings of the three Western ambassadors were held with Stalin on 2 and 23 August, as well as drafting sessions and talks with Molotov on 6, 9, 12, 16, 27 and 30 August. The talks ended with an agreement in the form of a communiqué and a directive to the four military governors to decide on measures for 'practical implementation' of the agreement.[136] Whatever contemporary or later interpretations in the West may say, the agreement must have been regarded by Stalin as a significant success and a clear indication that the policy of pressure was paying off. Some detail is appropriate.

In the first place, the direct approach from the Soviet point of view and the ensuing protracted talks in Moscow had the advantage of further removing the threat of the use of military force by the Western powers. Stalin undoubtedly thought that time, with autumn and winter approaching, could not but work against the viability of the Western sectors and the allied presence in Berlin – no matter what the outcome of the negotiations, and no matter on what level they were conducted.

When the three Western ambassadors in Moscow finally did manage to see Stalin on 2 August (only after some display of no urgency and playing hard to get on the Soviet side), [137] the first thing he wanted to know was whether his counterparts had the authority to open negotiations. To this the American ambassador replied, in accordance with his instructions, that they were there to discuss practical measures to work out a formula which might *lead* to negotiations. Secondly, Stalin said that, assuming the most acute questions concerning Berlin could be settled, were the three Western representatives prepared to discuss questions of Germany as a whole? The American ambassador replied that they had no authority to commit the three Western governments to specific proposals, but that they were interested in learning Stalin's views on that problem. Thirdly, Stalin indicated that the reasons for the traffic restrictions were manifold, including (1) technical problems, (2) the removal of large quantities of equipment from Berlin, (3) the London decisions and (4), not to be forgotten, the currency reform in Berlin. which – in his view – had disrupted the economy of the Soviet zone. Fourthly, Stalin made a concrete proposal which provided for

(A)   the simultaneous abolition of restrictive transport measures by the SMA, together with the abolition of the special mark B in Berlin, and replacement of that currency by the Soviet zone Deutschmark;

(B)   assurance that the implementation of the London decisions would be suspended until such time as the four powers met (which he understood the three Western representatives had suggested) and tried to reach agreement on fundamental questions affecting Germany. [138]

In other words, Stalin wanted the talks to be considered negotiations; he gave a wide scope to the reasons for the imposition of the blockade, and he demanded far-reaching concessions for the lifting of the blockade.

It would be inappropriate to present too much detail of the extremely interesting and well-documented negotiations in Moscow. They almost warrant a case study on their own. Only the end result can be stated briefly. [139] In short, although the agreement did not accept the second point of Stalin's proposal, it did make provision for the first as follows.

(A)   Restrictions on communications, transport and commerce between Berlin and the Western zones and to and from the Soviet zone of Germany which have recently been imposed shall be lifted;

(B)   the German mark of the Soviet zone shall be introduced as the sole currency for Berlin, and the Western mark B shall be withdrawn from circulation in Berlin. [140]

These measures were to be put into effect simultaneously *provided* agreement was reached among the four military governors in Berlin on their practical implementation. The directives to the four military governors included several specific guidelines.

(1) No discrimination or action against holders of Western marks B in connection with the exchange of those Western marks issued in Berlin. These shall be accepted for exchange for German marks of the Soviet zone at the rate of one for one.

(2) Equal treatment as to currency and provision of fully accessible banking and credit facilities throughout all sectors of Berlin. The four military governors are charged with providing adequate safeguards to prevent the use in Berlin of the German mark of the Soviet zone from leading to disorganizing currency circulation or disrupting the stability of currency in the Soviet zone.

(3) A satisfactory basis for trade between Berlin and third countries and the Western zones of Germany. Modification of this agreed basis to be made only by agreement among the four military governors.

(4) The provision of sufficient currency for budgetary purposes and for occupation costs, reduced to the greatest extent possible, and also the balancing of the Berlin budget.[141]

Finally, currency in Berlin was to be circulated by the German Bank of Emission of the Soviet zone, and a Financial Commission of representatives of the four military governors was to be set up to 'control' the practical implementation of the financial arrangements.

The directives contained several potential advantages from the Soviet point of view. This was clearly recognized by Clay, who did 'not feel very happy' about them.

> First, the proposed establishment of a financial commission avoids acceptance of Berlin as a quadripartite city under Kommandatura; in effect our acceptance means a politically separate Berlin under Soviet currency . . .
>
> Secondly, the proposed trade agreement implies treating Berlin as part of [the] Soviet zone since it would place trade to third countries and western zones on [the] same basis. This of course means an even [that is, equal] exchange of raw materials for goods of [the] same value which will represent a great cost with food and coal subsidized by [the] Allies and West Germany . . .
>
> Thirdly, budgetary control of [the] city lies in Soviet hands.
>
> Fourthly, the occupation cost limitation [see point 4 of the directives] will be a great financial liability to [the] West.[142]

To this can be added a fifth point. By agreeing (in point 2, above) to provide safeguards to prevent the disorganization of currency circulation and the disruption of currency stability in the Soviet zone, the three Western powers had in fact accepted one of the major Soviet propaganda themes and major justifications for the blockade. They had agreed to a broad clause of 'safeguards' which could — even without a full-scale blockade — be used by the SMA for legitimizing a variety of restrictive measures. The fruit of Soviet pressure apparently was ripening. What happened to make the harvesting such a dismal failure?

The Fourth Phase (31 August to 14 September)

The main features of this phase of the crisis are the failure of the four military governors in Berlin to reach agreement on the 'practical implementation' of the guidelines worked out in Moscow, a Soviet threat to interfere with the airlift, and severe Soviet and German communist pressures against the Berlin legislative assembly and the city executive.

In a series of long meetings, held on 31 August and 1, 2, 4, 7 and 8 September, Marshal Sokolovsky's negotiating tactics conformed to the warning given by Clay at the beginning of the meetings: 'It is not [the] Soviet custom to give more in the field than in Moscow.' [143] In fact Sokolovsky asserted that his Western colleagues had a completely different interpretation of what Stalin and Molotov had or had not agreed to in Moscow, and he made new demands which had not been on the agenda in Moscow at all. Apparently Stalin believed that the gains made in Moscow were insufficient to ensure speedy control over the whole city and that even more could be won by maintaining the squeeze on life in the city. Thus Stalin overplayed his hand and lost what he had gained so far.

The crucial word which, more than anything else, was responsible for the failure of the four military governors to reach agreement was that of 'control'. According to Western interpretation, Stalin and Molotov had agreed, and the directives provided, that the projected quadripartite Financial Commission would have broad powers of control over all the subject matters enumerated in paragraphs (1) to (4) of the directives, including the circulation of currency and the extension of credit in Berlin. The Soviet negotiators rejected this and contended that Stalin and the directives meant the Financial Commission to have a much more limited function. [144] What became evident in the course of the protracted negotiations was the firm Soviet intention to replace any form of quadripartite control over finance in the city by *unilateral* Soviet control. In addition, Sokolovsky and his colleagues insisted on the control of *trade* by Soviet authorities and on the restriction of *air transport*. This was evidently too much for the West to accept. The series of meetings in Berlin had come to an end, and the American ambassador in Moscow was instructed on 12 September to 'seek immediately, together with your British and French colleagues, an interview with Stalin and Molotov'. [145]

Even at this late stage it does not seem that Stalin considered the breakup of the series of meetings of the four military governors a disadvantage. As Murphy reported, at the last stage in the negotiations in Berlin Sokolovsky was apparently 'well satisfied to record disagreement' and that he was not even interested in finding agreement 'even when differences were minor'. [146] Also the Western ambassadors' request to see Stalin yet again was denied on the ground that the Generalissimo was 'on vacation'. [147]

However, Stalin did consider it advisable to increase the pressure on the three Western allies. After the meeting of the military governors on 4 September had concluded its business of the day, Marshal Sokolovsky rose to make an announcement. He stated that Soviet air maneuvers on an extensive scale would be held beginning on 6 September for several days, and that it would be necessary for these maneuvers to extend into the air corridors over

Berlin.[148] In conjunction with the imminent breakup of the talks in Berlin, and new pressures at the local level (see below), Sokolovsky's announcement seemed to foreshadow direct Soviet interference with the airlift. In Western perceptions a new, more dangerous, juncture of the crisis appeared to have been reached. A session of the National Security Council was called on 7 or 9 September; on 10 September Forrestal talked to Marshall about the problem of whether or not to use atomic weapons in war, and a few days later the American President was to make a decision of principle on that matter.[149]

At the same time the Soviet Union increased the pressure in Berlin, in particular on the elected city assembly (*Stadtverordnetenversammlung*) and the city government (Magistrat). This pressure was facilitated by the fact that both institutions held their sessions in the *Soviet* sector and that at that time the SMA controlled the police (in all of Berlin). In line with international practice, the city assembly had adopted a law banning demonstrations from a specified area around the building where it held its meetings. The Soviet commandant, however, had never given effect to this law. When the assembly met on 6 September, under the protection of specially appointed auxiliary personnel, demonstrators rushed into the building, overpowered the auxiliaries, manhandled Western delegates and journalists, and occupied the hall. With 'anti-Soviet' and 'anticommunist' assembly members removed, the SED (East German communists) and their sympathizers took over the chair and declared the assembly session open.[150]

On the same day police broke into the office of the American liaison officer and arrested German employees of the Magistrat. Other employees took refuge in the offices of the British and French liaison officers. On 8 September Sokolovsky gave the French military governor his word of honor that the city employees in question would be allowed to leave freely; however, when they left the building they were arrested by Soviet soldiers and police waiting outside.[151]

Although these events led to a *de facto* division of the city into two assemblies and two city governments, it is doubtful whether the Soviet Union in September 1948 was working under the assumption of such a split being more than a temporary state of affairs, the desired end result of pressure still being communist control of the whole city.

The Fifth Phase (14 September 1948 to 31 January 1949)

Complete deadlock locally and internationally characterizes this phase of the crisis. The basic irreconcilable positions are stated again and again in aides-mémoire and notes from the Western powers on 14, 22 and 26 (27) September and from the Soviet Union on 18, 25 September and 3 October.[152] On 29 September the scene of frustrating and unproductive discussion was transferred, by a formal Western request, to the United Nations where the two sides proceeded to confront each other verbally throughout October and into November.[153] During that time the airlift took on the character of a perfectionist, large-scale operation; however, despite Sokolovsky's implied threat of 4 September, Soviet interference with the airlift remained marginal. Increasingly a Western counterblockade, preventing shipments of goods from Western to Eastern Germany, began to make itself felt in the economy of the Soviet zone.

Communist mass action 'from below' became increasingly counterproductive in its effect on the population as a whole. In these conditions the SED and its satellite parties on 30 November convened an extraordinary meeting of the city assembly (with the delegates of the noncommunist parties absent) to transform the *de facto* division of the city into a *de iure* division of sorts by electing a new 'democratic' Magistrat. The Berlin problem and its relation to the future of Germany as a topic in the Soviet press gave way to a broad discussion of 'Lysenkoism' and 'Titoism'. Conditions were ripe for a Soviet initiative to break the deadlock and to end the blockade.

In an interview with a *Pravda* correspondent at the end of October Stalin had still presented an unconciliatory image.[154] He summed up the proceedings at the UN Security Council as an 'expression of the aggressiveness of policy of the Anglo-American and French ruling circles'. He also deplored – perhaps with some regret of gains lost – that an agreement had already been reached in Moscow at the end of August, but that the Western governments had disavowed their ambassadors, 'i.e. had broken it [the agreement]', and that all this could be explained by the fact that in reality the Anglo-American and French ruling circles were 'not interested in agreement and cooperation with the USSR'.[155] However, the very fact of the interview, the extensive reports on the reception it was given internationally,[156] and the Soviet commentary stressing Soviet readiness for agreement[157] – all this can be taken as an indication that dissatisfaction with the evolution of events in the Berlin crisis was beginning to make itself felt in Soviet policy.

This is confirmed also by the about-face on the official Soviet view of American domestic politics. President Truman had been contemplating another direct approach to Stalin, this time in the form of sending Chief Justice Vinson to Moscow – a plan which did not materialize, in part because of premature disclosure in the press on 9 October;[158] in any event, initially it had not helped to improve Truman's and the Democrats' standing in Soviet official reports as compared to Wallace and the Progressive Party. But after the elections of 2 November there was a significant change of tack. A TASS report from Washington quoted American newspapers to the effect that Truman's victory was due, among other things, to his 'adherence to the principles of Roosevelt'.[159] In his address at the thirty-first anniversary of the October Revolution, Foreign Minister Molotov explained Truman's victory as having been due to the rejection by the people of the 'openly reactionary and most aggressive program' of Dewey and the Republican Party.[160] Ilya Ehrenburg and *Pravda* commentator Marinin were to elaborate on this theme and set off the Democrats from the 'clique of Dewey-Vandenberg-Dulles'.[161] From this and other indications the American ambassador in Moscow concluded, correctly, that 'the current signs of shift may be the prelude to a further "peace" move'.[162]

The Final Phase (January to May 1949)

The decompression of the crisis began when Stalin replied to a series of questions by the American newspaperman J. Kingsbury Smith at the end of January 1949. Provided the Western allies 'agreed to postpone the establishment of a separate Western German State, pending a meeting of the Council of Foreign Ministers to consider the German problem as a whole' (Kingsbury Smith's question), Stalin saw 'no obstacle to lifting transport restrictions, on the understanding, however, that transport and trade restrictions, introduced by the Three Powers should be lifted simultaneously'.[163] Two weeks later at the United Nations, Ambassador Phillip G. Jessup, acting under instructions of the United States government, approached Ambassador Jacob Malik of the Soviet Union with the question whether the omission of the currency question as a condition of the settlement of the blockade had been intentional.[164] On 15 March Malik informed Jessup that the omission had not been accidental – the road to a compromise solution was thus opened exactly along the lines laid down in Stalin's reply to Kingsbury Smith's questions. By that time Western confidence and Western interests in a speedy formation of a West German government had been strengthened to such an extent that Stalin settled on the minimal demand of a meeting of the Council of Foreign Ministers. On 4 May agreement was reached in New York, and on 5 May a four-power communiqué was issued, announcing that the blockade and counterblockade would be lifted and that the Council of Ministers would meet at a later date.[165] After eleven months the Berlin blockade and the first major superpower crisis after World War II was brought to an end.

Notes: Part Two, Chapter 7

1   *The Times*, Review of the Year 1947, 2 January 1948. The conference itself is amply documented in US Department of State, *Foreign Relations 1947, Vol II*, pp. 676–830. The next meeting of foreign ministers of the four powers was to take place only in May 1949 in significantly changed conditions.

2   *Pravda* and *Izvestiia*, 31 December 1947.

3   ibid.

4   Memorandum of the conversation (presumably prepared by Frank K. Roberts, private secretary to Foreign Minister Bevin), Top Secret, 18 December 1947, in Smith (ed.), *The Clay Papers*, doc. 306, pp. 514–8.

5   *The Times*, 8, 9 and 30 January 1948.

6   Teleconference between Clay in Berlin and Secretary of the Army Royall and Under Secretary Draper in Washington, Top Secret, 12 January 1948, in Smith (ed.), *The Clay Papers*, doc. 316, p. 537.

7   Cable to Under Secretary of War, Draper, Eyes Only, Top Secret, 3 November 1947, ibid., doc. 288, p. 476.

8   Cable to Draper, Personal, Secret, 16 January 1948, ibid., doc. 320, p. 545.

9   *The Times*, 17, 23 and 24 January 1948 and 4 February 1948; the *New York Times*, 17 January and 4 February 1948.

10 For instance, the TASS reports of 8 January, published in *Pravda* and *Izvestiia*, 10 January 1948.

11 *Tägliche Rundschau*, 11 January 1948.

12 *The Times*, 21 January 1948.

13 Order No. 32 of the SMA, in Ministerstvo inostrannykh del SSSR, Ministerstvo inostrannykh del GDR, *Za antifashistskuiu, demokraticheskuiu Germaniiu: Sbornik dokumentov, 1945–1949 gg.* (Moscow: Izdatel'stvo politicheskoi literatury, 1969), pp. 494–5. There is some doubt as to whether this devolution of power to the DWK took place at that time.

14 ibid., pp. 495–6. The conference ultimately opened on 23 February.

15 Communiqué published in *Pravda* and *Izvestiia*, 19 February 1948.
16 Twenty years after the fact Czech historians, writing during the Prague Spring, revealed that Valentin Zorin, Soviet Deputy Minister for Foreign Affairs, had not (as many people suspected at that time) come to Prague on 19 February merely for the reason of checking on grain deliveries. In fact he came to check (and help direct?) events during the crisis. More specifically, he promised Gottwald that 'the Soviet Union would not allow the West to interfere', a message that was reiterated in *Pravda* of 22 February 1948. For more detail see Pavel Tigrid, 'The Prague *coup* of 1948', in Thomas T. Hammond (ed.), *The Anatomy of Communist Takeovers* (New Haven, Conn., and London: Yale University Press, 1975), pp. 429–30.
17 This is so despite a report by the American ambassador in Prague, Steinhardt, of 30 April 1948, which summarized the seizure of power by the Communist Party and stated that 'There was no evidence of any Soviet troop concentrations on the borders of Czechoslovakia' and that 'There was no direct evidence of Soviet interference' (US Department of State, *Foreign Relations 1948, Vol. IV*, p.750).
18 *The Times*, 8 March 1948.
19 ibid., 18 March 1948.
20 *Pravda* and *Izvestiia*, 19 March 1948.
21 The Treaty of Friendship, Cooperation and Mutual Assistance between the Soviet Union and Finland was signed on 6 April 1948. See below, pp. 86–7.
22 The note to the three Western powers was published in the Soviet press on 9 March 1948. For a complete text see also MID SSSR, MID GDR, *Sbornik dokumentov, 1945–1949*, pp. 501–10. The West had replied to the previous Soviet note (13 February, see above) on 21 February.
23 MID SSSR, MID GDR, *Sbornik documentov, 1945–1949*, doc. 211, pp. 517–9.
24 *The Times*, 24 March 1948.
25 *Tägliche Rundschau*, 24 and 28 March 1948; *Neues Deutschland*, 24 and 28 March 1948; and *Pravda* and *Izvestiia*, 30 March 1948. It is important to note in this context that the Soviet press earlier had reported the existence of a difficult food problem and the increase in strikes and demonstrations in Western Germany. In fact *Pravda* correspondent Yu. Korol'kov in a report from Stuttgart had even given an exaggerated impression of the scope of the problem, asserting that the population in the Ruhr at the beginning of 1948 began to receive 'a mere 500 calories a day' (actually they were around 1,120 calories) and that a wave of strikes was gathering momentum throughout the Bizone with hundreds of thousands out on strike in the Ruhr in January, 2 million at the end of the month in Bavaria and more than 3 million workers and employees taking part in mass demonstrations in the Bizone at the beginning of February (*Pravda*, 18 February 1948; for comparison of these data with Western figures see above, p. 80).
26 Teleconference TT-9218, Top Secret, 17 March 1948, in Smith (ed.), *The Clay Papers*, doc. 349, p. 580.
27 ibid.
28 *The Times*, 15 April 1948.
29 Teleconference TT-9286, Top Secret, 31 March 1948, in Smith (ed.), *The Clay Papers*, doc. 357, p. 602. Kenneth Royall was Secretary of the Army in 1948. The uncertainty in Washington about Western rights apparently extended beyond the problem of access. This is indicated by the full text of Royall's query to Clay. Royall asked: 'Do you know of any documentation of agreement with [the] Russians as to our rights to occupy [sic] and have access to Berlin?' The two sets of rights, of course, are covered in separate agreements, the right to occupy Berlin being codified in an agreement by the European Advisory Commission in London in 1944.
30 Clay and Sir Ronald Weeks were standing in for their senior commanders, General Eisenhower and Field Marshal Mongomery, according to an editorial note by Smith, ibid, doc. 16, p. 26.
31 Notes of a Conference between Marshal Zhukov and Soviet Representatives, General Clay and US Representatives, General Weeks and British Representatives at Marshal Zhukov's Headquarters on 29 June 1945, Beginning at 14.30 Hours, ibid., doc. 16, pp. 31–2. See also Clay, *Decision in Germany*, pp. 24–7.
32 Smith (ed.), *The Clay Papers*, pp. 31–2.
33 The content of the letter was transmitted by Clay to Washington in a teleconference on 31 March 1948 between Clay (in Berlin) and Secretary of the Army, Kenneth Royall; Chief of Staff, General Omar Bradley; Deputy Chief of Staff, General J. Lawton Collins; and the

Director of Plans and Operations, US Army, Lieutenant General Albert C. Wedemeyer, Teleconference TT-9286, Top Secret Eyes Only, 31 March 1948, in Smith (ed.), *The Clay Papers*, doc. 357, pp. 600–1.

34   For the benefit of his interlocutors in Washington, who appeared to be quite puzzled by the complexity of the technical problems of access, Clay said that 'If we permit entry [of Soviet officers to inspect documents], it will be only a day or two until one of our people is pulled off [the train] on trumped-up charges'. Concerning the problem of cargo, Clay explained that 'we cannot be forced to request permit from Soviet commander each time we bring in supplies' (ibid., p. 603). The introduction of the new controls and their effects were reported in *Pravda* and *Izvestiia*, 7 April 1948.

35   In an explanation to Secretary Royall and General Bradley, Teleconference TT-9300, Top Secret Eyes Only, 2 April 1948, in Smith (ed.), *The Clay Papers*, doc. 363, p. 613.

36   Teleconference TT-9341, ibid., doc. 371, p. 624. Clay added that 'This is a complete embargo', but of course at that time it was not.

37   *The Times*, 7 May 1948.

38   ibid., 9 April 1948; *Pravda* and *Izvestiia*, 7 April 1948. The Soviet deputy commandant was pressed by his Western colleagues to present a list of the firms concerned, but this list was never produced.

39   Interview of Lieutenant General Luk'ianchenko with a correspondent of the newspaper *Vorwärts* in Berlin on 30 March 1948, published in *Izvestiia*, 2 April 1948. Soviet assertions of a large-scale pillage of Berlin were reported in *The Times*, 3 April 1948.

40   As reported in ibid., 5 April 1948. General Hays at that time was US Chief of Staff.

41   ibid., 3 and 21 April 1948.

42   ibid., 2 April 1948. It is not clear whether General Clay, in his report to Washington on 2 April (where he reported air traffic as being 'normal'), included buzzing or frolicking of Western aircraft as part of the new normality, or whether 2 April was a quiet day in the air.

43   According to eyewitness reports, the British passenger plane was preparing to land when the Soviet fighter plane passed underneath, then rose steeply and hit the British plane. A joint British-Soviet commission set up to investigate the cause of the air crash broke down after the Soviet representatives refused to admit German witnesses (*The Times*, 14 April 1948). Evidently embarrassed by the accident the USSR kept silent on this matter. But when the Soviet newspapers finally did break silence it was to attack violently the findings of the by then exclusively British commission of inquiry, which had laid full responsibility for the accident on the Soviet pilot. The Soviet attacks were published in *Pravda* and *Izvestiia*, 21 April 1948.

44   Clay's report to General Bradley, CC 3745, Top Secret, 6 April 1948, in Smith (ed.), *The Clay Papers*, doc. 366, pp. 618–9.

45   *The Times*, 8 April 1948; see also ibid., 6 and 9 April 1948.

46   *Tägliche Rundschau*, 24 April 1948, and *Neues Deutschland*, 25 April 1948.

47   *The Times*, 26 April 1948.

48   ibid., 2 April 1948. British units surrounded and isolated the Russian post and it later withdrew.

49   ibid., 9 and 14 April 1948.

50   ibid., 30 April 1948.

51   ibid., 26 April 1948.

52   Clay [in London] Personal and Eyes Only for Draper [Assistant Secretary of War], 73255, Secret, 7 May 1948, in Smith (ed.), *The Clay Papers*, p. 649. Clay's reference about the international train concerns the Nord Express between Paris and Berlin. This train service was regulated by international agreement in Venice in 1946 at a conference attended by the Soviet Union.

53   Clay, *Decision in Germany*, p. 362 (my italics).

54   Robert Murphy, *Diplomat Among Warriors* (Garden City, NY: Doubleday 1964), p. 321.

55   *The Times*, 18 May 1948.

56   ibid.

57   Stalin proposed the conclusion of such a treaty in a letter received in Helsinki on 23 February 1948. On 5 March 1948 Molotov is reported as having had a rough and unpleasant meeting with the Finnish Foreign Minister, in the course of which Molotov accused the Finnish government of aligning itself with Britain for anti-Soviet purposes; Molotov closed the meeting abruptly by walking out of the Finnish Foreign Minister's office with the cryptic remark 'we shall see'. See telegram by the American Minister in Finland (Warren) to the

US Secretary of State, Secret, 6 March 1948, in US Department of State, *Foreign Relations, 1948*, Vol. IV, pp. 770–1.

58 The French Minister in Helsinki, Coulet, for the first quotation, and the Social Democratic Chairman of the Finnish Diet, Fagerholm, for the second, both quoted in a telegram by the American Minister in Finland (Warren) to the Secretary of State, Secret, 20 February 1948, ibid., pp. 763–4.

59 So, for instance, the Finnish Foreign Minister, Enckell, and the French Minister in Finland, Coulet, as quoted in the telegram by the American Minister in Finland (Warren) to the Secretary of State, 28 February 1948, ibid., p. 765.

60 See the TASS reports based on foreign press reports in *Pravda* and *Izvestiia*, 22 April 1948. Concerning the first point, 'large-scale' is relative in the Italian electoral context and should be measured against the offenses of other parties, including the parties of the Popular Front. However, the existence of a 'special secret fund' was correctly reported then and has subsequently been confirmed (US Department of State, *Foreign Relations, 1948*, vol. III); see also *International Herald Tribune*, 13 February 1975.

61 The Acting Secretary of State to the embassy in the Soviet Union, Top Secret, Washington, 24 April 1948, in US Department of State, *Foreign Relations, 1948*, Vol. IV, pp. 834–5.

62 The ambassador in the Soviet Union (Smith) to the Secretary of State, Top Secret, 4 May 1948, ibid., p. 845.

63 ibid.

64 *Pravda* and *Izvestiia*, 11 May 1948.

65 ibid., 13–17 May 1948. Authoritative commentary was provided by V. Kudriavtsev in *Izvestiia*, 16 May 1948.

66 ibid. and *Pravda*, 13 May 1948.

67 ibid., 18 May 1948. Also included in Stalin's reply was a general invocation of the principle of coexistence and the necessity of peaceful settlement of disputes between the United States and the Soviet Union.

68 The chargé d'affaires in Greece (Rankin) to the Secretary of State, Secret, 4 June 1948, in US Department of State, *Foreign Relations, 1948*, Vol. IV, p. 101.

69 ibid. Earlier the executive secretary of the National Security Council had correctly noted in a position paper that 'the Greek Army may be able to eliminate the guerrillas as a major obstacle to Greek recovery' but that the USSR retained 'the capability of causing an augmentation of satellite aid sufficient to render doubtful the achievement of a military decision' ('The position of the United States with respect to the use of US military power in Greece', Top Secret, 25 May 1948, ibid., p. 94).

70 *Pravda*, 9 June 1948. The other ingredients of the Soviet 'peace offensive' were reported in an editorial in *The Times*, 14 June 1948.

71 It is interesting to note that, in keeping with the past practice of largely excluding France and the French zone in Germany from propagandist attack, the first TASS reports about the announcement of the currency reform in the three Western zones spoke of 'panic and chaos in the *Bizone*' (*Pravda*, 19 June 1948, my italics).

72 Clay for Noce [Director, Civil Affairs Division, War Department], Confidential, CC 4675, 12 June 1948, in Smith (ed.), *The Clay Papers*, doc. 422, pp. 676–7.

73 ibid.

74 Clay for [Brigadier General Charles K.] Gailey, Top Secret, 13 June 1948, ibid., doc. 423, p. 677.

75 *The Times*, 14, 15 and 16 June 1948. It does not speak for the logical consistency of the explanations put forward by a Soviet author when he argues on the one hand that the USSR was forced to adopt 'additional measures on communications between the Western zones of occupation and Berlin' (in reference to the full imposition of the blockade on 23–4 June) while on the other hand rejecting inferences that the closure of the autobahn bridge was anything but part and parcel of the continuing preparations for the blockade. The Soviet author still quotes in support the rationale put forward by Sokolovsky in a letter to General Robertson on 17 June 1948, to the effect that 'the Soviet military authorities have taken all the necessary measures to have the Hohenwarth[e] bridge repaired as quickly as possible'. See V. Vysotsky, *West Berlin*, trans. David Fidlon (Moscow: progress Publishers, 1974), p. 80, fn. 1, and p. 82; V. N. Vysotskii, *Zapadnyi Berlin i ego mesto v sisteme sovremennykh mezhdunarodnykh otnoshenii*, pp. 149–50, fn. 3, and p. 155. It took eleven months to reopen the bridge, but repairs apparently had not been carried out.

76 *The Times*, 8 June 1948.

77   Clay for Gailey (see above, note 74). See also Murphy, *Diplomat among Warriors*, p. 311.
78   Clay Personal for Echols [Director, Civil Affairs Division, War Department], Confidential, CC 5635, 23 May 1946, in Smith (ed.), *The Clay Papers*, doc. 119, p. 210; see also ibid., docs 133, 140, 151 and 165.
79   ibid., doc. 138, p. 244.
80   Clay Personal for Noce [Director, Civil Affairs Division, War Department], Secret, CC 7679, 17 January 1947, in Smith (ed.), *The Clay Papers*, doc. 182, p. 303.
81   In the session of the Allied Control Council of 11 February 1948, ibid., doc. 331, p. 561.
82   This, in fact, has proved to be one of the fundamental obstacles to monetary union in the EEC – despite the fact that all the economic systems concerned are market-type economies.
83   Marshal Sokolovsky's letter to General Clay, 22 June 1948, as published in *Pravda*, 23 June 1948. Corresponding letters were sent to General Robertson and General Koenig.
84   The official in question is V. N. Beletsky who was attached to the Soviet embassy in East Berlin at the end of the 1960s and the beginning of the 1970s as an expert on the Berlin problem. His book, *Zapadnyi Berlin i ego mesto v sisteme sovremennykh mezhdunarodnykh otnoshenii*, and the English 'translation' appeared under the name of 'V. N. Vysotskii' and 'V. Vysotsky' respectively (see above, note 75). The two books are based on a 'candidate' thesis which Beletsky submitted in 1968 to the Institute of International Relations at the Central Committee of the SED. I am indebted for this information to Gerhard Wettig of the Bundesinstitut für ostwissenschaftliche und internationale Studien in Cologne. Some of the differences – a number of them of considerable political importance – between the English and Russian versions can be found in my book review in *Survival*, vol. 17, no. 6 (November/December 1975), pp. 309–10. The support for the thesis concerning the improvised nature of the Soviet reaction to the Western currency reform appears on p. 152 of the Russian version and p. 81 of the English 'translation' of Beletsky's (Vysotsky's) book.
85   *Tägliche Rundschau*, 4 February 1948.
86   Clay for the Department of the Army, Top Secret, CC 4140, 2 May 1948, in Smith (ed.), *The Clay Papers*, doc. 387, p. 643.
87   ibid., p. 644. It is also perhaps because the editor of Clay's papers found it difficult to believe that such a cable could actually have been sent by Clay himself that he adds in a footnote: 'The cable probably was prepared by Jack Bennett, Clay's financial adviser.'
88   ibid.
89   Yalizarov's refusal to attend the Kommandatura meeting as reported in *The Times*, 19 June 1948. The next stage in the dissolution of this body was an article in *Tägliche Rundschau*, 24 June 1948, claiming that the control mechanism in Germany *and Berlin* had collapsed (see below, p. 94). Finally, the Soviet commandant announced on 1 July 1948 that he would no longer attend the meetings of the Kommandatura because that body had 'for all practical purposes ceased its activity'. *Documents on Berlin, 1943–1963*, ed. Wolfgang Heidelmeyer and Guenter Hindrichs (Munich: R. Oldenbourg Verlag for the Forschungsinstitut der Deutschen Gesellschaft für Auswärtige Politik, 1963), pp. 67–8).
90   *The Times*, 19 June 1948; *Tägliche Rundschau*, 19 June 1948.
91   ibid.; *Pravda* and *Izvestiia*, 20 June 1948.
92   The exchange of letters is published in *Documents on Berlin, 1943–1963*, p. 58 and pp. 62–5. Only Sokolovsky's letters of 19 and 22 June (not those of the Western military governors) were published in the USSR, *Pravda* and *Izvestiia*, 22 and 23 June 1948.
93   As reported by the news agency of the Soviet zone, and published in *Tägliche Rundschau*, 23 June 1948; also quoted in *The Times*, 23 June 1948. This is confirmed by Clay who reported to Washington that the Soviet delegation had 'threatened severe economic measures in the event of issuance of a separate currency in Berlin' (Smith, ed., *The Clay Papers*, doc. 438, p. 695).
94   For the complete text see MID SSSR, MID GDR, *Sbornik dokumentov, 1945–59 gg.*, pp. 554–60.
95   As reported by *The Times*, 23 June 1948.
96   Smith (ed.), *The Clay Papers*, doc. 438, pp. 694–5.
97   *Documents on Berlin, 1943–1963*, p. 66; *The Times*, 24 June 1948.
98   ibid., 26 June 1948.
99   This cursory survey of the stages and phases of the crisis is supplemented by more detail in Chapter 4, 'Crisis and Risk in International Relations'.

100 *Tägliche Rundschau*, 24 June 1948.

101 ibid.

102 Text published in *Pravda*, 25 June 1948; for a Soviet view of the conference see Trukhanovskii (ed.), *Istoriia mezhdunarodnykh otnoshenii*, p. 220. For additional data concerning the content of the Warsaw statement of the eight foreign ministers see above, pp. 68–9.

103 The reference is to Sokolovsky's proclamation to the German population of 24 June (tele-conference between Clay in Berlin and Secretary Royall and General J. Lawton Collins in Washington, Top Secret, TT-9667, 25 June 1948, in Smith (ed.), *The Clay Papers*, doc. 442, p. 700). Smith's reference to Sokolovsky's proclamation of 19 June (ibid., fn. 1, p. 699) is erroneous; see *The Times*, 25 June 1948 and Clay, *Decision in Germany*, p. 366.

104 Clay Personal and Eyes Only for Draper [Assistant Secretary of War], Top Secret, CC 4910, 27 June 1948, in Smith (ed.), *The Clay Papers*, doc. 444, p. 708.

105 Robert Murphy in the *Saturday Evening Post*, 22 February 1964, p. 48.

106 Walter Millis (ed.), *The Forrestal Diaries*, pp. 454–5.

107 ibid., p. 454.

108 Clay, *Decision in Germany*, pp. 365–6. Clay mentions a number of about a hundred C-47 aircraft, seventy Dakotas and an unspecified number of C-54s in a dispatch to Draper, Personal and Eyes Only, Top Secret, CC 4910, 27 June 1948, in Smith (ed.), *The Clay Papers*, doc. 444, pp. 707–8. The carrying capacity of the C-47 was about 2·5 tons of cargo, that of the C-54 about 10 tons.

109 Clay, *Decision in Germany*, p. 365 in Smith (ed.), *The Clay Papers*, doc. 444, p. 708. Among other things the 'minimum economy' excluded domestic heating; electricity supplies would be available only for a few hours a day.

110 ibid.

111 ibid.

112 *The Times*, 26 June 1948.

113 *Pravda* and *Izvestiia*, 1 July 1948. General Robertson's letter was not published in the Soviet Union.

114 Clay Personal for Noce, Top Secret, CC 4979, 1 July 1948, in Smith (ed.), *The Clay Papers*, doc. 450, p. 715.

115 *The Times*, 3 July 1948.

116 Clay for Royall and Bradley, Top Secret, CC 5027, 3 July 1948, in Smith (ed.), *The Clay Papers*, doc. 454, p. 723.

117 *Pravda* and *Izvestiia*, 5 July 1948.

118 Smith (ed.), *The Clay Papers*, doc. 454, p. 724 (see above, note 116).

119 As mentioned above, initially there was still a trickle of supplies coming into Berlin by barges. This was to stop entirely by 4 August.

120 *Documents on Berlin, 1943–1963*, pp. 69–70 (my italics), from the US and British notes, which were identical in tenor. The French note was different in some aspects.

121 MID SSSR, MID GDR, *Sbornik dokumentov, 1945–1949 gg.*, pp. 574–8. *Izvestiia*, 16 July 1948, published both the Anglo-American note(s) of 6 July and the Soviet reply.

122 *New York Times*, 1 July 1948.

123 *The Times*, 2 July 1948.

124 Frank Howley, *Berlin Command*, p. 209.

125 Millis (ed.), *The Forrestal Diaries*, p. 485.

126 Clay Personal for Bradley, Top Secret, CC 5109, 10 July 1948, in Smith (ed.), *The Clay Papers*, doc. 461, p. 730.

127 *New York Times*, 24 July 1948.

128 *The Times*, 9, 10 and 19 July 1948.

129 ibid., 12 July 1948.

130 Clay Personal for Bradley, Top Secret, CC 5118, 10 July 1948, in Smith (ed.), *The Clay Papers*, doc. 464, p. 734.

131 Teleconference TT-9768 between Colonel R. W. Mayo, Department of the Army, Plans and Operations, *et al.*, in Washington and Brigadier General V. E. Pritchard, EUCOM, Plans and Operations in Berlin, Top Secret, 13 July 1948, ibid., p. 737.

132 Clay Eyes Only for Bradley, Top Secret, FMPC 336, 15 July 1948, ibid., p. 740. The cable was sent from Frankfurt.

133 Editorial note in US Department of State, *Foreign Relations, 1948*, Vol. II, p. 977.

134 The Secretary of Defense (Forrestal) to the Secretary of State, Top Secret, 28 July 1948,

ibid., p. 994. For a more detailed study of this problem in the context of American decision-making see Millis (ed.), *The Forrestal Diaries*, pp. 459–60; Clay, *Decision in Germany*, p. 368; and Truman, *Memoirs, Vol. II: Years of Trial and Hope*, pp. 124–6.

135 US Department of State, *Foreign Relations, 1948*, vol. II, pp. 971 and 973. Secretary of State Marshall's telegram to the embassies was sent on 20 July 1948.

136 Text of the directive as published in US Department of State, *The Berlin Crisis*, p. 40–1. The content of the agreement will be discussed below. Molotov was also present in the meetings of 2 and 23 August.

137 It was first reported that Molotov was absent 'on vacation'. Deputy Foreign Minister Zorin, who substituted for Molotov, indicated in a meeting with the three Western ambassadors on 30 July that a discussion with Generalissimo Stalin and Foreign Minister Molotov was not profitable as there had been no change in the position of the United States; see communication from the ambassador in the Soviet Union (Smith) to the Secretary of State, Top Secret, 30 July 1948, in US Department of State, *Foreign Relations, 1948*, Vol. II, p. 995.

138 This summary draws on the report sent by Ambassador Smith to the Secretary of State on 3 August, ibid., pp. 999–1006.

139 It is also worth mentioning that, in contrast to the ill-fated exchanges between Ambassador Smith and Molotov on 4 May, the Soviet newspapers *completely ignored* the ongoing meetings. The TASS reports of 2 and 23 August merely mentioned that Stalin and Molotov had received the three Western ambassadors for talks, but not even a hint of the subject discussed was given (*Pravda* and *Izvestiia*, 3 and 24 August 1948).

140 US Department of State, *The Berlin Crisis*, pp. 40–1.

141 ibid. In the original, the points (1) to (4) are given capital letters (A–D); this leads to some confusion with the main points (A) and (B) immediately above.

142 Teleconference TT-1080, Top Secret, 24 August 1948, in Smith (ed.), *The Clay Papers*, doc. 502, pp. 781–2. The significance of the point about limitation of occupation costs is to be seen in the fact that the Western powers subsidized food, coal and other basic materials at great cost. Stalin and Molotov implied that these imports should not be part of the current budget but should be recoverable separately as a 'debt' or 'charge' against the city; see Ambassador Smith's report to the Secretary of State of 24 August 1948, in US Department of State, *Foreign Relations, 1948*, Vol. II, pp. 1066–7.

143 Teleconference TT-1113 between Clay in Berlin and Under Secretary of State Draper in Washington, Top Secret, 30 August 1948, in Smith (ed.), *The Clay Papers*, doc. 511, p. 794.

144 US Department of State, *Foreign Relations, 1948*, Vol. II, pp. 1099–140.

145 The Secretary of State to the embassy in the Soviet Union, Top Secret, 12 September 1948, ibid., p. 1151.

146 ibid., p. 1136.

147 ibid., p. 1157, fn. 1. Molotov was to substitute for Stalin. The three Western ambassadors presented an aide-mémoire.

148 ibid., p. 1121.

149 Truman, *Memoirs, Vol. II: Years of Trial and Hope*, p. 128; Millis (ed.), *The Forrestal Diaries*, pp. 486–7. The date for the meeting of the National Security Council is given as 7 September in Forrestal's diaries and as 9 September in Truman's memoirs. See also the discussion by Herbert Feis, *From Trust to Terror: The Onset of the Cold War, 1945–1950* (London: Blond, 1971), pp. 351–2. For details of the President's decision see below, p. 138.

150 *Berlin: Behauptung von Freiheit und Selbstverwaltung, 1946–1948*, series 'Berliner Zeitgeschichte', Vol. II (West Berlin: Duncker & Humbolt for the Berlin City Government, 1959), pp. 226–8.

151 ibid.

152 US Department of State, *Foreign Relations, 1948*, Vol. II, pp. 1152–97, and *The Berlin Crisis*, pp. 46–50. The date of 26 or 27 September respectively is due to the fact that the Western powers did not present their notes simultaneously.

153 Young, *Politics of Force*, p. 119. The Berlin question at the United Nations is well documented in an entirely separate section in US Department of State, *Foreign Relations, 1948*, Vol. II, beginning on p. 1197.

154 Text of the interview as published in *Pravda* and *Izvestiia*, 29 October 1948.

155 ibid. Stalin's version, perhaps needless to say, does not conform to the facts. The

agreement was to come into force 'subject to agreement being reached among the four military governors in Berlin for their practical implementation'. There is no ambiguity about this: the version published in US Department of State, *The Berlin Crisis*, pp. 40–1, is the same on this point as that rendered by MID SSSR, MID GDR, *Sbornik dokumentov, 1945–1949*, pp. 580–1. For the context of the agreement see above, p. 100.

156 As published in *Pravda* and *Izvestiia*, 30 and 31 October and 1 November 1948.
157 For instance, the articles by M. Marinin in *Pravda*, 2 and 3 November 1948.
158 Truman, *Memoirs, Vol. II: Years of Trial and Hope*, pp. 213–19.
159 *Pravda*, 5 November 1948.
160 ibid. and *Izvestiia*, 7 November 1948.
161 *Pravda*, 6 and 7 November 1948.
162 The ambassador in the Soviet Union (Smith) to the Secretary of State, Secret, 9 November 1948, in US Department of State, *Foreign Relations, 1948*, Vol. IV, p. 933.
163 *Pravda*, 31 January 1949. The final phase of the crisis is discussed by Feis, *From Trust to Terror*, pp. 354–9, and Shulman, *Stalin's Foreign Policy Reappraised*, pp. 69–70.
164 ibid.
165 ibid., pp. 70–3.

8
Factors of Risk-Taking

I IDEOLOGY

The assumption made here is that the Berlin crisis is woven into a complex ideological context and can be analyzed from several different angles. First, because of the nature of the confrontation as an East—West conflict, the general inflection of 'peaceful coexistence' and the main line adopted by the Soviet Union towards the major capitalist countries will be considered. Secondly, questions will be raised as to the specific social, political and ideological conditions applying in the crisis area, the role played by the East German Socialist Unity Party (SED) and communist mass action during the crisis and the scope of Soviet attempts for achieving a 'revolutionary transformation' of the social and political system in Berlin and Germany. Thirdly, assuming the existence of linkages between Soviet security perceptions, ideology, and the socioeconomic system in the USSR and the areas under Soviet control after World War II, the problem will be examined as to whether there is a consistent ideological framework integrating Soviet domestic, intra-bloc, interparty and international relations – a framework in which the Berlin crisis would appear as but one of the manifestations of a general pattern.

The Berlin Crisis and (Peaceful?) Coexistence

The Soviet historian Roy Medvedev, author of an authoritative book from Marxist perspectives on the origins and consequences of Stalinism published in the West, correctly, but somewhat euphemistically, summarizes the general ideological and political context of the Berlin crisis in the following manner.

> Toward the major capitalist states Stalin took a very hard line, beginning in 1947–8. The struggle for peaceful coexistence was not the chief task of Soviet foreign policy in that period. *The clearest example of this hard line was Stalin's policy with respect to Germany, especially the so-called Berlin crisis*, which greatly exacerbated the situation in Europe.[1]

Evident in Medvedev's assessment is the relation of the Berlin crisis to a change in Soviet policy toward the major capitalist states in 1947. The Soviet historian no doubt took as one of the starting points of his interpretation the highly significant speech by CPSU Politburo member, Andrei A. Zhdanov, at the founding meeting of the Cominform in Wilniza Gora (Upper Silesia) on 22–3 September 1947, in which a new inflection of peaceful coexistence was enunciated. Zhdanov said:

Soviet foreign policy proceeds from the fact of the coexistence for a long period of the two systems – capitalism and socialism. From this it follows that cooperation between the USSR and the countries with other systems is *possible*, provided that the principle of reciprocity is observed and that obligations once assumed are honored. Everyone knows that the USSR has always honored the obligations it has assumed.[2]

The omission by Zhdanov of 'peaceful' from the composite term 'peaceful coexistence' may be an important fact in itself but should perhaps not be overrated. More important are the conditions he requires for coexistence. The essence of his elaborations is the view that while coexistence is theoretically 'possible' it is practically impossible in the present era.

Britain and America are pursuing the very opposite policy [to coexistence] in the United Nations. They are doing everything they can to renounce their commitments and to secure a free hand for the prosecution of a new policy, a policy which envisages not cooperation among nations, but the hounding of one against the other, violation of the rights and interests of democratic nations, and the isolation of the USSR.[3]

This is to say, Zhdanov left no doubt about the complete absence of conditions for genuine peaceful coexistence. He thus reiterates the interpretation enunciated earlier by Stalin in an interview with Harold Stassen in May 1947 where he expressed the view that while he believed cooperation between the two systems was possible, there did exist the reality of 'capitalist encirclement and danger of attack on the USSR. *If one party does not wish to cooperate then that means that there exists a threat of an attack.*'[4]

Even before Marshal Sokolovsky's dramatic walkout from the Allied Control Council on 20 March 1948 Soviet officials had made it clear that they did not see any indication of a Western desire to cooperate. In the autumn before the Berlin crisis the Soviet representative at the United Nations, Andrei Vyshinsky, had singled out the Truman Doctrine and the Marshall Plan as 'particularly glaring examples of the manner in which the principles of the United Nations are violated' and charged the West with an attempt 'to make use of Western Germany and German heavy industry (the Ruhr) as one of the most important economic bases for American expansionism in Europe' and 'to split Europe into two camps'.[5]

If it is correct that the Western powers had not, according to Soviet perspectives, shown any desire to cooperate and to carry out the obligations which they had assumed under the Yalta and Potsdam Agreements; if it is correct, consequently, that the preconditions for peaceful coexistence did not exist but instead the threat of an attack; and, finally, if Lenin's fundamental assumption of an 'inevitable' and 'frightful' series of 'collisions between the Soviet Republic and the bourgeois states' remained as valid in the post-World War II era as after World War I when Lenin enunciated this doctrine,[6] then it must be said that the Soviet Union created dangerous preconditions for the very clash over Berlin and Germany which it was trying to avoid. There is hardly a better justification for preventive war for an adversary to whom it has been communicated that cooperation is at an end, and war inevitable.

However, Stalinist, or Zhdanovist, ideological formulations sharply contrast not only with actual Soviet crisis behavior but also with Soviet communications during the crisis. Soviet officials took care not to convey the slightest impression that in the specific international conditions of 1948 they considered war to be likely, not to speak of 'inevitable'. On the contrary they made sure to emphasize Soviet openness to compromise solutions and renewed cooperation. The Western powers were told time and again that 'the Soviet Command has consistently displayed and is displaying concern for the well-being of the Berlin population' and that it was assuring the population of Berlin 'normal supplies in all essentials'.[7] At one time Marshal Sokolovsky even went so far as to express 'full understanding' of the measures taken by the United States and Britain 'to maintain traffic with the Western zones by air'.[8] Soviet officers in Berlin made some attempts to maintain social contacts with their Western counterparts and revive some of the old, wartime cordiality. And in the discussions in Moscow in August Stalin denied the danger of war, saying, 'After all, we are still Allies'.[9]

All this suggests a discrepancy between general ideological formulations and actual crisis behavior. It points to the validity of Western crisis theory which posits objective processes and dynamics, requiring the effective handling of techniques no matter what the ideological and political preconceptions of the decision-maker.

The 'Impending' Crisis of Capitalism

Concerning formalized ideological perceptions toward the major capitalist countries, there is, however, a second major element of Zhdanovist ideology – the thesis of a 'deepening' or 'impending' economic crisis of capitalism – which did seem to have had cognitive and operational significance. Again Zhdanov's authoritative speech at the founding meeting of the Cominform has to be taken as a starting point of analysis. On the surface there is a fundamental contradiction. Zhdanov points to the fact that the United States 'emerged from the war not only unweakened, but even considerably stronger economically and militarily': but at the same time he speaks of an 'impending economic crisis'.[10] However, in accordance with Lenin's *Imperialism: The Highest Stage of Capitalism* and the explanation furnished there, that fundamental, antagonist contradictions and crises in and among capitalist countries arise because 'export of capital has acquired pronounced importance' and because 'the territorial division of the whole world among the greatest capitalist powers is completed',[11] Zhdanov sets out to reconcile Leninist theory with Stalinist dogma and bring into harmony the view of an 'impending economic crisis of capitalism' with an 'economically and militarily stronger' United States. He states that

> the end of the war confronted the United States with a number of new problems. The capitalist monopolies were anxious to maintain their profits at the former high level, and accordingly pressed hard to

prevent a reduction of the wartime volume of deliveries. But this meant that the USA must retain foreign markets which had absorbed products during the war, and moreover, acquire new markets, inasmuch as the war had substantially lowered the purchasing power of most of the countries.[12]

As a result of the necessity to acquire new markets – to continue Zhdanov's argument – 'the United States proclaimed a new, frankly predatory and expansionist course'.[13] The linkage of the predicament of United States capitalism and foreign policy (imperialism) is thus established. When Zhdanov says that the 'broad aim' of American capital is to bring 'Europe into bondage', he could have expressed conclusions which were ultimately pronounced by Stalin in his *Economic Problems of Socialism in the USSR* in 1952 and adopted at the Nineteenth Party Congress of the CPSU in the same year, that war between capitalism and socialism was now less likely than war among capitalist states, the latter still remaining 'inevitable'.[14] As shown above, in 1947–8 the opposite conclusion was drawn, that of an increased danger of attack emanating from the 'division of the political forces operating in the world arena into two major camps' and 'the creation in peacetime of numerous bases and vantage grounds ... designed to be used for aggressive purposes against the USSR and the countries of the new democracy'. In this context it is significant that Zhdanov speaks of France and Great Britain as United States 'allies'.[15]

Without doing so directly, Zhdanov thus continues the attack on Eugene S. Varga, head of the Institute of World Economy and World Politics which had been launched in May 1947 at a public discussion of Varga's book, *Izmeneniia v ekonomike kapitalizma v itoge vtoroi mirovoi voiny* (Changes in the Economy of Capitalism Resulting from World War II), published in September 1946.[16] In essence Varga had argued that the crisis of capitalism might be deferred for as much as ten years through the increasing intervention of the state in capitalist economic processes; he foresaw the possibility of social reform without revolution and implied that war was not inevitable even while imperialism continued to exist.[17] Several of the books published under the auspices of the Institute of World Economy and World Politics supported Varga's views.[18]

However, in 1947–8 these views and their exponents were severely criticized. In October 1947 Varga's institute was abolished by means of a merger with the Institute of Economics; Varga himself henceforth was to play only a subordinate part as one of the members of that institute; and his journal, *Mirovoe khoziastvo i mirovaia politika* (World Economy and World Politics), after having published the stenographic protocol of the discussion of his book of May 1947 in which he had been unrepentant on many aspects of his theses, was forced to cease publication.[19] Clearly in the course of 1948 the predominant line was that Varga's book and others of its kind were 'unMarxist', were written under the influence of 'bourgeois methodology' and objectively constituted support for the Marshall Plan.[20]

The doctrinal concepts pronouncing an impending economic crisis of capitalism could be a matter of complete indifference to the analyst of the Berlin crisis were it not for the possibility that genuine Soviet perceptions are at issue here. This *possibility* must be considered a high *probability* when the consistency of Soviet policy in exploiting 'revolutionary opportunities' allegedly existing in 1947–8 in the imperialist camp is taken into account.

One of the major indications of this lies in the intensification of the class struggle as evident in the series of large-scale, violent strikes staged by communist labor unions in Italy and France at the end of 1947 and then again in the summer and fall of 1948. The origins of this new policy of the two most important Communist Parties in Western Europe can be traced to the founding meeting of the Cominform, where Jacques Duclos and Luigi Longo found themselves – as one of the co-victims later put it – *au banc des accusés*.[21] Their 'crime': lack of revolutionary zeal. In his opening presentation the French party leader had been perceptive and courageous enough to warn that a campaign of violence would surely play into the hands of the bourgeoisie.[22] This had turned out to be true by the end of the first series of strikes in 1947, and it showed itself in the further isolation of the party domestically.[23] In foreign policy, militancy of the CPF may very well have contributed to the increasing French support for a joint Western allied policy in Germany and in the Berlin crisis. But these disadvantages may have been outweighed in Stalin's view by the fact that the strikes were damaging the prospects of rapid economic growth in Western Europe. The balance sheet of costs and benefits, therefore, may have appeared unclear.

No such ambiguity applied to the results produced by the militancy of the Czech communists in February 1948. Almost by any definition Czechoslovakia in January 1948 was by and large a democratic, multiparty state with a capitalist economy. At that time President Beneš anticipated a 'calm' development of the country, elections to be held in the spring (which, he thought, 'the Communists [would] lose and rightly so') and the absence of any danger of a putsch by the communists ('they cannot afford it').[24] The fact that mass demonstrations and strikes, the threat of armed insurrection and the pressures of an emerging superpower in close proximity to the country combined to shatter the optimistic assumptions of the Czechoslovak President within a month cannot be underestimated in its significance for the unfolding of events in the Berlin crisis, for the continuation of strikes in Italy and France, and for the persistence of Stalin's erroneous opinion that he only needed to 'shake his little finger' and Tito would fall.[25] If militancy and left-wing radicalism could not be dismissed *a priori* as an 'infantile disorder' but could, under favorable conditions, serve to break the capitalist adversary's will to resist, and if these conditions seemed to present themselves during the period of an 'impending economic crisis of capitalism', was it not – in Stalin's perspective – worth the risk to repeat the successful tactics of the Czechoslovak type elsewhere? Seen in this light the Berlin blockade would indeed have to be considered as a consistent application of a general line, as but one of many other manifestations of 'left' policies. Is this interpretation supported by local communist tactics?

'Infantile Disorder' in Berlin

In the course of 1948 tactics in the Soviet occupation zone and in the Soviet sector of Berlin moved from broad alliance and national appeals to militant sectarian 'mass action'. More slowly than in Eastern European countries the hard line laid down at the founding meeting of the Cominform in the fall of 1947 was transferred to Germany, notwithstanding fundamental differences in conditions applying there. If Stalin hoped to influence German politics as a whole he could not dispense with the need to formulate a coherent and attractive program which would appeal to broader 'progressive forces' in East as well as in West Germany. But much of the appeal had already been lost by the blatantly exploitative nature of reparation deliveries from the Soviet zone to the Soviet Union, and by the forced merger of the Communist Party of Germany (KPD) and the Social Democratic Party (SPD) in April 1946 to form the Socialist Unity Party (SED).

Nevertheless at the end of 1945 several theses were enunciated by Anton Ackermann, a high-ranking party functionary of the KPD before the merger with the SPD, to the effect that the possibility existed of a 'German road to socialism' with transitions 'on relatively peaceful lines'.[26] They were still echoed at the First German People's Congress, a numerically impressive gathering of 2,215 delegates (most of them from the Soviet zone) held in East Berlin on 6 and 7 December 1947. In accordance with the spirit of Ackermann's theses, the congress issued appeals for the holding of a referendum for the preservation of national unity and the formation of a central German government. A similar appeal under the slogan 'Save the unity of Berlin' was issued by the congress on 15 January 1948.[27]

But as the movement towards a separate West German state gained momentum, it became evident, in the later view of two East German analysts, 'That the acute danger for Germany and her capital required a significantly stronger mobilization of all patriotic forces; national protest had to become a matter of national self-help'.[28] Increasingly, a contradiction between national appeals and militant tactics became apparent. On the one hand the People's Council (*Volksrat*), a kind of shadow government, elected at the Second People's Congress in March 1948, continued to deal with questions of a peace treaty, a German constitution, economics, justice, culture and welfare. But on the other hand on 12 March 1948, at the hundredth anniversary of the appearance of the Communist Manifesto, the chief of the information office of the Soviet military administration in Germany, Colonel Tulpanov, initiated a direct attack against the 'so-called Social-Democratic reformists', claiming that the Social Democratic Parties of Western Europe 'had abandoned Marxism and openly entered the camp of bourgeois ideology'.[29] Demonstrations, protests and labor strikes with political overtones became more frequent. On 14 June allegedly 'more than 100,000 labor union members demonstrated against the terror. In the Western Sectors there were sporadic protest strikes.'[30] In the words of the two East German authors: 'Everything pointed to the fact that *the struggle for Berlin had entered its decisive stage.*'[31]

The dichotomy of leftist radicalism and nationalist appeals continued throughout the blockade. Reporting on the Two-Year Economic Plan for the Soviet zone, the SED party leader, Walter Ulbricht, stated in obvious reference to the Marshal Plan and the London recommendations on 27 June: 'The Two-Year Plan is the only plan that can help the German people because it is a German plan.'[32] He did not reveal, however, that the plan was actually drafted by the SMA.[33] Ulbricht no doubt was conscious of the difficult terrain on which his party had to operate. Despite that, he reiterated a fundamental Stalinist dogma: '*Some working-class people think that the class struggle abates with progress in the building of a democratic order. The opposite is the case.*'[34] East German communist dilemmas were highlighted also by the hasty withdrawal of a statement by Hermann Matern, a high-ranking SED functionary. At the beginning of July 1948 he announced that Berlin, as a part of the Soviet zone, must be drawn into the economic system of Eastern Germany; only hours later, apparently upon reprimands from higher SED or Soviet authorities, Matern issued a denial and said that his previous statement was in error.[35]

As the blockade continued week after week, and as the SED remained incapable or unwilling to voice any criticism of Soviet policies, German communists, as communists elsewhere in Western Europe, appeared as mere tools of Soviet foreign policy, or, worse, as traitors to the national cause. As a consequence, the SED in a resolution of 3 July 1948 purported to draw the 'lessons of the mistakes made by the Communist Party of Yugoslavia' and demanded the creation of 'a politically coherent, visionary core of function-aries in the Party' having as its main task the 'struggle against all *enemies of the working class*, notably the Schumacher agents'.[36] For all practical purposes the campaign for a 'German road to socialism' was at an end. The orthodox concept of proletarian dictatorship in Germany, as in Eastern Europe, finally superseded the transitory concept of 'people's democracy'. Friendship with the Soviet Union and imitation of the Soviet example, in Ulbricht's words, became the *Prüfstein* (main test) for every true anti-fascist.[37] Following the blockade and the exclusion of the Yugoslav communists from the Cominform, former Social Democrats were being removed from the leading organs of the SED.

There is no point in tracing in detail the precise manifestations of a concer-ted Soviet and German communist campaign of terrorization and intimida-tion during the blockade such as militant demonstrations of 'workers' against democratic institutions; exertion of pressure on the *Stadtverord-netenversammlung* (city assembly) and Magistrat (city council); kidnapping of lower- and middle-echelon supporters of noncommunist parties and insti-tutions; the utilization of false confessions; the beating up of assembly members; the spreading of rumors by Soviet radio to create panic; and the sporadic military moves outside the Western sectors in plain sight of the Berliners.[38] It may suffice to summarize at this point that national appeals were ineffective invocations of a lost cause. As persuasion failed, left-wing radicalism became the 'infantile disorder' against which Lenin had argued in 1920.[39]

Ideology, Russian Nationalism and Foreign Policy

To return to the question as to whether Soviet and East German communist militancy in Berlin can be understood as but one element of a more general pattern of leftist militancy, it is worth noting that the transition from concepts and policies connected with 'people's democracy' to 'institutional and ideological uniformity' in East Central Europe was preceded by a turn towards ideological orthodoxy in the Soviet Union itself.[40] Although the conviction spread spontaneously in the USSR that now after the war there would be room for relaxation,[41] Stalin's election speech of 9 February 1946 left no illusions about the future directions of Soviet policy when he told his listeners:

> So far as plans for a longer term are concerned, the Party intends to organize a new upsurge of the economy, which will make it possible for us to something like treble the level of our industry compared with the pre-war period ... Only on this condition can we consider that our Motherland will be guaranteed against all accidents.[42]

Stalin thus established continuity with the justifications given at the Eighteenth Party Congress in 1939 when he addressed himself to the question: 'Will our state remain in the period of Communism also?' and when he replied: 'Yes, it will, unless the capitalist encirclement is liquidated, and unless the danger of foreign military attack has disappeared.'[43] In 1931, Stalin recognized that 'It is sometimes asked whether it is not possible to slow down the tempo a bit, to put a check on the movement'.[44] The reason why it was impossible then to slow down was because of the 'jungle law of capitalism. You are backward, you are weak – therefore you are wrong; hence you can be beaten and enslaved.'[45] With the defeat of German, Italian and Japanese fascism in 1945, as Stalin and Zhdanov elaborated, conditions had by no means changed. As a consequence, doctrinal justifications were found in order to legitimize a new phase of mobilization and revolutionary transformation of Soviet society and politics.

The extent of this reorientation again can only be highlighted here. It included a thorough reorganization of the training and indoctrination programs under the direction of the Higher Party School and the Academy of Social Sciences;[46] emphasis on labor discipline and heavy industry; a vast campaign against creativity in the arts and sciences which has come to be labeled *Zhdanovshchina* after its main exponent; the official sanctioning of a resurgence of anti-Semitism; a repressive nationality policy; and the restoration of tight party control over the military as evident, among other things, in the demotion in 1946 of Marshal Zhukov, hero of the Soviet victory in Berlin, and the avoidance of his name on 9 June 1948 at the third anniversary of German capitulation.

There is, however, one conceivable objection to the analytical framework positing a close interrelationship of domestic and intra-bloc revolutionary transformations from above and attempts in Berlin to evoke militant mass action from below: the emphasis on Russian nationalism and the increasing isolation of Soviet society and politics from foreign influences. As early as January 1945 the members of a Yugoslav delegation (Koca Popovic, Mijalko Todorovic, Svetozar Vukmanovic-Tempo and Milovan Djilas), during their stay in the Soviet Union, were 'bewildered and astonished at the marked Russification of public life' and 'taken aback by the arrogant attitude of the Soviet representatives', the 'attitude of a "superior race" and the conceit of a great power'.[47] Roy Medvedev confirms these impressions when he writes that in the period from 1946 to 1948:

> Signs of great-power chauvinism grew constantly stronger. The Russian element in the USSR was stressed to the point that a cult of the Russian nation was created. Orienting himself toward surviving Great Russian prejudices, Stalin increasingly replaced internationalism by a nationalist outlook.[48]

In line with this, contact with all things foreign was made much more difficult than ever before. In June 1947 a State Secrets Act was adopted which classified almost all information as secret and threatened Soviet citizens who provided such information to foreigners with severe penalties. A new decree was published in January 1948 outlawing direct contact, oral or written, between foreigners and Soviet citizens and organizations except through the Ministry of Foreign Affairs.[49]

Russian nationalism was reflected in Soviet statements on the exemplary nature of nationality policy as, for instance, in an editorial in *Bol'shevik* which claimed that

> Contemporary reality is brilliant testimony to the force and great progressive significance of the Leninist-Stalinist nationality policy. The successes of the Soviet Union in solving the nationality problem is an immensely inspiring example for all peoples of the world.[50]

and it was evident with regard to interparty relations and the international communist movement with assertions such as

> The Communist Party of the Soviet Union (Bolsheviks), created and educated by the great geniuses of revolutionary theory, Lenin and Stalin, serves as an *example to all fraternal Communist Parties* of how to approach the development of Marxist theory.[51]

All this, the practice as well as the doctrinal statements, objectively contradicted traditional Marxist precepts on the withering away of nationalism under socialism, but rather than receiving condemnation as a bourgeois remnant or revisionist deviation, nationalism had received doctrinal blessing in the 1930s with the acceptance of patriotism as a positive phenomenon; and potential objections which could have been raised by reference to the Marxist principle of internationalism and working-class solidarity were ruled out of court by the self-serving rationale that a true internationalist 'is ready to defend the USSR without reservation, without wavering, unconditionally'.[52] Under Stalin leftism had a distinctly nationalist flavor.

The overall picture which emerges from these considerations is unambiguous. The hardening of adversary relations in a 'two camp' concept, formalized perceptions of an impending crisis of capitalism, commitments to militancy and revolutionary transformations, the insistence on uniformity of socioeconomic structures of systems in East Central Europe and the retention of a particular definition of 'proletarian internationalism', permitting excesses of Russian nationalism without doctrinal contradiction to Marxist universalist ideals – all this constitutes a broad framework of leftist policies in which the Berlin crisis appears as part of a general pattern. While it is not possible to prove that leftist ideological commitments and the policies pursued on this basis inevitably led to the Berlin crisis,[53] it is fair to assume that the general framework established patterns of action which, once the Central European venture was launched, were difficult to deflect or arrest.

II SECURITY AND STATE INTERESTS

Traditionally, security has always had, apart from subjective factors such as threat perceptions, fundamental objective territorial and military dimensions. But while it is true that today, in an era of manifest revolution in military technology, international communication and intercontinental power, it is questionable whether it makes sense to go on dividing up the world into 'vital' and 'peripheral' geographical areas and spheres of influence,[54] the transition from traditional requirements of security to new forms had barely begun in 1948, and the implications of the change were to become fully visible only at the time of the Cuban missile crisis.[55] It therefore made a good deal of sense for the USSR in 1948 to approach security problems very much from a traditional perspective. But beyond that, domestic and international security for the Soviet Union has always been a function of social and economic factors. Soviet foreign policy has not been that of a traditional nation state; it has always been characterized by a mixture of national *and* ideological elements.

The problem at issue, therefore, is how Soviet security in its various dimensions – ideological, political, socioeconomic and military – could have been achieved *vis-à-vis* Germany in postwar conditions. The answer is probably by adopting any one of four broad options: (1) by a revolutionary transformation of the social and economic system of the whole of Germany under the leadership of a Communist Party controlled by the Soviet Union; (2) by a substantial weakening of the economic and military potential of Germany in conjunction with territorial reductions; (3) by division or dismemberment and the continued, long-term enforcement of such a state of affairs by four-power control; and (4) by striving for a unified, neutral Germany. Although these approaches are not mutually exclusive, each one of them affected Soviet interests in a different way and required different policies – and, as it was to turn out, each one of them seemed to fail in providing solutions to Soviet security dilemmas.[56]

The Revolutionary Transformation of Germany

According to classic Marxist theory, prospects for the revolutionary transformation of Germany in the early post-World War II period were bright indeed (as they had been in 1918–23), not only because of the doctrinal ruling that capitalism had reached its highest stage there and had become 'overripe' and because – as Stalin commented – Germany had 'an extremely qualified and numerous working class and technical intelligentsia'[57] but also because fascism (a variant of 'imperialism' in Marxist terminology) had been completely discredited and its collapse had set in motion far-reaching processes of socioeconomic change. After the war there was widespread feeling among the members of the two parties of the left, the SPD (Social

Democrats) and KPD (Communists), that it had been largely the disunity of the working class which had facilitated the rise of fascism in the 1930s. Many rank-and-file communists realized that it was necessary to base future policies on the decisions of the Seventh Comintern Congress which in 1935 had recognized the grave mistake they had made in labeling the Social Democrats 'social fascists' and, even more disastrously, in waging a 'principled' and merciless struggle against them. Then as now, broad alliance strategies, parliamentary roads to power and reconciliation of the parties of the left were called for to cope successfully with difficult tasks ahead.

Conditions for a socialist transformation of Germany could be considered as favorable also because in one part of Germany the Soviet Union exerted unchallenged control to impose its own policies; and in the other part of Germany the influx of several millions of migrants and refugees from the formerly German regions under Soviet and Polish control, Czechoslovakia and Hungary, as well as the large-scale destruction of housing during the war, had produced a fertile ground for social unrest. Mass demonstrations and strikes against inadequate living conditions and low food rations plagued the Western zones until as late as the spring of 1948.

There *was* to some extent a recognition by the SMA of the desire among the rank and file of German socialists and communists to make a fresh start. On 14 July 1945 a united front consisting of 'antifascist and democratic parties' was formed in the Soviet zone; in addition to the KPD and SPD it included the CDU (Christian Democrats) and the LDPD (Liberals). As if to broaden the antifascist consensus, the SMA authorized the foundation of two new political parties, the NDPD (National Democrats) and DBD (Democratic Peasants), as late as April and May 1948 respectively.[58] By that date, however, events had progressed too far, and the move was easily recognized for what it was: a propagandist device to demonstrate autonomy of political development and pluralism of political parties and ideologies where these no longer existed.[59]

All the worse for Marxist theory that the actual course of events in Germany in 1948, as in 1918–23, took a direction entirely different from the one it should have taken. For one thing, nationalism frustrated many hopes that might have been attached to a successful revolution or evolution in the postwar period, and something will be said about this later in this section. Equally important, the objective prerequisites of cooperation between Social Democrats and communists on German soil were lacking as the fundamental differences between the two parties as they had existed in the Weimar Republic – internal democratic structure and reformism on the one hand and Leninist-Stalinist orthodoxy in the form of democratic centralism on the other – had by no means disappeared. Such antifascist committees and democratic, socialist and communist organizations as had sprung up spontaneously after the war were quickly dissolved by the SMA in 1945. The *apparat* had begun to triumph over what might have proved to be a powerful independent socialist movement.[60]

Resented for its attempts to rally socialists around its flag in an organized as opposed to voluntary and spontaneous fashion, burdened by its association with an occupation power whose internal structure had been consistently rejected by German socialists as a model of development and guilty by association for the hasty and damaging reparations policy of that power (which will be examined later in more detail), the KPD was losing out in the race with the SPD for the political support of the German population. This led to an early reversal by the KPD of its initial preference for separate development of the two parties and, as noted, to the merger of the two parties in April 1946 – despite the fact that the majority of the SPD membership was against it. In that single instance where the merger proposal was put to a test among the members of the SPD, as in the three Western sectors of Berlin, it was rejected by a vast majority (82 percent).[61] And despite the fact that organizationally the SPD had ceased to exist in the Soviet zone and the SMA was heavily favoring the new Socialist Unity Party (SED), the latter party did not manage to win, as it thought it would, an absolute majority in the October 1946 elections for the regional parliaments in that zone. It fared even worse in the elections, held in the same month, for the city government in Berlin, where the SED received only 19·8 percent of the total vote as against 48·7 percent for the SPD, 22·2 percent for the Christian Democrats and 9·3 percent for the Liberals.[62]

If this was the fate of the political forces favored by the SMA in the area directly under its control (the Soviet zone), or acting in the shadow of its power (in Berlin), it is clear that the chances for a successful communist revolution, or even the hope of influencing the course of events through a strong Communist Party, were quite remote in the western parts of Germany.

But having said all that, it is only fair to state that from the very beginning Stalin did not seem to have placed much trust in the realization of the first option. At various times he had revealed that he was skeptical, some would say even cynical, about achieving communist revolutions abroad without the direct support of Soviet power. As far as Germany was concerned, this was shown by his comments to Djilas that 'you cannot have a revolution [there] because you have to step on the lawn';[63] or when he commented on a pre-1941 Soviet war film which showed rebellious elements of the German proletariat disrupting the rear of the German invaders, that 'the German proletariat did not rebel';[64] or when he is reported as having said to the Polish leader Mikolajczyk that communism fitted Germany 'as the saddle a cow'.[65] But although, as Stalin must have recognized, the option of the establishment of a communist regime in the whole of Germany no longer existed in 1948, other options perhaps still did.

Emasculation of Germany

Concerning the second possibility of safeguarding Soviet security interests and preventing future German aggression (the weakening of the economic and military potential of Germany and the reductions in its territorial base) there are several facets which need to be distinguished. As regards territorial questions, it was agreed at the Tehran conference that the northern part of East Prussia was to be transferred to the Soviet Union and a strong Poland was to be created with substantial territorial compensations in the north and west. Not only did this happen but Churchill's warning at Yalta not to 'overstuff the Polish goose' was completely ignored. Polish sovereignty was extended *de facto* to the *western* River Neisse, Stalin thereby presumably laying the basis for the most probable development in the circumstance: long-term Polish-German hostility and Polish dependence on the Soviet Union.[66] By 1948 events seemed to have drifted precisely in that direction because of the migration and expulsion of more than 10 million Germans from the areas east of the Rivers Oder and Neisse, the westward shift of several million Poles and the consolidation of Soviet and Polish administration in the new territories. In addition to the probable political consequences, the territorial changes in East Central Europe considerably weakened the power base of Germany and strengthened that of Poland and the Soviet Union at Germany's expense.

An important economic facet in the option of weakening Germany relative to the Soviet Union was contained in the Soviet demands for reparations. In accordance with the Potsdam Protocol, which provided that Soviet reparation claims should be met by removals from the Soviet zone of occupation and that the USSR would settle the reparation claims of Poland from its own share of reparations, the USSR – even before the war had ended – began transferring industrial equipment from its zone and removing German (and non-German) assets in Eastern Europe on a large scale.[67] Furthermore the Soviet Union was to receive (1) 15 percent of such usable and complete industrial capital equipment, in the first place from the metallurgical, chemical and machine-manufacturing industries, as was unnecessary for the German peace economy *in exchange* for an equivalent value of food, coal, petroleum products and other commodities as would be agreed upon and (2) 10 percent of such industrial capital equipment as was unnecessary for the German peace economy *without payment or exchange*. Removals of equipment as provided in (1) and (2) were to be made simultaneously, and the amount of equipment to be removed from the Western zones was to be determined within six months after the Potsdam conference.[68] As Clay observed correctly as early as September 1945, 'The Russians are clearly most anxious to get industrial facilities and equipment out of the Western zone[s] as quickly as possible'.[69] Moreover Soviet representatives at the Allied Control Council and in the various meetings of the Council of Ministers never tired of pointing out that the USSR, according to Soviet calculations, had suffered damage in World War II amounting to US$128 billion, and that in view of this it was entirely reasonable for the USSR to ask a total of US$10 billion in reparation from Germany in three forms – capital equipment, current production and services.[70]

The Soviet demands for German reparations were perfectly understandable from a practical economic point of view because of the desperate need for capital equipment in the reconstruction and modernization of Soviet industry.[71] However, it would be erroneous to ascribe vulgar Marxist ideas to Stalin in the sense that he looked only at the practical economic issue without regard to the political implications. The Soviet insistence on the breakup of trusts, syndicates, cartels and monopolies, the dismantling of German industry, demands for reparations in the three forms mentioned and international control over the Ruhr were all clearly connected with the overriding objective of weakening Germany and, in particular, emasculating her military-industrial potential. All this was, in fact, acknowledged quite frankly by Molotov when he said:

> *The aim of completely disarming Germany militarily and economically should also be served by the reparations plan.* The fact that until now no such plan has been drawn up, in spite of the repeated demands of the Soviet Government that the relevant decisions of the Berlin conference should be carried out, and the fact that the Ruhr has not been placed under inter-Allied control, on which the Soviet Government insisted a year ago, is a *dangerous thing from the point of view of safeguarding future peace and the security of nations.*[72]

Economic and security issues were thus very closely tied together by the Soviet Union into one propagandist package. In Soviet eyes the Marshall Plan was not designed to forestall a possible resurgence of German aggression but to encourage it;[73] The 'military-industrial system of the Ruhr' was to play a 'dominating role' in the formation of the Western European Union.[74] West Germany was to be transformed into a 'military-strategic springboard'.[75] The London recommendations, too, were interpreted in this fashion. The declaration of the Warsaw Conference of 24 June 1948 stated in summary fashion, without reference to the blockade which had come into force on the same day, that

> The London decisions are designed not to avert a repetition of German aggression, but to transform the western part of Germany, and particularly the heavy industry of the Ruhr, into an instrument for the rebuilding of Germany's war potential, to be used for furthering the strategic aims of the United States and Great Britain. It stands to reason that such a plan cannot but create favourable conditions for the recrudescence of German aggression.[76]

It could be argued that these Soviet statements are 'instrumental' rather than 'cognitive', that is, that they were entirely of a propagandistic nature and did not express genuine fears and anxiety of the Soviet leadership. It would be difficult to make a good case for this argument in view of Stalin's reported pessimism about the likely efficacy of political and economic measures to curb the military and industrial potential of Germany. As early as April 1945 Stalin assumed that defeated Germany would 'recover, and very quickly' because of its high level of industrialization and, as quoted, its 'extremely qualified and numerous working class and technical intelligentsia'.[77] Stalin drew the conclusion from this that the Germans would be 'on their feet again' in twelve to fifteen years.[78]

It would be equally difficult to argue that Stalin's assessment, which after all proved to be correct at least for the western – and more important – part of Germany, was completely unrelated to another statement which he made at the same time. At one point in the discussion, Djilas says, Stalin rose from the table, 'hitched up his pants as though he was about to wrestle or to box, and cried out almost in a transport, "The war shall soon be over. We shall recover in fifteen or twenty years, and then we'll have another go at it."'[79] It is fair to infer from all this that in Stalin's mind doubts about the viability of economic and political measures to control Germany, expectations of the speedy recovery of Germany and apprehensions about the possibility, or even inevitability, of another military conflict were all closely linked.

Soviet policies seemed to be conducted in such a way as if to make Stalin's perceptions a self-fulfilling prophecy. More specifically, the Soviet economic and reparations policy in Germany had come to a dead end, and it appears that the unfolding of the Berlin crisis was not unrelated to this fact. This is so because the exploitative reparations policy had not only produced negative political consequences for the 'competition between the two opposed social and economic systems on German soil' but it had also begun to affect the economic base of the Soviet zone itself to a lasting degree. In 1946 Soviet reparation demands and zonal production had both risen sharply and in 1947, when reparation demands had largely changed their form (the removal of capital stock was replaced to a great extent by the extraction of commodities from current production) and reached unprecedented heights, production after recovery from a setback in the winter of 1946–7 had still suffered only a slight overall reduction. But by March and April 1948 the volume of industrial production in the Soviet zone had reached its peak. It then dropped sharply and flattened out despite all efforts to make it rise again. As events were to show, neither the currency reform in the Soviet zone nor the ensuing Two-Year Plan (1949–50) achieved their stated purpose of substantially increasing production. Most important for the present argument, the rise that did occur during the course of 1949 appears to have been due entirely to the abatement of Soviet reparation demands. In fact industrial output rose almost exactly by the amount by which the Soviet Union reduced its demands and by what, above the previous levels, it allocated to the German economy from its stock companies (see Figure 8.1).[80]

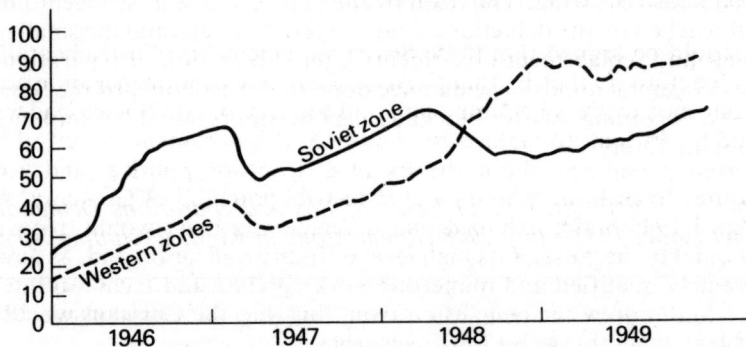

Figure 8.1   *Volume of Industrial Production 1946–9, as a Percentage of 1936, of Western Germany and Soviet Zone, (Including Reparations from Primary Products and Soviet Stock Companies).*

This point is important because it helps to demolish the astounding Soviet thesis that it was not only possible to eat the cake and have it too, but that in order to have the cake it was a *precondition* to eat it. This thesis was promulgated by Molotov, apparently in all seriousness, at the 12 December 1947 session of the Council of Foreign Ministers in London where he stated that '*reparations deliveries, far from hindering the rehabilitation of industry, facilitate it*'.[81] This was proved, according to Molotov, by United States statistical data which showed that the level of industry in the Anglo-American zone in mid-1947 was 35 percent of the figure for 1938, whereas in the Soviet zone the level of industry was 52 percent of the 1938 level.[82] This reasoning and the corresponding figures were not only given wide circulation (as, for instance, by the German communist leader Otto Grotewohl in an article for the Cominform journal)[83] but they were lent support in scholarly journals. Conveying the impression of favorable economic developments in the Soviet zone an article in *Voprosy ekonomiki* claimed:

> For the year 1948 the Soviet Military Administration [in Germany] has set up an exact plan for reparation deliveries and the lowering of occupation expenditures and at the same time provided for a growth rate of industrial production of 7–10 per cent. Simultaneously conditions have been created for the improvement of the economic situation and a significant rise in the standard of living of the working population of East Germany.[84]

It is very doubtful whether there was in fact such an exact reparations plan because all economic statistics, with the exception of a few niggardly percentages, were treated as secret by the Russians in the USSR as well as in Germany and *reparations* statistics were top secret; as the SMA was not responsible for reparations but a proliferation of other agencies it is even doubtful whether anyone in the Eastern zone or in the Soviet Union knew the precise data on this sensitive subject.[85] Also it was not only doubtful but quite incorrect to say that by 1948 favorable conditions had been created in the Soviet zone for the improvement of the economic situation and a rise in the standard of living. The truth of the matter was that stringent limits had been reached by the depletion of raw materials stocks and the small net total of new and replacement investments after subtraction of reparations in the form of capital goods. The damage done to the economy of the Soviet zone by the beginning of the blockade can be appreciated by looking at the following figures.[86]

Table 8.1 *Estimated Total Value of Soviet Reparations Demands in the Soviet Zone, 1945–July 1948 (Reparations in Kind, Excluding Services)*

		Reichsmark, 1936 value
(a)	dismantling of capital goods (replacement value)	4,100,000,000
(b)	reparations from current production and stocks	4,390,000,000
(c)	food	970,000,000
(d)	value of production from Soviet stock companies	2,010,000,000
Total		11,470,000,000

On the other hand the economic recovery of the Western zones had definitely begun in the latter half of 1947. Industrial production in the Western zones was catching up with that in the Soviet zone in relation to the 1936 level and in June 1948 surpassed it (see Figure 8.1, above, where the two lines cross over), only to be given an additional boost by the successful currency reform. As Germany was considered by many as the key to the success for European recovery, the prospects for the successful implementation of the European Recovery Program (Marshall Plan), which was signed on 3 April 1948, and of the objectives of the Organization for European Economic Cooperation (OECD), formed on 16 April 1948, appeared bright indeed.

As a consequence the Soviet Union was losing important points in the propagandist battle. In view of the strikes and demonstrations in the Western zones against low food rations, Soviet claims such as the following had perhaps not entirely lost credibility for everyone in the spring of 1948.

> [I]n connection with the famine in the Bizone the illegal movement of hungry people from the Western zones over the demarcation line into the Soviet zone has sharply increased in recent times, taking on a *mass character* with the onset of spring. Thousands of German inhabitants are crossing into the Soviet zone every day, hoping to find food and work there.[87]

Even then, of course, there was a net flow of Germans *from* the Soviet *to* the Western zones. Though problems of food supplies existed in the first quarter of 1948 and were acknowledged by the Western occupation powers, there was certainly no question of a famine; in any case conditions in food supply began to improve considerably in the spring of 1948 and the promulgation of the currency reform had a dramatic salutary effect. As it had been known that the Soviet Union had not been averse to taking food as reparations (see Table 8.1, above, item *c*), and as reparations deliveries from current production continued in 1948, a wide gap in the standard of living between the Western zones and the Soviet zone could easily be predicted. Soviet claims such as the one just quoted would soon no longer be tenable.

In the present context of the economic dimension of Soviet security policy two major points must still be noted. As American policy worked under the assumption that extensive reparations deliveries and speedy economic recovery were mutually contradictory, and as the assessment and delivery of reparations was based on the economic unity of Germany – a condition that no longer existed at the end of 1945 – the dismantling of capital equipment in the American zone and with it reparations deliveries to the Soviet Union (and also to Western claimants) were 'suspended' in May 1946. Molotov was to deplore this at the Moscow Foreign Ministers' Conference in March 1947, where he noted that since the Potsdam conference the Soviet Union had only received the insignificant equivalent sum of US$7·5 million in reparations deliveries in exchange for commodities (pursuant to category *a*) and US$5 million in reparations free of charge (category *b* of the Potsdam Protocol).[88] But as the cooperation of the prime ministers of the German *Länder* and other German political and economic leaders was needed for the implementation of the London recommendations it was simply no longer politically feasible to resume reparations deliveries to the Soviet Union unless very valid reasons could be presented. If reparations from *the whole of Germany* were meant to be an element of safeguarding Soviet security within the overall program of emasculating Germany, matters by 1948 looked bleak indeed.

Exactly the same is to be said for the controversy about 'international' control of the Ruhr. In the early four-power discussions such control, just like reparations, was conceived of only within the framework of the whole of Germany. From the Western point of view it therefore appeared objectionable and pretentious for the USSR to retain complete control over the economy in the Soviet zone and demand additional rights in the economy of the Western zones. Clay was in full agreement with predominant American and British (and on this issue also French) views when he stated bluntly that 'we should not enter into an agreement for international control [of the Ruhr] until we know that such an agreement will not involve Soviet representation in such control'.[89]

For all these reasons a fundamental conflict between economic and political priorities in Germany had to be resolved by the Soviet Union some time during the Berlin crisis. If Germany was to be preserved, or reestablished, as a single nation state the time to abandon a politically harmful economic policy had come. By mid-1948 the insistent Soviet knocks at the doors of the three Western zones for the payment of reparations and the demands for 'international' control of the Ruhr, in the sense of a Soviet share in such control, sounded hollow and anachronistic. A radical change in Soviet economic policy in Germany was required if a united Germany was to respect security interests of the USSR and cooperate economically with it in good faith.

Somewhat paradoxically a similar conclusion forced itself upon Soviet policy if the division of Germany was to be the operational principle during the Berlin crisis. If the creation of a West German state was to be answered by the formation of a counterpart in the Soviet zone, as it ultimately would, exigencies of the viability of such a state also necessitated abandonment of the counterproductive economic policy. What evidence is there that the course for the division of Germany was consciously adopted by the Soviet Union during the crisis?

Division and Dismemberment

In the light of all the facts available it would be erroneous to say that Soviet policy was consciously and consistently aimed at achieving the dismemberment or division of Germany. On the contrary as the end of the war approached Stalin had increasingly rejected this option, realizing, no doubt, that wartime coalitions in Europe historically have had a tendency to disintegrate rapidly after the achievement of victory and that therefore interallied agreements in general would be difficult to enforce over a long period of time. In particular the experience of Versailles had shown clearly that controls of Germany were ineffective. In fact the very issue of interallied control had been a powerful stimulus to revisionist and nationalist tendencies, even though the extent of territorial reductions of Germany then had been quite limited.

It was reasonable to assume therefore that division or dismemberment of Germany after World War II would result in unleashing the powerful forces of German nationalism and create new security risks. Stalin's recognition of this danger is reflected in his appreciation that 'The experience of history shows that Hitlers come and go but the German nation, the German state, remains';[90] in the appeals to German nationalism rather than to 'progressive forces' by founding, in July 1943, the Nationalkomitee Freies Deutschland (Free German National Committee) and the Bund Deutscher Offiziere (Federation of German Officers) in an attempt to bring about an early political solution to the war;[91] in his refraining from pushing the idea of dismemberment at Tehran, being reluctant about it at Yalta and declaring on Victory Day (9 May 1945) that the USSR 'has no intention of either dismembering or destroying Germany'.

The view that Stalin did not intend to divide Germany is supported also by the very extent of the transfer of German territory to Poland and the scale of the expulsion of German population. If Soviet policy at the end of the war had provided for an East German state under Soviet tutelage it would have been much better to establish a balance of size and potential between a future GDR or its equivalent on the one hand, and Poland on the other. For the USSR this would have meant agreeing to the *eastern* River Neisse as the border between the two countries rather than the western River Neisse; the area separated by the two rivers would have made an important difference not only with regard to East German production capacity (because of the large coal deposits of this region and the various types of industry which were integrated with the German economy) but also with regard to population (because of the 2·7 million people living there, almost all of them German). The problem of the viability of the GDR, which came to haunt the Soviet Union perennially but most acutely during the Berlin crisis of 1961, could have been alleviated to a considerable extent by adopting such a course of action.[92]

The realization of the resilience of German nationalism and the difficulty of enforcing a division of Germany is evident also in the period leading up to the Berlin crisis. In 1947 Vyshinski stated to the British war correspondent Alexander Werth that 'If there isn't a central German government, there will be before long a militarist and West German government. Don't quote me, but just remember what I said.'[93] In the same year Foreign Minister Molotov even opposed the idea of federalization of Germany as 'dangerous' because it would 'play into the hands of the militarists playing on the German people's longing for "German unity"'.[94]

In retrospect it appears that the stronger the momentum towards the creation of a separate West German government the more insistent the Soviet demands for the preservation of German unity. After the Foreign Ministers' Conference in London in Decemberr 1947 Molotov was reported in *Pravda* as having advocated a 'united, independent and democratic Germany', the formation of 'all-German economic departments' or, at the very least, 'the establishment of an all-German Consultative Council', but all this, according to Molotov, had been rejected by the West and 'instead Western Germany was being turned into the breeding ground for another world war'.[95]

These arguments were repeated in 1948. The note of the Soviet government to the three Western powers of early March and the justification provided by Marshal Sokolovsky for terminating Soviet participation at the Control Council at the end of March took issue with the London conference and charged the West with excluding the USSR from decision-making and even consultation on problems concerning Germany as a whole.[96] On 26 March, that is, only a few days after Sokolovsky's dramatic gesture, Lieutenant General Luk'ianchenko of the Soviet military administration in Germany stated for the historical record that 'The division of Germany is already an established fact' and that it was clear to all that 'this division was caused by the USA, Britain and France'.[97]

The fact that the USSR increasingly portrayed itself as the champion of German unity and even advocated the holding of a referendum on this question could be explained by the Soviet desire not to be held responsible in a court of history for the powerful drift towards the division of Germany – a drift which the Soviet Union itself had helped to set in motion. There is something to be said for this view. But at the same time division of Germany contained the threat of territorial revisionism and nationalism. From the Soviet point of view, even in 1948, it may still have appeared preferable to be included in the taking of decisions concerning Germany as a whole rather than be excluded and faced with a West German state hostile to the USSR by the very circumstances of its creation. Maintenance of unity may also still have appeared potentially advantageous to the Soviet Union as it did not seem to have given up hope of gaining access to reparations from the Western zones, and from the Ruhr in particular.

Neutralization of Germany

It would seem, therefore, that a detached analysis of the pros and cons of the German problem in 1948 advised a policy striving for the maintenance of a unified German state, neutralized, noncommunist in character, but ranged somewhere between socialism and capitalism in system structure, with a small army and police force for internal security and self-defense. This is the kind of policy suggested in essence by Stalin in his note to the three Western powers on 10 March 1952, in proposals made by his successors in 1954 and, as applied to Austria, in the State Treaty of 1955. This option probably was not foreclosed in 1948.

However, chances of success in carrying out this option required repudiation of the 'two camp' theory with all its implications of militant tactics. Equally important, it presupposed trust in the peaceful intentions of the Western powers. It also made it necessary to have confidence in a peaceful development of a united Germany. Above all, a nonrevisionist 'united Germany' seemed to pose as a precondition the return of the areas east of the Rivers Oder and Neisse, areas which many Germans – with Western allied encouragement – had already begun to consider as only 'temporarily under Soviet and Polish administration'.[98] Apart from this territorial issue, three years of Soviet occupation had done much to damage the possibility of reconciliation between Germans and Russians.

In the light of what was said in the context of the by 1948 obsolete option of a revolutionary transformation of the whole of Germany (the isolation of the KPD, the recognized hollowness of the claim that the Soviet zone was founded on democratic principles, pursued progressive and peaceful policies and acted in voluntary 'friendship with the Soviet Union') and the anti-Russian bias of German nationalism, the option of neutralization, if adopted in 1948, could not have meant anything but a Germany orienting itself towards the West in much the same way as Austria does today – though forbidden to ally itself formally with other powers, fundamentally remaining a Western country with a capitalist socioeconomic structure and a liberal parliamentary political system. The difference, however, between a neutralized Germany and a neutralized Austria (or Finland for that matter) was one of scale and vital importance. To prevent a country without a major industrial base and with a population of only about 7 million inhabitants from becoming a threat to Soviet security was a proposition quite different from living with a country with a heavy industrial base and a population of approximately 80 million inhabitants.

Nor was there much consolation or attraction in appealing to the old times of good Soviet-German relations in the 1920s. Rapallo was a temporary expedient from both the Soviet and the German points of view as defeated and ostracized nations. For Germany it had the major benefit of taking one major potential claimant of reparations off the waiting list and bringing moral pressure to bear on other countries to moderate their demands. At least on this score conditions had changed completely in as much as it was now the Soviet Union that figured as the most uncompromising claimant of reparations.

As the reestablishment of German unity in 1948, if it involved expression of preferences by the German people, would undoubtedly have led to a substantial defeat for the Soviet-type system in the Soviet zone there is much merit to the argument that Stalin, rather than risking developments of this kind, chose what appeared to him the lesser risk, namely, to hold fast to the area occupied by the Red Army, complete a series of pacts 'with all the states at its Western border, from the Black Sea to the Baltic and, after the conclusion of the Soviet-Finnish treaty, right up to the Arctic ocean' and so deal a 'powerful blow to all instigators of a new world war'[99] and to make the resulting sphere of influence safe for the USSR by incorporating the whole of Berlin in it – were it not for the equally valid argument that in Stalin's view, notwithstanding the desirability of incorporating Berlin in the Soviet zone, the enforcement of the division of Germany was impossible.

Given these apparently insoluble dilemmas for Soviet security in 1948 it would have been entirely understandable if Soviet policy had merely drifted into acceptance of the division of Germany as inevitable, trying to contain emerging dangers by pursuing conciliatory policies. Instead a strategy of coercion was adopted, utilizing local conventional superiority and Soviet leverage over progressive elements as means of forcing Western compliance to ill-defined Soviet demands. Perhaps this strategy cannot be explained entirely in rational terms, as a policy arrived at by the careful weighing of ends and means. Beyond the vague feeling or anxiety that Germany had been a threat to Soviet security in the past and that it was likely to be one in the future, Stalin may never really have had a clear conception as to how to approach, let alone solve, the German problem. This would explain much of the ultimate failure of the whole Berlin venture. But maybe the Soviet strategy – if it deserves this epithet at all – had much to do with the balance of military power in 1948.

III MILITARY POWER

The questions arising for the Berlin crisis and, more generally, post-World War II diplomacy in a context of Soviet strategic inferiority are primarily not whether Western revisionist historians are right in saying that 'the [atomic] bomb served to toughen the United States approach to disputed Central and Eastern European issues even before it was actually used' in Hiroshima and Nagasaki; or whether, thereafter, the American nuclear monopoly gave Truman sufficient confidence 'to attempt major reversals in negotiations over Poland, Germany, Hungary, Bulgaria and Rumania'.[100] Assertions such as these about US nuclear diplomacy (or 'blackmail' in Soviet parlance) have been discussed at length and largely dismissed by Western scholars if what is meant by 'nuclear diplomacy' is the systematic use of atomic power as an instrument of foreign policy *vis-à-vis* the Soviet Union as early as the period from 1945 to the onset of the Berlin crisis in 1948.[101]

Some light will be shed on these problems also. However, the questions to be dealt with here are primarily concerned with possible *Soviet* perceptions and behavior, notably: (1) did Stalin know and appreciate the military and political significance of the new weapon? (2) Is there any indication for believing that Stalin was sufficiently impressed by the strategic importance of the weapon to be restrained in his taking of risks in foreign policy? Only after these problems have been dealt with is it useful to examine further questions: (3) how, if at all, did nuclear issues enter into crisis bargaining in Berlin in 1948? And (4) what were the forms of interplay of military-strategic and local conventional power?

The American Nuclear Monopoly and its Political Significance

To begin with, the existence of the atomic bomb was a fact of which Stalin was informed 'casually' by Truman on 24 July during the Potsdam conference – if not earlier by Soviet intelligence. Stalin's reaction was as casual as the way in which he was informed. Truman thought that Stalin showed no special interest. 'All he said was that he was glad to hear it and hoped that we would make "good use of it against the Japanese".'[102]

It may be quite possible that Stalin at that particular point in time did not fully understand the historic significance of the new weapon. This may be so despite the fact that Igor N. Golovin, a Soviet physicist, disclosed in 1966 that the decision to build the atomic bomb was taken as early as the summer of 1942, and that after the first explosion of an atomic bomb had taken place in the United States at Alamogordo on 16 July 1945 Soviet scientists were ordered to speed up their efforts.[103] And it may be so despite the corroborating account by Marshal Zhukov, who wrote that when Stalin was informed by Truman about the new weapon of unusual destructive force, he (Stalin) remarked to Molotov on that evening that he was going to tell I. V. Kurchatov, the scientist responsible for the nuclear weapons program, 'to speed up our efforts'.[104]

The view that Stalin may at first not have grasped the full military and political significance of the new weapon is supported by General Shtemenko's memoirs. After accurately describing Truman's casual way of informing Stalin ('in an unofficial conversation, face to face') and complaining about his failure 'even to mention [any] plans to use such a weapon' against Japan, Shtemenko continues:

> Later Aleksei Innokent'evich [Antonov, Chief of the Soviet General Staff] said to me that Stalin had told him about the Americans' possession of a new bomb with very great destructive force. But Antonov, *apparently like Stalin himself, did not get from this conversation with Truman the impression that what was mentioned was a weapon that was new in principle.*[105]

The point to be made is simply that Stalin's instructions to speed things up are not necessarily inconsistent with underestimation of the actual explosive force and effects of the new weapon. Many Americans, too, were to appreciate only gradually the full scope of the changes in weapons technology.

But whatever the case may be as to the *testing* of the new weapon, there can be no reasonable doubt that the actual *use* of the weapon against Hiroshima and Nagasaki on 6 and 9 August, and the Japanese surrender thereafter, drastically impressed upon Stalin the tremendous importance of what had happened. In the middle of August the People's Commissar of Munitions, Boris L'vovich Vannikov, and his deputies were summoned to the Kremlin. They

> were sitting in Stalin's waiting room, rather puzzled why, after his return from Potsdam, he had summoned them. Suddenly, another person appeared at the door. This was I. V. Kurchatov. And at once it became clear to everyone what the conversation would be about.
>
> 'A single demand of you, comrades,' said Stalin, 'provide us with atomic weapons in the shortest possible time. You know that Hiroshima has shaken the whole world. The equilibrium has been destroyed (*ravnovesie narushilos'*). Provide the bomb – it will remove a great danger from us.'[106]

Considering Stalin's commitment in his election speech of February 1946 to give Soviet scientists proper assistance so that 'they will be able in the near future not only to overtake but to surpass the achievements of science beyond the boundaries of our country',[107] the huge energy requirements to separate U^{235} from U^{238} by means of gas diffusion, the complex engineering problems, the limited technological potential of a war-ravaged country and the fact that the first known Soviet test of a nuclear weapon took place much earlier (on 29 August 1949) than most Western scientists expected, it is justifiable to call the Soviet nuclear weapons program *a top priority project based on Stalin's recognition of the military and political importance of the new weapon and the determination to abolish the American nuclear monopoly as quickly as possible*. Much of this is still reflected in the comments Stalin was to make to Djilas in January 1948. At his dacha near Moscow,

> Stalin spoke about the atom bomb: 'That is a powerful thing, pow-er-ful!' His expression was full of admiration, so that one was given to understand that he would not rest until he, too, had the 'powerful thing'.[108]

Before that was to happen, however, attempts had apparently to be made to lessen in advance the psychological advantages which might accrue to the United States in crisis situations. The first major instance of such an attempt came in an 'interview' (replies to questions put in writing) with the British correspondent Alexander Werth in September 1946 which was published prominently in the Soviet press. In response to the question, 'Do you believe that virtual monopoly by the USA of the atomic bomb constitutes one of the main threats to peace?', Stalin answered:

> I do not believe the atomic bomb to be as serious a force as certain politicians are inclined to regard it. Atomic bombs are intended to intimidate the weak-nerved, but they cannot decide the outcome of war, since such bombs are by no means sufficient for this purpose. Certainly monopolist possession of the secret of the atomic bomb does create a threat, but at least two remedies exist against it: (a) monopolist possession of the atomic bomb cannot last long and (b) the use of the atomic bomb will be prohibited.[109]

In this short treatment of an important topic Stalin managed to put forward four elements of reassurance for the USSR, which are conversely four elements reducing the value of nuclear weapons for the United States. First, he implied that the USSR could hardly be counted among the 'weak-nerved' and that it could not be intimidated. Indeed, Stalin's most resourceful and uncompromising bargaining for maximum gain, during the Potsdam conference and thereafter, is virtually devoid of examples for retreat, and where there was retreat and compromise Stalin was careful not to convey the impression that it had occurred as a result of direct US military threats. This is valid even for the case still widely held to be the foremost example of Soviet retreat under direct US military pressure in the early postwar era: Iran, in March 1946. Undoubtedly there was diplomatic pressure. The evidence, however, for some sort of American military pressure, let alone ultimatum, is simply lacking.[110]

Secondly, if nuclear weapons could *not*, as Stalin argued, 'decide the outcome of war',[111] it followed that one should not make much ado about them. As if to underline this view, in the period from 1947 to 1953 not a single article on atomic weapons is known to have appeared in the Soviet military press, no matter whether in daily newspapers or periodicals, openly or in restricted circulation.[112] Also, to the extent that nuclear weapons were, as Stalin said, 'by no means sufficient' for deciding the outcome of general war, they fit seamlessly into Stalinist military doctrine as being merely 'transitory' or 'temporary' factors (as distinguished from 'permanently operating factors').

A third element to reduce the political utility of nuclear weapons for the United States was touched upon by Stalin in his interview with Alexander Werth. By saying that 'monopolist possession of the atomic bomb cannot last long' he clearly implied that the USSR was working on such a device and would soon be able to make it available to its armed forces. Injection of a degree of uncertainty about Soviet progress in producing an atomic bomb had begun even earlier, at a reception by the Soviet embassy after the conclusion of the London Foreign Ministers' Conference in September 1945. Molotov, drinking 'rather much even for him', according to Foreign Minister Bevin, had raised his glass and said: 'Here's to the Atom Bomb', and added, '*We've got it.*' [113] The very same impression was still to be conveyed more than two years later, when Molotov stated in a speech in Moscow on 6 November 1947 that

> among the expansionist circles of the United States of America has spread a new peculiar religion: lacking faith in its domestic forces [it has built up] faith in the secret of the atomic bomb, although *that secret has long ceased to exist*. (Prolonged applause.) [114]

But despite the 'prolonged applause' with which the editors of *Izvestiia* had greeted Molotov's announcement in Moscow, there was little sign in the West (and hence no consolation to the USSR for the course of the Berlin crisis) that the Soviet claims had made much of an impression. This is so not least because Molotov's use of the term 'secret of the atomic bomb' seemed to imply quite clearly that the USSR had not been able to *manufacture* an operational weapon. In fact Western scientists were publicly to voice the opinion as late as the spring of 1948 that even with successful espionage it would take the USSR 'at least five years to make a reasonable stock of atomic bombs'.[115]

Nor was there much advantage to be gained from a fourth element touched upon by Stalin in order to underplay the significance of nuclear weapons: the expressed hope that such weapons would be 'prohibited'. For the disappointment of this hope the Soviet Union itself was largely to blame. The Baruch Plan for the control of nuclear energy (and atomic weapons) had mainly been defeated because of the unrealistic and – if the Soviet Union really wanted an agreement – incomprehensible Soviet position that (1) the USA should first consent to the destruction of its nuclear weapons stockpile. (2) Only then could the USA count on the USSR to become a participant in an international authority for the control of atomic energy and weapons. (3) The veto principle, however, would have to be applied in such an authority.[116] No agreement, of course, was even marginally likely on such a basis. The problem of the American nuclear monopoly for the Soviet Union, therefore, did not go away.

Stalin's problem was made worse by not saying in his interview with Alexander Werth that the American public would not allow the use of nuclear weapons (because such a statement would have been incorrect) and by his explicit acknowledgment that the US nuclear monopoly *did* 'create a threat'. It is not surprising, therefore, that the sensitivity of the Soviet Union to the potential use of nuclear bombs as a weapon of war and an instrument of diplomacy reemerged shortly before the imposition of the blockade. This came in the form of a protest by the embassy of the USSR in Washington delivered to the US Department of State and dated 9 June 1948. In reference to a speech by General Kenney, commander of the Strategic Air Command, and an article published about it in an American magazine (*Newsweek*), the embassy complained that the article (and Kenney's speech) had

> set forth a plan to use American air forces, air bases and atomic bombs against the Soviet Union, particularly for the destruction of Soviet cities such as Moscow, Leningrad, Kiev, Kharkov, Odessa, and others. Speaking of plans for attack on the Soviet Union by American aircraft with atomic bombs, the magazine *Newsweek* states: 'Their targets: first Moscow – Moscow above all. Then the other large cities of European Russia – Kiev, Leningrad, Kharkov, and Odessa.' It is further stated in the article that American strategists are thinking in terms of 'closing the circle of air bases around Russia' in order to 'make it smaller and smaller, tighter and tighter, until the Russians are throttled'. This plan envisages combined air, naval, and ground operations from American bases located near the Russian mainland and their use for intensive bombing raids and attacks by guided missiles.
>
> The publication of this article, which is an example of unbridled propaganda for a new war against the Soviet Union, is a rude violation of the resolution of the Second Session of the [UN] General Assembly [condemning all forms of war propaganda].[117]

Apart from showing the Soviet sensitivity to the whole issue of nuclear weapons this protest also constituted a fifth element in the series of attempts at neutralizing the advantages accruing to the United States on account of its monopoly of nuclear weapons. In addition to the assertions that (1) the USSR could not be intimidated, (2) atomic bombs could not decide the outcome of general war, (3) the Soviet Union had, or was about to have, the bomb in any case and (4) nuclear weapons would soon be outlawed, a *moral* argument was put forward. Nuclear weapons, in the Soviet view, contradicted basic principles of the United Nations. None of this made much impact on American behavior in the Berlin crisis. On the contrary the nuclear monopoly played an important role in deterrence.

The attempt by the United States to improve its bargaining position *vis-à-vis* the Soviet Union through efforts at the military-strategic level began shortly after the communist *coup* in Czechoslovakia and the first troubles along the road and rail communications to Berlin when a demonstration flight of three B-29 (Superfortress) bombers around the world was authorized.[118] No in-flight, refueling capability was displayed and one of the planes crashed off the coast of Saudi Arabia; nevertheless the political purpose behind the demonstration was evident.

After the blockade had been imposed Clay reported to Washington after discussions with General Robertson that 'his [the British] Government strongly urges the dispatch of bombers from the United States to selected airdromes in France and England prior to the start of negotiations'.[119] Clay himself thought that the augmentation of air forces was 'urgent' because 'They [the Russians] are definitely afraid of our air might' and because 'the arrival of aircraft will be [a] deciding factor in sustaining Allied firmness'.[120] On the same day (27 June), at a meeting in Secretary of the Army Royall's office, Forrestal, Royall and others discussed the pros and cons of sending two air force groups of B-29 strategic aircraft (sixty in all) to Britain and on the next day President Truman made a decision of historic significance by approving the proposed transfer of such aircraft to Western Europe.[121] The process of American withdrawal from Europe was thus reversed in a most tangible and dramatic way.

On 2 July Secretary of State Marshall reported that B-29 strength in Germany had been increased from one squadron (ten aircraft) to a full group and that agreement had been reached with the British Foreign Minister, Ernest Bevin, permitting the transfer of two groups of B-29s to British soil.[122] As the latter transfer did not seem to proceed quickly enough, and in conditions where Clay and Robert Murphy were pressing for authorization to break the block-ade by means of moving a convoy along the autobahn,[123] Clay thought it important 'that the two B-29 groups now approved for movement into the UK be started at once, as it is my view that they should be in England when this con-voy movement is started'.[124] For the movement no approval of a convoy was forthcoming from Washington, but between 17 and 19 July the sixty scheduled B-29 bombers of the US air force arrived in Britain.[125] All this was on the assumption, as expressed by the American chargé d'affaires in Moscow, Foy Kohler, in September 1948, that 'our lead in atomic warfare possibilities is pre-sumably still a key factor in deterring [the] Soviets'.[126] As President Truman had authorized the use of atomic weapons before, Stalin could be under no illu-sions that he would not do so again. In fact in mid-September Truman took a decision of principle to use nuclear weapons in war 'if it became necessary'.[127]

But all this makes the problem even more puzzling as to why the United States did not abandon the expensive airlift and invoke its nuclear monopoly in a more direct form to back up an ultimatum to the Soviet Union to reopen at once the interrupted links between Berlin and the Western zones, or face the consequences. And all this also does not yet explain the apparent optim-ism on the Soviet side that the United States, in addition to the psychological advantages it could derive from its nuclear monopoly, would not resort to the actual use of force.

The Disparity of Conventional Power and its Significance

The reason why there was a sound military rationale for the Soviet Union to view the taking of risks in the Berlin crisis with greater relaxation than the adversary's possession of nuclear monopoly at first sight appeared to warrant has much to do with the huge disparity of military power at the conventional level, both locally and globally. As far as the 'correlation of forces' in Europe was concerned, Germany was defeated, disarmed and occupied. Britain was exhausted and so was France (and apart from that could not be relied upon to participate in any venture involving confronta-tion with the USSR). The United States had demobilized on a grand scale after the war, and its defense budget had fallen dramatically from US$81·2 billion in 1945, to US$14·4 billion in 1947 and US$11·7 billion in fiscal year 1948. By the spring of 1948 the total manpower of the armed forces had been reduced to 1,384,000 officers and men.[128]

As for the United States Air Force in Europe (USAFE) – a force that would have been immediately involved in any direct military clash with the Soviet Union over Berlin – plans for fiscal year 1948 showed how drastically the process of withdrawal of US forces from Europe was scheduled to continue; the number of military personnel attached to USAFE was to decline from 37,872 officers and men to a mere 9,790.[129] The significant reduction in available air power is demonstrated also by the fact that in the period between the end of the war and the beginning of the Berlin crisis the US air force had to abandon bases in Britain, Italy, Iceland and Greenland so that in the spring of 1948 air bases for training purposes only remained in the exposed American zone of Germany.[130] To take some more examples, at the beginning of the blockade the strength of US fighter aircraft in the whole of Europe was down to seventy-five aircraft,[131] and by as early as May 1946 there were no B-29 bomber aircraft in Europe except for those few (about a squadron) shuttled between the United States and training bases in Germany.[132] In the opinion of a Western analyst,

> it is safe to say that by May 1948 the United States had reduced its air power in Europe to the point that the Soviet Union might have questioned the American resolve to stand firm against Soviet pressures directed against Berlin.[133]

The power of the US army had shrunk equally dramatically in the period from 1945 to 1948. By March 1948 personnel of that branch of the armed forces was down to 544,000 officers and men of which only 92,000 were in Europe. Not only was the army plagued by recruiting difficulties, it also suffered from an almost total lack of modern equipment for the field forces, particularly modern tanks and armored vehicles.[124] It is fair to agree with General Omar Bradley's assessment that the condition of the army in 1948 was 'absolutely ineffective' and that Secretary Forrestal was right when he admitted that in the event of a Soviet attack on Western Europe, 'Our forces [in Germany], and particularly our ground forces, would be inadequate, quite inadequate'.[135]

In fact Western allied withdrawal during the spring of 1945 from territories in Czechoslovakia and Germany in compliance with the provisions for postwar occupation had surrendered considerable military advantage to the USSR: a concave rather than convex zonal frontier had been created, and the River Elbe was lost as a natural defensive obstacle. Moreover the United States had only one division in Central Europe, the Western allies six in all (three French and two British in addition to the one American). These few divisions, however, were strung out all along an arc stretching from Bavaria to the west, along the German borders with the Benelux countries rather than along the east/west divide in Germany. Hence when the Berlin crisis began not a single Western allied unit existed to cover the entire north German plain between Hanover and Hamburg – an area that lay in the axis of advance of two Soviet armies with eight divisions.[136] It is not surprising, therefore, to read in a top secret emergency war plan of the Joint Chiefs of Staff, dated 21 July 1948 and codenamed HALFMOON, the laconic statement:

It is contemplated that the initial withdrawal of Allied forces will be to the Rhine. Further withdrawal in the face of Soviet pressure must take advantage of all opportunities to delay Soviet advances . . . [I]t is probable that US forces will withdraw through France either to French ports or to the Pyrenees.[137]

In view of all the lamentary military deficiencies and grand withdrawal plans in the event of major hostilities in Europe, it was obvious that the hastily projected increases in the US defense budget in the spring of 1948, amounting to US$3 billion (later increased to US$3·48 billion) could not affect the American military posture in Europe *vis-à-vis* the Soviet Union at short notice.

In contrast the Soviet Union in 1948 maintained a huge military establishment estimated by a variety of sources as between 2,500,000 and 5,000,000 men, most of them in the ground forces.[138] As Soviet armed forces strength had been about 11,000,000 men in 1945, it is true to say that the Soviet Union, like the United States, *had* embarked upon large-scale demobilization in the early postwar years. However, the manner in which demobilization was carried out was different in the two countries: whereas the American measures seemed to have been guided by principles consistent with a prolonged period of peace and had resulted in the dismantling of military capabilities and effectiveness, the Soviet High Command had extensively reorganized and rationalized its forces – the Red Army – in a process of contraction, had withdrawn into a cocoon, transformed itself and reemerged, not as a butterfly but as a wasp under the new name of 'Soviet Army'. Its 175 reorganized divisions were given a much more flexible command and control structure, even more professional leadership, more firepower and greater mobility.[139]

According to estimates by General Clay, Soviet forces in Germany numbered over 300,000;[140] they had at their disposal several thousand tanks, and many of the units were part of 'guard' (*gvardia*) or 'shock' formations drawing on the best personnel and equipment available.[141] These forces (Group of Soviet Forces in Germany) and the Northern Group of Forces in Poland consisted of no less than seven armies with twenty-four maneuver divisions, thirteen supporting divisions (nine antiaircraft, two artillery and two internal security) and forty independent brigades or regiments. Although three of the six mechanized armies deployed in East Germany were merely on cadre status, Soviet reorganization had been implemented in such a way as to allow for rapid mobilization and conversion to combat strength.[142] But even without such measures the size, equipment and combat readiness of the forces actually deployed appeared (and was) entirely sufficient to overrun the weak defenses of Western Europe.

This capability appeared all the more credible as the Soviet air forces were estimated by the *World Aviation Annual* in July 1948 to comprise as many as 400,000 officers and men and 14,000 first-line aircraft.[143] Although this figure, as well as production estimates of jet aircraft and bombers, turned out to be exaggerated (a more realistic figure being fewer than 10,000 aircraft),[144] and although most of these planes consisted of light bombers and ground attack aircraft for tactical support of the ground forces, Soviet air strength could easily be concentrated in Western areas of deployment and from these positions be able – probably without major difficulty – to gain air superiority in Europe.[145]

Military Power and the Psychology of Risk

There is no doubt that the erosion of American military power in Europe, and the ensuing realization that Soviet forces had the capability of over-running that area, had a paralysing effect on United States behavior in the Berlin crisis. When President Truman had to deal with the agonizing prob-lem of deciding for or against an attempt to break the blockade by force he naturally looked to the Joint Chiefs of Staff for advice, and the advice he was given was that the United States would need eighteen months to build up the forces needed to cope with a Soviet military counterchallenge. In fact, as Robert Murphy observed,

> The most determined opposition to the use of force [in order to break the blockade] came from the JCS [Joint Chiefs of Staff] who viewed the problem in purely military terms. Secretary of State Marshall, who had been a soldier most of his life, was equally opposed to breaking the blockade.[146]

The picture, however, is still incomplete to the extent that so far the American nuclear monopoly has been portrayed as the ultimate *and* effective instrument not only of successful deterrence but also of war-fighting. But this is a picture that was not in the minds of those American theorists and military leaders who were thinking about general war. While it was acknow-ledged that strategic bombardment provided 'the one single most important element of our [United States] capability',[147] and while Air Force General Carl Spaatz testified to the Senate Armed Services Committee in 1948 that 'Without the atomic bomb, we cannot expect these attacks to be decisive', it was also generally agreed, as Spaatz continued, that

> The Air Force must be prepared to close with the enemy and win the air war. We must advance our air base areas so that all our air power operating from land bases can be projected against the future enemy in sustained mass operations.[148]

Given a combat radius of the B-29 of only 2,000 miles, sustained strategic operations from air bases in Alaska, Greenland and Newfoundland would have been ineffective against many important targets in the USSR, and this was true even for one-way strikes with a range of 4,000 miles under combat conditions. The only potentially promising air bases for sustained strategic missions against the USSR would have been in Britain, but even there would have been military problems if the Soviet air force exercised air superiority over the continent of Europe.

But there was another problem: the American delivery capability of nuclear weapons during that time was minimal. Only twenty-seven B-29 bombers modified to carry the atomic bomb existed in January 1946, and only five more were available for atomic weapons operations at the beginning of 1948.[149] During the initial phases of the Berlin crisis an additional hurdle had to be overcome. The Joint Chiefs of Staff (JCS), and particularly General Vandenberg, were of the opinion that the airlift was possible only by withdrawing virtually all the strategic aircraft from Supreme Air Command (SAC) for purposes of air transport. This would have denied *any* nuclear capability to the United States if the crisis over Berlin had erupted into war. At least this potentially crippling idea was overruled by President Truman.[150]

Even more important in this connection was yet another problem. In the period immediately after the war the number of assembled warheads in the American nuclear stockpile was zero or close to it. From public information long available but unnoticed in the official history of the US atomic energy program, it is known that in April 1947 the United States had *no* assembled weapons.[151] No military bomb assembly team was ready until December 1947 to replace the civilian teams which had been disbanded (in 1946). All this was at a time when there were very few matched sets of components to assemble and when it took twenty-four men nearly two days to prepare one weapon for combat.[152]

Truman was not even informed of the 'size' of the existing stockpiles until April 1947 and then was shocked to discover the actual state of affairs.[153] When growth of the atomic stockpile was finally decided upon afterwards, implementation of this decision was hampered because of both technical and political reasons. The technical reason lay principally in the general dismantling of the Los Alamos Scientific Laboratory after the war and the political constraint – valid at least until the summer or autumn of 1948 – in Truman's conviction that international control of atomic weapons would still be achieved. US war-planning, according to Truman, should not rely exclusively on nuclear weapons. Thus his reaction to the JCS's emergency plan, HALFMOON, which had called for a 'powerful air offensive designed to exploit the destructive and psychological power of atomic weapons against the vital elements of the Soviet war-making capacity', was to order the development of an alternative plan based on conventional forces.[154] No advice was offered as to how this alternative plan was to be put into effect within a reasonable time and without drastic budgetary increases. Inexplicably, in view of his own preferences, Truman announced on 13 May 1948, that he was intent on placing a ceiling of $14·4 billion on the fiscal year 1950 defense budget, and indeed he refused to raise the limit in the following eight months.[155] A deepening of United States dependence on nuclear weapons for the duration of the Berlin crisis and thereafter was the predictable result.

Let us return, however, to the actual numbers involved. The growth of the atomic stockpile from April 1947 onward was quite slow. General Spaatz recalled that during his tour of duty as air force chief, that is, until April 1948, there were only *about a dozen bombs*.[156] Similarly, the air force's plans for implementation of HALFMOON's 'powerful air offensive' called for dropping fifty atomic bombs – apparently all that were thought to be available in the near future.[157]

This, many scientists and strategists thought, was simply not enough for an effective strategy. According to some estimates, 'the damage done by strategic bombing of Germany was equivalent to 500 Atomic Bombs. But Germany did not surrender until her armies were defeated.'[158] Stefan

Possony wrote in the *New York Times* that 6,500 (!) bombs were probably needed for destroying the cities and industrial potential of a major military power such as the USSR;[159] even less hawkish analysts, like Patrick Blackwell, thought that several thousand atomic bombs were necessary for such a purpose.[160]

During the Berlin crisis of 1948, therefore, the Stalinist military doctrine of nuclear weapons as not being decisive for deciding the outcome of general war cannot be thought to have been as unrealistic as it appears at first sight. The doubts in the United States about the likely effectiveness of strategic bombing (given the marginal delivery capabilities and small atomic stockpile) had probably filtered through to Stalin. But nevertheless – again using the terminology of Stalinist military doctrine – there were 'permanently operating factors' which favored the United States. That country was virtually invulnerable to strategic attack by the USSR in 1948. It possessed great naval superiority over the Soviet Union. And its industrial and technological resources were incomparably greater. In the event of war, even given the Soviet capability of overrunning Europe, everything pointed to a protracted struggle during which the USA could successfully bring to bear its strategic invulnerability and strategic superiority over the USSR. Having acknowledged early on, in August 1945, that Hiroshima had 'destroyed the equilibrium', Stalin still recognized in February 1948, at a meeting with Bulgarian and Yugoslav communist leaders, that the United States was *'the most powerful state in the world'*.[161]

To sum up, one of the most important features of Soviet behavior in the Berlin crisis concerns the interrelationship between local conventional superiority and military-strategic inferiority. Most likely the gap in conventional power favoring the USSR over the USA and the tremendous disparity of forces existing in Europe constituted a strong temptation for the Soviet Union to initiate risky probes of Western determination and provided the Soviet leadership with the confidence that such probes would not be challenged by force. On the Western side, the deficiencies in effective military power in Europe had a paralyzing effect.

Secondly, in the light of the above considerations, it is difficult to accept the view that 'the era of the American monopoly of the atom bomb passed without any special advantage accruing to the United States on its account'.[162] True, the nuclear monopoly was not directly brought to bear on the Berlin crisis (as in Iran in 1946), whether in the form of an explicit threat or an ultimatum. But it was always there in the background – a constant reminder to Stalin not to overplay his hand. Beyond that the transfer of B-29 aircraft to Britain was an implicit threat, refreshing, if need be, everyone's memory about the cards which the United States could play if it came to the worst. To that extent American strategic power did not deter the Soviet Union from taking risks, but it almost certainly set stringent limits: it deterred the further exploitation of advantages in conventional forces and cautioned Stalin against any escalation of the conflict.

There is a final consideration which may be difficult to measure, but which may be quite important nevertheless: the disparity in domestic structure between the two main adversaries and the way it is connected with the military dimension of the Berlin crisis. On the one hand the openness of the Western political system had accurately conveyed to the opponent the anxiety inherent in apocalyptic images of Soviet mass armies advancing virtually unopposed to the Atlantic. This had strengthened the psychological advantages of the Soviet Union. The West on the other hand was put at a disadvantage in strategic bargaining by its memory of the efficiency of the Soviet military juggernaut once it had recovered from the initial reverses in 1941, by the apparent ease with which human lives were expended, and by the suspicion on this basis that Stalin could indeed not be counted among the 'weak-nerved', even in the face of nuclear weapons. Deterrence under such conditions appeared difficult to achieve. This is but one example of how Soviet domestic conditions affected the course of the Berlin crisis. Others need to be examined in more detail.

IV DOMESTIC POLITICS

As noted earlier, the relevance of domestic factors for Soviet risk-taking and crisis behavior can be analyzed under three different headings – the import-ance of the individual *personality* or personalities shaping the decisions; the significance of power struggle and the interplay of opposing forces and tendencies among the *leadership*; and the relevance of constraints and opportunities created by the *Soviet system*. [163]

This approach may have its merits as an analytical tool yet it raises the ques-tion whether, in the specific period and crisis under consideration, it is advan-tageous or even possible to follow this threefold differentiation in practice. When speaking of Stalinism or the Stalinist system a hidden assumption is already manifest, namely, that Stalin has left such an imprint on Soviet politics that person and system form an indissoluble, unified entity – a suggestion which is endorsed by Seweryn Bialer's view of Stalin not merely as a political leader but as an institution. [164] And although Soviet historiography continues to deny the existence of any such phenomenon as Stalinism, it does refer to a 'period of the personality cult', or (more recently and euphemistically) the 'cult of personality', [165] thus implying that Soviet domestic politics were shaped to a considerable degree by 'subjective' factors. For these reasons caution is advised with regard to taking the differentiations too far.

Stalin: a Pathological Risk-Taker?

In the view of George F. Kennan, who met Stalin on several occasions during his long service at the American embassy in Moscow, '*Stalin was not really a normal man*. Like Ivan the Terrible, he was a captive of a personal devil within his own soul.' [166] Not being a psychologist or psychiatrist by profes-sion, Kennan remains cautious in linking Stalin's presumably abnormal per-sonality to foreign policy, but many other Western analysts, although not knowing Stalin personally, have done so. Speaking about 'costly and risky ventures such as the aggression by proxy in Korea', Robert C. Tucker con-cludes: 'Few situations could illustrate more convincingly the potential importance of personality, and specifically the pathological personality, in foreign policy.' [167]

Similar views have been expressed in the Soviet Union. The former Commissar of the Soviet Navy, Admiral N. G. Kuznetsov, for example, speaks of Stalin's 'pathological mistrust'.[168] In the famous Secret Speech Khrushchev called Stalin a 'very distrustful man, sickly suspicious';[169] and in reference to the Yugoslav Affair of 1948, Khrushchev drew the lessons from Stalin's mania for greatness, saying that 'He [Stalin] had *completely lost consciousness of reality*; he demonstrated his suspicion and haughtiness not only in relation to individuals in the USSR, but in relation to whole parties and nations'.[170]

Medical professionals, both in the West and in the Soviet Union, have participated in the debate and thrown the weight of scientific language behind the proposition of Stalin's alleged mental illness. The British psychiatrist Anthony Storr establishes a link between schizoid tendencies and paranoia and introduces a comparison of De Gaulle and Stalin by saying that schizoid people may be notably successful and that, in politics, leaders of an apocalyptic, visionary type may attain power because they identify their own desire for it with the cause that they espouse. On this basis Storr makes the following comparison:

> The general [De Gaulle] has so far [1968] remained sane; but it is not unlikely that old age and the deterioration consequent upon cerebral arteriosclerosis might undermine his defences and release *paranoid ideas and behavior*. This remarkable leader could, *like Stalin*, become a *danger both to his country and to the world*.[171]

This remark, casual though it may be, reveals fundamental assumptions about influences of psychopathological traits on foreign policy. Soviet professionals have expressed views similar to those put forward by their colleagues in the West. N. A. Alekseev, for instance, a Communist Party member since 1897 and a physician by profession, argued at a meeting of old Bolsheviks with delegates to the Twenty-Second CPSU Congress in 1961 that Stalin was mentally sick and incompetent (*nevmeniaemyi*).[172]

In attempting to answer the question of how relevant psychopathological traits in Stalin's personality may have been for his behavior in foreign policy, I must confess my own ignorance of psychology and psychiatry and rely instead on the medical expertise compiled elsewhere and the extensive research done by Roy Medvedev on this subject.

Two terms recur in the expression of views about Stalin's abnormal personality – schizophrenia and paranoia. Concerning schizophrenia, the *Encyclopedia of Mental Health* offers no definition of the term at all, but lists instead various types and forms of illnesses such as 'simple type', 'hebephrenic type', 'catatonic forms' and 'paranoid forms' of schizophrenia.[173] Similarly the *Encyclopaedia Britannica* underlines the complexity of the term when it writes that the term 'schizophrenia' is used by psychiatrists 'to indicate a group of mental disorders in which the symptoms occur in varying combinations and with varying degrees of intensity'; psychiatrists have considered it 'either as a single disease entity or a collection of somewhat similar patterns of psychological reactions to life situations'.[174] In more detail, schizophrenia is explained as

A mental disorder characterized by a special type of disintegration of the personality: thought processes are directed by apparently random personal associations rather than logically to a goal, there is incongruity between the content of the thought and the corresponding emotion, and an impaired relation to reality.[175]

However, as far as this was possible to establish, not a single Western or Soviet individual who has come in contact with Stalin personally has ever seriously argued that Stalin did not proceed in a highly purposive, determined and logically consistent fashion according to reasonably well-defined goals. Also, on the basis of the extensive record of the wartime conferences and of the talks in Moscow in August 1948 on Berlin, it would be very difficult to argue the case that Stalin had somehow an 'impaired relation to reality', or – to put it in relative terms – that his sense of reality was less than, say, Roosevelt's in 1945 or Ambassador Smith's in 1948. Clearly, according to the present definition, schizophrenia as an explanation of Stalin's foreign policy and risk-taking propensities appears inadequate.

Concerning paranoia, the second possible explanation of Stalin's behavior on grounds of irrational personality influences, medical definitions list two main constituting elements – 'unrealistic feelings of self-overevaluation, grandeur or grandiosity' and 'unrealistic and irrational feelings of persecution'.[176] Particularly appropriate in reference to Stalin may be the link established between the two elements: processes of overcompensation of inferiority complexes and the attribution of blame to external conspiracies when aspirations fail.[177] And equally relevant in Stalin's case would be the explanation that paranoia is 'a chronic but otherwise benign form of paranoid schizophrenia' in which the individual suffers from 'delusional ideas of a superficial, but not grossly bizarre or irrational kind, while the personality remains fairly well preserved'.[178]

From this point on it is appropriate to follow the line of reasoning adopted by Roy Medvedev. The Soviet historian argues that medicine makes a distinction between a real mental illness in which the person is unaware of his behavior (and hence cannot be held responsible in law) and various abnormal states of personality in which a person is conscious of what he is doing. Applied to Stalin, this means that despite the presence of some features characteristic of paranoid psychopathology, and despite the fact that his behavior clearly shows traits of moral degeneration and perhaps even psychic derangement, Stalin must be considered beyond doubt as '*a responsible (vmeniaemyi) man*, and in most cases was *fully aware* of what he was doing'.[179]

So far it has been possible to follow Medvedev's line of reasoning. However, this is not where the matter can be laid to rest. Even assuming the presence of paranoid elements in Stalin's psyche, all inferences about foreign policy behavior must be considered as fundamentally ambiguous: fear of domestic and external conspiracies and exaggerated threat perceptions can, of course, give rise to aggressive attitudes and behavior (which is not necessarily the same as the actual taking of risks). But at the same time it would seem even more logical to expect *excessive caution* based on a constant preoccupation with real or imagined risks. It is the latter perspective which generally appears to be the more valid assumption about Stalin's foreign policy.

Secondly, and equally important, arguing from Marxist positions within the Soviet context, Medvedev remains highly insensitive to the possibility of what might be called political paranoia as opposed to individual, psychopathological paranoia, that is to say, to the possibility that Marxist-Leninist ideology and the Soviet system contain elements which facilitate, or perhaps even call forth, logically and inexorably, a man of Stalin's qualities. Thus there are stringent limits to the attempts at explaining important aspects of Stalin's foreign policy by psychological or psychopathological idiosyncrasies. It is appropriate to look more closely at political explanations.

Stalin and the Power Struggle of his Subordinates

A close look at possible manifestations of power struggle in 1948 is warranted because it may provide indications as to changes in policy – on the assumption that policies in the USSR are inextricably linked with personalities and political conflict with leadership conflict.

The starting point for a Kremlinological analysis of the Berlin crisis would be the changes in the relative power position of two major contenders for power, Georgi Malenkov (who could be called, with all the limitations inherent in such a term, an advocate of policies of the right) and Andrei Zhdanov (an exponent of policies of the left). No doubt, owing to the success in his role as defender of Leningrad, Zhdanov had again risen to prominence in the period after the war, whereas Malenkov ceased to be listed as Secretary of the Central Committee in 1946.[180] The trend of Malenkov's decline appears to have been accentuated in June 1947, when G. F. Aleksandrov, a close associate of Malenkov, was replaced by Suslov.[181] On the other hand Zhdanov's comeback was emphasized by the prominent role he played at the founding meeting of the Cominform in September 1947 and by the extensive repression of cultural and intellectual freedoms between 1946 and 1948 which carried his name (*Zhdanovshchina*).[182]

However, the changing composition of Soviet leaders in the negotiations with the Yugoslavs over a two-year period (1946 to 1948) provide clues as to the reversal in the relative fortunes of the two leaders. Whereas Zhdanov, Beria and Molotov had appeared at virtually all the important official or private meetings together with Stalin and other associates, 10 February 1948 marks the first time since 1946 that Malenkov (and Suslov) were included in the 'first circle' of Stalin's associates.[183] At the second meeting of the Cominform, held in Bucharest in June 1948, Zhdanov was still the official spokesman of the Soviet Union but with him were Malenkov and Suslov.[184] In July 1948 Malenkov returned to the secretariat and on 31 August Zhdanov died under circumstances which have given rise to suspicions and charges that he was poisoned or died of medical malpractice.[185]

In early 1949 a systematic purge of Zhdanov's followers and associates began, claiming as its victims Secretary Kuznetsov and all the other secretaries of the Leningrad party (Zhdanov's former stronghold); the chiefs of the big Leningrad industries; N. A. Voznesensky, chief of the State Planning

Commission; his brother, rector of Leningrad University; M. I. Rodionov, chairman of the Council of Ministers of the Russian Federated Republic; Colonel I. V. Shikin, head of the Red Army Political Directorate; and many more. All of them were demoted, many of them were arrested and imprisoned and some of them were shot.[186]

If these are the facts, what is their significance? Leonard Schapiro, presumably because of his expressed focus on the Communist Party of the Soviet Union, confines the relevance of Malenkov's ascendancy and Zhdanov's decline to the realm of Soviet *domestic* politics.[187] In contrast Robert Conquest writes that 'Malenkov and Suslov were being brought into the *international* field to counter Zhdanov' and that 'the main issue on which Zhdanovism failed in Stalin's eyes was that of foreign policy'.[188] Finally, Marshall Shulman argues – in reference to the Zhdanovist policy of dogmatism and militancy – that 'By the summer of 1948, the effectiveness of this policy seemed at best questionable', and he points to evidence such as the 'estrangement of Yugoslavia', the 'failure of potentialities in Germany, France and Italy to materialize', the 'unhappy involvement in the Berlin blockade' and the 'stimulus which Soviet militancy had provided to the mobilization and cohesion of the Western powers', the inference to be drawn from these examples presumably being (as in Conquest's analysis) that 31 August 1948 marks something like a turning point in foreign policy – irrespective of whether Zhdanov was murdered or died of natural causes.[187]

Whereas it was indeed objectively questionable whether the policy associated with Zhdanov's name was still effective, it is difficult to support the view of a major reappraisal of the theory and practice of Soviet foreign policy in the summer of 1948. The Berlin crisis had only begun, its outcome was uncertain at that time. Similarly, the policies of pressure *vis-à-vis* Yugoslavia after her expulsion from the Cominform in June 1948 had only begun. New strike waves were to shake France as late as the fall of 1948.[190] The concept of the 'imminent crisis of capitalism' was upheld, and the attacks on Varga and his economic and political theories were resumed in October 1948.[191] The first tangible evidence of the emergence of a new 'peace' offensive came only after the presidential elections in the United States when Truman was suddenly credited (or should one say discredited?) with 'adherence to the principles of Roosevelt'.[192] Shulman's own analysis provides substantive examples of reorientation in Stalin's foreign policy only for the spring of 1949. The connection of policy changes with changes in the political fortunes of Malenkov and Zhdanov in the summer of 1948 also does not sufficiently explain why, if this connection exists, Malenkov's rise began even *before* the Berlin crisis and *before* the Soviet break with Tito.

This still leaves the problem of lead time. It could be argued that there is a possibility of conceptual reappraisal in the summer of 1948 because allowance has to be made for a time lag necessary for the implementation of the new policies. Support for this point of view could be drawn from the notoriously slow and cumbersome mode of procedure of Soviet bureaucracy. This perspective, however, does not seem right. Even making due allowance for bureaucratic procrastination and delay, and for Stalin's need to find effective international channels for new policies, it is a bit much to believe that such a process would have lasted from July/August 1948 to the end of

January 1949, when the end of the Berlin crisis was foreshadowed by Stalin's replies to Kingsbury Smith's questions. Late autumn or early winter would be a much more realistic date for an 'agonizing reappraisal', and there would still have been enough time to think carefully about the forms in which new approaches should have proceeded.

All this leads to two major conclusions – first, that there was no triumph of a 'Malenkov line' over a 'Zhdanovist line' in foreign policy at such an early date as the summer of 1948 despite the (according to Kremlinological analysis) paradoxical possibility that the power position of Malenkov the person by that time had been strengthened, and that that of Zhdanov the person had declined (perhaps even to the ultimate point of physical liquidation). Secondly, and not entirely unconnected with this, the idea of a power struggle among Stalin's subordinates is only of very limited use in explaining the conduct of Soviet policy in the Berlin crisis.

This interpretation can be corroborated by the fact that the power constellation at the apex, almost by any criterion of comparison, remained remarkably, almost boringly, stable in the period from 1939, throughout the war and up to and including the Berlin crisis. This can be shown in Table 8.2.[193]

Table 8.2   *Composition of the Politburo*

1939 (after the Eighteenth CPSU Congress)	1949 (at the end of the Berlin Crisis)
Stalin	Stalin
Molotov	Molotov
Voroshilov	Voroshilov
Kaganovich	Kaganovich
Mikoyan	Mikoyan
Andreev	Andreev
Khrushchev	Khrushchev
Zhdanov	Zhdanov (died August 1948)
Kalinin (died 1946)	Malenkov (appointed 1941)
	Beria (appointed 1946)
	Bulganin (appointed 1946)
	Voznesensky (appointed 1947)

Table 8.2 shows that the only vacancy that did occur in the Politburo prior to Zhdanov's death was caused in like manner (though without attendant suspicion of murder), by the death of Kalinin in 1946.[194] For the rest, four new members were added but all the other members retained their seat on the Politburo.

This line of interpretation, in both of its conclusions, conforms to the views expressed by Ambassador Smith during the Berlin crisis. Reporting from Moscow about the possible implications of the vacancy in the Politburo, Smith thought that Zhdanov's death 'is not likely to have any effect on Soviet internal or foreign policies or [the] party's ideological lines upon which Zhdanov would not have dared to pronounce without full approval by . . . Stalin'.[195]

All this makes it appear appropriate to search for the influence of domestic factors on the Berlin crisis in the realm of interrelationships between Stalin, 'his' – the Soviet – system and the organizations over which he presided. First and foremost it is a question of the implications of the enormous concentration of power in one hand.

Decision-Making in the Stalinist System: Strengths and Weaknesses

As early as 1922, in the often quoted 'testament', Lenin had deplored that 'Comrade Stalin, on becoming General Secretary, concentrated enormous power in his hands, and I am not sure he always knows how to use this power carefully enough', and on the basis of Stalin's 'impatience' and 'infatuation with administrative fiat' Lenin had urged Stalin's removal from the office of general secretary.[196]

However, the concentration of power in Stalin's hands had only begun and was not completed until after the purges of the 1930s. While Khrushchev's remarks about Stalin's policies quite often may have been self-serving, one can accept his statement that 'Stalin thought that now [after the Seventeenth CPSU Congress in 1934] he could decide all things alone and all he needed were statisticians; he treated all others in such a way that they could only listen to and praise him'.[197]

Increasingly the preparation, taking, verification and control of decisions shifted away from the Central Committee and the Politburo to Stalin and a so-called special sector (*osobyi sektor*), which was nominally attached to the Central Committee but for all practical purposes was a private secretariat under the leadership of A. N. Poskrebyshev who, in turn, was directly responsible to Stalin.[198]

Yet the step from centralization to supercentralization was yet to come. During World War II – a crucial period for understanding decision-making processes in the Stalinist period, including the period of the Berlin crisis – a State Defense Committee (*Gosudarstvennyi Komitet Oborony*, GKO) was established under the chairmanship of Stalin. It remained small in size all during the war with a basic membership of eight but with far-reaching competence, empowered to issue decrees (with the force of law) superior to all state, party, local Soviet, *Komsomol* and military organs, responsible for the direction of the economy and military production and charged with matters relating to 'state security and public order'.[199] The GKO and the *Stavka* (the equivalent of the GHQ) were closely fused by giving GKO members the right to sit with the *Stavka* as part of it. However, as John Erickson summarizes in his analysis of the GKO-*Stavka* system, the unification of military and political direction 'produced in established Stalinist style that blurring of competences which may have promoted the "cult of the individual" but which riddled the command organs with inefficiency, procrastination, internal competition and external indecision'.[200]

A small part of the iceberg of administrative overlap and confusion (so characteristic also of the German equivalent to the Stalinist system, the

Führerstaat) in the conditions leading up to the Berlin crisis was evident in the conflict between the SMA and 'other' organs over policy in the Soviet zone of occupation in Germany. Matters of political organization were the primary responsibility of the SMA but it had no control whatsoever over reparations policy, the latter being a responsibility divided among various organizations, including the office of the Four-Year Plan and the Ministries of Foreign Trade, Defense and the Interior (NKVD, later – starting from April 1946 – MVD).[201] These organizations appear to have taken their job quite seriously, contrary to the preferences of the SMA. Wolfgang Leonhard reports that an officer of the main political administration of the Red Army, when driving with him through the Soviet sector of Berlin, referred to the authorities in charge of reparations as the 'reparations gang' and 'the enemy'[202] – for good reasons, because (as noted) dismantling and reconstruction, reparations and loyalty of the German population were policies which were in essence mutually exclusive.[203]

Seen from these perspectives, overcentralization must be regarded as a weakness and as having had some share in the dilemmas confronting the USSR in 1948. However, it would be wrong to see the problems of decision-making in the Stalinist system as *caused* by organizational autonomy – something these organizations clearly did not have. If the instructions from the center to the Milking Organization were to 'milk the cow' and to the Slaughtering Organization to 'slaughter it', the inevitable, messy result cannot be ascribed to ineffectiveness of, or mistakes made by, organizations at the local level (although this may be a convenient excuse invoked by those responsible at the top).

All this is to say that in a system of overcentralization ultimate responsibility rests with the center. This will be particularly true in conditions where the importance of the issue in hand requires immediate attention and decision, or where the center decides to act and interfere in an arbitrary manner.

An interesting example to that effect is provided by Malcolm Mackintosh.[204] The Soviet representatives in the Allied Control Commission in Bulgaria in 1945 had been meeting with their Western counterparts (in line with Stalin's work habits in Moscow) from late evening until the early hours of the morning for days on end and insisting on single lists for the scheduled elections. In the early morning of the very same day that the elections were due to be held Stalin rang Colonel General (later Marshal) Biryuzov, the commander of the Soviet forces in Bulgaria, to issue new instructions for elections to be held on multiple lists, thus at a stroke reversing previous policies.

One detail of Mackintosh's report is of particular interest. The officer who had answered the telephone prior to Biryuzof had fainted in terror upon hearing Stalin's voice – an indication of the fact that no matter how tough the officer, and no matter how high his rank, reporting to Stalin (as General Vasilevskii openly admitted) was an unbearable strain and a summons to Moscow had a very ominous ring.[205]

Facts of this kind are not of mere anecdotal and passing interest but are important to bear in mind when one begins to think about the possible relationships between Stalin on the one hand and the SMA in Germany on the other, or about the explanatory value of an organizational process model as against a model of unified, centralized or rational decision-making. On the one hand the strain of reporting to Stalin may to a large extent explain why there was so much Soviet persistence in an endeavour that had become increasingly counterproductive. In the face of Stalin's characteristic refusal to condone failure, who dared explain that the Berlin venture had come to a dead end? Although Khrushchev was speaking about another event (available intelligence information concerning the impending German attack on the Soviet Union in June 1941), his criticism of weaknesses in the Stalinist decision-making system may be much to the point also with regard to the Berlin crisis when he said that the failure to draw the necessary consequences from the available information happened 'because the leadership was conditioned against such information, such data was dispatched with fear and assessed with reservation'.[106]

It is reasonable to suppose that Stalin did not see a Sokolovsky in 1948 in any other way than a Vasilevskii in 1942 or a Biryuzov in 1945, and that – given the fact of an important confrontation with the United States – Stalin devoted maximum attention to the crisis and kept Sokolovsky on a tight rein. There is no direct evidence to verify this assumption. However, the description of the meeting between the three Western ambassadors and Stalin on 23 August in Moscow is in conformity with these views. The details provided are that that meeting (like the one in Bulgaria three years earlier, as described by Mackintosh) lasted from the late evening until the early hours of the morning. Stalin plunged his negotiating partners into a discussion much of which, it is fair to say, was beyond their full understanding, including matters of a technical nature, such as the balancing of the Berlin budget, the limitation of its size, the drawing of token occupation costs, and so on, all neatly designed to serve the overall purpose of insuring Soviet control over economic life in the whole of the city.[207] This knowledge of detail points to maximum attention devoted by Stalin to the Berlin problem and to the absence of conditions in which organizational processes had much chance to assert themselves against supercentralization.

In the final analysis the domestic processes at the root of Soviet policy in the Berlin crisis (notably the recourse to pressure and threat, the stubborn persistence in the face of adverse objective conditions and the ultimate drifting into the division of Germany and Berlin, rather than embarking on the experiment of a neutralist, and perhaps democratic socialist, Germany) depended a great deal on a unique interrelationship between Soviet ideology, Stalin's personality and the Stalinist system. Something of this reconstruction of reality can be found in Djilas' observation that 'Thanks to both ideology and methods, personal experience and historical heritage, he [Stalin] regarded as sure only whatever he held in his fist'.[208]

Notes: Part Two, Chapter 8

1   Roy A. Medvedev, *Let History Judge: The Origins and Consequences of Stalinism*, ed. David Joravsky and Georges Haupt, trans. Colleen Taylor (New York: Knopf, 1971), p. 479 (my italics).
2   *For a Lasting Peace, for a People's Democracy (Official journal of the Cominform)*, no. 1 (10 November 1947), my italics.

3 ibid.

4 *Pravda*, 8 May 1947 (my italics).

5 Speech to the UN General Assembly, UN General Assembly, *Official Records*, Plenary Meetings, Verbatim Record, 18 September 1947, pp. 86–8.

6 Lenin on 18 March 1919 at the Eighth Party Congress, in V. I. Lenin, *Selected Works*, Vol. VIII (New York: International Publishers, 1943), p. 33.

7 Note of the Soviet government of 14 July to the Western powers, 14 July 1948, *Pravda*, 15 July 1948.

8 Letter to the British General Robertson, ibid., 1 July 1948. See above, p. 96.

9 Smith, *My Three Years in Moscow*, p. 244. This is confirmed by Charles E. Bohlen, with the editorial assistance of Robert H. Phelps, *Witness to History, 1929–1969* (New York: Norton, 1973), p. 280. At the time of the Berlin crisis Bohlen was senior adviser on Soviet affairs to the Secretary of State.

10 *For a Lasting Peace*, no. 1 (10 November 1947).

11 V. I. Lenin, *Imperialism: The Highest Stage of Capitalism*, new edn. (New York: International Publishers, 1969), pp. 76–89.

12 *For a Lasting Peace*, no. 1 (10 November 1947).

13 ibid.

14 Joseph V. Stalin, *Economic Problems of Socialism in the USSR* (Moscow: Foreign Languages Publishing House, 1952), pp. 37–41 and Malenkov's report to the Central Committee in Leo Gruliow (ed.), *Current Soviet Policies: The Documentary Record of the Nineteenth Party Congress and the Reorganization after Stalin's Death* (New York: Praeger, 1953), p. 106; see also Shulman, *Stalin's Foreign Policy Reappraised*, pp. 240–5.

15 *For a Lasting Peace*, 10 November 1947.

16 The analytical importance of the Varga controversy was introduced above, pp. 71–2.

17 See the discussion of the Varga controversy by Marshall D. Shulman, *Stalin's Foreign Policy Reappraised*, pp. 32–5, and 'The discussions on E. Varga's book on capitalist war economy', *Soviet Studies*, vol. 1, no. 1 (June 1949), pp. 28–40.

18 Some of these included L. Eventov's *Voennaia ekonomika Anolii* (editor responsible, I. Trachtenberg), S. Vishnev's *Promyshlennost' kapitalisticheskikh stran vo vtoroi mirovoi voine* (editor responsible, L. Eventov) and M. Bokshitskii's *Teknniko-ekonomisticheskie izmeneniia v promyshlennosti SShA vo vremia vtoroi mirovoi voiny* (editor responsible, I. Trachtenberg), all published under the auspices of the Institute for World Economy and World Politics in 1946 and 1947.

19 The last issue of *Mirovoe khoziastvo i mirovaia politika* was no. 12 (1947). It was 'succeeded' in March 1946 by a new journal, *Voprosy ekonomiki* (Problems of Economics), of which K. Ostrovitianov of the Institute of Economics was the chief editor.

20 The unkind point about the Marshall Plan was made by I. Dvorkin in the October 1948 discussions at the enlarged session of the Learned Council of the Institute of Economics, *Voprosy ekonomiki*, no. 9 (1948), pp. 56–7. For the 'un-Marxist' label and the accusation concerning 'bourgeois methodology' see *Bol'shevik*, no. 3 (1948), p. 74 and no. 5 (1948) p. 74. The most puzzling part of the Varga controversy is the fact that Varga was allowed to remain a member of the Institute of Economics and even to participate in the October 1948 discussions *despite* the severe criticism.

21 Eugenio Reale, *Avec Jacques Duclos au banc des accusés à la réunion constitutive du Kominform* (Paris: Plon, 1948). Duclos and Longo were leader and deputy leader of the French and Italian Communist Parties respectively. They represented their parties at the founding meeting. Eugenio Reale was a member of the CPI until 1956. His account is confirmed by a Yugoslav eyewitness, Vladimir Dedijer, *Josip Bros Tito. Prilozi za biografiju* (Belgrade: Kultura, 1953), pp. 412–76.

22 Reale, *Avec Jacques Duclos*, pp. 85 and 87.

23 For the setbacks suffered by the CPI see above, p. 87.

24 Interview of 12 January 1948 with Josef Korbel, as quoted in Josef Korbel, *The Communist Subversion of Czechoslovakia, 1938–1948: The Failure of Coexistence* (Princeton, NJ: Princeton University Press, 1959), pp. 198–9.

25 Khrushchev in his Secret Speech of 25 February 1945, in *The Anti-Stalin Campaign and International Communism*, ed. Russian Institute, Columbia University (New York: Columbia University Press, 1956), pp. 62–3. This is confirmed by Dedijer who quotes Stalin as having said in the spring of 1948, 'As soon as I move my little finger, Tito will be thrown out', in Vladimir Dedijer, *The Battle Stalin Lost* (New York: Viking Press, 1970), p. 35.

25   Anton Ackermann, 'Gibt es einen besonderen deutschen Weg zum Sozialismus?', *Einheit* (Berlin), vol. 1, no. 1 (February 1946), p. 29.
27   *Neues Deutschland*, 16 January 1948.
28   Keiderling and Stulz, *Geschichte Berlins, 1945–1968*, p. 146.
29   Erich W. Gniffke, *Jahre mit Ulbricht* (Cologne: Verlag Wissenschaft und Politik, 1966), p. 293.
30   Keiderling and Stulz, *Geschichte Berlins, 1945–1968*, p. 149.
31   ibid., p. 150 (my italics).
32   Gniffke, *Jahre mit Ulbricht*, p. 320.
33   ibid.
34   ibid., p. 321 (my italics).
35   *Telegraf* (Berlin), 3 July 1948.
36   As quoted by Gniffke, *Jahre mit Ulbricht*, p. 325 (my italics). Kurt Schumacher was the leader of the Social Democratic Party of Germany at that time. A Soviet author writing in the Cominform journal called Schumacher a 'lackey of the German imperialists' who is 'often compared to Hitler, not without reason'. D. Kraminov, in *For a Lasting Peace*, 15 February 1948.
37   Gniffke, *Jahre mit Ulbricht*, p. 340.
38   Howley, *Berlin Command*, pp. 198–203, and Gniffke, *Jahre mit Ulbricht*, p. 316.
39   V. I. Lenin, *'Left-Wing' Communism, an Infantile Disorder: A Popular Essay in Marxist Strategy and Tactics* (New York: International Publishers, 1969).
40   Zbigniew K. Brzezinski, *The Soviet Bloc: Unity and Conflict*, rev. edn (New York: Praeger, 1961), pp. 3–150.
41   Djilas, *Conversations with Stalin*, p. 45.
42   *Pravda*, 10 February 1946.
43   Joseph V. Stalin, *Problems of Leninism* (Moscow: Foreign Languages Publishing House, 1947), p. 637.
44   Joseph V. Stalin, 'The tasks of building executives', ibid., p. 355.
45   ibid., p. 356.
46   *KPSS v resoliutsiiakh i resheniiakh s''ezdov, konferentsii i plenumov TsK*, Vol. III (Moscow: Politizdat 1954), pp. 476–84, as quoted by Brzezinski, *The Soviet Bloc*, p. 43.
47   Djilas, *Conversations with Stalin*, p. 120 and pp. 139–40.
48   Medvedev, *Let History Judge*, p. 492.
49   *Vedomosti Verkhovnogo Soveta SSSR*, 25 January 1948. Exempted from this prohibition were necessary contacts between foreigners and Soviet citizens such as bus conductors, shopkeepers and others providing essential services.
50   'Sovetskaia politika ravnopraviia natsii' (editorial), *Bol'shevik*, no. 9 (1948), p. 6.
51   *For a Lasting Peace*, 15 April 1948 (my italics), as quoted by Brzezinski, *The Soviet Bloc*, p. 71.
52   J. V. Stalin, *Sochineniia*, Vol. X (Moscow: Gosudarstvennoe izdatel'stvo politicheskoi literatury, 1948), p. 53.
53   The overall pattern of leftism, for instance, did not prevent a moderate policy towards Finland. As noted in the preceding chapter, not only was the treaty of 6 April 1948 far less severe in its provisions than had been feared, but the Finnish Communist Party also refrained from attempting extralegal action even after it had suffered defeat in the parliamentary elections of 1 and 2 July and was excluded from the government.
54   This is a point made by Marshall D. Shulman, 'What does security mean today?', *Foreign Affairs*, vol. 49, no. 4 (July 1971), pp. 607–18.
55   On the decline of territoriality as a factor of security see John H. Herz, *International Politics in the Atomic Age* (New York: Columbia University Press, 1959).
56   The conclusions of the following discussion of Soviet options and dilemmas very much coincide with, but do not draw on, those of Hans-Peter Schwarz, *Vom Reich zur Bundesrepublik: Deutschland im Widerstreit der aussenpolitischen Konzeptionen in den Jahren der Besatzungsherrschaft, 1945–1949* (Neuwied und Berlin: Luchterhand, 1966), pp. 201–70. Schwarz's study is probably the most comprehensive and analytically the soundest treatment of Germany in the international context in 1945–9.
57   Stalin as quoted by Djilas, *Conversations with Stalin*, p. 114.
58   The party programs of the NDPD and DBD and the approval of the activity of the two parties by the Soviet military administration are published in MID GDR, MID SSSR, *Sbornik dokumentov, 1945–1949*, pp. 531–5, 541–8 and 549–50.

59 This is so not least because of the fact that the two party leaders had been former members of the KPD.
60 Wolfgang Leonhard, *Child of the Revolution*, trans. C. M. Woodhouse (London: Collins, 1957), pp. 325–6.
61 In a ballot on 30 March 1946; see Eberhard Schneider, *Die DDR: Geschichte, Politik, Wirtschaft, Gesellschaft* (Stuttgart: Verlag Bonn Aktuell, 1975), p. 28.
62 To clarify this point: the SPD had only ceased to exist in the Soviet zone, not in Berlin. The two parties, SPD and SED, were therefore pitted against each other in the city elections.
63 Djilas, *Conversations with Stalin*, p. 79.
64 ibid., p. 103.
65 Charles Bohlen in a seminar session, Columbia University, 19 March 1970.
66 Herbert Feis, *Between War and Peace: The Potsdam Conference* (Princeton, NJ: Princeton University Press, 1960), pp. 221–74. This difference between the western and eastern Rivers Neisse, which was at issue at Yalta, was not negligible as it involved the fate of about 2·7 million ethnic Germans and hence the problem of future German revanchism. For further consideration of this point see also below, p. 130.
67 Concerning the impact on and the estimated magnitude of the losses incurred by the East German economy because of Soviet occupation policy see below, p. 127 and also the case study of the Berlin crisis of 1961, pp. 233–4.
68 US Department of State, *Foreign Relations of the United States: The Conference of Berlin (Potsdam)*, Vol. II (Washington, DC: Government Printing Office, 1960), pp. 1478–98.
69 Letter from Clay to McCloy, 3 September 1945, in Smith (ed.), *The Clay Papers*, doc. 30, p. 64.
70 The United States at Yalta had agreed on US$20 billion (half of which was to go to the USSR) as a *basis of discussion*. Soviet representatives took this to mean agreement in principle.
71 This point was apparently stressed by Vladimir Semenov, political adviser to Marshal Zhukov, and other officials of the Soviet Foreign Ministry *vis-à-vis* Rudolf Nadolny, a former ambassador of Germany in Moscow (1933–4) and an advocate of the pro-Russian section of the German diplomatic community, who had succeeded in establishing exploratory contacts with Soviet diplomats in Berlin. In 1946 a Soviet Foreign Ministry official reportedly commented to Nadolny during one of his visits to Soviet military headquarters in Berlin-Karlshorst that 'Germany should again become big and strong, and be friends with the Soviet Union. It should have the right to self-determination. The Soviet government in principle accepted the Weimar Constitution as a basis [for the political organization of] Germany but the constitutional question was one for Germany to decide. However, *the Soviet government could not compromise on the [question of] reparations from current production; Russia had to be rebuilt first, and then Germany, but not vice versa.*' See Rudolf Nadolny, *Mein Beitrag* (Wiesbaden: Limes Verlag, 1955), p. 179 (my italics).
72 At the 10 July 1946, meeting of the Council of Foreign Ministers in Paris: see V. M. Molotov, *Problems of Foreign Policy: Speeches and Statements, April 1945–November 1948* (Moscow: Foreign Languages Publishing House, 1949), p. 66 (my italics).
73 M. Marinin, in a two-part series about the Marshall Plan, *Pravda*, 5 and 6 March 1948.
74 ibid.
75 Yuri Zhukov in an article on the London conference of Western powers, ibid., 29 February 1948.
76 ibid., 25 June 1948.
77 Djilas, *Conversations with Stalin*, p. 114. See p. 121.
78 ibid. The Soviet Foreign Ministry official quoted above, note 71, expressed a very similar opinion to Nadolny. He told his German visitor that 'the Soviet government was not out to transform Germany into a Soviet satellite (*es zu sowjetisieren*). The Germans at the moment were hungry and downcast, but gradually they would recover, and then they would turn against Russia' (Nadolny, *Mein Beitrag*, pp. 178–9).
79 Djilas, *Conversations with Stalin*, pp. 114–15.
80 Reproduced from J. P. Nettl, *The Eastern Zone and Soviet Policy in Germany* (London: Oxford University Press, 1951), p. 241. The treatment of economic developments in the Soviet zone draws on ibid., pp. 240–1.
81 Molotov, *Problems of Foreign Policy*, p. 534 (my italics). A corollary to this thesis was the view that the 'so-called foreign aid' was harmful to the economic development and political

development of the Western zones. 'The German debt in the Western zones', Molotov stated at the same session, 'will soon reach several billions of dollars. For the German people, these obligations will be *harder to bear than any reparations*' (ibid., my italics).

82 ibid., p. 534.

83 *For a Lasting Peace*, 1 February 1948.

84 G. Gertsovich, 'Vosstanovlenie mirnoi ekonomiki v Sovetskoi zone okkupatsii Germanii', *Voprosy ekonomiki*, no. 1 (March 1948), pp. 93 and 100.

85 Nettl, *The Eastern Zone*, pp. 199–200.

86 ibid., p. 237. For comparison, the total budget of the Soviet zone for 1948–9 amounted to 8·657 billion Reichsmark. The total value of the above figure (11·47 billion Reichsmark) was close to US$4 billion at the then exchange rate.

87 *Pravda*, 7 April 1948 (my italics). Apart from making the point of 'misery in the Western zones' in its own right, claims such as these, as noted, had the additional purpose of justifying traffic restrictions on the access routes.

88 Yuri Zhukov, reporting Molotov's statements at the conference, *Pravda*, 31 March 1947. The figures may very well correspond to the facts.

89 Clay Eyes Only for Draper, Top Secret, CC 3129, 7 February 1948, in Smith (ed.), *The Clay Papers*, doc. 329, p. 556.

90 J. V. Stalin, *The Great Patriotic War of the Soviet Union*, 5th edn (Moscow: Foreign Languages Publishing House, 1950), p. 84.

91 See Bodo Scheurig, *Freies Deutschland: Das Nationalkomitee und der Bund Deutscher Offiziere in der Sowjetunion 1943–1945* (Munich: Nymphenburger, 1960).

92 In recognition of the importance of the border problem for the viability and legitimacy of a future East German state, the United States ambassador in Moscow, Walter Bedell Smith, wrote in August 1948 that 'If Western powers should be forced out of Berlin and, following establishment of Western German government, Communist-dominated government be established in northeastern Germany, latter's prestige and attracting power throughout the country might be vastly increased by return of part of this area [east of the River Oder and the Western River Neisse' (telegram to the Secretary of State [Marshall], Secret, 21 August 1948, in US Department of State, *Foreign Relations, 1948*, Vol. IV, p. 910).

93 Werth, *Russia: The Post-War Years*, p. 234.

94 At the Foreign Ministers' Conference in Moscow, March 1947, ibid., p. 236.

95 *Pravda*, 18 December 1947.

96 The Soviet government note to the three Western powers was published in *Pravda*, 9 March 1948; the Soviet version of the crucial events of 20 March (the walkout of the Soviet representation at the Control Council) according to *Pravda*, 22 March 1948.

97 TASS report from Berlin, ibid., 29 March 1948. The phrase 'The division of Germany is now an accomplished fact' was the line of the day carried verbatim by *Neues Deutschland* and *Tägliche Rundschau*, and it was amplified in an article by *Pravda* correspondent Yu. Korol'kov, *Pravda*, 1 April 1948. However, the Soviet Union's expert on German problems, Danil Mel'nikov, interpreted the separate *currency reform* of 18 June as completing the division of Germany, ibid., 20 June 1948; see also the *Pravda* report under the heading 'Separatnaia denezhnaia reforma – zaveshchanie raskola Germanii' (The separate currency reform – completion of the division of Germany), ibid., 21 June 1948. In other words there was some confusion among Soviet contemporary observers as to what precisely made the division of Germany an 'accomplished fact'.

98 Even Germans favorably inclined towards the Soviet Union like Nadolny (see above, notes 71 and 78) considered the return of most of the areas east of the Rivers Oder and Neisse an indispensable condition for an overall Russian-German settlement. This was clearly stated in his (Nadolny's) memorandum of 30 April 1947 to Molotov, where he reasoned as follows: '[T]he intended [*sic*] expulsion of nine million Germans from their traditional homeland and the *de facto* separation of the eastern German provinces [from the Reich] in favor of Poland have given rise to the greatest embitterment among the German people; [both of these measures] *will never be accepted by the German people*. However, the German people is prepared to sacrifice as much territory as would be necessary for Polish access to the sea. It is to be hoped that the Russian statesmen will find an appropriate solution' (Nadolny, *Mein Beitrag*, p. 180, my italics).

99 'Sovetskaia politika ravnopraviia natsii' *Bol'shevik*, no. 9 (1948), p. 5.

100 Gar Alperovitz, *Cold War Essays* (Garden City, NY: Doubleday, 1970), p. 70.

101 One convincing example for the rebuttal of the thesis of US nuclear diplomacy is Thomas T. Hammond, 'Did the United States use atomic diplomacy against Russia in 1945?', in Peter J. Potichnyj and Jane P. Shapiro (eds), *From the Cold War to Detente* (New York: Praeger, 1976), pp. 25–56.

102 Harry S. Truman, *Memoirs, Vol. I: Year of Decisions* (Garden City, NY: Doubleday, 1955), p. 416.

103 Arnold Kramish, *Atomic Energy in the Soviet Union* (Stanford, Calif.: Stanford University Press, 1959), pp. 100 and 106; Wolfe, *Soviet Power and Europe*, pp. 35–6. The discussion of Soviet nuclear weapons programs draws on Wolfe's book, Shulman's *Stalin's Foreign Policy Reappraised*, pp. 24–6, and the most thorough and detailed study of this problem so far, David Holloway, *Entering the Nuclear Arms Race: The Soviet Decision to Build the Atomic Bomb, 1939–45*, International Security Studies Program, Working Paper No. 9 (Washington, DC: The Wilson Center, 1979).

104 G. K. Zhukov, *Vospominaniia i razmyshleniia*, Vol. II, 2nd rev. edn (Moscow: Novosti, 1974), p. 418.

105 S. M. Shtemenko, *General'nyi Shtab v gody voiny*, 2nd rev. edn (Moscow: Voenizdat, 1975), p. 429 (my italics).

106 As quoted by A. Lavrent'eva, 'Stroiteli novogo mira', *V mire knig*, no. 9 (1970), p. 4. This article reviews a biography of Vannikov by G. Ustinov, *Narodnyi komissar*. The biography, however, does not seem to have been published. My attention was drawn to Lavrent'eva's article by Holloway, *Entering the Nuclear Arms Race'*, p. 41.

107 *Pravda*, 10 February 1946, as quoted by Shulman, *Stalin's Foreign Policy Reappraised*, p. 24.

108 Djilas, *Conversations with Stalin*, p. 153.

109 *Pravda*, 25 September 1946.

110 The Soviet news agency for once appeared to have been closer to the truth when it stated, immediately and bluntly after the publication of Truman's *Memoirs*, that the statement in Truman's book 'about some sort of "ultimatum" is an invention from beginning to end' (TASS, in English, 29 April 1952). It is doubtful that TASS would have taken the risk of exposing itself to the embarrassment of being proved wrong by publication of US documents to support Truman's case if such documents had in fact existed. Similarly the presence of the battleship *Missouri* in the eastern Mediterranean, which is also often taken as evidence of US military pressure in the Iranian crisis, was a coincidence rather than design: the Turkish ambassador to Washington had died and the battleship was carrying his body back to Istanbul. Foreign Secretary Byrnes had been asked by Forrestal, the Defense Secretary, whether a fleet should accompany the *Missouri* – this, however, with a view to strengthening Greece and Turkey, not to bring pressure to bear on the USSR in connection with Iran. In any case, the fleet was never sent. Hence the Soviet retreat in Iran has much more to do with Stalin's overall estimation of the 'correlation of forces' (see below, p. 143), as well as with his at that time not unreasonable assumption that the Soviet-Iranian agreement of 26 March 1946 provided the USSR with the opportunity to achieve its objectives in Iran *without* confrontation. These issues are carefully examined by James A. Thorpe, 'Truman's ultimatum to Stalin of the 1946 Azerbaidjan crisis: the making of a myth', *Journal of Politics*, vol. 40, no. 1 (February 1978), pp. 188–95; J. Philipp Rosenberg, 'The Cheshire ultimatum: Truman's message to Stalin in the 1946 Azerbaidjan crisis', ibid., vol. 41, no. 3 (August 1979), pp. 933–40; and Valerie Spencer, 'The Iranian crisis of 1945–46', unpublished paper, Royal Military College of Canada, May 1979.

111 Stalin's 'interview' with Alexander Werth, *Pravda*, 25 September 1946.

112 Raymond L. Garthoff, *Soviet Strategy in the Nuclear Age* (New York: Praeger, 1958), p. 64.

113 Dalton Diary, entries dated 5 October 1945 and 17 October 1945 (my italics). Hugh Dalton, at the time of the London Foreign Ministers' Conference, was Chancellor of the Exchequer and hence a colleague of Ernest Bevin in the Cabinet. The diary, here as quoted by Feis, *From Trust to Terror*, p. 98, can be consulted at the London School of Economics.

114 *Izvestiia*, 7 November 1947 (my italics).

115 *The Times*, 29 March 1948.

116 This clearly emerges from the records of discussions in the UN Commission on Atomic Energy and its subcommissions and the two volumes published by the US Department of

State, *The International Control of Atomic Energy: Growth of a Policy* (Washington, DC: US Government Printing Office, 1946) and *The International Control of Atomic Energy: Policy at the Crossroads* (Washington, DC: US Government Printing Office, 1948).

117   US Department of State, *Foreign Relations, 1948*, Vol. IV, p. 887. It took some time for the protest to be put in this form. General Kenney had made his speech on 7 May; the *Newsweek* report appeared on 17 May; the Soviet protest was dated 9 June 1948.

118   The demonstration flight is discussed by Ralph E. Mitchell, 'Atomic air power and American foreign policy: the period of nuclear monopoly 1945–49', PhD dissertation, University of Kentucky, 1965, p. 220. The proposal to demonstrate the United States long-range atomic bombing capability by sending B-29s around the world was made by Senator Stuart Symington as early as 1946, the *New York Times*, 13 October 1946.

119   Clay Personal and Eyes Only for Draper, Top Secret, CC 4910, 27 June 1948, in Smith (ed.), *The Clay Papers*, doc. 444, p. 707.

120   ibid., p. 708.

121   Millis (ed.), *The Forrestal Diaries*, p. 455.

122   ibid., p. 456; see also the *New York Times*, 16 July 1948.

123   See above, pp. 92–3.

124   Clay Eyes Only for Bradley, Top Secret, FMPC 336, 15 July 1948, in Smith (ed.), *The Clay Papers*, doc. 469, p. 740.

125   *The Times*, 19 July 1948. The delay, according to General Omar Bradley, was because of reasons of 'timing to secure maximum results' (Smith, ed., *The Clay Papers*, doc. 453, p. 722).

126   The chargé in the Soviet Union (Kohler) to the Secretary of State, Top Secret, 28 September 1948, in US Department of State, *Foreign Relations, 1948*, Vol. IV, p. 920.

127   Millis (ed.), *The Forrestal Diaries*, p. 487.

128   US Congress, Senate, Committee on Armed Services, 80th Congress, 1st Session, *Hearings, Universal Military Training* (Washington, DC: US Government Printing Office, 1948), p. 45. See also US Congress, Senate, Committee on Armed Services, 80th Congress, 2nd Session, *Hearings, Universal Military Training* (Washington, DC: US Government Printing Office, 1948), for facts and figures relating to the military balance in the period 1945–8.

129   Annual Report of the Secretary of the Air Force, 30 June 1948, as quoted by Mitchell, 'Atomic air power', p. 142.

130   ibid., esp. pp. 33–41.

131   *The Times*, 19 June 1948. It was announced then that the fighter strength would soon be doubled to the (still unimpressive) figure of 150 fighter planes.

132   Mitchell, 'Atomic air power', p. 142.

133   ibid.

134   *The Times*, 26 March 1948; HCA/MEAB, 1949, Part 3, Department of the Army, Supplemental, pp. 781–2, as quoted by Mitchell, 'Atomic air power', p. 192.

135   US Congress, Senate, Committee on Armed Services, 80th Congress, 1st Session, *Hearings, Universal Military Training*, pp. 45 and 50, as quoted by Mitchell, 'Atomic air power', p. 192.

136   Phillip A. Karber, 'The Central European arms race: 1948–1980', paper prepared for the Conference on Arms Control, Ebenhausen, 11–13 June 1980, p. 13, and the statistical data and graph on pp. 10–11. Karber's detailed study, when published, will fill a major gap concerning the quantitative aspects of the arms race in central Europe and lay the basis for a better understanding of its dynamics.

137   JCS 1844/13, Top Secret, Brief of Short Range Emergency War Plan (HALFMOON), 21 July 1948, Records of the Joint Chiefs of Staff, Modern Military Records Branch, in Thomas H. Etzold and John Lewis Gaddis (eds), *Containment: Documents on American Policy and Strategy, 1945–1950* (New York: Columbia University Press, 1978), p. 318.

138   Various Western estimates, as quoted by Wolfe, *Soviet Power and Europe*, pp. 10–11. These figures exclude security troops, estimated at between 400,000 and 600,000 men. Among the figures for the total strength of the Soviet armed forces, which Khrushchev provided in 1960, are the following: 11,365,000 men in 1945; and 2,874,000 in 1948 (source: *Pravda*, 15 January 1960). Alexander Werth states that 'the Soviet armed forces, which had been reduced from 11 million men in 1945 to 3 million at the beginning of 1947, were now [in the second half of 1947] being gradually increased to over 5 million' (Werth, *Russia*, p. 333). However, Werth does not document this assertion.

139   This is examined in more detail by Karber, 'The Central European arms race', pp. 4–7.
140   Dispatch by General Clay, Personal for Eisenhower, Top Secret, SX 3741, 6 November 1947, in Smith (ed.), *The Clay Papers*, doc. 292, p. 492.
141   Malcolm Mackintosh, *Juggernaut: The Russian Forces, 1918–1966* (New York: Macmillan, 1967), p. 272; see also Wolfe, *Soviet Power and Europe*, p. 39.
142   Karber, 'The Central European arms race', pp. 7–9.
143   *The Times*, 19 July 1948.
144   It took some time for these figures to be revised, see below, 'The Berlin Crisis of 1961', p. 254.
145   In the light of the seventy-five-odd US fighter aircraft stationed in Europe it is astonishing to read the assertion by the former American commandant in Berlin, General Howley, that the air corridor was open because the 'Reds couldn't close it' and that 'Moscow didn't control the skies' (Howley, *Berlin Command*, p. 205).
146   Murphy, *Diplomat Among Warriors*, p. 316. This is confirmed in Forrestal's report to Marshall, see above, p. 98.
147   Bernard Brodie and Eilene Galloway, 'The effects of the atomic bomb on national security', *Bulletin of the Atomic Scientists*, vol. 3 (June 1947), as quoted by Mitchell, 'Atomic air power', p. 36.
148   US Congress, Senate, Committee on Armed Services, 2nd Session *Hearings, Universal Military Training*, p. 391.
149   David Alan Rosenberg, 'American atomic strategy and the hydrogen bomb decision', *Journal of American History*, vol. 66, no. 1 (June 1979), p. 65. This study draws extensively on hitherto unpublished material.
150   David MacIsaac, *The Air Force and Strategic Thought, 1945–1951*, International Security Studies Program, Working Paper No. 8 (Washington, DC: The Wilson Center, 1979), pp. 36–7.
151   Letter from Albert Wohlstetter, 2 June 1980.
152   ibid. and Rosenberg, 'American atomic strategy', p. 65.
153   Letter from Albert Wohlstetter, 2 June 1980; David E. Lilienthal, *The Journals of David E. Lilienthal, Vol. II: The Atomic Energy Years, 1945–1950* (New York: Harper and Row, 1964), pp. 165–6, and Richard G. Hewlett and Francis Duncan, *A History of the United States Atomic Energy Commission, Vol. II: Atomic Shield, 1947–1952* (University Park, Pa: Pennsylvania State University Press, 1972), pp. 53–5, as quoted by Rosenberg, 'American atomic strategy', p. 65. Lilienthal was head of the Atomic Energy Commission from 1946 to 1950.
154   ibid., pp. 68–9.
155   ibid. The military, political and economic rationale (to the extent that it existed) of the FY1950 defense budget has been thoroughly examined by Warner R. Schilling, 'The politics of national defense: fiscal 1950', in Warner R. Schilling, Paul Y. Hammond and Glenn H. Snyder, *Strategy, Politics, and Defense Budgets* (New York and London: Columbia University Press, 1962), pp. 1–266.
156   Rosenberg, 'American atomic strategy', p. 65. The slow growth of the number of nuclear warheads in the American arsenal can be reconstructed also by looking at figures 2 and 3 of Albert Wohlstetter's article, 'Rivals but no "race"', *Foreign Policy*, no. 16 (Fall 1974), pp. 60–1. The graphs were drawn from the official, classified US stockpile figures showing the absolute numbers; they were cleared for publication in *relative* form.
157   Rosenberg, 'American atomic strategy', p. 68. On the basis of declassified papers of the JCS, papers of the Chief of Staff of the Air Force, and correspondence with Edward B. Giller (former head of the Research Directorate of the Air Force Special Weapons Center and similar positions at the Atomic Energy Commission), Rosenberg comes to the conclusion that a '*fifty-bomb stockpile in July 1948 [is] a reasonable estimate*' (my italics).
158   Rear Admiral V. Gallery, Assistant Chief of Naval Operations for Guided Missiles to the Deputy Chief of Naval Operations (Air), 17 January 1949, citing unidentified 'authorities', may very well have missed the point entirely. Two or three atomic bombs dropped, say, on Berlin, Hamburg and Düsseldorf in the course of the war, would very likely (as in the Japanese case) have precipitated immediate surrender by Nazi Germany.
159   *New York Times*, 3 July 1949.
160   Letter from Albert Wohlstetter to the author, 2 June 1980. Blackwell, a nuclear physicist, is the author of a book on the military and political consequences of atomic energy, published in 1948.

161   Djilas, *Conversations with Stalin*, p. 182 (my italics).
162   Ulam, *Expansion and Coexistence*, p. 497.
163   See pp. 59–62.
164   Seweryn Bialer, in a course on 'The dynamics of Soviet politics' at Columbia University.
165   The shift in terminology from the 'period of the personality cult' to 'cult of personality' was made with particular vigor at the Twenty-Third CPSU Congress in March 1966. Presumably the latter term is meant to emphasize that the seriousness of the distortion of Soviet social and political development in the USSR was less than had previously (under Khrushchev) been alleged.
166   George F. Kennan, *Russia and the West Under Lenin and Stalin* (New York and Toronto: Mentor Books, 1960), p. 284 (my italics).
167   Tucker, *The Soviet Political Mind*, p. 171.
168   N. G. Kuznetsov in an article in *Oktiabr*, no. 11 (1965), pp. 147–8 and p. 162.
169   Khrushchev's speech of 25 February 1956 at the Twentieth Party Congress, in *The Anti-Stalin Campaign*, p. 18.
170   ibid., p. 63 (my italics).
171   Anthony Storr, *Human Aggression* (New York: Atheneum, 1968), p. 98 (my italics). For a discussion of Stalin's personality and its possible influences on foreign policy see also Joseph de Rivera, *The Psychological Dimension of Foreign Policy*, pp. 193–5.
172   As quoted by Roy Medvedev, *Let History Judge*, p. 305.
173   *The Encyclopedia of Mental Health*, Vol. 5 (New York: Watts, 1963), pp. 1407–20.
174   *Encyclopaedia Britannica*, Vol. 19 (Chicago and London: Encyclopaedia Britannica, 1969).
175   *Butterworths Medical Dictionary* (London: Butterworth, 1965).
176   *The Encyclopedia of Mental Health*, Vol. 5, p. 1407.
177   ibid.
178   *Butterworths Medical Dictionary*, p. 1052.
179   Medvedev, *Let History Judge*, p. 306 (italics in the original).
180   Zhdanov's star had risen from 1934 onwards (after Kirov's murder) to the position of heir apparent to Stalin. By June 1941, however, Malenkov's ascendancy had begun. Although Zhdanov was a *full* Politburo member at that time, it was Malenkov, a *candidate* member, who was included in the State Defense Committee. On Malenkov's ascendancy and Zhdanov's demise see Harrison E. Salisbury, *The 900 Days: The Siege of Leningrad* (New York: Hearst/Avon Books, 1969), pp. 160–70. On the State Defense Committee (GKO) see above, pp. 150–1.
181   Leonard Schapiro, *The Communist Party of the Soviet Union* (London: Eyre & Spottiswoode, 1960), pp. 507–8.
182   See above, p. 119.
183   Robert Conquest, *Power and Policy in the USSR* (London: Macmillan, 1961), pp. 92–3.
184   ibid.
185   This charge was made in the so-called Doctor's Plot of 13 January 1953 which has been interpreted as the opening move by Stalin to initiate a new wave of purges shortly before his death; on the controversy over Zhdanov's death and the charges arising from the Doctor's Plot see *The Anti-Stalin Campaign*, pp. 63–5; Salisbury, *900 Days*, pp. 665–6; Djilas, *Conversations with Stalin*, p. 155; Shulman, *Stalin's Foreign Policy Reappraised*, pp. 46–50; and Conquest, *Power and Policy*, pp. 95–111.
186   Salisbury, *The 900 Days*, p. 666.
187   Schapiro, *The Communist Party*, pp. 507–8.
188   Conquest, *Power and Policy*, p. 93 (my italics).
189   Shulman, *Stalin's Foreign Policy Reappraised*, p. 47. The idea of a turning point (or the beginning of a reappraisal) in Soviet foreign policy in the summer of 1948 is not explicitly stated by Shulman. However, the inference is strong. It is mentioned that the Zhdanovist policy was 'questionable' and that, as if as a consequence, 'Malenkov returned to the Secretariat' and 'Zhdanov died'.
190   ibid., p. 16.
191   See note 20, above. Other examples of continuation of Zhdanov's policies could be cited. Concerning the repression of cultural and intellectual freedoms, Shulman writes that 'After Zhdanov's death in August 1948, the campaign continued no less virulently, but with a somewhat different inflection. The main target of attack became "homeless cosmopolitanism", a formula which combined elements of anti-Semitism and anti-Americanism' (Shulman, *Stalin's Foreign Policy Reappraised*, p. 42).

192 See above, p. 103.
193 Table 8.2 is based on R. W. Pethybridge, *A History of Postwar Russia* (London: Allen & Unwin, 1966), p. 51.
194 Similarly there was only one vacancy caused in the ranks of alternate members of the Politburo in the period from 1945 to 1948, that of Colonel General Shcherbakov, head of the main political administration, who died – presumably also of natural causes – in 1945.
195 The ambassador in the Soviet Union (Smith) to the Secretary of State, Confidential, 4 September 1948, US Department of State, *Foreign Relations, 1948*, Vol. IV, pp. 917–18.
196 These statements form part of a collection of various remarks and comments on the state of the party and political affairs written by Lenin in 1922, printed in *Kommunist*, no. 9 (1956) and in Lenin, *Sochineniia*, Vol. XXXVI, 4th edn (Moscow: Izdatel'stvo politicheskoi literatury, 1957), pp. 543–7; for an interpretation see E. H. Carr, *A History of Soviet Russia: The Interregnum, 1923–1924* (Baltimore, Md: Macmillan/Penguin, 1954), pp. 256–76.
197 Khrushchev's Secret Speech, in *The Anti-Stalin Campaign*, p. 24.
198 Captain N. Ruslanov, *Sotsialisticheskii vestnik*, nos. 7–8 (July–August 1953), pp. 128–9.
199 John Erickson, *Stalin's War with Germany, Vol. I: The Road to Stalingrad* (London: Weidenfeld & Nicolson, 1975), pp. 138–9.
200 ibid., p. 139. If this was true for centralization during the war the situation was presumably not helped by the formal breakup of this system after the war. (In September 1945 the GKO was abolished and in January 1946 the Higher Military Council (*Vysshii voennyi sovet*) was formed, consisting of members of the Politburo, Central Committee and leaders of the armed forces.) The main argument here is that, no matter how high the degree of centralization, bureaucratic confusion continued to exist.
201 Nettl, *The Eastern Zone and Soviet Policy*, p. 199.
202 Leonhard, *Child of the Revolution*, p. 345.
203 See above, pp. 125–30.
204 In conversation with me.
205 Erickson, *The Road to Stalingrad*, p. 373.
206 Khrushchev's Secret Speech, in *The Anti-Stalin Campaign*, p. 44. Dmitri Shostakovich mentions a similar instance from the realm of music. Stalin had listened to a piano concerto by Mozart and asked for the record. There was none. No one, however, dared to tell Stalin – '*they were afraid to say no [because] no one ever knew what the consequences might be*'. In the end, in record time, a new record was made – one single copy. This excerpt is taken from Shostakovich's memoirs, the *New York Times Magazine*, 7 October 1979 (my italics).
207 US Department of State, *Foreign Relations, 1948*, Vol. II, pp. 1066–7. It is interesting to note that whereas Clay in Berlin immediately recognized the important gains made by the Soviet Union in the talks in Moscow in August 1948, Ambassador Smith reported to the Secretary of State that 'practically every safeguard on which we have insisted has been included in the final draft [of the communiqué and directives to the four military governors] (ibid., p. 1068, see also above, pp. 99–100).
208 Djilas, *Conversations with Stalin*, p. 82.

9
Process Analysis

The imposition of the blockade and the acceptance of risks appears to have been based on the following four major calculations made by the Soviet leadership. (1) In a period of 'impending crisis of capitalism' the determination of the Western powers to resist pressures and stay in Berlin is low. (2) The supply of Berlin by air is impossible over a prolonged period of time; the Western powers, therefore, will be forced to leave Berlin or make significant political concessions on the German problem. (3) The West does not want war and is therefore unlikely to use force unless attacked militarily; it is therefore also necessary to prevent military incidents of any sort from getting out of control. (4) Even if the Western powers were willing in principle to resist pressure, Soviet and German communist pressure on the local population in Berlin would serve to undermine the very social, economic and political basis on which the Western powers could hope to maintain their presence in the city.

Each one of these calculations could have been a miscalculation. There was the possibility that Western determination was unexpectedly high. The 'success' of the airlift could force the Western powers into a tight corner from which the only way out was the use of force. The confidence to be able to control the force of events could be unwarranted. And the local population could turn spontaneously against the Soviet occupation forces.

The matter is complicated by constant change in the mix of objective conditions during the crisis. Nevertheless it is fair to say that while the tactical implementation of the Soviet coercive strategy in Berlin can be viewed as skillful, the venture as a whole was still doomed to failure because of major miscalculations. It is useful, therefore, to look more closely at each and every point.

Soviet Probing and Western Determination

Regarding the first possible calculation, it could indeed appear as a matter of conjecture whether the West was determined to stay in Berlin and accept the risks connected with it. As Clay noted, correctly in my view, the question '*Mourir pour Berlin?*' was answered in the negative by most Frenchmen in the early phases of the Berlin crisis.[1] Clay also asserts, with some exaggeration, that among the British in Berlin and London the opinion was that 'We should pull out while we can still do so without much loss of prestige'.[2] Nevertheless before the full imposition of the blockade there was hesitation and doubt and these feelings were shared by Americans in Germany, but particularly in Washington. This was enhanced by the Joint Chiefs of Staff, who were aware of the militarily 'indefensible' position in Berlin.[3]

Soviet assumptions that Western determination to resist pressures was low could have been confirmed by the consistent failure to challenge by force the

Soviet probes in the period prior to the imposition of the blockade. On 1 April five trains entered the Soviet zone, three of them American, the other two British (the latter stocked with food for several days). One American train commandant, 'who apparently lost his nerve' and later was to be questioned, permitted Soviet representatives to board his train and was permitted to proceed. All the other trains, however, were stopped in one way or another and had to back out of the Soviet zone.[4] A replay of the procedure on 21 June did not lead to any other result: a US military freight train with armed guards was ordered to proceed to Berlin via the regular authorized corridor Helmstedt–Berlin. The train was stopped, and when the American officer in charge attempted to force the train through it was prevented from proceeding further due to the removal of a section of rail or by some other mechanical device.[5] This train, too, withdrew from the Soviet zone.

The possibility of a discrepancy between Western determination and its effective communication to the Soviet Union was manifest also in much of the official reaction on the verbal level prior to the blockade. When the SMA had refined a complex system of inspection and validation of transit documents in the spring of 1948, a high-level meeting of American officials explicitly rejected the idea of a strongly worded communication to Stalin 'because it would add disproportionate emphasis on this incident and might convince the Russians that they had secured precisely the effect they were after'.[6]

In view of facts of this kind on the verbal and nonverbal level, it is interesting to ask whether Moscow would ever have imposed the blockade if Washington had adopted the course of action advocated by Clay. In detail, as early as 1 April he told General Bradley, 'I am giving some thought to sending a guarded truck convoy through, since this could force the issue' – a rather surprising 'thought' on the surface as there was no blockade of road traffic, the restrictions affected rail traffic only and Clay admitted that 'rail traffic cannot be moved [by us] with others [the Soviet authorities] controlling the signal system'.[7] The main reason for Clay's overall approach was to respond to every kind of Soviet challenge, and as early and vigorously as possible, so as to stop the probes from becoming ever more severe.

For him to accept the rules of the game as defined by Stalin and to avoid provocation was to invite the very disaster which early resistance was designed to prevent. Although the question of whether the imposition of the blockade would have been prevented by the early demonstration of force can never be answered in confidence, Clay's reasoning appears sound. Murphy, too, seems to see much of the reason for the blockade ever having taken place as being lack of vigorous responses in the stage of Soviet probing of Western determination. 'They [the Soviet leaders] had tested our will to insist upon access rights, and the three Western powers had not been able to conceal their doubts and hesitations.'[8]

However, changes in American determination to assert Western interests in Berlin once the blockade was imposed could not have been overlooked by Stalin. Indeed there was an enormous difference between annoyances and inconveniences of all sorts on the one hand and the complete isolation of the city on the other. The blockade increasingly came to be recognized in the United States as an important test of wills. In April Clay was still out of tune with prevailing opinion in Washington when he put forward a domino theory for Western Europe (the first domino having fallen with Czechoslovakia, the next to be Berlin, then Western Germany and then Western Europe) and his dramatic plea that 'If we mean that we are to hold Europe against communism, we must not budge'.[9] Washington went as far as accepting the principle that it was desirable to stay in Berlin, but what was controversial was the degree of commitment and the level of risk that was to be accepted to assert this principle. The discrepancy between the two – desire and commitment – was still evident in the president's decision, as quoted, 'to stay [in Berlin]. Period' but to maintain an 'unprovocative but firm stand'.[10]

In contrast it could be argued that there are numerous examples which do not bear out the assertion that, in essence, weakness had been conveyed to Stalin and encouraged him to embark on the venture of the blockade. In March a demonstration flight of B-29s had taken place. The new regime of identification and documentation required by the SMA on the access routes was never accepted. A Soviet military post had been established in the British sector on 2 April; it was surrounded and then withdrawn under pressure. The Western reaction to the air accident of 5 April had been swift and vigorous. Finally, to conclude the argument, on 10 June the American military command had intervened with armed guards to stop Soviet representatives from removing locomotives and railroad cars from the American sector in Berlin.[11] While this was apparently not enough to convince Stalin that he was overstepping the limits when he decided on the blockade, the instances of Western resistance and counterchallenge, though at a low level, were important enough to convince Stalin not to interfere with the airlift. Such an interpretation appears even more valid if the examples of resistance and counterchallenge are seen in conjunction with the clear manifestations of American resolve, shared by both political parties *after* the blockade had been imposed. To take a representative example, on 19 July Senator Vandenberg, a Republican, wrote:

> The 'calculated risk' evidently is becoming more 'risky' – and probably deliberately so. But I do not see how we can yield our basic position without total sacrifice of every chance we have for peace in Europe, or in the world.[12]

Such statements were strong enough to induce second thoughts about interfering in the airlift. But what may have been the Soviet calculations with respect to this matter?

Soviet Calculations and the Airlift

Concerning the second possible Soviet calculation (the view that the airlift would prove an impractical and ineffective measure to undercut the blockade on the ground), only hindsight can make Soviet optimism appear completely unfounded. Those in a position to know, like Western air specialists, were quite pessimistic about the prospects of supplying a city of more than two million inhabitants by air. The air force chiefs in Washington were 'flabbergasted' by such an idea.[13] General Curtis LeMay, the US air force commander in Europe, asked about the possibilities of coal supplies by air, dryly commented to Clay on the phone: 'We must have a bad phone connection.'[14] The British commandant in Berlin, General Herbert, believed that if the Soviets imposed a blockade, 'we could never hold out'.[15] Many others shared this view.[16] And even Clay, a perennial optimist, estimated that 500 to 700 tons of supplies a day was the maximum of what would be 'a very big operation'.[17] Such a small volume, needless to say, was completely inadequate to maintain the viability of West Berlin.

The question which figured foremost in Western, and almost certainly in Soviet calculations, was not *whether* Berlin could hold out, but for *how long*. The best estimate in the United States State Department was that food could be supplied to West Berlin for a maximum of two or three months.[18] There is every reason to believe that the Soviet estimations were similar. This is evident, for instance, in Sokolovsky's letter to General Robertson (29 June) in which he expressed his confidence that it was possible for the West 'to provide for the continued supply of goods to the population for the *next few weeks*'.[19] In Howley's assessment, Sokolovsky 'thought we had only two weeks' supply of food'.[20] TASS reported from Berlin on 4 July: 'Every day the food situation in the three Western Sectors of Berlin grows more and more critical',[21] and in what may have been genuine expression of estimates, TASS quoted a 'British aviation specialist' as saying that the supply of coal via air to Berlin was 'impossible'.[22] It is not at all surprising, then, that Clay received the impression in a meeting of the four military governors in Germany on 3 July that Marshal Sokolovsky was confident that 'we would be forced to leave Berlin'.[23] Even as late as mid-September, perhaps in anticipation of the hardships of the coming winter, the Soviet German expert, Danil Mel'nikov, attempted to show that it was a 'legend' that the airlift worked, that 'reality' had disproved Western claims.[24]

The conclusion appeared inescapable to Frank Howley that the USSR had 'badly underestimated' the extent of Western preparations for withstanding a siege as well as the potentialities of an airlift.[25] The question must be asked: what would have been the consequence if the airlift had in fact turned out to be the failure which most specialists at first expected? With little 'breathing space and essential time to think' for the West,[26] did Stalin do nothing but confront the three Western powers with the precarious alternative of capitulation or the use of force? This may have been the case objectively. However, the answer to the question is most likely that Stalin was confident of his ability to prevent events from getting out of hand.

Soviet Control of the Force of Events

On 27 June a Western observer noted that 'Where troops of two antagonistic powers are in close contact as they are in Berlin, the possibility of the type of "incidents" which lead to war is always present'.[27] On 19 July Vandenberg worried about the 'rapidly complicating conditions' in the Berlin air corridors that could 'precipitate a miscalculated accident almost at any time'.[28] Truman, in his memoirs, reasoned that there was the 'possibility that Russia might deliberately choose to make Berlin the pretext for war', but 'a more immediate danger was the risk that a trigger-happy Russian pilot or hot-headed Communist tank commander might create an incident that could ignite the powder keg'.[29] These observations are at odds with the objective conditions in the crisis.

In particular, reasoning of this kind must have appeared utterly alien to Stalin. It would have been strange for him to think that there could occur a breakdown in the normal channels of command. The consequences of disobedience were well known. No one, including Sokolovsky, was exempt from them. But what if an accident had happened, what then? It is not necessary to engage in much conjecture because the air accident of 5 April can be regarded as a test case. It was clearly understood by all sides that this event was, in fact, nothing but an accident. It was a source of embarrassment for the SMA and an opportunity for the Western allies to demonstrate the unacceptable consequences of further Soviet harrassment in the air corridors. But this is as far as matters went. All this is to say that it is very difficult to see any contingency of accidents of this type leading to war. There are other considerations pointing in the same direction.

When it became apparent that the airlift had been underestimated in its potentialities, it immediately produced the effect of relieving the actors of time pressure. This served to contain immediate risks of military actions to a considerable degree. From the Soviet point of view this development could only be considered as advantageous because the blockade could be retained as a constant source of pressure, but these pressures would be at lower levels of risk. On the assumption that the airlift was no more than a temporary expedient, Stalin could hope to win Western concessions for the ultimate lifting of the blockade. Again, if this reasoning did indeed play a role in Soviet calculations, it cannot be dismissed as entirely unfounded. From this perspective military incidents were unwelcome and the Soviet Union could be expected to avoid them.

In the final analysis it must have appeared to Stalin that there was a tremendous margin of safety built into the confrontation over Berlin. The reason for saying so is the apparently sheer inexhaustible patience and restraint displayed by the Western policy-makers, enhanced by the differences of opinion and the difficulties of coordination in the Western camp. Despite the negative experiences with the direct approach tried out in May 1948 (Smith–Molotov), and despite the Western claim in the notes of 6 July not to engage in negotiations prior to the lifting of the blockade, Stalin succeeded in involving the three Western powers in almost a full month of protracted negotiations in Moscow (the ambassadors' talks with Stalin and Molotov, 2 to 30 August), for another two weeks in Berlin (at the level of the military governors, 31 August to 14 September), then in another exchange of notes and aides-mémoire, only to learn of yet another proposal for a direct approach in the form of Truman's idea to send Chief Justice Vinson to Moscow (at the beginning of October).[30] It was reasonable to assume that, faced with such an adversary, incidents of all sorts could be defused relatively easily.

But having said all that, there is one exception to the general picture of the low probability of the force of events making an impact in the crisis – sporadic confrontations between a more and more hostile population and the Soviet military in Berlin. During the initial phase of the blockade, when Soviet and East German police attempted to interfere in black market activities, they were attacked by an angry German crowd, shooting broke out, and an unidentified number of German civilians were killed. Soviet troops felt compelled to take up positions along the sectorial borders.[31] A similar, potentially even more explosive, situation developed at the beginning of September. More than 300,000 Berliners assembled at the Platz der Republik close to the Brandenburg Gate. Describing these events the American commandant writes: 'Some of the mob surged over into the Russian side of the gate, yelling, "Let's drive the Russians back to Moscow!".'[32] Soviet soldiers again felt compelled to use force in order to contain the danger of events getting out of control.

Incidents of this kind, involving not the restrained calculations of Western policy-makers but irrationality, emotionalism and the 'subjectivism' of the populace, are probably something any Soviet leadership least likes to have to deal with. At the same time the very fact that these constraints made themselves felt acutely point to one of the most important Soviet miscalculations in the whole venture.

Soviet Pressures and the Population of Berlin

The fourth possible Soviet calculation — expectations that the morale of the Berliners was rather low and that the Western powers would be forced to leave Berlin as a consequence of social, economic and political transformations in the city — could have been based not only on the admittedly precarious military position of the city surrounded by several Soviet élite (*gvardia*) tank and motorized divisions, but also on the fact that the Germans in 1948 were still a demoralized people and easily manipulable by the victorious powers. As a defeated and occupied city, resistance on its own would have remained hopeless and was, to many, unthinkable. Of course to the average Berliner 'Berlin is worth a war',[33] but how could he expect it to be worth it for the Parisian, Londoner or New Yorker?

It is not surprising, therefore, that a survey of editorials in noncommunist newspapers published in West Berlin revealed three principal causes of concern — 'fear of war, fear that the Western powers would desert Berlin, and fear that the airlift would fail to bring in sufficient supplies'.[34] Since the extent of determination and the spirit to resist on the part of the local population in Berlin, up to the present day, is very much a function of the extent of Western determination and Western support, doubts about the full extent of Western resolve could have served to reinforce Soviet calculations that the venture might be successful if it were carried on long and far enough.

Finally, the idea that a capitalist adversary should have strong morale, that his will could not be broken by severe pressure and that he would not in the long run submit to superior power must have appeared unlikely. It would have contradicted Soviet ideological preconceptions and actual experience in postwar international affairs up to that date.

Clay sensed that the linchpin of the Berlin crisis was the morale of the population in Berlin. The 'principal danger' was not that of an escalation of military incidents but the activity of 'Russian-planned German Communist groups' which, in conjunction with the deprivations of the land blockade, could lead to a serious demoralization among the population and make the Western allied position untenable even if they were willing to maintain it.[35] Only today with the benefit of hindsight is it possible to dismiss these considerations as unfounded.

What remains to be said is that the recognition of this 'principal danger' contributed a good share to the failure of Soviet tactics. Clay insisted that 'We must not destroy their [the Germans'] confidence by any indications of departure from Berlin'.[36] As early as 2 July, Under Secretary of State William Draper, who was then on visit to Berlin, reported to Washington (quite to the point) that 'The constant buzz of food planes overhead has raised the Allied and German morale to a high level'.[37]

Verbal Communications

In 1948 the tenor of Soviet communications regarding the risk of war and the seriousness of the crisis can be summarized best under the heading of 'much ado about nothing'. The fact of a full-scale blockade was never admitted; there was only a gradual shift of explanations away from purely technical grounds to economic and political justifications, but the temporary nature of the blockade measures was always stressed. The Soviet government assured the Western powers that it was striving 'for the speediest elimination of the difficulties which have arisen recently'.[38] Stalin personally assured the Western ambassadors on 2 August that it was 'not the purpose of the Soviet Government to force the Western Governments from Berlin' and that the USSR and the West were still 'Allies';[39] Molotov thought that Moscow and the West were still 'partners in Germany'.[40]

These communications were well suited to serve several distinct purposes: to enhance the legitimacy of Soviet actions, to facilitate a Soviet-American compromise and to persuade the Western powers that it would be wrong for them to interpret the blockade as a hostile act directed against them. (In fact, clearly denying the full scope of the blockade, Sokolovsky – in one of his letters to General Robertson – spoke only of 'restrictions of movements of the *German population*' as if movements of the Western allies had never been restricted, or were unrestricted at the time.[41] Finally, such communications were well designed to permit the lifting of all the restrictions, or of a part of them, without loss of prestige in case of vigorous Western counteraction.

On the other hand, the content and purposes of verbal communications which were advantageous, or even necessary, for the *control* of risks, served to undermine the *effectiveness* of risk-taking. The Soviet Union maneuvered itself into the position of a blackmailer refusing to state the exact amount of money to be paid, while at the same time retaining the innocuous and polite manners of a gentleman. In a study of three post-World War II crises, the conclusion has been advanced that for a coercive strategy to be effective, there must be 'clarity concerning the precise terms of settlement'.[42] If this view is correct, Soviet communications, by their very ambiguity in content and cordiality in style, did not facilitate the achievement of a settlement.

The lack of clarity of demands is closely linked to the violation of another important principle of coercive diplomacy, 'the carrot and the stick' approach, the requirement that open or veiled threats be coupled with plausible and binding promises of acceptable compromises.[43] In his memoirs Smith writes that the main political demands were never 'approached directly or made an outright condition for the lifting of the blockade'.[44] This view is both right and wrong. It is wrong because on 2 August Stalin put his cards on the negotiating table with the three Western ambassadors (including Smith) by putting forward the proposal of a lifting of the blockade in exchange for the abolition of the special mark B in the Western sectors of Berlin and postponement of the implementation of the London recommendations.[45] What Stalin did not say, and could not say, was that what he wanted was unilateral control over the whole of the city and, preferably, concessions on other aspects of the 'German problem'. To that extent the true nature of the demands was never stated directly.

But there was another problem. Once agreement on specific proposals appeared to have been reached, it came to be interpreted in such a way as to make the agreement meaningless, and at the same time new demands were added to old ones. Thus it would be correct to summarize that — because of the presence of substantial Soviet military forces in Berlin and in the surrounding areas — the stick as a nonverbal instrument of coercion always loomed large. Yet the carrots were not only withheld from the Berlin population in a literal sense but also, figuratively, from the Western allies; or, when they were offered, they turned out to be inedible. All this served to reinforce Western suspicions that Soviet objectives, in principle, were unlimited and that any compromise would only evoke new Soviet demands.

Limits and Failure of Soviet Risk-Taking

Once the airlift had become 'reality in the first week of July' and proved its effectiveness beyond reasonable doubt, the failure of Soviet coercion and risk-taking became increasingly apparent. Stalin's display of an attitude of cordiality and compromise did not convince the three Western powers that their vital interests were not threatened. After the decision had been taken in Washington 'to stay [in Berlin]. Period' and made credible by the large-scale airlift, the main overt target of Soviet coercion, the Berlin population, was largely immunized against pressures. Thus a stalemate developed which became increasingly disadvantageous for the Soviet leaders, forcing them to think of new moves if they wanted to secure any of their original objectives. At any time after the manifestation of failure a decision had to be made to withdraw or to adopt a higher risk strategy.

Such a strategy could have consisted of three possible measures: (1) an armed takeover of the Western sectors of Berlin, (2) a combination of 'mass actions from below' and Soviet military intervention, and (3) interference with the airlift.

Because of the presence of Western military forces in Berlin, the first alternative was to be considered nothing but the beginning of military conflict. There is no evidence to support a theory that the Soviet leaders ever considered this option seriously.

The second alternative reportedly was under discussion. According to an American journalist with informants in East Berlin, there were to be 'spontaneous' protest demonstrations in the Western sectors against the 'occupants'. Armed communists were to provoke shooting incidents with the German civilian police. On the basis of the claims advanced by Moscow and the SMA that Berlin was part of the Soviet zone, Soviet troops would then intervene to restore order.[46] If this account is to be regarded as more than just a piece of the general Soviet campaign to spread demoralizing rumors, it still remains a fact that the plan was never implemented – for very good reasons, because the only distinguishing element compared with the armed takeover is the meager addition of a rather shaky law-and-order argument. In 1948 the individual sector commandants were (and still are today) responsible for security in their respective sectors. In all likelihood the Western commandants would have rejected Soviet arguments as pretexts and resisted the unwarranted intervention with force.

The last alternative for achieving the original objective was to stop the airlift. For that purpose it was probably not even necessary to start shooting down American, British and French planes; so-called passive measures, such as radar jamming and putting chaff into the atmosphere, might have been effective enough. But this course of action was rejected too. According to American sources there was a total of 162,275 flights of US planes between June 1948 and June 1949, but less than 1 percent of these flights were reported to have been molested by buzzing, close flying, jamming, radio interference, and so on.[47] Western sources do not show that even one single accident was caused directly by Soviet interference with Western air operations. As mentioned, the fatal accident at Gatow in the British sector, where an irresponsible Soviet pilot had frolicked an incoming British plane, occurred on 5 April 1948, that is, *before*, not during, the blockade.

All this can only point to a Soviet conviction that denial of the airlift as a course of action would have left open only two alternatives for the West: to break the blockade by force or to surrender the position in Berlin. As those were the only two apparent alternatives available to the West on the very day when the blockade was imposed, it follows that once the venture was launched Stalin must have immediately reconsidered – almost as if he had suddenly become very anxious about the daring step he had taken with potentially far-reaching consequences.

Considering the fact that Soviet behavior showed great restraint in the use of violence against Western military personnel and operations, rejecting all alternatives that would have involved even lower-level military clashes between units of the superpowers, two conclusions appear inescapable: (1) the Soviet leaders excluded war as a means to further their objectives; (2) the limit of risk-taking was the occurrence of violence between military units of the superpowers. Since the Soviets did not want to *initiate* violence, the reasoning appears sound that they would also not have *reacted* with violence to Western attempts at securing land access by force. In the terminology of this thesis, all indications point not only to calculated risk-taking, but also to the existence of what Triska and Finley call a 'risk-reducing emergency strategy'.[48] Some of the most perceptive contemporaries of the Berlin crisis, General Clay and the former mayor of Berlin, Ernst Reuter, argue along these lines. 'The care with which the Russians avoided measures which would have been resisted with force' had convinced Clay that the Russians 'did not want war;' although no armed convoy could have crossed the border without the possibility of trouble, 'the chances of such a convoy being met by force with subsequent developments of hostilities were small'.[49] Reuter agreed with this assessment.[50] This view is confirmed also by the fact that the Soviet authorities were always ready to withdraw from a *competition* in risk-taking on issues about which the Western powers had felt strongly or where they threatened to take retaliatory measures.

Notes: Part Two, Chapter 9

1 Clay, *Decision in Germany*, p. 362.
2 ibid.
3 Murphy, *Diplomat among Warriors*, p. 315; see also *Department of State Bulletin* (DOSB), vol. 19, no. 487 (31 October 1948), pp. 541–3. On the role of the JCS see above, pp. 98 and 141.
4 Clay Personal for Chief of Staff [Bradley], Top Secret, 1 April 1948, in Smith (ed.), *The Clay Papers*, p. 607. In his memoirs Clay appears to have confused this event with the one on 21 June. His description fits the events of the latter date, not the former: 'The train progressed some distance into the Soviet Zone but was shunted off the main line by electrical switching to a siding where it remained for a few days until it withdrew rather ignominiously' (Clay, *Decision in Germany*, p. 359). Smith, *The Defense of Berlin*, p. 104, accepted this version. However, *The Clay Papers* can be considered as more reliable. The same applies to the events of 21 June as reported by Murphy to Washington, see note 5, below.
5 The United States Political Adviser for Germany (Murphy) to the Secretary of State, Top Secret, 21 June 1948, in *Foreign Relations, 1948*, Vol. II, pp. 911–2.
6 Millis (ed.), *The Forrestal Diaries*, p. 408.
7 Clay Personal for Chief of Staff, Top Secret, CC 3681, 1 April 1948, in Smith (ed.), *The Clay Papers*, doc. 359, p. 607.
8 Murphy, *Diplomat among Warriors*, p. 316.
9 Teleconference TT-9341 between Clay and Bradley, Top Secret Eyes Only, 10 April 1948, in Smith (ed.), *The Clay Papers*, doc. 371, p. 623.
10 See p. 176.
11 Clay for Noce [Director, Civil Affairs Division, War Department], CC 4675, Confidential, 12 June 1948, in Smith (ed.), *The Clay Papers*, doc. 422, p. 676. *Reichsbahn* (railroad) property and operation was not, and still is not, in the hands of the Western commandants. All the other examples in the above context were mentioned previously.
12 Vandenberg, Jr (ed.), *The Private Papers of Senator Vandenberg*, p. 453.
13 Murphy, *Diplomat Among Warriors*, p. 318.
14 ibid.
15 As quoted by Howley, *Berlin Command*, p. 201.
16 *New York Times*, 21 July 1948.
17 C. J. Murphy, 'The Berlin airlift', *Fortune*, November 1948, p. 90. See also above, p. 95.
18 *New York Times*, 21 July 1948.
19 *Pravda*, 1 July 1948 (my italics).
20 Howley, *Berlin Command*, p. 200.
21 *Pravda*, 5 July 1948.
22 ibid., 4 July 1948.
23 Clay, *Decision in Germany*, p. 367.
24 Danil Mel'nikov, 'The "airlift": legend and realities', *New Times* (Moscow), 15 September 1948.

25   Howley, *Berlin Command*, pp. 200–1.
26   ibid., p. 201.
27   Drew Middleton in the *New York Times*, 27 June 1948, as quoted by Young, *Politics of Force*, p. 97.
28   Vandenberg, Jr (ed.), *The Vandenberg Papers*, p. 453.
29   Truman, *Memoirs, II: Years of Trial and Hope*, p. 124.
30   All these examples were mentioned in Chapter 7.
31   Howley, *Berlin Command*, p. 211.
32   ibid., pp. 217–18; see also the East German authors' account confirming these events, Keiderling and Stulz, *Geschichte Berlins 1945–1968*, pp. 171–2.
33   Editorial in the newspaper of the SPD, *Sozialdemokrat*, 17 August 1948.
34   Davison, *The Berlin Blockade*, p. 136.
35   Teleconference TT-9667 between Clay in Berlin and Secretary Royall and General J. Lawton Collins in Washington, Top Secret, 25 June 1948, in Smith (ed.), *The Clay Papers*, doc. 422, p. 700.
36   Clay, *Decision in Germany*, p. 366. Slightly different wording, but basically the same point was expressed by Clay in the teleconference quoted above, note 35.
37   Teleconference TT-9720 between Clay, Murphy and Draper in Berlin, and Secretary Forrestal, Secretary Royall and General Bradley in Washington, in Smith (ed.), *The Clay Papers*, doc. 453, p. 721. The SMA did not do so well at getting across its thesis that more was going out of Berlin than coming in and that, therefore, the 'real significance' of the airlift was not some sort of 'aid mission' but the 'plundering of Berlin' (editorial, 'Nicht Hilfsaktion sondern Ausplünderung Berlins', *Tägliche Rundschau*, 30 June 1948).
38   Note of the Soviet government to the Western powers of 14 July 1948, *Pravda*, 15 July 1948.
39   Smith, *My Three Years in Moscow*, p. 244.
40   The ambassador in the Soviet Union (Smith) to the Secretary of State, Top Secret, Urgent, 31 July 1948, in US Department of State, *Foreign Relations, 1948*, Vol. II, p. 998.
41   *Pravda*, 1 July 1948 (my italics).
42   Alexander L. George, David K. Hall and William F. Simons, *The Limits of Coercive Diplomacy: Laos, Cuba, Vietnam* (Boston, Mass.: Little, Brown, 1971), p. 26.
43   ibid., pp. 25–6.
44   Smith, *My Three Years in Moscow*, p. 253.
45   See above, pp. 99–100.
46   Curt Reiss, *The Berlin Story* (New York: Dial Press, 1952), pp. 197–8.
47   Robert Rodrigo, *Berlin Airlift* (London: Cassell, 1960), p. 214. The basis of the percentage is 733 reported incidents for the period of August 1948 to August 1949.
48   Triska and Finley, 'The Soviet Union, reckless or cautious?', p. 322.
49   Clay, *Decision in Germany*, p. 374.
50   Davison, *The Berlin Blockade*, p. 105.

10
Consequences, Conclusions and Lessons

The brilliant handling of techniques of crisis management, the effective control of risks and the 'restraint and skill of Soviet diplomats' that averted a breach of peace in those alarming months cannot be considered as an achievement in itself. The failure of the coercive strategy in Berlin had become not merely a matter of – as Soviet diplomats are reported as saying in the spring of 1949 – having 'gambled and lost'; what remained was not simply 'to liquidate the adventure'.[1] Crises tend to unleash powerful forces of change; important lessons are drawn, no matter whether they correspond to reality in an objective manner, and these conditions combine with lingering psychological shock waves of heightened anxieties in the aftermath of crises to make it difficult to revert to a mere restoration of the former status quo. Far from succeeding in winning a lever or a prize, the taking of risks was counterproductive. 'The attempt to "starve out" Berlin gained the Russians nothing. Indeed, they lost a great deal.'[2] Roy Medvedev underlines this view. Comparing the Berlin crisis and the Korean War, he concludes:

> In both cases the Soviet Union and its allies were finally obliged to retreat to their original positions. The struggle ended formally in a draw, but under the circumstances the result favored our opponents far more than ourselves.[3]

The realization that coercive strategies and the crises in their wake not only give rise to immediate and direct *risks of war* but may entail significant and potentially long-range political *costs*, was clearly expressed by Soviet spokesmen during the Khrushchev era and by Khrushchev himself. Defending major policy changes at the height of his de-Stalinization campaign in domestic, intra-bloc and foreign policy, at the Twenty-Second Party Congress in 1961 Khrushchev said that failure to restore Leninist principles of leadership 'would have led to a weaker position for the Soviet Union in the world arena, and to a worsening of relations with other countries, which would have been fraught with serious consequences'.[4]

In a similar vein the authors of an authoritative history on international relations, edited by Nikolai Inozemtsev in 1963, criticized Stalin's approach to foreign policy and his 'subjective and dogmatic' theoretical assessments which 'hindered the development of Marxist theory on questions of international relations, led to an alienation between theory and foreign-policy practice and in the end resulted in an unacceptable situation'. Stalin's successors, however, had taken the steps necessary to 'reduce international tension' and to 'assure that the conduct of Soviet foreign policy would take full account of the concrete particulars of the situation and the actual correlation of forces'.[5] As a result, 'thanks to the consistent peaceful foreign policy of the countries of the socialist camp, the tension in international relations fraught with great danger, was replaced by a certain détente'.[6]

The full extent of the political costs which had to be borne by the USSR as a consequence of the Berlin crisis (and similar ventures undertaken within the general framework of militancy and left-wing 'infantile disorders') can only be sketched very briefly here. On a very general level the Berlin crisis had raised fundamental questions of *morality and legitimacy*. The attempt to starve out Berlin and use its population as a hostage for ill-defined political goals touched Western sensitivities in a deep and lasting way and had significant repercussions. Cold war images of communist totalitarianism and Soviet aggressiveness and perceptions of international relations as being similar to the conditions of the 1930s became widely accepted. Concurrent with an increasingly uncompromising bargaining stand in early 1949 and the lifting of the blockade without major preconditions, the lessons for the West appeared to be the same as those won from dealing with Nazi Germany: aggression has to be stopped at an early stage; negotiations can only be fruitful from positions of strength.

To provide some examples, for Dean Acheson, Secretary of State at the time of the lifting of the blockade, the prime lesson of the Berlin crisis was that the Soviets 'are not moved to agreement by negotiation – that is by a series of mutual concessions calculated to move parties desiring agreement to an acceptable one'.[7] For Charles Bohlen, senior adviser on Soviet affairs to the Secretary of State during the Berlin crisis, 'The principal lesson of the Berlin blockade was that if the Western Allies were prepared to stand firm on their rights, they had better than a fifty-fifty chance of winning'.[8] And in a context directly related to the Berlin crisis, Truman wrote in retrospect:

> I had learned from my negotiations with the intransigent Russian diplomats that there was only one way to avoid a third world war, and that was to lead from positions of strength. We had to rearm ourselves and our allies and, at the same time, deal with the Russians in a manner they could never interpret as weakness.[9]

In this way the consequences of the Berlin crisis extended to the *military sphere*. During the crisis, the United States (as noted) never explicitly threatened to use nuclear weapons pursuant to a specified contingency. But the transfer of heavy bombers to bases in Germany and Britain in July was not only to be interpreted as an unambiguous warning signal to Stalin; at the same time (1) it foreshadowed the reintroduction of American forces to the European continent and (2) it reflected the beginning of a shift in Washington – and elsewhere in the West – to consider the use of nuclear weapons against the Soviet Union as justified on grounds of expediency *and* morality. In a climate of opinion in the West in which a Bertrand Russell could find it morally justified to urge nothing less than preventive war,[10] it is not surprising to read that Secretary of Defense Forrestal felt in July 1948 that

> It was difficult for me to carry out my responsibilities without resolution of the question whether or not we are to use the A-bomb in war. I

observed also that it seemed to me that the Secretary of State had a deep interest in this, because if there were any questions as to the use of this weapon, he was automatically denied one of the most potent cards in the negotiation.[11]

The question of whether or not to use nuclear weapons in war was resolved, as mentioned, by the American President, who made a decision of principle to use them 'if it became necessary'.[12] The extent of support for the resolution of the nuclear issue in this way is manifest also in the assurances given by Prime Minister Clement Attlee (Labour) to John Foster Dulles in November 1948. Attlee emphasized that 'there is no division in the British public mind about the use of the atomic bomb – they [are] for its use. Even the church in recent days has taken this position.'[13]

As a corollary to the reconsideration of nuclear power and its potential use as a political instrument, the discussions of *Western defense integration* received new stimuli. Prior to the blockade, on 11 June Senator Vandenberg had secured passage of a resolution opening the way for American participation in external alliances. This, for the time being, did not mean much in practice. The Berlin crisis, however, acted as a constant rumbling noise in the background, warning of the possibility of a major volcanic eruption. It reminded the Western negotiators during the several months of protracted negotiation not to lose sight of the necessary safety measures to be agreed upon. It may have contributed to the fact that the blockade was not yet over when the North Atlantic Treaty was signed (on 4 April 1949).

Dramatic as these responses may have seemed at the time, or seem in retrospect, the deficiencies remained as severe as ever; the most obvious military lessons of the Berlin crisis were never recognized; and moreover, some of the lessons drawn were simply wrong. The leaders of the emerging military-political alliance reacted to the threatening tremors of the Berlin crisis mainly with organizational charts and declarations but very little substantive preparation. And where preparations were made they were designed to deal with eruptions which were unlikely to take place.

Above all one would have thought that the most realistic contingencies implied in the rumblings of Berlin were conflicts *short of all-out war*, requiring mobile, flexible and readily available power – forces in being and/or rapid deployment forces which could cope with limited conflict. With the exception of some far-sighted analysts (Kennan among them at that time), American officials and academic specialists alike were painfully slow to wake up to the need to deter Soviet risk-taking at lower levels, to balance at least to some degree the Soviet preponderance in conventional strength and to reduce the temptations inherent in local conventional inferiority of the West. Most Americans responsible for various aspects of national security continued to regard war and peace as two entirely separate and distinct states.

Charles Bohlen is right, therefore, when he summarizes the effects of the Berlin crisis by saying, 'The blockade certainly did *not* lead to any rearmament by the United States'.[14] In essence the strength of the US ground forces and fighter aircraft in Central Europe did not change until after the outbreak of the Korean War. 'With the lifting of the Berlin blockade a tranquillity settled over Europe. There was no crisis in sight',[15] and hence there appeared to be no justification to make appropriations for war rather than peace. But even prior to that, during later stages of the Berlin crisis, the 'possible explosive points in the world' to which Truman had called attention in February 1948 – Greece, Italy, Korea and Palestine – had virtually been forgotten in military and budgetary planning.[16] The JCS had estimated that a defense budget of $21–3 billion, or about $17 billion at the very minimum, was necessary to maintain some foothold in Europe and that everything short of that meant cutbacks in conventional forces;[17] and an influential article in *Fortune* of December 1948, programmatically entitled 'The arms we need', had similarly argued that 'if the US intends to continue its present foreign policy, it will in all probability need a greater military force than it now possesses' and called for a budget of approximately $18 billion.

All this was to no avail. Expenditure for the armed forces for the years immediately prior to and after the Berlin crisis remained essentially the same: $11·8 billion in fiscal year 1947; $10·5 billion in FY1948; $11·3 billion in FY1949; and $11·6 billion in FY 1950.[18] If one were to look only at these figures and actual deployments in Europe and elsewhere one could gain the impression that the Berlin crisis had never taken place. What can explain this astonishing state of affairs?

First and foremost, there was the (most likely correct) notion that the American nuclear monopoly had been the prime factor in deterring the Russians from escalating the conflict over Berlin. However, it was also thought that the atomic bomb created for the West some sort of 'window of opportunity', seemingly making it unnecessary to embark on a major effort at rearmament, reorganization and modernization of the armed forces. The two firmly held assumptions that made the view out of the window seem so promising were: (1) the Soviet Union would probably not be able to build an atomic bomb before 1952, and (2) the countries of Europe could be expected increasingly to look after their own defense. Within little more than a year after the end of the Berlin crisis these notions and all the other main assumptions which had shaped national security discussions in 1948–9 – strategic, scientific, military, diplomatic and economic – had been shown to be false.[19] The Europeans did not rally to their own defense, the Soviet bomb exploded in August 1949 and the guerrilla wars in Asia and the North Korean invasion of the south demonstrated the sorry state of Western capabilities to cope with limited military conflict.

Apart from general political and military consequences, there were also a number of consequences affecting specific countries and problem areas. First, the *German problem* took on a new form. The trends towards the formation of a West German state, 'provisionally' representing the interests of Germany as a whole, increased in momentum during the Berlin crisis. By 8 April 1949 the three Western allies had reached agreement among themselves as to the principles for the formation and control of a federal republic, and little more than two weeks later the major parties and political leaders in the Western zones consented to the scheme; a new German government was formed in September. Not least because of Soviet occupation policy and the pressures on the population during the blockade, the new German state, and West Berlin to an even higher degree, were staunchly anticommunist, thus creating a real security problem in more immediate terms than had existed before.

Militant, direct tactics by communists in Europe and coercion by the Soviet state in Berlin led to a serious, if only temporary, weakening of left-wing forces in *France*. The strikes there and the declaration, in February 1949, by Maurice Thorez, general secretary of the French Communist Party, that the PCF would support the Red Army even if it should enter French territory, outraged the National Assembly, led to demands for Thorez's prosecution for treason, to police raids upon communist installations and to arrests, and seemed to condemn French communism to a similarly insignificant role in national politics as that of its sister party in West Germany. [20] On the state level, 'For the French, the blockade had the effect of making them, *nolens volens*, nervous partners in the airlift operation'. [21] By April 1949 France had become a signatory of the North Atlantic Treaty.

Finally, there is the *Yugoslav Affair*, related to the Berlin crisis in time, conceptual approach and methods of Soviet foreign policy. Khrushchev was explicit as to its consequences only to the point of saying: 'We have paid dearly for this "shaking of the little finger".' [22] The costs to which Khrushchev alluded lay in the response of Yugoslavia – mobilization of powerful forces of resistance and national cohesion and, on the international level, the quest for American support to safeguard economic viability and military security. [23]

In sum, the Zhdanovist policy of militancy, pressure and coercion, pursued first with and then without Zhdanov after his death, had collapsed by the spring of 1949. The 'impending crisis of capitalism' had not materialized, but the policies pursued on its basis had led to a crisis of Soviet foreign policy. The doctrines of two camps and capitalist encirclement, artificial as they may have been in the spring of 1948, had turned out to be self-fulfilling prophecies containing real dangers of an emerging united Western bloc by the spring of 1949. Are there any lessons Stalin learned from these developments?

Soviet Foreign Policy and Ideology Reappraised?

There are signs of a new flexibility and experimentation in Soviet foreign policy during and after the termination of the Berlin blockade in the spring of 1949. The peace movement is a case in point. Two congresses of peace which were held in Paris and Prague in April 1949 set the stage for the Communist Parties to begin some courtship display towards Western intellectuals and progressive bourgeois elements. A renewed emphasis was ushered in on problems of peace and disarmament. Neutralist tendencies and forces were encouraged to assert an independent role in world politics. [24]

As an example of these new tendencies, Soviet Foreign Minister Vyshinskii, in his opening address to the General Assembly of 23 September 1949, expressed a strong belief in peaceful coexistence and businesslike relations with all countries, and in this context he evoked the period of the Popular Front in the 1930s. [25] In November the Cominform confirmed the new line when it adopted a resolution officially declaring the struggle for peace 'the pivot of the entire activity of the Communist Parties and democratic organizations'.[26]

It is during this phase of Soviet foreign policy that some misconceptions about the thesis of the fatal inevitability of war were set right. This was not an easy task and the end result left much to be desired. Lenin's thinking and writing on this subject had been absolutely clear. He had considered war as inevitable both in relations among the capitalist states (because of constant redivision of markets and influence) and between 'the Soviet republic and the bourgeois states'.[27] World War II, moreover, could still have been taken as proof for the validity of his ideas: it was both an interimperialist war and a war between imperialism and the Soviet Republic.

It must have been extremely bewildering for novices in the art of dialectical interpretation and reinterpretation, therefore, suddenly to read in the authoritative party journal *Bol'shevik* that the thesis on the fatal inevitability of war was some kind of 'misanthropic preaching disseminated by the imperialists, and their right socialist and Titoist agents'.[28] The journal of the Cominform, too, no longer seemed to adhere to the view that Lenin's thesis had been the result of correct, scientific and farsighted analysis; it exposed the notion of fatal inevitability of war as 'one of the main propaganda theses of the Anglo-American imperialists'.[29]

This important transformation of an important part of Leninist theory in the period of the peace movement, that is, from the spring of 1949 throughout the early 1950s, occurred not without reason. However, the challenge of Leninism was more apparent than real. First, without making the precise differentiation one would have hoped for, the 'inevitability of war' was something that concerned primarily the relations among *capitalist* states, not those between imperialism and socialism. This was a doctrinal shift that was to be made explicit by Stalin at the Nineteenth Party Congress in 1952. Secondly, Lenin (as was to be expected) was still right. He had spoken of a *long-term trend*, whereas the Anglo-American imperialists, right socialists and Titoists were spreading the lie of war as an inevitable event of the immediate future.[30]

This view of what Lenin had really meant also betrays something of the probable reasons for the complex dialectical contortions. Stalin must finally have drawn the right conclusions from the Berlin crisis and the deterioration of East – West relations: effective crisis control and propagation of a theory on the fatal inevitability of war are mutually exclusive; to communicate to an adversary that one considers war to be inevitable is, in essence, inviting him to embark on preemption.[31] There is a second reason for the doctrinal 'clarification'. The 'struggle for peace and disarmament as the central focus of activity of the international communist movement' required steering between two equally undesirable states of mind: defeatism and complacency. If war really was fatalistically inevitable it simply made no sense even to try to do something about it. But if war was already banished from the history of mankind there was no rationale for a peace movement.

Yet despite these doctrinal shifts and portents of new directions in Soviet foreign policy there was little substantive change. The peace movement was still primarily an instrument to bring pressure on Western governments, although in a more subtle form. While there were signs of flexibility and broad alliance tactics towards Western Europe, Eastern Europe was about to be subjected to new waves of purges and patterns of orthodoxy and uniformity. In the military sphere the Soviet Union did what the West should have done but did not do. It added nearly 80,000 men and new equipment to its forces in Germany, thereby bringing its cadred units up to an active strength of no less than 70 percent of wartime manning and tilting the conventional imbalance even further in favor of the Soviet Union.[32]

Finally, the explosion of the first Soviet nuclear device in August 1949, the victory of communism in China in the fall, anticolonialist and nationalist uprisings in Indonesia and Indochina, guerrilla wars in Burma, Malaya and the Philippines with communists in the forefront, and unrest in the French and British territories of North Africa and the Middle East were taken partly as a reflection, partly an anticipation, of a more favorable distribution of the 'correlation of forces in the world arena', apparently justifying a more assertive foreign policy. Only after the Korean War had created even more negative consequences than the Berlin crisis and threatened to bring a rearmed West Germany into the Western alliance, did Stalin and his successors set in motion a long-overdue and more fundamental reorientation of Soviet foreign policy.

Lessons for this Study

The main lessons and conclusions emerging from the study of the Berlin crisis of 1948 can be summarized as follows.[33]

(1) Undoubtedly the beginning of Western allied political and economic cooperation in Germany, the dangers attached to the creation of a viable, potentially powerful and strongly anticommunist and anti-Soviet West German state created conditions which required Soviet *defensive* responses. But at the same time the blockade of Berlin, used successfully as a lever, or won as a prize, would have served in turn to continue the momentum of Soviet *offensive* political moves in Central Europe.

To generalize from this specific point: it would appear that it is always difficult, if not impossible, to say whether risk-taking in any instance is a case of self-defense, unprovoked aggression, semi-aggression, or – to use a recent addition to the American political-military vocabulary – protective reaction. Even if there *is* an unambiguous case of self-defense it may not be perceived as such by the adversary. Moreover the legitimacy of self-defense may be abandoned at some point by the use of disproportionate measures. This interpretation would be in keeping with the model of this thesis. A player who decides to invite disaster for defensive reasons may improve his position so radically that he could win the game. In the real world of 1948 the adversary felt called upon to resort to countermeasures which in turn amplified original dilemmas and created new ones for the side which had initiated the crisis in the first place.

(2) There were serious *deficiencies in Stalin's conceptual approach* to the crisis. This is apparent in the shifts of explanation for imposing the blockade, in contradictory communications, in the failure to spell out acceptable compromise proposals for terminating the blockade and in the apparent

absence of clearly defined objectives. While such ambiguity was conducive to the control of risks, always providing for an easy retreat in the event of vigorous Western military counteraction, it did not serve the achievement of Soviet aims. Ambiguity came to be regarded by the West as proof that the Soviet Union showed no realistic limitation of objectives.

(3) While Soviet policy may have been based on a correct assessment of *risks*, it showed an underestimation of political *costs*. When the Soviet Union terminated the blockade in the spring of 1949 without any gain, conditions did not merely revert to the former status quo. The outcome rather served to demonstrate the validity of propositions advanced in the theoretical part of this study, namely, that crises are often watersheds of history; that, once they occur, they give rise to increased threat perceptions; and that these perceptions may last and affect political behavior for a long time. The Berlin crisis, in conjunction with the Korean War, set in motion powerful forces of United States—European cooperation which, for the first time in the history of Soviet foreign policy, transformed the mere doctrinal ghost of capitalist encirclement into a reality.

(4) Concerning the four possible *determinants of Soviet risk-taking* and crisis behavior, it would be difficult, as well as artificial, to construct a precise hierarchy or rank ordering of factors according to their relevance. All four variables can be isolated for analytical purposes, but in the end they must be considered in conjunction with each other to receive a more accurate picture of reality. Three of the factors examined are so closely interrelated that they make the Berlin crisis appear almost as a logical result of the main tendencies in force at the time. These factors are: a highly militant, leftist or Zhdanovist line in ideological formalized perceptions and doctrinal codifications; a narrow interpretation of Soviet security interests in the Soviet Union itself and in the areas under Soviet control; and a phase of repression and restoration of party controls in Soviet domestic politics.

(5) Concerning Soviet *ideology*, doctrinal codifications warning that war was still inevitable and that there was always a danger of 'capitalist encirclement' and the risk of serious accidents could have advised Soviet restraint and the rejection of risk-taking ventures. However, the opposite conclusion was drawn. Dangers seemed to be met best by a militant stance. Moreover history appeared to be in need of a push to speed up the 'impending crisis of capitalism'. In this sense there is a positive correlation between leftist ideological commitments and high risk-taking propensities in foreign policy.

(6) As for the relevance of *security interests*, the Soviet Union was faced not with a direct and acute problem in 1948 but with emerging dilemmas and potential threats. On the one hand a divided Germany was likely to produce German nationalist tendencies and a rearmed West Germany as a spearhead of American imperialism in Europe; such a country could easily yield to the temptation of setting out to revise the still tenuous results of World War II. On the other hand a neutralized united Germany required continued four-power control and cooperation (which, as history and life itself had shown, was difficult to maintain), and in all likelihood it would have turned out to be an industrially advanced and economically powerful country, anti-Soviet and anti-Russian as well and probably also irredentist (because of substantial losses of territory in the East). As the first development, a separate West

Germany as a spearhead of American imperialism, appeared to take concrete shape in the spring of 1948, some initiative seemed well in place. However, the approach used to check emerging threats was counterproductive and in any case no ready-made solution for solving the potential security problems was available. This may be one of the reasons why Soviet policy during the Berlin crisis showed so little clarity and consistency.

(7) Concerning *domestic* factors of Soviet policy in the Berlin crisis of 1948, there is no evidence of the power struggle or bureaucratic politics significantly shaping Soviet crisis behavior. The crisis shows all the attributes of an ill-conceived venture embarked upon and maintained in its momentum by Stalin himself. But the crude attempts of pressure on the Western powers and on the population in West Berlin are related to domestic politics in the sense that, to Stalin, intimidation of domestic opponents had proved successful (and that such intimidation had proved effective also in Czechoslovakia). The autocratic and arbitrary manner of decision-making in all likelihood also serves to explain why the increasingly counterproductive nature of the blockade was not recognized more quickly. Information, accurate or inaccurate, which contradicted the fundamental assumptions of a policy in progress was likely to be assessed with fear and thus unlikely to reach Stalin. To that extent there is some validity to aspects of the organizational process model. For the most part, however, elements of centralization and unified, rational decision-making appear to have been dominant.

(8) *Military factors* have to be considered both as serious limitations on Soviet risk-taking as well as temptations. The militarily indefensible position of Berlin and the significant withdrawal of American conventional power from Europe in the immediate postwar period may have been instrumental in Soviet calculations assuming a low probability of military challenges to the blockade. However, superior American economic and technological resources and mobilization potential, American naval supremacy and, last but not least, American nuclear monopoly cautioned against the persistence in a competition in risk-taking with even higher risks of war. In this sense there is an inverse correlation between military-strategic inferiority and the acceptance of risks of war in Berlin.

Notes: Part Two, Chapter 10

1   As quoted by Murphy, *Diplomat Among Warriors*, p. 321.
2   Smith, *My Three Years in Moscow*, p. 257.
3   Medvedev, *Let History Judge*, p. 479.
4   N. S. Khrushchev, Report to the Central Committee, 17 October 1961, *Pravda*, 18 October 1961.
5   Inozemtsev (ed.), *Mezhdunarodnye otnosheniia posle vtoroi mirovoi voiny*, Vol. II (1963), pp. 55 and 58, as quoted by Wolfe, *Soviet Power and Europe*, pp. 56–8.
6   ibid., p. 58.
7   Dean G. Acheson, *Present at Creation: My Years in the State Department* (New York: Norton, 1969), as quoted by Gaddis Smith, 'The Berlin blockade', p. 53.
8   Bohlen, *Witness to History*, p. 287.
9   Truman, *Memoirs, Vol. II: Years of Trial and Hope*, p. 171.
10 Wolfe, *Soviet Power and Europe*, p. 20.
11 Millis (ed.), *The Forrestal Diaries*, p. 462.

12   See above, p. 138.
13   As quoted by Gaddis Smith, 'The Berlin blockade', p. 53.
14   Bohlen, *Witness to History*, p. 287 (my italics).
15   ibid.
16   Schilling, 'The politics of national defense: fiscal 1950', p. 211.
17   Rosenberg, 'American atomic strategy', p. 69.
18   Schilling, 'The politics of national defense: fiscal 1950', p. 222. Actual spending, not Presidential requests or (planned) Congressional appropriations at the beginning of the fiscal year.
19   ibid., p. 209.
20   On Thorez's attack on nationalism and its consequences see Shulman, *Stalin's Foreign Policy Reappraised*, pp. 58–64.
21   ibid., p. 20.
22   Khrushchev's Secret Speech, *The Anti-Stalin Campaign*, p. 62.
23   For details of Yugoslav-American cooperation in the wake of the 1948 Yugoslav-Soviet break see John C. Campbell, *Tito's Separate Road: America and Yugoslavia in World Politics* (New York: Harper & Row for the Council on Foreign Relations, 1967), notably pp. 10–29.
24   Concerning the origin, role, and consequences of the peace movement see the detailed discussion by Shulman, *Stalin's Foreign Policy Reappraised*, pp. 80–103.
25   Text in the *New York Times*, 24 September 1949, as quoted in ibid., p. 78.
26   *For a Lasting Peace*, no. 55 (1949).
27   See above, p. 113. The subject of redivision was discussed at length by Lenin in *Imperialism: The Highest Stage of Capitalism*.
28   'Mira ne zhdut – mir zavoevyvaiut' (editorial), *Bol'shevik*, no. 22 (November 1950), p. 3. My attention was drawn to the editorial in *Bol'shevik* by Paul Marantz, 'Soviet foreign policy factionalism under Stalin? A case study of the inevitability of war controversy', *Soviet Union*, vol. 3, pt. 1 (1976), p. 100.
29   *For a Lasting Peace*, no. 79 (1950); see also no. 56 (1949). All examples and many others are provided by Marantz, 'Soviet foreign policy factionalism under Stalin?', pp. 99–100.
30   ibid.
31   See above, pp. 113–14.
32   Karber, 'The Central European arms race', p. 9.
33   This summary will be kept very brief so as to avoid repetition in Part Three, 'Comparisons and Conclusions'.

11

Interpretations, Ambiguities and Questions

Less than a decade after the abandonment of the dramatic attempt to win political advantage a new leadership decided to reignite the crisis. Why did it happen? What is it that led Khrushchev to believe that it was possible now to change the status quo to the Soviet Union's advantage and not merely repeat the previous pattern of events? Was there simply an important flaw in Stalin's coercive diplomacy and his manipulation of risks that could be remedied by using different means or adopting new tactics, or had conditions changed within the past ten years to such a degree that a second attempt would have to be considered in a completely different light? Soviet and Western analyses provide a variety of answers to these questions.

Defensive Measures

Whatever the emphasis on particular issues by Soviet and East German government spokesmen and scholars, the major theme expressed in their interpretations of the origin and dynamics of the Berlin crisis of 1961 is that the authorities in West Berlin and Bonn, with the support of certain factions of the ruling circles in other imperialist countries, had taken a variety of monetary, economic, political and military measures of an openly aggressive intent, or of a more subtle, subversive character, which had done great harm – and threatened to do more harm – to the German Democratic Republic (GDR) and to the socialist system as a whole.

This in fact is the main argument advanced in the declaration of the Warsaw Pact member states on 13 August 1961. Subversive activities directed from West Berlin had 'greatly increased of late'; and, to make matters worse, this had occurred 'right after the Soviet Union, the GDR and other socialist countries [had] advanced proposals for an immediate, peaceful settlement with Germany'.[1] The declaration then summarizes: 'This subversive activity has not only inflicted damage on the GDR but also affects the interests of other countries of the socialist camp'. For this reason,

the Warsaw Pact member states cannot but take necessary measures to guarantee their security and, primarily, the security of the GDR in the interests of the German people themselves ... [Therefore, they] address the People's Chamber and Government of the GDR, and all working people of the GDR, with the proposal to establish an order on the borders of West Berlin which will securely block the way to the subversive activity against the socialist camp countries, so that reliable safeguards and effective control can be established around the whole territory of West Berlin, including its borders with democratic Berlin.[2]

This official explanation by the member countries of the Warsaw Pact can only be considered as lavish in comparison with the very terse treatment contained in a Soviet history of international relations published in 1964. In what is reminiscent of some Soviet analyses of the Berlin crisis of 1948 as a smokescreen created artificially by the West, the book merely states:

In conjunction with measures carried out by the Soviet Union to safeguard world peace, the GDR, acting on recommendations by the member states of the Warsaw Treaty, put into effect defensive measures at the border between the GDR and West Berlin on August 13, 1961.[3]

According to the version of the Institute of World Economy and International Relations, published approximately one year after Khrushchev's fall, it was the 'unleashing of military measures by Western powers and West German reaction' which had 'called for countermeasures by the socialist states in order to strengthen security and the defense of interests of their peoples'.[4] Finally, a history of international relations, published in 1971, states that in the summer of 1961 imperialist forces had created 'an extremely dangerous situation' so that only a 'resolute rebuff could bring the imperialists to reason and safeguard the interests of the socialist states'.[5] What is evident in all three histories of Soviet foreign policy after World War II is the shift away from the theme of subversive activities, which was advanced almost exclusively in 1961, to the argument that it had been *military-political* pressures by imperialist forces which had prompted the socialist countries to take firm action.

However, Soviet and East German scholarship has not entirely abandoned the original explanation. In the most comprehensive study of the Berlin problem, written by Viktor Vysotskii and published in 1971, the general theme of subversive activity is explained and analysed in detail according to different issues. Regarding *monetary* issues, Vysotskii writes that although the value, or purchasing power, of the East German mark, DM(East), was almost equivalent to that of the West German mark, DM(West), the authorities in West Berlin and Bonn conspired in a scheme to keep the exchange value of the DM(East) artificially low. One DM(West) was exchanged at rates varying between DM(East) 3·7 and 8·0. He then continues saying that the East German marks, supplied cheaply to black marketeers, served as the means to create special trading centers in West Berlin which bought up industrial products, antiques, works of art and foodstuffs.[6] 'All this cost the German Democratic Republic dearly', writes Vysotskii.

According to the estimates of the American professor of economics, [Hans] Apel, the harm done to the GDR [in the period] from its foundation until August 13, 1961, by currency machinations and different kinds of speculation alone amounted to no less than 13 billion marks.[7]

In addition to monetary issues, Soviet and East German sources stress the importance of other *economic factors*, notably the manpower drain of the GDR economy. They have given substance to East German propagandistic word creations of the late 1950s and early 1960s, conveying the image of a large-scale scheme to disrupt the economy of the GDR: *Abwerbung, Grenzgängertum, Menschenhandel* and *Republikflucht*.[8] Vysotskii writes that the drain of qualified labor had not only depleted the ranks of important contributors to the national economy of the GDR; it had also slowed down technical progress and the implementation of plans and created difficulties in regular services for the population. He then goes on to say: 'The well-known West German economist, Professor Baade, estimated that the recruitment [*verbovka*] of qualified labor and the luring away of the technical intelligentsia inflicted even greater harm to the GDR than the machinations in exchange rates and different forms of speculation. He estimated it in the magnitude of 22·5 billion marks.'[9]

By listing more and more measures under the heading of 'economic aggression', Soviet and East German authors gradually increase the total sum of economic losses incurred by the GDR. They mention approximately 63,000 workers who lived in East Berlin but worked in West Berlin (*Grenzgänger*). These people, the authors charge, 'did not make any contribution to the development of the GDR' but at the same time 'they made use of all the benefits of social legislation in the GDR' such as free medical services, kindergartens, schools, cheap communal services, old age and disability pensions, and so on.[10]

All this taken together, and additional schemes of economic espionage and economic sabotage, serve as the basis for the claim that total economic losses of the GDR between 1949 and 1961 'added up to the colossal sum of 83·3 billion marks' – a sum that was increased later by the GDR to 120 billion marks.[11] The two East German authors summarize: 'The twelve years of open borders had demanded high losses, too high losses, and had put the GDR into a role of involuntary blood donor.'[12] The conclusion which is drawn from this is obvious: it all had to be stopped at some point.

The origins of the Berlin crisis are also to be found in *ideological factors*, according to Soviet and East German sources. They charge that various concepts were advanced in the West such as 'demonstrating the superiority of the capitalist system', 'underlining the attraction of the West' by 'making West Berlin a showcase of the Free World' lodging it as a 'thorn in the flesh' of the GDR and using it as a 'lever with which to open the door to the East'. Thus the only place at the junction of two worlds and two opposed social systems was not made a test case for peaceful coexistence but a 'center for subversive activity against the socialist countries' – a springboard and bridgehead for interference in Eastern European developments.[13]

Finally, there were important *military factors* allegedly necessitating countermeasures by socialism. Vysotskii establishes a link between ideology and military plans by Western imperialism by saying that West Berlin was also to serve as an important operational point for organizing so-called resistance movements in the GDR, preparing the way for a 'police action in intra-German conflict' as the first stage for a general 'rollback of communism'. By the time of August 1961 these plans had ripened to such an extent that their implementation seemed imminent.[14] Keiderling and Stulz link economic and military issues and arrive at the same conclusion: 'The ruling circles of the Federal Republic [of Germany] considered economic warfare as the preparatory stage for the military liquidation of the GDR.'[15] In sum, it would be a fair characterization of the main arguments of Soviet and East German interpretations that the measures of 13 August 1961 were not only of a defensive nature, but also *preventive*, taken to maintain peace in Central Europe.

Berlin: a Lever or a Prize?

Regarding Soviet and East German interpretations, it would be highly inappropriate to consider only those statements made in the summer of 1961 and thereafter. The Berlin crisis did not begin in 1961 nor did it appear to end in that year. In order to appreciate the full scope of the crisis, it should be remembered that the East German party leader, Walter Ulbricht, asserted at the end of October 1958 that '*All of Berlin* lies on the territory of the GDR'; that 'The Western powers have *destroyed the legal basis for their presence in Berlin*'; and that '*they no longer have any legal, moral, or political justification for their continued occupation of West Berlin*'.[15] Clearly the thrust of the demands here is directed against the Western presence and Western access rights.

Similar themes were taken up two weeks later by Khrushchev, on 10 November 1958, at a friendship meeting at the Polish embassy in Moscow, honoring a state visit by Wladislaw Gomulka. Khrushchev said that the Western powers had

> violated the Potsdam Agreement repeatedly and with impunity, while we have remained loyal to it as if nothing had changed. *We have every reason to set ourselves free from obligations under the Potsdam Agreement, obligations which have outlived themselves* and which the Western powers are clinging to, and to pursue with regard to Berlin a policy that would spring from the interests of the Warsaw Treaty.[17]

Khrushchev also argued that 'if the Western powers are interested in any questions regarding Berlin' they should 'build their relations with the German Democratic Republic'.[18] Implied here is the threat of a unilateral Soviet renunciation of the Potsdam Agreement and the establishment of a system that would take into account vaguely defined interests of the socialist countries and include the GDR as a sovereign, internationally recognized state.

All this is spelled out in more detail in the Berlin ultimatum of 28 November 1958 – that is, in the identical notes sent by the Soviet government to the three Western powers and a similar note addressed to the Federal Republic of Germany.[19] The central point advanced in the note to the three Western powers is the proposal:

to solve the West Berlin question at the present time by the conversion of West Berlin into an independent political unit [*samostoiatel'naia politicheskaia edinitsa*] – a free city, without any state, including both existing German states, interfering in its life. Specifically, it might be possible to agree that the territory of the free city be demilitarized and that no armed forces be contained therein. The free city, West Berlin, could have its own economic, administrative, and other affairs.[20]

As such this proposal could be regarded as quite limited in scope. However, the political importance and the extent of subject matter is broadened considerably by declarations of the Soviet government that it regarded all the wartime agreements relating to zones of occupation, administration and control machinery in Germany and Berlin as null and void; that it proposed for six months only 'not to make any changes in the present procedure for military traffic' of the three powers between West Germany and West Berlin; and that if the grace period would not be utilized to reach an acceptable agreement, 'the Soviet Union will then carry out the planned measures through an agreement with the GDR'.[21]

In a very strict sense West Berlin was the primary topic of the note. But at the same time, the 'free city' proposal, the renunciation of wartime agreements and the announced Soviet intention to conclude a separate agreement with the GDR in order to carry out ill-defined measures if the West did not comply – all this immediately touched upon a whole range of issues such as the extent of four-power control, rights and responsibilities in Germany and Berlin; relations between West Berlin and Bonn; access to West Berlin for West German and Western allied personnel and goods; recognition of the GDR, *de facto* or *de iure*; the role of East Germany in European politics; the nature of relations between East and West Germany; and, finally, the whole question of European security and superpower relations. While it was theoretically possible to separate West Berlin from larger issues, in practice it was impossible.

This interrelationship of issues can be shown by comparing the Berlin ultimatum of November 1958 with the Soviet draft peace treaty of 10 January 1959.[22] The draft, as well as the note of November 1958, demanded a settlement of the Berlin question. However, as a Western analyst of the Berlin crisis points out correctly, 'The November note proposed narrow negotiations on Berlin only; the January note made a bid for broad negotiations on the narrow basis of a prior Berlin solution'.[23] While linkages with broader objectives of Soviet foreign policy were to be played down by Soviet and East German sources in 1961 and thereafter, Soviet Foreign Minister Gromyko did emphasize them during the Geneva Foreign Ministers' Conference in July 1959 when he stated:

We have repeatedly tried to explain to our colleagues in the negotiations that there is a *logical link* between the question of West Berlin and the question of an all-German committee [composed of representatives from the GDR and the FRG] and its work [to prepare a German peace treaty], and that *this link is by no means artificial*.[24]

Let us take other Soviet statements in the period before the critical events of 1961. On 10 June 1959 Gromyko said at the Geneva conference that the

Soviet government could agree 'to the *provisional* maintenance of certain occupation rights of the Western Powers in West Berlin' under the condition that 'such a situation would exist only for a *strictly limited period*, namely one year'.[25] That is to say, a Berlin settlement would lead to the consideration of much broader issues, including the conclusion of a peace treaty. The communiqué of the Warsaw Pact countries of 4 February 1960 reverses the sequence:

> If the efforts toward the conclusion of a peace treaty with both German states do not meet with support and if the solution of this question comes up against attempts at procrastination, the states represented at the present conference will have no alternative but to conclude a peace treaty with the German Democratic Republic . . . and *to solve on this basis the question of West Berlin as well*.[26]

It is not the place here to treat Soviet policy on Berlin and the German problem comprehensively, But this much is evident by a comparison of various Soviet and East German sources in the period from the fall of 1958 to the spring and summer of 1961. Such comparison establishes very well the interrelationship between various issues and the ambiguity of Soviet demands and intentions. This justifies a closer look at Western interpretations.

Soviet Intentions and Expectations: Western Analyses

Adam Ulam is one of the Western analysts of Soviet foreign policy asking the question 'What, in fact, *were* the Russian motives?' His answer is unambiguous: 'To us *now*, it is clear that the main Soviet objective was to secure an agreement that would make it impossible for West Germany to obtain nuclear weapons.'[27] But then, later on in the same book, we find the explanation that Khrushchev had 'originally' raised the whole problem of Western rights in Berlin 'in order to pry out of the United States and her allies the *recognition of East Germany*'.[28] Continuing his analysis of the Berlin crisis Ulam states in the same context that the problem of Western rights 'became increasingly the object of dispute in and of itself'.[29] But, finally, a completely different version is given later on when he writes, equally unequivocally, that 'the only reasonable explanation' for the proclaimed 'readiness to risk nuclear war over Berlin' was Khrushchev's feeling that 'a militant posture toward the West and a success in Germany would enable him to resume *some degree of control over China's foreign policy* and to reduce the Chinese incentive to acquire nuclear weapons'.[30] If all this does not show contradictions it does at least suggest that more than one reasonable explanation may be possible.

A similar test of Western scholarship on Soviet foreign policy can be made with respect to the very voluminous book by Slusser on the Berlin crisis of 1961.[31] Despite the emphasis which Slusser puts on the interpretation that Soviet actions in the Berlin crisis were often the product of hard-line policies forced upon Khrushchev against his will, he also writes that

For Khrushchev the West Berlin question, together with the demand for a German peace treaty, was a *lever* which could be used to force the West to acknowledge a shift in the international *balance [of power] in favor of the Soviet Union*.[32]

However, with reference to Khrushchev's radio and television address of 7 August 1961, Slusser infers – incorrectly in my view – that Khrushchev had 'publicly acknowledged that the *basic issue* in the Berlin crisis was the question of *national prestige*'.[33] This theme recurs later on when Slusser states that Khrushchev had 'identified *national prestige as the underlying factor in Soviet strategy*'.[34]

As noted, one of Ulam's interpretations of Soviet objectives in the Berlin crisis was that the Soviet Union wanted to secure an agreement that would make it impossible for Germany to acquire nuclear weapons. The then ambassador of the Federal Republic of Germany in the USSR, Hans Kroll, shares this view,[35] and it recurs in the analysis by Schick. In Schick's words, 'Berlin crises are Moscow's way of opposing Bonn's policies: in 1958 it feared nuclear weapons acquisition; in 1948 it opposed the resurgence of German economic power.'[36] He then elaborates on this interpretation of Soviet defensive motives as follows.

> The Berlin crisis began and ended with a missile crisis. In 1958, Khrushchev objected to the Eisenhower Administration's decision to deploy American IRBM's [intermediate-range ballistic missiles] to Western Europe in response to Khrushchev's own 'missile gap' charges. He feared that the NATO agreement of December 1957 – reflecting Eisenhower's decision – would allow Bonn to gain access to nuclear weapons. Thus he stimulated the Berlin crisis to persuade the United States to reverse its plan and prepared a draft peace treaty to win recognition for a nuclear-free zone in Central Europe embracing West Germany.[37]

However, Schick's own analysis – concerned mainly with Western policies during the Berlin crisis between 1958 and 1962 – does not adduce much (if any) evidence for the proposition that the origins of the Berlin crisis are to be found in nuclear weapons issues. Indeed it is very difficult to believe that the Berlin crisis would *not* have occurred if West Germany had acceded to a non-proliferation treaty in 1958. If the assumed danger of German nuclear armament really was instrumental in setting the stage for the Berlin crisis, a good explanation is needed as to why this issue did not play an at all prominent part in the summit talks between President Eisenhower and Khrushchev at Camp David in September 1959. According to Eisenhower, 'Numerous problems were brought up somewhat haphazardly, but again and again we seemed to come back to Berlin and the latest Soviet ultimatum'.[38] The 'gist of a separate peace treaty', in Eisenhower's interpretation of the conversations at Camp David, was that 'the existence of West Berlin as an unwelcome irritant in the body of "peace-loving" East Germany was growing intolerable' – that is, not that Khrushchev was particularly concerned about Bonn's access to nuclear weapons at the time.[39] More than one and a half years later, at the Kennedy–Khrushchev summit in Vienna, it was again the theme of unwelcome irritant that featured prominently in the controversies, not that of nuclear weapons.

Without prejudicing here the results of later arguments, it would seem that the explanation of Soviet motives in the Berlin crisis as wanting to prevent German access to nuclear weapons is far too limited in scope. It would be more valid to formulate the problem in more general terms, as presented by Malcolm Mackintosh, who sees the Berlin crisis as another 'stage of Soviet counteroffensive in reply to NATO's decision to increase its military, political, and economic effectiveness on the Continent of Europe'.[40] Also Schick himself puts the significance of the nuclear weapons issue into perspective when he says that at some point, as the crisis evolved, the test of wills 'between Washington and Moscow over the immediate issue of Berlin assumed a life of its own'.[41]

Contextual Factors of Behavior and Decision-Making

Western analysts of the Berlin crisis have tended to de-emphasize ideology as a factor shaping Soviet behavior. It is as if they conformed to the general characterization advanced by William Zimmerman that they – Western analysts of Soviet affairs – had formed

> a well-founded judgment that what had seemed to make Soviet foreign policy unique, namely the role of ideology in the explanation of it, in fact explained very little of Soviet behavior in the post-war period. Indeed, with the exception of East Europe, where the Soviet Union has had the ability to enforce the norms of an 'international relations of a new type', it has very seldom followed the course which the postulated role of ideology would seem to imply.[42]

Although Zimmerman does not address himself specifically to the Berlin crisis, his and other writers' categories of analysis concerning the waning of ideology in Soviet foreign policy do raise important questions in the present context. Given the fact that the GDR is part of the 'exception' – East Europe – and that relations of the USSR with the GDR, according to Soviet definitions, follow norms of 'international relations of a new type', is it not essential to make allowances for the possibility that Soviet policies towards West Berlin and West Germany (and the Western allies as guarantee powers) are influenced to a high degree by requirements of intra-bloc cohesion? If Soviet commitments for maintaining the then existing political regime and socio-economic system in the GDR are inextricably linked with ideology, it would be unwise to evade an analysis of these issues.

This would also entail consideration of the precise meaning of the Soviet claim that 'subversive activities' played a role in inducing, or perhaps even forcing, the member states of the Warsaw Pact to take action and accept risks of superpower confrontation. It would necessitate a sharpening of awareness to the problem of interrelationships between Soviet state and security interests and the general ideological cohesion and unity of the Soviet bloc and their relevance for the Berlin crisis.

Apart from problems of ideology, and linkages between ideology and

Soviet security interests, military factors of Soviet behavior will have to be examined closely, too. Their relevance has been stressed primarily by current and former members of the Rand Corporation, to such an extent in fact that it is perhaps not too much of an exaggeration to speak of a Rand theory of the Berlin crisis. In the analysis by Thomas Wolfe, Khrushchev made Berlin 'the specific target of his efforts to convert the successes of Soviet technology into meaningful political gains'; the Berlin crisis of 1958–61 stood out as the 'prime example of the miscarriage of Khrushchev's belief that the forbidding image of Soviet strategic power, together with local pressures, would bring the West to concede positions previously impervious to Soviet diplomatic assault'.[43] For Wolfe, as for many other military analysts, Soviet and Western military measures and countermeasures between the spring and fall of 1961 appear as a purposive action–reaction pattern, as part and parcel of crisis bargaining.

The same theme recurs in the study by Hans Speier, another member of the Rand Corporation, who analyzed Soviet policy toward Berlin in the period from the November 1958 ultimatum up to and including the Vienna Summit of June 1961. Speier relates Soviet conduct in the Suez crisis of 1956, the Turkish-Syrian crisis of 1957, pressures against European member states of NATO and the crises of 1958 in the Middle and Far East to 'Soviet political blackmail' in Berlin.

> In all these situations, the Soviet Union tried to make strategic and political gains by means of menacing reminders of its nuclear power and delivery capabilities, by freely uttered predictions that general war might result from the behavior of the Western powers, and by carefully veiled conditional threats of military action in defense of Communist interests.[44]

Similar conclusions about the interrelationship of Soviet strategic power and risk-taking in Berlin (and later also in Cuba) have been drawn by Horelick and Rush.

> No doubt the Soviet leaders were bound to exaggerate their ICBM capabilities even without a Berlin campaign. Indeed, such exaggeration had been going on for a year when the Berlin campaign began. After early 1959, however, the effort to deceive the West became more contrived and systematic, and *it is not unlikely that this intensification resulted from initiation of the Berlin crisis some weeks earlier.*[45]

While almost all of the explanations mentioned so far, both those of Soviet and Western origin, conform to rational actor models, nonrational explanations have increasingly supplemented – and sometimes even supplanted – the classic approach. In the most recent book on Soviet policy in the Berlin crisis of 1961 the picture is drawn of a

> process of foreign policy formation [in the Soviet Union] in which an opposition faction could play Russian roulette with the peace of the world by taking actions which *deliberately risked nuclear war*, and in which a struggle for internal political power was successfully masked from the outside world.[46]

The author, Robert Slusser, asserts that an opposition faction in the Kremlin not only *could*, but actually *did*, play Russian roulette with international peace.

> At the outset of the period [beginning in the first week of September 1961], Frol Kozlov and his supporters appeared to be firmly in control of the levers of power in the Kremlin; their actions and decisions during the final week of August had *sharply altered the course of Soviet foreign policy* and by a series of risky and provocative moves had brought the Soviet Union dangerously close to a direct military confrontation with the West.[47]

The conceptual framework underlying Slusser's analysis is made explicit at one point. The author writes:

> Any attempt to impose unity on the expression of Soviet policy during this period can be successful only at the cost of ignoring the tangled welter of policy statements and selecting only those which support a simplistic, rationalized interpretation.[48]

However, it is not at all evident whether the tangled welter of policy statements is due to *conflicting outputs* from struggling factions in the Presidium, or whether these vacillations are not deliberate and inevitable manifestations of a *unified approach* by Khrushchev and the Presidium, offering alternatively the carrot and the stick, threatening on the one hand strong counteraction in the event of Western opposition to Soviet measures in Berlin, and conveying at the same time the image of a leadership disposed to reasonable solutions and compromise.

A concrete example for conflicting claims to the correct interpretation of facts concerns the resumption of the testing of nuclear weapons by the Soviet Union on 1 September 1961. Carl Linden, who approaches decision-making processes from conceptual perspectives similar to those of Slusser, starts from the assumption that Khrushchev 'was under powerful pressure to show that he was a tough and effective Communist leader who could win victories in power-political struggles with the leading power of the "capitalist" world',[49] and then concludes that 'The timing of the nuclear test resumption which scuttled the Geneva test-ban negotiations was another sign of pressure on Khrushchev from within the leadership'.[50] Slusser puts the case even more strongly when he characterizes the resumption of nuclear testing as a 'trump card' played by Khrushchev's opponents to escalate the Berlin crisis.[51] All this is a clear challenge to widely held views in the West that the resumption of nuclear testing (as well as a series of other military measures) had to be seen as a purposive act of Soviet crisis bargaining.

Approaching the origins and dynamics of the Berlin crisis from these angles of analysis, it is not surprising to find another eminent analyst, Michel Tatu, speculating about the problem 'whether it was the Berlin crisis that brought about an increase in military expenditure, as the official version has it, or conversely whether the need of the military to strengthen the armed forces prompted the crisis'.[52] While Tatu does not give a definite answer to this question, it would appear that his preferences lie with the latter view.

Domestic alliances (groupings) in communist systems frequently have looked for support in the international Communist Party system forming what political science terminology has called 'transnational' political alliances. These alliance relationships and their influence on domestic decision-making can most appropriately be analyzed within the scope of the governmental politics model. Ulam, as cited above, did include in one of his interpretations of the Berlin crisis the assumed Soviet desire to resume some degree of control over China and to reduce the Chinese incentive to acquire nuclear weapons without, however, dwelling on more general, theoretical implications of this analysis. Isaac Deutscher is more explicit in that respect. He writes,

> The need to compete with Mao [Tse-tung] for leadership in the communist camp has been an important factor in Khrushchev's decision to take action over Berlin. He has to refute Mao's charges. He has to show himself tough and determined. He has to demonstrate that he is not 'appeasing Western imperialism'. He has to calculate his diplomatic moves with an eye to their effect on the intense Russo-Chinese contest for the allegiance of so many Communist parties in Asia, Africa, Europe and Latin America.
> *This makes it difficult for him to engage in genuine bargaining with the West*, and imposes on him that diplomatic rigidity which so surprised President Kennedy in Vienna [in June 1961].[53]

This approach, evidently, is a corollary of the arguments about the relevance of domestic power struggles for Soviet decision-making in the Berlin crisis. It postulates that actions in foreign policy are not, or not always, taken on the merits of the issue in hand, but are an outcome of conflict relations. For this reason the possibility needs to be analyzed as to whether there was substantial support for hard-line policies advocated by the Chinese and by the East German leadership and whether – to put it in Kremlinological categories – there is any evidence for influence exerted on the pursuit of Soviet foreign policy by a Chinese faction or an Ulbricht faction.

The Dynamics of Crisis

Another possible approach to the explanation of Soviet policy in the Berlin crisis postulates the existence of an action–reaction process. It sees Soviet behavior determined primarily by external factors, not by static determinants; and it perceives Soviet objectives as flexible, depending on the degree of resistance and counteraction by the adversary. An extreme example is Elizabeth Barker's assumption that

> Khrushchev started the Berlin crisis without any real preparation, without any clear idea about the extent of his demands, the lengths to which he was prepared to go in order to achieve them, or even the methods and arguments he intended to employ.[54]

This interpretation may have been stated too strongly. But it is perhaps less difficult to agree with the analysis by Richard Lowenthal who writes that

Khrushchev and his associates differed from their Western adversaries in their confident, militant pursuit of an ideologically defined, worldwide and long-term *aim* – an aim to which the Bolshevik leaders had clung for more than forty years and three revolutionary generations. However, they did not and indeed cannot follow a long-term *plan*:

> Just like their opponents, they have to react to unforseen situations all the time. The difference – and it is a big difference – is merely that as they become stronger, the vision of their world-wide aims enables them to react less and less to dangers, and more and more to opportunities.[55]

Similar views of the dynamics of crisis are implied in the already mentioned interpretation by Schick, namely, that the Berlin crisis had undergone significant changes from 1958 to 1961: whereas problems of nuclear proliferation dominated Soviet thinking initially, the issue of Berlin came to assume a life of its own.[56] They recur in a different form in the analysis by Windsor, who writes that after the Paris Summit of May 1960 and Khrushchev's following visit to East Berlin,

> there were two distinct crises, not inherently related, but both acting on each other, each rendering the other uncontrollable, until they became so dangerous that a wall was built across Berlin to separate the two. The first was the general upheaval in the political and strategic relationships between the two blocs; the second was the imminent collapse of the East German state.[57]

To sum up, interpretations of Soviet behavior in the Berlin crisis range from the simplistic to the complex; from assumptions of a clear design to the absence of even any clear idea whatsoever; from views of basically defensive to offensive motives; from analyses of rational to nonrational behavior. Not all of these interpretations are mutually exclusive (although some of them certainly are). Before considering the relative validity of various arguments in a more systematic fashion (and following the standard pattern), some of the basic facts relating to the Berlin crisis will be presented first.

Notes: Part Two, Chapter 11

1   *Pravda*, 14 August 1961.
2   ibid.
3   Trukhanovskii (ed.), *Istoriia mezhdunarodnykh otnoshenii*, p. 732.
4   N. N. Inozemtsev (ed.) *Mezhdunarodnye otnosheniia posle vtoroi mirovoi voiny, Vol. III, 1956–1964 gg.* (Moscow: Izdatel'stvo politicheskoi literatury for the Institute of World Economy and International Relations, Academy of Sciences of the USSR, 1965), p. 210.
5   B. N. Ponomarev, A. A. Gromyko and V. M. Khvostov, *Istoriia vneshnei politiki SSSR, 1917–1970 gg., Vol. II, 1945–1970 gg.* (Moscow: Izdatel'stvo 'Nauka', 1971), p. 332.
6   Vysotskii, *Zapadnyi Berlin*, p. 197.
7   ibid.; Vysotskii's figures as quoted in *Neues Deutschland*, 5 March 1964. For a discussion of Apel's estimates see below, pp. 232–4. See also the repetition of this argument by G. M. Apokov, *Zapadnyi Berlin: problemy i resheniia* (Moscow: Izdatel'stvo 'Mezhdunarodnye otnosheniia', 1974), p. 142.
8   These terms are used extensively in official GDR documents as well as in East German scholarship, for instance, by Keiderling and Stulz, *Geschichte Berlins, 1945–1968*,

pp. 468–71. In detail: (1) *Abwerbung* conveys an active effort at recruitment, of luring away people who are settled in their socioeconomic or political environment. The term is thus more negative than *Anwerbung* (recruitment or hiring) in as much as it implies a change of loyalty and allegiance that is stimulated externally. (2) *Grenzgängertum*, literally translated, would simply mean 'border crossing'; however, the suffix *-tum* conveys the idea of a whole system, or elaborate network, of border crossings. It refers specifically to GDR citizens who crossed the borders to West Berlin before 13 August 1961 in order to work there. (3) *Menschenhandel*, 'man trade' or trade in human beings, is a broader category than 'slave trade'. It preserves the connotation of a gross violation of accepted norms of international law. Underlying this term is the communist claim that a high premium was paid to anyone who had successfully induced a citizen of the GDR to leave the state and work in the West. (4) *Republikflucht*, or 'flight from the republic', is punishable under GDR criminal law. A *Republikflüchtiger* is a person who leaves the republic (German Democratic Republic) illegally. In the linguistic battles between East and West Germany, this addition to the stock of German vocabulary has been rejected in West Germany: Germans leaving the GDR are by West German definition mere *Flüchtlinge*, 'refugees'.

9   Vysotskii, *Zapadnyi Berlin*, p. 199.
10 ibid., p. 199; see also Keiderling and Stulz, *Geschichte Berlins, 1945–1968*, pp. 468–71.
11 Vysotskii, based on *Neues Deutschland*, 13 August 1964, and other 'official data of the GDR', gives a range of between 83·3 and 100 billion marks and compares this figure with the gross national product of the GDR for 1961 of 141 billion marks (Vysotskii, *Zapadnyi Berlin*, p. 201). The figure of 120 billion marks was advanced at the Ninth Plenum of the Central Committee of the SED in April 1965, according to *Neues Deutschland*, 27 and 28 April 1965.
12 Keiderling and Stulz, *Geschichte Berlins, 1945–1968*, p. 493.
13 Vysotskii, *Zapadnyi Berlin*, p. 193 and pp. 209–10.
14 ibid., p. 218.
15 Keiderling and Stulz, *Geschichte Berlins, 1945–1968*, p. 461.
16 *Neues Deutschland*, 28 October 1958 (my italics).
17 *Pravda*, 11 November 1958 (my italics).
18 ibid.
19 The full text of the notes and Khrushchev's comments on them are published in *Pravda*, 28 November 1958.
20 ibid.
21 ibid.
22 The latter as published in *Pravda*, 11 January 1959.
23 Jack M. Schick, *The Berlin Crisis: 1958–1962* (Philadelphia, Pa: University of Philadelphia Press, 1971), p. 21.
24 US Department of State, *Foreign Ministers Meeting: May–August 1959, Geneva*, Publication 6882 (Washington, DC: US Government Printing Office, 1959), pp. 404–8, as quoted by Schick, *The Berlin Crisis*, p. 92 (my italics).
25 *Foreign Ministers Meeting, May–August 1959*, p. 260 (my italics).
26 *Pravda*, 5 February 1960 (my italics).
27 Ulam, *Expansion and Coexistence*, p. 620 (emphasis in the original).
28 ibid., p. 639 (my italics); similarly, Philip Windsor, in his analysis of the Berlin crisis of 1961, writes that the ultimate Soviet objective was that of 'persuading the West to recognize the division of Germany' (Philip Windsor, *City on Leave: A History of Berlin, 1945–1962* (London: Chatto & Windus, 1963), p. 252.
29 Ulam, *Expansion and Coexistence*, p. 639.
30 ibid., p. 655 (my italics).
31 Robert M. Slusser, *The Berlin Crisis of 1961: Soviet-American Relations and the Struggle for Power in the Kremlin, June–November 1961* (Baltimore, Md, and London: Johns Hopkins University Press, 1973).
32 Slusser, *The Berlin Crisis of 1961*, p. 9 (my italics).
33 ibid., p. 112 (my italics).
34 ibid., p. 114 (my italics); it should be pointed out that Slusser's main argument is that there was no consistent 'Soviet strategy' but an outcome of processes connected with the 'struggle for power in the Kremlin'.
35 Hans Kroll, *Lebenserinnerungen eines Botschafters* (Cologne: Kiepenheuer & Witsch, 1967), p. 388.

36   Schick, *The Berlin Crisis*, p. xvi.
37   ibid., p. 233.
38   Dwight D. Eisenhower, *The White House Years: Waging Peace, 1956–1960* (Garden City, NY: Doubleday, 1965), p. 444.
39   ibid., p. 446.
40   Malcolm Mackintosh, *Strategy and Tactics of Soviet Foreign Policy* (New York and London: Oxford University Press, 1962), p. 218. Mackintosh's reference to the 'Berlin crisis' applies to Soviet policy towards Berlin and Germany only in the period from the November ultimatum of 1958 to the abortive summit of May 1960.
41   Schick, *The Berlin Crisis*, p. 233.
42   William Zimmerman, 'Soviet foreign policy in the 1970s', *Survey*, vol. 19, no. 2 (Spring 1973), pp. 193–4; see also pp. 56–7, above.
43   Wolfe, *Soviet Power and Europe*, p. 89.
44   Hans Speier, *Divided Berlin: The Anatomy of Soviet Political Blackmail* (London: Thames & Hudson, 1961), pp. 28–9.
45   Arnold L. Horelick and Myron Rush, *Strategic Power and Soviet Foreign Policy* (Chicago: University of Chicago Press, 1966), p. 119, (my italics).
46   Slusser, *The Berlin Crisis of 1961*, p. xi (my italics).
47   ibid., p. 179 (my italics).
48   ibid., p. 231. Slusser's analysis at this point refers primarily to the period of mid-September to October 1961, but it is indicative of his general conceptual approach to Soviet policy in the Berlin crisis.
49   Carl A. Linden, *Khrushchev and the Soviet Leadership*, (Baltimore, Md: Johns Hopkins University Press, 1966), p. 114.
50   ibid., p. 115.
51   Slusser, *The Berlin Crisis*, p. 148 and pp. 157–70.
52   Michel Tatu, *Power in the Kremlin: From Krushchev to Kosygin* (New York: Viking Press/ Compass Books, 1971), p. 171.
53   Isaac Deutscher, *Russia, China, and the West, 1953–1966* (London: Oxford University Press/Penguin, 1970), p. 233 (my italics).
54   Elizabeth Barker, 'The Berlin crisis: 1958–1962', *International Affairs* (London), vol. 34, no. 1 (January 1963), p. 61. The only 'evidence' offered for this view is the fact that Khrushchev, in his speech of 10 November 1958, made the mistake of deriving Western rights in Berlin from the Potsdam Agreement, instead of from relevant four-power agreements of September 1944 and May 1945.
55   Richard Lowenthal, 'The impossible defensive', *Encounter*, vol. 17, no. 98 (November 1961), p. 21.
56   See pp. 189–90.
57   Windsor, *City on Leave*, p. 221.

12
Evolution of the Crisis: Events, Perceptions, Risks and Stages of Development

No doubt one of the reasons why there is such a wide range of differing interpretations of Soviet policy in the Berlin crisis is concerned with the selection of time intervals of analysis. It does make a difference for the validity of various arguments whether November 1958, or February or June 1961, is taken as a starting point. And it matters whether the termination of the crisis is held to be in late August 1961, October 1961 (at the time of the Twenty-Second Party Congress) or as late as the Cuban missile crisis in 1962. However, Soviet and Western writers agree that the period of greatest risk to peace was between June and October 1961. This is the period on which this study is focused. At the same time the background of facts and events must include key developments from November 1958 onward. However, the smoldering of the Berlin fuse and the important problem of interrelationships between Berlin and the Cuban missile crisis can only be touched upon here.

The protracted Soviet attempt to change the status quo in Berlin can perhaps best be summarized in six phases: (1) from November 1958 to March 1959; (2) May 1959 to August 1959; (3) September 1959 to May 1960; (4) May 1960 to February 1961; (5) February 1961 to June 1961; and (6) June 1961 to October 1961.[1] The details are as follows.

The first phase, from November 1958 to March 1959 – often referred to as the 'deadline crisis' – is characterized by the USSR in its note of 27 November 1958, setting a time limit of six months for solving the West Berlin question,[2] and by Western attempts to defuse the ultimatum. The phase ends with the withdrawal of the deadline on 2 March 1959 by the Soviet Union (after British Prime Minister Harold Macmillan's visit to Moscow) and Soviet-Western agreement to hold negotiations on Berlin and Germany.

The second phase is that of negotiations at the Geneva Foreign Ministers' Conference (11 May to 20 June and 13 July to 5 August 1959) with representatives of the two German states participating in a consultative role at two adjoining tables. Various compromise proposals were considered, including reductions of the Western allied military presence in West Berlin, curtailment of 'subversive activities', the internationalization of Berlin and, perhaps most important, the possibility of recognizing East German authorities as agents of the USSR empowered to control access routes to Berlin, with the understanding, however, that the right of free access be safeguarded. Although the Western negotiators thought that they had gone a long way towards meeting Soviet demands, the conference ended in failure to reach agreement. Shortly before it was recessed, President Eisenhower announced plans for a bilateral Soviet-American summit meeting.

The third phase is that of the elusive spirit of Camp David, lasting from the opening of talks between Eisenhower and Khrushchev at the President's retreat in Maryland on 25 September 1959 to the dramatic collapse of the projected four-power summit conference in Paris in May 1960. In this period there were no negotiations of substance, only commmitments on both sides to resume negotiations. Concerning East–West negotiations on Berlin it was agreed that 'no time limit should be fixed for them but that they should not be protracted indefinitely'.[3] It is also during this phase that Soviet-American bilateralism increasingly became an issue of alliance politics – China and the GDR expressing reservations about the Soviet Union's theme of détente, and France and West Germany warning against the pitfalls of summitry and concessions to the Soviet Union. As the West seemed to retreat from many of the compromise proposals offered at Geneva; as the French government, on 21 October, formally requested a delay in convening the four-power summit conference because of the absence of an effective reduction of tensions; and as all sides merely reiterated their basic, incompatible positions, the chances for a successful settlement of controversial issues waned considerably.

On 4 February 1960 the member countries of the Warsaw Pact still noted 'with satisfaction' that 'certain changes towards the improvement of the international situation' had taken place since the previous meeting of the Political Consultative Committee of the Warsaw Pact in May 1958. The communiqué only hinted vaguely at troubles with the negotiation tack when it charged that the Federal Republic

> interferes with the successful negotiations among the Powers and the solution of controversial international problems. An attempt is even made to undo [positive] results such as, for instance, the approximation of [different] points of view by the participants in the Foreign Ministers' Conference in Geneva in 1959.[4]

The still rather optimistic interpretations of the state of affairs as regards East–West relations, Germany and Berlin that prevailed among the Warsaw Pact countries stood in some contrast to the changes of mood in the West. Reflecting a more widespread disenchantment with the spirit of Camp David, Douglas Dillon, United States Under Secretary of State, stated in a speech in New York on 20 April that the Soviet view of Berlin was 'far removed from the facts'; that the GDR was but 'one of the outstanding myths in a vast Communist web of prodigious mythology'; and that while the situation in Berlin was indeed, as Khrushchev had frequently asserted, 'abnormal', it was nevertheless a 'monstrous' abnormality for which, in essence, the kind of political and social regime existing in the GDR was to blame. Dillon stressed that the United States was 'determined to maintain [the Western] presence in Berlin and to preserve its ties with the Federal Republic'.[5]

Dillon's speech evoked acrimonious responses in the Soviet Union. Mikoyan, for example, commented that although he knew Dillon to be a 'sensible man', in his speech he had uttered 'incredible things', including the thesis that 'the principle of coexistence should be thrown overboard' and that it was necessary to 'rearrange world order in his own way';[6] and Khrushchev inferred from Dillon's speech that the United States government was apparently unwilling to come to any settlement unless its views on Berlin were accepted.[7] However, notwithstanding these reactions in the Soviet Union, Eisenhower explicitly supported Dillon's statement at a press conference on 27 April.[8]

Tensions increased further when, on 1 May, an American reconnaissance plane of the U-2 type was shot down after it had penetrated approximately 1,000 miles into Soviet airspace. On 5 May, addressing the Supreme Soviet, Khrushchev turned the embarrassing espionage incident into a major political issue that was to disrupt the projected four-power summit conference in Paris. Khrushchev wondered whether the flights had been taken 'in order to exert pressure' on the Soviet Union, to 'frighten us with their military superiority', and to undermine détente. If so, this would have had 'no effect' on the Soviet government. But the impression was being formed that the incident was a 'foretaste of the summit meeting'.[9] Following denials and half-admissions on the part of the American administration, Eisenhower finally accepted responsibility for the reconnaissance flights. This, in turn, prompted Khrushchev, on 11 May, to rule out a return visit by the American President to the Soviet Union by stating that 'The Russian people would say that I was mad to welcome a man who sends spy planes over here like that'.[10]

The attempt to solve those issues, which Khrushchev had raised in 1958, by meaningful negotiations at the summit meeting in Paris failed on 16 May 1960 when Khrushchev demanded prior fulfilment of several conditions which President Eisenhower was unwilling to meet. However, the collapse of the summit conference did not lead (as many in the West had feared at the time) to the implementation of Khrushchev's earlier threats to sign a separate peace treaty with East Germany. Returning to Moscow via East Berlin, Khrushchev merely stated on 20 May:

> We are realists and we will never pursue a gambling policy. Under present conditions, it is worthwhile to wait a little longer and try to find a solution for the long-since ripe question of signing a peace treaty with the two German states. This will not escape our hands. We had better wait, and the matter will get more mature.[11]

The fourth phase (May 1960 to February 1961) is characterized by unveiled personal attacks on President Eisenhower in the Soviet press organs, calling him incompetent and deceitful and attributing to him the responsibility for the collapse of the summit conference; by the refusal on the part of the Soviet leadership – as evident in these personal attacks – to negotiate with the outgoing American administration; and by an increase in the scope of Soviet and East German attempts to change the status quo in Berlin by various measures of a gradualist nature, often referred to as 'salami tactics' by Western commentators.

On 23 May 1960, in a bitter exchange in the United Nations Security Council, Soviet Foreign Minister Gromyko and Ambassador Henry Cabot Lodge blamed each other for what had happened in Paris. Khrushchev denied that internal pressures in the USSR had forced him to sabotage the summit conference and pointed instead to militaristic pressures in the United States which had forced Eisenhower into a disastrous sequence of events. The strained international atmosphere contained Soviet threats, repeated several times in May and June, that the USSR would strike at overseas bases from which future overflights might be launched. They were exacerbated further when, on 1 July, Soviet fighter aircraft shot down an American RB-47 reconnaissance aircraft in the Barents Sea over international waters.[12]

As in the case of the first Berlin crisis, the onset of the second Berlin crisis is full of examples of Soviet probings and attempts to change the status quo unilaterally at the local level. These attempts go back as far as November 1958, but they increased in frequency and became more serious in the period after the collapse of the Paris Summit Conference. For example, in July 1960 the Federal Republic planned to hold its regular opening session of the Bundestag, the lower house of parliament, in Berlin – a practice established since 1954. Since 1959, however, Soviet and East German authorities had attacked these sessions as provocative, and their attacks were resumed now. But this time the West retreated before the verbal barrage. Whereas the United States took the position that this was a problem for the West Germans to decide, France and Britain made no secret of the fact that they opposed the meeting. As a consequence the projected Bundestag sessions were cancelled.[13]

Perhaps encouraged by this success, a planned rally by West German refugee organizations, scheduled to be held in West Berlin from 1 to 4 September 1960, was taken as an opportunity by the GDR authorities to challenge the West on two other issues of importance – unimpeded *access to* Berlin and freedom of *movement within* the city. On the first issue, the Ulbricht regime initiated a series of selective stoppages of West German civilian traffic, based on an announcement of 30 August that passage to Berlin would be prohibited to all West Germans who intended to take part in the meeting. Although the East German move did not affect allied traffic, it was nevertheless held to be 'the most stringent Communist interference with Western rights of access to West Berlin' since the Berlin blockade,[14] because by establishing the right to deny access to one particular group of revanchists, a right to grant or deny access in principle could easily be deduced. On the second issue, GDR authorities succeeded in virtually closing the sectoral border in the direction from West to East Berlin by announcing and implementing a decree that prohibited entry into East Berlin to all West Germans without a special pass issued by the GDR Ministry of the Interior. (Significantly, the decree was signed by the very same ministry rather than, as previously, by the mayor of East Berlin, thus giving notice of another step in the direction of the abrogation of the four-power status of the city.)

In September the two-pronged series of measures against access to Berlin and free movement within Berlin were continued. On 5 September the GDR authorities halted on technical grounds twenty-three barges bound for West Berlin from Hamburg, forcing the West to comply with new East German regulations. In Berlin itself, on 13 September 1960, the GDR extended the successful measures of 30 August and chipped away another piece of the status quo. The Ministry of the Interior began to issue new permits for West Germans and West Berliners planning to enter East Berlin. The significant feature of the new system was that residents of West Berlin now had to present their identity cards. No permit would be issued to a Berliner with a West German passport. This meant to convey – and still does in East German and Soviet interpretations – that West Berlin had separate legal status.[15]

The GDR authorities maintained pressure in various forms even after the successful introduction of new regulations applying to movement within Berlin: they attempted to prevent allied diplomatic personnel from entering East Berlin, claiming a right of inspection of their documents; refused entry into East Berlin to the apostolic nuncio in Germany; and on 26 September, in supposed reaction to a rally being held near the sector border by evangelist Billy Graham, they again virtually closed the East Berlin border for nearly twenty-four hours in a West–East direction.

Following an announcement by the West German government that in reaction to the series of East German moves it would void the interzonal trade agreement just negotiated in August and scheduled to take effect on 1 January 1961, the issues of free access to Berlin, free movement in Berlin and economics became interrelated. In November 1960 the GDR retaliated to the West German announcement with measures of potentially disastrous consequences for the viability of West Berlin, reserving a right to inspect, and consequently a right to refuse transit for, certain manufactured goods originating in West Berlin. The legal instrument for that action, by referring to the Potsdam Agreement, was to classify the goods in question as 'war materials'. Bonn in turn reconsidered and suggested implementation of the interzonal trade agreement in exchange for restoration of free movement in Berlin (and probably hoping that the issue of 'war materials' would disappear as well), but this was rejected in East Berlin; beyond that, *Neues Deutschland* now asserted that the cancellation of interzonal trade had invalidated the agreements of 1949 (ending the Berlin blockade) and that if agreement on the trade issue could not be reached, the GDR would 'propose to the Commandants of the occupation troops conclusion of special machinery [*Sonderregelung*] for their transports'.[16] In the end Bonn's attempt to achieve restoration of free movement in Berlin failed. A compromise was reached in late December whereby West Germany undertook to implement the interzonal trade agreement in exchange for East Germany's promise to abandon its measures against 'war materials'.

To sum up, in the period following the collapse of the Paris Summit Conference there was a lack of substantive negotiation between the major powers. Soviet spokesmen attempted to isolate West Germany in the Western alliance and made it clear that they would not do serious business with an American administration that – in their interpretation – had seriously discredited itself by the U-2 and RB-47 affairs. At the local level a series of measures were taken which undermined the status quo:

(1) The GDR had established precedents for refusing access to persons in transit from West Germany to West Berlin on political grounds.
(2) It had established precedents of setting rules and regulations on technical grounds.
(3) It had demonstrated its power to control entry of West Germans, West Berliners and civilian foreign nationals to East Berlin.

(4)   It had on occasion closed the border for movement in a West–East direction.

(5)   It had further substantiated its theory that West Berlin was an 'independent political entity' located 'on the territory of the GDR' by refusing to recognize Federal German passports issued to citizens of West Berlin.

(6)   It had, in conjunction with the Soviet Union, demonstrated that the West would retreat under pressure in certain cases (as shown, for instance, by the cancellation of the Bundestag meeting and the flights of C-130 aircraft.) [17]

All these measures had increased the general sense of insecurity in Berlin, in the West and, most important, among the East German population. Yet, paradoxically, whereas the GDR now exerted control over civilians *entering* East Germany and East Berlin, it was still powerless to check the movement of those *leaving* the GDR in increasing numbers as a consequence of increased insecurity. This, in turn, was to provide one of the major elements in the acceleration of events leading to the Berlin crisis in the summer of 1961.

The fifth phase (February to June 1961) is characterized by an increased sense of urgency about Berlin and the German problem conveyed by Khrushchev to West Germany (only indirectly at first to the new American administration); by an increasing flow of East Germans to the West; and by developments on the international level which may have influenced the timing of the Soviet decision to build the Berlin wall.

The first major indication that the USSR was now prepared to resume its political offensive after President Kennedy had formally taken office in January came in the Soviet aide-mémoire of 17 February to the Federal Republic. [18] It stated that:

> The Soviet Government is of the opinion that the question of a peace treaty with Germany has top priority in Soviet-West German relations at the present time; it places utmost value [*samoe pervostepennoe znachenie*] on the solution of this question without delay. [19]

In essence the note attempted to convey the impression that the Soviet government's patience had run out with Western dilatory tactics and that it had become weary of Western arguments of delay. Of course, it continued, the USSR did not exclude the 'possibility of an interim solution of the West Berlin problem'. But this was only with the understanding of 'fixing in advance a clearly delimited time span for the conclusion of the treaty'. [20]

Significantly the aide-mémoire was not explicitly addressed to the United States and it did not set a specific time limit for the conclusion of a peace treaty (although reference to the German parliamentary elections in September could have been interpreted as a new target date). Khrushchev proceeded as if he had accepted the request put to him by the American ambassador to the USSR, Llewellyn Thomson, acting on President Kennedy's instructions, to give the new administration enough time to prepare for Berlin negotiations. [21] The fact is that Khrushchev waited until 4 June, the second and last day of the bilateral Soviet-American summit talks at Vienna, to impress directly upon President Kennedy the urgency of concluding a peace treaty.

At the local level the difficulties for the GDR increased considerably. The number of East Germans officially registering in West Germany had risen from 30,273 in the first two months of 1961 to 42,636 persons in the following two months (the latter figure amounting to an annual equivalent of more than a quarter of a million inhabitants), the majority of whom were making use of the open borders in Berlin.[22] On the basis of these alarming figures, Ulbricht, at a plenary meeting of the SED Central Committee on 16 March, reportedly suggested closing the borders in Berlin and at the same time sought and received authorization to approach the Soviet leadership with this proposal.[23] It is only a conjecture, although a very plausible one, that Ulbricht did press the Soviet leadership to make an early decision on the border problem. What is *not* in dispute is that a meeting of the Political Consultative Committee of the Warsaw Pact member countries took place in Moscow on 28–9 March and that the meeting discussed the Berlin problem.[24] But again there is no reliable information as to the content and procedures of decision-making at the Moscow meeting. The assumption underlying the present analysis is that the decision to build the Berlin Wall was not taken at this meeting; that it was agreed to try out all available options of stopping the flow of refugees short of a dramatic confrontation; and that the effectiveness of measures taken at the local level should be evaluated in conjunction with developments at the international level, including the outcome of summit talks with the new American president.[25]

Important developments in the interim period between February and June 1961 at the international level include, first, the dramatic successes of the combined (communist) Pathet Lao and neutralist forces under Kong Le in Laos. As they won control of the Plain of Jars in early March they came into a position to threaten the security of both Vientiane and Luang Prabang. The Kennedy administration's response to these developments was to advocate a 'political solution' and make some moderate military gestures – a policy that was interpreted by American observers, and perhaps also by the Soviet leaders, as a 'tactical retreat under cover of a show of American strength, which may save face but will not save Laos'.[26] Secondly, and perhaps more important for shaping Soviet perceptions of the degree of American determination and resolve, there was the halfhearted support given by the Kennedy administration to the ill-fated invasion attempt by Cuban exiles in the Bay of Pigs in April 1961. For an adversary disposed to look for signs of irresolution it could easily have appeared that a president unwilling to act in a determined fashion close to his own territory would perhaps be even less disposed to display resolution in more remote areas.[27]

It is against this background of local and international events that President Kennedy agreed to Khrushchev's proposal of holding a summit meeting in Vienna, 3–4 June[28] – despite the fact that he (Kennedy) preferred lower-level negotiations by experts and diplomats.[29]

The sixth phase (June to October 1961) is the time interval during which – according to the concepts used here – risks of crisis turn into risks of war. It is characterized by another imposition of a deadline for the 'long-since ripe question of West Berlin'; by a rapidly accelerating flow of East Germans to

West Berlin; by various attempts of the Ulbricht regime to stem that flow; by a cycle of *military* moves and countermoves (which stand in contrast to all previous phases of the Soviet-East German policy of *diplomatic* pressure since 1958); by mutual assertions of determination to meet commitments which had been undertaken earlier; and by increasing apprehensions on all sides about a military conflict in Central Europe.

The new phase began with the Kennedy–Khrushchev summit meeting in Vienna of 3–4 June. Judging from the President's report to the American people on 6 June, as well as from later writings by Kennedy's associates, the Vienna meeting was characterized by clashes over a number of issues, but the 'most somber talks' were held on the Berlin problem.[30] The aide-mémoire which Khrushchev presented to Kennedy on 4 June did not state in precise terms that the Berlin and German problem would have to be solved by a particular date; but it did stress the necessity of an 'immediate' peace treaty and spoke of giving the rival German governments six months to reach agreement on internal German questions involved in such a settlement.[31] It was only after his return to Moscow, in his radio and television address to the Soviet people on 15 June, that Khrushchev flatly declared: 'We ask everyone to understand us correctly: *The conclusion of a peace treaty with Germany cannot be postponed any longer. A peaceful settlement in Europe must be attained this year.*'[32]

Publication of the aide-mémoire on Berlin, and another one on disarmament which Khrushchev had handed to Kennedy in Vienna, by *Pravda* on 11 June, and the forum which Khrushchev chose on 15 June to set a new deadline, indicated that the Soviet party leader intended to give maximum publicity to the Berlin issue and exert maximum pressure.[33] Pressure was also exerted in the Soviet notes (of 8 June) to the three Western powers and the Federal Republic, which contained strongly worded protests against scheduled meetings of the Bundesrat (the upper chamber of West Germany's parliament) in Berlin in mid-June.[34] Following the precedent of the cancelled Bundestag meetings of the previous year, the Bundesrat sessions in Berlin were rescheduled to be held in the Federal Republic proper.

On the very same day that Khrushchev announced the new deadline for the conclusion of a peace treaty (15 June) Ulbricht made an important reference to the possibility of separating the two parts of Berlin by a wall – although, of course, he denied that any such plans actually existed. This occurred at a press conference where a West German correspondent asked him: 'In your opinion, does [the proposal] to establish a Free City mean that a state border will be set up at the Brandenburg Gate? And are you determined to accept all the consequences which may follow from this fact?' Ulbricht replied:

> I take your question to mean that there are people who would like us to mobilize the construction workers of the capital of the GDR to build a wall. I am not aware that such an intention exists. The construction workers of our capital are occupied primarily with the construction of housing, and their labor is fully utilized for it. Nobody has the intention to build a wall.[35]

Considering the fact that in modern times no state border has ever presupposed the existence of a wall, Ulbricht's interpretation of the original question is quite extraordinary, posing the problem of whether Ulbricht made a *lapsus linguae*, whether he said it deliberately to reassure the population, or whether he said it to increase the general sense of insecurity, to stimulate even further the outflow of refugees and thereby to force the hands of his reluctant alliance partners so that they would endorse the very plan whose existence he so emphatically denied.

The period after the Vienna Summit meeting is characterized by increasing reliance of both sides on military moves and countermoves but also by an abundance of verbal communications on the topic of Berlin and problems of disarmament. They include important speeches by Khrushchev on 21 and 28 June, 8 July, 1, 7, 9, and 11 August; Kennedy's press conferences of 28 June and 10 August and his speech to the nation of 25 July; an exchange of notes on disarmament (United States note of 17 June and the Soviet reply of 4 July) and Berlin (replies to the Soviet Berlin memorandum of 4 June by the Federal Republic on 12 July and by the three Western allies on 17 July). There were also numerous face-to-face contacts between Western and Soviet leaders, diplomats and journalists, notably between President Kennedy and a group of Soviet journalists, including Adzhubei, Khrushchev's son-in-law and editor of *Izvestiia* in Washington on 26 June; between Kennedy and the Soviet ambassador to the United States, Menshikov, and the chief Soviet negotiator at the Soviet-American disarmament talks, Zorin, at the White House on 30 June; between Khrushchev and Sir Frank Roberts, the British ambassador in Moscow, on 2 July; Gromyko and Hans Kroll, the West German ambassador, in Moscow on 12 July; Khrushchev and John McCloy, chief United States negotiator at the bilateral disarmament talks, in Sochi from 25 to 27 July at Khrushchev's request; and Khrushchev and the Italian Prime Minister, Fanfani, in Moscow from 2 to 5 August.

While these notes, messages and meetings vary somewhat in content and significance, there are broad common features which could be summarized as follows. On Berlin, the Soviet side is pressing hard, putting the West on the defensive. Skepticism is expressed on problems of disarmament because of the tense international situation, notably in Central Europe. Khrushchev and other Soviet spokesmen reiterate that 'no threats will intimidate us and we will sign a peace treaty with Germany this year'. If the 'imperialists unleash war, the USSR will be forced to respond with crushing blows'. However, the West would 'not fight to defend occupation rights in Berlin' and would 'not risk war'.[36]

The Western response, in essence, was to stress its interest in maintaining the status quo; to warn the Soviet Union against taking unilateral action and creating a *fait accompli*; but to emphasize at the same time (quoting from the United States note of 17 July) that the 'United States is not wedded to one particular arrangement for Berlin'. (The note significantly and explicitly reverted in this context to the discredited Western proposals made at the 1959 Geneva conference.)[37] Another major Western response was contained in President Kennedy's speech of 25 July which, on the military side, contained yet another request for additional defense appropriations – US\$3·5 billion in addition to US\$3·4 billion requested in the spring of the same year; proposals for an increase of 225,000 men in armed forces strength; substantial increases in the draft; authorization to call up additional reserves; increases in the airlift capability of the air force; and reactivation of aircraft and naval vessels. On the political side, Kennedy's speech reiterated the position outlined in the note of 17 July; its tone was firm, warning against the danger of miscalculating American determination; at the same time it limited American commitments to *West* Berlin by putting forward what has come to be known as the 'three essentials' – the right of Western military presence; access and egress for the American garrison; and security and viability of the city.[38]

To return briefly to events at the local level, in the final weeks before 13 August the GDR authorities took a series of measures which were designed to restrict freedom of movement in and out of Berlin even further.[39] In late June Communist Party officials visited the homes of residents in East Berlin who worked in West Berlin, advising them to find jobs in the GDR; and on 3 July *Neues Deutschland* forecast that punitive measures would soon be taken against the *Grenzgänger*. On 6 July Ulbricht demanded in a three-hour speech to the GDR Assembly (*Volkskammer*) that the disruptive influence of West Berlin come to an end. On the following day East Berlin city officials announced that an earlier law, requiring persons working in the West to register with communist authorities, would be vigorously enforced; violators would be evicted from their houses. On 11 July the government of the GDR announced that henceforth *Grenzgänger* would not be allowed to purchase major consumer goods in the East. These restrictive measures were followed up by reports in the press about incidents of smuggling and illegal activities conducted across the East/West border. On 22 July rigorous curbs were placed on passenger rail traffic into East Berlin from the surrounding countryside. On 26 July the government announced that anyone detected trying to flee from the GDR would be subject to two years' imprisonment. On 1 August the GDR Ministry of Health suggested that all travel between East and West Germany and Berlin be suspended because of what it considered to be a polio epidemic in West Germany. On 2 August East Berlin border guards were increased sixfold at all crossing points and persons crossing the border were subjected to rigorous questioning, long delays and often confiscation of identity cards. But in terms of actually stopping the flow of East German citizens to the West, the restrictive and punitive measures taken by the GDR were unsuccessful and probably even counterproductive.

There can be little doubt that the next event of crucial importance for the more dramatic measures of 13 August and thereafter is what is described in the Soviet press as a 'meeting of the First Secretaries' of the member states of the Warsaw Pact (excluding Albania) on the German problem from 3 to 5 August in Moscow.[40] There was no prior announcement of the meeting[41] and no welcoming ceremonies were held for the participants upon arrival. Yet given the long duration of the meeting, and the fact that only little more than a week remained before the construction of the wall, it is entirely credible, as is believed in the West, that the actual list of participants included not only the First Secretaries, but also government representatives, the Ministers of Defense and the commanders of the armies and air forces of the Warsaw Pact.[42] And if the assumption made here is correct, that no definite decisions had been taken during the preceding meeting of the Warsaw Pact member countries in March, it would have had to be at the three-day meeting in

August that the final decisions for sealing the sectoral borders in Berlin were taken – perhaps including adoption of the declaration of the Warsaw Pact powers and several decrees of the GDR Council of Ministers and the GDR Ministry of the Interior, which were all made public on 13 August.[43]

A report, based perhaps on informants in the SED hierarchy, provides some interesting information concerning the proceedings at the meeting. According to this account – Ulbricht and Khrushchev were the main exponents of effective measures in Berlin on the first day of the meeting (3 August), arguing that the West was unlikely to take countermeasures. On the second day a vote was taken, the participants unanimously endorsing measures which would close the sectoral borders; since a concrete wall would have permanent character and could harm the prestige of the socialist community, Khrushchev suggested delaying the construction of solid structures until clarity could be gained about how the West would react. On the last day of the meeting (5 August) procedural questions were discussed: Marshal Konev was put in charge of military operations; in the event of Western counteraction, the border fortifications would be retracted twice by 100 meters by East German border forces, and if the West persisted in removing the obstacles, Soviet forces would safeguard them.[44]

The communiqué issued at the end of the meeting did not give any indication that unilateral measures were about to be taken. In it the meeting expressed 'firm determination (*nepreklonnaya reshimost'*) of all its participants to achieve a peace settlement with Germany before the end of this year'. It also stated that

> should the Western powers continue to evade the conclusion of a German peace treaty, the states concerned will be forced to conclude a peace treaty with the German Democratic Republic, which will draw a line under the last war and safeguard conditions, for stabilization of the situation in that part of Europe.[45]

In other words the threat of unilateral action was portrayed as *not* being immediate. First, there still seemed to be time for negotiations until the winter of 1961. Secondly, the measures to be taken in order 'to safeguard conditions' in Central Europe were to be based on the prior conclusion of a peace treaty with the GDR.

On 7 August, speaking on Soviet radio and television, Khrushchev was only slightly more specific about the impending unilateral measures. He said that the existing situation in Berlin had given the imperialists a 'convenient loophole' (*udobnaya lazeika*) with which they can 'place obstacles in the way of the GDR's development as a socialist state'.[46] However, according to Khrushchev,

> they [the imperialists] are being told: 'Stop, gentlemen. We know very well what you want, what you are aiming at; we are going to sign a peace treaty and close your loophole into the GDR.'[47]

But in this context, too, Khrushchev seemed to make the adoption of unilateral measures dependent on the prior conclusion of a peace treaty with the GDR, and only in retrospect did his repeated reference to West Berlin as a loophole that had to be closed take on particular meaning.

Khrushchev's speech coincided with the two-day (6–7 August) flight of the second manned earth satellite, that of *Vostok-2*, piloted by Major German Titov.[48] Both the regular and a special edition of *Pravda* described the new space venture enthusiastically and in detail, calling it 'unprecedented in human history' and implying strongly that the feat showed the superiority of socialist science (and the socialist system) over capitalism.[49] An appeal signed by the Central Committee of the CPSU, the Presidium of the Supreme Soviet and the Soviet government linked the flight of *Vostok-2* to international politics, but in a very general form, by invoking the need for peace and at the same time warning against unidentified 'enemies of peace' who were 'fanning military hysteria'.[50]

Whereas Khrushchev had not yet exploited the space flight explicitly for foreign political purposes, he did so unambiguously on 9 August during a reception in the Kremlin and in a speech from the speaker's rostrum overlooking Red Square, addressing a big crowd of people.[51] Khrushchev skillfully, though in an unsystematic, disorderly fashion, linked the Soviet preeminence in space with the capacity to develop a rocket with a warhead of 100 megatons ('Our rocket forces have said that they can send it aloft') with general international problems ('Our powerful rockets, which are unequaled by any country, help in solving peaceful tasks') and more specifically with the Berlin problem (saying that 'no threats will intimidate us and we will sign a peace treaty' and that 'Only a fool could respond with war to the conclusion of a peace treaty').[52]

On 11 August, addressing a Soviet-Romanian friendship meeting, Khrushchev delivered a final speech before the taking of unilateral physical measures two days later. The speech combined threats to destroy NATO military bases in Italy ('even if they are in orange groves'), in Greece ('reportedly located among olive groves') and West Germany ('the very existence of the population of West Germany will be placed in question' if Adenauer unleashed war) with the view that it was a 'fairy tale' that the Western powers would fight for the rights of Germans in Berlin.[53] After the speech, according to a report in the *New York Times*, Khrushchev 'sought out the Canadian, British, French and Italian ambassadors and chatted good-humoredly with them for about twenty minutes. Without referring to his earlier speech he flatly said there would be no war.'[54]

On Sunday 13 August, shortly after midnight (Central European time), units of the East German People's Army (*Volksarmee*), People's Police (*Volkspolizei*) and factory militia (*Betriebskampfgruppen*) began taking up positions at various crossing points between the sectoral borders in Berlin and the borders between West Berlin and the GDR. East German workers, under the close supervision of armed units, began placing double strands of barbed wire and light obstacles at the various crossing points all along the borders, tearing up cobbled streets and wooden barriers. Surface and underground rail transport between the sectors (S-Bahn and U-Bahn) was shut down.

Extensive troop movements and concentrations of Soviet and East German military units had already taken place in the days preceding 13 August; a full alert was now ordered, the units moving into their predetermined deployment areas throughout the GDR. Also shortly after midnight

East German radio announced that the border had been closed. The East German news agency ADN released the declaration of the Warsaw Pact member countries officially requesting the GDR to establish 'reliable safeguards and effective control' around the whole territory of West Berlin. It also made public a decree by the GDR Council of Ministers which, 'in accordance with' decisions by and 'in the interests of' the Warsaw Pact member countries, announced that such control was to be introduced on the borders of the GDR 'as is usually introduced along the borders of every sovereign state'.[55] Specifically this meant that GDR citizens were allowed to cross these borders 'only with special permission'. (Significantly, as a gesture to the special status of East Berlin, 'citizens of the capital of the German Democratic Republic' were listed separately but subjected to the same provision.) Another decree, this one signed by the GDR Minister of the Interior, specified details, conveying the idea that (1) permits could, in fact, be received from the competent *Volkspolizei* offices and (2) that for the purpose of visits to West Berlin, thirteen crossing points at the sectoral borders (out of a previous eighty-seven, approximately) remained open 'to motor cars and other vehicles and to pedestrians'. In addition the decree of the ministry asked GDR citizens 'who do not work in [East] Berlin . . . to refrain from traveling to Berlin until further notice'. Finally, a third East German decree, signed by the East Berlin city government, prohibited East Berliners from holding jobs in West Berlin.[56]

On 14 August the GDR closed the Brandenburg Gate, reducing the number of crossing points from thirteen to twelve. It also severed telephone and telegraph communications between East and West Germany (those between the two halves of Berlin had been cut a decade earlier). By 15 August the wooden barriers and barbed wire obstacles were beginning to be replaced by prefabricated concrete blocks. Buildings at the sectoral borders were being evacuated and bricked up a few days later. Ten days after the initial measures the division of Berlin and Germany was deepened further by a decree of the GDR Ministry of the Interior. Starting from 23 August residents of West Berlin had to apply for entry permits to visit East Berlin. Applications were to be made, 'stating the reasons for the visit, at two branches of the German Travel Bureau of the German Democratic Republic in West Berlin'.[57] A combination of popular resentment by West Berliners and determination by West Berlin, West German and allied officials not to tolerate a disguised form of GDR consular functions led to the immediate closure of the offices. Thus, after the population of the GDR had been locked in West Berliners were now locked out.[58] Finally, at the international level the Soviet Union seemed to extend and exacerbate the crisis still further in its note of 23 August to the United States by making an issue of allied access by air, charging that:

> the United States, Britain and France are plainly abusing their position in West Berlin, taking advantage of the absence of control over air communications. This represents a flagrant breach of the agreement reached in 1945. As is known, under this agreement air corridors were set aside for the three Western powers on a temporary basis to insure the needs of their military garrisons, not for the subversive and revanchist purpose of West German militarism.[59]

In the United States the predominant response was that of surprise, uncertainty and hesitation, but also relief,[60] and these attitudes, mixed with some indignation, soon found their expression in public statements. For instance, on 13 August at noon (5.00 p.m. Central European time), the Secretary of State, Dean Rusk, issued a statement which conveyed the impression that the United States government felt that vital Western interests had *not* been threatened and that, consequently, no physical counteraction was being contemplated. Among other things Rusk said that: 'Available information indicates that [the] measures taken thus far are aimed at residents of East Berlin and East Germany and not at the allied position in West Berlin or access thereto.'[61] And although Rusk deplored the violation of the four-power status of Berlin, he merely stated that 'These violations of existing agreements will be the subject of vigorous protest through appropriate channels'.[62]

Concerning this protest, a corresponding note to the Soviet military headquarters in Karlshorst was drafted by the three Western commandants in West Berlin on 13 August but was held up, pending consultations in Washington, until two days later. It was then delivered by messenger to Karlshorst, but the content was accurately described later by one writer as 'exceedingly mild and polite'[63] and another observer expressed the view that: 'It did not take on the appearance of a formal protest, and was merely descriptive of what had taken place.'[64] Even such measures as might have contributed to strengthening the morale of the population of Berlin were rejected.[65]

In Berlin itself the situation initially was tense and explosive. Crowds gathered at both sides of the sectoral borders. In West Berlin up to 10,000 people assembled at the Brandenburg Gate. At other points along the border youths, mainly workers and students, were throwing rocks at the East German armed units, and attempts were being made to remove barbed wire and other obstacles. Calls for unspecified 'action' were supported by the daily press. However, the overriding feature of the situation was the restraining influence exerted by the city government, instructing the police to prevent incidents which might have led to violence. In order to contain the dangers of spontaneous action, the Senat (city government), after some hesitation because of the risks involved, organized a big demonstration on 15 August in front of the Schöneberger Rathaus (city hall). At this mass meeting of about 250,000 people Willy Brandt divested himself of the delicate task of expressing sharp condemnation of the East German measures while being careful not to incite the population to take matters into their own hands. At the same time, Brandt suggested several measures, most of them depending on allied consent, in order to prevent a crisis of confidence erupting between West Berlin and the West.

Yet in Washington the mood of excessive caution persisted until Thursday 17 August. Only then did Kennedy heed some of Brandt's suggestions. He agreed to send Vice-President Lyndon Johnson to Berlin, to be accompanied by the 'hero of the Berlin blockade', General Lucius D. Clay. Also, as another symbolic measure, the President directed an increase of the US garrison in Berlin. A battle group of approximately 1,500 men was to proceed by way of the Helmstedt–Berlin autobahn and to arrive in the city on Sunday 20 August.

These measures achieved the purpose of raising morale in West Berlin. Several hundreds of thousands of enthusiastic people lined the streets to welcome Vice-President Johnson and General Clay. Several hundreds of thousands participated in another emotional gathering with the American visitors and Willy Brandt at the Schöneberger Rathaus. The battle group, according to its commander, was given 'the most exciting and impressive reception I've ever seen with the possible exception of the liberation of France'.[66]

Perhaps encouraged by the new mood, Britain, too, now made some demonstrative military gestures. In response to movements by the *Volks-armee* it sent infantry and tank units to the sector borders (21 August). This kind of response was continued when, on 23 August, the GDR Ministry of Interior issued a decree banning all persons in East and West from approaching the Wall closer than at a distance of 100 meters. All three Western powers countered this move by immediately dispatching troops to the sector borders. Another measure announced by the ministry, however, remained unchallenged: the reduction of the number of crossing points into East Berlin from twelve to seven.[67]

The effort to classify the phases and stages of the Berlin crisis and order events accordingly has arrived at a difficult point. What stands out in the minds of many observers is not only the dramatic hours and days following the border closure, but also the confrontation of American and Soviet tanks at Checkpoint Charlie. However, the latter event took place as late as October 1961 and not, as many assume from memory, in August. In the minds of many people the date of 13 August is deeply engraved as a dividing mark, separating a period of Soviet and East German pressures and international crisis on the one hand from consolidation of the status quo, restraint and reduction of anxiety on the other. However, this retrospective view scarcely does justice to the continuing tension in the more than two months between the middle of August and the end of October 1961. It neglects a number of important military measures taken by the Soviet Union and the fact that Khrushchev's threat to conclude a German peace treaty by the end of the year still remained in force. From the point of view of the Western public and political leaders in 1961, and objectively, the Berlin crisis was by no means over.

In fact the series of probes, challenges and counterchallenges which had characterized the period before 13 August continued after that date. At the local level the already-mentioned East German decree of 23 August on a safety zone of 100 meters on both sides of the Wall was followed on 24 August by the holding-up of United States army buses and demands by the East German police to inspect identity papers of allied military personnel; the firing of warning shots by East German police over the heads of a crowd in the French sector on 25 August; the shooting of refugees trying to escape; the harassment of commercial aircraft flying into Berlin at night and 'buzzing' of United States aircraft in daylight on 14 September; and the initiation by General Clay, on 21 September, of helicopter flights between West Berlin and Steinstücken, an enclave in East Germany, resulting in GDR threats to shoot down the helicopter.

These events at the local level found their counterpart at the international level. The Soviet challenge of the West on air access on 23 August [68] was followed on 28 August by an editorial in *Pravda* which stated that a peace treaty with Germany would be signed before the end of the year. An interview by *Novosti* correspondent Boris Burkov with Walter Ulbricht, which was published in the same issue of *Pravda*, carried a headline explaining the significance of the measures of 13 August as the 'First successful steps in preparation for the peace treaty'. On 29 August Radio Moscow announced that there was to be a 'temporary deferment' of servicemen due for release to the reserve 'until the conclusion of a peace treaty with Germany'. One day later the Soviet government declared that it would resume nuclear testing; it proceeded to do so almost immediately, exploding nuclear devices in the low- to intermediate-kiloton range. In a note to the Western allies on 2 September the Soviet Union reiterated its challenge of 23 August to Western air access. And on 8–9 September the first publicly announced meeting of Warsaw Pact defense ministers was held in Moscow. [69]

Although pressures and probing figured prominently in the Soviet and East German score, provision was also made for intermittent tunes of conciliation and negotiation. For instance, in a letter to Italian Prime Minister Fanfani on 24 August, Khrushchev declared the willingness of the Soviet Union to negotiate with the West on Berlin and Germany. [70] On the same day Khrushchev received the American newspaper columnist Drew Pearson, the text of the interview asserting that the Soviet Union was 'ready at any moment to meet with leaders of the Western powers on this matter [of Berlin and Germany] provided they have a sincere desire to achieve a realistic settlement of the German problem on a mutually acceptable basis'. [71] According to reports of an interview with two visiting British Labour Members of Parliament, Sir Leslie Plummer and Konni Zilliacus, on 31 August, Khrushchev explained the decision to resume nuclear testing as a measure 'to shock the Western powers into negotiations over Germany and disarmament'. [72] On 2 September the Soviet ambassador in Rome, Kozyrev, delivered yet another message from Khrushchev to the Italian Prime Minister, Fanfani, expressing the readiness of the Soviet Union to enter into negotiations. [73] On 5 September, on precisely the same day that Kennedy was quite gloomy about the prospects of negotiation, Khrushchev granted an interview to Cyrus L. Sulzberger of the *New York Times* in the course of which he was reported as saying that he would 'always be glad to meet the United States President to resolve pressing international problems'; he also reportedly stated that if all questions at issue between the two countries were solved, 'the possibility would present itself for me to invite President Kennedy to this country as our guest'; finally, Khrushchev gave Sulzberger a confidential message for Kennedy, suggesting the establishment of private contacts 'to find a means, without damaging the prestige of the United States, to reach a settlement – but on the basis of a peace treaty and a free Berlin'. [74]

The first indications that the Soviet Union would be prepared to lift the deadline on the conclusion of a peace treaty with Germany by the end of the year came in mid-September – first by Presidium member Frol Kozlov who stated in Pyongyang on 12 September that 'Our proposals are not an ultimatum'. [75] Similar hints were given to the former French Prime Minister, Paul Reynaud, and the Belgian Prime Minister, Paul Henri Spaak, when they visited the Soviet Union on 15 and 19 September.[75] Also in three meetings, or 'exploratory talks', between Dean Rusk and the Soviet Foreign Minister, Gromyko, on 21, 27 and 30 September, at the occasion of the opening of the UN General Assembly, the United States was assured by Gromyko that the deadline would be lifted if negotiations began in earnest.[77] Simultaneously, Khrushchev pursued the matter of private contacts with Kennedy 'without damaging the prestige of the United States' via two intermediaries in New York, Soviet officials Georgi Bolshakov and Mikhail Kharlamov, some of the essential points being Kharlamov's remark to Kennedy's press secretary, Pierre Salinger, on 23 September that 'The storm is over', and the delivery of a twenty-six-page personal letter from Khrushchev to Kennedy dated 29 September.[78] The 'exploratory talks' were continued also in a conversation between Gromyko and Kennedy on 6 October.

Unfortunately even today little is known of the substance of the 'exploratory talks' and the private contacts. Concerning the correspondence initiated by Khrushchev's letter, Sorensen writes that 'Although the publication of this correspondence could no longer affect the power or plans of either man, it is important that future Soviet leaders feel free to make private proposals via this channel without fear of their future use'.[79] This implies that perhaps important new proposals *had* been made which, if they had been taken up seriously, might have altered the course of events to a significant degree. This, however, is doubtful. In general terms Sorensen admits as much when he writes that 'Substantively the correspondence accomplished very little that was concrete'; the arguments exchanged 'did not differ in essence, though they did sometimes in tone, from the arguments their [Kennedy's and Khrushchev's] envoys or even speeches exchanged'.[80]

Also events, even in late September and October, did not point exclusively in one direction, that of negotiation and compromise. Not only did the Soviet nuclear tests continue; naval maneuvers were held in the Barents and Kara Seas involving the Soviet northern fleet, rocket troops and the air force; and in early October the first large-scale joint Warsaw Pact field maneuvers took place with Soviet, Polish, East German and Czechoslovak units participating. At the diplomatic level, in the talks held with Rusk in New York, Gromyko was reported as having restated 'the Soviet position as given by Mr Khrushchev at his Vienna meeting with Mr Kennedy'.[81] If so, this implied that Khrushchev merely held out the prospect of negotiations without wanting to abandon far-reaching demands which were unacceptable to the West. This impression is reinforced by the unsuccessful meeting between Kennedy and Gromyko in New York on 6 October, in the course of which Gromyko reportedly had restated the Soviet position in an uncompromising manner, leading Kennedy to complain: 'You've offered to trade us an apple for an orchard. We don't do that in this country.'[82]

Similarly Khrushchev and Brezhnev (the latter in his capacity as Chairman of the Presidium of the Supreme Soviet) stated in a message to Ulbricht and other East German leaders on 6 October, at the occasion of the twelfth anniversary of the founding of the GDR, that dangerous developments in West Germany 'urgently required' (*nastoiatel'no trebuiut*) the conclusion of a peace treaty and that it was to be hoped that this would occur 'in the immediate future' (*v samoe blizhaishchee vremia*).[83] On the same occasion, in East

Berlin, Walter Ulbricht and Soviet Politburo member Anastas Mikoyan repeated the demand for the conclusion of a peace treaty.[84] This contradictory pattern of apparent conciliation, diplomatic pressure and military demonstration continued during the Twenty-Second CPSU Congress (17–31 October).

On the opening day of the congress Khrushchev made the announcement which many people in the West had anxiously been awaiting.

> Some Western spokesmen say [Khrushchev stated] that our proposals that a German peace treaty be concluded this year are an ultimatum. But this is an erroneous contention. After all, the Soviet Union's proposals on concluding a peace treaty and on that basis settling the question of West Berlin, turning it into a free city, were put forward as early as 1958. A good deal of time has passed since then. We have not rushed settlement of the question, hoping for the achievement of mutual understanding with the Western countries. Where, may I ask, is the ultimatum?[85]

Khrushchev then continued that if the Western countries showed a readiness to settle the German problem: '*we shall not in that case absolutely insist on signing the peace treaty before December 31, 1961.*'[86] For all practical purposes the deadline was thus officially withdrawn. But then Khrushchev asserted also in the same speech that 'A German peace treaty must and will be signed, with or without the Western powers'.[87] He also reverted to a theme which he had raised with Sulzberger on 5 September – the testing of a superbomb in the 100-megaton range. Digressing from the written text he announced that the series of nuclear tests would 'probably' be completed at the end of October by detonating a hydrogen bomb in the 50-megaton range. It was true, he continued, 'We have said that we have a 100-megaton bomb'. But the Soviet Union was not going to explode it because 'we might knock out all our windows . . . However, in exploding the 50-megaton bomb we are testing the device for triggering a 100-megaton bomb'.[88]

Although events in Berlin failed to be mentioned at the Twenty-Second Party Congress, they now moved towards a new high point of tension.[89] On 22 October the deputy chief of the United States mission in Berlin, Mr Allen Lightner, was stopped by East German police at the Friedrichstrasse checkpoint (Checkpoint Charlie). According to customary practice, passengers of cars bearing license plates of any of the four allied powers in Germany, no matter whether in military or civilian clothes, had passed unimpeded between the sector borders. Now, however, Lightner was refused entry, the *Volkspolizei* explaining that henceforth all persons in *civilian* clothes entering the capital of the GDR would have to show identification. The Berlin Command and General Clay, in his capacity as President Kennedy's personal representative in Berlin, considered the issue of unimpeded access important enough to react with a show of determination. Several tanks and armored personnel carriers were dispatched to the checkpoint and when Lightner returned, and was again refused entry, he was escorted into East Berlin by eight men with fixed bayonets. When Lightner made the third trip of the day to East Berlin, he was allowed to pass uninspected. The Soviet and East German authorities, however, took up the challenge. On the next day,

23 October, the East German news agency ADN issued a statement of the GDR Interior Ministry to the effect that all civilians entering the GDR had to produce identification.[90] The issue was further complicated by the fact that on the very same day two British diplomats had shown their identification papers to East German police when they entered East Berlin. But General Watson, the United States commandant, was authorized by Washington, upon Clay's urging, to protest against the East German announcement and, failing to receive satisfaction, to demonstrate once more American determination to maintain customary practice.

On 25 October, therefore, probing and counterprobing continue at a higher level of tension. East German police again refuse entry to cars with American officials in civilian clothes; again tanks and armored personnel carriers are dispatched to the checkpoint; again officials are escorted by armed men; Soviet officers cross over to the Western side of the checkpoint to monitor movements; an American convoy is escorted to East Berlin; more American tanks appear on the Western side and Soviet officers appear on the Eastern side of the checkpoint; General Watson returns from an unsuccessful protest mission in Karlshorst with Colonel Solovyev, the Soviet commandant. In the evening the American tanks return to their barracks.

The following day, 26 October, was one of relative respite. However, activity of Soviet military units in East Berlin was reported, as well as the stationing of about thirty Soviet T-54 tanks near Unter den Linden, less than one mile away from Checkpoint Charlie.

On 27 October events moved to a climax. American tanks again appeared at the checkpoint, and armed escorts were again used to force uninspected entry. But shortly after, the Soviet Union intervened. Seven Soviet T-54 tanks were dispatched to the scene. They stopped about a hundred yards from the barriers, their guns pointing at American tanks on the other side. The American tanks moved closer and were reinforced. More Soviet tanks followed. Thus for the first time in post-World War II history the superpowers were facing each other militarily in a most direct fashion, both apparently willing to engage in a competition in risk-taking over what to many appeared to be a relatively unimportant issue. Both sides seemed to maintain their positions. The United States ambassador in Moscow, Llewellyn Thompson, was instructed to protest against the harassment of American officials to Foreign Minister Gromyko, and this protest was rejected. Nevertheless the danger of direct military conflict at the local level was quickly averted. The United States did not attempt to force uninspected entry of diplomats against Soviet military units. The Soviet Union withdrew its tanks in the morning of 28 October, sixteen hours after their appearance at the checkpoint, and the United States followed suit.

Notes: Part Two, Chapter 12

1 This ordering of phases draws on Barker, 'The Berlin crisis', p. 62.
2 For excerpts of the note see above, pp. 186–7.
3 *New York Times*, 29 September 1959.
4 *Pravda*, 5 February 1960.
5 *New York Times*, 21 April 1960.

6   *Pravda*, 24 April 1960.
7   ibid., 26 April 1960.
8   *New York Times*, 28 April 1960.
9   Speech by Khrushchev at a session of the Supreme Soviet, *Izvestiia*, 6 May 1960. For materials concerning the U-2 affair and its aftermath see US Congress, Senate, Committee on Foreign Relations, 86th Congress, 2nd Session, *Report: Events Relating to the Summit Conference* (Washington, DC: Government Printing Office, 1960); for more detailed analysis see also David Wise and Thomas B. Ross, *The U-2 Affair* (New York: Random House, 1962) and Horelick and Rush, *Strategic Power*, pp. 71–7.
10   *Pravda*, 13 May 1960.
11   *Pravda*, 21 May 1960.
12   Khrushchev said that 'the Soviet government limited itself to destroying the aircraft' because intrusion had been stopped at the very beginning, *Pravda*, 13 July 1960.
13   This account, as well as the enumeration of the following examples of Soviet and East German attempts to change the status quo unilaterally and gradually, draws on Jean Edward Smith, *The Defense of Berlin* (Baltimore, Md: Johns Hopkins University Press, 1963), pp. 224–6 and Schick, *The Berlin Crisis*, pp. 130–2.
14   *New York Times*, 31 August 1960.
15   See, for instance, Keiderling and Stulz, *Geschichte Berlins*, p. 456.
16   *Neues Deutschland*, 19 December 1960.
17   The case of the C-130 aircraft (which was not mentioned above) is yet another example of Soviet probing in the phase in question. The issue developed as follows. As a matter of habit, United States aircraft flying from West Germany to West Berlin had observed a 10,000-foot ceiling. With the advent of new aircraft that performed better and more cheaply at higher altitudes (for example, the C-130 aircraft), an attempt was made during the Eisenhower administration in March 1959 to fly above the customary ceiling. The USSR protested and interfered with the flights of a C-130 aircraft on 27 March 1959. The American probes were discontinued, and when the matter was suggested again in March 1960 the USSR again protested and declared that if the United States wished to conduct flights at the altitudes required, they would have to negotiate with the GDR. The United States then abandoned the plan (Schick, *The Berlin Crisis*, p. 110, and Smith, *The Defense of Berlin*, pp. 218–19).
18   The analysis of the background of the Soviet aide-mémoire to Bonn by Robert Slusser, 'The Presidium meeting of February, 1961: a reconstruction', in Alexander and Janet Rabinowitch with Ladis K. D. Kristof, (eds), *Revolution and Politics in Russia: Essays in Memory of B. I. Nicolaevsky* (Bloomington, Ill.: Indiana University Press, 1972), p. 290, is that 'a majority in the Presidium, led by the opponents of Khrushchev's policy of rapprochement with the United States, presented him with a clear-cut alternative: either obtain within six months a major concession from the West over Berlin, or accede to the resumption of nuclear testing by the Soviet Union. The Soviet note [handed] to West Germany on February 18 marked the launching of this propaganda offensive.' There is no evidence for this bold assertion.
19   *Pravda*, 4 March 1961.
20   ibid.
21   Sorensen, *Kennedy*, p. 542.
22   See the detailed statistics compiled by the government of the Federal Republic, *Die Flucht aus der Sowjetzone und die Sperrmassnahmen des kommunistischen Regimes vom 13. August 1961 in Berlin* (Bonn and Berlin: Bundesministerium für gesamtdeutsche Fragen, 1961), esp. pp. 15–16.
23   Hermann Zolling and Uwe Bahnsen, *Kalter Winter im August* (Oldenbourg and Hamburg: Gerhard Stolling Verlag, 1967), pp. 101–2.
24   See the communiqué in *Pravda*, 31 March 1961.
25   According to Soviet interpretations the decision to seal the borders was taken later, at the meeting of the first secretaries of the Warsaw Pact Communist and Workers' Parties in Moscow, 3–5 August 1961. See, for example, Vysotskii, *Zapadnyi Berlin*, p. 224, and Inozemtsev (ed.), *Mezhdunarodnye otnosheniia*, Vol. III, p. 210. However, the communiqué of the August meeting, as published in *Pravda*, 6 August 1961, did not – for obvious reasons – reveal that any measures had been agreed upon. Two West German analysts of the Berlin crisis give the following account of the meeting of 28–9 March 1961. Ulbricht strongly argued for immediate and effective closure of the borders with the help of East

German border police and by means of barriers and barbed wire. The party leaders of Hungary (János Kádár), Romania (Georghiu-Dej) and Bulgaria (Todor Zhivkov) argued that these measures would harm the prestige of the socialist community and that the West would take countermeasures so that there was a risk of military conflict. The party leader of Czechoslovakia (Antonín Novotný) warned that the West might tear down the border obstacles. Khrushchev argued that an aggravation of the Berlin crisis should be avoided at the present time and that it had to be established first whether Kennedy's Berlin policy was different from that of his predecessor. This left Ulbricht isolated at the Moscow meeting. The only measure taken was to strengthen Soviet troop deployments in East Germany and Poland (Zolling and Bahnsen, *Kalter Winter im August*, pp. 102–4). While this account is plausible, it is not necessarily reliable. No source is given by the two authors.

26 *Saturday Evening Post* (n.d.), as quoted by Roger Hilsman, *To Move a Nation: The Politics of Foreign Policy in the Administration of John F. Kennedy* (Garden City, NY: Doubleday, 1967), p. 134. A detailed analysis of the Laos problem as an issue in East–West conflict cannot be attempted here; for references see ibid., p. 104–55 and Arthur J. Dommen, *Conflict in Laos: The Politics of Neutralization* (London: Pall Mall Press, 1964).

27 The Bay of Pigs disaster received extensive coverage in *Pravda* and *Izvestiia*, 18–24 April 1961. Kennedy's biographers and associates stress that the Soviet leadership could easily have misinterpreted the limited United States support for the Cuban venture as irresolution. See, for example, Hilsman, *To Move a Nation*, p. 134. Horelick and Rush, *Strategic Power*, p. 123n., put the case perhaps too strongly when they write: 'In view of the importance of the subjective element in Khrushchev's campaign on Berlin, that is, his assessment of the opponent, it is arguable that Khrushchev might not have renewed the offensive in 1961 had it not been for the United States failure in Cuba in April.'

28 Kennedy's agreement to meet Khrushchev was announced by the White House on 19 May.

29 Sorensen, *Kennedy*, pp. 551–2.

30 Kennedy in his report to the American people on the Vienna summit meeting in the *New York Times*, 7 June 1961.

31 US Congress, Senate, Committee on Foreign Relations, *Documents on Germany, 1944–1961* (Washington, DC: Government Printing Office, 1961), pp. 642–5; Russian text in *Pravda*, 11 June 1961.

32 For the text of Khrushchev's speech of 15 June 1961 see *Pravda*, 16 June 1961 (my italics).

33 Tass released the text of the aides-mémoire on 10 June. The United States Secretary of State, Dean Rusk, had suggested to the NATO Council that publication of the 4 June aide-mémoire on Berlin would mean that a serious crisis had to be expected (*New York Times*, 12 June 1961).

34 *Pravda*, 9 June 1961.

35 *Neues Deutschland*, 16 June 1961. The *Leipziger Volkszeitung* must have enhanced anxieties among the population by giving the following subtitle to Ulbricht's press conference: 'We're not building a wall' (Carola Stern, *Ulbricht: A Political Biography*, New York, Praeger, 1965).

36 See especially Khrushchev's speeches of 8 July and 7 and 11 August, *Pravda*, 10 July and 8 and 11 August 1961; the meetings between Gromyko and Kroll, in Kroll, *Lebenserinnerungen*, pp. 500–3; and the meeting between Khrushchev and McCloy, the *New York Times*, 11 August 1961.

37 For the full text of the United States note, see *DOSB*, vol. 40, (1961), pp. 224–30.

38 Text in *Documents on Germany, 1944–1961*, pp. 694–701. For analysis and interpretation see Slusser, *The Berlin Crisis*, p. 80; Wolfe, *Soviet Power and Europe*, p. 94; and Schick, *The Berlin Crisis*, p. 151.

39 This enumeration of restrictive and punitive measures by the GDR draws on Smith, *The defense of Berlin*, pp. 258–60.

40 *Pravda*, 6 August 1961.

41 Concerning the secrecy of the meeting, arrival and composition of participants, Slusser mentions that Radio Prague, on 3 August 1961, stated that Antonin Novotny, the First Secretary of the Czechoslovak Communist Party, had flown to Moscow to 'spend his vacation' in the Soviet Union (Slusser, *The Berlin Crisis*, p. 100).

42 Zolling and Bahnsen, *Kalter Winter*, p. 111.

43 It is interesting to note in this context that Vysotskii, *Zapadnyi Berlin*, p. 224, states that 'the meeting [of 3–5 August 1961] took the decision to carry out the necessary measures in order to safeguard the security of the countries of the socialist commonwealth'. Although

Vysotskii refers in his footnote to *Pravda*, 6 August 1961, there is nothing in that issue of the paper that would have given an indication that any decision had in fact been taken at that meeting. What is more, Vysotskii also quotes in the same context from the Warsaw Pact Declaration, released on 13 August, making it appear that it too was adopted at the 3–5 August meeting. Concerning the timing of the decision to 'take effective measures' in Berlin, Kroll, *Lebenserinnerungen*, p. 510, contains a reference that a meeting of Warsaw Pact chiefs of government and foreign ministers took place 'at the end of June'. If so, this lower-level meeting suggests another review of the situation in Berlin and East Germany; it would not appear to have been an occasion where final decisions were taken. (In parenthesis it should perhaps be mentioned that the West German ambassador's memoirs should be treated with greater reservations than memoirs generally. While the facts may be more or less correct, Kroll clearly overestimates his and West Germany's potential for influencing events.) Slusser, *The Berlin Crisis*, pp. 95–6, presents as a fact that Khrushchev decided on the 'Soviet Union's minimum objective' (sealing the border) on 27 July 'as soon as he learned of the US military build-up, announced in Kennedy's speech of July 25' and that a Presidium meeting 'ratified' Khrushchev's decision before the 3–5 August meeting of the Warsaw Pact.

44   Zolling and Bahnsen, *Kalter Winter*, pp. 111–15. The recall from retirement of Marshal Ivan S. Konev was reported in the *New York Times*, 11 August 1961; according to the Foreign Minister of the GDR, Lother Bolz, on 11 August, the appointment of Konev was one of the measures which had to be seen in the context of Warsaw Pact preparations for the conclusion of a peace treaty between the USSR and the GDR (*Washington Post*, 12 August 1961, as quoted by Slusser, *The Berlin Crisis*, p. 101). For an interpretation of the significance of Konev's appointment see below, pp. 245–6.

45   *Pravda*, 6 August 1961.

46   ibid., 8 August 1961.

47   ibid.

48   The first flight, that of *Vostok-1*, had taken place some months earlier, on 12 April, piloted by Major Yuri Gagarin.

49   *Pravda*, nos 219 (15 709) and 220 (15 710), 7 August 1961.

50   ibid., no. 220 (15 710), 7 August 1961.

51   Khrushchev's speech and his remarks at the reception were reported in *Pravda*, 10 August 1961; additional information is provided by the report in the *New York Times*, 11 August 1961.

52   See preceding footnote.

53   *Pravda*, 12 August 1961.

54   *New York Times*, 12 August 1961.

55   Russian original of the Warsaw Pact Declaration as published in *Pravda*, 14 August 1961; the East German decrees as published in *Neues Deutschland*, 13 August 1961.

56   ibid.

57   Decree of the GDR Ministry of the Interior of 22 August, 1961, *Neues Deutschland*, 23 August 1961.

58   Theo Sommer in *Die Zeit*, 17 August 1961.

59   *Pravda*, 25 August 1961. This statement was quoted in full in order not to contribute to the proliferation of historical myths. Schick's interpretation is conducive to that when he writes that 'In a note to the United States on August 23, *Moscow abruptly threatened to interrupt air access*, inflaming the crisis still further' (Schick, *The Berlin Crisis*, p. 168, my italics).

60   The sequence of events in Washington is described in detail by biographers, advisers and officials of the Kennedy administration, notably Theodore C. Sorensen, Arthur M. Schlesinger, Jr, Roger Hilsman and Pierre Salinger and – drawing on additional information – in the analyses of Western policy by Schick, Jean E. Smith, Eleanor Lansing Dulles and Richard Merritt. There is no major disagreement concerning the basic facts as described here.

61   US Department of State, *Berlin – 1961* (Washington, DC: Government Printing Office, 1961), pp. 41–2.

62   ibid.

63   Smith, *The Defense of Berlin*, p. 279.

64   Eleanor Lansing Dulles, *The Wall: A Tragedy in Three Acts* (Columbia, SC: University of South Carolina Press, 1972), p. 76. The protest of the three Western commandants is published in *Documents on Germany, 1944–1961*, pp. 729–35.

65   For instance, President Kennedy reacted angrily to a letter sent to him by Willy Brandt
     (then mayor of West Berlin) suggesting several measures designed to achieve this purpose.
66   Colonel Grover S. Johns, as quoted by Smith, *The Defense of Berlin*, p. 292.
67   The decrees as published in *Neues Deutschland*, 24 August 1961. Of the seven remaining
     crossing points four were to be used by West Berliners, two by West Germans and one by
     non-German citizens and allied personnel (the last one mentioned is the checkpoint at
     Friedrichstrasse or, in United States usage, Checkpoint Charlie).
68   See p. 209.
69   The military measures will be discussed more systematically; see below, pp. 214–5.
70   *New York Times*, 28 August and 4 September 1961.
71   *Pravda* and *Izvestiia*, 28 August 1961; published also in N. S. Khrushchev, *Kommunizm –
     mir i schast'e narodam*, Vol. I (Moscow: Izdatel'stvo politicheskoi literatury, 1962),
     pp. 347–54; an English text of the interview is published in *Documents on Germany,
     1944–1961*, pp. 548–63.
72   *The Times* and the *New York Times*, 2 September 1961.
73   *The Times*, 5 September 1961.
74   Materials relating to the well-prepared interview were published in *Izvestiia*, 9 September
     1961, and *Pravda*, 10 September 1961, after they had been published in the *New York
     Times* on 8 September 1961; Khrushchev's confidential message was published in ibid., 6
     November 1966, the purpose being, according to Sulzberger, to clarify the issue raised by
     Kennedy's press secretary, Pierre Salinger, in his book *With Kennedy* (Garden City, NY:
     Doubleday, 1966); a lengthy discussion is provided by Slusser, *The Berlin Crisis*,
     pp. 190–210.
75   *Pravda*, 13 September 1961.
76   Reported by all major Western newspapers at the time.
77   According to Dean Rusk, as reported in the *New York Times*, 1 October 1961. Other details
     of the contents of the Gromyko–Rusk talks were not reported; no communiqué was issued;
     Sorensen, *Kennedy*, pp. 598–9 and Arthur Schlesinger, Jr, *A Thousand Days: John F.
     Kennedy in the White House* (Boston, Mass.: Houghton Mifflin, 1965), p. 360, though
     mentioning the talks, are even less explicit than some of the newspaper accounts published
     at the time.
78   Salinger, *With Kennedy*, pp. 190–9, and Sorensen, *Kennedy*, pp. 552–5, are the two
     sources on the issue of personal contacts.
79   ibid., p. 552.
80   ibid., pp. 553–4.
81   *The Times*, 23 September 1961.
82   *New York Times*, 7 October 1961; Sorensen, *Kennedy*, p. 599.
83   *Pravda*, 7 October 1961; the message was also published prominently in *Neues Deutsch-
     land*, 7 October 1961.
84   *Pravda*, 7 October 1961 and *Neues Deutschland*, 9 October 1961.
85   *Pravda*, 18 October 1961, as quoted in Leo Gruliow (ed.), *Current Soviet Policies, Vol. IV:
     The Documentary Record of the Twenty-Second Congress of the Communist Party of the
     Soviet Union* (New York: Columbia University Press, 1962), p. 51.
86   ibid. (my italics).
87   ibid.
88   ibid. To Sulzberger, Khrushchev had mentioned the existence of several bombs in the
     100-megaton range as a fact, but he had then requested a change in wording so that the final
     version of the interview read that 'we *will have* a bomb with a power equivalent to 100
     million tons of TNT' (*New York Times*, 8 and 11 September 1961, my italics).
89   The following events were described in detail by all major Western newspapers and also, to
     a significant extent, in the East German press. The account here follows Smith, *The
     Defense of Berlin*, pp. 319–24, and Zolling and Bahnsen, *Kalter Winter*, pp. 182–93.
90   *Neues Deutschland*, 24 October 1961.

13
Factors of Risk-Taking

I IDEOLOGY

Analysis of the Berlin crisis of 1961 in the light of ideology makes it necessary to pick up the threads from the doctrinal reorientation initiated after the Berlin crisis of 1948 and to ask, first, in what respects there has been an evolution concerning the theory of peaceful coexistence, likelihood of war and forms of competition and conflict between socialism and imperialism; it requires asking questions as to how ideological codifications interpret the main trends of the epoch, the existing correlation of forces and the primary tasks for Soviet policy (the analytical aspect of Soviet ideology); and it necessitates looking at the problem of whether the stated priorities and commitments are in contradiction to or conformity with actual policy (the operational aspect). Secondly, a more limited focus has to consider the relationship of Soviet formalized attitudes and perceptions towards the crisis area – West Berlin and West Germany – to the general ideological framework. Thirdly, East Berlin and East Germany are part of the socialist system, those elements of Soviet ideology pertaining to cohesion and Soviet control in East Central Europe and their possible influence on Soviet behavior in the Berlin crisis have to be examined.

The Prevention of War and the Berlin Crisis

An attempt to reconstruct the main doctrinal developments in the period leading up to the Berlin crisis should concentrate on two major documents: the speech Khrushchev delivered on 6 January 1961 at a joint meeting of the party organizations of the Higher Party School, the Academy of Social Sciences and the CPSU Central Committee's Institute on Marxism-Leninism;[1] and the Draft Program of the Communist Party of the Soviet Union, adopted at the June 1961 plenary meeting of the CPSU Central Committee.[2] The declared purpose of the former was to report to the assembled party theoreticians on the 'results' of the World Conference of Eighty-One Communist and Workers' Parties held in Moscow in November 1960. This was to be a highly important and politically sensitive endeavor due to the controversial nature of the world conference, as had been evident in extensive preparatory meetings in Moscow presided over by the CPSU's chief theoretician, Mikhail Suslov, in September and October 1960; the reported allegations that the conference had to be called earlier than originally planned, according to the Soviet view, because of Chinese violations of the declaration adopted at the previous world conference in 1957; the unusually long duration of the conference (almost three weeks); the secrecy of the proceedings; and the abundance of leaks and semiofficial and official statements by various participants subsequently, showing that the meetings were often characterized by acrimonious charges and countercharges on a broad spectrum of ideological and political issues, with crystallizations around two main interpretations – Soviet and Chinese – but also with a variety of modified or independent positions.[3] Given the fact that the Moscow Declaration[4] inevitably constituted a compromise, full of ambiguities and qualifications, it was highly relevant from the Soviet viewpoint to 'clarify' some of the controversial issues and provide a 'correct' interpretation of the document. This, in essence, should be regarded as the main purpose of Khrushchev's report.

The second document is equally important. It is a full statement of the then current Soviet conceptions of socialism and the building of communism in the Soviet Union (to be achieved within twenty years), as well as a coherent set of prescriptions to be adopted so as to enable the Soviet Union to cope with changes in the international environment. This Draft Program was to incorporate many of the ideas contained in Khrushchev's report of 6 January. It formed the basis of extensive discussion in party meetings, newspapers and journals. And it was to be adopted – with several modifications – at the Twenty-Second Party Congress in October.

The most general summary of doctrinal developments prior to the Berlin crisis on problems of war and peaceful coexistence, based on the two documents, is the stereotype and, on the face of it, almost meaningless assertion that the main decisions of the two previous congresses, the Twentieth (1956) and Twenty-First (1959) were still valid. Somewhat more to the point, Khrushchev noted in his report of 6 January that 'the participants [in the world conference] were very well aware that the problem of preventing a thermonuclear war is the most burning and vital problem for mankind' and that therefore the conference had 'disclosed and outlined ways of making even more effective use of the new possibilities for preventing a world war'.[5]

This is only a rather veiled reference to the thesis of the Twentieth Party Congress that 'war is not fatalistically inevitable'.[6] However, many of the issues which had been defined without much clarity by Stalin in 1952 (at the Nineteenth Party Congress), and by Khrushchev in 1956 and 1959, did receive some refinement in 1961. This applies primarily to the codifications concerning different types of war and differing probabilities attached to their occurrence.

'In present-day conditions', Khrushchev explained, 'it is necessary to distinguish between the following kinds of war – world wars, local wars and wars of [national] liberation, or popular uprisings.' As regards the question of world war, Khrushchev develops four main theses. First, he declares that in present-day conditions *'wars among the capitalist, imperialist countries'*, into which, presumably, as in World War II, the socialist countries could be drawn, *'are not the most probable'*.[7] This is a surprising but clear departure from the thrust of Stalin's arguments as expressed in his *Economic Problems of Socialism* in the USSR and the proceedings of the Nineteenth Party Congress.[8]

Stalin had still asserted then that the doctrine on 'the inevitability of wars between capitalist countries remains in force'.[9] The 'contradictions' between the capitalist countries were seen as being stronger than the 'contradictions' between socialism and imperialism. (He predicted, for example, that West Germany and Japan would refuse to languish forever 'in misery under the jackboot of American imperialism'.)[10] Contrary to that, Khrushchev appears to have been impressed, as early as 1956, by the increase in cooperation between Western Europe, Japan and the United States and the reduction of conflicts among them. Hence when he had declared war not to be fatalistically inevitable, he undoubtedly had this in mind. The thesis of 1961 – wars among the capitalist countries as 'not [being] the most probable' – therefore must be considered as a consistent evolution of his thinking.

Khrushchev's second thesis follows logically from the first: as interimperialist wars are not the most probable, the imperialists could be expected to be preparing for war primarily not against each other: they *'are preparing for wars primarily against the countries of socialism*, above all against the Soviet Union as the most powerful of the socialist states.'[11] It would be wrong, however, to infer from this statement that Khrushchev was turning back the clock to March 1919, to Lenin and his fear of an 'inevitable' series of 'frightful collisions between the Soviet republic and the bourgeois states'.[12] Such wars, too, could still be prevented. (How, in Khrushchev's view, this could be done will be discussed below.)

The third thesis is the at first sight rather obvious assertion that *'a world war in contemporary conditions would be a nuclear-rocket war'* and that such a war would be 'the most destructive in the history of war'. Yet the latter part of the statement deserves elaboration. In his report of 6 January Khrushchev dealt at length with this problem, quoting Western scientists to the effect that within sixty days of nuclear war 500 to 600 million people could perish; that whole countries could be wiped out; and that, apart from the casualties of direct attack, many more would die as a result of radioactive contamination. Even more important, 'the working people and their vanguard, the working class, would be the first to suffer'.

All this scarcely fitted into a systematic campaign of threat in connection with the Berlin crisis. It was most likely designed to counteract the Chinese, their professed sanguine opinion about the atomic bomb as a paper tiger and, related to that, their advocacy of a more forward-oriented, more revolutionary, policy of world communism.

Doctrinally much more consistent, and much more useful as a device for enhancing the Soviet bargaining position in Berlin, is a fourth thesis on world war: *'if the imperialist madmen unleashed a world war, capitalism would be swept away and destroyed by the peoples.'*[13] Or, as the Draft Program puts it,

> Peaceful coexistence or catastrophic war – that is the alternative offered by history. Should the imperialist aggressors nevertheless dare to unleash a new world war, the peoples will no longer tolerate a system that drags them into devastating wars. They will sweep imperialism away and bury it.[14]

In this way doctrinal formulations steer clear of any acknowledgment that nuclear war would mean, or could mean, the destruction of mankind (as Malenkov had prematurely contended in 1953). This is not to say that nuclear war was regarded as a legitimate device to further world revolution.

The crux of the matter lies in the dialectical refinement that it is not war itself that would be instrumental in destroying capitalism but that the 'peoples' would rise up against the 'madmen' who unleashed war and sweep capitalism away as a system.

Theoretically a world war could grow out of a regional military conflict. Turning, therefore, to the category of *local wars*, care must be taken not to confuse Khrushchev's definitions with those widely accepted in the West. According to Western concepts, local wars are conflicts among 'third actors', that is, they do not involve the superpowers or states directly allied with them (for example, wars between the Arab states and Israel, or between India and Pakistan).[15] What Khrushchev has in mind corresponds to what is widely understood in the West as 'limited war' – wars directly involving one of the two superpowers, or a state closely allied with one of them, limited in geographical scope and in the use of weapons. (Examples for the latter category would be the Korean War and the Vietnam War and, according to some definitions, also the French and British attack on Egypt in 1956.) That this is, in fact, Khrushchev's understanding is shown by his remarks that there is 'talk now in the imperialist camp about local [that is, limited] wars'; that 'small-caliber nuclear weapons are even being made for use in such wars'; that a 'special theory of local [that is, limited] wars has been devised'; and that, finally, the 'aggression of Britain, France and Israel against Egypt' had to be considered as 'an example of local [that is, limited] war unleashed by the imperialists'.[16]

What is not altogether clear in this typology of wars, perhaps deliberately so, is the place of a local, or limited, war in *Europe*, or, quite appropriately in the present context, a small-scale military conflict in Berlin. On the military-doctrinal level the Soviet attitude in this period remained rigidly opposed to the concept of 'flexible response' in Europe, emphatically ruling out the very possibility of mutual restraints in this potential theater of war. The inference to be drawn from that is that this is deliberate and that it is intended to serve deterrent purposes. This is evident in the general statement by Khrushchev in the report of 6 January that 'A small imperialist war, no matter which of the imperialists starts it, might develop into a global thermonuclear, rocket war'. Finally, what remains to be said is that Khrushchev does not rule out the occurrence of such wars: 'There have been local wars in the past, and they may occur in the future.'[17]

Whereas the occurrence of local or limited war is portrayed as a probability, the occurrence of *national liberation wars* – the third and final category of Khrushchev's typology – is considered a certainty: 'Such wars are not only possible but inevitable.'[18] This straightforward formulation is another example of the consistent evolution of Khrushchev's thinking since the Twentieth Party Congress.[19] There is still a further clarification. 'These uprisings or national-liberation wars must not be identified with wars among states', Khrushchev went on to say. Examples given include the struggle of the Viet Minh and the Algerian FLN against the 'French colonialists' and Castro's 'uprising against a tyrannical internal regime, backed by American imperialism'.

If the occurrence of national liberation wars is inevitable, outbreaks of local or limited war probable and the likelihood of escalation high (particularly in Europe), how is it at all possible to avoid a world war? The doctrinal prescriptions – ideological and military – are quite clear on that point. Not passively to avoid or evade (*izbezhat'*) war, but actively to avert or prevent (*predotvrashchat'*) it, must be the overriding operational principle: 'The possibility of preventing war (*predotvrashcheniia voiny*) is not a gift from Heaven. Peace cannot be begged for. It can be safeguarded only by an active purposeful struggle.' [20] Khrushchev's report on the communist world conference and the Draft Program of the CPSU enumerate some of its salient features: (1) strengthening of the military and economic potential of the Soviet Union and the socialist camp; (as the Draft Program put it, it is the 'growing superiority of the forces of socialism over the forces of imperialism' that is leading to a 'real possibility of excluding world war from the life of society even before the complete victory of socialism on earth and while capitalism survives in part of the world'); (2) striving for greater unity of action among communists (which is first and foremost an appeal to China not to jeopardize the chances of coordinated policies towards the Western countries, globally and regionally); (3) enlargement of the '"zone of peace", including both socialist and nonsocialist peace-loving states in Europe and Asia'; (4) utilization of 'contradictions' among the imperialist countries; (5) sharpening of the awareness of 'the masses' and political leaders in the capitalist countries as to the consequences of nuclear war; and (6) the use of threats in order to 'sober up' Western political leaders and 'bring them to their senses'.

One line of argument in explaining the relevance of ideology for Soviet behavior in the Berlin crisis could be as follows. The Twentieth Party Congress and its ideological reorientation had ushered in a broad spectrum of rightist policies in the USSR (emphasis on consumer goods, reduction of the armed forces, de-Stalinization, and so on) and strong commitments to détente policies abroad. As Khrushchev wanted to stand by these principles and policies, the pressures on the Western powers in Berlin, and the emphasis on threats and military power, are entirely out of keeping with the general ideological line. This, to conclude the argument, is yet another example of the wide gap between doctrine and practice in Soviet foreign policy.

This reasoning cannot be supported. The creation of anxiety and risk awareness among social and political forces in the West, and the use of military pressures and threats, *were* solidly founded in theory. Evidence for this lies in operational principles (5) and (6) above. It is to be found in the assertions that: 'After all, even the mere understanding of the threat of a destructive war strengthens the determination of the masses to struggle against war' and that: 'Consequently, it is necessary to warn the masses of the very dangerous consequences of a new world war and thereby rouse the righteous wrath of the peoples against those who are preparing this crime.' [21] It is corroborated by the frank admission that: 'We are warning of the threat of war in order to heighten the vigilance and activity of the peoples and to mobilize them for the struggle to prevent world war.' [22] It is supported by the claim that

> The present correlation of forces in the international arena enables the socialist camp and the other peace-loving forces, for the first time in

history, to set themselves the entirely realistic task of forcing the imperialists, under threat of seeing their system destroyed (*prinudit' imperialistov pod ugrozoi gibeli ikh stroia*), to refrain from unleashing a world war.[23]

This evidence of a more general nature is complemented by evidence as it applies to specific policies and regions. In the Middle East, according to Khrushchev, it was Soviet 'intervention', or 'interference' (*vmeshatel'stvo*) in the Suez crisis, notably the Soviet government's 'stern warning to Eden and Guy Mollet [that had] stopped the war'.[24] In 1957 'we stopped an attack on Syria from Turkey, which was being pushed into this reckless act by the US imperialists'.[25] And in 1958, after the Iraqi revolution, when the 'American and British brought up their forces preparing for an attack on Iraq', their plans 'misfired' and they did not dare to carry out their plans 'due to the stern warning given by the Soviet Union'.[26]

Finally, the evidence applies to Central Europe, Germany and Berlin. The argument made for this regional context is that the struggle for peace in Europe and against 'revived West German militarism' is waged by the Soviet Union, the GDR, Poland, Czechoslovakia and the other socialist countries along various lines; that the most important of these is the struggle for a peace treaty; and that this campaign so far has helped in many ways to expose the aggressive circles in the USA, the Federal Republic and in other NATO countries, strengthened the international position of the GDR and revealed that the positions of the three Western allies in Berlin are 'especially vulnerable'.[27] From this, the following conclusion is drawn: '*It is necessary step by step to continue bringing the aggressive imperialist circles to their senses, to compel* [zastavliat'] *them to reckon with the real situation.*'[28]

Economic and Military Dimensions of Peaceful Coexistence and the Berlin Crisis

Yet another variation on the theme of the possibilities of preventing war while at the same time achieving objectives of Soviet foreign policy is the formulation: 'In the conditions where there exists a mighty socialist camp possessing powerful armed forces, the peoples can undoubtedly prevent war *and thereby ensure peaceful coexistence.*'[29] The statement in this form implies an entirely negative content to peaceful coexistence. It is seen as a state of affairs forced upon imperialism and characterized merely by the mutual interest to avoid nuclear war. The Draft Program of the CPSU also stresses competitive rather than cooperative elements of peaceful coexistence. It defines peaceful coexistence as a 'specific form of class struggle' (that is, not the highest form of class struggle) and contains the qualification that the socialist countries, while 'consistently pursuing a policy of peaceful coexistence, are steadily strengthening the positions of the world socialist system in its competition with capitalism'.[30]

Of course all the important documents make reference to the desirability of developing economic and cultural *cooperation*. However, if one compares these references to similar statements of the late 1960s and early

1970s, with their far-reaching doctrinal commitments to broad cooperation between the systems and the wide spectrum of US-Soviet agreements concluded on their basis, the invocation of cooperation as an aspect of peaceful coexistence does appear overly cautious, hortatory and halfhearted.

It is with all these qualifications and clarifications that it is right to say that economic competition is identified as the most important form of class struggle. This theme had been clearly stated as early as the Twenty-First Party Congress, where Khrushchev, in his key address, announced that 'The economy is the main area in which peaceful competition between socialism and capitalism is unfolding' and that the Soviet Union wanted to 'win this competition in an historically short period'.[31] It was also at that congress where the thesis was promulgated that the October Revolution of 1917 was indeed a challenge to capitalism, but that 'it was not a military challenge; it was a challenge of peaceful competition'. The Soviet Union did not want to compete 'in the arms race and the production of atomic and hydrogen bombs, but in the production of manufactured goods, meat, butter, milk, clothing, footwear and other consumer goods'.[32]

Two dimensions are thus distinguished in this new setting of priorities, one international, the other domestic. The first stresses the competitive aspect with capitalism, the United States in particular, and declares the outcome of the struggle on this front as decisive for the ultimate victory of socialism. The second emphasizes the need to make greater progress in the development of the consumer and agricultural sectors of the Soviet economy at the expense of slowing down in relative terms the expansion of heavy industry and military production. Both dimensions are clearly present in the period leading up to the Berlin crisis.

In Khrushchev's report of 6 January 1961 the two dimensions are treated as follows. First, concerning the international aspect:

> Victory of the USSR in *economic competition* with the USA, and victory of the whole socialist system over the capitalist system will be *a major turning point in history* and will exert an even more powerful revolutionizing effect upon the workers' movement of the whole world.[33]

The reason why victory of socialism over capitalism in the economic sphere is seen as of supreme political importance is stated also.

> The faster we advance in economic development, the stronger we will be economically and politically and the greater will be the influence of the socialist camp on the direction and pace of historical development, on the destinies of the world.[34]

At the same time data are furnished to show that the Soviet Union was well on the way to catching up with and surpassing the United States. The average rate of growth in industrial production in 1957–9 was 2·3 percent in the United States, according to Khrushchev; it dropped to 2 percent in 1960; and it was expected to show a negative growth rate of 3·7 percent in 1961 ('according to American sources'). In contrast to that the average rate of growth in industrial production in the USSR was said to have been 10·9 percent on average in 1957–9 and 10 percent in 1960. More and more comparative figures are adduced, culminating in the assertion: '*Economists estimate that in 1965 [at the end of the Seven-Year Plan, 1959–65] the USSR will surpass the USA in volume of production, and approximately by 1970 in per capita output.*'[35] This prediction was to be reiterated time and again,[36] and it found its way into the Draft Program of the CPSU in the following form.

> *In the current decade* (1961–1970) the Soviet Union, creating the material and technical base of communism, will surpass the strongest and richest capitalist country, the USA, in per capita production . . .
> *In the following decade* (1971–1980) the material and technical base of communism will be created and there will be an abundance of material and cultural benefits for the whole population . . . [emphasis in the original].

Turning to the domestic economic and political implications of the general ideological concept, the argument is as follows. 'We have a powerful industry, and our armed forces have the most modern armament. Why should we deny a man what he can receive without harm to the further development of our socialist state?' Although great strides forward were to be made in the period of the Seven-Year Plan in expanding iron and steel production, it was not intended to develop these two industries to the utmost: 'Communism cannot be built only by offering machines and non-ferrous metals.'[37] For these reasons capital investments in agriculture and light industry were to be expanded.

Both the international and the domestic dimensions of the new priorities conceal the potential for sharp contradictions. Thus the Draft Program in essence skirts important issues and obviously seeks to avoid domestic controversy by declaring that 'the chief task of heavy industry is to meet the needs of the country's defense in full *and* [my italics] to satisfy the requirements of man, of Soviet society, better and more fully'. Khrushchev was promising guns and butter, and it remained to be seen whether his promise could be kept.

Even more seriously, the question arises whether it was in fact possible to pursue a policy of threat and pressure, as evident in the renewal of the Berlin ultimatum in June 1961, *and* curtail defense efforts (and meeting the country's defensive needs 'in full'). How realistic was it to think that it would be possible to gain access to Western credits, technology and knowhow, and expand East–West trade, all of which could help in the fulfillment of the ambitious economic goals set forth, while at the same time challenging the West on a vulnerable and important issue in Central Europe?

One must begin to wonder whether these contradictory tactics and mutually exclusive objectives reflect cynicism or naïveté. In the course of the Berlin crisis it would almost inevitably become apparent that something had to give. How and when this happened, whether Khrushchev himself adjusted to necessities emanating from the Berlin crisis, or whether changes of tack were forced upon him by domestic opponents, still needs to be discussed.

Erosion of Soviet Ideology in the GDR?

A good indication of the acute dilemmas facing the GDR in 1961 is given by the two East German authors.

> The sharpness of class struggle on the economic front, intensified psychological warfare and the effects of an open border made ideological work and economic organization difficult, notably in the region of Berlin . . . In many fields the projected plan targets were not fulfilled as a consequence.[38]

The most interesting point of this account is the linking of ideological and economic issues. In fact, this linkage is so close that it appears almost impermissible to separate the two.

Economically, many of the problems started with the ill-conceived extension of Khrushchev's plans for the 'building of communism in the USSR' and 'catching up with and surpassing' the United States to the GDR. To catch up with and surpass the Federal Republic in per capita productivity, production and private consumption was one of the main themes of the Fifth Party Congress of the Socialist Unity Party (SED) in July 1958 and it became the 'main economic task' of the GDR Seven-Year Plan (1959–65) – a plan which was, moreover, closely modeled on the Soviet Seven-Year Plan. Based on considerable economic success of the economy in 1957 and 1958, with growth rates of the net material product of 7 and 12 percent respectively, East German economic planners hoped to achieve the goal of surpassing West Germany in per capita private consumption as early as 1961.[39] Ultimately the consumer was to be a major beneficiary of economic progress. Yet in order to meet the planning targets a substantial rise in productivity was required. This in turn could only be achieved by increases in investments and by raising the work norms, that is, by a 'temporary' economic policy of belt-tightening. The problem of 'ideological work' in the GDR for purely economic reasons thus became an important issue in the origins of the Berlin crisis.[40]

These acute problems must be seen in conjunction with problems of a more fundamental nature, although this means entering a more subjective and speculative realm. They concern the legitimacy of the communist regime in the GDR, the likely degree of identification of the East German population with their state, and the chances for consolidation of the system in the conditions of open borders.

First, there is the persistence of *Nationalbewusstsein* (national consciousness) in the GDR, the awareness of Germany as one nation divided into two parts. Given the fact that the eastern part was internationally isolated except within the Soviet bloc, containing only the smaller portion of resources and population and enjoying lesser prosperity than the western part, the West German claim of *Alleinvertretung* (sole representation) always constituted an external threat to the national legitimacy of the communist regime. This threat had important implications for the Soviet Union because its twenty divisions stationed in the GDR continued to be seen as the main pillar maintaining the division of Germany. In these conditions any assertion of nationalism could not fail to be directed against the Soviet Union. Although the

Draft Program of the CPSU does not deal specifically with the danger of *German* nationalism, it does address itself in general to the phenomenon of nationalism in the *world system of socialism*, calling it the 'basic political and ideological weapon used by international reaction and the remnants of the domestic reactionary forces against the unity of the socialist countries'. It then goes on to say:

> Nationalism is detrimental to the common interests of the socialist commonwealth, and above all it harms the people of the country in which it appears, since alienation from the socialist camp retards the country's development, deprives it of the possibility of making use of the advantages of the socialist system and encourages attempts by imperialist powers to utilize nationalist tendencies for their own purposes.[41]

As this negative verdict implied, the 'imperialist powers' might attempt to 'utilize nationalist tendencies' also in Germany. In a crisis it could potentially be an explosive force. Khrushchev seemed to have been precisely under this impression as he felt it expedient, in his radio and television broadcast on 7 August 1961, to assuage in advance a possible anti-Russian and anti-Soviet eruption of German nationalism by saying 'The Soviet Union well understands how dear the cause of Germany's national unity is to the German people', adding, however, that unity could only be achieved by the Germans themselves.[42]

Secondly, the persistence of *Nationalbewusstsein* and the rival claim to national legitimacy by West Germany had found an equivalent in the inadequately developed *Staatsbewusstsein* (literally, 'state consciousness') of citizens in the GDR. On the surface this seems to be contradicted by the relative loyalty shown by the East German armed forces, police and factory militia. The Ulbricht regime, on the other hand, had avoided for more than a decade the introduction of obligatory military service – a deficiency that was quickly corrected almost immediately after the building of the wall. Prior to that, many young people, when pressed to join the armed forces of the GDR, had simply made their way to the West.

The two East German authors therefore frankly admit in retrospect that the open borders and economic measures taken in the West, apart from inflicting economic damage on the GDR, had greatly 'impaired the consciousness (*Bewusstsein*) of many citizens'.[43] There was good reason to believe that steady economic progress and the mere passage of time would ultimately lead to greater cooperation and adjustment to the reality of a separate East German state, as it had in West Germany. But in 1960 and 1961, as will be shown, there were severe economic setbacks, and the identification of the population with the GDR suffered as a consequence.

The third and perhaps the greatest problem from the point of view of the Soviet and East German leaderships was the inadequately developed *sozialistische Bewusstsein* – identification with and acceptance of the ideological belief system in the GDR. Even those people who were quite willing to serve the community in various functions, as scientists, medical doctors, engineers, managers, and so on, often could not be relied upon to be ideological supporters of the Soviet-type system. In fact attitudes among the technical and nontechnical intelligentsia outside the SED were such that the achievements made by the GDR in various fields were attributed quite frequently to 'German national characteristics', such as organizing abilities and hard work, rather than to efforts by the party. This was frequently expressed in the comment that progress was made in East Germany in spite of the socio-economic and political system, not because of it.

There are, of course, many reasons for the lack of *sozialistisches Bewusstsein*. Some of the more important ones include memories of the punitive character of Soviet behavior in the last phases of the war and the early post-war period (as mentioned in the discussion of the Berlin crisis of 1948); resentment against the repressive features of the system itself; the existence of family ties and the establishment of new contacts, which were cutting across the ideological divisions; and access to information via.private letter exchanges, visits (notably in Berlin) and reception of radio and television broadcasts from West Germany and West Berlin – all of which were quite unimpaired by linguistic barriers.

In the light of these three factors the SED did indeed face irreconcileable dilemmas in its 'ideological work'. Openness to broader forces of society, democratization and liberalization, as one option, would have encouraged the *Geist des Sozialdemokratismus* (spirit or ghost of Social Democracy) among the lower echelons of the party and the population at large – a ghost that was hoped to have been exorcised successfully in 1946 with the forced merger of the Communist Party (KPD) and Social Democratic Party (SPD), but which, even in more favorable conditions twenty years later, in 1966, at the occasion of an abortive speakers' exchange between leaders of the SED and the West German SPD, was to reappear unexpectedly in a most threatening posture. 'Administrative measures' to help along the ill-developed *sozialistische Bewusstsein* and eradicate national aspirations, as a second option, would have provided new stimuli to the by 1961 typical evasion of pressure – migration to the West. It was not advisable to take this course of action. Sealing of the borders was a third option, but its adoption could produce serious domestic and international 'complications', including the risk of popular revolt and international armed conflict. Any decision as to which one of these options was to be chosen depended to a large extent on the Soviet Union and its perception of interests in Germany.

II SECURITY AND STATE INTERESTS

As a starting point for this discussion, it is appropriate to refer again to the Draft Program of the CPSU. The part dealing with 'The World System of Socialism' claims that

> The experience of the peoples of the world socialist commonwealth has confirmed that their fraternal *unity and cooperation* [italics in original] conform to the *supreme national interests [vysshie natsional'nye interesy]* of each country. The strengthening of the unity of the world socialist system on the basis of proletarian internationalism is an *absolute requirement [nepremennoe uslovie]* for the further successes of all the states belonging to it.

The socialist system must overcome certain difficulties arising mainly from the fact that in the past most of the countries of this system had a medium or even a low level of economic development, and also from the fact that *world reaction is doing its utmost to impede the building of socialism.*[44]

These formulations read as if they were tailor-made for the Berlin crisis – and well they might have been. Cohesion of the socialist commonwealth as a 'supreme national interest' and an 'absolute requirement' for the further progress of each member country, yet the existence of 'certain difficulties', such as different levels of economic development and efforts by 'world reaction' (presumably the capitalist countries) to 'impede the building of socialism', can be described as a pattern into which the Soviet Union was weaving the main strands of the Berlin crisis. Success or failure of the Soviet and East German Seven-Year Plans with their ambitious economic goals depended crucially on whether or not it would be possible to 'overcome certain difficulties' manifesting themselves so acutely in 1961 in the GDR and in Soviet-East German economic relations.

The Importance of the GDR for the Soviet Economy

In the course of the 1950s the GDR and the Soviet Union had established a complementary economic relationship, whose main feature was (and still is) GDR dependence on Soviet raw materials, energy and semifinished products on the one hand, and Soviet reliance on GDR high-technology products and equipment, such as machine-building tools, chemical products, optical instruments and electrical appliances on the other. The importance of the GDR for the national economy of the USSR is demonstrated by the fact that an impressive 34·5 percent of Soviet total imports of machinery and equipment in 1960 originated in the GDR.[45] It is of course true that the share of foreign trade in the GNP of the Soviet Union, as of the United States, is quite marginal generally, estimated at less than 4 percent. But to draw from this the conclusion that foreign trade, and particularly the importation of industrial machinery and equipment in the case of the USSR, is relatively unimportant for the economy is similar to saying that a bobbin is only a small part of a sewing machine and, consequently, is 'relatively unimportant'.

By late spring and early summer 1961 severe strains were making themselves felt in the Soviet-East German special economic relationship. This is shown among other things by the development of trade imbalances from 1960 to 1961. While Soviet exports to East Germany *rose* from US$1,051·7 million in 1960 to US$1,209·1 million in 1961, Soviet imports from East Germany *fell* from US$929·3 million to US$875·9 million in the same period. Also in the same period the share of GDR machinery and equipment in total Soviet imports of these products fell from the 34·5 percent mentioned above to 28·4 percent.[46]

Even in retrospect it is difficult to measure precisely the degree to which these imbalances were caused by the lagging performance of the East German economy. Yet it is appropriate to interpret them against the background of general economic malaise in the GDR, evident above all in the consistent decline of growth rates of the social product (*Gesellschaftliches Gesamtprodukt*): from 12 percent (1958) to 11 percent (1959), to 6 percent (1960) and, finally, to 4 percent (1961).[47] These low figures, needless to say, contrasted sharply with the targets of 9 to 10 percent average annual growth (11 percent industrial growth) as provided for in the East German Seven-Year Plan.[48] Also these developments could hardly have been interpreted by the Soviet political leadership and economic planners as a unique or short-term phenomenon. They had deeper roots in the GDR economy threatening to disrupt Soviet-East German economic relations for a long time to come.

The Acute Economic Crisis in the GDR

By the late spring of 1961 several factors had converged to contribute to a general economic crisis in East Germany. First, as a factor of cardinal importance, there was an increasing *shortage of skilled labor*, due primarily to the westward migration of people from the Soviet Zone and the GDR (the 'refugee problem'). According to official West German statistics,[49] in the period from the end of World War II to 1961 a total of 3·8 million people had migrated to West Germany, but only 565,000 had migrated east from West Germany. This constitutes a net loss of 3·25 million inhabitants for the GDR. Expressed differently, and taking a narrower period of account, in the years from 1949–61 the population of the GDR had decreased from slightly more than 19 million to little more than 17 million inhabitants. The net loss of 2 million people in this period represented not only more than 10 percent of the population – an enormous figure by any standard – but constituted also a loss of 15 percent of the working population. Moreover an American economist who divided the last category into three groups estimated that at least one-quarter of the most highly qualified group had migrated to the West in the period from 1949–61.[50] Apart from that, the official West German statistics also show a disproportionally high share of young people who had migrated from East Germany.

Concerning the primary motivations of this extensive westward migration, it has been argued convincingly that they were economic and material, and only to a lesser degree ideological and political; that it is appropriate for this reason – as I have done – to speak of a problem of population migration, rather than of a refugee problem; that even on the basis of a close look at official West German statistics, as compiled in *Die Flucht aus der Sowjetzone*, the percentage of people who left the GDR for economic and material reasons would seem to be closer to 60 percent than, as stated in the government publication, 15 percent; and that on the basis of independent analyses it is more realistic to raise this figure to about 75 percent.[51]

In the light of the overall trends a critical point could be expected to occur where the loss of a single engineer, a highly skilled mechanic or a foreman in the construction industry would produce extremely serious disruptions of the whole complex production process as qualified replacements simply ceased to be available. A mere stagnation of trends in westward migration would then be inadequate to avert economic disintegration. In the past there had been fluctuations. In 1953, the year of the June workers' rising, more than 330,000 persons had left the GDR – the highest annual figure at any time in the period of the state's existence. After a decline in 1954 and 1955 the numbers rose to about 279,000 in 1956. They then fell again to approximately 144,000 in 1959. But despite the by then lower basic figure of the population, the number of migrants increased in 1960 to nearly 200,000 people. In the last months of 1960 and first six months of 1961 the monthly rates rose to between 20,000 and 30,000 persons. Undoubtedly, the critical point had been reached.

A second major factor contributing to the acute economic crisis in the GDR concerns *problems of investment and scarcity of capital reserves*. As these problems were setting narrow parameters to any program of catching up with and surpassing West Germany, it is appropriate to probe more deeply here. This requires an examination of the probable causes of the significant disparity in economic development and standard of living between East and West Germany and the political and (not so) academic controversies surrounding the issue.

Taking into account disproportionally higher wartime destruction in East Germany than in West Germany, greater dismantling of equipment by the occupying power, reparations extracted from current production, greater losses due to unequal trade, monetary transfers, loss of population, and 'indirect' or 'relative' losses incurred because East Germany, unlike West Germany, had not received aid under the Marshall Plan and other aid programs, Hans Apel estimates the total relative loss of capital suffered by East Germany as compared to West Germany in the period from 1945–61 to be 107·2 billion marks.[52] However, Apel strongly emphasizes that in calculating the loss to the East German economy the period from 1945–50, as compared to the period from 1951–61, 'is by far the more significant, because it prevented the formation of a sound foundation of capital'. The average annual burden to the East German economy was '9 billion marks in the early period, but only 6 billion marks thereafter'; in relation to national income, 'the losses of the first five post-war years weighed three times more heavily than in the following decade'.[53]

It would therefore be intellectually dishonest to use some of these figures, put them into a different time scale, and neglect the political implications. But this is precisely what happens in Vysotskii's treatment where, in reference to Apel's analysis, it is stated that a loss of 83·3 billion marks was 'sustained by the GDR *from the day it was founded to the day when the borders with West Berlin were taken under control*'.[54] Apel's two periods of accounting (1945–50 and 1951–61) are thus dissolved, and a new period (1949–61) is introduced which conveniently deletes the effects of Soviet occupation policy. Whereas Apel stressed the significance of relative damages incurred directly by East Germany due to the dismantling of industrial equipment, reparations and unequal trade, and indirectly due to aid received by West Germany in the early postwar period, Vysotskii (and other Soviet and East German sources) inaccurately convey the impression that Apel's figures are the net result of 'exchange machinations', 'various kinds of speculation', 'black market activities', 'economic espionage' and 'various indirect forms of economic warfare such as the blocking of deliveries, sabotage, economic boycott, creation of additional difficulties in its foreign trade and so forth'.[55]

There is, moreover, one important paragraph which addresses itself squarely to the origins of Warsaw Pact measures in the summer of 1961. But this paragraph has been deleted from the English 'translation' of Vysotskii's book. The Russian version reads:

> The damage incurred by the German Democratic Republic in this period of the existence of open borders with West Berlin strongly impeded the development of the GDR. If the GDR had not sustained such great losses, its rates of economic development, in the opinion of Professor Apel, might have been by far higher than those of the FRG. [56]

The deletion of this paragraph in the revised, English version appears to reflect (1) the reluctance to reveal explicitly that growth rates in West Germany had in fact surpassed those of East Germany and that the whole idea of 'catching up with and surpassing' the former country was a questionable objective from the very start of the Seven-Year Plan; (2) an attempt to shift attention away from economic to military-political justifications for taking 'countermeasures', as evident, for instance, in Vysotskii's assertion that 'After the unsuccessful provocations of 1953 and 1956, the FRG concentrated on preparing a counterrevolutionary putsch coupled with direct invasion of the GDR by the Bundeswehr'. [57]

But to complete the argument, no matter what the precise figures, the fact remained that the GDR was still suffering from an enormous shortage of capital even at the end of the 1950s. The Seven-Year Plan, therefore, set out to create *new* capacities and to create them *rapidly*. (This is shown by, among other things, the enormous size of the projected increases in investment for the seven-year planning period, namely 142 billion marks; [58] to allow comparison, the net material product of the GDR in 1961 was 141 billion marks.) From an economic point of view it was therefore almost logical that the plan put the emphasis on expansion of *heavy industry* – despite the consumer-oriented rhetoric accompanying the launching of the plan in 1958–9. It was perhaps equally predictable that the party leadership would have to act as it did, to demand greater efforts of the working population, decree increases in work norms, tighten labor discipline and enforce cutbacks in private consumption.

The third major factor contributing to the general and acute economic crisis in the GDR in 1961 is connected with a second, final wave of *collectivization in agriculture* and a severe decline in growth rates of agricultural production. At the end of 1958 as much as two-thirds of the total agricultural area was still in private hands. The pace of collectivization had remained slow. In fact if the conversion rates of 1953–59 had been maintained, the process of collectivization could have lasted up to seventy years. [59] In 1959, however, the SED leadership decided to make greater efforts in 'socialist construction in the countryside'. Pressure on private farmers to join collectives of various types increased, still somewhat gradually in 1959, with 300,000 enterprises joining collectives, but taking on explosive proportions in the first four months of 1960 when another 300,000 units were affected. [60] The result was that, in a comparatively short period of time, private agricultural production virtually ceased to exist in the GDR.

It is difficult to assess the precise repercussions of collectivization on the volume of agricultural production in the years 1959–61. During these years bad harvests due to unfavorable weather conditions also plagued West Germany. (In contrast to the GDR, however, the Federal Republic could easily maintain supplies by increased imports of agricultural products. The GDR did not have the necessary hard currency reserves to buy on capitalist markets, and no emergency aid from COMECON countries was forthcoming.) Also the problem of capital and labor shortages again played a significant role which is difficult to measure in relation to the effects of collectivization. Although the negative effects of collectivization on agricultural production in the GDR are denied in a study for the Institute for Social Sciences at the CC of the SED, the study also states that

> those cases, where production fell temporarily, can be attributed for the most part to conditions where some farmers had reduced their livestock before joining the LPG [agricultural collective], had not brought in their seeds or had badly organized collective work. In some cases collective democracy could develop only with difficulty because of deficiencies in leadership, because qualified cadres were not available everywhere, and because some organs of Party and state gave unsatisfactory support to the new LPGs.[61]

In other words, there were plenty of problems.

Inadequate labor supply, shortages of capital in industry and agriculture, high growth rages for heavy industry at the expense of consumption, collectivization, and bad harvests – all of these factors interacted forcefully, reducing supplies to the population of necessary foodstuffs, swelling the stream of people moving west, exacerbating the labor shortages still further and completing a vicious circle which, somehow, had to be broken.[62]

There is, conceivably, yet another factor which contributed to the acute economic crisis in the GDR in 1961 – interruption of intra-German trade flows by West Germany. Vysotskii broadly refers to this problem when he speaks of the 'creation of additional difficulties for its [the GDR's] foreign trade'.[63] An authoritative article in *Voprosy istorii* on the Berlin crisis is more specific: 'In 1960, the FRG [Federal Republic of Germany] in its attempt to "force on its knees" the German workers' state, invalidated the trade agreement with the GDR which had been in existence since 1951.'[64]

On the one hand it is correct that intra-German trade was both important and advantageous to the GDR, important because in 1961 it accounted for 11 percent of its total foreign trade (as against only 2 percent of West Germany's foreign trade)[65] and because, as the two East German authors Keiderling and Stulz put it – 'continuity of production of many enterprises depended on West German deliveries of steel, special steels, chemical products and machine-building equipment'.[66] Intra-German trade was also advantageous because it was (and is) cleared on the basis of a one-to-one exchange rate of East German for German marks and because the GDR could, within certain limits, draw on interest-free credits to finance imports. Given these facts it was indeed possible that negative economic repercussions could have resulted from a decision adopted at the Eleventh Plenum of the CC of the SED (December 1960) launching a program of *Störfreimachung* (that is, 'safeguarding the planned economy of the GDR against interfering measures', 'to safeguard it once and for all'),[67] because it implied a further orientation of trade flows and costly investments to supplant deliveries from West Germany.

But this would have been a self-inflicted injury. West Germany had reconsidered its decision, and an intrazonal trade agreement was duly concluded at the end of December 1960. As a result, despite the building of the Wall and the East German program of *Störfreimachung*, intra-German trade was only marginally less in 1961 (872·9 million units of account) than 1960 (959·5 million units of account).[68]

Acknowledgment of a Critical Situation

The economic crisis in the GDR, which ultimately led to the complete abandonment of the Seven-Year Plan (in early 1962), found its expression in actions and statements of the SED leadership. At the Twelfth Plenum of the CC of the SED in March 1961, the chairman of the state planning committee, Bruno Leuschner, no longer stressed the theme of 'catching up with and surpassing' West Germany but merely demanded 'hard and concentrated work'.[69] The idea of introducing a five-day week, as put forward by workers in May and June 1961 at electoral meetings of the labor unions (FDGB), was rudely dismissed. The East German newspaper *Tribüne* of 2 June 1961 explained in this context that 'Of course, needs grow faster than possibilities for their satisfaction' and that it was difficult to meet demands for a five-day week because of 'bad discipline at work and *Republikflucht*'.

Finally, Politburo member Erich Honecker reported to the Thirteenth Plenum of the CC of the SED (3−4 July 1961) that the goals of the Seven-Year Plan were in the process of revision.

> The refusal by the West German government soberly to consider the proposals for the conclusion of a peace treaty, as well as the announcement [by that government] to respond to the conclusion of a peace treaty with increasing interference in trade relations with the German Democratic Republic and other socialist countries, makes it necessary at present to adopt several measures in the economic sphere which were not provided for in the Seven-Year Plan.[70]

Having thus put the blame for plan revisions on the West German government and its refusal to cooperate in the solution of problems, Honecker proceeded to elaborate on the nature of economic problems, deploring the fact that 'difficulties still exist in some sectors of the economy'; 'certain raw materials are still lacking'; 'not in all the fields yet has industry reached the required technical level'; there were still 'gaps in supplies to the population'; and it was impossible 'at all times rapidly to increase production of consumer goods without creating, at the same time, the necessary material basis'.[71]

This public acknowledgment of severe problems, an unusual step in any one-party state, and the allocation of blame to external influences apparently had several purposes. It helped to legitimize the sealing of the borders, before and after the fact, in the face of the population of the GDR. More important, if the Soviet leadership had not yet made up its mind whether or not to take drastic measures, the GDR's open complaints served to bring pressure to bear on the USSR for a speedy decision; after all, its interests were most affected next to East Germany's.

Implications for Soviet Security

In the discussion of Soviet security interests in the Berlin crisis of 1948 it was argued that the prospects for maintaining the division of Germany for long appeared to be quite slim – a conviction that must have impressed itself even more strongly on the minds of Soviet leaders in 1949 as the policy of finger- and fist-shaking conducted by the SMA had proven ineffective. Indeed, the *Zeitgeist* in the late 1940s blew strongly against the theme of 'beyond the nation state' (vigorously, as noted, also in the USSR in the form of Great Russian chauvinism), and to no detached observer would it have appeared a spent force in Germany.

It is quite possible that the note sent by Stalin to the three Western powers on 10 March 1952 proposing the reestablishment of German unity reflected the continuing Soviet sense of unease with the unsolved German problem and apprehensions about the security threat implicit in a resurgence of German nationalism. Stalin's successors seemed to have shared such apprehensions. This is shown by the instructions issued by the Soviet High Commissioner in Germany, Semenov, to the SED at the beginning of June 1953 to work out (within a week!) detailed plans for the extension of Beria's and Malenkov's 'new course' to the GDR;[72] the demand to submit lists for the formation of a new Central Committee, Secretariat and Politburo;[73] and the charges later made by Ulbricht, the prime target of the Soviet demand for personnel changes, and Khrushchev that Beria had conducted a 'capitulationist policy' which would have led to the 'restoration of capitalism' in the GDR.[74]

Whether or not the introduction of the new course in the GDR would have led to the restoration of capitalism is entirely conjectural. Reform of East German politics and society along the lines demanded by Semenov would, however, have made it easier to construct a security system in Europe *not* requiring large Soviet military forces to enforce the division of Germany. This possible reasoning behind the Soviet proposals was hinted at even by the (unreformed) Politburo of the SED. By way of an explanation of policy changes adopted on 9 June 1953, it stated that one of the purposes underlying them was to facilitate the 'establishment of German unity' and the 'rapprochement of the two parts of Germany'.[75]

The workers' rising of 17 June 1953, however, marks a turning point in the Soviet Union's German policy. Beria's and Malenkov's plans for a thorough purge of the SED and 'liberalization' of the GDR were apparently blamed for conveying Soviet weakness and encouraging popular revolt in East Germany. From this point onward the Soviet Union based its policies on a concept envisaging the long-term existence of two German states.

It would be interesting to know what it was that gave Stalin's successors the confidence to think that this concept was viable. A belief in the effectiveness of the Soviet Union's growing arsenal of nuclear weapons to discourage any military challenge of the Soviet position in Europe may have been at the root of it. This may have been combined with a feeling that time was working for the consolidation of East Germany as a separate state and reinforced by the realization, after June 1953, that a crisis situation of potentially disastrous consequences for the fate of the SED and the Soviet position in the GDR had turned out to have been relatively easily manageable.

If, in this way, the Soviet leaders had been responding to opportunities and hopes, they also had to react to challenges and potential threats. The 1950s saw an ever closer cooperation between the United States and Western Europe, as well as increasing trends of Western European integration, which were ultimately to culminate in the formation of the EEC. The firm course steered by Chancellor Adenauer with regard to the strengthening of the Western alliance (and the corresponding 'policy of strength' adopted towards the Soviet Union) banished any idea of 'neutralization' or 'third road' for a reunited Germany (within the 1937 borders as was still the official West German position) from the practical realm of politics. Under the circumstances the Soviet Union could not but react with firm commitments and guarantees to the viability of a socialist East Germany as a full member of the Soviet bloc.

The dangers were amplified in 1960 and 1961. The EEC was making an important, positive impact on economic growth of its member countries (or so it seemed to observers) and, by implication, was enhancing the power potential of NATO's European arm. Precisely at the same time the Soviet Union and the westernmost area of the bloc were experiencing a weakening of their current and, thereby, future military potential, not least because of the open borders in Berlin. All this, in conjunction with the dissipation of the 'missile gap' myth (which will be discussed presently), could have inspired new confidence for the Western 'policy of strength', and set back the Soviet hopes for international recognition of the GDR and ultimate vindication of the 'two states' concept.

Finally, the Soviet leaders' firm commitments to the viability of the GDR as a full member of the socialist community had found their counterpart in Ulbricht's strong invocation of the 'special relationship GDR–USSR' and his determination not to waver in the 'construction of socialism' in the GDR, with additional proof provided by forced collectivization. In these conditions it was evident that a Soviet refusal to uphold often proclaimed principles of intra-bloc relations, such as 'proletarian' or 'socialist internationalism' and 'fraternal assistance', would have seriously undermined confidence among other party leaderships, and encouraged dangerous misconceptions among the population of other member countries in the Warsaw Pact. All this must have weighed heavily in Soviet calculations.

III MILITARY POWER

The main research problems of this section are concerned with Soviet capabilities in 1961, the degree to which military disparities existed between the superpowers and how they might have influenced Soviet behavior. The employment of implicit or explicit threats and the sequence of military actions and counteractions in various stages of the crisis will have to be examined and attempts will have to be made to distinguish military measures which are connected with *political* objectives of crisis bargaining and the manipulation of risk, measures which may be related to long-term *military* requirements with a view to future employment of military power for deterrence and defense, and measures which may be the result of *domestic* pressures exerted, for instance, by the Soviet military or hard-liners in the top political leadership.

As these are complex questions, many of which perhaps cannot be answered with full confidence, it is necessary to go beyond the general political background provided in the second chapter and add more information concerning the specific aspect of military measures (verbal and nonverbal) taken by the Soviet Union.

Measures prior to and during the Most Acute Phase of the Crisis

It may be appropriate to begin this enumeration of measures with the large-scale maneuvers of Soviet and GDR troops conducted on East German territory in June, after the Vienna Summit, in the presence of the Soviet Defense Minister, Marshal Malinovsky, and the commander-in-chief of the Warsaw Pact armed forces, Marshal Grechko.[76] Next, a carefully stage-managed demonstration of Soviet military preparedness and national unity was given on 21 June, on the twentieth anniversary of Nazi Germany's invasion of Soviet Russia: Khrushchev appeared at the Great Kremlin Palace wearing the uniform of lieutenant general – the rank he had held as political adviser on the Stalingrad front. Directly behind the speaker's rostrum were lined up the military and political leaders (in that order) of the Soviet Union.

The speeches which were delivered – by Khrushchev, Malinovsky, Marshal Chuikov (commander-in-chief of the Soviet ground forces), General Krylov (commander of troops of the Moscow Military District), and Major General Saburov (a former commander of a partisan unit in the Ukraine) – added up to one single major line of argument: the Soviet armed forces had utterly defeated German aggression and militarism in World War II; but today German revanchism and militarism again was rampant, West Berlin was being used to increase tension, and the ruling circles of the Western powers showed tendencies to enter upon a dangerous path – 'they would like to make the German question the object of a test of strength' (Khrushchev's speech); however, nothing could deflect the Soviet Union from its stated goal of signing a separate peace treaty with the GDR by the end of the year should the Western powers refuse to consider the Soviet proposals in a more sober frame of mind.[77]

Beyond that Khrushchev hinted at three measures, all of which were to be endorsed only little more than two weeks later. The first two concerned future increases in the Soviet defense budget and the numerical strength of the Soviet armed forces. To quote directly from the 21 June speech, Khrushchev said that increased military expenditures and expansion of armed forces in Western countries

may confront the Soviet Union with the necessity of increasing allocations for armaments, too, in order to strengthen and improve our
defenses and, if necessary, also increasing the numerical strength of
our armed forces in order, on the basis of our might, to ensure peace
and peaceful coexistence.[78]

A third measure foreshadowed in the same speech was the warning that:
'The moment the USA resumes nuclear explosions, the Soviet Union will
immediately begin testing its nuclear weapons.'[79]

Endorsement of the first two measures was expressed on 8 July by Khrushchev in his speech to graduates of the military academies of the Soviet armed
forces. Pointing to 'such facts as the building up of armed forces in the
Western countries', notably in the United States, 'steps to increase considerably the number of strategic bombers, which are constantly kept in the air',
'stepping up the program of developing rocket-missile strategic weapons',
and the proposal to increase military expenditures by more than US$3·5
billion so that total United States 'military expenditures in fiscal year
1961−2 will exceed US$53 billion' (as contained in Kennedy's messages to
Congress of 28 March and 25 May), Khrushchev drew the following conclusion.

> Taking into account the existing situation, the Soviet government has
> been forced to instruct the Ministry of Defense to suspend temporarily,
> pending special orders, the reduction of armed forces planned for
> 1961. In view of the growing military budgets in the NATO countries,
> the Soviet government has taken a decision to increase defense expend-
> itures in the current year by 3,144 million [new] rubles, thereby increas-
> ing the total military expenditures in 1961 to 12,399 million rubles.[80]

Both measures – the suspension of the troop reduction program and the
announcement of a significant increase in defense expenditures by about
one-third – constituted dramatic reversals of the commitments and priorities
of the latter half of the 1950s, and they contradicted the program of further
reductions in manpower and defense expenditures as announced at the
beginning of 1961.

On 9 July a big military air show was held at Tushino, where the latest
Soviet achievements in tactical and strategic aircraft were displayed, the
significant point being that such demonstrations had not been held for four
years.[81] On the same day, an article signed by Air Marshal Vershinin
appeared in *Pravda* drawing attention to the equipment of Soviet aircraft
with missiles of all types. On 27 July *Izvestiia* turned to naval armaments and
declared that the USSR now possessed a 'sufficient quantity' of nuclear-
powered submarines armed with powerful missiles of all types and traveling
at speeds 'exceeding those of American submarines'. On the same day,
Khrushchev boasted to McCloy (the chief American negotiator at the
Geneva disarmament talks) that the Soviet Union had the ability to build
and deliver by missile on United States territory a 100-megaton superbomb.[82]

Also on the same day (27 July), in the already-mentioned interview with
McCloy, Khrushchev had reacted strongly to Kennedy's speech of 25 July,
which among other things had contained the request for additional defense

appropriations and the proposal to increase United States military capabilities, particularly in the conventional sphere. Presumably in reference to these measures, Khrushchev claimed in his radio and television address of 7 August that the United States was 'in effect carrying out mobilization measures and threatening to unleash war'; he mentioned also – correctly – that Britain and France were 'going to transfer additional forces to West Germany'. This was the context into which Khrushchev put his warning about Soviet countermeasures (*otvetnye mery*).

> As you already know, the Soviet government has decided to increase expenditures on the country's defense and to discontinue the reduction of our armed forces which, until now, we had been carrying out unilaterally [see Khrushchev's speech of 8 July, quoted above]. In short, the necessary measures are being taken to make the defensive might of the Soviet Union still greater and more reliable. We shall keep an eye on the further course of events and act as the situation warrants. [Now, the key sentences:] *We may later have to increase the numerical strength of the army on the western frontiers* with divisions that will be transferred from other areas of the Soviet Union. In this connection *we may perhaps be forced to call up part of the reserves* so that our divisions are at full strength and prepared for any contingencies.[83]

Khrushchev's announcement clearly implied that after the trend of troop reductions in progress in the USSR since 1955 had first been *arrested*, it was now being considered to *increase* total Soviet troop strength (by the call-up of reserves).[84] Moreover, Khrushchev left open the option to announce further increases in defense expenditures because it was allegedly only the 'tentative view of the Central Committee and the government that this should not be done'.[85] As to the announced possibility of a later increase in the 'numerical strength of the army on the western frontiers [of the USSR] with divisions that will be transferred from other areas of the Soviet Union', no information is available to this writer as to whether this ultimately took place. However, according to one report, additional Soviet units seem to have been transferred to and deployed in *Eastern Europe*, in Poland, in the spring of 1961.[86]

On 6–7 August *Vostok-2* was in orbit, and this event – as noted – was skillfully exploited by Khrushchev when he linked claims of Soviet preeminence in the space race with claims of preeminence in rocket development, the capacity to develop and deliver a 100-megaton nuclear weapon and the necessity of concluding a peace treaty.[87]

On 10 August information was made available to Western press representatives in Moscow that Marshal Konev had been appointed commander-in-chief of the Group of Soviet Forces in Germany (GSFG); in addition, it was thought that he had been given operational command of the GDR armed forces and units of the CSSR and Polish armed forces as well.[88] Finally, in the week before the closing of the border, and during the building of the Berlin Wall on and immediately after 13 August, there was a substantial increase in military movements and readiness measures of GDR and Soviet units in East Germany.

Measures after the Most Acute Phase of the Crisis

The renewal, or continuation, of Soviet pressures on Berlin was evident in the Soviet note of 23 August to the United States charging 'flagrant breaches' of agreements on air access to Berlin.[89] This was followed by a series of measures, warnings and announcements which came in rapid succession at the end of August and beginning of September.

On 28 August Radio Moscow broadcast a statement by TASS noting that foreign submarines had recently committed 'a number of violations of the state seacoast of the Soviet Union'; the submarines had been 'making observations for intelligence purposes' and in view of this, the Soviet government had instructed the Defense Ministry 'to take measures to destroy the violators'.[90]

On the next day (29 August), the Central Committee of the CPSU and the Soviet government made a dramatic announcement. The Soviet Defense Ministry had been instructed

> to issue orders on the temporary deferment, until the conclusion of a peace treaty with Germany, of the transfer to the reserve of the necessary numbers of soldiers, sailors, sergeant majors, and non-commissioned officers, whose term of service expires in 1961.[91]

Put more simply, an unspecified number of servicemen (draftees born in 1940 and due for release in 1961) were to be retained in service. This represented one step forward in the direction of increasing rather than decreasing the total strength of the Soviet armed forces which Khrushchev had said to be under consideration before the building of the Wall.

Moreover on 30 August the Soviet government announced its decision to resume testing of nuclear weapons,[92] despite the fact that Khrushchev had stated on several occasions that to break a moratorium the country first would take upon itself an enormous moral and political responsibility and expose itself in the eyes of all nations.[93] This decision was taken also despite expressly stated assurances by the Soviet government that the USSR 'has decided not to resume nuclear explosions in the Soviet Union if the Western powers do not resume the testing of atomic and hydrogen weapons' and that the Soviet government would be 'freed from this self-imposed undertaking' only if the West resumed testing first.[94] To add to the embarrassment, the beginning of the test series coincided with the opening of the conference of nonaligned countries in Belgrade.

The tests themselves followed each other in rapid succession: the first explosion occurred on 1 September, the next ones on 4, 5 and 6 September; all of them were in the low- to intermediate-kiloton range. The first nuclear explosion in the megaton range occurred on 10 September. In all, the Soviet Union carried out twenty-two nuclear tests between 1 September and 22 October 1961. (During the whole of the period from 1949, when the first Soviet atomic bomb was exploded, to March 1958, when the USSR had halted nuclear tests, the number of such explosions had been no more than about sixty.)[95] All this appeared to be consistent with the Soviet government's announcement of 30 August that 'The Soviet Union has worked out plans for developing a series of nuclear bombs of higher yield – 20, 30, 50 and 100 megatons' and of deploying 'powerful rockets capable of lifting these nuclear bombs and delivering them to any point on the globe'.[96]

The same issue of *Pravda* which carried the Soviet government's announcement concerning the resumption of nuclear testing also contained a warning that maneuvers would be held jointly by the Soviet northern fleet, rocket troops and units of the Soviet air force in the Barents and Kara Seas. These areas were declared dangerous to shipping and aircraft between 10 September and 15 November.

Marshal Malinovsky, writing in *Pravda* on 14 September, justified the many recent efforts made by the USSR to strengthen its defense potential – including the resumption of nuclear testing – and appeared to justify future efforts by pointing to the exigencies of international politics and the military measures taken in the West.[97] In fact Malinovsky's article must probably be regarded as a preface of sorts to the decree by the Soviet Defense Ministry, dated 14 September and published one day later, announcing that the contingent of draftees born in 1942 was to be called up for military service and that *all* releases from active service were cancelled until further notice.[98] Thus the troop reduction program as outlined in January 1960 had undergone a complete reversal in three successive stages: the reductions planned for 1961 were first suspended (8 July); next, the contingent of draftees born in 1940 was retained in service (29 August); finally, those born in 1942 were drafted in the normal way (14 September).

Concerning claims of missile capabilities and developments in missile technology, the Deputy Minister of Defense and commander-in-chief of the rocket troops, Marshal Moskalenko, stated in an article in *Krasnaia zvezda* on 13 September that the Soviet Union now possessed rockets with an explosive force of several megatons, each of which could not be intercepted or deflected from their target by any defensive means now existing. These statements were evidently related not only to the ongoing series of nuclear tests in the USSR but also to the announcement by TASS of 10 September that missile tests would be held over the central Pacific area in the period from 13 September to 15 October.[99] The first in a series of reports on ICBM test flights was carried by *Pravda* on 15 September, which stated that a multistage missile had been successfully launched over a distance of more than 12,000 kilometers in the central Pacific. Yet the ICBM tests and the reports about them in the Soviet newspapers continued beyond the time when the series was to have been completed. On 14 October, while publicizing another ICBM test, the Soviet Union announced that the ongoing test series would be extended to 30 October (that is, until after the conclusion of the Twenty-Second Party Congress).[100]

The period from mid-September to the beginning of October was also characterized by a flurry of articles by Soviet military leaders. In addition to Defense Minister Malinovsky and the commander-in-chief of the missile forces, Moskalenko, numerous other high-ranking military figures participated in this campaign, including Marshal Vershinin, commander-in-chief of the Soviet air force; Marshal Biriuzov, commander-in-chief of the anti-aircraft forces; Army General Zhadov; and Admiral Golovko.[101] The theme expressed with modifications was that a 'real threat has been created to the

Soviet Union' and 'military hysteria' was rampant in the West, Marshal Vershinin even going so far as to say that 'the aggressors have set their course towards unleashing a third world war';[102] in these conditions the USSR 'cannot sit with folded hands and look on with indifference' – measures had to be taken in order to strengthen the defense potential and readiness of the Soviet armed forces.[103]

There are yet two more innovations in the series of military measures which need underlining. First, the defense ministers of the Warsaw Pact member countries held their first publicly announced meeting from 8 to 9 September in Warsaw with the chiefs of staff of the member states' armed forces participating and Marshal Grechko acting as chairman of the meeting.[104] Secondly, TASS announced on 25 September that the Warsaw Pact would hold military maneuvers some time in October and November on the territories of its member countries with land, air, airborne and naval forces participating.[105] Joint Warsaw Pact maneuvers had been held once before, in 1958, but they had not been publicly announced. The maneuvers of 1961 did take place in early October with Soviet, Polish, GDR and Czechoslovak forces participating.

To sum up, Soviet military and military-related measures in the period between June and October 1961 included

(1)   Soviet and Warsaw Pact maneuvers involving all types of forces at various times;
(2)   a flurry of 'military preparedness' speeches by Soviet military leaders;
(3)   a substantial increase rather than, as originally planned, a decrease in the defense budget;
(4)   a substantial expansion of the strength of the armed forces rather than, as originally planned, a reduction of armed forces;
(5)   the resumption of nuclear tests after a moratorium in force since March 1958, the USSR thereby abandoning the 'self-imposed obligation' to resume testing of nuclear weapons only if the West did so first;
(6)   the continuation of the space program (*Vostok-2*);
(7)   a series of ICBM tests, lasting from mid-September to the end of October.

Analysis

If an attempt is made to explain these measures in terms of the rationality of Soviet behavior as a response to requirements of the Berlin crisis a sequence of three major purposes can be distinguished. First, as the most ambitious objective, *compellence*[106] of the Western powers to accede to Soviet demands for the conclusion of a peace treaty in which the West would have had to make major concessions; ultimately, given the nature of the problems outlined in the previous two sections (ideology, and security and state interests), this would have required Western cooperation in curbing the flow of GDR citizens to West Berlin. As no cooperation on this issue was forthcoming, two other major purposes would then have had to become increasingly important – *deterrence* of Western counteraction against unilateral action by the

Soviet Union and the GDR; at the same time, because of the risk that deterrence of Western counteraction might fail, or that the population of East Germany would rise in revolt, some measures would have had to serve the requirements of *military intervention* and *war-fighting*.

There is much to be said for the validity of such an interpretation. But there are problems. Assuming that the period of most acute danger for the Soviet Union had passed some time during or after the week beginning 13 August it was to be expected that the Soviet Union would significantly reduce its military and threat profile on both the verbal and nonverbal levels. This, however, did not occur. Far from reducing its threat posture after the maximum danger point had safely passed, the Soviet Union even enhanced it.

This difficulty concerns in particular the resumption of nuclear testing: if all measures had to be seen in the context of bargaining related to the Berlin crisis, it would have been logical to assume that the test series ought to have begun before 13 August, not afterward. The explanation offered by Wolfe to uphold the argument of rational behavior related to the crisis is not entirely convincing. Wolfe writes that the period between 'mid-August and about mid-October' – a period 'during which Soviet military demonstrations reached their peak [and] many of the top military leaders joined in a concerted speech-making campaign' – seemed to show 'the Soviet Union's concern over a possible Western military reaction to the *fait accompli* of the Berlin Wall'.[107] It does appear odd to postulate Soviet concern about Western military reaction long after the Berlin Wall had indeed become a *fait accompli*.

Perhaps it is appropriate to begin by asking whether there are any indications at all that the Soviet leadership, or lesser Soviet spokesmen, acknowledged at any time that military power in general, or any of the measures in particular, were intended to serve foreign policy objectives. There is a general statement to this effect by Khrushchev in his memoirs: 'When we established control on the borders of the GDR [in August 1961], we relied heavily on our own armed forces which were stationed in Germany after the war.'[108]

Another acknowledgment that at least some of the military measures were directly related to the Berlin crisis is contained in his assertion that 'our appointment of Marshal Konev as commander was actually just an "administrative" appointment to demonstrate to the West that we regarded the situation as seriously as they did'.[109] This is spelled out in even more detail in the second volume of Khrushchev's memoirs:

> I suggested to the leadership that we appoint Konev commander-in-chief of our own troops in Germany. To use the language of chess, the Americans had advanced a pawn, so we protected our position by moving a knight . . . Konev went to Berlin and took over as commander-in-chief from General Yakubovsky, who became Konev's deputy. However, we stressed to Marshal Konev that his appointment was temporary and symbolic, and that as soon as the situation returned to normal he would return to Moscow.[110]

As Konev had played a prominent role in World War II, ranging from his helping to blunt the German advance to Moscow in the winter of 1941/2 to his participation in the siege of Berlin in 1945, it is possible fully to accept

Khrushchev's explanation of Konev's appointment as having been of a 'symbolic' nature.[111]

There are other admissions. In July 1962, when the USSR again resumed testing of nuclear weapons (a significant fact in itself, considering the emerging Cuban venture), an editorial in *Pravda* asserted that a similar resumption of tests in the autumn of 1961 had inhibited the reactions of Soviet adversaries to the Berlin Wall.[112] Later sources were to elaborate on that issue and state that the testing of supermegaton weapons had a 'sobering effect' on Western leaders, who did not dare 'to risk unleashing a military conflict with the Soviet Union in the autumn of 1961'.[113]

All the explanations cited so far are explanations provided *ex post facto*. But, significantly, the explicit acknowledgment that some of the military measures (or military power in general) were used for political purposes can be found also in contemporary pronouncements, for instance, when Khrushchev, as quoted, said at the skillfully stage-managed celebrations honoring cosmonaut Titov that 'Our powerful rockets, which are unequaled by any country, help in solving peaceful tasks' – one of those tasks being, as Khrushchev had made clear in the same context, the conclusion of a peace treaty with Germany.[114] Similarly, concerning the increase in military expenditures, the suspension of the troop reduction program, the retention of servicemen due for release to the reserve and the resumption of nuclear testing, the Soviet political and military leaders alike maintained in each and every case, with only slight variations, that these measures had been 'forced upon' the Soviet Union; the Soviet measures were 'necessary' and 'unavoidable' due to 'international circumstances' (that is, the 'fanning of war hysteria in the West', the Western powers 'stepping up the arms race to unprecedented proportions', their 'bringing additional forces and armaments into West Berlin' and 'increasing the numerical strength of their armies', and the like).

The announcement of 29 August concerning the retention of servicemen due for transfer to the reserve in 1961 was linked explicitly to the Berlin crisis ('until the conclusion of a peace treaty with Germany'). The resumption of nuclear testing was also explained to the two left-wing British parliamentarians, Zilliacus and Plummer, in a rather direct and straightforward fashion; Plummer reported in a telephone conversation from Yalta that Khrushchev 'appeared convinced that it was only by threats he had made that negotiations [on Germany] would be resumed' and that he had said, 'I knew that it [the resumption of testing] would cause alarm, but I have had enough and I am going to do something about it. We are not going to go on with the present situation.'[115] Semyon Tsarapkin, the Soviet delegate at the three-power test stop negotiations, stated that the resumption of nuclear testing by the Soviet Union might prove a deterrent to 'warmongers and those playing with fire'.[116]

Similarly on 9 September the Soviet government issued a statement rejecting a proposal made by Kennedy and Macmillan to renew the test ban negotiations and continue the moratorium on nuclear tests in the atmosphere. The statement deplored that the Western proposal made

> no mention whatever of the critical nature of the time we are living through, of the tension in the international situation, although one

would think it would be clear to them [the Western powers] that the state of affairs with regard to nuclear testing cannot possibly be considered in isolation from the international situation.[117]

All these examples of how Soviet political leaders and diplomats, between June and October 1961, linked military measures taken by the Soviet Union to international problems support the theory that Khrushchev considered the building of the Berlin Wall only as the beginning of more far-reaching changes in Europe to be helped along by military pressure. Their primary rationale, then, appears to have been the achievement of Soviet aims in *foreign policy*. Two of the three possible explanations mentioned earlier, however, still have to be examined. Were these measures forced upon Khrushchev by the perennial exigencies of power in the Kremlin, that is, are they the outcome of *domestic politics*? Or is the reason for their adoption to be found in the *military* realm, in the 'action–reaction pattern' of the Soviet-American arms competition? It is necessary, therefore, to look in some detail at the East–West military balance in 1961 and its significance for Soviet behavior in the crisis.

The Military Balance: Strategic Power

Put in summary fashion, the overall military balance in 1961, as in the 1950s, was composed of imbalances and asymmetries – United States preponderance in strategic power, but Soviet superiority in long-range theater nuclear forces and conventional power in Central Europe. Although in January 1960 Khrushchev had put forward what appeared at the time to be a comprehensive program of minimum deterrence and military sufficiency, requiring nothing less than a thorough transformation of Soviet military strategy and force structure, this program was never fully implemented.

First and foremost, the Soviet Union never embarked upon mass production of first-generation ICBMs. Whatever the reason – constraints of cost, serious technical deficiencies, an 'amazing mistake of judgment', the 'ganging up' of the older branches of the Soviet services against new missile projects,[118] or the Soviet leaders' 'confidence in the extreme disinclination of the United States, despite its great and increasing preponderance of intercontinental power, to initiate or provoke general war'[119] – the fact remains that the Soviet Union never even came close to opening the much-feared, much-anticipated and much-talked-about 'missile gap'.

The point about the missile gap, as summarized concisely by Alsop,[120] does have some significance for the Berlin crisis. In the wake of the successful launching of the Sputnik and further Soviet space exploits American intelligence analysts estimated that the Soviet Union would produce about 150 ICBMs by 1961. As no antimissile warning system was expected to exist at that time and as the United States strategic forces had a relatively narrow base, presenting no more than about fifty targets, the Soviet Union would have been in a position to destroy most of the US strategic power in a first strike by 1961. The U-2 overflights gave no hint that the Soviet Union was exploiting its initial advantage, but both laterally and longitudinally the U-2 viewing range was limited, and the flights themselves had to be stopped after the débâcle of May 1960 when one U-2 plane was shot down and the Paris Summit Conference wrecked. The ambiguities and uncertainties were dispelled to a much greater degree only at the end of November 1960 when the first reconnaissance satellite, which was programmed to look at the areas missed by the U-2, confirmed the very limited scope of the Soviet ICBM effort. As early as January 1961, in his farewell message to Congress, President Eisenhower said that 'the "missile gap" shows every sign of being a fiction'.[121]

Nevertheless press reports all through 1961 cited estimates of between thirty-five to seventy-five Soviet ICBM launchers, but even these estimates may have exaggerated the actual size of the Soviet ICBM force at the time of the Berlin crisis because, in 1964, the Department of Defense stated that the Soviet Union had by 1961 deployed only 'a handful' of ICBMs.[122]

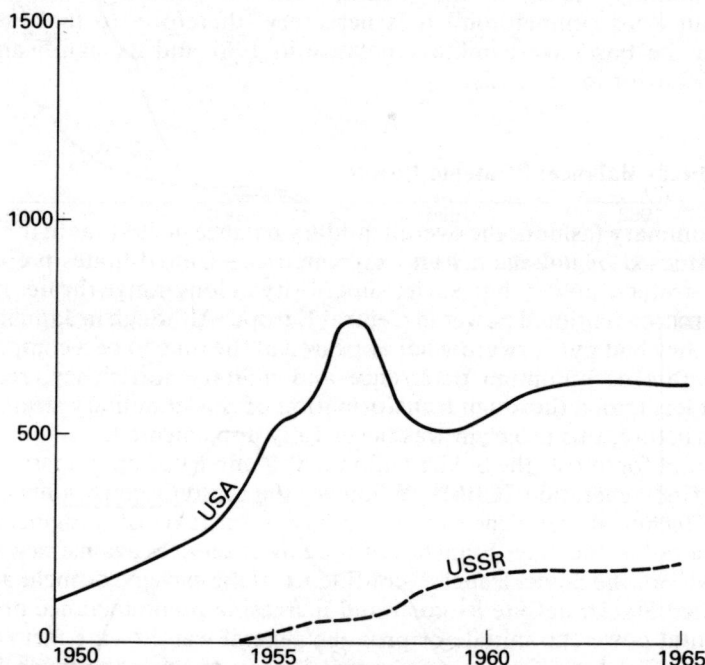

Figure 13.1   *US and Soviet Long-Range Bombers, 1950–65.*

The United States preponderance in strategic power at the time of the Berlin crisis in 1961 can be appreciated at a glance by looking at Figures 13.1 to 4.[123] Most pronounced is the commanding lead of the United States in strategic aircraft with 600 American as against 190 Soviet long-range bombers; and although the USSR led the USA in medium-range bombers (1,050 Soviet as against 1,000 American bombers), this asymmetry still added to the American strike capability against the Soviet Union because only the United States was able to employ these bombers against the adversary power due to its extensive network of air bases around the world. The

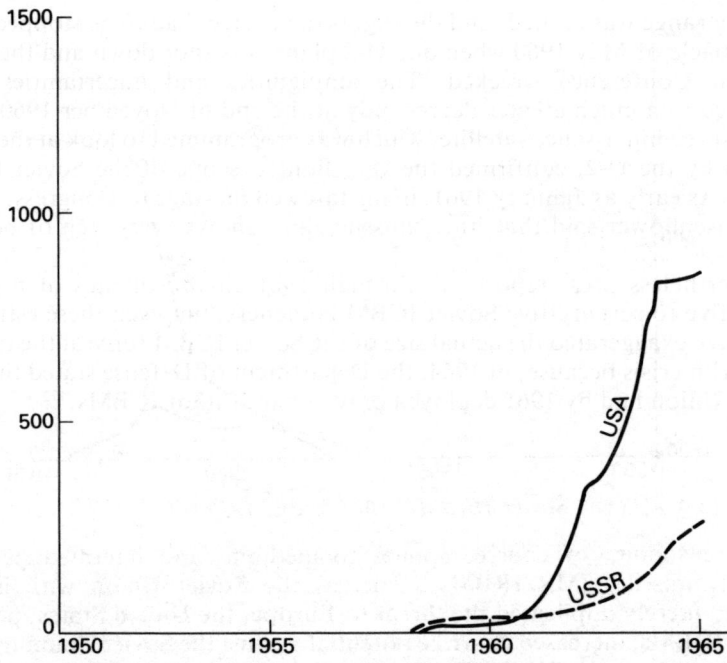

Figure 13.2   *US and Soviet ICBMs, 1950–65.*

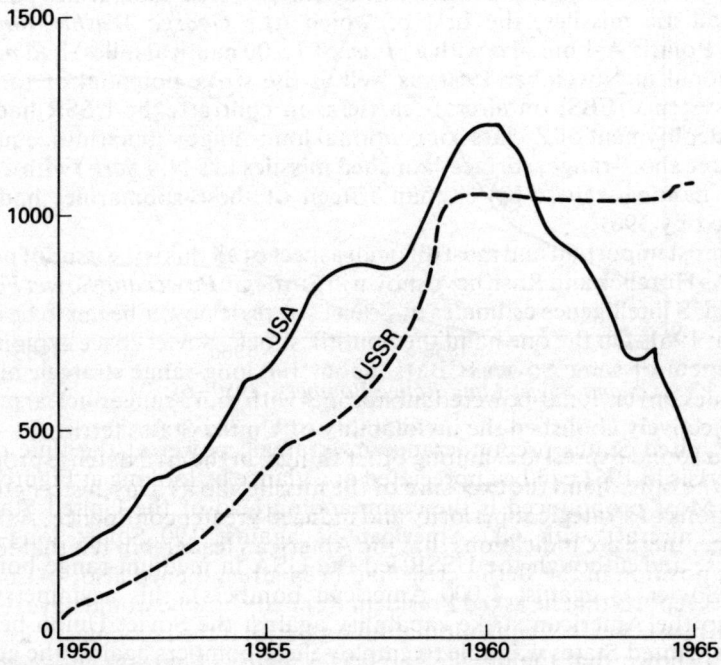

Figure 13.3   *US and Soviet Medium-Range Bombers, 1950–65.*

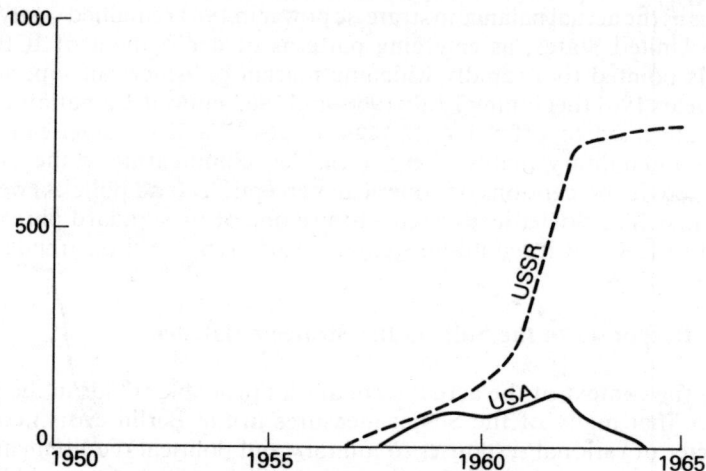

Figure 13.4   *US and Soviet MRBM/IRBM forces, 1950–65.*

same reasoning, of course, applies to medium- and intermediate-range ballistic missiles (MR/IRBMs): whereas the Soviet Union with its 270 missiles merely duplicated the threat to Europe, the United States, possessing 90 IRBMs, increased its strike potential against the Soviet Union from its launching sites in Italy and Turkey.

A more complete picture of United States strategic superiority must take into account also the deployment of nuclear-powered submarines equipped with ballistic missiles, the first of which (the *George Washington* with sixteen Polaris A-1 missiles with a range of 1,200 nautical miles) had become operational in November 1960, as well as the strike potential of forward-based systems (FBS) on aircraft carriers. In contrast, the USSR had only begun deployment of Z-class conventional long-range submarines, equipped with three short-range, surface-launched missiles (SS-N-4 *Sark*) with a range of 350 nautical miles. Fewer than fifteen of these submarines had been deployed by 1961.

The most important and most difficult aspect of all this is the issue of perceptions. As Horelick and Rush have shown in *Strategic Power and Soviet Foreign Policy*, US intelligence estimates of Soviet strategic power began to be scaled down in 1961. On the one hand the Sputnik shock, Soviet space exploits, the deployment of some Soviet ICBMs, about 190 long-range strategic aircraft and some conventional-powered submarines with short-range nuclear missiles had objectively abolished the inviolability of United States territory – a fact that had found expression, among other things, in the civil defense program. But on the other hand the exposure of the missile gap as a myth strengthened perceptions of strategic superiority and induced greater confidence. As a consequence, there are indications that the American leadership felt that its bargaining position in the Berlin crisis had been strengthened also. (Alsop, for instance, reports that he asked President Kennedy how he would have responded to Khrushchev's Vienna ultimatum on Berlin if the reconnaissance satellites had shown that the missile gap was a reality. Kennedy answered that whenever he began to think about it he had too much trouble sleeping.) [124]

Thus as the actual balance in strategic power in 1961 remained vastly in favor of the United States, as emerging patterns of deployment of ICBMs and SLBMs pointed to a rapidly widening margin of American superiority, as fiscal years 1961 (beginning 1 July 1960) and 1962 showed dramatic increases in funds allocated to offensive strategic forces,[125] and as American political leaders and military analysts were extensively commenting on these developments, Soviet perceptions of American perceptions (and policies) were likely to change. The Soviet leadership – to use one of its standard phrases – was bound to feel that it 'could not remain indifferent' to these trends.

Soviet Responses to the Shift in the Strategic Balance

It is in the context of the actual state of and probable trends in the strategic balance that many of the Soviet measures in the Berlin crisis take on the character of rational responses to military and political requirements. First, because of strategic inferiority *vis-à-vis* the United States it would be useful from the Soviet point of view to enhance as much as possible the sense of vulnerability of the United States' European allies. This, in turn, could serve to induce these countries to bring pressure to bear on the USA not to engage in any risky ventures in Berlin. These purposes are undoubtedly part of the explanation for the 'orange grove' and 'olive grove' statements, the reminders that the Soviet Union had the potential to wipe certain countries 'from the face of the earth', that six H-bombs would be quite enough to annihilate the British Isles and nine would take care of France,[126] and that if Adenauer and the *Bundeswehr* thought that they could achieve reunification of the German nation by war, in that case 'Germany will be reduced to dust'.[127]

Interestingly, Khrushchev thought this aspect of deterrence or intimidation to have been quite successful:

> 'If a third world war is unleashed,' Adenauer often said, 'West Germany will be the first country to perish.' I was pleased to hear this, and Adenauer was absolutely right in what he said. For him to be making public statements like that was *a great achievement on our part. Not only were we keeping our number one enemy in line, but Adenauer was helping us to keep our other enemies in line, too.*[128]

Secondly, as satellite reconnaissance filled the gaps in United States information about Soviet ICBM deployments, or lack thereof, it would also be reasonable to expect from the Soviet Union a toning down of superiority claims (as they were now questionable) and a stance more in line with actual capabilities. There is evidence for that. In his speech of 21 June Khrushchev spoke of *parity* in military power, not Soviet superiority, when he said that 'Even the representatives of the imperialist powers themselves now say that an equilibrium of forces has now formed in the world between the Western states and the socialist countries'.[129] Similarly, and perhaps even more cautiously, he told graduates of the Soviet military academies on 8 July:

> Today it is acknowledged in the West that the forces of the Soviet Union and other socialist countries are not inferior to the forces of the

Western powers. However, the proper conclusions are not drawn from this fact: where there are equal forces, there must also be equal rights and equal opportunities. Yet our partners, acknowledging that the balance of power (*sootnoshenie sil*) has not shifted in their favor, nevertheless want to dominate in international agencies and impose their will there.[130]

In his speech of 7 August on radio and television Khrushchev made only passing reference to ICBMs ('we have been developing a diversity of rockets: intercontinental ballistic missiles and also rockets of various ranges . . . Our rocketry is moving along well'),[131] but perhaps there was no reason to speak loud words because of the even louder action of the ongoing *Vostok-2* flight (6−7 August). Nevertheless the 'equilibrium of forces', Soviet forces 'not being inferior' to those of the West and alleged acknowledgments by the Western countries that the balance of power had 'not shifted in their favor' are a far cry from the bold superiority claims made earlier by Khrushchev.

A third type of response that the Soviet Union could have been expected to make after shifts in the strategic balance had become apparent was to stress alternative means of delivery (for example, strategic bombers), qualitative improvements in missile technology not subject to detection by satellite reconnaissance (for example, improvements in payload and accuracy of ICBMs) and increases in the destructiveness of weapons (for example, increases in the size of nuclear weapons). There is no evidence of an upgrading of the strategic bomber forces (*dal'naia aviatsiia*). In fact, although he reassured the various branches of the military establishment that the 'strengthening of the defense of the Soviet Union depends on the perfection of all the types of troops of our Armed Forces', he immediately contradicted this statement in the same address (21 June) by saying that 'exceptionally great responsibility lies with the rocket troops, especially the units which service the ballistic rockets of various ranges, from tactical to intercontinental'.[132] (In essence Khrushchev was saying that the branches of the armed forces were equal, but some were more equal than others.) However, aspects of the strategic balance other than quantity of ICBMs *were* stressed, and particularly so after Kennedy's speech of 25 July.

On 27 July − according to reports in the *New York Times* and by Schlesinger − Khrushchev told McCloy in Sochi that if war broke out it would be decided *by the biggest rockets* and that the Soviet Union had them (that is, Khrushchev made no mention of numerical advantages); and in the same context, for the first time, he boasted that the Soviet Union had the ability to build and deliver by missile on United States territory a 100-megaton nuclear bomb.[133] These boasts were repeated by Khrushchev on 9 August at the reception for cosmonaut Titov.[134]

If the interpretation here is valid (that shifts in the strategic balance largely explain the kind of claims made by the Soviet leadership) the actual resumption of nuclear tests itself must be regarded as a corresponding response on the hardware side. Evidently the Soviet decision was not taken on the spur of the moment. One of the chief American negotiators of the Test Ban Treaty is convinced that the new (1961) round of Soviet-American talks, which had been conducted at Geneva, the United Nations and through private diplomatic channels, 'had been deliberately misused [by the USSR] as a screen for test preparations – a situation which we had begun to suspect early in the spring of 1961'.[135] In the closed game of strategic competition the resumption of testing was one of the ways of moving rationally according to the rules of the game, and such a move appears even less surprising given the continuing political confrontation over Berlin.[136]

Space exploits, the quality of Soviet missiles, the test series of nuclear weapons, including the 'superbombs', and the series of flight tests of ever 'more powerful rockets' (always proving successful and always demonstrating great accuracy, according to TASS announcements) were thus linked skillfully for military and political reasons – to improve the Soviet military posture in real terms and to contain the potentially adverse psychological and political effects of changed and changing Western perceptions of the strategic balance. A similar reasoning can be applied with regard to the military balance at the conventional level.

Conventional Power

In view of United States superiority in strategic power it is probably not an exaggeration to say that the success of the Soviet measures of 13 August (in terms of Western acquiescence and the failure of the German population to engage in active resistance) depended to a large extent on the Soviet conventional superiority at the local level.

The forces available to the Soviet leadership during the Berlin crisis included the following components: (1) the Group of Soviet Forces in Germany (GSFG), consisting of twenty divisions – ten tank divisions (about 4,000 tanks) and ten mechanized (about 2,500 tanks), and the 24th Air Army, composed of two or three air corps with an estimated total of 900 planes; (2) the East German *Volksarmee*, with six to seven divisions – two tank and four to five motorized divisions (in all about 1,700 tanks) – and air forces of up to 370 planes; (3) Czechoslovak armed forces, comprising fourteen divisions, of which two tank and twelve motorized (in all about 3,400 tanks).[137] In addition to these forty to forty-one divisions, the Soviet Union could reinforce its armed strength in the area with elements of the six Soviet divisions stationed in Hungary and Poland, and of the forty to fifty divisions from the western border regions of the USSR. At the time the Soviet Union was credited with possessing 175 divisions and this was considered as giving it an almost inexhaustible reservoir of conventional power with which to reinforce its strength in Central Europe; it was also credited with being capable of bringing a substantial portion of its tactical air force into operation, said to consist of an estimated 10,000 planes.[138]

According to official Western figures at the time, the NATO command had at its disposal in Central Europe a total of nineteen to twenty-two divisions, including five American, three British, seven to eight West German, two to three French, and two to three belonging to other NATO members.[139] The reinforcement potential of the United States would have consisted of about four divisions and the transfer to the European theater of a large number of American aircraft. But, in all, not counting the much greater Soviet reinforcement potential, the USSR was credited at the time of the

Berlin crisis with a superiority of two to one in divisions and more than two to one in tanks.

Some of these estimates were inaccurate and some of the assumptions unfounded. First, from 1962 onward, detailed reviews indicated that at least half of the 175 Soviet divisions were cadre divisions (that is, essentially paper units) and that it was these units which were being compared with combat-ready divisions of the USA and other NATO countries. It was only later on in the 1960s that the counting of Soviet and NATO divisions on a one-to-one basis, taking into account the differences in manpower, firepower and other capabilities, was abandoned, so that a ratio of 1:1·7 of American to Soviet divisions ultimately came to be accepted as more realistic.[140] Secondly, it also turned out that the figure of 10,000 Soviet tactical aircraft was grossly exaggerated, later estimates putting the total figure at no more than 4,000.[141] Thirdly, it also did not make much sense to adopt a one-to-one ratio for comparing East European and, particularly in the conditions of the Berlin crisis, East German divisions with NATO divisions.

However, even making allowance for a somewhat distorted view of individual aspects of the conventional balance, globally and in Central Europe, and making the point that things at this level did not look nearly as bleak for the West as they did in 1948, the autopsy of the actual state of affairs still shows impressive superiority of the Warsaw Pact in 1961. Four years earlier the Soviet Union had withdrawn two divisions from East Germany but at the same time converted two mechanized divisions to tank divisions and four infantry divisions to fully mechanized divisions, and deployed all six of them forward within the immediate proximity of the East/West German border.[142] All this was part of a general pattern of reorganization in the course of which manpower reductions were compensated by the introduction of tactical nuclear weapons, including surface-to-surface missiles – a development described by Wolfe under the heading of 'nuclearization of the theatre forces'[143] – but also by increased mechanization and modernization of existing units, the addition of large quantities of tanks, armored personnel carriers, rocket launchers, and so on.[144]

Redeployments, reorganization, modernization and nuclearization of the Warsaw Pact forces had thus increased the threat posed to NATO in Central Europe and military analysts in the West were to draw quite pessimistic conclusions from this. They argued that 'in a cold war as in a military conflict, success on the battlefield is decided by the relative strength of the two sides, not throughout the world, but on the battlefield itself'.[145]

Khrushchev made every effort to enhance such perceptions. He emphasized to the graduates of the Soviet military academies that: 'it is a [separate] *peace treaty* to which some people are threatening to respond by force and by provoking a dangerous international crisis.' However, 'Many of you will be serving in the forces which, under the Warsaw Treaty, are stationed in the German Democratic Republic, so you will be called upon to repel aggressive forces should they have a mind to wreck the peace settlement by force of arms'.[146] Later in the month (27 July) Khrushchev was even more direct. He told McCloy, according to a report in the *New York Times*, that 'if the Western powers wanted to shoot their way through to West Berlin they should remember that the Soviet Union had *superiority in arms and divisions* and was *nearer to the field of battle*.[147] (This statement harked back to what Khrushchev earlier, in July 1959, had told another American visitor, Averell Harriman. American generals, Khrushchev had said, 'talk of maintaining your position in Berlin with force. That is bluff. If you send in tanks, they will burn and make no mistake about it'.)[148]

By comparing the claims Khrushchev had made since the Suez crisis, both as regards military-strategic power and the conventional balance, and no matter whether they involved overall assessments of superiority or inferiority, or more detailed matters such as quantitative aspects, accuracy, destructiveness or range, one conclusion stands out most of all: *all these claims, and the threats on their basis, were carefully calibrated, taking into account the actual state of affairs, future trends and American perceptions.*[149] Khrushchev, therefore, could not have been ignorant of developments in NATO which, if they were to have been implemented in full, could have seriously eroded Soviet advantages. The fact is that tendencies to strengthen NATO's conventional and theater nuclear capabilities had begun to take tangible form. The underlying strategy of flexible response and graduated deterrence, designed to give the West 'a wider choice than humiliation or all-out nuclear war', had been part of the *credo* of the Kennedy administration from the very outset but it received considerable impetus in the course of the Berlin crisis and found its most dramatic expression in the measures announced by Kennedy on 25 July, notably the big increases in US armed forces strength by 225,000 officers and men. The continuing build-up of the West German armed forces fitted closely into the general concept.

The program of armed forces reductions in the Soviet Union, therefore, stood in sharp contrast to the trends in NATO – visibly and, from Khrushchev's point of view, painfully so.[150] Cuts in force levels had been carried out in 1955–7 (resulting in reductions of about 1·8 million men from a peak of 5·7 million men in 1955), and a second reduction had taken place in 1958–9 (involving already a much lesser number, about 300,000 men, but also including withdrawal of some forces from Eastern Europe). At the time of the Berlin crisis the Soviet Union was in the middle of a third stage of reductions: as codified in the Law on a New Large Reduction of the Soviet Armed Forces of 15 January 1960, troop levels were to be cut *by the fall of 1961* by 1·2 million men to bring down the total number to 2·4 million.[151] But if the estimate is correct that by 8 July 1961, 'only about half of the projected 1·2 million cut had been made',[152] the program was already running behind schedule. It is therefore probably no exaggeration to say that the troop reduction program had *de facto* been suspended before the official announcement to that effect.

Soviet Military Power and the Berlin Crisis

To sum up, during the Berlin crisis of 1961 the Soviet Union was forced to act in conditions of military-strategic inferiority (and the prospect of a widening margin of this inferiority) in relation to the United States. Soviet *public* pronouncements gave no indication that the Soviet leadership was in any way aware of constraints being placed on its political actions. They stressed instead that parity existed and that in some aspects of strategic power the USSR was even superior to the United States, for instance, as regards bigger missiles and bigger nuclear warheads. However, United States military-strategic superiority must be considered as one of the most important restraining influences on further Soviet advances in the Berlin crisis.

At the same time the American side did not draw the conclusion that it was able to use its strategic superiority in an attempt to stop or reverse the change in the status quo in Berlin. This was due to perceptions of the Kennedy administration that the United States had ceased to be invulnerable and that the Soviet Union possessed significant superiority at the local level as a result of its having maintained, despite the reductions, superior armed forces strength (number of divisions, tanks and aircraft), the nuclearization of the Soviet theater forces since 1958, and the build-up of MR/IRBM and medium-range bomber forces at the Soviet Union's western periphery. The USSR in turn made the most of these military assets by enhancing the sense of vulnerability in the United States, and in particular by heightening anxieties of the United States's European allies in the series of military measures described above. To the extent that there was no Western counterchallenge to the Soviet *fait accompli* in Berlin, the Soviet military posture was effective and successful.

Another conclusion may be more controversial. In the present analysis, the program of Soviet armed forces reductions was bound to be terminated in any case, given (1) the prospect of a widening gap in military strategic power in favor of the United States and (2) the build-up of the *Bundeswehr* and renewed emphasis on conventional power in the context of the NATO strategy of flexible response. As in the case of some of the United States measures in the conventional sphere, the Berlin crisis only dramatized and accelerated the taking of these measures.

This, evidently, is an explanataion which conforms to the rationale of the closed game of military competition and exigencies of crisis bargaining. It is challenged by the theory that domestic opponents *nolens volens* forced Khrushchev to reconsider his priorities – not only to suspend the reduction of armed forces but also to increase defense spending, concentrate on priority growth of heavy industry, resume nuclear testing, take a harder line in foreign policy, and so on. It is appropriate, therefore, to analyze these problems more closely in their proper domestic context.

IV   DOMESTIC POLITICS

Analysis of the domestic dimension of Soviet policy in the Berlin crisis has remained a hazardous endeavor likely to touch sensitivities of various schools of thought about the likely impact of Khrushchev's personality on policy, the nature of Khrushchev's power, the influence of interest groups and, more broadly, the extent of changes in the Soviet system initiated in the Khrushchev era. As summarized by Carl Linden, one school of thought emphasizes the stability of Khrushchev's leadership. After the resolution of succession struggles, in particular after the June 1957 leadership crisis, Khrushchev, according to this school, is said to have acquired all the levers of power necessary to ensure his dominance in the leadership and put him beyond the reach of effective challenge. The opposite school sees leadership politics under Khrushchev as dynamic and unstable, treats conflict as a continuous process of Soviet political life and hence is aware of the possibilities, or even necessity, of compromise.[153]

As in the debate between traditionalists and scientists in political science the debate about the extent of Khrushchev's power has been useful in as much as it has sharpened important issues,[154] but it also has had more disagreeable features, such as personal attacks, artificiality and sterile scholasticism.[155] Thus it could appear that no useful purpose can be served in restaging a somewhat contrived ballet, featuring the same academic primadonnas and their known caprices, were it not for the fact that there are not only disagreements of substance but also many issues which have not been explored in detail at all. First, little attempt has been made to relate analysis of domestic politics to foreign policy, and to the 1961 Berlin crisis in particular. And the only book-length study in which such an attempt has been made, with its emphasis on an opposition faction being able to play Russian roulette, 'taking actions which deliberately risked nuclear war' and 'sharply alter[ing] the course of Soviet foreign policy', is more likely to obscure important issues, than to illuminate them.[156]

Rather than skating immediately on the thin ice of analyzing assumed or actual leadership struggles it may be more appropriate to begin by looking at an important set of interrelated issues. Such an interrelationship was first explicitly stated at the Twentieth CPSU Congress, refined at the Twenty-First Congress and restated in variations in 1960 and 1961 as follows. (1) A more vigorous pursuit of peaceful coexistence and relaxation of tension abroad makes it possible to freeze or even reduce defense expenditures. (2) The reduction of armed forces, made possible by the relaxation abroad, contributes to savings in the defense budget and provides for an expansion of the productive labor force. (3) Curtailment of military expenditures makes it possible to increase investment in the civilian sector of the economy, particularly in agriculture and consumer industry. (4) The diversion of funds from the military sector into the civilian sector, and the transfer of manpower from the armed forces to the labor force, has an important effect on overall economic growth and will lead to a breakthrough in the main arena of conflict between the two systems – economic competition.

These four elements have all the attributes of being part of a 'grand design', setting clear priorities in domestic and foreign policy. The problem is only that this grand design was never implemented.

The Budget in Domestic and International Perspective

Let us take the issue of the budget first. As shown in Table 13.1, overt defense expenditures had been reduced significantly in 1956 and 1957 and had remained virtually constant at a lower level. The budget for 1961 provided for yet another, though slight, decrease in defense expenditures. But the difficulty of separating Khrushchev's declarations from intent, and programs from policies, begins precisely at this point: there may be no correlation

Table 13.1 Explicit and Estimated USSR Military Outlays, 1955–62

	1955	1956	1957	1958	1959	1960	1961	1962
					(billion rubles)			
1 Defense outlays	10·74	9·73	9·12	9·36	9·37	9·30	11·6	12·7
2 Estimated military component of other outlays								
I Science	0·45	0·59	0·81	1·00	1·17	1·40	1·6	1·8
II Budget residuals								
(a) low	1·27	1·79	1·59	1·23	4·23	3·02	0·1–9·2	0·0–5·0
(b) high	3·81	4·49	4·46	4·27	7·46	6·45	3·8–12·9	2·1–8·9
3 Estimated total military outlays								
(a) low	12·46	12·11	11·52	11·59	14·77	13·72	13·3–22·4	14·5–19·5
(b) high	15·00	14·81	14·39	14·63	18·00	17·15	17·0–26·1	16·6–23·4
					Indexes (1958 = 100)			
4 Defense outlays	114·7	104·0	97·4	100·0	100·1	99·4	123·4	135·1
5 Estimated total military outlays								
(a) low	107·5	104·5	99·4	100·0	127·4	118·4	114·7–193·1	125·0–168·1
(b) high	102·5	101·2	98·4	100·0	123·0	117·2	116·4–178·8	113·7–160·3

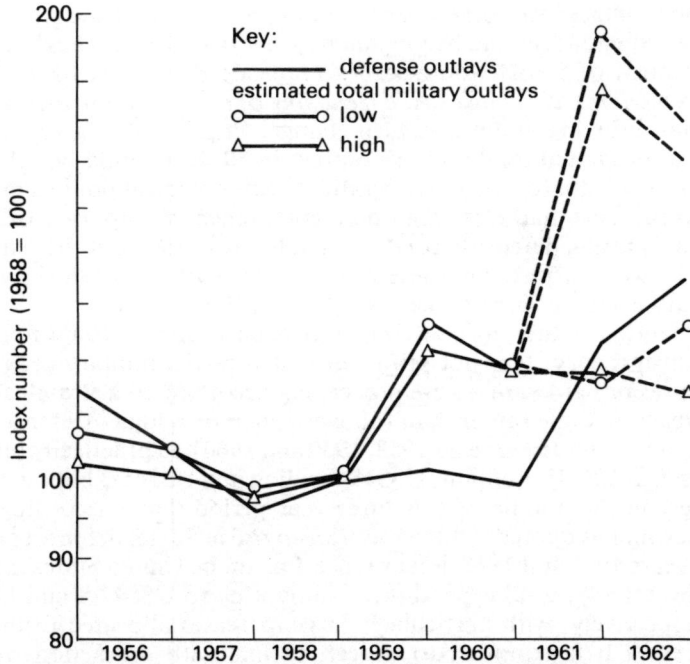

Figure 13.5 *Indexes of Defense and Estimated Total Military Outlays, 1956–62 (1958 = 100).*

Note: 'low' and 'high' refer to the absolute value series of Table 13.1. As this figure uses a relative scale, 'low' may appear above 'high'.

whatsoever between overt Soviet defense expenditures as a proportion of the budget and actual military outlays. There is no doubt that the former is a gross understatement of reality. As for the latter value, it simply is not known with any degree of precision – estimates based on complicated economic calculations which cannot possibly be reproduced here can only give a rough idea of expenditures.

Even bearing in mind these qualifications, there is some agreement among Western analysts concerning broad trends. Of particular importance for the present context is the observation that in some years, notably in 1959–60, 'the explicit defense allocation remained constant, at a time when Western experts were convinced that Soviet military hardware production was increasing'.[157] Abraham Becker, an analyst of Soviet economics at the Rand Corporation, argues similarly. Official Soviet claims are that no real increase in defense expenditures took place from 1957 to 1961, whereas estimated values of total military outlays show a sharp rise in 1959, with some small decline in 1960; in his view it was still unclear what had happened in 1961–2, but military expenditures 'may have at least held their own or nearly so in 1961; possibly they increased further and perhaps even more sharply than in 1959. The 1962 data almost defy comparison with earlier years.'[158] These trends, which are confirmed by other analysts,[159] are shown in Table 13.1 and Figure 13.5.[160]

If these estimates are correct, one major conclusion emerges: the increase in defense expenditures had begun much earlier than Khrushchev's dramatic announcement of 8 July would seem to indicate. It is more likely that *the announcement merely confirmed a trend line of rising defense expenditures*, rather than bringing about a sudden change. In particular, given the large increase of estimated total military outlays in 1959, it would be difficult to argue – as advocates of the bureaucratic/Kremlinological politics model do – that Khrushchev had embarked on a comprehensive program of détente abroad and cutting defense expenditures at home in 1959 but that suddenly, in 1961, he was frustrated in these worthy endeavors by political rivals and the military using the Berlin crisis as a pretext.[161]

Some caution is therefore advisable as regards conventional notions of arms control theory. It is not self-evident that Soviet military programs – expenditures *or* hardware – were proceeding according to a straightforward action–reaction cycle rather than following their own logic. Defense spending in United States fiscal years 1958, 1959 and 1960 had practically remained *unchanged*, at US$45·1 billion, US$45·8 billion and US$45·3 billion.[162] Yet it is precisely in the middle of this three-year period that – according to the Western estimates quoted – there was a *steep rise* in Soviet defense spending. In fiscal years 1961 and 1962 defense spending in the United States increased quite substantially, total expenditures amounting to US$47·8 and US$52·4 billion respectively, with particularly large increases allocated to the strategic forces.[163] It is tempting to expect, in line with the action–reaction theory, that Soviet spending rose equally sharply. This, however, cannot be confirmed. The margin of uncertainty concerning the actual size of Soviet increases in these two years is too great to allow for any confident conclusions.[164]

More confidence is warranted as regards the following proposition: the official Soviet version of 'no real increases in defense expenditures' in the period from 1956 up to July 1961 (a false version because there *were* increases according to the estimates), as well as the announcement of a big increase on 8 July (a correct message only in the sense that it confirmed existing trends of expenditures and did not initiate a sudden change), are both to be taken as *signals* rather than precise reflections of the actual state of affairs. But signaling of what to whom?

It is doubtful that Khrushchev intended to appease the top military leadership, which had probably been made aware of the previously (in 1959) initiated *de facto* rise in defense spending. It would be more correct to say that society at large in the Soviet Union and foreign countries, notably the Western powers, were meant to be the recipients of the signal: domestically, it could be used as a convenient excuse for explaining the disappointing performance of the economy in general, and consumer industry in particular (more of this later); and, internationally, the signal could be used for 'proving' that the Soviet Union accepted the challenge of increased defense expenditures in the United States (to which Khrushchev had explicitly referred in his announcement),[165] and that the USSR was not retreating under American pressure from its stated goals in the Berlin crisis.

Horelick and Rush arrive at the same conclusion, though adopting a different approach. They argue that even taking the official Soviet figures on defense spending and Khrushchev's announcement of 8 July at face value, 'an increase [in the official budget by almost one-third] could not be spent on a rational program within that year' and hence 'a major purpose of the announcement must have been to demonstrate the seriousness of Soviet intentions with regard to Berlin'.[166]

The Suspension of Armed Forces Reductions

The argument about defense spending (one aspect of Khrushchev's announcement of 8 July) can now be linked to the problem of troop reductions, the second major aspect of the announcement: in the former case it was suggested that existing trends were merely confirmed or reinforced, and in the latter case it was submitted that the program of armed forces reductions was already running behind schedule and that a *de facto* suspension was merely announced publicly. Evidently there is some connection. But there is also a broader issue involved, perhaps a contradiction. How realistic is it really to assume that the Western estimates of rises in total military outlays are correct, or approximately correct, considering the contraction of the size of the Soviet armed forces from 5·76 million in 1955 to about 3 million in July 1961? Was there really *no* saving in defense expenditures despite large-scale armed forces reductions?

One answer to this question must be that even the official Soviet data on defense expenditure show the absence of any direct relation between reductions in manpower and reductions in the military budget (see Table 13.2).[167]

Table 13.2 *Soviet Manpower and Military Expenditures*

Year	Ground forces	Total armed forces	Defense budget (billion rubles)[a]	Defense budget as percentage of state budget
1955	3,200,000	5,763,000	10·7	19·9
1956	?	5,120,000	9·75	17·3
1957	2,500,000		9·12	15·0
1958	2,500,000	3,920,000	9·36	14·6
1959	2·35−2,500,000	3,620,000	9·37	13·3
1960	2·24−2,500,000		9·30	12·7
1961				
planned	?	2,420,000	9·26	11·9
July	2·2 −2,500,000	3,000,000	12·4[b]	16·0[b]
December		3,800,000	11·6	15·2

  [a] In new (1961) rubles. There are minor differences between *actual* defense expenditures, the latter usually being slightly lower than the former; all figures relate to actual defense spending as provided in the annual issue of *Narodnoe khoziaistvo SSSR*.
  [b] Planned according to Khrushchev's announcement of 8 July 1961 (*Pravda*, 9 July 1961).

As Galay points out in an analysis of this problem, only the first reduction of 640,000 men in 1955 resulted in a significant cut in the overt defense budget. The much larger reduction of 1·2 million men in 1956−8 produced a smaller cut in the budget than in 1955, the reduction of 300,000 men in

1958—9 hardly affected the budget at all, and the same would have been true for the planned manpower reductions in the 1960—1 period.[168]

However, the more realistic assumption, namely, that there was in actual fact an *inverse* relation — increased defense expenditures despite troop reductions — is not at all unrealistic considering that the Soviet Union not only continued to retain the largest standing army in the world, but continued to modernize its equipment, spending substantial sums on space technology, deploying large numbers of MR/IRBMs and at the same time (in May 1960) building up an entirely new branch of the armed forces, the strategic rocket forces. As France's later experience was to confirm, the decision to build up a strategic striking force (the *force de frappe*) is likely to increase rather than decrease the defense burden on the economy despite cutbacks in armed forces strength.[169]

The problem, then, as it most likely confronted the military establishment in the USSR was not stagnation or reduction in defense expenditures but allocation and reallocation of resources within and among the different branches of the Soviet armed forces, the scope of manpower reductions and their psychological and social consequences. These issues alone were bound to create heated debates and social dislocation. However, there is little evidence that the first two troop reduction programs met with serious opposition from the traditionalist elements in the military establishments;[170] it was only after the announcement of the third stage of reductions that signs of difficulty and controversy became more apparent. On the one hand Defense Minister Malinovsky felt constrained to warn the officers affected by reductions not to make 'unrealistic demands on local authorities and seek highly paid top positions' and to explain that 'leading positions in the economy and the administration generally are occupied by deserving Soviet citizens who cannot [simply] be dismissed to make room for officers'.[171] On the other hand it was pointed out by other officers that the relation between troop reductions and improvement of economic performance was not as direct as the political leadership seemed to believe. This argument was confirmed to a certain extent by the Minister of the Merchant Marine, Bakaev, who pointed out that sailors could not automatically be received into the merchant marine but had to go to school first to receive proper training.[172]

But although Malinovsky (as well as Marshal M. V. Zakharov who nevertheless was later to be dismissed) expressed support for the program of armed forces reductions at the meeting of the Supreme Soviet which discussed Khrushchev's proposals, he also warned against overreliance on 'one type of weapon' and called for a 'reasonably balanced' mix of forces.[173] It is also interesting to note that two of Malinovsky's senior aides, Marshals V. D. Sokolovsky (Chief of General Staff) and I. S. Konev (then commander of the forces of the Warsaw Pact), failed to support the program of armed forces reductions at that session or later. They both lost their posts in April 1960 in a reshuffle of the military command.[174] It is quite reasonable to infer that they were opposed to the principle or procedure of manpower reductions. Another high figure affected by the reshuffle was S. K. Timoshenko (commander of the Byelorussian Military Region). However, whereas Sokolovsky and Timoshenko were demoted to less prestigious posts, Konev was assigned no duties whatever from 1960 to August 1961.

To revert from this to the question of the reasons for the suspension of the troop reductions program as announced on 8 July – is it likely that the military were now making a comeback and forcing Khrushchev to change his plans? More specifically, was Konev's appointment to the post of commander of the GSFG a move not related to the international crisis at all but to a new turn in the ongoing controversy between Khrushchev and the traditionalists in the military?

In his analysis Boris Nicolaevsky cautiously summarizes Konev's appointment as representing 'a victory for Konev's *policy*'.[175] He also makes the interesting point that Konev still figured as a participant in all kinds of military conferences even after his dismissal in April 1960.[176] This fact could be interpreted as additional proof for Khrushchev's weakness *vis-à-vis* the military or, more likely, it could be an indication of a more limited adversary relationship between the political and the military leadership than Western perceptions of a perennial *kto-kogo* struggle would seem to allow.

An equally interesting point is mentioned by Nicolaevsky in the same context. Marshal Zhukov, who was dismissed as Defense Minister in 1957 and had not reappeared in public since, did appear at the French industrial fair in Sokolniki Park (Moscow) which had opened on 15 August.[177] Again, is this confirmation of the growth in power of the military, or did Khrushchev try to enlist Zhukov, too, for a show of national unity during the international crisis? The latter appears more plausible. This is confirmed by the Penkovsky Papers. After presenting detailed material concerning controversies between Khrushchev and various military leaders after Zhukov had been dismissed, and confirming that Marshals Timoshenko, Rokossovsky, Konev and Sokolovsky had argued against Khrushchev's policy of cutting the numerical strength of the armed forces and the pay and supplementary allowances of officers, the Penkovsky Papers continue:

> Later, in 1961, during the Berlin crisis Khrushchev proposed that Zhukov, Sokolovsky and Konev, to prove their loyalty to the Party and the country, should return to active work with him. Sokolovsky and Konev agreed, but Zhukov refused although he is still fit and active.[178]

But in any case, the point to be emphasized here is that both events – Konev's reappointment to active duties and Zhukov's reappearance in public – which could conceivably demonstrate the increased power of the military *vis-à-vis* Khrushchev, occurred *after* the announcement of 8 July. If, contrary to Soviet tradition and contrary to all available evidence, Bonapartism really had raised its head, and if the measures announced on 8 July are to be considered a result of successful military pressure, it would be logical to look for evidence of this *before* that date.

There is an additional, broader, consideration. The question of what conventional force levels are 'sufficient' or 'adequate' to meet requirements of deterrence, compellence, or war-fighting involves a certain measure of arbitrariness, and in such a situation it is indeed fairly safe to assume that a substantial section of the military leadership would tend to suggest higher levels than some sections of the political leadership. Nevertheless Khrushchev was able to reduce the size of the armed forces to a considerable extent (from 5·76 million in 1955 to about 3 million in July 1961).[179] Why? It is fair to argue that the force levels in the mid- and late 1950s were oversize. The nuclearization of the theater forces, begun in 1958, had made it possible to substitute firepower for manpower. Moreover, not only was the military divided on this issue on professional grounds, according to branch of service and outlook, into what are called traditionalists and modernists in the West, but officers were also divided on political grounds, according to the relative strength of their dependence on Khrushchev's patronage and their relative willingness to tie their career to his.

But a critical point had probably been reached. After an initial cut in the first stage of reductions the strength of the ground forces had remained virtually unchanged at 2·2 to 2·5 million men throughout the second and initial part of the third stage. In order to maintain a balance among the various branches it was now, in 1961, to be expected that it was going to be the turn of the ground forces to contract in size.[180] Given an international political crisis, worsening relations with China and tendencies for strengthening conventional armaments in NATO, nothing could have come at a politically more inconvenient time. Perhaps it is useful to remember that in the 1970s, in a period of détente and approximate military-strategic parity, the total strength of the Soviet armed forces was estimated at 3·57 million men.[181] How realistic was it to implement a program of reductions to a level of 2·4 million men in a period of high political tension and military-strategic inferiority? In the game of military competition and political confrontation the facts were so compelling that even mediocre political leadership (or, in the later words of Marshal M. V. Zakharov, the reinstated Chief of General Staff, even persons who 'claim strategic farsightedness' but lack a 'rudimentary knowledge of military strategy')[182] could not have been blind to them. It is unrealistic to assume that Khrushchev was in fact blind to them and it is unlikely that a conspiracy of the military and political hard-liners was needed to open his eyes.

Heavy Industry versus Agriculture and Consumer Goods Production

Turning to the third issue in the interrelated set of policies, the controversy of heavy industry versus agriculture and the production of consumer goods, it would be an important substantiation of the more dramatic, and perhaps academically more fashionable, argument about an opposition faction asserting its power in order to change Khrushchev's policies if it could be shown that those policies had actually been pursued since 1959 but that they had then been dramatically reversed in 1961. It will be shown that this was in fact not the case.[183]

First, if the estimates of huge increases in actual military outlays in 1959 and possibly thereafter are broadly accurate it would appear that the contradictions mentioned above, of Khrushchev wanting to have the cake and eat it too,[184] is even more severe than originally assumed. The nature of the flaw of wanting to meet the ambitious economic goals of the Seven-Year Plan (1959–65) while engaging in an ambitious foreign policy venture in Central Europe, and for that reason having to maintain an effective military posture, was not that of a potential contradiction (as assumed earlier) but *a*

contradiction in actual fact as early as 1959. In essence, and put in the simpli-
fied form of Western discussions, Khrushchev was promising more butter,
but more guns were actually produced.

Secondly, warnings against assumptions of dramatic change in 1961 are
contained also in general trends of industrial production. New and more
realistic indices were constructed at that time in the West which brought out
the point that the Soviet performance had been overestimated. A significant
slackening of growth rates in industry had become evident. The rates were
now estimated to have been about 10 percent or more in the period 1950 to
1957; 9·1 percent in 1958; 8·4 percent in 1959; 6·3 percent in 1960; and in the
range of 6·9 percent to 5 percent in 1961.[185] It would lead too far to analyse
the possible reasons for this slackening of growth rates. Suffice it to say that
there is a long-term trend in which 1961 does not at all appear atypical and
that there were good reasons for the political leadership to be concerned
about finding ways of improving the overall economic performance.

Thirdly, the issue of agriculture and consumer goods production appears
to be far more complex and far more economic in nature than is implied in
the political explanation, that is, the postulated disruption of Khrushchev's
programs by a hard-line opposition. The general starting point in 1961 was
indeed an agonizing one for the Soviet leadership. During the period 1954–8
Khrushchev had on the whole been successful in introducing a better balance
in the economy by increasing the rate of agricultural investment relative to
industrial investment, raising government purchasing prices for farm
products and expanding the development of new lands, and these measures
had combined with better than normal weather conditions to lift agriculture
out of its stagnant position. However, by the time the Seven-Year Plan was
launched, the rate of agricultural investment relative to industrial investment
(whatever the reason) had already begun to decline, acreage expansion had
decreased, the initial benefits of this program had petered out and weather
conditions had returned to normal or worse than normal. With little
progress in agricultural output in the first two years of the Seven-Year Plan,
the problem of raising the level of agriculture without impairing industrial
growth again became acute in 1961.[186]

There is little doubt that Khrushchev wanted to make a determined effort
to overcome the return to stagnation and decline in agriculture. At the
important plenary session of the CPSU Central Committee on agriculture in
January 1961, which was concerned with this topic, Khrushchev stated that
'we must make up for lost time and in the remaining five years of the Seven-
Year Plan attain a far higher rate of development in agricultural production'.[187] He also laid down the principle of how this was to be done. 'Funds
accumulating as a result of overfulfilment of the Seven-Year Plan must be
diverted towards the further and still greater development of the consumer
goods industry and agriculture.'[188] In essence, industry (that is, heavy
industry) was henceforth to finance agricultural development instead of the
reverse, as formerly. Moreover Khrushchev's speech to the Central Committee contained controversial remarks such as the suggestion that 'all branches
of the economy must be developed in definite proportion', that they should
'develop evenly' and, more polemically, that 'eating increases the appetite'
so that 'some comrades have now developed an appetite for giving the

country as much metal as possible'. What seemed to be implied here was a revision of the time-honored priority development of production of capital goods (group A in Soviet terminology) over production of consumer goods (group B).

In detail, what Khrushchev probably had in mind was not the utilization of funds resulting from overfulfillment of the Seven-Year Plan *per se*, but overfulfillment in *group A*. For instance, the annual plan for the previous year (1960) had set an increase for group A at 8·8 percent but output in this category actually was said to have risen by 11 percent. The planned rate for group B was 6·4 percent and the actual rise was given as 7 percent.[189] Seen in this light there was indeed good cause for reallocating resources to agriculture and consumer industry and for the decision of the Supreme Soviet at the end of 1960 (to which Khrushchev pointed in his speech to the January 1961 CC plenum) to assign an additional 2·5 to 3 billion (new) rubles to consumer industry.[190]

However, allocations destined for agriculture had been cut before, in 1959 and in 1960, as Khrushchev himself had stated,[191] and 1961 was to prove no exception. Although Khrushchev had warned in January that the proposed reallocation in favor of agriculture and light industry would be insufficient to cover capital investments in the production of artificial fertilizers and agricultural machinery, by as late as May the Soviet government had not taken any steps to implement the scheme and as late as March the Soviet press was still stating that only 7·8 percent (!) of the industrial plants due to go into production would serve the consumer industries.[192] All this occurred before the Vienna Summit and before the summer crisis, not during or after it. If there was an opposition faction wrecking Khrushchev's plans in agriculture and consumer goods production it must have been active, as well as successful, ever since the promulgation of the Seven-Year Plan.[193]

The case of scepticism and caution towards the view that the military and a hard-line faction in the Kremlin forced the reversal of priorities on Khrushchev is strengthened by Khrushchev himself, in his memoirs. Speaking at some length about the problem of allocation of funds and economic, social and military priorities he says that 'Apparently the control of military spending is a universal problem' – a point well taken – and that unfortunately there was a 'tendency for people who run the armed forces to be greedy and self-seeking'.[194] He also writes that he commiserated with President Eisenhower on this issue (during his visit to the United States in 1959) who had told him that his military leaders always came to him and asked for more money pointing to the Soviet Union and arguing that if they did not get the funds they needed they would fall behind. Khrushchev, according to his recollections, then replied,

> It's just the same. Some people from our military department come and say, 'Comrade Khrushchev, look at this! The Americans are developing such and such a system. We could develop the same system, but it would cost such and such.' I tell them there's no money; it's all been allotted already. So they say, 'If we don't get the money we need and if there's a war, then the enemy will have superiority over us'. So we discuss it some more, and I end up by giving them the money they ask for.[195]

This does sound like the exposé of a universal problem where the political leadership hesitatingly yields to military opinion. But in the same context Khrushchev also makes a far stronger case for his own responsibility and initiative.

> When I was the leader of the Party and the Government, I decided that we had to economize drastically in the building of homes, the construction of communal services, and even in the development of agriculture in order to build up our defenses. [Khrushchev then mentions some examples of cuts in investment, and goes on to say,] I think I was right to concentrate on military spending, even at the expense of all but the most essential investments in other areas. If I hadn't put such a high priority on our military needs, we couldn't have survived.[196]

Even bearing in mind all the known limitations of memoirs in general, and Khrushchev's memoirs in particular, it would be unwise to dismiss as irrelevant the main points which Khrushchev makes in this context. In his own understanding he does not appear as a victim of pressures exerted by the military and a hard-line faction in the Kremlin, but as a political leader who places high value on military power.

Conflict and Decision-Making

But having said all that, the central point still needs to be made. In the final analysis it does not really matter too much for the present inquiry when the defense budget increased, and by how much, what the precise degree of opposition by the military to Khrushchev's program of troop reductions was, and whether or not the 'metal-eaters' won some victories over Khrushchev in 1961 in the battles between agriculture and consumer industry versus heavy industry and defense spending. A much more important point is whether it is correct to assume that (1) those political leaders favoring priority growth of group A and higher defense spending and (2) those military leaders who, perhaps naturally, support this priority and in addition resented Khrushchev's military policies, are both, by virtue of their positions, to be considered adherents to a course of collision and confrontation, direct, militant tactics and risk-taking in international affairs. In other words, the crucial problem concerns the precise nature of the relationship between domestic politics and foreign policy.

Unfortunately, systematic study of this problem is lacking. But at the outset it is useful to warn against drawing the battle lines between two opposed camps in Soviet domestic politics too clearly. Even Khrushchev himself felt constrained to emphasize repeatedly that tractors and agricultural machinery are made of metal, too, and that 'a powerful advance in agriculture cannot be achieved without heavy industry'.[197] However, contrary to widely held assumptions there does *not* appear to be a direct correlation between orthodox views on ideology, military policy and economics on the one hand, and high proclivities for risk-taking in foreign policy on the other.

Several examples pointing to the absence of such direct correlations can be provided. Molotov in the 1950s could rightly be regarded as a Stalinist at heart, as an advocate of heavy industry, who even went so far as to suggest that only the foundations of socialism had been built in the USSR and who is not at all known for his sympathies for agriculture and consumer industry, yet he appears to have been strongly *against* the expansion of commitments in the Middle East.[198] Secondly, concerning the Cuban missile crisis, it is not altogether clear what role the military leadership played in this venture, but there appears to have been opposition to Khrushchev's plans at least by the head of the strategic rocket forces, General Moskalenko.[199] Thirdly, Brezhnev who ever since 1964 had been instrumental in tightening party control over society, maintaining ideological orthodoxy in the USSR and Eastern Europe, including Czechoslovakia in 1968, who has strictly adhered to priority production of heavy industry, and who has cultivated special relations to the military, has at the same time been averse to taking risks in foreign policy.

But what about the Berlin crisis? As usual, evidence on these sensitive matters is scanty. To turn to the Soviet military first, from the Penkovsky Papers there emerges the picture of a basically opportunist military leadership, interested in career advancement and higher budgetary allocations for defense but abstaining from playing a direct role in foreign policy. As regards the military's attitude toward Khrushchev's policy in the Berlin crisis, exactly the opposite of widely held assumptions would seem to have been prevalent. Far from egging Khrushchev on, the military leaders seem to have been apprehensive about the state of the country's defenses and the 'big risk' Khrushchev appeared to be embarking upon.[200] This, in retrospect, would have been a perfectly natural attitude to take if one had first-hand knowledge of the true extent of Soviet military-strategic inferiority in relation to the United States.

There was more reason for the military to be apprehensive. Khrushchev had shown a remarkable tendency for sudden moves and ill-advised initiatives ('subjectivism' and 'harebrained scheming' in Soviet terminology). This was evident in de-Stalinization, the Zhukov affair, the discovery of the 'anti-party group', in party and economic reform, in agriculture and, last but not least, in military affairs and foreign policy. As Marshal Zakharov was to say after Khrushchev's fall, 'subjectivism is dangerous in any activity', but 'particularly dangerous in military affairs which deal with problems of the country's defense'.[201] For instance, as the Penkovsky Papers show, after having downgraded conventional weapons, Khrushchev suddenly – because of the Berlin crisis 'attaches a great deal of importance to tank troops'. The account continues that, in fact,

> So much importance is attached to tanks in connection with the Berlin crisis that controversy has already broken out in the General Staff over finances. They are afraid that too much money has been allotted to the tank troops and that there will not be enough for missiles, electronics, and other types of equipment.[202]

Given these 'dangerous' tendencies of 'subjectivism' as seen by the military, it is even possible that this group exerted some *restraining* influence on Khrushchev's foreign policy. What should be ruled out with some confidence is the thesis that the military actively supported Khrushchev's more far-reaching designs in the Berlin crisis.

Turning to the political leadership, it is appropriate to begin with the accepted interpretations by members of what Linden called the 'conflict school'. Ploss writes that Presidium members Frol Kozlov and Mikhail Suslov led an austerity group in the Soviet hierarchy[203] and that both of them were neo-Stalinists;[204] Nicolaevsky, writing in 1961, considers Suslov simply a Stalinist;[205] Linden explicitly states that Suslov's views on several issues were similar to those of Molotov,[206] and that both Suslov and Kozlov had orthodox views and showed preference for heavy industry and defense.[207] This is woven by Slusser into the foreign policy context. Suslov and Kozlov are singled out as the 'leading oppositionists',[208] who, at every turn of the screw in the crisis, are behind the 'work of authorities in Moscow who were willing to push the Soviet offensive [in Berlin] to the limit'[209] – not too successfully, apparently, because Kozlov realized in the end that there was only 'one path open to him – clandestine conspiratorial opposition'.[210]

Tatu writes that at the January 1961 CC plenum Kozlov was appointed rapporteur to the forthcoming party congress on the subject of the reform of statutes – a role Khrushchev had assumed at the Nineteenth Party Congress. Although this post was only of a longstanding tradition without any basis in law, Kozlov in essence thereby assumed the position as potential successor to Khrushchev at the head of the party; for the time being he functioned as general supervisor of cadres.[211] Kozlov also showed interest in armament production and appears to have had close links with Dmitri Ustinov, the leading figure in defense industry, these links dating back as far as the period from 1936 to 1944 when Kozlov was active in organizing the war industry in the same city (Izhevsk) in which Ustinov was consistently elected deputy to the Supreme Soviet.[212] All this is confirmed to some extent by the Penkovsky Papers, which provide the important detail that 'Kozlov frequently attends the meetings of the Supreme Military Council together with Khrushchev, Mikoyan, and Suslov' and the observation that 'Kozlov is very much interested in military matters. He sticks his nose into everything, and wants to know all the details.'[213] The Penkovsky Papers also mention the 'possibility of a split in the top [political] echelon, for instance on the Berlin question'.[214]

But before drawing any rash conclusions from all this, a closer look at published evidence is warranted. As far as the chief alleged hard-liner on Soviet policy in the Berlin crisis, Kozlov, is concerned, he appears to have made only two speeches in the period between June and October 1961: on 11 July, at a reception in the Mongolian embassy in Moscow, marking the fortieth anniversary of the founding of the Mongolian People's Republic; and on 12 September, in Pyongyang, at the Fourth Congress of the North Korean Communist Party. What did he say that might conceivably justify the inference that his position on the Berlin and the German problem was 'harder' than that of Khrushchev? In the first speech he did not mention Berlin or Germany at all (or even the United States for that matter).[215] In his second speech he anticipated Khrushchev's 'official' lifting of the Berlin ultimatum (at the Twenty-Second Party Congress, see p. 214) by about a month. In fact Kozlov's wording of 12 September was almost the same as Khrushchev's of 17 October. This is the crucial passage:

Our proposals are not an ultimatum. The Soviet Union is prepared, together with interested countries, to consider and discuss any reasonable comments and amendments to our draft peace treaty.[216]

If anything, this stand on the German problem puts Kozlov in the ranks of advocates of restraint (unless, of course, it is to be supposed that Kozlov's position was not at all as powerful as it has variously been described and that he was forced to adopt a stand that contradicted his beliefs). And if so, it does not at all have to invalidate the view that he, as well as Suslov, were advocates of increased military readiness and heavy industry. At one time (in 1954–5), for tactical reasons in the succession struggle, Khrushchev himself had advocated this position only to abandon it at his convenience.

What is more, although the Penkovsky Papers confirm the hypothesis of controversies in the top political leadership about Berlin policy, it is Khrushchev who is seen as the driving force behind the hard line. Hence the battle lines between hawks and doves are drawn quite differently from what adherents to the conflict model would make us believe. According to rumors the account reads: 'Khrushchev has frequent quarrels with Mikoyan'; according to Viktor Churaev, head of the Central Committee's Bureau for the RSFSR, 'there are many foreign policy questions on which Mikoyan disagrees with Khrushchev'; and in Penkovsky's own opinion (or according to his own information) the reason why there are these controversies is because 'Mikoyan is against the hard policy on Berlin'.[217] Thus the approximate state of affairs regarding Berlin was probably as follows: Khrushchev, as on previous occasions, taking the initiative, creating anxiety among elements of the military and the political leadership that he might be embarking on harebrained scheming and adventurism, and leading to a conviction that he needed to be restrained in order to prevent a catastrophe.[218]

If this picture is an accurate representation of the real state of affairs, as this writer believes it is, one might expect Khrushchev to reassure actual or potential critics as to the necessity of Soviet pressures on the German problem. (After all, from the point of view of the Soviet public, including middle-echelon and lower-echelon party officials, everything had been quiet on the 'western front' prior to the launching of the 1958 Berlin ultimatum. The true extent, that is, the mass character, of the East Germans' exodus from the GDR was for obvious reasons never revealed in the Soviet Union. Khrushchev, therefore, could easily have been blamed for creating unnecessary risks.) Various examples of such reassurance could have been selected. The most striking is that which was provided less than a week before the taking of physical action in Berlin, in his radio and television address to the Soviet people of 7 August, in which Khrushchev not only referred to West Berlin as a 'convenient loophole',[219] but also introduced hypothetical inquirers.

There are those who might say: 'But is it at all necessary to sign a peace treaty with Germany now? Why not wait another two or three years or even longer? Perhaps that would eliminate tension, remove the danger of war.'[220]

To these concerned people he replies that the Western countries would regard further delay as a 'strategic breakthrough and would at once broaden the range of their demands'. They would demand liquidation of the socialist system in the German Democratic Republic, try to annex the lands restored to Poland and Czechoslovakia under the Potsdam Agreement and finally attempt to abolish the socialist system in all countries of the socialist camp.[221]

As a final consideration, no matter what the extent of personal preferences of Khrushchev's colleagues in the Presidium and in the party at large, it remains very doubtful that active factional conflict interfered in Khrushchev's handling of the Berlin crisis. The Presidium had been purged in Khrushchev's favor in 1957 and consisted not only of the four major protagonists mentioned so far (Khrushchev, Kozlov, Suslov and Mikoyan) but a total of fourteen members (the ten others being Brezhnev, Kosygin, Podgorny, Furtseva, Polyansky, Kuusinen, Shvernik, Aristov, Ignatov and Mukhitdinov), many of whom could still be considered loyal to or dependent on Khrushchev. Again it may be useful to refer to the Penkovsky Papers on this issue. The reader is told that 'there is smouldering opposition within the leadership'; however, 'it is not allowed to come out into the open for fear that Khrushchev may yet again announce the existence of some new anti-Party group'.[222]

In sum, the thesis of powerful domestic political pressures egging Khrushchev on in the Berlin crisis, either before or after 13 August, is difficult to reconcile with all (or, if one prefers, the little) that is known about Soviet domestic politics in 1961. But what about alliance pressures which – as described in the theoretical part – can be considered as one of the facets of the bureaucratic politics model?

Decision-Making and the Socialist Community

A good case can be made for arguing that Ulbricht was a major driving force behind hard-line policies of the Warsaw Pact member countries on the German problem in 1961. Statements by the GDR on the question of Berlin and Germany were more uncompromising than those emanating from the Soviet Union. In fact some of Ulbricht's pronouncements often anticipated new Soviet moves, they tended to continue pressure where the Soviet Union had already indicated a desire to compromise, and other statements were even of a blatantly provocative nature. For example, already prior to Khrushchev's ultimatum of November 1958, on 27 October 1958, Ulbricht reverted to the position formulated by Marshal Sokolovsky during the 1948 Berlin crisis, (only exchanging 'GDR' for Sokolovsky's 'Soviet Zone of Occupation'), by saying at a mass rally in East Berlin, 'All of Berlin is located on the territory of the German Democratic Republic. All of Berlin is under sovereignty of the German Democratic Republic.'[223] And when asked by a Western correspondent about what would happen if the allies chose not to bow to Soviet proposals and a second airlift were instituted, Ulbricht replied provocatively that such a move 'would be considered a military threat' to the GDR and would be answered accordingly.[224]

It is also noticeable that Ulbricht was more direct than Khrushchev in attacking positions of the Western allies in Berlin and that he displayed a greater attitude of unconcern about likely international consequences of these direct challenges. For instance, asked about details concerning GDR control over communications to Berlin after the signing of a peace treaty, in particular whether this meant that Tempelhof Airport – the biggest airport in West Berlin – would be closed down, Ulbricht replied flippantly that 'perhaps the airport will close itself down';[225] two weeks later, the GDR announced that by 1 August foreign aircraft would be required to register with a GDR 'safety center' on entering and leaving East German airspace.[226] However, when the Soviet Union took up this matter it was at a later date (in its note of 23 August) but also in an ambiguous way, charging that the West was violating agreements reached in 1945 'for the subversive and revanchist purpose of West German militarism'. The Soviet Union also did not challenge in principle the right of the three Western powers to use these air corridors which served 'to insure the needs of their military garrisons'.[227]

Differences of emphasis in the GDR and Soviet attitudes towards Berlin and Germany are confirmed in a study of major statements of these two countries in the period from January to August 1961.[228] Using content analysis as a research technique, the study concludes that the Soviet Union and the GDR pursued increasingly divergent goals. With the mounting crisis, the Soviet materials showed greater concern for possible international complications and the maintenance of peace, whereas the GDR continued to advocate the conclusion of a separate peace treaty as vigorously as ever. Finally, echoes of this divergence of official attitudes could be heard as late as December 1961. With seventeen days left for Khrushchev to implement his threat made in June (but retracted in October) to conclude a separate peace treaty by the end of the year, Ulbricht announced that Khrushchev had decided to sign a separate peace treaty after all. There was no word of confirmation from the Soviet Union.[229]

In many ways the more uncompromising East German position can be regarded as an asset from the Soviet point of view: by pointing to the demands of an allegedly reckless ally obsessed with immediate and local issues, it can portray itself as a responsible superpower disposed favorably to compromise solutions (which, from the Western point of view, may still be unacceptable). To that extent there is a tacit or explicit division of labor. However, it also stands to reason that there were genuine differences of interest between the Soviet Union and the GDR and that Ulbricht, who felt his own position directly threatened, actively pressed Khrushchev to take drastic steps in order to improve the worsening conditions of the GDR. One of these steps – and probably not the only or last one – was the building of the Wall.

Heinz Lippmann, a former secretary at the Central Council of the FDJ (the East German equivalent of the KOMSOMOL) and deputy to Erich Honecker from 1949 until late 1953, who later defected to the West, reports that discussions of plans to seal off the borders dated back to the early 1950s.[230] During the World Youth Festival in 1951, when many young people had crossed over to West Berlin, it was found that all checks of subway and metropolitan trains by police and FDJ auxiliaries at sector crossing points had proved ineffective. In 1952 and 1953, when the number of people leaving East Germany had increased considerably, discussions took place in the East

German leadership about how to stop the exodus. Later, plans were discussed to issue special permits and keep a close watch on the main traffic routes; some of these measures were tried out but none of them had proved effective either. It is on the basis of these experiences that the thought of constructing a wall ripened in the minds of the SED leadership. [231]

It has already been mentioned that it is plausible that Ulbricht received authorization from the plenary meeting of the SED Central Committee (16–19 March 1961) to approach the Soviet leadership with the proposal to construct a wall in Berlin, that the Moscow meeting of the Political Consultative Committee of the Warsaw Pact (28–9 March) discussed this proposal, but did not endorse it at that point. [232] On this basis it could be argued that Ulbricht's famous denial of 15 June, to the effect that nobody in East Germany had any intention of building a wall, [233] was quite deliberate so as to stimulate even further the outflow of citizens and to increase the pressure on Khrushchev to act. [234] This view could be supported by the fact that Ulbricht is not known for having committed many Freudian slips during his long party career (although, like Khrushchev, he seemed to lose his temper at times), but for skillful manipulation of propaganda techniques.

Heinz Lippmann, however, disagrees with this interpretation. In his view Ulbricht's statement was inadvertent, showing that 'at that time the wall was a discussion topic' and that 'Ulbricht did not yet have [Khrushchev's] final approval'. [235] Carola Stern also thinks that Ulbricht committed a *lapsus linguae*. [236]

But no matter whether Ulbricht's remark was deliberate or inadvertent, the fact that it was made at all would seem to indicate at the very least that Ulbricht was already preoccupied with preparations for building the wall and merely waiting for final approval from Khrushchev and endorsement by the Warsaw Pact countries. This is confirmed by Kroll. Khrushchev reportedly mentioned to him that

> I don't want to conceal from you the fact that in the final analysis it was me who gave the order [to build the Wall]. Ulbricht had indeed put pressure on me for quite some time, and in the final months had urged me ever more vehemently [to act]. However, I do not want to hide behind his back. It is much to small for me. [237]

But having said all that, does it follow that the course of events shows the expanded role and influence of the GDR in the socialist bloc, or of an Ulbricht faction within the Presidium of the CPSU? Both propositions are doubtful – the first because the very instability and vulnerability of the GDR in 1961 made that country more dependent on the Soviet Union and the other members of the Warsaw Pact than ever before, the second because – as argued above – Khrushchev's policies in the Berlin crisis appeared risky enough to fellow members of the Presidium to require caution and restraint rather than further encouragement.

To sum up, the significance of pressures from the GDR (or China) [238] may be similar to that of pressures from the Soviet military concerning the increase in the Soviet defense posture during the Berlin crisis: if policies are consistently advocated which ultimately turn out to be compelling on their merits, the adoption of these policies cannot necessarily be interpreted as proof of these actors' 'power' over the policy-making process in the Soviet Union. It rather goes to show the validity of what German political science calls *die normative Kraft des Faktischen* – the power of facts to set norms of action.

Notes: Part Two, Chapter 13

1   *Pravda*, 25 January 1961.
2   *Pravda* and *Izvestiia*, 30 July 1961.
3   For details see, among many other sources, Donald S. Zagoria, *The Sino-Soviet Conflict, 1956–1961* (Princeton, NJ: Princeton University Press, 1962); William E. Griffith, *Albania and the Sino-Soviet Rift* (New York: Atheneum, 1967), and his article 'The November 1960 Moscow meeting: a preliminary reconstruction', *China Quarterly*, no. 11 (July–September 1961); and Richard Löwenthal, *World Communism: The Disintegration of a Secular Faith* (New York: Oxford University Press, 1966), esp. pp. 188–202.
4   Published in *Pravda*, 6 December 1960.
5   ibid., 25 January 1961.
6   Khrushchev's report to the Twentieth Party Congress, ibid., 15 February 1956.
7   ibid., 25 January 1961 (my italics).
8   Stalin's book is a collection of comments on a draft for a new textbook on political economy written in February, April, May and September of 1952, that is, shortly before the Nineteenth Party Congress (October 1952). The complete Russian text was published in *Pravda*, 3 and 4 October 1952. Reference is made here to an English edition, Joseph Stalin, *Economic Problems of Socialism in the USSR* (Moscow: Foreign Languages Publishing House, 1952).
9   ibid., p. 40.
10 ibid., pp. 38–9.
11 *Pravda*, 25 January 1961 (my italics).
12 see above, p. 113.
13 Khrushchev's report of 6 January 1961, *Pravda*, 25 January 1961 (my italics).
14 ibid. and *Izvestiia*, 30 July 1961.
15 See above, p. 45.
16 Khrushchev's report of 6 January 1961.
17 ibid.
18 ibid.
19 In his report to the Twentieth Party Congress, Khrushchev had observed that 'To preserve and – in some places to re-establish – their domination, the colonial powers are resorting to the suppression of colonial peoples by force of arms, a method which has been condemned by history' (*Pravda*, 15 February 1956). Although this method may have been condemned by history, the Western powers, in Khrushchev's eyes, *were* still resorting to it and likely to do so in the future.
20 Khrushchev's report of 6 January 1961.
21 ibid.
22 ibid.
23 ibid.
24 ibid. This was a standard theme, which was to be repeated time and again; see, for instance, Khrushchev's speech at the Third Congress of the Romanian Workers' Party (*Pravda*, 22 June 1960).
25 ibid.
26 ibid.
27 Khrushchev's report of 6 January 1961.
28 ibid. (my italics).
29 ibid. (my italics).
30 *Pravda* and *Izvestiia*, 30 July 1961.
31 *Pravda*, 28 January 1959.
32 ibid.
33 ibid., 25 January 1961 (my italics).

34 ibid.
35 ibid.
36 See, for instance, Khrushchev's speeches in Alma Ata on 15 and 24 June 1961, and his speech to Soviet military graduates in Moscow on 8 July 1961.
37 Khrushchev's report of 6 January 1961. These ideological themes are very closely related to military and domestic issues of the Berlin crisis; see the relevant chapters below.
38 Keiderling and Stulz; *Geschichte Berlins*, p. 460.
39 Deutsches Institut für Wirtschaftsforschung (ed.), *DDR-Wirtschaft: Eine Bestandsaufnahme* (Frankfurt aM: Fischer Verlag, 1971), pp. 56–7.
40 Maintenance of the economic viability of the GDR will be considered as one major state interest of the Soviet Union and be treated in more detail on pp. 231–7.
41 Draft Program of the CPSU, *Pravda*, 30 July 1961.
42 ibid., 8 August 1961.
43 Keiderling and Stulz, *Geschichte Berlins*, p. 460.
44 Draft Program of the CPSU, *Pravda*, 30 July 1961 (my italics except where indicated otherwise).
45 Ministerstvo vneshnei torgovli SSSR, planovo-ekonomicheskoe upravlenie (ed.), *Vneshnaia torgovlia Soiusa SSSR za 1959–1963 gody* (Moscow: Vneshtorgizdat, 1965), pp. 214–31; see also Deutsches Institut für Wirtschaftsforschung (ed.), *DDR-Wirtschaft*, table 88, p. 355.
46 ibid., tables 85 and 86, pp. 352–3, and table 88, p. 355.
47 ibid., p. 57.
48 *Gesetzblatt der Deutschen Demokratischen Republik*, pt I (1959), p. 745.
49 *Die Flucht aus der Sowjetzone.*
50 Hans Apel, *Wehen und Wunder der Zonenwirtschaft* (Cologne: Verlag Wissenschaft und Politik, 1966), p. 29.
51 ibid., pp. 75–92.
52 ibid., pp. 46–50, and pp. 251–67.
53 ibid., p. 50.
54 Vysotskii, *Zapadnyi Berlin*, p. 21; see also above, p. 184.
55 ibid., pp. 199–200, and Vysotsky, *West Berlin* pp. 109–10.
56 Vysotskii, *Zapadnyi Berlin*, p. 201.
57 Vysotsky, *West Berlin*, p. 120.
58 *Gesetzblatt der Deutschen Demokratischen Republik*, pt I (1959), p. 745.
59 Apel, *Wehen und Wunder*, p. 153.
60 ibid.; see also Stern, *Ulbricht*, pp. 206–9.
61 Hans Müller and Karl Reissig, *Wirtschaftswunder DDR: Ein Beitrag zur Geschichte der ökonomischen Politik der Sozialistischen Einheitspartei Deutschlands* (East Berlin: Dietz Verlag for the Institut für Gesellschaftswissenschaften beim ZK der SED, 1969), p. 323.
62 The decline in the production of foodstuffs in the GDR in 1960 and 1961 is shown in *Bericht der Bundesregierung und Materialien zur Lage der Nation, 1971* (Bonn: Bundesministerium für innerdeutsche Beziehungen, 1971), p. 102.
63 Vysotsky, *West Berlin*, p. 110.
64 A. S. Grossman, 'Granitsa mira', *Voprosy istorii*, no. 10 (1969), p. 199.
65 Horst Mendershausen, *Interzonal Trade in Germany, Pt I: The Trade and Contractual Relations*, RM-3686 (Santa Monica, Calif.: Rand Corporation, July 1963), pp. 15–29.
66 Keiderling and Stulz, *Geschichte Berlins*, p. 458.
67 Walter Ulbricht's report and resolution of the eleventh plenary session of the CC of the SED, 15–17 December 1960, as quoted in ibid., p. 459; see also *Neues Deutschland*, 21 and 22 December 1960.
68 *Bericht der Bundesregierung*, 1971, p. 234, table A3. One unit of account corresponds to one German mark.
69 *Neues Deutschland*, 19 March 1961, as quoted by Konstantin Pritzel, *Die Wirtschaftsintegration Mitteldeutschlands* (Cologne: Verlag Wissenschaft und Politik, 1969), p. 83.
70 *Neues Deutschland*, 9 July 1961, as quoted in ibid., pp. 83–4.
71 ibid.
72 Heinz Brandt, *Ein Traum der nicht entführbar ist: Mein Weg zwischen Ost und West* (West Berlin: Verlag 'Europäische Ideen', 1977), p. 209. The author was secretary of the party committee of Berlin in June 1953. He defected to West Berlin in 1958. The Soviet military administration was replaced in November 1949 by a Soviet control commission and then, in

May 1953, by a (civilian) high commission and the supreme commander of the Group of Soviet Forces in Germany.

73   ibid. The implication of the last demand was obviously that Ulbricht had to go.
74   Khrushchev in a speech on 3 March 1963, *Pravda*, 10 March 1963; Ulbricht at the fifteenth plenary session of the CC of the SED, *Die Neue Zeitung*, 23 August 1953. The charges should not be taken too literally. Both Khrushchev and Ulbricht – although for different reasons – had axes to grind against Beria. Neither the report by *Pravda* on Beria's arrest (10 July) nor the text of his indictment (published on 24 December 1953) mentioned any accusations related to Germany or to any question of foreign policy; see the detailed account by Victor Baras, 'Beria's fall and Ulbricht's survival', *Soviet Studies*, vol. 27, no. 3 (July 1975), pp. 381–95.
75   *Neues Deutschland*, 11 June 1953. Note the reference to two parts (*Teile*) of Germany rather than to two German states (*Staaten*).
76   N. Galay, 'Berlin: on the eve of dénouement', *Bulletin of the Institute for the Study of the USSR*, vol. 8, no. 10 (October 1961), p. 23.
77   All of these speeches were published in *Pravda*, 22 June 1961.
78   ibid.
79   ibid.
80   ibid. and *Izvestiia*, 9 July 1961. Unless otherwise indicated, all ruble values are expressed in new rubles, introduced in 1961. One new ruble equals ten old rubles.
81   *Pravda*, 10 July 1961; this enumeration draws on Galay, 'Berlin', pp. 23–5.
82   Schlesinger, *A Thousand Days*, p. 454; for details, interpretation and other references see Slusser, *The Berlin Crisis*, p. 91.
83   *Pravda*, 8 August 1961; *Izvestiia*, 9 August 1961 (my italics).
84   In the end the procedure adopted was, first, to defer the release of an unspecified 'necessary number' of servicemen to the reserve (according to the announcement by the CPSU Central Committee and the Soviet government of 29 August 1961, *Pravda*, 30 August 1961) and thereafter to cancel the release from active duty of all servicemen and the calling up of the contingent born in 1942 (*Pravda*, 15 September 1961). See below, p. 242.
85   *Pravda*, 8 August 1961 and *Izvestiia*, 9 August 1961.
86   Zolling and Bahnsen, *Kalter Winter*, p. 107.
87   See pp. 207–8.
88   Galay, 'Berlin', p. 24; see also above, p. 207.
89   See p. 209.
90   Text published in *Pravda*, 29 August 1961.
91   Text published in *Pravda*, 30 August 1961, p. 1, in big headlines across the whole page: 'O Tsentral'nom Komitete KPSS i Sovete Ministrov SSSR: O vremennoi otsrochke uvol'neniia v zapas soldat, matrosov, serzhantov i starshin, vysluzhivshikh sroki deistvitel'noi voennoi sluzhby.'
92   Text published in *Pravda*, 31 August 1961, p. 1, also in big headlines across the whole page: 'Zaiavlenie Sovetskogo pravitel'stva.'
93   For instance, in a letter to President Eisenhower, 22 April 1958, in US Department of State, *Documents on Disarmament, 1945–1959*, Vol. II (Washington, DC: Government Printing Office, 1960), p. 999, and in his address to the Supreme Soviet, 14 January 1960, in *Pravda*, 15 January 1960. This is discussed by Arthur H. Dean, *Test Ban and Disarmament: The Path of Negotiations* (New York and Evanston: Harper & Row, 1966), pp. 89–90.
94   Announcement by the Soviet government on 28 August 1959, (*Izvestiia*, 29 August 1959); see also Khrushchev's speech of 21 June 1961, quoted in part on p. 240.
95   Galay, 'Berlin', p. 25.
96   *Pravda*, 31 August 1961.
97   'Zashchita sotsialisticheskogo otechestva – nash sviashchennyi dolg', *Pravda*, 14 September 1961.
98   'Prikaz Ministra oborony Soiuza SSR', *Pravda*, 15 September 1961.
99   ibid. and *Izvestiia*, 11 September 1961.
100 The ICBM tests were completed at the end of October (as scheduled in the 14 October announcement) and shipping and air traffic in the area of the central Pacific was again declared safe (*Pravda*, 30 October, 1961).
101 *Krasnaia zvezda*, 16, 20, 22 and 29 September 1961, and *Sovetskaia Rossiia*, 3 October 1961.

102   *Krasnaia Zvezda*, 16 September 1961.

103   *Pravda*, 14 September 1961.

104   *Izvestiia*, 12 September 1961.

105   *Pravda*, 26 September 1961.

106   For the distinctions between deterrence, coercion, compulsion and 'compellence' see Schelling, *Arms and Influence*, pp. 69–78.

107   Wolfe, *Soviet Power and Europe*, p. 95.

108   *Khrushchev Remembers* [Vol. I], trans. and ed. Strobe Talbott, with an introduction, commentary and notes by Edward Crankshaw (Boston, Mass.: Little, Brown/Bantam Books, 1970), p. 506. Khrushchev's memoirs may not be an accurate guide to the facts because inaccuracies, rationalizations and half-truths are mixed with accurate information and the obvious. Perhaps the foremost benefit to the scholar is the insights it affords into the general mood and mode of thinking by Khrushchev. In this respect Khrushchev's reference to the role of the armed forces in Germany is quite enlightening.

109   *Khrushchev Remembers*, Vol. I, p. 508.

110   *Khrushchev Remembers: The Last Testament* [Vol. II], trans. and ed. Strobe Talbott, with a foreword by Edward Crankshaw and an introduction by Jerrold L. Schecter (London: Deutsch, 1974), pp. 504–5. Characteristically, the wheat has to be separated from the chaff: Khrushchev's reference to the Americans advancing a pawn refers to the appointment of General Lucius D. Clay, whereas the Russians moving a knight (*kon'*) refers to Konev's appointment. However, Konev's appointment was announced on 10 August (and, as noted, probably decided upon earlier, at the meeting of Warsaw Pact leaders, 3–5 August but Clay was asked to be the President's special envoy to Berlin only on 18 August – in other words, Khrushchev confuses the sequence of moves. The editor of Khrushchev's memoirs points out the pun – *kon'*, of course, being the root of Konev's surname – but fails to correct Khrushchev's error.

111   In this context Smith draws the parallel that the symbolic nature of the move would have been similar if the United States had at some point in time after the Korean War recalled General Douglas MacArthur to command American forces in South Korea (Smith, *The Defense of Berlin*, p. 264).

112   *Pravda*, 23 July 1962.

113   P. A. Nikolaev, *Politika Sovetskogo Soiuza v Germanskom voprose* (Moscow: Izdatel'stvo 'Nauka', 1966), pp. 290–4, and Nikolai N. Inozemtsev (ed.), *Mezhdunarodnye otnosheniia posle vtoroi mirovoi voiny*, Vol. I (Moscow: Izdatel'stvo 'Mezhdunarodnye otnosheniia', 1962), p. 211, as quoted in Wolfe, *Soviet Power and Europe*, p. 95.

114   *Pravda*, 10 August 1961; see above p. 208.

115   *The Times* 2 September 1961; see also above, p. 212.

116   ibid., 1 September 1961.

117   *Izvestiia*, 9 September 1961.

118   Joseph Alsop in *Foreign Policy*, no. 16 (Fall 1974), pp. 86–7, in his comment on Wohlstetter's article, 'Rivals but no "race"', ibid., pp. 48–81.

119   Horelick and Rush, *Strategic Power*, pp. 105–6.

120   *Foreign Policy*, (Fall 1974), pp. 84–7.

121   *New York Times*, 12 January 1961.

122   'Department of Defense statement on US military strength', 14 April 1964, and the *New York Times*, 15 April 1964, as quoted by Horelick and Rush, *Strategic Power*, p. 37. However, if by a 'handful' is meant a total of no more than five ICBMs, the accuracy of the Defense Department's statement must be doubted. More likely it was to emphasize, in an offhand manner, the very modest deployment effort of the USSR at that time.

123   Based on Bloomfield, *et al.*, *Khrushchev and the Arms Race: Soviet Interests in Arms Control and Disarmament, 1954–1964* (Cambridge, Mass.: MIT, 1966), pp. 94–5; various issues of *The Military Balance* (London: International Institute for Strategic Studies, 1959–73); and Charles M. Perry, 'Major US-Soviet strategic nuclear delivery vehicles, 1946–1973', in Geoffrey Kemp, Robert L. Pfaltzgraff, Jr, and Uri Ra'anan (eds), *The Superpowers in a Multinuclear World* (Lexington, Mass., and Toronto: D. C. Heath, 1974), pp. 275–85.

124   Alsop in *Foreign Policy* (Fall 1974), p. 87.

125   See the graphic illustration and analysis of US spending for strategic forces by Wohlstetter, 'Rivals but no "race"', ibid., fig. 6, p. 62, and pp. 65–71. The second large

increase for strategic forces in FY 1962 (beginning 1 July 1961) was in essence decided upon *in the fall of 1960*.

126   See above, p. 208; the last assertions (about the H-bomb, the British Isles and France) were made by Khrushchev to the British ambassador, Sir Frank Roberts, on 2 July in Moscow, as reported by Alsop in the *Washington Post*, 12 July 1961.

127   As stated by Khrushchev in his speech of 7 August 1961 (*Pravda*, 8 August 1961 and *Izvetiia*, 9 August 1961).

128   *Khrushchev Remembers*, Vol. I, p. 569 (my italics); similarly, Vol. II, p. 361. Although Khrushchev did not specifically make this point with reference to the Berlin crisis, it is appropriate to use the quotation in this context as it underlines the purposive character of Khrushchev's nuclear threats as a general phenomenon.

129   *Pravda*, 22 June 1961, and *Izvestiia*, 23 June 1961. Khrushchev had made the same point almost verbatim in a speech on 23 June at a Soviet-North Vietnamese friendship meeting in the Kremlin (*Pravda*, 29 June 1961).

130   *Pravda*, 9 July 1961.

131   *Pravda*, 8 August 1961; *Izvestiia*, 9 August 1961.

132   *Pravda*, 22 June 1961 and *Izvestiia*, 23 June 1961.

133   *New York Times*, 1 and 11 August 1961; Schlesinger, *A Thousand Days*, pp. 392 and 454.

134   As reported by the *New York Times*, 11 August 1961. Khrushchev again appeared to stress qualitative advantages when he said on the same occasion, 'The Americans do not launch any sputniks. They hop up and fall down into the ocean' (ibid.).

135   Dean, *Test Ban and Disarmament*, p. 90.

136   This is confirmed fully by Penkovsky, *The Penkovsky Papers*, p. 238, who provides interesting detail on technical matters about missile testing as well. The view that there were military reasons for the resumption of testing is supported also by the fact, as noted on p. 242, that the first tests were only in the low and intermediate kiloton range. If political pressure had been the *only* reason for the resumption of tests the USSR might have begun by exploding some of the bombs in the megaton range first.

137   This enumeration draws on Galay, 'Berlin', pp. 27–8.

138   *Wehrkunde* (Munich), no. 2 (1961), pp. 98–9; see also Wolfe, *Soviet Power and Europe*, p. 169.

139   Galay, 'Berlin', p. 27.

140   Alain C. Enthoven and K. Wayne Smith, *How Much is Enough? Shaping the Defense Program, 1961–1969* (New York and London: Harper & Row, 1971), pp. 134–7.

141   Wolfe, *Soviet Power and Europe*, p. 169.

142   Karber, 'The Central European arms race', p. 40.

143   Wolfe, *Soviet Power and Europe*, pp. 173–8.

144   Karber, 'The Central European arms race', p. 40. The quantitative and qualitative aspects of these developments are shown in detail in Karber's third chapter with the aid of graphs and tables.

145   Galay, 'Berlin', p. 29.

146   *Pravda* and *Izvestiia*, 9 July 1961 (italics in the original).

147   *New York Times*, 1 August 1961 (my italics).

148   Interview of 23 June 1959, as published in *Life*, 8 July 1959.

149   This is shown also by Horelick and Rush's analysis, *Strategic Power and Foreign Policy*, esp. pp. 35–125.

150   Khrushchev's sensitivity to these issues was demonstrated in comments he made to the British ambassador, Sir Frank Roberts, at a reception in the Kremlin on 2 July (that is, less than a week before the announcement of the suspension of troop reductions). According to John Alsop, Khrushchev told Sir Frank that an increase in NATO's strength of ground forces in Germany, say, by one division, could be answered a hundredfold by the Soviet Union, the *Washington Post*, 12 July 1961.

151   *Pravda*, 16 January 1960; *Krasnaia zvezda*, 20 January 1960.

152   Wolfe, *Soviet Power and Europe*, p. 165; see also Nikolai Galay, 'The numerical strength of the Soviet armed forces', *Bulletin of the Institute for the Study of the USSR*, vol. 9, no. 5 (May 1962), pp. 41–3; and Bloomfield, *et al.*, *Khrushchev and the Arms Race*, pp. 99–100.

153   Linden, *Khrushchev and the Soviet Leadership*, pp. 1–9.

154   This debate was conducted in a series of articles and comments in *Problems of Communism*, in the September–October 1962, September–October 1963 and November–December

1963 issues; it flared up again after Khrushchev's fall in the January–February, May–June and July–August issues of 1965 in the same journal. Participants in the debate in *Problems of Communism* at one time or another were Thomas H. Rigby, Robert Conquest, Carl Linden, Robert C. Tucker, Wolfgang Leonard, Michel Gordey, Merle Fainsod, Richard Lowenthal, Uri Ra'anan, Adam Ulam, Leon Smolinski, Seweryn Bialer and J. W. Cleary.

155 Linden, for instance, deplores the fact that adherents to what he calls the 'conflict school' have earned for themselves the not always complimentary title of 'Kremlinologists' but sees no problem in charging that the followers of the opposite view belong to the 'totalitarian school' of Soviet leadership politics (Linden, *Khrushchev and the Soviet Leadership*, p. 4). Apart from the not very complimentary label attached to the latter school, the main problem with this categorization is that it does not do justice to the nuances of interpretation. (Certainly I decline at the outset to be put into any of the categories. In Linden's view, among those who have adopted the broad outlook of the conflict school are Robert Conquest, Robert Tucker, Sidney Ploss, David Burg, Peter Wiles, Boris Meissner, Wolfgang Leonhard and Victor Zorza. If there is merit in this list, Michel Tatu and Robert Slusser should be added to it. Linden makes it clear that he is an adherent of this distinguished camp.) To take an example of the problem of categorization: whereas I find myself in *agreement* with Linden's working definition – that Khrushchev's power at any given point in time should be regarded as variable, depending among other things on policy successes and failures and the balance of forces in the domestic and international political environment – I find myself in *disagreement* with the thrust of Linden's argument concerning the Berlin crisis of 1961. Secondly, when Linden writes that those who stressed the stability of Khrushchev's leadership turned to concepts in contemporary political science and modern sociological and behavioral studies, he ignores the fact that in many ways Kremlinology is at the heart of the bureaucratic politics model and thus has an intellectual affinity to many of the modern concepts of political science theory. Thirdly, Linden confidently asserts that 'the conflict school has moved beyond the initial Kremlinological tendency to play down the policy dimension of Soviet politics, that is, the question of power for what?' (ibid., p. 6). This, to my mind, is more wishful thinking than reality. Many adherents of the conflict school as defined by Linden have not abandoned the original preoccupation with the concept of power for the sake of power.

156 See above, p. 191. For a criticism of Slusser's interpretation of Soviet domestic politics and the Berlin crisis in addition to the one made in this book, see the appendix of my PhD dissertation, 'Soviet risk taking and crisis behavior: a theoretical and empirical analysis', Columbia University, 1977, my review in *Soviet Studies*, vol. 26, no. 1 (April 1974), pp. 289–91, and Arnold L. Horelick, *et al.*, *The Study of Soviet Foreign Policy*, p. 44.

157 Franklyn D. Holzman, *Financial Checks on Soviet Defense Expenditures* (Lexington, Mass., and Toronto: D. C. Heath, 1975), p. 11.

158 Abraham S. Becker, *Soviet Military Outlays since 1955*, RM-3886-PR (Santa Monica, Calif.: Rand Corporation, July 1964), p. 70.

159 Stanley H. Colh, 'Economic burden of defense expenditures', in US Congress, Joint Economic Committee, *Soviet Economic Prospects for the Seventies* (Washington, DC: Government Printing Office, 1973), p. 151; J. D. Godaire, 'The claim of the Soviet military establishment', in ibid., *Dimensions of Soviet Economic Power* (Washington, DC: Government Printing Office, 1962), pp. 39–40; and Bloomfield, *et al.*, *Khrushchev and the Arms Race*, pp. 52–3.

160 Reproduced from Becker, *Soviet Military Outlays*, pp. 36 and 40.

161 Slusser, for instance, writes that the sudden increase of 8 July was 'forced upon' Khrushchev by the military between 4 and 6 July 'as the price of their support for Soviet policy in the Berlin crisis' (Slusser, *The Berlin Crisis*, p. 60).

162 *The Military Balance, 1972–73*, p. 73. The three fiscal years cover the period from 1 July 1957 (beginning of FY1958) to 30 June 1960.

163 ibid. On the rises in allocations to the US strategic forces see above, p. 251.

164 The deficiencies of traditional arms control theory in providing a convincing explanation of trends in Soviet defense spending and military deployments extends above all to the *steady* increase in Soviet defense expenditures and military power throughout the period from 1964 to 1980. Nothing even remotely comparable occurred in NATO, Japan or China. It may also be recalled that the significant increase in Soviet capabilities in Central

Europe, which took place after the Berlin crisis of 1948, was not at all prompted by equivalent or similar developments in the West; see p. 261.

165 See p. 240.

166 Horelick and Rush, *Strategic Power*, p. 124.

167 For the figures on the Soviet armed forces the following sources were used: Bloomfield, *et al.*, *Khrushchev and the Arms Race*, p. 100, and N. Galay, 'The burden of Soviet military expenditure', *Bulletin of the Institute for the Study of the USSR*, vol. 8, no. 3 (March 1961), p. 31. The figures of the defense budget were compiled from various issues of *Narodnoe khoziastvo SSSR*.

168 Galay, 'The burden of Soviet military expenditure', p. 31.

169 Military expenditures in France rose from US$3·9 billion in 1960 to US$5·4 billion in 1966. In the same period the strength of the armed forces decreased from 781,000 officers and men to 500,000 (*The Military Balance, 1972–73*, pp. 73–4.

170 Wolfe, *Soviet Power and Europe*, p. 161, and *Soviet Strategy at the Crossroads* (Cambridge, Mass.: Harvard University Press), pp. 139–52.

171 In the debate concerning the third stage of reductions (1960–1), *Krasnaia zvezda*, 20 January 1960.

172 *Sovetskii flot*, 11 February 1960. This subject does not appear to have been researched very well; it would be interesting to be able to have a more comprehensive picture of this debate. Unfortunately such a picture is not provided by Wolfe's studies (cited in note 169, above). I am indebted to G. E. Hudson of Wittenberg University for references to the discussion in the naval press and to Bakaev's article.

173 *Pravda*, 4 January 1960.

174 This account draws on Tatu, *Power in the Kremlin*, pp. 70–1.

175 Boris Nicolaevsky, *Power and the Soviet Elite*, ed. Janet D. Zagoria (London: Pall Mall Press, 1965), pp. 251–2 (my italics).

176 ibid.

177 ibid., p. 252. The opening of the exhibition was reported in *Pravda* and *Izvestiia*, 16 August 1961, and for its duration of about one month received a fair amount of press coverage. To my knowledge, Zhukov's appearance was not officially reported (understandably).

178 Penkovsky, *The Penkovsky Papers*, p. 237. This account of events also serves to explain why the more appropriate counterpart to Lucius Clay, Marshal Zhukov, failed to appear in Berlin in 1961 and why it was Konev who did. Colonel Penkovsky (or Penkovskii in transliteration) was an officer of the chief intelligence directorate (GRU) of the Soviet General Staff who provided the West with secret information until he was arrested in October 1962. He was later shot. Whereas it is now clear – after the US Senate Committee's report on intelligence activities and the rights of Americans (the Church Committee) – that it was not Penkovsky himself who wrote the book, it would be wrong to consider the Penkovsky Papers a forgery and hence useless for scholarly purposes. The Senate Committee report itself states that the book was prepared and written by 'agency assets' (agency meaning the CIA) on the basis of 'actual case materials'. It is not difficult to guess that these case materials originated with Penkovsky. Much of the information presented in the Penkovsky Papers is so detailed and so much of it has been confirmed later that it is possible to agree with Robert Conquest that the case for authenticity remains incomparably stronger than the counterarguments (*The Times*, 18 May 1976). John Erickson also does not doubt the authenticity of the materials (interview in Edinburgh, 24 May 1976).

179 See Table 13.2, p. 261.

180 ibid.

181 *The Military Balance, 1975–1976*, p. 8. This figure excludes border troops and internal security forces.

182 *Krasnaia zvezda*, 4 February 1965.

183 The Kremlinological/bureaucratic political argument in this context is developed systematically by Sidney I. Ploss, *Conflict and Decision-Making in Soviet Russia: A Case Study of Agricultural Policy, 1953–1963* (Princeton, NJ: Princeton University Press for the Princeton Center of International Studies, 1965). Slusser's conceptual approach very closely follows the images conveyed by Ploss. Linden, *Khrushchev and the Soviet Leadership*, pp. 106–16, applies his 'conflict model' to this problem; Tatu, *Power in the Kremlin*, pp. 164–75, approaches the problem from similar perspectives.

184 See p. 421.
185 The new indexes as developed by the American economists Rush Greenslade and Phyllis Wallace; estimates and discussion by Willard L. Thorp and G. Warren Nutter in US Congress, *Dimensions of Soviet Economic Power*, pp. 20, 51–2, 56 and 65.
186 Joseph W. Willett, 'The recent record in agricultural production', *Dimensions of Soviet Economic Power*, p. 95, and Hans Kohn in ibid., pp. 228–9. For instance, the Seven-Year Plan required Soviet grain harvests to increase at a rate of 2·2 percent per annum over the record harvest in 1958. Yet 1961 was the third successive year in which the grain harvest failed to reach the 1958 total. According to Willett, ibid., p. 99, Soviet claims for the 'barn yield of grain production were exaggerated; nevertheless, the trend of decline, which is quite pronounced in the Western estimates, is apparent also in the Soviet claims (figures in millions of metric tons):

Year	Soviet claims	Western estimates
1958	141	125
1959	126	100
1960	134	100

To round off the picture, production of milk, according to Soviet figures, had reached a point of stagnation (61·7 million tons in 1959 *and* in 1960), and meat production even showed a decline (8·92 million tons in 1959 and 8·68 million tons in 1960).
187 Khrushchev's speech of 17 January 1961 to the CC plenum of the CPSU, *Pravda* and *Izvestiia*, 21 January 1961.
188 ibid. This idea of course was not a new one. For instance, Khrushchev had proposed this redistribution of investment allocations on 29 October 1960 (N. S. Khrushchev, *Stroitel'stvo Kommunizma v SSSR i razvitie sel'skogo khoziastva*, Vol. IV, Moscow: Izdatel'stvo politicheskoi literatury, 1963, p. 162). See also Tatu, *Power in the Kremlin*, p. 167.
189 Plan fulfillment report in *Pravda* and *Izvestiia*, 26 January 1961.
190 *Pravda* and *Izvestiia*, 20 January 1961.
191 In a note to the CPSU Presidium of 29 October 1960 he explained that the investment program under the Seven-Year Plan was already cut by 1·3 billion (new) rubles (N. S. Khrushchev, *Stroitel'stvo Kommunizma*, Vol. IV, p. 181). See also Tatu, *Power in the Kremlin*, p. 169.
192 G. A. Vvedensky in *Bulletin of the Institute for the Study of the USSR*, vol. 8 no. 5 (May 1961), p. 22.
193 Perhaps it should be mentioned at this stage that in the final analysis the plan for growth of group A was overfulfilled and the plan for group B was not fulfilled. Group A was to increase by 9·5 percent but actually rose 10 percent. Group B was to rise 6·9 percent, but increased only by 6·6 percent. See *Pravda*, 21 December 1961 (plan and budget report), and ibid., 23 January 1962 (plan fulfillment report).
194 *Khrushchev Remembers*, Vol. I, p. 571.
195 ibid., pp. 571–2.
196 ibid., pp. 567–8.
197 For instance, in his speech to the CC plenum of the CPSU, 17 January 1961 (*Pravda*, 21 January 1961).
198 Uri Ra'anan, *The USSR Arms the Third World: Case Studies in Soviet Foreign Policy* (Cambridge, Mass.: MIT, 1969), pp. 102–7 and 123.
199 He was dismissed in April 1962, which is at a point when the decision to deploy missiles on Cuba must have been made. Shortly after the failure of the Cuban venture, Moskalenko returned to his position as a Deputy Minister of Defense (Tatu, *Power in the Kremlin*, pp. 236–7).
200 Penkovsky, *The Penkovsky Papers*, pp. 131–2, 136–8, 142 and 161.
201 *Krasnaia zvezda*, 4 February 1965.
202 *The Penkovsky Papers*, p. 142.
203 Ploss, *Conflict and Decision-Making*, p. 209.
204 ibid.
205 Nicolaevsky, *Power and the Soviet Elite*, p. 275.
206 Linden, *Khrushchev and the Soviet Leadership*, p. 113.
207 ibid., pp. 105–6.

208   Slusser, *The Berlin Crisis*, p. 72.
209   ibid., p. 147, in reference to the Soviet note of 23 August 1961.
210   ibid., p. 377, in reference to the origins of the Soviet-American confrontation at Check-point Charlie in October. Echoes of the argument about Kozlov can be found in the inter-pretation offered by Samuel B. Payne, Jr, concerning the Test Ban Treaty negotiated in 1963. To Payne it seemed that 'this treaty was far more the result of Frol Kozlov's stroke in April 1963, which greatly weakened the conservative opposition to Khrushchev, than of the missile crisis' (Samuel B. Payne, Jr, 'The Soviet debate on strategic arms limitation: 1968–72', *Soviet Studies*, vol. 27, no. 1 (January 1975), p. 44, fn. 71.
211   Tatu, *Power in the Kremlin*, pp. 131 and 137.
212   ibid.
213   *The Penkovsky Papers*, p. 133. The case for authenticity of the material contained in the Penkovsky Papers is strengthened by the fact that the very existence of the Supreme Military (or Defense) Council (*Sovet oborony*) was officially confirmed on 9 May 1976 when a decree, conferring the title of 'Marshal of the Soviet Union' on Brezhnev, mentioned that Brezhnev was also 'Chairman of the Defense Council' (*Pravda*, 9 May 1976).
214   ibid., p. 131.
215   *Pravda*, 12 July 1961. Inexplicably Slusser, *The Berlin Crisis*, p. 74, asserts that Kozlov's speech 'was much more menacing [than a speech by Suslov] in its treatment of the United States'.
216   *Pravda*, 13 September 1961. Kozlov's next recorded speech was not until late in the proceedings of the party congress, on 28 October, when he reported on the new party statutes.
217   *The Penkovsky Papers*, p. 131.
218   As far as Suslov is concerned, the case of ideological orthodoxy being tantamount to proclivities for aggressiveness, interventionism and hard-line policies abroad is seriously undermined by uncharacteristically good evidence to the effect that Suslov was on the side of those members of the Politburo in 1968 who were against or wanted to delay interven-tion in Czechoslovakia as long as possible. See Jiri Valenta, 'Soviet decisionmaking and the Czechoslovak crisis of 1968', *Studies in Comparative Communism*, vol. 8, nos i and 2 (Spring/Summer 1975), pp. 147–73, and Dimitri K. Simes, 'The Soviet invasion of Czechoslovakia and the limits of Kremlinology', ibid., pp. 174–80, esp. p. 175.
219   See p. 207.
220   *Pravda*, 8 August 1961.
221   ibid. The idea of a strategic breakthrough may have been what Khrushchev had in mind *vis-à-vis* the West.
222   *The Penkovsky Papers*, p. 131.
223   W. Ulbricht, *Zur Geschichte der deutschen Arbeiterbewegung*, Vol. VII (East Berlin: Dietz Verlag, 1964), p. 647.
224   *New York Times*, 30 November 1958.
225   *Neues Deutschland*, 16 June 1961. Ulbricht made the remark at the same press conference at which he spoke of any lack of intention by the GDR to build a wall.
226   *New York Times*, 29 June 1961. The demand was rejected by the United States and nothing ever came of it.
227   For text of the whole paragraph concerning this issue see p. 209.
228   Anita Dasbach Mallinckrodt, *Propaganda hinter der Mauer: Die Propaganda der Sowjet-union und der DDR als Werkzeug der Aussenpolitik im Jahre 1961* (Stuttgart and Berlin: W. Kohlhammer, 1971). Unfortunately, however, the study has only a very narrow data base (eight documents) for content analysis. The more enlightening parts of the book are reached where the confining framework and language of content analysis is abandoned.
229   *Neue Zürcher Zeitung*, 16 December 1961, as quoted by Windsor, *City on Leave*, p. 253.
230   Heinz Lippmann, *Honecker and the New Politics of Europe* (London: Angus & Robertson, 1973), p. 187. Erich Honecker during that time was first secretary of the FDJ (Freie Deutsche Jugend). In addition he was nominated candidate-member of the Polit-buro at the Third Congress of the SED in July 1950.
231   loc. cit.
232   See p. 203.
233   See pp. 204–5.
234   Zolling and Bahnsen, *Kalter Winter*, p. 105, write that Ulbricht knew how alert the

population in East Germany was to subdued notes in a tune and that he realized that a denial would fan rumors about the closing of the border.

235 Interview by Anita Dasbach Mallinckrodt with Heinz Lippmann, 22 August 1967, quoted in Mallinckrodt, *Propaganda hinter der Mauer*, p. 81.

236 Stern, *Ulbricht*, p. 188. Carola Stern's further interpretation, namely, that Ulbricht was interested in a 'peaceful settlement' but that Khrushchev opposed such a settlement and 'decided in favor of the wall', is rather odd.

237 Kroll, *Lebenserinnerungen*, p. 512.

238 Although the Sino-Soviet conflict is an important topic, the problem at issue here is to show how it affected Soviet policy-making in the Berlin crisis. To me this seems a fruitless task except perhaps to the extent that it can reveal some problems. For instance, it is possible to agree with Deutscher's view that the need to compete with Mao Tse-tung for leadership in the communist camp may have been one factor in Khrushchev's decision to take action over Berlin (see above, p. 193), though it is already doubtful whether this was, as Deutscher writes, an 'important' factor; however, it is even more problematic to suggest that the need to compete with Mao Tse-tung 'made it difficult for him [Khrush-chev] to engage in genuine bargaining with the West' and that it imposed on him 'that diplomatic rigidity which so surprised President Kennedy in Vienna' (ibid.). If this is a valid framework of analysis, how is it to be explained that Khrushchev *did* in fact compromise in Vienna, on an issue, however, that was of more direct concern to China, namely, Laos? Even more fanciful is Ulam's idea that the success of Soviet policies in Germany would have enabled Khrushchev 'to resume some degree of control over China's foreign policy' (see above, pp. 188-9). It is difficult to see how this could have happened. In essence Soviet policy in Berlin follows its own logic, and so does the Sino-Soviet conflict – there may be an interrelation between the two issues, but the extent and forms of this remain highly conjectural. For some comments concerning possible ramifications of a triangular political and ideological relationship between the Soviet, Chinese and East German leadership and the Berlin crisis see also Zagoria, *The Sino-Soviet Conflict*, p. 396

14
Process Analysis

In order to appreciate more fully the characteristics and limits of Soviet risk-taking, the likely purposes of verbal communications, the way in which instruments of crisis control were used, possible changes in objectives, and the problem of whether the Soviet policy in Berlin in 1961 should be considered a success or failure, it is necessary first to examine two questions: what sort of complications, if any, did the Soviet military and political leaders expect? Were these expectations (perceptions of risk) justified or unjustified?

Risks and Perceptions of Risk

The official version of Soviet risk awareness was given as early as November 1958. The note sent to the United States at that time deplored the fact that Berlin had become a 'dangerous center of contradiction between the Great Powers' and went on to say,

> Its role in the relations between the Powers may be compared to a smoldering fuse that has been connected to a powder keg. Incidents arising here, even if they seem to be of local significance, may, in an atmosphere of heated passions, suspicion, and mutual apprehensions [that is, in a crisis], cause a conflagration which will be difficult to extinguish.[1]

This theme, that there might be a dangerous development leading from a general adversary relationship via increased tension and crisis to a 'conflagration', was pursued intermittently for more than two years and it was stressed particularly in the two last phases (the fifth and sixth) leading up to the building of the Wall. For example, in his report on radio and television on 15 June 1961, concerning the results of the Vienna meeting, Khrushchev expressed the apprehension that transitions between crisis and war may be rapid and the boundary fluid: '[W]ho can say', Khrushchev asked, 'where lies the borderline between cold war and a war in the full sense of the word?'[2] Somewhat more optimistically he stated that he had received the 'impression [at Vienna] that President Kennedy understands the great responsibility that lies with the governments of two such powerful states', adding, 'I should like to hope that the awareness of this responsibility will remain in the future'.[3] Similarly, in the radio and television address of 7 August Khrushchev said that 'Kennedy took a sober view of things and displayed definite realism'.

> Life demands, however [he continued], that statesmen not only express

sensible judgments but that *in their policy, too*, they do not venture to overstep the line beyond which the arguments of reason fall silent, and blind and dangerous gambling with the destinies of peoples and states begins.[4]

Khrushchev thus acknowledged that discrepancies between sensible judgment and policy were possible. But how could this 'blind and dangerous gambling' occur? It could happen, for instance, as a result of internal or external pressures – a possibility which Khrushchev did not mention specifically in this context – or it could occur because of irrational behavior under stress. In the same speech Khrushchev recalled an incident in World War II when a confused general had committed suicide before his very eyes. 'This tragedy occurred', Khrushchev reasoned, 'because the man was thoroughly unnerved. He no longer knew what he was doing and lost his self-control.' It was not a direct analogy, but some people in the West were losing their self-possession and self-control. In the example mentioned it was only one man who perished. 'But under present conditions, were some Western leaders to act recklessly and push the world into a new war, such a suicidal act would spell death to millions upon millions of people.'[5]

On the basis of these and similar remarks a strong case could be made showing Soviet risk awareness during the Berlin crisis. Such an endeavor, however, would be questionable if not naïve. There can hardly be any doubt that the *open* discussion of risks of war and dangers of escalation was primarily an instrument of deterrence of Western action or counteraction. What is more, the statements quoted above, which seem to imply risk awareness, ought to be read in conjunction with those which imply a serious underestimation of risk, so, for example, when the Soviet ambassador in Washington, Mikhail Menshikov, is reported as saying, 'In the final analysis, when the chips are down, the American people won't fight for Berlin',[6] or when Khrushchev expressed the opinion that the American generals' talk of maintaining the position in Berlin by force was 'bluff';[7] or when he said that Western leaders' claims that they would 'fight for the freedom of the Germans in West Berlin' were but a 'fairy tale'.[8]

This contradictory, or perhaps more appropriately, complementary pattern of statements and the difficulty of distinguishing between genuine perception and instrumental purposes severely limits the scope of generalization. The fact remains tha Khrushchev did find it necessary to embark on a protracted campaign, using apocalyptic images and a variety of psychological means of pressure and persuasion. This very fact speaks for the presence of risk awareness and genuine apprehension about the possibility of Western counteraction. But there is other evidence pointing in the same direction.

Considering the possible contingencies under which the measures of 13 August could lead to a major military conflict, three main threats existed from the Soviet (and East German) point of view. (1) Anger, frustration and panic of the East German population could result in a popular uprising. (2) An emotionally charged anti-Russian and anticommunist populace in West Berlin, perhaps incited by politicians at mass rallies, could take matters into their own hands. (3) The three Western powers in Berlin, perhaps motivated by pressures from West Berlin and West German authorities, could take the calculated risk of removing the obstacles placed in the way of freedom of movement within Berlin. Worst of all, elements of all three worst cases could combine.

In particular, as in June 1953, it was possible that young people from West Berlin would merge with construction workers in East Berlin to form an explosive mixture of people threatening to unleash forces with unpredictable consequences. In these conditions who was to guarantee the reliability of the military units of the *Volksarmee*, the *Betriebskampfgruppen* (factory militia) or, for that matter, the construction workers mobilized in force for the purpose of sealing themselves into their own country. After all, young East German workers had made up the highest proportion of 'refugees' before 13 August. It is also important to remember that superior military force is not necessarily sufficient for inducing rational behavior – the Hungarian popular revolt was doomed to failure from the start against superior Soviet military power, yet it had occurred nevertheless. Would the Western powers stand idly by in the case of a bloody suppression of a popular revolt? And, if so, would not the possible scale of the uprising in itself make the execution of the planned measures impossible and merely speed up the collapse of the East German regime?

As during the Berlin crisis in 1948 even a low probability of any of these contingencies taking place must have given the Soviet and East German leaderships cause for serious concern. It would be surprising if it had been otherwise. According to the account by Heinz Lippmann, 'the surprise move of August 13 involved considerable uncalculated risk for Honecker' (who was then a full member of the SED Politburo and Central Committee secretary for party organization, cadres and security matters and thus in charge of carrying out the measures). Lippmann continues:

> Moving the frontier troops and workers' task forces up to the sector frontier was hazardous enough in itself. They had of course taken part in maneuvers and exercises, but they had never been put to the test in an operation of this kind. There was no knowing how they would conduct themselves if it came to a clash with Allied troops or the West Berlin police. Honecker was very well aware of the physical and psychological strain the troops would be under.[9]

Apprehensions in the CPSU Presidium about Khrushchev's policy with regard to Berlin were already mentioned.[10] In his memoirs Khrushchev confirms that there was serious concern about how far the German units could be relied upon to be involved in the measures of 13 August. He writes,

> We had our doubts about the ability of the [East] Germans to control their own borders. The guards were equipped with firearms, but it's not so easy for a soldier to shoot a fellow German. We expressed this concern to our German comrades, and they [reassured us].[11]

The troops, as Khrushchev writes, were equipped with firearms, but were they issued with live ammunition? Smith asserted in 1963 that testimony from defecting officers of the East German armed forces had subsequently 'revealed that Communist forces in East Berlin on August 13 were issued only blank ammunition and were under orders to give way should Allied troops intervene'.[12] Windsor wrote in the same year that 'it is now known that the heavily armed troops who occupied the frontier on the night of the 12th had no ammunition' but he also stated that 'Not only did the NCOs [noncommissioned officers] and officers carry ammunition: the tanks and armored cars were loaded with live shells.'[13] Later writings, by Zolling and Bahnsen, for instance, extend this view and say that the men were also given live ammunition;[14] and more recent studies, too, claim that 'The rumor that there was no issue of ammunition to the East German military has not been substantiated'.[15] My own inquiries with city officials and members of the United States mission in Berlin[16] indicate that it is quite possible that not all the units of the *Volksarmee* and *Betriebskampfgruppen* were issued with live ammunition. This could mean that there was no consistent pattern of implementation, which would not be too unusual; or it could confirm the view that the East German political leaders, or even individual commanders of units, were uncertain about the reliability of the armed forces. The point about live ammunition for the men remains unclear.

Even bearing in mind this gap in our knowledge, much is to be said for a reconstruction of the course of events as follows: the East German leadership, itself still uncertain of the loyalties of its population and armed forces and relying – as in 1953 – on the allied superpower to come to its aid in the event of trouble, reassured Khrushchev; whereas Khrushchev, relying on the judgment of his German ally and his own, reassured some of his colleagues in the Presidium. Both the East German leadership and Khrushchev must have been enormously relieved by the failure of serious opposition to break out in East Berlin and East Germany.

The same applies to the other two possible events which could have led to serious military conflict – violent reactions by the West Berliners and the Western allies. *The Times* special correspondent reported in early September that he was assured frequently in East Germany that the

> East German Government never expected to get away with the sealing of East Berlin so easily, and was very nervous, when it did decide to go ahead, over possible allied countermeasures. But these did not come, and nervousness gave way to overwhelming self-confidence.[17]

The sigh of relief which ultimately was to lead to 'overwhelming self-confidence' was clearly, almost pathetically, expressed in the headline of the *Neues Deutschland* editorial of 15 August: 'Fantastic, how everything worked out!'[18] No doubt the Soviet government must have been equally nervous about the possibility of countermeasures from West Berlin or the Western allies, and equally relieved when it failed to materialize.

The counterargument to this, based on hindsight, could be that Kennedy had explicitly limited American guarantees to West Berlin and to the access routes, not to freedom of movement within Berlin, and that this was known to the Soviet and East German leaderships. However, had not Dean Acheson specifically excluded South Korea from the United States defense perimeter in the Far East, and had not war taken place nevertheless? What is more, one of Kennedy's 'three essentials' included the viability of West Berlin. Was

West Berlin viable without unrestricted communication between the two parts of Berlin? Indeed, there was still a large margin of uncertainty. It is therefore easy to believe Kroll's account that Khrushchev had given Marshal Konev strict orders to avoid local incidents and that there were reports in Moscow (as elsewhere) that Khrushchev and Ulbricht 'expected a harsh reaction by the Western powers and [that] they were quite surprised by their compromising [and] excessively passive attitude'.[19]

There are still other indications pointing to Soviet apprehension. They include the long delay in taking action and the thoroughness with which the measures were prepared at the local and international levels.[20]

This links up to the next major question: how was it possible that the West was surprised by the measures of 13 August to such a degree, and how was it possible that the Western reactions turned out to be so weak? In as much as this involves analysis of Western decision-making, it is not the purpose here to deal with it. What is of interest is the role which Soviet crisis diplomacy may have played in eliciting this particular kind of reaction.

Content and Purposes of Verbal Communications

Soviet verbal communications, backed by an elaborate web of nonverbal communications,[21] served to create a favorable psychological climate for taking the measures of 13 August as well as for extracting further concessions from the Western powers thereafter. In particular, the following aspects conducive to Western surprise and inaction in August 1961 can be filtered out from the flood of messages contained in public speeches by Khrushchev and other political and military leaders; diplomatic notes and memoranda; the output of the Soviet press; conversations between Khrushchev and various Western visitors; and the private correspondence between Khrushchev and Kennedy.

(1) Creation of a sense of personal (Khrushchev's) and national commitment and the impression that the USSR was determined to 'solve the Berlin problem' at high cost and risk.

(2) Communication of the warning that any Western countermeasures to Soviet unilateral action, once it became necessary because of Western 'procrastination', would be opposed by force and would lead to a major military conflict in Europe.

(3) Creation of a sense of urgency – evident particularly in the justifications of the two time limits or ultimatums imposed by the Soviet Union – conveying the impression that the status quo had to be changed, that inaction could no longer be tolerated, and that 'grave dangers' were attendant on any further delay.

(4) Creation of a sense of anxiety in the West by a rapid succession of veiled and unveiled threats and invocation of the dangers of nuclear war.

(5) Skillful exploitation of 'interimperialist contradictions' by attempting to isolate West Germany as the presumed driving force behind hardline policies on the German problem; by carefully selecting specific targets of intimidation, namely, the European allies of the United

States; and by emphasizing direct contacts and responsibility of the two superpowers and their leaders.

(6) Deception of the West as to the timing and nature of the measures of 13 August. (In the last ultimatum, that of June 1961, the Soviet Union seemed to envisage unilateral measures only *after* the end of December, that is, after all other avenues to a solution of the Berlin problem had been exhausted.)

(7) Creation of a sense of compromise (in addition to the preference for Soviet-American bilateralism mentioned in point 5) by stressing that not all the proposals put forward by the Soviet Union had to be adopted in the form presented, that – as far as the immediate context of 13 August is concerned – Soviet objectives were limited, and that in essence nothing dramatic was happening.

Sufficient material covering the first four points has been presented throughout this thesis, so it is possible to concentrate on the last three.

Concerning the fifth point, utilization of interimperialist contradictions, strong prescriptions for their application can be found not only in such basic writings as Lenin's *Imperialism: The Highest Stage of Capitalism* but also in Khrushchev's reinterpretations of Lenin. In his important speech of 6 January 1961 Khrushchev wanted to leave no doubt that although the 'capitalist world is not now split into two imperialist camps, as was the case on the eve of the two world wars', and although – as quoted – 'wars among the capitalist, imperialist countries are not the most probable', the imperialist camp nevertheless was 'far from united'; it was 'rent by bitter internal struggle'.[22] Even more important in the present context, Khrushchev reminded his distinguished audience that the Soviet Union, in defeating Hitler, 'also used the contradictions among the imperialist states'.[23]

In fact, the Soviet Union could count not only on differences of attitude and approach among the Western countries involved in the Berlin crisis, but also on differences *within* these countries. Both types of differences – 'interimperialist' and 'intra-imperialist' in Soviet terminology – existed as to the degree to which the Western powers should deal with the East German government without loss of prestige and undue damage to the position of West Germany; the timing (if not the principle) of summit conferences, as well as the scope of prior consultation; the extent to which Soviet and East German salami tactics' including occasional serious harassment, should be opposed; the degree to which the rights of the Western allies in all of Berlin should be safeguarded, including the freedom of movement of civilians between the two parts of the city; the question of whether concessions should be made on the Soviet and East German demands to curb 'subversive' activity in West Berlin; and the problem of how far the links between West Germany and West Berlin should be allowed to develop.

This leads directly to the point about the isolation of West Germany. As the country most affected by the Soviet demand for a German peace treaty, most vulnerable to domestic pressures not to give way to 'the Communists' and most interested in maintaining close links between West Berlin and West Germany, it would naturally be forced to take a hard line. The Soviet Union and the GDR could observe this in particular on the question of holding

Bundesrat and Bundestag meetings in West Berlin – an issue where the three Western allies repeatedly refused to back West Germany. The problem was complicated by personal animosities between Chancellor Adenauer and President Kennedy.

Even without these animosities there was a rich field for Soviet propagandist influence on Western opinion, with charges ranging from the claim that Bonn was trying 'to take maximum advantage of the war psychosis artificially created around the "Berlin problem" in order to achieve a further militarization' of the countries participating in the EEC and 'to subordinate them to Bonn's policy',[24] to personal attacks on Chancellor Adenauer and the charge that he 'stubbornly drags his allies onto the path of threats and intensification of the war danger'.[25]

It is in the context of exploiting interimperialist contradictions that the Soviet Union tried to derive maximum advantage from the vulnerability of the United States's European allies to Soviet nuclear strike capabilities. The purpose of this campaign was evidently to force them to exert a restraining influence on NATO's overall policy on Berlin. Italy, Greece, Turkey, Britain and West Germany were, literally, the target countries which were singled out most of all.

At the same time there were appeals to superpower responsibility. Soviet spokesmen, beginning with Khrushchev, repeatedly stressed the need for Soviet-American cooperation to reduce the risk of war. They made – in their view – a logical and consistent claim to political equality based on the (false) claim to military-strategic parity. The Vienna Summit is an example of this. Part of the thesis of superpower responsibility for world peace is the professed need to restrain reckless or adventurist allies – in the concrete case of Berlin in Soviet perspectives, the leaders of West Germany and West Berlin. It is highly instructive on this point to read Khrushchev's memoirs carefully. Before leaving Vienna, Khrushchev remembers, he had a meeting with Bruno Kreisky, then Austria's Foreign Minister.

> To tell the truth [Khrushchev said], I recounted for Kreisky everything I'd told Kennedy. I knew that what I said would get back to Kennedy – and it would also be passed on to Willy Brandt. I hoped that by underscoring our determination not to abandon our intentions we might succeed in encouraging these leaders toward rational discussions and ultimately a reasonable agreement – all, hopefully, without raising temperatures to the boiling point.[26]

This *ex post facto* reasoning is entirely consistent with Khrushchev's preference for superpower bilateralism exerting a restraining influence on local actors.

Concerning the sixth point contributing to Western surprise and inaction, successful deception as to the timing and nature of the measures of 13 August, the important thing to remember is that unilateral Soviet action, according to the Vienna memorandum, was not threatened until *after* the expiry of the six-month deadline, that is, until after the end of 1961. Western misreading of the timing of Soviet actions is expressed in Kennedy's statement after the Vienna Summit that 'It will be a cold winter'[27] as opposed to the hot summer that actually occurred. The idea that the conclusion of a

German peace treaty was urgent, but that the USSR would not act until after the end of the year, was left to stand – as noted – as late as in the communiqué of the meeting of the Warsaw Pact member countries in Moscow (3–5 August).[28]

Related to the misreading of the timing of the Soviet and East German measures (encouraged by Soviet verbal communications) is the miscalculation about the nature of the threat. Foremost in the Western mind remained the fear of a new blockade. This was evident not only before 13 August but also afterward. It is shown in the sighs of relief of President Kennedy about the limited nature of the measures on 13 August, in the United States ambassador to the Soviet Union, Llewellyn Thomson's, reaction to the measures that 'it could have been worse',[29] and in Kennedy's 'most anxious moment during the prolonged Berlin crisis', which was not on 13 August but on 20 August, when the battle group of about 1,500 men was proceeding toward West Berlin. In Sorensen's description this was Kennedy's 'first order of American military units into a potential confrontation with Soviet forces'. Kennedy postponed his usual weekend plans and kept his military aide in constant touch with the convoy's commander. 'When the first group of sixty trucks turned unimpeded into West Berlin, he felt that a turning point in the crisis had been reached.'[30] Undoubtedly, the protracted Soviet campaign of emphasizing risks of war and creating anxiety had produced its desired effect. The failure of worst-case assumptions to materialize was greeted with a sigh of relief.

The final point, creation of a sense of compromise and good will, is the counterpart to intimidation in successful crisis bargaining (the carrot supplementing the stick). To this effect, the 'After all, we are still allies' theme of the Berlin crisis of 1948 was invoked again in 1961. During a reception in the Kremlin in honor of a delegation from Romania on 11 August, and after having delivered an unconciliatory speech, Khrushchev made a point of singling out many of the Western ambassadors and talking with them in an amicable way.[31] It is also in this vein that Marshal Konev gave a reception for the three Western allied commandants in Potsdam on 10 August, during which he assured his guests that the Western rights 'will not be touched' and that future action would 'not be directed against West Berlin'.[32] (In fact Khrushchev claims that he told Konev specifically, before he left for Berlin, 'Try to establish contacts with the US general [Albert Watson II, the American commandant]'.)[33] Also to be seen in this context is the visit which the Soviet ambassador to West Germany, Smirnov, paid to Chancellor Adenauer on 16 August and during which Smirnov delivered a personal message from Khrushchev, assuring the Chancellor that Soviet aims underlying the measures of 13 August were limited.[34]

As in Berlin in 1948, the theme of 'much ado about nothing' was advanced by Soviet and East German authorities in 1961. This is evident not only in the gesture of the announcement of Khrushchev's vacation plans (no matter whether he did in fact go on vacation or not) but also in the decree of the GDR Council of Ministers stating euphemistically that 'such control is to be introduced on the borders of the German Democratic Republic, including the border with the Western sectors of Greater Berlin, which is usually introduced along the borders of every sovereign state'; that the measures taken by the GDR 'do not affect the visits of citizens of other states' to East Berlin; and that they 'in no way revise former decisions on transit between West Berlin and West Germany'.[35] It is shown also in the declaration of the Warsaw Pact member countries, furnishing the understatement of the Berlin crisis with the phrase that, regrettably, 'the protective measures along the borders of West Berlin will somewhat inconvenience (*sozdaet izvestnve neudobstva*) the population'.[36]

Characteristics and Limits of Soviet Risk-Taking

The Berlin crisis of 1961, just as the crisis of 1948, constitutes a clear example of calculated risk-taking. It has all the attributes of such action as manifest in long deliberation, delay of action and attempts to remedy the problem by various means involving lesser risk. There are, however, several important differences between the two crises, concerning the characteristics and limits of risk-taking. The main difference lies in the determination of the Soviet leadership in 1961 to accept higher risks than in 1948 and to proceed with the venture even if Western counteraction occurred. Several lines of reasoning support this assessment.

First and foremost, in the Berlin crisis of 1961 there was clarity as to the Soviet demands and objectives. This in itself made it more difficult to embark on a retreat. Whereas in June 1948 Soviet and East German authorities had stressed the temporary nature of the 'traffic restrictions' and later on provided monetary, economic and political objectives but still left obscure the overall purpose, in August 1961 Soviet and East German demands remained essentially limited and were unambiguous on one point: the new border regime was vital to the interests of the two countries and hence was here to stay. Only one vague, almost meaningless, verbal concession was made in the declaration of the Warsaw Pact: the necessity of the defensive measures would disappear 'when a peaceful settlement with Germany is achieved and the questions awaiting their solution are settled on this basis'. Yet even this dim ray of hope was deleted in the decree of the GDR Council of Ministers.

Secondly, the clarity and decisiveness of the measures of August 1961, in contrast to those of June 1948, is underlined not only by the fact that a meeting of the Warsaw Pact member countries was called to ratify decisions for a new border regime in Berlin, but that these countries openly assumed responsibility for the measures by giving the GDR a mandate.[37] The device of a multilateral conference to enhance the legitimacy of risk-taking was, of course, not a new device. It had been used also in June 1948. However, the differences are obvious. The conference of Soviet bloc countries in Warsaw (23–4 June 1948) involved the foreign ministers only. More important, no direct link was ever established by the conference between its own proceedings and any joint action to be taken, the impending blockade included.

There is a third line of reasoning to support the proposition that the Soviet Union was prepared to accept higher levels of risk in 1961 than in 1948. By the time the Berlin crisis approached its climax in the summer of 1961, Soviet prestige and Khrushchev's personal standing both abroad and at home had become deeply involved. The threat of ultimatum had been used repeatedly by Khrushchev and the Soviet government, quite explicitly and emphatically in the period between November 1958 and March 1959, and then again following the Vienna Summit in June 1961. At various other times reference had been made to the urgency of the situation and less explicit deadlines were set for the termination of Western rights in Berlin with or without voluntary agreement by the West. At the press conference of 27 November 1958 announcing the Soviet intentions for Berlin and Germany, Khrushchev significantly throughout the entire ninety-minute session not once referred to any of the advisers who accompanied him, nor did he use any notes, and his answers frequently paraphrased or quoted the text of the ultimatum directly. All this convinced many of those present during the press conference that Khrushchev himself had been the author of the November 1958 note.[38] In the view of President Eisenhower at that time: 'There seemed to be no avoiding a showdown because Khrushchev had apparently laid his prestige on the line'.[39] Dulles, too, 'believed that Khrushchev would probably move soon to carry out his threat [of signing a separate peace treaty with the GDR]'.[40] Khrushchev reportedly told Macmillan during his visit to Moscow in February 1959 that there was no room for maneuver or for retreat from his intention to sign a peace treaty with East Germany.[41]

In 1961, even before the setting of another deadline, Soviet prestige was committed even further to a major change in the status quo in Berlin and Germany. For example, in conversations with Khrushchev on 10 April 1961 Walter Lippmann gained the impression that Khrushchev was absolutely determined to proceed with the separate peace treaty.[42] If all this is read in conjunction with repeated threats of intervention, though in an ambiguous form, in the Middle East in 1956, 1957 and 1958 and in the Taiwan Straits crisis in 1958, yet another failure in Berlin to make action match words could seriously undermine the credibility and effectiveness of Soviet foreign policy. And if it is true that Khrushchev personally was the architect of the diplomacy of threat and deadline, failure to achieve significant gain would affect his political power at home and in the international communist movement.

One counterargument to the view of Soviet and East German determination to proceed with the border closure even if the Western powers had attempted to resist it by tearing down the obstacles is based on the fact that, initially, only barbed-wire fencing and wooden barriers were put up; that more solid structures of concrete (the Wall) began to appear only on 15 August; that the number of crossing points was only gradually reduced; and that access restrictions for citizens of West Berlin came only later (on 15 August, in the form of the requirement to obtain special permits for vehicles entering East Berlin, and on 23 August, in the form of demanding special entry permits for individuals to be issued by GDR authorities in West Berlin).

However, this gradualist procedure testifies more to tactical flexibility and to Soviet and East German apprehension about countermeasures than to a wavering on the principle of a drastic revision of the border regime. If the construction of obstacles *at* the border had been resisted, the Wall could easily have been built a few yards *inside* the Soviet sector.[43] If the West had then complied, this would have created a no-man's-land between the Wall and the sector borders, but it would not have changed the overall result of the Soviet and East German measures. If the West had persisted (presumably invoking freedom of movement between the four sectors as legal justification) it would have encroached on Soviet sovereignty in its own sector. Unless the Western allies wanted to dissolve the Soviet sector entirely – a contingency which would have been difficult to contemplate for any of the four occupation powers – it would have had to be prepared intermittently to organize raids into the Soviet sector for the forcible removal of the obstacles. For such an endeavor of intermittent violence, if agreement to proceed in this fashion could ever have been reached, the Western allies were ill-prepared, militarily and psychologically. Owing to months of preparation, the Soviet Union was fully prepared in both respects and there is little reason to doubt that it would have responded vigorously to the counterchallenge. As Geoffrey McDermott, the political adviser to the British commandant in Berlin, put it:

> If General Clay had been in Berlin I have little doubt the tanks would have rolled that day. And this course of action was discussed at length at our meeting. But we decided against it and I do not believe it would have done any lasting good even though it might have boosted the Berliners' morale for a time. For though there was no actual wall to knock down that first day, we should have had to mow down ranks of scruffy-looking but quite well-armed East Germans, and their barbed wire. Whether the East Berlin population had then risen or not the Russians could not possibly have allowed us to occupy their sector of Berlin. Their powerful forces, very much at the ready, would have gone into action. There would have then ensued at best a battle, in which the Western garrisons were bound to be defeated and forced to retreat to their sectors; at worse, a war.[44]

Changes in Objectives

By late spring and early summer 1961 the Soviet Union was far from winning a substantial improvement in the status quo by accepting risks and exploiting alleged 'changes in the correlation of forces in favor of socialism'; it was faced instead with a rapid deterioration of the status quo. To put it pointedly: rather than exploiting favorable trends and taking risks on this basis to achieve a dramatic breakthrough 'in the historic competition between the two systems' – a notion still prevalent in 1958 – risk-taking had become a matter of reversing disadvantageous trends, if not of sheer necessity. Related to this is a change in Soviet objectives.

To begin with, it is realistic to abandon the idea of a 'most reasonable', or even the 'only reasonable', objective pursued by Khrushchev during the prolonged campaign for the conclusion of a peace treaty, and to posit instead the existence of a *range of objectives*, subject to change of emphasis as domestic, intra-bloc and international conditions changed. Some of the most important of these objectives can be listed as follows: to induce the Western powers to yield their position in Berlin (the most unlikely to be realized); to enhance the domestic stability and the international status of the

GDR; to limit the influence of West Berlin as a showcase of the West by increasing its sense of vulnerability and decreasing its ties with West Germany; to win final and irrevocable acceptance of the postwar political and social order in Europe, in particular to neutralize the threat to this order emanating from West Germany and her declared policy of nonrecognition of the GDR (and the borders) and her desire to see Germany reunited.

The achievement of any one of these major objectives would have opened up a number of additional prospects, including, as Wolfe summarizes, the creation of

> an acute sense of insecurity and betrayal in West Germany while helping to repair the instability of the East German regime; lending new weight to Soviet influence over Central European affairs; slowing down the momentum of economic and defense integration in Western Europe; undermining European confidence in the American commitment; and not least, demonstrating the emergence of a new balance of power, under which the West would have to be prepared to make further concessions on disputed issues.[45]

It is quite possible that the Soviet demand for the conclusion of a peace treaty, with or without the Western powers, had been made in all seriousness in 1958–9. By 1961, however, it had taken on the character of an ossified, yet still threatening, formula, which was to be used for the achievement of less ambitious goals. The idea of forcing the Western powers out of Berlin, above all, had definitely been shelved. Developments in the GDR had put the Soviet Union into an unwanted position: to act unilaterally and, to make matters worse, to act unilaterally in conditions of relative (and growing) military-strategic weakness *vis-à-vis* the United States. The measures of 13 August, consequently, have to be regarded as emergency measures. Some Soviet sources do regard them as such. The measures of 13 August, in their view, 'were important because they made it possible to solve a series of urgent questions which were then facing the USSR and other socialist countries, chiefly the GDR'.[46]

The October Confrontation: a Case of Ritualism

Little mention has so far been made of an event that is easily recalled, owing to its dramatic aspects, but often confused with the events of August 1961 – the confrontation of Soviet and American tanks at the Friedrichstrasse checkpoint in October 1961. It is justifiable, however, not to focus much attention on the tanks of October because the fundamental question of whether the Western allies would 'swallow the bitter pill'[47] of the East Germans being effectively locked in, and the West Berliners being effectively locked out, was settled by that time. For all practical purposes, a new game was played – under the same rules, but at a lower level of risk. The object in this new game was to find out, on the Soviet side, whether the West would be prepared to make further concessions, willingly or under pressure. On 17 October, Khrushchev, as noted, withdrew the *ultimatum* for the conclusion of a peace treaty with Germany by the end of the year, thereby opening up new possibilities for negotiation and compromise. But he did not put aside the *principle* for the conclusion of a peace treaty and, as events at the local level a few days later (22–8 October) were to show, this did not mean that the USSR had stopped probing Western determination.

The immediate cause of the confrontation of Soviet and American tanks at the Friedrichstrasse checkpoint – the problem of whether civilians in official vehicles of the three Western allies had to produce identification to East German police upon entering East Berlin – was slight almost by any standard. It looked like a mere trifle, apparently, to the British diplomats, who did show their identification papers; and from the point of view of international law authority (delegated by another power at that!) to inspect papers contributes very little to international legal recognition, which is what the GDR wanted most. Only customary practice had been abandoned and General Clay chose to make an issue of it.

Once this had happened it was precisely the relative insignificance of the issue which allowed a confrontation to develop: a venture that 'really isn't worth it' can be abandoned quickly and without loss of face. Only confrontations over matters of vital importance to two competitors are difficult to scale down. Moreover the problem of popular emotions did not apply here as the controversy concerned only the armed units of both sides. The confrontation, therefore, was a confrontation without substance, involving the semblance of risk, not its reality. It was an example of 'ritualized aggression' as ethologists might call it – a game in which two contestants, sometimes literally, engage in a show of force in order to impress a rival rather than to warn him of an imminent attack.

Khrushchev knew the rules of this game. He writes:

> They [the Americans] had taken the initiative in moving up to the border in the first place, and therefore they would, so to say, have been in a difficult moral position if we forced them to turn their backs on the barrels of our cannons. Therefore we decided that at this point we should take the initiative ourselves and give the Americans an opportunity to pull back from the border once the threat of our tanks had been removed. My comrades agreed with me.[48]

General Clay showed himself satisfied that the purpose of the demonstration had been served: 'The fiction that it was the East Germans who were responsible for trying to prevent Allied access to East Berlin is now destroyed.'[49] Apart from the problem of establishing with confidence who actually initiated the probe (Ulbricht as well as Konev was in Moscow for the Twenty-Second CPSU Congress at the time), the main point is rather that the United States had demonstrated its apparent willingness not to swallow a succession of further pills. As Soviet and East German probing was to continue beyond October 1961 there was a case for overreacting and 'melodramatizing'.[50]

Notes: Part Two, Chapter 14

1   *Pravda*, 28 November 1958.
2   ibid., 16 June 1961.

3 ibid.

4 *Pravda*, 8 August 1961 (my italics).

5 ibid. Khrushchev had mentioned the analogy that 'some unreasonable person may commit suicide' in a speech on 21 June 1961 at the twentieth anniversary of Hitler's invasion of the Soviet Union (*Pravda*, 22 June 1961).

6 *New York Herald Tribune*, 16 July 1961, as quoted by Slusser, *The Berlin Crisis*, p. 64; see also Sorensen, *Kennedy*, p. 586.

7 Khrushchev in an interview with Averell Harriman on 23 June 1959, *Life*, 8 July 1959.

8 Khrushchev in a speech at the Soviet-Romanian friendship meeting on 11 August 1961 (*Pravda*, 12 August 1961). Khrushchev expressed the same opinion several times to the German ambassador in Moscow (Kroll, *Lebenserinnerungen*, pp. 461–85).

9 Lippmann, *Honecker*, pp. 187–8.

10 See pp. 269–71.

11 *Khrushchev Remembers*, Vol. II, p. 508.

12 Smith, *The Defense of Berlin*, p. 276, fn.

13 Windsor, *City on Leave*, pp. 240–1.

14 Zolling and Bahnsen, *Kalter Winter*, p. 124.

15 Dulles, *The Wall*, p. 34, fn. Another source asserts, 'To limit the risk of shooting incidents with the Western Allies – for there was no telling just how they would react – the police units charged with blocking the intersector border were going to be issued two five-bullet clips of blanks, and three clips of live ammunition for their carbines. The first clips were to be fired, if necessary, for purposes of warning or intimidation; the others were to be used only if absolutely necessary.' Other units were 'plentifully supplied with live ammunition' (Curtis Cate, *The Ides of August: The Berlin Wall Crisis, 1961*, London: Weidenfeld & Nicolson, 1978, p. 223).

16 In 1969 working for the press and information office of the Federal Government in Berlin.

17 *The Times*, 11 September 1961.

18 'Grossartig, wie das alles geklappt hat!', editorial in *Neues Deutschland*, 15 August 1961.

19 Kroll, *Lebenserinnerungen*, pp. 511 and 514.

20 One of the pieces of evidence used for showing that Khrushchev was not really worried very much about any of the above-mentioned three contingencies is the idea that he left Moscow at a time that could be considered critical. (According to Soviet reports, Khrushchev was in Kiev from 13 to 14 August, *Pravda*, 14 August 1961). I have a suspicion, however, that no matter whether or not Khrushchev had in fact gone on vacation the announcement itself, far from being 'strong evidence that the Soviet leadership was confident that there was no real risk of international conflict' (Slusser, *The Berlin Crisis*, p. 132), may be an indication of shrewd Soviet crisis diplomacy – a signal to the Western powers that the Soviet Union, doing 'business as usual', did not consider the measures of 13 August to be in any way dramatic.

21 See above, especially the military measures listed on pp. 286–7.

22 *Pravda*, 25 January 1961; see also above, pp. 220–5.

23 ibid. The Draft Program reiterated these doctrinal points by asserting that the 'contradictions between the principal imperialist powers are growing deeper'. Whereas old key points of imperialist rivalry were being revived, new contradictions would inevitably arise and deepen (*Pravda* and *Izvestiia*, 30 July 1961).

24 Article by V. Mikhailov in *Pravda*, 20 July 1961.

25 Khrushchev in his speech at a Soviet-Romanian friendship meeting on 11 August (*Pravda*, 12 August 1961). On 1 August *Pravda* quoted the British historian A. J. P. Taylor as saying that 'We [in the West] are all the slaves of Adenauer'. The campaign to isolate West Germany had begun in earnest in 1958. In the course of it such absurd assertions were made as the claim – in a review of a Soviet book on the history of World War II – that Hitler had attacked the Soviet Union after having attacked the Western countries first, that today 'the West German revanchists might direct their arms against, say, France' first and then turn against the East, and that those who are encouraging West Germany's rearmament 'should think about this' (Major General N. Pukhovsky, in *Pravda*, 24 July 1960).

26 *Khrushchev Remembers*, vol. II, pp. 500–1.

27 As quoted by Hilsman, *To Move a Nation*, p. 136.

28 See p. 207.

29 Kroll, *Lebenserinnerungen*, p. 510.

30 Sorensen, *Kennedy*, p. 594.

31 *New York Times*, 12 August 1961.
32 As quoted by Zolling and Bahnsen, *Kalter Winter*, p. 120; see also the *New York Times*, 17 August 1961; and Windsor, *City on Leave*, p. 240. As noted, TASS announced Konev's appointment on 10 August. It is probable that Konev arrived in Berlin earlier, on 7 August, as Zolling and Bahnsen report.
33 *Khrushchev Remembers*, Vol. II, p. 505.
34 *New York Times*, 17 August 1961. See also Kurt L. Shell, *Bedrohung und Bewährung Führung und Bevölkerung in der Berlin Krise* (Cologne and Opladen: Westdeutscher Verlag, 1965), p. 53. A communiqué was released after the meeting.
35 Decree of the GDR Council of Ministers of 12 August 1961 (*Neues Deutschland*, 13 August 1961).
36 *Pravda*, 14 August 1961.
37 This is contained in the declaration of the Warsaw Pact member countries of 13 August 1961, which stated that these countries 'address the People's Chamber and Government of the GDR, and all the working people of the GDR, with the proposal to establish an order on the borders of West Berlin which will securely block the way' (*Pravda*, 14 August 1961).
38 Smith, *The Defense of Berlin*, p. 184, based on a report in the *New York Times*, 28 November 1958.
39 Eisenhower, *Waging Peace*, p. 334.
40 ibid., p. 331.
41 ibid., p. 345.
42 Walter Lippmann, *The Coming Tests with Russia* (Boston, Mass.: Little, Brown, 1961), p. 23.
43 If the information of the two West German authors, Zolling and Bahnsen, is correct, there was discussion of this procedure at the Moscow meeting of the Warsaw Pact member countries; see p. 207.
44 Geoffrey McDermott, *Berlin: Success of a Mission?* (New York: Harper & Row, 1963), pp. 33–4. Similarly, the former West German Chancellor, Konrad Adenauer, writes in his memoirs that De Gaulle had told him in December 1961 that Berlin would already be under Soviet control if the West had used force on 13 August 1961; see Konrad Adenauer, *Erinnerungen, 1959–1963* (Stuttgart: Deutsche Verlagsanstalt, 1968), p. 123.
45 Wolfe, *Soviet Power and Europe*, pp. 89–90.
46 Vysotskii, *Zapadnyi Berlin*, p. 237; Vysotsky, *West Berlin*, p. 160.
47 This is a phrase used by Khrushchev in *Khrushchev Remembers*, Vol. II, p. 509, and the same metaphor occurs frequently in *The Penkovsky Papers*; it is most important in the contex on p. 161 where Khrushchev is said to have been content that the Western countries 'swallowed their first pill on 13th August 1961, when Berlin was closed off' and that he hoped that they would swallow a 'second pill' – the conclusion of a separate peace treaty with the GDR.
48 *Khrushchev Remembers*, Vol. I, p. 510. In both volumes of his memoirs, however, Khrushchev could not resist the temptation to make his light shine more brightly by claiming that the Soviet leadership had received information that the West was planning 'to break down our border installations' (ibid., p. 508) and 'forcibly to restore unrestricted passage in and out of the city' (ibid., Vol. II, p. 507). A similar assertion is made by Grossman in his article in *Voprosy istorii*, no. 10 (1969): 'at the end of October 1961, General Clay, together with the West German "ultras" [extremists], planned to break through with tanks to the center of the capital of the German Democratic Republic.'
49 General Lucius D. Clay on 27 October 1961, as quoted by Smith, *The Defense of Berlin*, p. 323.
50 A phrase of unidentified 'officials' in Washington wondering about the wisdom of the action, as reported by E. W. Kenworthy in the *New York Times*, 5 November 1961.

15
Consequences, Conclusions and Lessons

The consequence of the measures of 13 August, when the population of East Germany was locked in, and of 23 August, when West Berliners were locked out, became apparent only in retrospect. The Western political leaders were still under the impression that a turning point had not yet been reached and that the Wall was but a prelude to more far-reaching changes advocated in the Soviet draft peace treaty. In fact the continuing series of military measures (ICBM test flights, nuclear testing, increases in armed forces strength, maneuvers and threatening speeches by military leaders) as well as the continuing sequence of political probes (concerning air access to West Berlin, access of allied civilians to East Berlin, attempts to limit the four-power status of the city to West Berlin and demands for the withdrawal of Western troops) did not point in the direction of relaxation of tension after the crisis, but to an increase in tension with the possibility of a new flare-up always present. The confrontation of October 1961 appeared to be an example of this.

Soviet Conclusions

Between August and October 1961 Soviet political leaders and commentators were careful to avoid claims that the situation in Berlin had dramatically changed. Of course coverage of events supported the measures of August as 'timely and necessary'. But at the same time it asserted that the 'voices of realism' in the West had not yet won the upper hand – Western 'provocations' in Berlin had not been stopped, and Adenauer and Brandt were still talking about 'countermeasures'.[1]

At the Twenty-Second Party Congress, which could have been expected to provide some authoritative analysis of the historic decisions that put an end to the deplored 'subversive activities' from West Berlin, the events of 13 August were virtually ignored, first and foremost by Khrushchev. It was left to Ulbricht to state at the congress as a matter of fact that the GDR had been forced to build a 'protective wall against fascism'. The main part of his speech, however, dealt with the *continuation* of subversive activity from West Berlin for the purpose of which 'billions of marks' were still being spent by the imperialists. The only point that was underlined by Ulbricht in this context was the statement that *'the conclusion of a peace treaty with Germany is the most urgent task'*[2] – a statement that was endorsed by Khrushchev in equally uncompromising words (despite the removal of the deadline).[3] Thus analysis of the consequences remained subordinated to the tactical requirement of understatement, so as not to present the West with any argument for letting the matter of the peace treaty rest.

There is another, equally important, reason for the understatement of the consequences of the August measures in the immediate aftermath of the crisis. The Wall had to be built, Soviet sources had asserted, primarily because of ideological subversion and economic disruption from West Berlin, but the precarious state of the social and economic system of the GDR in the summer of 1961, as well as the disastrously large scale of emigration from East Germany to West Berlin and West Germany, had never been revealed.[4] Thus there was a noticeable reluctance, which still has not disappeared completely in contemporary Soviet sources, to present the full range of consequences and their significance.

However, as the Cuban missile crisis put a drastic end to Khrushchev's policy of winning Western concessions by means of pressure, including in Berlin, the tactical requirement of restraint on analysis disappeared to a large extent. This became evident in Khrushchev's speech of 16 January 1963 at the Sixth Congress of the SED in East Berlin,[5] and even more so after the conclusion of the GDR–USSR Treaty of Friendship, Mutual Assistance and Cooperation of 12 June 1964, which for all practical purposes can be regarded as a substitute peace treaty. As a consequence the problem of summing up an important phase in postwar history was made easier.

Two major aspects are distinguished in Soviet sources when the 'historic significance' of the 'protective measures' of August 1961 are being analyzed. The first, which receives considerably more emphasis than the second, is the assertion that 'the rug was pulled out from under the feet of the adventurist elements who had hoped to kindle a military conflict at the open border between the GDR and West Berlin'; the second is the observation that 'the events of August 13 significantly consolidated the domestic situation in the GDR and contributed to the successful building of socialism in that country'.[6] Not much can be gained from looking at the standard histories of international relations and Soviet foreign policy, which devote only a few terse remarks to these themes (in the unbalanced fashion noted above).[7] It remains for Vysotskii's analysis to provide more detail. In his view, which is an important one because of his former attachment to the Soviet embassy in East Berlin:[8]

> it can be said for certain that the socialist countries won this battle, and that the erection of a defensive wall against militarism and revanchism on the border with West Berlin was a major achievement by the entire socialist community and an event of truly historic significance.

In addition to elaborations on the theme of 'cooling the heads of overzealous strategists' (the first aspect), Vysotskii distinguishes the following results which directly or indirectly enhanced the domestic and international position of the GDR (the second aspect):

(1)   The attitude of the Western powers towards the German problem changed. They no longer actively supported demands for free elections and the reunification of Germany. These demands were no longer made 'prerequisites for settling other international problems'.

(2) There was increasing differentiation of political forces in West Germany. That country was forced to abandon positions on the German problem to which it had clung stubbornly for a long time. The 'Adenauer era' was about to come to an end, as shown in the elections to the Bundestag on 17 September 1961, in which the CDU/CSU lost its absolute majority.

(3) Difficulties were created for the population of West Berlin. As a consequence the Senat was forced to enter into direct negotiations with the GDR.

(4) A new chapter in the history of the GDR was opened. The GDR was able to begin the 'large-scale construction of socialism', introduce a new system of economic planning and administration and develop the economy at a faster pace.[9]

The consequences, as seen by the East German authors' collective in its history of foreign policy of the GDR, complement Vysotskii's analysis. In its view, too, the West German ruling circles and their supporters overseas had suffered a 'significant defeat' and the measures of 13 August 1961 constituted a 'turning point in the class struggle between socialism and imperialism in Germany'.[10] In addition to the points made by Vysotskii, the East German authors' collective adds:

(5) The GDR was put into a more favorable position to win acceptance for the principles of peaceful coexistence between the two German states. New possibilities were opened up for the establishment of normal relations between the two German states.[11]

The summary of the consequences, as expressed in these Soviet and East German sources, is basically sound — notwithstanding the self-righteous and polemical way in which it is put. Concerning the broad heading of 'consolidation of the GDR', it is correct, as *The Times* correspondent reported from East Germany in September 1961, that nervousness about the possibility of allied countermeasures or a popular uprising gave way to 'overwhelming self-confidence'.[12] This was reflected in Ulbricht's claim of as early as 18 August 1961 that 'our measures have shown, even to those who did not believe it before, the true balance of power in the world' and in his prediction, or warning, that

> After the radical limitation of the influence of the West Berlin front-line swamp (*Frontstadtsumpf*) a few things will advance at a faster pace. We can devote ourselves without interference to the real tasks, the implementation of which will benefit the whole population of the German Democratic Republic. Many of us will have received a new consciousness of strength — a very favorable asset for carrying out our work.[13]

This new sense of self-confidence was reflected also in the way in which the Ulbricht regime set out to restore party control over society. Recalcitrant peasants, earlier *Grenzgänger* and members of the FDJ who had not volunteered for military service were beaten up by picked squads of young factory guards. 'It was a systematic and extensive operation, which *Neues Deutsch-land* glorified as "education by the fists of the workers".' [14] As the way to West Berlin was barred to young people it was now possible for the GDR to introduce compulsory military service.[15] Of the East German population only the desperate and daring, in numbers too insignificant to have negative repercussions in the economy, were still able to find their way to the West. The rest had to adjust to the new realities and find their place in the GDR. The Western countries, too, had to adjust to the new realities. Before looking at this process it is essential to summarize Khrushchev's conclusions and lessons.

Khrushchev's Lessons

What is striking in both volumes of Khrushchev's memoirs is the explicit comparison of the Berlin crisis of 1948 with that of 1961 and the insistence, as in official sources, that the Soviet Union and the GDR scored a major victory in 1961. 'Stalin had tried to take advantage of the West Berlin issue, but he suffered a defeat.' [16] Costs had to be paid because

> The West had managed to exploit the tension generated by the block-ade and to impose conditions on East Germany which were even more constraining and one-sided than the ones set by the Potsdam agree-ment.[17]

In contrast, concluding the description of the confrontation of October 1961, as well as the chapter on the Berlin crisis, Khrushchev stated that

> Thus the West had tested our nerve by prodding us with the barrels of their cannons and found us ready to accept their challenge. They learned that they couldn't frighten us. *I think it was a great victory for us, and it was won without firing a single shot.*[18]

Success was made up of the following ingredients: the Soviet Union 'guaran-teed the GDR's right to control its own territory and its own borders'; 'The GDR's economic problems were considerably relieved . . .'; and 'Further-more, the establishment of border control in Berlin had a very positive effect on the consciousness of the people'.[19]

This favorable summary of events, as well as the equally favorable – and at times almost enthusiastic – official Soviet accounts, could be dismissed as putting on a good show after the failure to compel the West to sign a peace treaty. But this would be unwise. There is good reason to assume that a peace treaty might not have given the Soviet Union and East Germany all they had wanted. Khrushchev for one seems to have thought so.

> Of course, even if we had [had] a peace treaty, it wouldn't have solved these problems [of manpower drain and the easy access of West Berlin-ers to commodities in the GDR] because Berlin's status as a free city would have been stipulated in the treaty and the gates would have remained open.[20]

In other words, the demand for the conclusion of a peace treaty was not an absolute one, but a demand relative to the achievement of specific Soviet objectives. For this reason, Khrushchev continues,

> I would say that we didn't quite achieve the same sort of moral victory that a peace treaty would have represented, but on the other hand we probably received more material gains *without* a peace treaty. If the West had agreed to sign a treaty, it would have meant concessions on our part, particularly with regard to movement of people across the border.[21]

In the light of this realistic assessment, stressing the instrumental nature of the demand for the conclusion of a peace treaty,[22] it is possible to summarize the lessons which Khrushchev may have drawn, as follows. Significant material gain was made without the conclusion of a peace treaty and 'without firing a single shot'. The taking of unilateral action and the creation of a *fait accompli* was successful because the West was taken by surprise, because the action was carefully prepared and because a strong deterrent posture accompanied the measures. As this success was achieved even in conditions of military-strategic inferiority, it was likely that further advances could be made in conditions of parity, in particular by creating a more credible threat *vis-à-vis* the United States. At the same time the growing awareness in the United States of a growing strategic preponderance over the Soviet Union had already prevented, for the time being, the achievement of further gains in the period between late August and October 1961.

If these were indeed the lessons which Khrushchev had drawn from the Berlin crisis they would go a long way toward explaining the origins of the Cuban missile crisis – not only with regard to its substance (that is, the attempt to create strategic parity by an ingenious shortcut) but also with regard to the dynamics and techniques of the crisis (that is, the attempt to take the United States by surprise, the long preparation and the adoption of a strong deterrent posture in the hope of creating a successful *fait accompli*). To that extent there is what may be called a 'dialectic' relationship between the two crises: by applying the techniques used in the Berlin crisis to the Cuban environment, the Cuban missile crisis was to make the conditions ripe for further advances in Berlin.[23]

As manifest in the significant failure of the venture, there were flaws in this application of the lessons of Berlin to Cuba. No doubt one of the reasons why the lessons were inadequate is connected with the fact that the West had a different idea of the outcome of the Berlin crisis.

Western Conclusions

Taking into account that there is little disparity between Soviet and Western views of the outcome of the Berlin crisis of 1948, it is a matter of great interest and consequence to see, quite in contrast to Soviet sources, a fairly broad consensus of interpretation in the West speaking of a 'failure' of Soviet policy in Berlin in 1961,[24] a 'failure of the Berlin campaign',[25] a 'strategic failure',[26] and even assertions to the effect that: 'It was no secret in late 1961 that Khrushchev's most glaring failure was in Berlin.'[27]

Details of the case have been argued differently by different authors but there is a common denominator of two major elements: (1) Khrushchev had proposed far-reaching changes, summarized in the draft peace treaty of January 1959, yet in fact a peace treaty was never signed. (2) 'Actual rights were not affected [by the measures of 13 August], only a Four-Power Status that had existed only on paper.'[28] These two themes are woven by some Western scholars into a context showing, in addition, 'positive aspects' of the outcome of the Berlin crisis. Speaking of 'legal rights that had long since ceased to exist in fact' and seeing 'no reason [for the West at that time] to initiate countersteps that could catapult the world into war', one scholar of this positivist school goes on to say:

It turned out that the East German action had its positive side, too. For one thing, it dramatically demonstrated the bankruptcy of the GDR's political system. This fact would prove to be of great propagandistic value. More important, the closure of the Berlin border resolved one of the West's most serious dilemmas: how to achieve a relaxation of tension in the Berlin area without actually taking steps in the West to halt the flow of refugees. By cutting the Gordian Knot of the refugee problem, the East Germans also enabled the Soviet Union to postpone the conclusion of a separate peace treaty, in effect putting on ice the nagging question of Berlin's future.[29]

All this appears very much as an awkwardly argued rationalization of an unambiguous Western retreat. First, it is not obvious why there is less 'propagandist value' – if this was an important issue – in tens of thousands of East Germans leaving the GDR every month but more propagandist value in the existence of the Wall. Secondly, it is not evident why any Western country was under any moral, legal or political obligation to assist a state lacking legitimacy in acquiring stability or, worse, in helping it to circumvent a universally recognized right (namely, the right of emigration for its citizens). Thirdly, it is not apparent whether it was the Wall that 'enabled the Soviet Union to postpone the conclusion of a separate peace treaty' or whether it was the demand for the conclusion of a peace treaty that enabled the Soviet Union to build the Wall. Fourthly, it is not sound legal sense to argue that only 'paper rights' were breached as if the free movement of persons in Berlin had not become, in addition to being a paper right, a *customary* right exercised daily by thousands of people. It would seem that paper rights in this understanding are defined, curiously, as rights that exist *de jure* and *de facto* but cannot be enforced.

The case for minimizing the significance of the Soviet and East German success (but still not for speaking of a Soviet 'failure') becomes more convincing if it is argued that the West, in full anticipation of the risks inherent in maintaining legal rights and customary practice, had already defined and accepted psychologically a state of affairs that did not yet exist. This, indeed, is the essence of the three essentials put forward by Kennedy in his speech of 25 July and adopted by the NATO ministerial meeting in Paris in early August 1961. It is in the light of this limitation of interests to West Berlin that a significant *change* in the status quo could appear to the West as mere *confirmation* of the status quo, and that the Wall could be (and still is) seen as the mere physical embodiment of post-World War II 'realities'.[30]

Although there is reluctance to state this fact plainly, even in scholarly analyses, the net sum of this account – the real lesson – is that Soviet military power had been successfully transformed into political gain in Central Europe.[31] When Fulbright, in his frequently quoted statement of 30 July 1961, thought that the East Germans 'have a right to close it [the border]', he was mistaken, but he was right when he said, 'I think the Russians have the power to close it in any case'.[32] It was this realization which, to a great extent, induced the West *ex ante* not to challenge in advance Soviet measures yet to be taken.

This retreat in the face of Soviet military pressure was to show clearly the hollowness of concepts aimed at forcing the Soviet Union to change its policies. This affected primarily the West German concept of policy from positions of strength (*Politik der Stärke*). However, somewhat paradoxically at first sight, the process of normalization of relations between East and West Germany was set back in the immediate aftermath of the crisis. The unprecedented act of dividing a city by a concrete wall, as well as the shooting of people trying to escape or emigrate, made it even more difficult to establish direct contacts with the Ulbricht regime on any level. Thus the immediate aftermath of the crisis gave a new impetus to the West German claim of sole representation (*Alleinvertretungsanspruch*) of the German people and the elaborate attempt on its basis to isolate East Germany. Only after the formation of the Grand Coalition (CDU/SPD) government in 1966 did some of the principles of a new *Ostpolitik* evolve, and only after a further change of government in 1969, under the Little Coalition (SPD/FDP), did the process of normalization really begin to get under way.

At the international level, too, the employment of strategic threats by the Soviet Union, the increase in Soviet armed forces strength, the announcement of an increase in defense expenditures, the movement of troops in East Germany, the measures of 13 August and, later on, the resumption of nuclear testing all contributed to an exacerbation of superpower relations. Militarily, some substance was put into programs under way, or under discussion, for a strengthening of conventional forces in NATO. On 19 September 1961 the United States Secretary of Defense, Robert McNamara, announced at a press conference that 73,000 reservists, including two divisions of the National Guard, would be called for duty on 15 October.[33] Also in September the West German government announced a three-month extension of military service for 6,000 volunteer officers and noncommissioned officers and 30,000 men.[34] France and Belgium increased the size of their forces in Germany, and so did Britain. Before the Berlin crisis it was expected that the numerical strength of the British Rhine Army (BAOR) would be reduced from its level of 55,000 men; the planned reduction was suspended during the crisis, and in September additional forces were sent.[35]

These additions to Western conventional power were partly in implementation of NATO's new doctrine of flexible response (later to be adopted officially) and partly symbolic gestures in the continuing controversy with the Soviet Union over the German problem. They may have done their share to increase stability and enhance deterrence. However, they did not lead to a qualitative change in the military balance, globally or regionally. In Central Europe the Soviet Union retained its large margin of superiority in conventional power and in medium- and intermediate-range nuclear systems. As a compensation, the United States was rapidly about to build up a considerable lead in strategic power. The Berlin crisis, however, did not seem to have had an appreciable effect on the US strategic weapons program: the basis for serial production of ICBMs and SLBMs had been laid before 1961, and there is no evidence that the deployment rate of these two weapons systems was increased in response to the crisis.

Lessons for this Study

The main lessons of the Berlin crisis of 1961 which need to be drawn so as to lay the basis for the overall conclusions and comparisons of the two crises with each other and other crises can be summarized as follows.

   (1) The Berlin crisis of 1961 (June to October as defined here) appears to be the most acute point of a longer-term Soviet campaign of pressure lasting from November 1958 to November 1962. During that time important *shifts of emphasis* took place. In 1958 the Soviet Union started out with a display of strength and confidence in the wake of the Sputnik shock, conscious of accelerating processes of decolonization and in anticipation of improved economic performance. It presented to the West an image of solidarity with China and of a dynamic country and leader[ship] prone, at times, to reckless action in foreign affairs. To that extent the origins of the Berlin crisis contain offensive elements. They are symbolized, most of all, in the challenge to the Western allied presence in the city.

   However, as the rift with China could no longer be concealed, as the assumed advances in Soviet strategic power turned out to be exaggerated, and as the Soviet economic performance failed to match the hopes and ambitions expressed in the Seven-Year Plan, more defensive elements had come to prevail in 1961. This trend was enhanced by the dramatically deteriorating situation in the GDR. In that way the USSR's position shifted from that of a player exploiting advantageous trends in the game to one forced to accept risks in order to prevent a significant defeat. This is the essence of the measures of 13 August.

   Once, however, it had become apparent that the situation had been improved at least to the extent of satisfying the immediate interests and needs of the socialist bloc, the Soviet Union reverted to the original, more long-range objectives of the campaign of pressure. Yet the overall correlation of forces, as manifest in the exacerbated rift with China and the increased sense of confidence derived in the West from an increasing margin of military-strategic superiority, worked against further success of pressure.

   (2) The question of whether West Berlin, and the Western allied presence there, was *a lever or a prize* – a question that was a valid one to ask in the context of the Berlin crisis of 1948 – had probably been settled by as early as 1958, when the first ultimatum was put forward. Berlin, the Western allied presence included, could only be a lever. It could be used effectively because

of the very vulnerability of the city. The prizes to be won in the period from 1958 to 1962 were greater stability of the GDR and the 'socialist commonwealth', an increase in the international standing and international recognition of the GDR, a more far-reaching acceptance of the territorial, political and socioeconomic status quo in Europe, and other benefits. West Berlin itself entered in this spectrum of overall Soviet objectives in two ways: its unique role as an escape hatch had to be drastically curbed or terminated; and its attractiveness and, therefore, potential for what Soviet official sources call 'subversion' had to be limited. The measures of 13 August, seen from this perspective, constitute only the most dramatic aspects of a campaign that was consistent in its objectives from 1958.

(3) The question of whether Soviet risk-taking in 1961 is to be considered a *success or a failure* is of crucial importance. Certainly it was a failure if it is to be assumed that the demands of the draft peace treaty of January 1959 accurately reflected the expectations of the Soviet leadership. However, if it is accepted – more realistically – that the demands summarized in the draft peace treaty constituted an instrument for the achievement of the more limited objectives outlined in the previous point, that the Soviet and East German leaderships were apprehensive about the possibility of Western counteraction and popular unrest, and finally that the status quo was not only fixed more rigidly and effectively (receiving a 'physical embodiment'), but changed in favor of the Soviet Union and the GDR, it becomes evident that the Soviet leadership most likely considered the results of the Berlin crisis of 1961 a success and that it also assumed that this success could lead to new concessions and compromises by the West if pressure were maintained. The latter expectation proved incorrect in the immediate aftermath of the crisis of 1961, but the crisis laid the objective conditions for the ultimate achievement of Soviet aims as defined in point (2).

(4) Concerning *ideology* as one of the factors shaping Soviet policy in the Berlin crisis of 1961, the issue is more complex than the three standardized dichotomies – left versus right commitments and priorities, the gap of theory and practice and the idea of ideology versus national interest – would suggest.[36] Although elements of the right dominated major doctrinal formulations in 1961 there was at the same time a broad justification of the policy of threat and pressure as pursued by the Soviet Union in the period from the November 1956 ultimatums in the Suez crisis to the ultimatums of 1958 and 1961 on Berlin (elements of the left). Although the theme of peaceful coexistence was stressed, its main content remained limited to the express need to avoid war. Competition and conflict, rather than cooperation, were still the main organizing principles of the concept. In summary, therefore, we may conclude that there was *no congruence* of domestic, intra-bloc and international policies and doctrines in 1961. Instead, there were numerous ideological threads and policies difficult to weave into a consistent pattern. Undoubtedly this was a reflection of the increased complexity of Soviet and international politics.

The issue of ideology is complicated further by the problem of whether there is a gap between Marxist-Leninist theory and practice and, if there is such a gap, whether it is accepted cynically by the Soviet leadership, or whether the gap is in reality one of expressed expectations which founder on the rocks of lagging Soviet performance in various fields. The last-mentioned explanation appears to be the most accurate one in the specific conditions of 1961.

The importance of ideology was unambiguous in one respect: the need to safeguard the viability of the socialist community, of which the GDR by then had become an integral part. To that extent the Berlin crisis of 1961 underlines the importance of ideology for Soviet security; and at the same time it makes nonsense of a rigid dichotomy between ideology and national interests.

Liberalization of many facets of life in East Germany – for example, allowing more trade with the West, encouraging human contacts between the two parts of Germany, abandoning forced collectivization, supporting small enterprises, and so on – would have alleviated to a large extent the problem of westward migration of the East German population and would have helped the Soviet Union out of the dilemma of having to act unilaterally and under pressure. However, the SED leadership was not ready for it, and – apart from some tendencies in this direction in 1953 – the Soviet Union never pushed the SED to adopt a 'new course' of de-Stalinization, relaxation and liberalization.

(5) As mentioned in the previous point, it is practically impossible to disentangle Soviet ideological and *state interests* in the Berlin crisis: both reinforced each other and formed a unified entity. The 'refugee problem', from the Soviet vantage point, was not merely an ideological embarrassment but, because of the deepening crisis of the GDR economy, a serious setback to the ambitious targets of the Seven-Year Plan of the USSR and a severe handicap in the main declared arena of East–West competition: economic performance.

Because of the issues of intra-bloc cohesion and Soviet control, the dynamics of Soviet policy in the Berlin crisis closely resembled that of Soviet interventions in Eastern Europe. However, there was a major difference, touching directly on Soviet security: popular discontent and economic crisis in the GDR combined with the open borders to West Berlin, the contacts between East and West Berliners and the presence of the Western allies in the city to make the Berlin crisis an inseparable part of the East–West conflict.

(6) The constellation of *military power* in 1961 showed significant advantages for the Soviet Union at the local level – in conventional power, as well as in medium- and intermediate-range bombers and missiles capable of delivering nuclear warheads against targets in Western Europe. Also the United States was (and felt) vulnerable to Soviet nuclear strikes by various means of delivery (including less than 'a handful' of ICBMs and close to two hundred long-range bombers). In contrast the reintroduction of American troops in Europe and the build-up of the *Bundeswehr* after the Korean War, from NATO's point of view, had somewhat lessened the imbalance at the conventional level. The USA still retained a significant lead over the USSR in all indicators of military-strategic power and was capable of inflicting considerably more damage on the territory of the Soviet Union than *vice versa*.

It is safe to conclude from this distribution of military power that it set stringent limits to the use of force for both superpowers: it discouraged any direct interference with access to West Berlin and the Western military presence by the Soviet Union, and dissuaded the United States from challenging the unilateral Soviet measures of 13 August. However, such a stalemate invariably favors the side (the USSR in this case) which is bent on creating a *fait accompli* and which thereby burdens the adversary with the responsibility for initiating violence.

In the course of the crisis the Soviet Union relied heavily on military measures both of a verbal and nonverbal variety. Some of these measures clearly had political and psychological significance in increasing Western anxiety about war and enhancing the Soviet deterrent posture; other measures were specifically related to the requirements of conducting a military intervention or coping with a local military conflict; yet further measures served to improve the overall conventional and military-strategic power of the Soviet Union *vis-à-vis* the West in conditions of American advances in strategic power and renewed emphasis on usable conventional power for local and limited war. It is not possible to say precisely in each case whether *military* requirements or *political* purposes of crisis bargaining prevailed. But precision on this point would be artificial anyhow because both aspects in the Berlin crisis complemented each other. However, there is little reason to assume that the measures adopted were somehow a nonrational outcome of the domestic power struggle – a point to be summarized next.

(7) Examination of the *domestic dimension* of Soviet behavior in the Berlin crisis of 1961 did not inspire confidence to apply a bureaucratic politics model. There is no evidence for the existence of a hard-line faction, alone or in conjunction with the Soviet military, pushing, forcing or egging on the political leadership to take reckless action. There is no evidence of such a faction even temporarily taking over and hence bearing responsibility for such measures as the suspension of the troop reductions program, the announcement of an increase in the defense budget or the resumption of nuclear testing. There *is* evidence of various Soviet officials expressing views in favor of greater emphasis on heavy industry, but no evidence that these officials, or their protégés, successfully conspired to effect a change in Khrushchev's priorities away from agriculture to defense; nor, for that matter, that these officials with certain views on defense and agriculture also had something to say on problems of foreign policy *and* that they had the power to assert their views. It is more convincing to believe that individual military leaders and members of the party Presidium were concerned that Khrushchev might be going too far in his challenge of the West on Berlin, or that he might act too impulsively.

Notes: Part Two, Chapter 15

1 See especially the daily reports by V. Kuznetsov in *Pravda*, and by V. Bai and O. Yakovlev in *Izvestiia* in the period from mid- to late August 1961.

2 *Pravda*, 21 October 1961; emphasis in the original.

3 'A German peace treaty must and will be signed, with or without the Western powers'; see p. 214.

4 As mentioned above, the concealment of the true magnitude of the problems facing the GDR also may have presented some problems for Khrushchev in legitimizing his Berlin policy at home; see pp. 270–1. Leo Gruliow has summarized the extent to which the Soviet press

failed to give an accurate representation of the origins, content and consequences of the measures of 13 August. The events *not reported* by the Soviet press included, among other things, the fact that East Germans had left for West Berlin in increasing numbers; that the 'protective measures' consisted of a solid wall of concrete and bricks; that the closure of the borders made it impossible for relatives on both sides of the sectoral borders to visit each other (after 23 August); that Soviet forces had been deployed around Berlin in combat readiness and that Marshal Konev was appointed commander of the GSFG; that the East German police used tear gas and water hoses to disperse demonstrators on the Western side of the sector borders; that big protest demonstrations took place in West Berlin (these were only alluded to as 'provocations'); and that the measures met with a negative response also in countries of the Third World, including India. See Leo Gruliow, 'Nuclear testing and the Soviet press', *International Press Institute (IPI) Report* (October 1961), p. 1. Because the East Germans were aware of the problem, and because they could listen to West German radio and television stations, reporting in the GDR was more extensive and reflected the drama more accurately.

5   At the Sixth Congress of the SED in East Berlin Khrushchev was to declare: 'And now, if we view the matter from the standpoint of the immediate interests of the socialist countries, the problem of the German peace treaty is not really what it was before the defensive measures were taken on the GDR border with West Berlin' N. S. Khrushchev, *The New Content of Peaceful Coexistence in the Nuclear Age* (New York: Crosscurrents Press, 1963), p. 19.

6   A. S. Grossman, 'Granitsa mira', *Voprosy istorii*, no. 10, (1969), p. 201.

7   Trukhanovskii (ed.) *Istoriia mezhdunarodnykh otnoshenii*, Vol. III pp. 547–9; Inozemtsev (ed.), *Mezhdunaroonye otnosheniia posle vtoroi mirovoi voiny*, Vol. III, pp. 211–12; and the recently appeared fifth volume of A. A. Gromyko *et al.* (eds), *Istoriia diplomatii*, Vol. V (Moscow: Izdatel'stvo politicheskoi literatury, 1974), pp. 523–4.

8   See p. 168. Both the Russian and the English ('translated') version of Vysotskii's book contain a section entitled 'The importance of the August 13 measures'.

9   Vysotskii, *Zapadnyi Berlin*, pp. 237–45; Vysotsky, *West Berlin*, pp. 160–6. The points are not enumerated in that order but scattered over various pages. Point (4) is cautiously prefaced: 'As the GDR press pointed out . . . '

10 Peter Klein *et al.* (eds), *Geschichte der Aussenpolitik der Deutschen Demokratischen Republik: Abriss* (East Berlin: Dietz Verlag, 1968), pp. 233–7.

11 ibid., p. 237.

12 See p. 287.

13 Ulbricht's radio and television address of 18 August 1961 (*Neues Deutschland*, 19 August 1961).

14 Windsor, *City on Leave*, p. 244.

15 On 20 September 1961 (*The Times*, 21 September 1961).

16 *Khrushchev Remembers*, Vol. II, p. 501.

17 *Khrushchev Remembers*, Vol. I, pp. 500–1.

18 ibid., p. 510 (my italics).

19 ibid., pp. 504 and 510.

20 ibid., p. 503.

21 *Khrushchev Remembers*, Vol. II, pp. 507–8 (italics in the original).

22 Even more frankly than Khrushchev, the History of Foreign Policy of the German Democratic Republic makes the point that the 'resolute demands by the German Democratic Republic and the other socialist countries' for the conclusion of a German peace treaty no later than the end of 1961 'contributed' (!) significantly to the success of the measures of 13 August 1961 (Klein *et al.*, *Geschichte der Aussenpolitik*, p. 235).

23 John Erickson's account of the logistical preparations for the Cuban missile crisis constitutes an important piece of evidence confirming this dialectical relationship between Berlin and Cuba. According to his information the Soviet Union began to plan actively for the Cuban contingency as early as the *autumn of 1961* (rather than the spring of 1962, as most Western writers hold) by moving supplies, large quantities of oil in particular, to ports at the Black Sea. These movements were unconnected with the ongoing large-scale autumn maneuvers (interview with Erickson in Edinburgh on 24 May 1976).

24 Judson Mitchell, 'The revised "two camps" doctrine in Soviet foreign policy', *Orbis*, Spring 1972, p. 21.

25 Wolfe, *Soviet Power and Europe*, p. 230.

26 Helmut Dahm, *Abschreckung oder Volkskrieg: Strategische Machtplanung der*

Sowjetunion und Chinas im internationalen Kräfteverhältnis (Olten and Freiburg: Walter-Verlag, 1968), p. 27.

27 Hyland and Shyrock, *The Fall of Khrushchev* (London: Pitman, 1968), p. 5.
28 Theo Sommer, 'Die bitteren Realitäten', *Die Zeit*, 24 August 1971.
29 Richard L. Merritt, 'A transformed crisis: the Berlin Wall', in Roy C. Macridis (ed.), *Modern European Governments* (Englewood Cliffs, NJ: Prentice-Hall, 1968), p. 149.
30 On this point – notwithstanding the significant differences in analysis – there is some convergence of Soviet and Western interpretation. To Vysotsky, 'The assertions in Western propaganda that the border wall divided the city and perpetuated the split of Berlin and Germany are nothing more than a clumsy fabrication. Germany had long ago [*sic*] been replaced by the GDR and the FRG and Greater Berlin by West Berlin, which is a special entity, and by Berlin, the capital of the GDR . . . *Consequently, the border wall was merely a physical embodiment of the situation which arose as a result of the splitting up of Germany and Berlin by the Western Powers*' (Vysotsky, *West Berlin*, pp. 165–6; Vysotskii, *Zapadnyi Berlin*, pp. 244–5, my italics).
31 The History of Foreign Policy of the German Democratic Republic put this point bluntly: 'Thus the German Democratic Republic, in conjunction with the USSR and its other allies, [and] taking into account the correlation of forces in world politics, succeeded in utilizing certain realistic features of Kennedy's foreign policy, whose aim it was to avoid a direct military confrontation of the main nuclear powers in Europe' (Klein *et al.* (eds), *Geschichte der Aussenpolitik*, pp. 234–5.
32 *New York Times*, 3 August 1961.
33 *The Times*, 20 September 1961.
34 ibid., 13 and 21 September 1961.
35 ibid., 14, 15 and 21 September 1961.
36 For details see pp. 328–34.

PART THREE
Comparisons and Conclusions

16
Operational Principles of Soviet Risk-Taking and Crisis Behavior

Three main conclusions emerge from the study. The first is the limited relevance of much of the literature on crises for the analysis of Soviet behavior in the two Berlin crises. The second is the surprising degree to which Soviet behavior in the two cases reflected operational principles of the traditional Bolshevik belief system. The third shows the player at the international board to have a distinct personality which is well suited to manipulate risks in the chess game named disaster and which, when he plays the game, allows him to do so in a purposive and determined fashion.

The reason why so many elaborations on the topic of international crises leave much to be desired is not only to be found in the state of affairs mentioned in the introduction to this thesis, namely, that empirical studies of Soviet risk-taking and crisis behavior are rare, and that generalizations on international crises are based primarily on empirical studies of American foreign policy. More important, much of the literature has been overshadowed by one single crisis of major importance – the Cuban missile crisis. Most of the works on crisis management appeared within the scope of a few years after the crisis, and not many of them succeeded in ridding themselves of the fixation on the dramatic aspects of the hectic thirteen days in October 1962. Policy-making, too, was (at least initially) overshadowed by the missile crisis, as is evident in McNamara's statement, made shortly after the crisis, that 'There is no longer any such thing as strategy, only crisis management'.[1]

All this would not matter very much were it not for the fact that the framework of analysis derived from the Cuban missile crisis has been superimposed on Soviet crisis behavior. The problem with this is that Soviet behavior in the Cuban missile crisis appears in retrospect as one major *exception* to traditional (and subsequent) patterns of Soviet risk-taking, rather than as a confirmation of such patterns. This is so despite the fact that in the theoretical part of this work the two Berlin crises and the Cuban missile crisis have been separated from all other cases and grouped together in a separate category of analysis.[2] In order to understand Soviet crisis behavior it is appropriate to consider with care the more protracted character of the Berlin crises.

Certainly, in the Berlin crisis of 1948 there is very little to support the idea of processes assumed to be the rule, the image that 'each power tries to outbid the other by some margin in its verbal or material commitment at each stage' and that:

Moderately worded notes are followed by stiff notes. Notes are followed by movements of ships, troops, or airplanes in locations close to
the theater of the quarrel, and perhaps some forces are infiltrated or
landed overtly. Shots are fired, followed by a more-than-equal retaliation from the other side. Allied nations step into the picture. And so
on, through threat and counterthreat, retaliation and counterretalia-
tion, right up to the brink of all-out war – and perhaps, across it.[3]

Although there were warning signals at the local level, both of a verbal and
material kind, the image of the escalation ladder just does not fit. At the
diplomatic level the Soviet Union in 1948 adopted a stance of conciliation
and compromise. And when one major step up the ladder was taken by the
imposition of the blockade it was accompanied by mixed and ambiguous
verbal communications – lame excuses, expressions of regret, invocation of
the old wartime spirit as well as some moderately worded statements conveying the idea that compromises on Berlin and Germany are possible and desirable. Reality presented itself as much more complex than was made allowance
for in many Western writings.

On the surface the 'outbidding of each power by the other by some margin
in its verbal or material commitment at each stage' in the Berlin crisis of 1961
appears to apply more easily. On both sides – Soviet and American – a
number of moves and countermoves were taken, including maneuvers of
various types of forces, speeches emphasizing military preparedness,
announcements of increases in defense expenditures, strengthening of
conventional forces, and improvements in the strategic posture. This has
been enumerated in much detail. However, these measures were spread out
over a relatively long period of time (from about May to October 1961);
many of them – paradoxically from the point of view of classic crisis
management theory – were taken *after* the gravest danger point was safely
past; finally, the image of escalation does not fit very well in this case either
for the reason that it was never quite clear what the military measures were
all about, whether they were to be considered part and parcel of the arms
race (or arms 'competition'), whether they were designed to improve the
overall bargaining positions, whether (on the Soviet side) they were meant to
be instruments of compellence forcing the Western powers out of Berlin and
establishing a radically different regime on the access routes, or whether –
more modestly – they were designed for purposes of deterrence of Western
counteraction to the measures of 13 August. In the Cuban crisis no such
ambiguity applied. Verbal and material moves on the American side were
unambiguous to the extent that the missiles had to come out. Verbal and
material moves on the Soviet side were unambiguous in their intention to
keep them in, if possible. There was no middle way of keeping medium-
range missiles in Cuba and withdrawing intermediate-range missiles, or
withdrawing only half or a third of them.

Another important deviation from the classical model of crisis management concerns time constraints. In an age of rapid communication and high
speeds of strategic and conventional delivery systems this is indeed an
important issue to consider, and reference to the hypothetical crisis dynamics produced by such constraints has been made in the theoretical part. However, in practice the issue did not play an important role in either of the two

crises examined here. In 1948 the 'technical difficulties' alleged by the SMA made it appear that the blockade was not final and required some time of watchful waiting. It was even agreed by all in principle that the important road bridge over the River Elbe and some of the railway bridges were in need of repair because of wartime damage. So there was no immediate pressure to act for this reason. As the airlift developed, the need to act was removed even further because the position of the Western powers and essential activity of the German civilian population could be maintained for the time being; finally, at the international diplomatic level the Soviet Union was maneuvering itself into an increasingly awkward position, pushing the thought of military action further into the background.

In 1961 things were different only to a certain extent. There *was* pressure on the West to act quickly *if* action was to be taken. To that extent there are parallels to the Cuban missile crisis. In 1961 and 1962 a *fait accompli* was being created that could only be removed by deciding quickly and acting forcefully. But as the point of contention in Berlin in 1961 had already been yielded to the Soviet Union in advance, as the population refrained from acting rashly on its own and was actively being discouraged from venting its anger and resentment, time constraints were removed in the first days after 13 August. The Soviet Union had to revert to re-creating a sense of urgency in a quite artificial manner so as to win more concessions in round two of the resumed pressure.

These are only some of the differences between the two crises examined and the assumed classic case. Others emerge in an examination of individual characteristics of Soviet risk-taking. For this purpose it is appropriate to return to some of the instrumental beliefs or operational principles of Soviet foreign policy mentioned in the theoretical part,[4] suggest some additional beliefs, principles or axioms, and see how much validity there is to each one of them.

(1) *Do not embark on forward operations against an opponent which are not carefully calculated in advance and move forward only after careful preparation.* There is overwhelming evidence in both crises examined that this proposition is valid. In 1948 the first serious examples of selective interference with access to and egress from Berlin came after Marshal Sokolovsky's dramatic walkout from the Allied Control Council (20 March). These 'warning signals of crisis' continued in one form or another until the very day of the imposition of the blockade (23–4 June). It was also evident that the blockade was related clearly and unambiguously to the currency reform in the Anglo-American zone. As shown by the severe restrictions adopted by the SMA at the weekend preceding the currency reform (11–12 June), obviously taken under the assumption that that weekend would see the announcement of the reform, there is no hint of any improvisation or spontaneous move on the Soviet side. The claim that the currency reform of 18 June came as a surprise to the USSR – a theme advanced by Soviet spokesmen then and repeated in Soviet sources ever since – is completely unwarranted as the newspaper of the SMA had already appeared on 4 February with a correct Soviet report to the effect that printed notes for a separate monetary reform were already available in the Western zones.[15] This is not to say that the calculations were sound, or that the result was successful, but only that

the measures adopted showed careful preparation and came only after a series of tests of the American determination to respond to more severe challenges.

Calculated risk-taking and careful preparation is apparent also in the Berlin crisis of 1961. In that case the probing of the extent of Western determination and resolve can be said to have started as early as when the first ultimatum on the Berlin problem was issued, but certainly it was well under way at the time of the second ultimatum in June 1961. This probing could help to reveal the extent to which the Western powers were united on the issues in dispute and to show where action could be taken without risking Western countermeasures. But the most important feature in the present context is the surprisingly long period of delay in taking physical measures. The evidence available points to pressures exerted by Ulbricht on Khrushchev starting from mid-March 1961. A meeting of the Political Consultative Committee in Moscow on 28–9 March probably discussed the problem, but the course of events justifies the conclusion that the procedure adopted there was only to try out all available options of stopping the outflow of East Germans at the local level and avoid the sharpening of conflict at the international level. By June this procedure had turned out to be inadequate. In part as a consequence of this, and in part as a response to diplomatic opportunities seemingly been offered by an apparently weak, inexperienced and irresolute American leadership, the pressure was increased also at the international level, at the Vienna Summit. But even then two more months were to pass, filled with preparations at the local and international levels, before the risk of taking physical measures was decided upon by the Soviet Union, to be endorsed finally at the meeting of the first secretaries of the member countries of the Warsaw Pact, on 3–5 August. Another ten days were left to complete the material preparations in East Germany, carefully camouflage the impending action and prepare for all the contingencies which might arise.

It is instructive to compare this type of Soviet behavior with that shown in other crises and in other situations where there was only a risk of superpower crisis. As regards the conflicts in the Middle East in 1956, 1967 and 1973, the principle of 'do not embark on forward operations against an opponent which are not carefully calculated in advance' is only of limited applicability as the USSR was primarily *responding* to local events. Of course there were some elements in the Soviet response which had the characteristics of a forward operation in the late stages of the local conflict – as evident in the nuclear threats made by Khrushchev (through Bulganin as head of government) on 5 November 1956;[6] the use by Kosygin of the hot line on 10 June 1967, threatening that unless Israel halted its military operations the Soviet Union would take 'necessary actions, including military';[7] and the alert of Soviet airborne divisions (approximately 45,000 operational troops) between 8 and 16 October 1973, other signs of build-up for military intervention and a strongly worded letter sent by Brezhnev to President Nixon on 24 October of the same year.[8] But all these examples appear to have had as a primary function (1) to bring pressure to bear on the United States to restrain its presumptive ally, Israel, and (2) to demonstrate to the Soviet Union's presumptive allies, the Arab countries, that the USSR was acting resourcefully on their behalf. To that extent, all of these moves were of limited purpose and limited risk. But even if one adopts the view that these instances are examples of Soviet forward operations in conditions of international conflict, the element of careful calculation, as evident primarily in the precise timing of the threats, is nevertheless confirmed.

A similar reasoning applies to Soviet intervention in Czechoslovakia in 1968. Although the events in Czechoslovakia – even more so than those in the Middle East – produced only risks of crisis in superpower relations, it is useful to consider Soviet behavior in that instance, too, as the risks and costs involved (though of a different type than in superpower crises) were high, including among other things the possibility of armed resistance by the Czechoslovak armed forces, negative political and economic repercussions in the Soviet bloc, problems in the international communist movement and exposure of Soviet forces to the animosity of 'fraternal workers'. If this is granted, the degree to which Soviet behavior in Czechoslovakia in 1968 conformed to a general pattern of behavior as manifest in the Berlin crises of 1948 and 1961 is striking. The first harbingers of action to be taken later came at the meeting of the Warsaw Pact member countries (with the exception of Romania) in Dresden, on 23 March 1968, and in a speech by Brezhnev at the end of March in which he warned that 'renegades cannot bank on going unpunished'.[9] Yet it was to take many more bilateral Soviet – Czechoslovak meetings and multilateral conferences, several more months of pressure by diplomatic, economic and military means and explicit and implicit threats, for actual intervention to take place on 21 August 1968. Intervention was delayed for a long time but when it did take place it caught the Czechoslovak leadership and most Western analysts by surprise. No doubt because of long and careful preparation, the tactical implementation of the measures was skillful, swift and effective.[10]

But what about Cuba? Is Soviet behavior there also to be regarded as an exception to the general pattern, that is, as a *violation* of the axiom under consideration here? It would be difficult to believe that there was no calculation in advance, although it may not deserve the distinction of 'careful'. But Soviet behavior there was certainly a blatant violation of the axiom of careful preparation. This applies first and foremost to technical preparation. Surface-to-air missiles were not operational until after the arrival and construction of strategic offensive missiles, the radar system for detection of U-2 planes and guidance of antiaircraft missiles was built too late, there was no camouflage prior to the detection of the missiles by the United States, and the missile sites were all built in a pattern familiar to US Intelligence.[11] It is of course possible to consider all these errors and oversights as examples of an organizational process model, as Allison does (see Part One of this book), but as regards the axioms of Soviet crisis behavior they are simply a violation of the principle of 'move forward only after careful preparation'.

But there is more to the axiom of careful preparation than the technical aspect. More important is the international *political* aspect which can be said to include the rules: '*carefully prepare the ground psychologically*', '*make every attempt to demoralize the adversary*' and '*soften his potential resistance by an alternation of severe pressure and holding out the prospect of compromise*'.

These rules were followed closely in Berlin in 1948 and 1961 and in Czechoslovakia in 1968, but again the Cuban missile crisis appears as a significant exception to the rule. The classic procedure would have required getting the adversary used to the idea of a big Soviet military establishment in the Caribbean, it would have meant increasing the level of forces and armaments in the familiar 'salami tactics' procedure, to try to drive home the point that from the Soviet point of view tactical (or any other) nuclear weapons and delivery systems in Cuba were as normal and natural as American nuclear weapons and delivery systems in West Germany, rather than declaring officially that 'the Soviet Union has such powerful missiles for delivering . . . nuclear warheads that there is no need to seek sites for them beyond the boundaries of the Soviet Union' [12] and even reassuring the United States privately on various occasions that no offensive missiles would be emplaced in Cuba. [13] Deception, as argued in the discussion of the Prisoner's Dilemma as a frame of reference, implies the admission that one's cause is unjust precisely because it cannot be pressed openly; it is therefore likely to endow the adversary with a sense of moral indignation and his cause with legitimacy. [14] Of course, in the process of increasing pressure it might have appeared quite clearly that the United States would under no circumstances have been prepared to tolerate the planned scheme. But this is what probing and careful preparation is really all about. The required action would then have had to conform to another axiom, which will be examined presently.

(2) *'Push to the limit', 'engage in pursuit' of an opponent who begins to retreat or make concessions, but 'know when to stop' (in conditions of challenging an adversary); 'resist from the start' any encroachment by the opponent, no matter how slight it appears to be, but 'don't yield to enemy provocations' and 'retreat before superior force' (in conditions of responding to a challenge by an adversary).* [15] In both cases examined the axioms of behavior for Soviet leaders taking the initiative were confirmed without qualification. In Berlin in 1948 the Soviet Union had been pushing against access, the Western allied presence and the viability of the Western sectors. However, the pressures were unsuccessful, among other reasons because the Western allies were determined to stay in the city and because the German population failed to be demoralized; both depended to a large extent on the unexpected effectiveness of the airlift in supplying the allies and the city. In the resulting conditions, as mentioned, three alternatives were available to Soviet policy: to interfere with and seriously disrupt the operation of the airlift; to take over the Western sectors directly by the use of military force; or to adopt a more indirect approach to the same effect by organizing civil disturbances in the Western sectors with the help of local communists and then intervening to 'restore order' and to 'safeguard the security of the Soviet zone of occupation'. [16]

Soviet interference with the airlift would have resulted in direct military clashes in the air. In the course of probing it had become evident that both the United States and Britain were quite sensitive on the issue of air access and had reacted strongly to the single air accident caused by a Soviet pilot on 5 April. The SMA was made aware of the fact that fighter protection was being contemplated on the runs to Berlin. Any repetition of such an air accident would almost with certainty have led to the adoption of such a course of action. At the same time the extension of the blockade to air communications by the USSR would have forced the hand of the American President to authorize Clay's proposed scheme of reopening ground access by force. (As noted, in Clay's and Murphy's opinion Stalin had already over-stepped the limits by imposing a blockade on the ground.) Evidently, one of the rules of the game was, on both sides, avoidance of the use of force, even at low levels.

This injunction against low-level clashes of military units applies also to the instances of probing on ground communications and in Berlin itself. In each and every instance of pressure on *ground access* a form of probing was selected by the SMA that did not need direct backup by military force, and at times it strongly discouraged the use of force by the adversary as it would have been ineffective (for example, the shunting of locomotives to sidings).

In those instances of pressure *in Berlin* where armed units of the Western allies appeared on the plan in response to low-level Soviet challenges, Soviet units were withdrawn as a consequence without getting embroiled (for example, the erection of a barrier in the British sector on 2 April and the withdrawal of Soviet units after British forces had isolated the post).

It would also have been a violation of the principle of 'knowing where to stop' if Stalin had decided to adopt any of the other two remaining alternatives. Particularly if faced with a direct military takeover of the Western sectors, the pressures on the American President to take military counter-action would have been enormous. At a stroke all the Soviet Union's World War II advances would have been put at risk. However, everything short of a massive takeover could have been and almost certainly *would* have been resisted by Clay in Berlin by invocation of the legal principle, upheld in low-level counterchallenges, that the allies were sovereign in their respective sectors.

All these considerations apply with equal validity to the Berlin crisis of 1961. Ground access was beset by problems and challenges, but these challenges were not at all comparable in their importance to the blockade. In fact it is fair to say that the challenges to access were primarily verbal. Where selected stoppages were involved they affected Germans only, they were taken much earlier than in the crisis months of 1961 and they were made in the form of using East Germany as a proxy. There was no interference with the reinforcement of the American forces which proceeded to Berlin on the autobahn on 20 August. As in 1948 there was some buzzing or frolicking of aircraft but even more care was taken in 1961 to avoid accidents. In Berlin itself the picture in 1961 was similar to that of 1948. Wherever possible GDR police and armed units and border guards were used as a buffer to prevent confrontation, no matter whether it applied to the East German attempts to check identity papers of allied military personnel (for example, on 24 August 1961), or of civilians (for example, in late October 1961) or, most important, to the measures of 13 August.

The discussion of the main axiom as it applies to the two Berlin crises shows the operation of subsidiary rules which can be called *'avoid the direct use of military force'* and *'use proxies wherever possible'*. In fact the use of proxies for the purpose of avoiding the direct use of Soviet military personnel and scaling down the level of risk is a common feature of Soviet foreign policy, which applies not only to East Germany in the Berlin crises, but also to North Korea (and China) in the Korean War, North Vietnam in the Vietnam War, the Arab countries in Middle East conflicts, Egypt in the Yemen in 1967, and Cuba in Angola in 1975–6.[17] To that extent the Cuban missile crisis is yet again a contradiction of preferred patterns of Soviet behavior. The installment of missiles was, and was declared by Kennedy to be, a direct Soviet challenge directly involving Soviet military weapons and personnel. American naval forces were directly moved in position against Russians. Russian technicians and military personnel on the missile sites were directly exposed to American air strikes.

However, one important aspect of the set of axioms *is* confirmed by Soviet behavior in the Cuban missile crisis, the principle 'know when to stop' or (under the assumption that the United States had actually gone over to the offensive) 'retreat before superior force'. Although it was at a late stage, it was not too late to avoid direct clashes of the military forces of the two superpowers.

There are, of course, instances where the Soviet Union used military force directly. When this happened security interests or the territorial integrity of the Soviet state were, or appeared to be, at stake, and in all of these instances force was used massively, swiftly and with determination. This was evident in the large-scale bloody clashes between Japanese and Soviet armed forces in the summer of 1938 and 1939, and it was shown in the Ussuri clashes in March 1969. In these instances the USSR used armed force in the manner described for the limited political purpose of teaching the adversary a severe lesson. But the determined, massive and swift use of force is also an important feature of Soviet behavior in Eastern Europe in conditions where its supremacy in any particular country appeared to be threatened; and it is a feature in the expansion of Soviet power along its periphery, the latest example of this being the occupation of Afghanistan in December 1979. Hence as regards the *direct* use of force the Soviet leaders act as if they were in full agreement with a principle formulated by the German General Guderian for the use of tank forces in war, namely, that if these forces are to be used, not to use them piecemeal and sporadically, but massively and in concentrated fashion (*Nicht kleckern, sondern klotzen*).

However, so far there have been no examples where the Soviet Union committed forces directly against the United States or any of its allies in the American treaty system. To generalize from this, any Soviet decision for the commitment of forces appears to be based on three calculations or expectations: no resistance (military involvement) of the adversary superpower; low resistance locally; and a high probability that political power can quickly be handed over by the Soviet intervention forces to local political forces. There are still other recurrent patterns of Soviet behavior which can be observed.

(3) *Before engaging in forward operations 'carefully construct a fall-back position' so as to meet unexpectedly high resistance by the adversary*. Indeed it does appear quite clearly that in 1948 and in 1961 the Soviet Union had skillfully constructed a road for tactical retreat in the event of serious complications. In the Berlin crisis of 1948 the measures were described as being of a technical nature and local significance. Although no one could miss the point of why the first multilateral conference of foreign ministers of

the USSR and the countries of the Soviet bloc was held at the very same time when the blockade measures were put into effect (23–4 June 1948), the statement of that conference did *not* establish any direct link between larger political demands on the German problem (which it did mention) and the physical measures at the local level (which it did not mention). In conformity with the present axiom, this had the effect of giving the USSR an easy way out: if the United States had reacted immediately by issuing an ultimatum for the reopening of communications, some of the technical difficulties could have been made to disappear as quickly as they had appeared – without loss of face, without making it necessary to shelve the political demands, and even without making it necessary to abandon some form of pressure. If, however, the United States had gone beyond that and used force, it could have been accused of acting rashly, without justification and provocatively, but still would have found itself in the uncomfortable position of having to keep the access routes open on a long-term basis, presumably by establishing a military presence along the access routes – a course of action that was clearly ruled out, even by Clay.

Similarly, in 1961 the physical measures initially were easily retractable. At first only barbed-wire fencing and wooden barriers were used (the construction of a concrete wall beginning only on 15 August, after it had turned out that the West would not take resourceful counteraction) and the number of crossing points was only gradually reduced.[18] Also, as noted in the discussion of the previous axiom, Soviet military units were not directly involved in the operation. These elements combined provided the Soviet Union with the tactical flexibility needed to cope with an (unlikely) vigorous Western response. Various options were then still available to achieve the stated purpose of establishing a new border regime and stopping the flow of people from East to West, for instance, the taking of 'border measures' not *at* but *inside* the Soviet sectors. Both crises, therefore, validate a subsidiary axiom of Soviet behavior, the rule: *'do not settle for a single probability estimate of unwanted risks' that may develop in the future, but 'engage in sequential analysis.'*[19]

Again, it is the Cuban missile crisis that appears to be an exception to the general rule of Soviet risk-taking and crisis behavior. If the assumption had been made by Khrushchev that the United States would react vigorously (as it did), with what sort of tactical flexibility would he have been left in the calculation? It is difficult to find any at all at the local level. Conceivably some flexibility would have been restored to Khrushchev if he had acted elsewhere, for instance, if he had responded to the naval quarantine of Cuba with a land blockade of Berlin. It is even possible that someone on the Soviet side seriously suggested such a course of action during the crisis, or that it was raised after the fact by Khrushchev's critics. But most likely this would have compounded the problems for the Soviet Union rather than alleviated them. Foreign Minister Gromyko implied as much when he reported to the Supreme Soviet in December 1962 that already the Cuban missile crisis 'had brought the world one step, perhaps only half a step, from an abyss'; it also made 'many people think how the whole matter might have developed if yet another crisis in Central Europe had been added to the critical events around Cuba'.[20] This refusal to widen the scope of East–West conflict over Cuba by re-igniting the Berlin crisis is linked to yet another principle of Soviet behavior.

(4) *Never lose sight of the political objectives to be achieved, and in pursuing them do not let yourself be diverted by false notions of bourgeois morality*. This is not to argue that the Soviet leaders are insensitive to moral issues but that their morality is different from ours. It is measured not against the aspirations of the individual but against history. In 1948 to resort to a medieval siege operation of sorts with the purpose (as the West saw and portrayed it) of starving out a city of more than two million inhabitants was problematic not because it offended Stalin's or the SMA's sense of morality but because it provided the adversary in the historic competition between the two systems with a convenient propaganda slogan and an instrument to bring about alliance cohesion. It is not surprising, therefore, that Marshal Sokolovsky and the Soviet government were quick to express 'concern for the well-being of the Berlin population by assuring them normal supplies in all essentials' and offering to resume food deliveries to the Western sectors – on Soviet terms.[21] In 1961, too, the human consequences of the border closure was something the West, in Soviet perspectives, was sure to exploit in their propaganda (the 'walling in' of people, the transformation of East Germany into a 'concentration camp', and so on). But this changed nothing as regards the perceived (and so legitimized) overall historic requirement of making the GDR and the socialist community more stable internally.

If, finally, the first phases of the Soviet occupation and control of Afghanistan showed only modest use of the huge arsenal of military power available, moderate (though deliberate and carefully selected) application of terror and – quite in contrast to Amin's rule – almost an absence of brutality, it is not because of moral abhorrence for the perpetration of such acts but because of the overriding objective to facilitate the formation of a political basis broad enough to support a workable administrative framework.

To this could be added the subsidiary axiom of *resist false bourgeois notions of pride and prestige*. Again, it would be wrong to picture the Soviet leadership as impervious to considerations of prestige. Only such considerations are not of an abstract, classless content but tied to the safeguarding or new assertion of Soviet interests. Setbacks are by definition temporary. One step back will lead to two steps forward.

These principles could be seen in force in 1967, when the Soviet Union's Arab protégés were thoroughly defeated, and when many an officer in the Soviet General Staff must have thrown up his arms in frustration at the seemingly complete Arab military incompetence. Nevertheless the loss of weaponry was quickly made good, the political commitments became stronger (up to and including the conclusion of a friendship treaty), and the military involvement became deeper, finally leading to the dispatch of Soviet pilots and antiaircraft personnel to help with the air defense of Egypt in the summer of 1970. A similar dynamic was at work between 1972 and 1973: the embarrassing expulsion of the Soviet military presence in the summer of 1972 and deteriorating Soviet–Egyptian relations from this point onward did not prevent the USSR from lending considerable military support to the Arab countries in the October 1973 war (in the form of large-scale supplies delivered during the emergency) as well as political support (in the form – as mentioned above – of adopting a 'ready to intervene' posture).[22] In all these sequences of events the pursuit of objective interests was more important than the nurturing of hurt pride.

Nothing could demonstrate better the importance of the axiom under discussion than the Soviet failure to respond vigorously to the blockade of North Vietnamese harbors by the US navy in May 1972. Respectable observers, Soviet specialists among them, then feared a confrontation more serious than that of the Cuban missile crisis. This was based on the assumption that the Soviet Union, having achieved rough military-strategic parity and superpower status, would simply not put up with the humiliating measures directed against a socialist ally, Soviet ships and Soviet logistical operations. Yet apart from the difficulty for the Soviet Union of how to challenge US naval supremacy successfully at the local level – a problem of which the USSR must have been painfully aware also in Cuba in 1962 – there was the equally important consideration of Soviet goals and interests. By the spring of 1972 it had become obvious that American withdrawal from South Vietnam was only a matter of time. The mining of the North Vietnamese harbors, like the bombing of Cambodia, was only the last convulsion before the final end of US involvement in Southeast Asia. As time was working in favor of the Soviet Union and North Vietnam there was no need to intervene.

Objectives and Outcomes in 1948 and 1961

If it is correct to say that so many operational principles of Soviet risk-taking made an impact on the Berlin crisis of 1948 *and* the Berlin crisis of 1961, what is it that explains the difference in the result – the fact that the blockade failed to achieve anything and led to a deterioration of the Soviet position, whereas the construction of the Berlin Wall went unchallenged and induced the Soviet Union to continue with the pressure? Most likely there is more than one answer to this question. But as 'failure' or 'success' are relative matters which can be measured only by comparing objectives with results, it is reasonable to assume that an important part of the answer lies in differences in objectives.

In 1948 the objectives pursued by the Soviet Union for all practical purposes could only be interpreted by the West as unlimited – and it is probably fair to say that they were. Stalin clearly acted in accordance with another maxim of Soviet behavior: *gains can be made, even against a stronger opponent, by limiting the means on behalf of objectives, which may be quite ambitious*.[23] Although for the political leaders in the United States and Britain in 1948 it was a valid question to ask whether Berlin was a lever or a prize in Soviet objectives, under the assumption of flexible, and in the final analysis unlimited, objectives, *any* answer would have yielded the same unacceptable result. By winning Berlin as a *prize* the Soviet Union at a stroke would have improved its own and the German communists' position in East Germany to a considerable degree. But what guarantee was there that the Soviet demands on the 'German problem' (reparations, heavy industry, the status of the Ruhr, the social, economic and political development of the Western zones, the plans for the creation of a separate West German state) would suddenly have disappeared? In fact these demands might have been put forward even more vigorously. Conversely, the successful use of Berlin as a *lever* on the issue of the formation of a separate West Germany would most likely have encouraged Stalin to try harder in Berlin and probably much more successfully in the then changed conditions as the morale of the population of Berlin – one of the crucial factors in the crisis – would have suffered a shock at the realization of Western retreat.

In Berlin in 1961 Soviet objectives were unlimited, too, to the extent that in the period from November 1958 to August 1961 Khrushchev pursued a whole *range of objectives* – in Berlin, in Germany and in Western Europe.[24] But there was one crucial difference. When the measures of 13 August were taken they were tied specifically to one limited objective, the establishment of a new regime at the borders between East and West Berlin. Western access to Berlin, another important issue in the protracted Soviet campaign of pressure, was specifically excluded from the justification and explanation of the measures. The limitation of Soviet objectives, and Western perceptions that the status quo was merely being defined more clearly, appeared to rule out the acceptance of risks to stop the USSR and the GDR from proceeding with the border measures. But the basic pattern of Soviet behavior, the working of the principle of 'push to the limit' and 'engage in pursuit', was demonstrated soon after 13 August, when the old demands on the 'German problem' were put forward and new ones added.

Notes: Part Three, Chapter 16

1   Bell, *Conventions of Crisis*, p. 2.
2   See pp. 45–7 and Table 4.1, p. 46.
3   Karl W. Deutsch, *The Analysis of International Relations* (Englewood Cliffs, NJ: Prentice-Hall, 1968), p. 113.
4   See pp. 53–4; see also my 'Consensus versus conflict: the dimension of foreign policy', in Seweryn Bialer (ed.), *The Domestic Context of Soviet Foreign Policy*, Studies of the Research Institute on International Change, Columbia University (Boulder, Co, and London: Westview Press/Croom Helm, 1981).
5   See p. 91.
6   *Pravda*, 6 November 1956.
7   As reported by Lyndon Baines Johnson, *The Vantage Point: Perspectives from the Presidency* (London: Weidenfeld & Nicolson, 1971), p. 302; for details see Adomeit, *Soviet Risk-Taking and Crisis Behaviour*, p. 13–14.
8   Galia Golan, 'Soviet aims and the Middle East War', *Survival*, vol. 16, no. 3 (May/June 1974), pp. 106–14.
9   *Pravda*, 30 March 1968.
10 In the case of Czechoslovakia, 1968, it is highly probable that the delay had a second dimension (in addition to the dimension of operational principles): a sound majority in the Politburo for intervention was very slow in the making. At times it seemed that the Soviet leaders were genuinely prepared to tolerate the Prague reformist course. This is argued convincingly in Jiri Valenta, 'Soviet decisionmaking and the Czechoslovak crisis of 1968'.
11 These examples are mentioned by Allison, *Essence of Decision*, pp. 106–8.
12 TASS declaration of 11 September 1962, published in *Izvestiia*, 12 September 1962.
13 Several examples for the time period of 4 September to 13 October are listed by Allison, *Essence of Decision*, pp. 40–1.
14 See pp. 31–3, esp. p. 32.
15 George, 'The "Operational Code" ', pp. 181–2, as quoted above, p. 53.
16 See p. 170.

17 This is not to say that these proxies did not pursue their own interests, or that proxies are to be equated with dependent satellites dancing to the tune of the Soviet leadership's flute. These examples merely serve to show that, wherever possible, the Soviet Union has preferred indirect involvement to direct superpower confrontation.
18 See p. 208 and pp. 299–300.
19 George, 'The "Operational Code"', pp. 180–81; see also above, point (6), p. 53.
20 *Pravda*, 14 December 1962.
21 See p. 96.
22 See Chapter 4, note 20, and p. 318.
23 George, 'The "Operational Code"', p. 183; see also above, point (4), p. 53.
24 See pp. 294–6.

17
Factors of Soviet Risk-Taking and Crisis Behavior

'L'Idéologie est morte! Vive l'idéologie!'

If it is correct that the deductive approach (adopted by Leites and George) and the inductive method (followed here) coincide in their end result, namely, that there are operational principles and recurring patterns of behavior which are specifically Soviet, what is it that accounts for it? 'Soviet ideology' must be an important part of the answer – a conclusion that is likely to contradict conventional wisdoms in American scholarship.[1] It may be useful, therefore, to look more closely at the arguments put forward in support of the thesis that Soviet ideology need not be taken all too seriously in the analysis of post-World War II Soviet foreign policy and to state in more detail why, in the argument of this study, ideology continues to matter.

One reason for the reluctance in American scholarship to attribute a significant role to Soviet ideology in shaping Soviet behavior very likely has something to do with the image in the mind of the analyst associating 'ideological' with 'irrational', 'reckless', 'adventurist', and the like, but contrasting it with 'pragmatic', 'opportunist', or 'realistic'.[2] Ideology as a factor shaping Soviet behavior is as a consequence being eroded in the mind of the analyst when he is faced with instances where Soviet representatives display diplomatic skill, act as shrewd and calculating businessmen or pay much attention to military power as an instrument of furthering state interests.

Another possible explanation for the Western diagnosis of the erosion of ideology in Soviet foreign policy is to be found in a very narrow – and hence inadequate and misleading – definition. 'Ideology' is often conceived of as nothing but the equivalent of the degree of Soviet support for world revolution, and sometimes even this is measured by the degree to which the Soviet Union is willing to employ military force on behalf of local communists in various areas of the world. As a consequence, the importance of ideology in Soviet foreign policy is being reduced for the Western analyst when the Soviet leaders apparently close their eyes to the oppression of local communists while engaging in cooperation with the oppressors at the state level (as in many countries of the Arab world), stand by with folded arms as Marxist regimes are being crushed (as in Chile) or fail to exploit alleged or real advantages for deepening the 'crisis of capitalism' (as in the wake of the oil crisis after 1973).

Other explanations have much to do with the philosophical preconditioning of the Western analyst. To scholars reared in the Anglo-Saxon tradition of empiricism and pragmatism, the very thought that leaders in the practical realm of politics in the twentieth century should be guided in their actions by a rigid belief system appears incredible or inconceivable.[3] They find the Hegelian form of Soviet ideology difficult to grasp, and 'the pronouncements of Soviet ideologists appear to them similar to the chants and litanies of some esoteric religious cult'.[4]

These basic tendencies of analysis have been much reinforced recently. On the one hand there are many scholars now who have had some form of contact with their Soviet counterparts, and an increasing number of them are able to read the Soviet scholarly output of the various institutes of the Academy of Sciences of the USSR in the original. Many of their Russian counterparts appear to be (and often are) men of reason and many of the scholarly analyses, give or take some of the obligatory references to Lenin, resemble Western modes of analysis. Hence the conclusion, noted above, that Western and Soviet perspectives on the international system are essentially similar.[5] On the other hand the basic tradition of empiricism and pragmatism has found specific expression recently in the behavioral revolution in the social sciences with the generation of pressures, often justified, for more stringent measurement and higher standards of verification. These pressures have been extended to Soviet studies. But there are tremendous problems of 'operationalizing' a research problem such as the influence of ideology in Soviet foreign policy. As a result it often appears more appropriate to delete a factor such as ideology altogether than to lay open a research plan to the charge of being unscientific because an immeasurable factor has been introduced. Ideology, therefore, has often been eroded by default rather than design.

In order to arrive at a realistic assessment of ideology as a factor of Soviet behavior it is necessary to abandon some faulty distinctions altogether, to recognize that the term has a broad scope and to acknowledge that what matters most are not so much the perceptions and products of the *institutchiki*, or the thin apologias and rationalizations of lower- and middle-level *apparatchiki* one is allowed to meet, but the probable belief system and actual, observable behavior of the political leadership.

The broad *scope* encompassed by Soviet ideology needs to be considered first. As summarized by Alfred Meyer, Soviet ideology can be said to include, among other parts, a philosophy called dialectical materialism; generalizations about man and society, past and present, called historical materialism; an economic doctrine called political economy, which seeks to explain the economics of capitalism and imperialism on the one hand and of socialist construction on the other; and a body of political thought, or guidelines, now called scientific communism, which deals, first, with the strategy and tactics of communist revolutions and, secondly, with political problems of socialist states.[6]

The next stage in the examination of the problem of ideology is to assume that there may be a variety of *functions* played by each individual part of Soviet ideology, to make allowance for the possibility that the manifold activities in politics and society may be influenced by ideology to differing degrees, and to be aware of the problem that the relative importance of various aspects of ideology may change over time. The precise delimitation of functions of ideology may be a matter of preference (there will always be overlaps to a certain extent), but their existence itself has not been in dispute.[7] They could be called as follows:

(1)   analytical or cognitive function;
(2)   operational or tactical function;
(3)   utopian, revolutionary or missionary function;
(4)   legitimizing function;
(5)   socializing function.

Briefly, the analytical function refers to a conscious process and asks questions such as 'How do the Soviet leaders see the world?' and 'What, in the view of the Soviet leadership, are the basic structural elements of the international system, the sources of conflict, the factors accounting for stability or change, and so on?' The second function is more difficult to define. It can be taken as meaning (a) that the Soviet leadership is acting on the basis of the results of analysis (the impact of perception on behavior); (b) that the Soviet leadership codifies and formalizes the main line of a partic- ular era in world affairs, defines the scope of peaceful coexistence, sets forth its view on the correlation of forces and the like, and arrives from there at the main tasks to be pursued (that is, the impact of doctrine on behavior); or (c) that there exist deeply engrained operational principles formed by ideology (the impact of socialization and experience on behavior). It is within this function of ideology that the left/right dichotomy finds its proper place of discussion.

The third function of ideology – the utopian, revolutionary or missionary function – is often (but incorrectly) taken to be the only one that matters. It is also the one that is at the basis of the dichotomy of ideology versus 'the national interest'. By referring to it the analyst asks questions such as 'To what extent is world revolution still a goal of Soviet foreign policy?', 'To what extent is the Soviet leadership committed to supporting local commun- ists and their bids for power?' and 'What is the role of the USSR within the international communist movement?'

The fourth function has two important dimensions – one domestic, the other international. Legitimacy of power in the USSR is based on Marxism- Leninism; although other forms of legitimacy may eventually emerge, at the present stage of development it would appear that any Soviet leader, or leadership, attempting to deviate from that basis would be destroying the very ground on which he or it is operating. By extension this applies to the legitimacy of Soviet rule in Eastern Europe, where the Soviet system has been transplanted and where it is being protected by the various means of control available to the Soviet Union.

The last function rests in the dialectical interplay between ideology and the education, upbringing, experience and career patterns of the top leadership. This must lead an open-minded analyst to ask: 'What kind of psychological makeup of the leadership results from socialization processes in the Soviet Union?' Behind such a question would lie the assumption that the exper- iences in the control and organization of society, and the criteria of success or failure in the domestic *kto-kogo* struggle, are apt to be transplanted by the successful leaders to the international arena.

To return to the conclusions of this study. As regards Soviet behavior in the two crises in Central Europe, nothing could be further from the truth, therefore, than the statement, 'ideology had nothing to do with it'. Combined operational, legitimizing and socializing aspects of Soviet ideology (functions 2c, 4 and 5 of the above categorization) have much to do with the existence (and persistence) of the operational principles summarized in the previous section and with the shaping of Soviet interests affected in the crises.

Concerning the operational aspect, some of the axioms summarized above could have been taken straight from Lenin's *'Left-Wing' Communism, an Infantile Disorder*, for instance, the admonition that 'To tie one's hand beforehand, openly to tell the enemy, who is at present better armed than we are, whether we shall fight him, and when, is stupidity and not revolutionariness'[8] or the advice that

> The more powerful enemy can be conquered only by exerting the utmost effort, and by necessarily, thoroughly, carefully, attentively and skillfully taking advantage of every, even the smallest 'rift' among the enemies.[9]

When Lenin adds in characteristic polemical fashion that those who did not understand this 'do not understand even a particle of Marxism' he makes a charge that to some degree also applies to adherents of the 'erosion of ideology' view when they juxtapose as antitheses 'ideology' on the one hand and 'opportunism' or 'pragmatism' on the other, thereby overlooking the fact that rigidity in doctrine does not by any means imply rigidity in tactics.[10] Attention must be paid to the Leninist distinction between short-term considerations and long-range ideological goals. In a certain sense, as Leo Labedz has argued, all politics, ideological or not, tend to be concerned first of all with short-term considerations.

> But there is a difference between policies which appertain to nothing else, and those which take long-term considerations, ideological or other, as their frame of reference. To confuse the two as 'pragmatic' in the same sense is to misunderstand the character of Soviet policies in the past, and . . . at present.[11]

The view that the education, upbringing, experience and career patterns ('socialization') of the Soviet leaders account for specific behavioral patterns in domestic and international politics impinges on the argument that the Soviet leaders are cynical with regard to ideology, in particular to the aspect of a universal classless society. Well they might be. Revolutionary idealism and romanticism may very well be regarded as a thing of the past, and 'Ideological evolution during six decades of Soviet history can be summarized as a reluctant retreat from the utopian and universalistic claims of Marxist doctrine *without, however, their abandonment*'.[12] In addition to that, other aspects of ideology have become more pronounced (legitimacy, for instance, which will be dealt with presently), and still others have been retained. To be counted among them are the ideas that life, including 'international life', is an unending struggle, that this struggle can only end with the victory of one socioeconomic system over the other, and that to stand still, and not to plan for advances and gains, means falling behind and to be thrown on the rubbish heap of history. In Western societies, by analogy, processes of secularization have progressed far but the influence of Protestantism and Catholicism will tend to affect even the cynic's behavior (as does the influence of ideology in the USSR) because he will not be able to rid himself of unquestioned assumptions and ideas which he takes as given or erroneously holds to be self-evident.

Even if the credibility of Soviet ideology is wearing thin and, in international politics, is becoming more of a liability than an asset, it is still a fallacy to argue that ideology is 'nothing but *ex post facto* rationalization' (*Rechtfertigung*) and has nothing to do with motivation (*Antrieb*). Rationalization and motivation, for an individual, a political leadership or a state (and particularly when it comes to a state conforming to the notion of 'an ideology in power'), can be *mutually reinforcing* mechanisms.[13] This leads directly to the problem of legitimacy.

No matter whether it is the power of the Soviet leadership, the power of institutions (the party, the armed forces, the police, the courts, and so on), relations among the countries of the socialist community (that is, the exercise of Soviet control and influence in the ruling communist states), or Soviet claims – open or tacit – to preeminence in the international communist movement, all of this is justified in terms of ideology. Criteria of achievement and well-being, too, are used by the Soviet leadership to elicit cooperation and compliance. Such criteria, however, belong to the realms of practical politics and expediency. They are only subsidiary to and derivative of the basic ideological principles.

Marxism, as Robert Wesson has argued, would probably have been 'effectively if not overtly left behind as the new state settled down after the revolution, to be replaced by a straightforward faith of patriotism, Russianism and loyalty to the new rulership', but it was 'indispensable because the new Soviet state undertook to govern a multinational domain'.[14] Marxist internationalism was practically dropped during the war but it became important again as the Russian armies recovered the Ukraine and other minority areas. 'As Soviet forces asserted hegemony over nations of Eastern Europe, the role of ideology became still more vital.'[15] This much, at least, seems to be granted also by adherents to the 'erosion of ideology' school. Although, in their view, ideology has come to play a much lesser role in Soviet foreign policy in general, Eastern Europe is nevertheless being regarded as an exception.[16]

The fallacy of this view can be shown quite simply, and quite legitimately, by substituting 'Soviet sphere of influence' or 'socialist community' for 'Eastern Europe'. As Cuba, Mongolia and Vietnam belong to it, as Angola, Ethiopia and South Yemen are allied with it and as strenuous efforts are made to integrate Afghanistan in it the (as they perceive it) 'limited' and 'regional' importance of ideology is immediately transformed into a phenomenon of global significance. For all these reasons, to say that the USSR is only a 'new name for old Russia' would be to convey the wrong idea; to assume that Soviet foreign policy is merely Russian imperialism in a new garb would be, as Vernon Aspaturian put it, 'a catastrophic mistake'.[17]

Certainly these considerations are valid with regard to East Germany and the Berlin crises. To assert that the GDR was but a new name for old East Germany would not only have been anathema to the SED leadership in 1961, but it would have been an idea extremely alien to *all* Germans, no matter what their political orientation, because in their conception old East Germany (*Ostdeutschland*) used to begin east of 'East Germany' – odd as this may sound in English. [18] But the legitimizing function of Soviet ideology enters forcefully into both crises because the type of system in the making on German soil in 1948 and the system as it existed in 1961 derived their tenuous claim to legitimacy neither from German history nor from achievement but exclusively from ideology. The problems for the Soviet Union were complicated by the fact that ideology had not only to swim against *currents of nationalism* in Germany and cope with a singular *lack of socialist achievement* there but also to contend with strong rival variants of *German Marxism* as opposed to Russian Bolshevism.

This threefold challenge to ideological legitimacy of the Soviet zone of occupation, and later the GDR, took different forms in the two crises, but in both cases the challenge is inseparable from important or (if one prefers) vital Soviet interests as defined by the respective leaderships. In 1948 options other than confrontation were still open to the Soviet Union. In recognition of nationalism as a strong political force some form of neutralized Germany might have been preferable to an irredentist, hostile West Germany as a spearhead of 'American imperialism'; in recognition of Marxism and independent socialism as a strong current in Germany some form of third road for that country could have prevented its inclusion in schemes of 'capitalist encirclement' such as NATO. With such a Germany, neutralized and democratic-socialist, some form of friendship and cooperation was possible. But all this could have happened only *if* there had been dramatic change in Soviet ideology towards the genuine acceptance of 'many roads to socialism' externally and the opening up of the Soviet system to a kind of 'socialism with a human face' internally. It is in large measure because of the rigidity and the unacceptable face of Stalinist ideology that these theoretical alternatives had no chance of being tried out in practice.

In 1961 the threefold challenge to ideological legitimacy had by no means disappeared. The challenge was evident in the form of an economically successful West Germany and its claim of sole representation, in West Berlin as a center of attraction for East Germans and East Europeans and in the rising attractiveness of social democracy as a political force. It was evident also in the fact that the Soviet-type system on German soil had been thoroughly discredited and was suffering a worsening political and economic crisis. But by then the GDR had become so much bound up with the USSR, and economically and politically had become so much part and parcel of the Soviet bloc, that alternatives other than physical action to remedy this state of affairs no longer seemed to exist.

In sum, Marxist-Leninist ideology furnished important portions of the analytical and perceptual framework, operational principles and legitimation of Soviet behavior in both crises. These are the constant features. However, when comparing the role of ideology in the two Berlin crises there is also one feature of change. In 1948 a broad congruence of elements of the left still existed, both in doctrine and in actual policy. But in 1961 such congruence was absent, as demonstrated by the fact that the predominant elements of the right coexisted with confrontation.

Two explanations can be offered for this development. First, by 1961 the greater complexity of international relations and the increasing diversity in the international communist movement and of Soviet society and politics almost inevitably had led to inconsistencies and contradictions in the various elements of Soviet theory and practice. Congruence of left/right priorities and commitments had become a thing of the past. Secondly, in 1948 Soviet doctrine still clung to leftism not only in the form of the 'two camps' theory but also the Leninist thesis on the 'fatal inevitability of war'. This thesis, as argued above, was a dangerous thing for crisis diplomacy, and it is not surprising that it was first 'clarified' and then modified by Stalin and finally abandoned by Khrushchev.[19] By 1961 it had become standard Soviet practice to try to combine a rightist ideological approach of the 'carrot' toward the West with that of a military and political 'big stick'.

The Balance of Interests

The discussion of ideology as a factor shaping Soviet behavior in the two Berlin crises underlines the fact that it is difficult to uphold the distinction between 'Marxist-Leninist ideology' and 'the Soviet national interest'. Even authors who subscribe to the validity of such a dichotomy for analytical purposes hasten to add the reservation that this is a 'crude antithesis'.[20] This is true not only because Soviet ideology is a complex phenomenon but also because 'the Soviet national interest' (like any national interest) is a highly subjective and ambiguous concept, capable of manipulation and almost limitless reinterpretation, so that in reality political leaders are faced with a complex tangle of interests (in the plural), always changing according to specific social, economic, military, political *and* ideological conditions, both of an international and domestic dimension, and making it necessary every time to distinguish between costs, benefits and risks of a long-term or short-term nature.

Despite these complexities one must be wary of worrying about a tautological trap that in reality does not exist. It could be argued that 'national interests', vital or peripheral, can be defined only *ex post facto*: more specifically, that the relative importance of particular interests can be measured only in retrospect by the degree of commitment made by a particular state on their behalf. However, this argument resembles recent criticisms of Darwin's theory of natural selection. By defining fitness as 'differential reproductive success' (that is, by considering evolution as a change in numbers, not as a change in quality) a vacuous tautology results because natural selection is no more than 'the survival of those who survive'. However, certain morphological, physiological and behavioral traits can be considered *a priori* superior as designs for living in new environments. Certain traits 'confer fitness by an engineer's criterion of good design, not by the empirical fact of their survival and spread'.[21]

Similarly, in international relations political leaders and analysts are able to make their own *a priori* judgments as to the degree to which a particular state's interests are involved, whether they are of primary or secondary importance and whether the design to safeguard the various interests is adequate, effective, legitimate and the like. The mutually perceived balance of interests thus comes to be of crucial importance for the origin, course and outcome of international crises. For an actor to succeed in conveying the idea that vital interests are at stake for himself, and only secondary interests for the adversary, confers to him tremendous advantages in the bargaining process. However, a good deal will usually be known about his 'utility function',[22] and although any state actor will tend to enhance the legitimacy of risk-taking by constructing an asymmetry of perceived interests, there will be limits within which such claims will appear credible.

It is on this issue that there are important differences between the two Berlin crises. In 1948 the balance of interests was tilted against the Soviet Union. There was some recognition in the United States and Britain of Soviet political interests (security from Germany) and also of economic interests (reparations from Germany), but both were *not* to be granted at the expense of the economic and political recovery of Western Europe or at the expense of its security *vis-à-vis* the Soviet Union. The USSR was seen as challenging the Western powers not only directly in Berlin, but also interfering in their affairs in their own zones in Western Germany. This, to the West, was evident in the circulation of currency notes from the duplicate set of printing plates in the Soviet zone; the Soviet demands for *one* currency despite the existence of two entirely separate economic systems on German soil; the claims for a share in the control of the Ruhr while denying any similar share for the Western powers in the Soviet zone; the disruption of recovery in Western Europe by communist-organized strikes; and, finally, the Soviet charges that the social, economic and political provisions of the Potsdam Agreement had been carried out in the Soviet zone but not in the Western zones of Germany. In sum, the Soviet Union – according to Western perceptions – was engaged in a broad offensive to *change* an ill-defined status quo, in Berlin, in Germany and in Europe, and as Soviet objectives were held to be practically unlimited the need to 'put a stop to Russian pretensions' became an important factor in the crisis.

All these conditions had changed dramatically by 1961. Despite the verbal challenge to the existence of the GDR, primarily by West Germany, and despite the strong moral reservations of the regime – as of other regimes in Eastern Europe – the West *de facto* included the GDR and East Berlin in the Soviet sphere of influence. It had made no attempt to interfere in the riots in June 1953 (as in Poland and Hungary in 1956 and later in Czechoslovakia in 1968). It recognized the importance of the GDR and its technological potential for the Soviet economy. It realized that the GDR and its territory had been integrated politically and militarily in the Warsaw Pact. Finally, because of the instability of the GDR it feared for the stability of Europe. In conjunction with the limitation of Soviet objectives, the balance of interests was strongly favorable for the kinds of risks the Soviet Union was taking on 13 August. At a crucial juncture of the protracted crisis over Berlin the USSR was seen as wanting to *maintain* the status quo.

The same point can be made by looking in more detail at the economic dimension of Soviet interests in the two crises. It is true that in 1948 a separate West Germany with the Ruhr as its strong industrial base could form the potential basis for a military threat to the USSR of formidable proportions, particularly if this state were allied with the American economic and military potential. It is also true that, conversely, a unified Germany with its vast technological and economic potential would most likely be a formidable center of attraction for the smaller countries in the Soviet sphere of influence; ultimately it, too, could become a security threat. But no matter whether Germany was to be divided or united, a policy of confrontation with the Western powers was unlikely to help in solving the dilemma.

The problems were compounded in the spring of 1948 when the exploitative reparations policy had begun to make itself felt adversely in the economic performance of the Soviet zone and had become counterproductive in the ideological and economic competition between the two systems on German soil. Whatever the previous net benefit of reparations for the Soviet economy, the importance of the small eastern part of Germany for the Soviet Union's recovery now appeared to be even more marginal. Moreover, on this issue there was a significant difference of interest by the major protagonists. In Western perceptions the recovery of the Western zones of Germany was seen as the precondition of the recovery of Western Europe. In exchange for abandoning the plans for the political unification of the Western zones (a precondition in turn for economic recovery), the US and Britain expected far-reaching Soviet concessions on economic and political unity of Germany. The fact that the Soviet Union was far from making these concessions, but seemingly demanded more from the West, could only increase the perceived imbalance of interests.

Probably contrary to original Soviet expectations, the GDR by 1961 had come to play an important part in the economy of the Soviet Union and in Comecon – despite the damage done by reparations, reorientation of trade, exclusion of the industry and population of West Berlin from GDR territory and the incessant manpower drain. This was evident in the fact that in the year preceding the construction of the Wall the GDR's proportion in the Soviet Union's total imports of machinery and equipment was more than one-third. The GDR was therefore an important factor in the concrete conditions of the early 1960s for the realization of the Soviet Union's ambitious plans for catching up with and overtaking the United States in economic performance. All this was tacitly acknowledged in the West. It was tacitly conceded that there existed an asymmetry of interests in favor of the Soviet Union.

Although there is a significant difference in mutually perceived economic and political interests in the two crises, there is at the same time a fundamental similarity. An important reason for the dilemmas with which the Soviet Union was faced both in 1948 and 1961 can be found in the USSR's low level of industrial development as compared to that of the industrialized countries of the West. In one form or another the fear of 'backward Russia' that it might lose control over at least part of the technological potential of 'advanced Germany' loomed large in the origins of both crises. Yet the Soviet Union was rejected by the vast majority of Germans as a model of development. It was never accepted by them as a country of superior culture or civilization, and the unacceptable face of Stalinism in its original (Soviet) and derived (East German) variety merely served to confirm these perceptions. But despite these tremendous handicaps the Soviet Union has managed nevertheless to hold on to its part of Germany. The reason for this success is connected with the interaction between the balance of interests and the balance of forces.

The Balance of Forces

There were strong similarities in the military balance in the two crises. In both 1948 and 1961 the United States had a significant lead over the USSR in military-strategic power, naval armaments and overall industrial and technological resources. In both cases the major form of compensation for these deficiencies on the Soviet side was to make its military posture in Europe as effective as possible by means of maintaining quantitatively and qualitatively superior conventional forces over its potential adversaries. In both crises – tacitly in 1948, and very bluntly and explicitly in 1961 – Europe was effectively held hostage to American restraint.

But despite this basic similarity in the distribution of power, important changes had taken place in the period from 1948 to 1961. In 1948 the territory of the United States had for all practical purposes been invulnerable to strategic attack from the Soviet Union. The USSR had no nuclear weapons then and it lacked the kind of long-range strategic aircraft and naval power necessary to inflict damage on US territory even with conventional weapons. These conditions, however, had changed by 1961. The territory of the United States by then was and (as the public and private civil defense efforts revealed) felt vulnerable to strategic attack by the Soviet Union by means of ICBMs (though they were very few in number), long-range strategic aircraft and also by submarine-launched guided missiles and nuclear-armed torpedoes. Although there was some compensation for this Soviet advantage in the fact that the USA in 1961 was in a position to operate from a number of bases all around the periphery of the USSR, and also with strike aircraft from aircraft carriers, and that it possessed a vast number of operational nuclear bombs obtained from serial production, the fundamental fact remained that the Soviet Union in 1961, as compared to 1948, could enter the crisis with a much improved military-strategic posture and confidence *vis-à-vis* the United States. Whereas in 1948 what Stalin had said three years earlier was still true, namely, that the 'equilibrium' had been 'broken', it was by and large restored by 1961.

There had also been changes in military power at the local level. In conventional forces the USA had improved its bargaining position by the stationing of more than 400,000 troops in Europe, and this was helped along by the process of West German rearmament which was then well under way. But these improvements were not enough to outweigh the Soviet superiority in conventional forces. For this reason NATO's doctrine of 'flexible response', which had emerged shortly prior to the outbreak of the second Berlin crisis, posited the need for relying on tactical nuclear weapons in the event of a massive Soviet attack with conventional forces. But even then the credibility of this strategy of flexible response (officially adopted by NATO in 1967) was undermined. The nuclearization of theater forces in NATO and the Warsaw Pact was only in its first stages (to reach its climax only in the late 1960s) but the Soviet Union had the double advantage that NATO thinking envisaged the use of tactical nuclear weapons primarily on NATO (that is, West German) territory, and that the psychological sensitivities this produced in West Germany were enhanced by the Soviet Union's considerable nuclear capabilities in its medium- and intermediate-range missiles and bombers poised against targets in Western Europe. If *all* these elements of the balance – conventional, theater nuclear and intercontinental – are seen in conjunction, it is possible to summarize again that in 1961 a more equal distribution of military checks and balances existed between East and West than in 1948.

A difficult, though important, problem arising from this discussion is the question of whether *Soviet military-strategic superiority* – had it existed – would have made a difference in the two crises. The answer must of necessity be conjectural. But it would appear as indisputable that a Soviet nuclear monopoly, in addition to Soviet conventional superiority in Europe, would have been politically disastrous for the West in 1948. The American determination to respond vigorously to the Soviet challenge was impaired to a large extent by its realization of the tremendous gap in conventional military power in Europe and the deplorable state of readiness of the US armed forces in general. Despite the moral outrage which the blockade produced in the West, and despite the repeated urging by Clay and Murphy to send an armed convoy along the autobahn in order to break the blockade by force, a laborious and expensive evasion of confrontation was kept up until the very end. That is to say, if a gap in strategic power had been added to the gap in conventional power the temptation for the Soviet Union to escalate its measures in the contest for Berlin, and presumably also the temptation to push harder in Finland, Greece, Yugoslavia, Turkey and Iran, would have been almost irresistible; the Western determination in responding would have been weaker.

The question of whether superiority of the Soviet Union over the United States in strategic power would have made a difference to Soviet behavior in Berlin in 1961 cannot be answered unless one knows what 'strategic' is meant to include, how wide a margin of 'superiority' is assumed to exist, and whether 'everything else' (for example, the distribution of conventional and theater nuclear forces) is posited to exist at the level at which it existed in 1961. Looking at the problem with Soviet eyes – that is, considering any nuclear system capable of reaching the Soviet Union a strategic weapon – and positing only a relatively small margin of superiority in intercontinental delivery systems and 'everything else' as being equal, the outcome of the Berlin crisis might not have been much different from what it actually was. Berlin in the heart of Europe would probably still not have been perceived by the Soviet leaders as an Afghanistan of sorts which could be taken over without grave risks of superpower military conflict or risks of rapid escalation to nuclear levels.

Four points can be said to follow from all this. First, it is unwise to establish artificial correlations in the strategic sphere alone. Mechanistic correlations of American and Soviet strategic power with the evolution of Soviet foreign policy since World War II yield the conclusion (a false one) that 'military-strategic inferiority induces risk-taking' (for example, the Soviet initiatives in the Berlin crises and Cuba) and 'military-strategic parity induces restraint' (for example, the early abandonment of probing in Cuba in 1970 and the failure of the Soviet Union to challenge the American block-ade of North Vietnamese harbors in May 1972). *What is evidently necessary is to see strategic power in conjunction with conventional power, the global balance together with the local or regional balance and to consider tactical or theater nuclear weapons along with strategic nuclear weapons.* As demon-strated clearly by the two Berlin crises, this is particularly true for Europe. But, in essence, the same applies to the Cuban missile crisis, the blockade of North Vietnamese harbors in 1972, as well as the conflicts in the Middle East, including the October 1973 war.

Secondly, marginal or moderate changes in the respective arsenals do not matter very much for risk-taking provided the overall 'balance of terror', 'essential equivalence', 'mutually assured destruction', or whatever term is preferred, remains intact. It is doubtful whether Soviet (or American) political leaders have in mind precise comparisons of numbers for various contingen-cies such as: 'If the USA launches a first strike, x millions of Russians will be killed. Our response will kill x millions of Americans'; or 'If we launch a first strike, we will be able to destroy y cities, whereas . . .'. In both crises examined (and probably in all crises in the nuclear age), it is fair to assume that the polit-ical leaders on both sides were restrained in their willingness to use force, even at low levels, by the realization that to drift into large-scale war would have been a catastrophic mistake, and that 'victory' in the end might not have looked much different from defeat.[23] For this reason the concept of military superiority or *supremacy is likely to be of little operational value in crises unless this superiority is clear-cut in all categories of military power.* (As a reflection on the past, in the years from 1964 to the early 1980s the Soviet Union made stringent efforts to achieve clear-cut advantages both in the US-Soviet strategic competition as well as locally and regionally, particularly in Europe and Southwest Asia, including the Persian Gulf. These attempts were success-ful to a considerable extent. As for the present, they can be said to have influ-enced the behavior of local actors in terms of a greater adaptation to Soviet power. Whether or not they are – as a reflection on the future – sufficient to change the behavior of the superpowers in a crisis must remain controversial.)

Thirdly, in both cases the propositions advanced in Chapter Two of this book, in the section 'Risks and the State of the Game', received practical verification. A player faced with a change in the status quo to his disadvant-age and probable defeat will tend to accept risks of disaster in order to prevent the threat of defeat from becoming a fact. In the real life of interna-tional relations these risks may be accepted despite existing disparities in power favoring the adversary. Of course the perceived distribution of milit-ary power will affect crisis behavior of the respective powers but under the assumption of a balance of power (balance in the sense of 'essential equival-ence' or 'mutual assured destruction') *what will be of even greater import-ance is the mutually perceived balance of interests.* On this will depend to a large extent the respective degrees of determination to engage in a competi-tion in risk-taking.

Fourthly, in conditions of rough military-strategic parity weaknesses in conventional power on the Western side and a distribution of interests that is not thoroughly lopsided (that is, where the Soviet Union would clearly violate vital Western interests), *the temptation for Soviet leaders will be great to act in the expansion of power along the model of Berlin in 1961, Cuba in 1962 and Afghanistan in 1979: to try to create a* fait accompli *quickly and attempt to get away with it under a strong deterrent posture.* The advantage of this strategy under the umbrella of the nuclear stalemate is to burden the adversary with the decision to use violence first and with the difficulty of dislodging a power in place. But the adoption of such a strategy of *fait accompli* presupposes a correct diagnosis of the balance of interests and determination in the issue under dispute. Whether or not such a diagnosis is properly made depends a lot on the domestic processes and the nature of interrelationships between domestic politics and foreign policy in the Soviet Union.

Crisis Decision-Making

One of the most surprising conclusions to be drawn from the examination of the two crises is the basic similarity of Soviet crisis behavior *despite* extensive differences on all three levels of analysis of domestic politics. In some ways the contrast between Stalin and Khrushchev could not be more pronounced, the former known to have been more restrained, calculating, conservative, systematic and ruthless, with an astounding memory for detail, but also a man of narrow intellectual horizon and limited experience abroad, the latter generally regarded as more flamboyant, imaginative, inventive and optimistic, more willing to take risks, but also more open to new ideas and schemes and prepared to learn from foreign contacts and travel.

Similarly the contrast in the basic structure of the leadership is tremendous, Stalin in the post-World War II period ruling without any known major challenge to his supreme authority, the period up to and including the Berlin crisis even being devoid of changes in the composition of his subordinates in the Politburo owing to power struggle. Khrushchev, on the contrary, had to fight hard to win the upper hand in the post-Stalin succession struggle, defend his position against challenges by powerful colleagues in the Presidium in 1955 and 1957 and was finally ousted by a leadership conspiracy in 1964.

There were also significant differences in the structure of the Soviet system. In the 1930s and 1940s the system had relied to a great extent on terror and repression and been able to concentrate on basic tasks of industrialization. But in the course of the 1950s the complexity and differentiation of politics, society and economics made it necessary to search for transitions from coercion to political participation and material incentives, from extensive to intensive growth and from mobilization to modernization; because of recurrent leadership conflict there was increased scope for the influence of interest groups in the policy-making process.

There were, finally, some differences in style or method of threat employed by the two leaders. Stalin adopted a low-key approach to confrontation; he never resorted to direct and open threats, there was no saber-rattling campaign by his generals, no warnings of the enormous destruction which the Soviet armed forces could wreak in Europe, and no skillful construction of rationales of how the United States might be vulnerable to strategic attack. In contrast Khrushchev hardly missed an opportunity, after the device had been tried out in the Middle East in 1956, to issue dire warnings and threats, conjure up apocalyptic consequences of general war and brag about the sophistication, destructiveness, quantity and reliability of the Soviet arsenal, particularly in strategic weaponry.

Nevertheless, fundamentally, Stalin's implicit threats, enhanced by troop movements, were just as effective in inhibiting the West from using force as Khrushchev's explicit threats in 1961, and the same is true of the image of ruthless determination which surrounded Stalin and the image of impulsiveness and impetuousness conveyed by Khrushchev. Moreover both Stalin and Khrushchev put on a good show of joviality and displayed an attitude of being rather good-natured people of solid stock. Both hastened to tell their senior commanders – Sokolovsky and Konev respectively – to establish contacts with their American military counterparts, be sociable (up to a point) and avoid incidents, and both treated some of their important visitors with tact and conciliatory remarks – devices which were effective to such an extent that at different times the two leaders were seen as being respectively a 'prisoner of the Politburo' [24] and the 'exponent of the doves', with whom it was better to arrive at a compromise quickly lest a more dangerous faction took over. As a 'senior advisor' on Soviet affairs was to say about Khrushchev during the Berlin crisis of 1961:

> We must give him an out. If we do this shrewdly, we can downgrade the tough group in the Soviet Union which persuaded him to do this. But if we deny him an out, then we will escalate this business into a nuclear war. [25]

This type of advice is just one example of awareness of the second level of analysis in Soviet domestic politics – leadership conflict and the power struggle. The assumption that Soviet behavior in the two crises was influenced by factors of this kind is shared by a number of political leaders and analysts. Although the view of Stalin as a prisoner of the Politburo would have appeared unacceptable to most serious observers of the Soviet Union in 1948, some American diplomats did see Soviet politics as the outcome of a struggle between two factions, a tough one headed by Molotov, and a conciliatory one headed by Stalin; in the view of political leaders and analysts, Kozlov and Khrushchev were to assume the respective roles in 1961.

Despite the persistence of these and similar views, [26] and perhaps their increasing attraction among scholars, the two crises have not furnished direct or indirect evidence in support of images of nonrational decision-making and crisis behavior as an outcome of power struggle. Particularly as regards the Berlin crisis of 1948 it is easy to agree with the US ambassador in Moscow, Smith, who – even prior to his lengthy discussions with Molotov and Stalin in August which very much confirmed the validity of his views – thought that the 'hawk and dove' image of politics in the Stalinist system was not only misleading, but deliberately fostered as a Soviet bargaining technique.[27]

> Tough 'McCarthy' Molotov makes exaggerated demands which kind, pipe-smoking 'Bergen' Stalin whittles down into so-called concessions which temporarily relieve anxiety of [the] foreign statesman until he wakes up to [the] reality of [the] tough bargain he has been forced to accept.[28]

Contrary to that it could be argued that it is one thing to de-emphasize the significance of group conflict for the Berlin crisis in the Stalin era, but quite another to assert the very same for the Berlin crisis in the Khrushchev era. Nevertheless it is quite legitimate to stress the importance of 'rational actor' assumptions also in 1961 because the question at issue is not whether there was power struggle or leadership conflict, but whether there is evidence for the influence of such conflict in *foreign policy*.

The evidence for influence of this kind in 1961 is weak indeed. And unconvincing are the attempts to cast Kozlov in the role of *enfant terrible* in the Berlin crisis who, at the head of the 'tough' group in the Presidium and in conjunction with the military, was responsible for the reversal of many of Khrushchev's priorities and for pushing Soviet policy toward the brink of war. If anything, the influence of leadership politics in the Berlin crisis worked the other way and much more diffusely, many of Khrushchev's colleagues and also some of the high-ranking officers being apprehensive about the potentially hazardous effects of Khrushchev's subjectivism in foreign and military affairs.

To include the third level of analysis in the summary – if the tributaries of conflict are found to be foul it is not to be expected that the actual pool of organizational process and bureaucratic politics approaches will be of such clarity that it is possible to explore more accurately the depths of Soviet decision-making in crises. Some muddying of the waters has already been observed in the theoretical context,[29] and colors darken even further when the results of the case studies are added to the pool.

Concerning organizational processes there is not much to say in either of the cases examined, except that in 1948 the SMA was responsible for political organization in the Soviet zone of occupation and for the measures related to the blockade of Berlin and that, making allowance for the adverse objective conditions in which it had to operate, it did act with skill, circumspection and a good feel for the limits of pressure. At the same time there was a proliferation of organizations carrying out a politically ill-advised reparations policy. If these policies were working at cross purposes with regard to the overall competition for the future orientation of Germany, it is no use blaming the organizations for it; the responsibility must lie squarely with the policy-makers at the center. In 1961 it is reasonable to assume that the Soviet embassy in East Berlin and Marshal Konev were fully informed about all the impending measures and were keeping a close eye on their implementation by the GDR. Undoubtedly it would be interesting to know more about the nature of these interrelationships, if only for their intrinsic interest, but it would be problematic to distill from this knowledge much of relevance to the 'essence of decision' in the crisis.

As regards the bureaucratic politics model, great care has to be taken not to superimpose standard assumptions about Western policy on each and every case of Soviet (foreign) policy. In the first place, it is doubtful whether the key which unlocks the secret of who advocates what sort of policy is the aphorism, 'where you stand depends on where you sit'.[30] (Even in the Western context there is the problem of how to explain why, of all the occupants of particular seats, it was the Secretary of Defense (McNamara) who after the discovery of the missiles in 1962 adopted the stand of 'a missile is a missile'.) In the Soviet context it may be quite convenient to put together on one big bench the 'military-industrial complex', the advocates of heavy industry and the hard liners of the party; and the 'agricultural lobby', the advocates of consumer industry and the supporters of détente on another,[31] but such a seating arrangement may exist only in the speculative mind of the observer in the West, and the same applies to the Western assumption that each particular bench subscribed to a 'totality of interlocking views'.

The way in which such conceptual approaches are superimposed on particular events, with dubious validity, is evident in the daring assertion that there is 'considerable and detailed documentation' that in the early 1960s Kozlov and Suslov sat on the former bench and Khrushchev on the latter, and that: 'Almost invariably the zig-zags in resource allocation can be correlated with clearcut and congruent changes in foreign policy, be it relations with Tito, polemics with China, or incidents on the road to Berlin.[32] As regards resource allocation, even such an organization as the CIA, which for decades has made it its business to estimate one major item of expenditures, namely, defense spending, has seen it fit suddenly to claim that it has probably consistently underestimated the Soviet defense budget by the not negligible margin of about 100 percent; hence, any clear-cut claim (including any Soviet claim) on that issue alone should be regarded with much suspicion. With even more suspicion must be regarded the claim that there is solid documentation demonstrating the congruence of zig-zags in resource allocations with issues in Soviet foreign policy, above all in the Berlin crisis.

This is not the place to engage in an extensive criticism of some of the applications of the bureaucratic politics model to Soviet foreign policy.[33] However, in the context of the analysis of Soviet behavior there is particular validity in concluding with some brief remarks about another facet of the model, the influence of interest groups, in particular the likely influence of the military on Soviet crisis behavior.

Under the two interrelated assumptions of 'where you stand depends on where you sit' and the 'totality of interlocking views' the matter is quite simple. The military can always be counted to sit on the bench of the hardliners. On many issues of domestic politics, economics and foreign policy it can be expected to be in conflict with the main core of the party. Certainly it is likely that there will be party−military conflict over questions such as budgetary allocations for the various branches among the armed forces, the size of the ground forces, the role and functions of the Soviet navy, the technical and political implications of armed forces reductions in Central Europe, SALT and other matters. However, the preoccupation with party−

military conflict must not overlook the basic *similarities in objectives and attitude of the party and the military*, just as it must not underrate conflict *within* the military establishment and *within* the party.

In domestic politics, military-patriotic education, discipline, devotion to duty, conservatism and ideological orthodoxy are preferences which are shared by the military as well as by the party *apparatchiki*. To assume that the military is always the advocate of a high degree of professionalism and technical expertise evades the question of whether it is not often the party that utilizes the central *apparat* to give military science and its introduction into the armed forces a push, perhaps *against* conservative and traditional elements of the military. In fact it would seem that the high level of technological innovation in the military sphere is as much a consequence of the high priority attached by the party to military power as it is an instrument of Soviet foreign policy because of pressures exerted by the military.

It is on the basis of these considerations that the question of the attitudes and influence of the Soviet military in foreign policy could most appropriately be analyzed. Roman Kolkowicz writes that in what 'may be described as generic to all military establishments', one of the 'functional interests' of the Soviet military is the 'Maintenance of a certain level of international political tension in order to provide the rationale for large military budgets and allocations'.[34] While this may be correct it explains nothing about attempts by the military to exert influence on Soviet foreign policy, about the effectiveness of these attempts when they are made, or about the problem of whether hard-line attitudes imply support of the military for ventures which require the acceptance of military risks, as in Berlin in 1948 and 1961, or in Cuba in 1962, or whether they work for or against military commitments as, say, in the Middle East, the Horn of Africa, or Afghanistan.[35]

In addition to that, the analyst comes up against the same problem in foreign policy as in Soviet domestic politics, that is, of distinguishing between preferences of the military and the political leadership. Soviet political leaders have gone out of their way to stress that, détente notwithstanding, there remains not only a certain level of international political tension, but a 'fundamental contradiction between imperialism and socialism in the world arena' and hence the necessity for vigilance, military preparedness and military budgets. Détente has been explained by the military and the political leadership as the direct result of significant changes in the 'correlation of forces in favor of socialism', that is, primarily by the growth of Soviet military power.

What all this means for the analysis of Soviet decision-making in international crises is pointed out by Malcolm Mackintosh who concludes on the basis of three case illustrations that 'when a foreign policy adopted by the leadership coincides with military views, it is difficult to distinguish whether the policy was initiated by the Party or by the military'; that in cases where the views of the armed forces might differ from those of the party leaders, 'there is nothing to suggest any diminution of the Party's ultimate primacy in foreign policy decision-making'.[36]

Mackintosh's conclusions may well be representative of differences between British and American scholarship or of the beginning of a more general disenchantment with the concept of interest group participation in Soviet foreign policy. As regards the American context, Gallagher and Spielmann write that the

> attraction for the pluralistic rather than the monistic features of Soviet society can be ascribed to the fashions of political science, particularly to the great interest that developed in the 1950s on the theoretical and empirical analyses of group and institutional impacts on the political process . . . to keep the picture in perspective, it is necessary to consider the opposing characteristic of the Soviet political system, i.e., the strong centralizing tendencies that work to concentrate political initiative and power at the top.[37]

This is a view that is strongly supported by the analysis of Soviet behavior in the two Berlin crises and it is likely that it is equally valid for the analysis of Soviet risk-taking and crisis behavior in general.

Notes: Part Three, Chapter 17

1 See above, pp. 56–8.
2 The image also often implies that the more 'pragmatic' the Soviet Union becomes, the easier it will be to deal with it, and the greater the tendency for the Soviet Union to become a status quo-oriented power.
3 This is a point made by Alfred G. Meyer, 'The functions of ideology in the Soviet political system', *Soviet Studies*, vol. 17, no. 3 (January 1966), p. 273.
4 loc. cit.
5 See p. 57.
6 Meyer, 'The functions of ideology in the Soviet political system', p. 273. Meyer also included the official history of the CPSU and pronouncements made by the party concerning the interpretation of current affairs and the setting of goals and priorities.
7 The first four of the five functions named above conform roughly to distinctions made by Marshal Shulman. Similar distinctions have appeared in print, for example, Zimmerman, *Soviet Perspectives on International Relations*, pp. 282–3.
8 V. I Lenin, *'Left-Wing' Communism, an Infantile Disorder: A Popular Essay in Marxist Strategy and Tactics* [written in 1920] (New York: International Publishers, 1969), p. 59.
9 ibid., p. 53.
10 This is a point made long ago by Brzezinski and Huntington, *Political Power*, p. 66, but it is still right.
11 Leo Labedz 'Ideology and Soviet policies in Europe', paper delivered at the Twentieth Annual Conference of the International Institute for Strategic Studies (IISS), 7–10 September 1978, p. 3. See also my paper, 'Ideology in the Soviet view of international affairs', delivered at the same conference, which very much agrees with Labedz's approach and conclusions. Both papers are published in Christoph Bertram (ed.), *Prospects of Soviet Power in the 1980s* (London: Macmillan, 1980).
12 Labedz, 'Ideology and Soviet policies in Europe', p. 6.
13 ibid., p. 3.
14 Robert G. Wesson, 'Soviet ideology: the necessity of Marxism', *Soviet Studies*, vol. 21, no. 1 (July 1969), p. 69.
15 loc. cit.
16 See pp. 36 and 190.
17 Vernon V. Aspaturian, 'Ideology and national interest in Soviet foreign policy', in *Process and Power in Soviet Foreign Policy*, p. 331.
18 The West Germans, and politically indifferent 'East Germans', have always referred to 'East Germany' as *Mitteldeutschland* (Central Germany). If the SED rejected this label it

was not because of its disagreement with the geographical distinction, but because what it wanted was to see the official political term of 'German Democratic Republic' implanted in the consciousness of the Germans.

19   See pp. 113–14, 177–80 and 221–2.

20   Edmonds, *Soviet Foreign Policy*, pp. 153–4. The author also concedes that 'Soviet historians and statesmen are guilty neither of dishonesty nor cynicism when they claim, in effect, that what is good for their country is good for world communism'. To this can be added the view that 'Soviet ideology itself defines "national interest", "power", and "world revolution" in such a way as to make them virtually as indistinguishable as the three sides of an equilateral triangle' (Aspaturian, 'Ideology and national interest', p. 333). Finally, there should be little disagreement with the argument that 'Depending on the perceptions of fact and value among these people [the Soviet leaders], Soviet national interest may be served by the aggressive pursuit of power by Communist Parties in all countries. Or, Soviet national interest may not be served by such a course at all. The national interest is a *conclusion*, derived logically from premises of fact and value, some of which may have been drawn from, or conditioned by, the precepts of Marxism-Leninism' (Triska and Finley, *Soviet Foreign Policy*, p. 114).

21   Stephen Jay Gould, 'Darwin's untimely burial', *Natural History*, vol. 85, no. 8 (October 1976), p. 26. To demonstrate the point the author adds that 'It got colder before the mammoth evolved his shaggy coat.'

22   The term and its significance was explained on pp. 20–2.

23   For the difference between 'defeat' and 'disaster' and its implications see pp. 21–3.

24   In a speech on 11 June 1948, President Truman was reported as saying: 'I like Old Joe. He's a decent fellow but he's a prisoner of the Politburo' (as quoted by Shulman, *Stalin's Foreign Policy Reappraised*, p. 31).

25   Averell Harriman who, in the recollections of Arthur Schlesinger, Jr, at the height of the Berlin crisis called the White House from the United States UN mission in New York to make this point. No exact date of Harriman's call is given (Schlesinger, *A Thousand Days*, pp. 821–2).

26   Another leadership dichotomy assumed to have made a difference for Soviet policy in the Berlin crisis of 1948 is that between Zhdanov ('tough') and Malenkov ('soft'); see pp. 147–50.

27   For other examples of this technique within the theoretical context see pp. 36–7.

28   The ambassador in the Soviet Union (Smith) to the Secretary of State, Secret, 6 March 1948, in *Foreign Relations, 1948*, Vol. IV, p. 819. The reference is to the American ventriloquist Mr Edgar Bergen and his wooden dummy named Charlie McCarthy. The telegram was sent in response to a cable from Budapest to the State Department which had contained the view of different lines advocated by Molotov and Stalin.

29   See pp. 33–40.

30   This is one of the central assumptions of Allison, *Essence of Decision*, p. 176, quoting Sorensen, *Kennedy*, p. 686.

31   Dallin, 'Domestic factors influencing foreign policy', pp. 42–3.

32   ibid., p. 43.

33   For a more detailed examination of domestic factors of Soviet risk-taking and the problem of the extent to which Soviet behavior in crises may be different from Soviet behavior in foreign policy in general (the 'level of analysis' problem) see my article, 'Consensus versus conflict', and Hannes Adomeit and Robert Boardman (eds), *Foreign Policy Making in Communist Countries: A Comparative Approach* (Farnborough: Saxon House, 1979).

34   Roman Kolkowicz, 'The military', in H. Gordon Skilling and Franklyn Griffiths, *Interest Groups in Soviet Politics* (Princeton, NJ: Princeton University Press, 1971), p. 141.

35   There is a general problem here: the analysis of interest groups in Soviet politics has focused primarily on their possible influence on *domestic* rather than *foreign* policy; so, for instance, Joel J. Schwartz and William R. Keech, 'Group influence and the policy process in the Soviet Union', *American Political Science Review*, vol. 62, no. 3 (September 1968), pp. 840–51, on the 1958 Educational Reform Act; Philip D. Stewart, 'Soviet interest groups and the policy process', *World Politics*, vol. 22, no. 1 (1969), pp. 29–50, on Khrushchev's plans for 'production education' in 1964; and Ploss, *Conflict and Decision-Making in the Soviet Union*, on agricultural policy under Khrushchev.

36   Malcolm Mackintosh, 'The Soviet military: influence on foreign policy', *Problems of Communism*, vol. 22, no. 5 (September–October, 1973), pp. 10–11. These conclusions,

de-emphasizing conflict between the party and the military, find a counterpart in Stephen White's warning not to exaggerate cleavages between the party and economic managers or technocrats. He writes: 'An examination of the educational and occupational composition of the CPSU membership and of its leading bodies suggests that no sharp distinction can be made between the two groups; and that the relation between managers and *apparatchiki* may more accurately be seen as one of interpenetration and mutual absorption'. See his 'Contradiction and change in state socialism', *Soviet Studies*, vol. 26, no. 1 (January 1974), p. 42.

37 Gallagher and Spielmann, *Soviet Decision-Making for Defense*, pp. 23–4.

Bibliography

The first part of the bibliography contains all the documentary materials, memoirs and secondary sources pertaining to the two Berlin crises in general and to Soviet policies in the two crises in particular. Compiled in the second part is the literature on risk and crisis in general and all the materials on Soviet risk-taking and crisis behavior in the context of Soviet foreign policy; included in this part are also the books and articles on ideological, economic, military and domestic political factors of Soviet behavior

A. THE BERLIN CRISES

SOVIET AND EAST EUROPEAN SOURCES

I Collections of Documents and Speeches. Diplomatic Histories

Academy of Sciences of the USSR, Institute of History (ed.), *A Short History of the USSR, Part II* (Moscow: Progress Publishers, 1965).

Gromyko, A. A., *et al.* (eds), *Istoriia diplomatii* (History of Diplomacy), Vol. V (Moscow: Izdatel'stvo politicheskoi literatury, 1974).

Hänisch, Walter, *Aussenpolitik und Internationale Beziehungen der DDR, Vol. I: 1949–1955* (Foreign Policy and International Relations of the GDR) (East Berlin: Staatsverlag der Deutschen Demokratischen Republik, 1972).

Inozemtsev, N. N. (ed.), *Mezhdunarodnye otnosheniia posle vtoroi mirovoi voiny, Vol. III: 1956–1964 gg.* (International Relations after World War II, Vol. III: 1956–1964) (Moscow: Izdatel'stvo politicheskoi literatury for the Institute of World Economy and International Relations, Academy of Sciences of the USSR, 1965).

Khrushchev, N. S., *Kommunizm – mir i schast'e narodam* (Communism – Peace and Happiness for the Peoples), Vol. I (Moscow: Izdatel'stvo politicheskoi literatury, 1962).

Khrushchev, N. S., *Stroitel'stvo Kommunizma v SSSR i razvitie sel'skogo khoziastva* (The Building of Communism in the USSR and the Development of Agriculture), Vol. IV (Moscow: Izdatel'stvo politicheskoi literatury, 1963).

Khrushchev, N. S., *To Avert War: Our Primary Task* (Moscow: Foreign Languages Publishing House, 1963).

Khrushchev, N. S., *The New Content of Peaceful Coexistence in the Nuclear Age* (New York: Crosscurrents Press, 1963).

Klein, Peter, *et al.* (eds), *Geschichte der Aussenpolitik der Deutschen Demokratischen Republik: Abriss* (History of Foreign Policy of the German Democratic Republic: A Short Course) (East Berlin: Dietz Verlag, 1968).

Lenin, V. I., *Selected Works*, Vol. VIII (New York: International Publishers, 1943).

Lenin, V. I., *Imperialism: The Highest Stage of Capitalism*, new edn (New York: International Publishers, 1969).

Lenin, V. I., *'Left-Wing' Communism, an Infantile Disorder: A Popular Essay in Marxist Strategy and Tactics* (New York: International Publishers, 1969).

Lenin, V. I., *Sochineniia* (Works), Vol. XXXVI, 4th edn (Moscow: Izdatel'stvo politicheskoi literatury, 1957).

Ministerstvo inostrannykh del SSSR, Ministerstvo inostrannykh del GDR, *Otnosheniia SSSR s GDR, 1949–1955 gg.: Dokumenty i materialy* (Relations between the USSR and the GDR, 1949–55: Documents and Materials) (Moscow: Izdatel'stvo politicheskoi literatury, 1974).

Ministerstvo inostrannykh del SSSR, Ministerstvo inostrannykh del GDR, *Za anti-fashistskuiu demokraticheskuiu Germaniiu: Sbornik dokumentov, 1945–1949 gg.* (For an Anti-Fascist, Democratic Germany: A Collection of Documents, 1945–49) (Moscow: Izdatel'stvo politicheskoi literatury, 1969).

Ministerstvo vneshnei torgovli SSSR, Planovo-ekonomicheskoe upravlenie (ed.), *Vneshnaia torgovlia Soiusa SSSR za 1959–1963 gody* (Foreign Trade of the USSR in 1959–1963) (Moscow: Vneshtorgizdat, 1965).

Molotov, V. M., *Problems of Foriegn Policy: Speeches and Statements, April 1945–November 1948* (Moscow: Foreign Languages Publishing House, 1949).

Ponomarev, B. M., Gromyko, A. A., and Khvostov, V. M., *Istoriia vneshnei politiki SSSR, 1917–1970 gg., Vol. II: 1945–1970 gg.* (History of Foreign Policy of the USSR, 1917–1970, Vol. I: 1945–1970) (Moscow: Izdatel'stvo 'Nauka', 1971).

Stalin, Joseph V., *Problems of Leninism* (Moscow: Foreign Languages Publishing House, 1947).

Stalin, Joseph V., *Economic Problems of Socialism in the USSR* (Moscow: Foreign Languages Publishing House, 1952).

Stalin, Joseph V., *Sochineniia* (Works), Vol. X (Moscow: Gosudarstvennoe izdatel'stvo politicheskoi literatury, 1948).

Stalin, Joseph V., *The Great Patriotic War of the Soviet Union*, 5th edn (Moscow: Foreign Languages Publishing House, 1950).

Trukhanovskii, V. G. (ed.), *Istoriia mezhdunarodnykh otnoshenii i vneshnei politiki SSSR, Vol. III: 1945–1963 gg.* (History of International Relations and Foreign Policy of the USSR, Vol. III: 1945–1963 (Moscow: Izdatel'stvo 'Mezhdunarodnye otnosheniia', 1964).

Ulbricht, W., *Zur Geschichte der deutschen Arbeiterbewegung* (On the History of the German Workers' Movement), Vol. VII (East Berlin: Dietz Verlag, 1964).

II Books, Monographs and Memoirs

Apokov, G. M., *Zapadnyi Berlin: problemy i resheniia* (West Berlin: Problems and Solutions) (Moscow: Izdatel'stvo 'Mezhdunarodnye otnosheniia', 1974).

Dedijer, Vladimir, *Josip Bros Tito. Prilozi za biografiju* (Josip Bros Tito: Contributions to a Biography) (Belgrade: Kultura, 1953).

Dedijer, Vladimir, *The Battle Stalin Lost* (New York: Viking Press, 1970).

Galkin, A. A., and Mel'nikov, D. E., *SSSR, Zapadnye derzhavy i germanskii vopros, 1945–1965 gg.* (The USSR, the Western Powers and the German Problem, 1945–1965) (Moscow: Izdatel'stvo 'Nauka' for the Institute for World Economy and International Relations, Academy of Sciences of the USSR, 1966).

Keiderling, Gerhard, and Stulz, Percy, *Berlin 1945–1968: Zur Geschichte der Hauptstadt der DDR and der selbständigen politischen Einheit Westberlin* (Berlin: 1945–1968: On the History of the Capital of the GDR and the Autonomous Political Entity West Berlin) (East Berlin: Dietz Verlag, 1970).

Khrushchev Remembers [Vol. I], trans. and ed. Strobe Talbott, with an introduction, commentary and notes by Edward Crankshaw (Boston, Mass: Little, Brown/Bantam Books, 1970).

Khrushchev Remembers: The Last Testament [Vol. II], trans. and ed. Strobe Talbott, with a foreword by Edward Crankshaw and an introduction by Jerrold L. Schecter (London: Deutsch, 1974).

Müller, Hans, and Reissig, Karl, *Wirtschaftswunder DDR: Ein Beitrag zur Geschichte der ökonomischen Politik der Sozialistischen Einheitspartie Deutschlands* (Economic Miracle GDR: A Contribution to the History of Economic Policy of the Socialist Unity Party of Germany) (East Berlin: Dietz Verlag for the Institut für Gesellschaftswissenschaften beim ZK der SED, 1969).

Nikolaev, P. A., *Politika Sovetskogo Soiuza v Germanskom voprose* (Moscow: Izdatel'stvo 'Nauka', 1966).

Protopopov, A. C., *Sovetskii Soiuz v Organisatsii Ob''edinennykh Natsii* (The Soviet Union in the United Nations), Vol. I (Moscow: Izdatel'stvo 'Nauka', 1965).

Shtemenko, S. M., *General'nyi Shtab v gody voiny* (The General Staff in the Years of the War), 2nd rev. edn (Moscow: Voenizdat, 1975).

Varga, Eugene S., *Izmeneniia v ekonomike kapitalizma v itoge vtoroi mirovoi voiny* (Changes in the Economy of Capitalism Resulting from World War II) (Moscow: OGIZ, 1946).

Vysotskii, Viktor Nikolaevich, *Zapadnyi Berlin i ego mesto v sisteme sovremennykh mezhdunarodnykh otnoshenii* (West Berlin and its Role in the System of Contemporary International Relations (Moscow: Izdatel'stvo Mysl, 1971).

Vysotsky, Viktor, *West Berlin*, trans. David Fidlon (Moscow: Progress Publishers, 1974).

Zhukov, G. K., *Vospominaniia i razmyshleniia* (Reminiscences and Reflections), Vol. II, 2nd rev. edn (Moscow: Novosti, 1974).

III Articles

Ackermann, Anton, 'Gibt es einen besonderen deutschen Weg zum Sozialismus?' (Is there a special German road to socialism?), *Einheit* (Berlin), vol. 1, no. 1 (February 1946, pp. 23–32.

Dvorkin, I., 'Nemarksistkaia kniga o promyshlennosti kapitalisticheskikh stran' (An unmarxist book on industry in the capitalist countries), review of a book by S. Vishnev, *Bol'shevik*, no. 5 (1948), pp. 74–80.

Gatovskii, L., 'V plenu burzhuaznoi metodologii' (In the service of bourgeois methodology), review of a book by I. A. Trakhtenberg, *Bol'shevik*, no. 5 (1948), pp.74–80.

Gertsovich, G., 'Vosstanovlenie mirnoi ekonomiki v Sovetskoi zone okupatsii Germanii' (The establishment of a peaceful economy in the Soviet zone of occupation), *Voprosy ekonomiki*, no. 1 (March 1948), pp. 93–101.

Grossman, A. S., 'Granitsa mira' (Border of peace), *Voprosy istorii*, no. 10 (1969).

Lavrent'eva, A., 'Stroiteli novogo mira' (Builders of a new world), *V mire knig*, no. 9 (1970), pp. 4–5.

Mel'nikov, Danil, 'The "airlift": legend and realities', *New Times* (Moscow), 15 September 1948.

'O nedostatkakh i zadachakh nauchno-issledovatel'skoi raboty v oblasti ekonomiki' (On the shortcomings and tasks of scientific research work in the sphere of economics), Meeting of an Enlarged Session of the Learned Council of the Institute of Economics at the Academy of Sciences of the USSR, *Voprosy ekonomiki*, no. 8 (1948), pp. 66–110; no. 9 (1948), pp. 52–116.

Shneerson, A., 'Obostrenie obshchego krizisa kapitalizma' (The sharpening of the general crisis of capitalism), *Planovoe khoziaistvo*, no. 4 (July–August, 1948), pp. 76–91.

'Sovetskaia politika ravnopraviia natsii' (The Soviet policy of equality of nations), *Bol'shevik*, no. 9 (1948), pp. 1–6.

Thomas, S., 'Die sowjetische Deutschlandnote vom 10. März 1952: Eine verpasste Chance' (The Soviet note on the German problem of 10 March 1952: a lost opportunity), *Deutsche Aussenpolitik* (East Berlin), special issue (1967), pp. 91–96.

WESTERN SOURCES

I Documents, Official Publications and Diplomatic Papers

The Anti-Stalin Campaign and International Communism, ed. Russian Institute, Columbia University (New York: Columbia University Press, 1956).

Bericht der Bundesregierung und Materialien zur Lage der Nation, 1971 (Bonn: Bundesministerium für innerdeutsche Beziehungen, 1971).

Berlin: Behauptung von Freiheit und Selbstverwaltung, 1946–1948, series 'Berliner Zeitgeschichte', Vol. II (West Berlin: Dunker & Humblot for the Berlin City Government, 1959).

[The Clay Papers], The Papers of General Lucius D. Clay: Germany 1945–1949, 2 vols, ed. Jean Edward Smith (Bloomington, Ill., and London: Indiana University Press, 1974).

Die Flucht aus der Sowjetzone und die Sperrmassnahmen des Kommunistischen Regimes vom 13. August 1961 in Berlin (Bonn and Berlin: Bundesministerium für gesamtdeutsche Fragen, 1961).

Documents on Berlin, 1943–1963, ed. Wolfgang Heidelmeyer and Guenter Hindrichs (Munich: R. Oldenbourg Verlag for the Forschungsinstitut der Deutschen Gesellschaft für Auswärtige Politik, 1963).

Documents on Germany under Occupation, 1945–1954 (London and New York: Oxford University Press for the Royal Institute of International Affairs, 1955).

Etzold, Thomas H., and Gaddis, John Lewis, (eds), *Containment: Documents on American Policy and Strategy, 1945–1950* (New York: Columbia University Press, 1978).

Gruliow, Leo (ed.), *Current Soviet Policies: The Documentary Record of the Nineteenth Party Congress and the Reorganization after Stalin's Death* (New York: Praeger, 1953).

Gruliow, Leo (ed), *Current Soviet Policies, Vol. IV: The Documentary Record of the Twenty-Second Congress of the Communist Party of the Soviet Union* (New York: Columbia University Press, 1962).

US Congress, Joint Economic Committee, 87th Congress, 2nd Session, *Dimensions of Soviet Economic Power* (Washington, DC: Government Printing Office, 1962).

US Congress, Joint Economic Committee, *Soviet Economic Prospects for the Seventies* (Washington, DC: Government Printing Office, 1973).

US Congress, Senate, Committee on Foreign Relations, 86th Congress, 2nd Session, *Report: Events Relating to the Summit Conference* (Washington, DC: Government Printing Office, 1960).

US Congress, Senate, Committee on Foreign Relations, *Documents on Germany, 1944–1961* (Washington, DC: Government Printing Office, 1961).

US Congress, Senate, Committee on Armed Services, 80th Congress, 1st Session, *Hearings, Universal Military Training* (Washington, DC: Government Printing Office, 1948).

US Congress, Senate, Committee on Armed Services, 80th Congress, 2nd Session, *Hearings, Universal Military Training* (Washington DC: Government Printing Office, 1948).

US Congress, Senate, Subcommittee of the Committee on Appropriations, 80th Congress, 2nd Session, *Hearings, Supplemental Defense Appropriations Bill, 1948* (Washington, DC: Government Printing Office, 1948).

US Department of State, *The Berlin Crisis: A Report on the Moscow Discussions, 1948* (Washington, DC: Government Printing Office, 1948).

US Department of State, *Berlin – 1961* (Washington, DC: Government Printing Office, 1961).

US Department of State, *Documents on Disarmament, 1945–1959*, Vol. II (Washington, DC: Government Printing Office, 1960).

US Department of State, *Foreign Relations of the United States, 1947, Vol. II: Council of Foreign Ministers; Germany and Austria*, Department of State Publication 8530 (Washington, DC: Government Printing Office, 1972).

US Department of State, *Foreign Relations of the United States, 1948, Vol. II: Germany and Austria*, Department of State Publication 8674 (Washington, DC: Government Printing Office, 1973).

US Department of State, *Foreign Relations of the United States, 1948, Vol. IV: Eastern Europe, the Soviet Union*, Department of State Publication 8743 (Washington, DC: Government Printing Office, 1974).

US Department of State, *Foreign Relations of the United States: The Conference of Berlin (Potsdam)*, Vol. II (Washington, DC: Government Printing Office, 1960).

US Department of State, *Foreign Ministers Meeting, May–August 1959, Geneva*, Department of State Publication 6882 (Washington, DC: Government Printing Office, 1959).

US Department of State, *The International Control of Atomic Energy: Growth of a Policy* (Washington, DC: Government Printing Office, 1946).

US Department of State, *The International Control of Atomic Energy: Policy at the Crossroads* (Washington, DC: Government Printing Office, 1948).

II Books, Diaries and Memoirs

Adenauer, Konrad, *Erinnerungen, 1959–1963* (Stuttgart: Deutsche Verlagsanstalt, 1968).

Alperovitz, Gar, *Cold War Essays* (Garden City, NY: Doubleday, 1970).

Apel, Hans, *Wehen und Wunder der Zonenwirtschaft* (Cologne: Verlag Wissenschaft und Politik, 1966).

Becker, Abraham S., *Soviet Military Outlays since 1955* RM-3886-PR (Santa Monica, Calif.: Rand Corporation, July 1964).

Bloomfield, Lincoln P., Clemens, Jr, Walter C., and Griffiths, Franklyn, *Khrushchev and the Arms Race: Soviet Interests in Arms Control and Disarmament, 1954–1964* (Cambridge, Mass.: MIT, 1966).

Bohlen, Charles E., with Phelps, Robert H., *Witness to History, 1929–69* (New York: Norton, 1973).

Brandt, Heinz, *Ein Traum der nicht entführbar ist: Mein Weg zwischen Ost und West* (West Berlin: Verlag 'Europäische Ideen', 1977).

Brzezinski, Zbigniew K., *The Soviet Bloc: Unity and Conflict*, rev. edn (New York: Praeger, 1961).

Campbell, John C., *Tito's Separate Road: America and Yugoslavia in World Politics* (New York: Harper & Row for the Council on Foreign Relations, 1967).

Carr, E. H., *A History of Soviet Russia: The Interregnum, 1923–1924* (Baltimore, Md: Macmillan/Penguin, 1954).

Cate, Curtis, *The Ides of August: The Berlin Wall Crisis, 1961* (London: Weidenfeld & Nicolson, 1978).

Clay, Lucius D., *Decision in Germany* (Garden City, NY: Doubleday, 1950).

Conquest, Robert, *Power and Policy in the USSR* (London: Macmillan, 1961).

Crankshaw, Edward, *Khrushchev: A Career* (New York: Viking Press, 1967).

Dahm, Helmut, *Abschreckung oder Volkskrieg: Strategische Machtplanung der Sowjetunion und Chinas im internationalen Kräfteverhältnis* (Olten and Freiburg: Walter-Verlag, 1968).

Dallin, David J., *Soviet Foreign Policy After Stalin* (Philadelphia, Pa: Lippincott, 1961).

Davison, W. Phillips, *The Berlin Blockade: A Study in Cold War Politics* (Princeton, NJ: Princeton University Press, 1958).

Dean, Arthur H., *Test Ban and Disarmament: The Path of Negotiation* (New York and London: Harper & Row for the Council of Foreign Relations, 1966).

Dedijer, Vladimir, *The Battle Stalin Lost* (New York: Viking Press, 1970).

Deutscher, Isaac, *Russia, China and the West, 1953–1966* (London: Oxford University Press/Penguin, 1970).

Deutsches Institut für Wirtschaftsforschung (ed.), *DDR-Wirtschaft: Eine Bestandsaufnahme* (Frankfurt aM: Fischer Verlag, 1971).

Djilas, Milovan, *Conversations with Stalin*, trans. Michael B. Petrovich (New York: Harcourt Brace & World, 1962).

Dulles, Eleanor Lansing, *The Wall: A Tragedy in Three Acts* (Columbia, SC: University of South Carolina Press, 1972).

Dulles, John Foster, *War or Peace* (New York: Macmillan, 1950).

Eisenhower, Dwight D., *The White House Years: Waging Peace, 1956–1960* (Garden City, NY: Doubleday, 1965).

Enthoven, Alain C., and Smith, K. Wayne, *How Much is Enough? Shaping the Defense Program, 1961–1969* (New York and London: Harper & Row, 1971).

Erickson, John, *Stalin's War with Germany, Vol. I: The Road to Stalingrad* (London: Weidenfeld & Nicolson, 1975).

Feis, Herbert, *From Trust to Terror: The Onset of the Cold War, 1945–1950* (London: Blond, 1971).

Feis, Herbert, *Between War and Peace: The Potsdam Conference* (Princeton, NJ: Princeton University Press, 1960).

Garthoff, Raymond L., *Soviet Strategy in the Nuclear Age* (New York: Praeger, 1958).

Gniffke, Erich W., *Jahre mit Ulbricht* (Cologne: Verlag Wissenschaft und Politik, 1966).

Griffith, William E., *Albania and the Sino-Soviet Rift* (New York: Atheneum, 1967).

Hilsman, Roger, *To Move a Nation: The Politics of Foreign Policy in the Administration of John F. Kennedy* (Garden City, NY: Doubleday, 1967).

Holloway, David, *Entering the Nuclear Arms Race: The Soviet Decision to Build the Atomic Bomb, 1939–45*, International Security Studies Program, Working Paper No. 9 (Washington, DC: The Wilson Center, 1979).

Holzman, Franklyn D., *Financial Checks on Soviet Defense Expenditures* (Lexington, Mass., and Toronto: D. C. Heath, 1975).

Horelick, Arnold L., and Rush, Myron, *Strategic Power and Soviet Foreign Policy* (Chicago: University of Chicago Press, 1966).

Howley, Frank, *Berlin Command* (New York: Putnam, 1950).

Kemp, Geoffrey, Pfaltzgraff, Jr., Robert L., and Ra'anan, Uri (eds), *The Superpowers in a Multinuclear World* (Lexington, Mass., and Toronto: D. C. Heath, 1974).

Kennan, George F., *Memoirs: 1925–1950* (Boston, Mass., and Toronto: Little, Brown, 1957).

Kennan, George F., *Russia and the West Under Lenin and Stalin* (New York and Toronto: Mentor Books, 1960).

Korbel, Josef, *The Communist Subversion of Czechoslovakia, 1938–1948: The Failure of Coexistence* (Princeton, NJ: Princeton University Press, 1959).

Kramish, Arnold, *Atomic Energy in the Soviet Union* (Stanford, Calif.: Stanford University Press, 1959).

Kroll, Hans, *Lebenserinnerungen eines Botschafters* (Cologne: Kiepenheuer & Witsch, 1967).

Leites, Nathan, *The Operational Code of the Politburo* (New York: McGraw-Hill, 1951).

Leites, Nathan, *A Study of Bolshevism* (Glencoe, Ill.: The Free Press, 1953).

Leites, Nathan, *Kremlin Moods*, RM-3535-ISA (Santa Monica, Calif.: Rand Corporation, January 1964).

Leonhard, Wolfgang, *Child of the Revolution*, trans. C. M. Woodhouse (London: Collins, 1957).

Linden Carl A., *Khrushchev and the Soviet Leadership* (Baltimore, Md: Johns Hopkins University Press, 1966).

Lippmann, Heinz, *Honecker and the New Politics of Europe* (London: Angus & Robertson, 1973).

Lippmann, Walter, *The Coming Tests with Russia* (Boston, Mass.: Little, Brown, 1961).

Löwenthal, Richard, *World Communism: The Disintegration of a Secular Faith* (New York: Oxford University Press, 1966).

Mackintosh, Malcolm, *Strategy and Tactics of Soviet Foreign Policy* (New York and London: Oxford University Press, 1962).

Mackintosh, Malcolm, *Juggernaut: The Russian Forces, 1918–1966* (New York: Macmillan, 1967).

McDermott, Geoffrey, *Berlin: Success of a Mission?* (New York: Harper & Row, 1963).

MacIsaac, David, *The Air Force and Strategic Thought, 1945–1951*. International Security Studies Program, Working Paper No. 8 (Washington, DC: The Wilson Center, 1979).

Mallinckrodt, Anita Dasbach, *Propaganda hinter der Mauer: Die Propaganda der Sowjetunion und der DDR als Werkzeug der Aussenpolitik im Jahre 1961* (Stuttgart and Berlin: W. Kohlhammer, 1971).

Medvedev, Roy A., *Let History Judge: The Origins and Consequences of Stalinism*, ed. David Joravsky and Georges Haupt, trans. Colleen Taylor (New York: Knopf, 1971).

Mendershausen, Horst, *Interzonal Trade in Germany, Part I: The Trade and Contractual Relations*, RM-36-86 (Santa Monica, Calif.: Rand Corporation, July 1963).

Millis, Walter, (ed), *The Forrestal Diaries* (New York: Viking Press, 1951).

Murphy, Robert, *Diplomat among Warriors* (Garden City, NY: Doubleday, 1964).

Nadolny, Rudolf, *Mein Beitrag* (Wiesbaden: Limes Verlag, 1955).

Nettl, J. P., *The Eastern Zone and Soviet Policy in Germany: 1945–50* (London: Oxford University Press, 1951).

Nicolaevsky, Boris, *Power and the Soviet Elite*, ed. Janet D. Zagoria (London: Pall Mall Press, 1965).

Penkovsky, Oleg, *The Penkovsky Papers*, trans. P. Deriabin with an introduction and commentary by Frank Gibney and a foreword by Edward Crankshaw (London: Collins, 1965).

Pethybridge, R. W., *A History of Postwar Russia* (London: Allen & Unwin, 1966).

Ploss, Sidney I., *Conflict and Decision-Making in Soviet Russia: A Case Study of Agricultural Policy, 1953–1963* (Princeton, NJ: Princeton University Press for the Princeton Center of International Studies, 1965).

Pritzel, Konstantin, *Die Wirtschaftsintegration Mitteldeutschlands* (Cologne: Verlag Wissenschaft und Politik, 1969).

Reale, Eugenio, *Avec Jacques Duclos au banc des accusés à la réunion constitutive du Kominform* (Paris: Plon, 1958).

Reiss, Curt, *The Berlin Story* (New York: Dial Press, 1952).

Rodrigo, Robert, *Berlin Airlift* (London: Cassell, 1960).

Salinger, Pierre, *With Kennedy* (Garden City, NY: Doubleday, 1966).

Salisbury, Harrison E., *The 900 Days: The Siege of Leningrad* (New York: Hearst/Avon Books, 1969).

Schapiro, Leonard, *The Communist Party of the Soviet Union* (London: Eyre & Spottiswoode, 1960).

Scheurig, Bodo, *Freies Deutschland: Das Nationalkomitee und der Bund Deutscher Offiziere in der Sowjetunion, 1943–1945* (Munich: Nymphenburger, 1960).

Schick, Jack M., *The Berlin Crisis: 1958–1962* (Philadelphia, Pa: University of Philadelphia Press, 1971).

Schlesinger, Arthur, Jr, *A Thousand Days: John F. Kennedy in the White House* (Boston, Mass.: Houghton Mifflin, 1965).

Schneider, Eberhard, *Die DDR: Geschichte, Politik, Wirtschaft, Gesellschaft* (Stuttgart: Verlag Bonn Aktuell, 1975).

Schwarz, Hans-Peter, *Vom Reich zur Bundesrepublik: Deutschland im Widerstreit der Aussenpolitischen Konzeptionen in den Jahren der Besatzungsherrschaft, 1945–1949* (Neuwied und Berlin: Luchterhand, 1966).

Shell, Kurt L., *Bedrohung und Bewährung: Führung und Bevölkerung in der Berlin Krise* (Cologne and Opladen: Westdeutscher Verlag, 1965).

Shulman, Marshal D., *Stalin's Foreign Policy Reappraised* (New York: Atheneum, 1965).

Slusser, Robert M., *The Berlin Crisis of 1961: Soviet-American Relations and the Struggle for Power in the Kremlin, June–November 1961* (Baltimore, Md, and London: Johns Hopkins University Press, 1973).

Smith, Jean Edward, (ed.), *The Papers of General Lucius D. Clay: Germany 1945–1949*, 2 vols (Bloomington, Ill., and London: Indiana University Press, 1974).

Smith, Jean Edward, *The Defense of Berlin* (Baltimore, Md: Johns Hopkins University Press, 1963).

Smith, Walter Bedell, *My Three Years in Moscow* (Philadelphia, Pa: Lippincott, 1950).

Sorensen, Theodore, *Kennedy* (New York: Harper & Row, 1965).

Speier, Hans, *Divided Berlin: The Anatomy of Soviet Political Blackmail* (New York and London: Praeger/Thames & Hudson, 1961).

Stern, Carola, *Ulbricht: A Political Biography* (New York: Praeger, 1965).

Storr, Anthony, *Human Aggression* (New York: Atheneum, 1968).

Tatu, Michel, *Power in the Kremlin: From Khrushchev to Kosygin* (New York: Viking Press/Compass Books, 1971).

Truman, Harry S., *Memoirs, Vol. I: Year of Decisions* (Garden City, NY: Doubleday, 1955).

Truman, Harry S., *Memoirs, Vol. II: Years of Trial and Hope* (Garden City, NY: Doubleday, 1956).

Tucker, Robert C., *The Soviet Political Mind: Studies in Stalinism and Post-Stalin Change* (London: Pall Mall Press, 1963).

Ulam, Adam B., *Expansion and Coexistence: The History of Soviet Foreign Policy, 1917–67* (New York: Praeger, 1968).

Vandenberg, Arthur H., Jr, (ed.), *The Private Papers of Senator Vandenberg* (Boston, Mass.: Houghton Mifflin, 1952).

Werth, Alexander, *Russia, the Post-War Years* (London: Robert Hale, 1971).

Windsor, Philip, *City on Leave: A History of Berlin, 1945–1962* (London: Chatto & Windus, 1963).

Wise, David, and Ross, Thomas B., *The U-2 Affair* (New York: Random House, 1962).

Wolfe, Thomas W., *Soviet Power and Europe: 1945–1970* (Baltimore, Md, and London: Johns Hopkins University Press, 1970).

Wolfe, Thomas W., *Soviet Strategy at the Crossroads* (Cambridge, Mass.: Harvard University Press 1964).

Young, Oran R., *The Politics of Force: Bargaining during International Crises* (Princeton, NJ: Princeton University Press, 1968).

Zagoria, Donald S., *The Sino-Soviet Conflict, 1956–1961* (Princeton, NJ: Princeton University Press, 1962).

Zolling, Hermann, and Bahnsen, Uwe, *Kalter Winter im August* (Oldenbourg and Hamburg: Gerhard Stolling Verlag, 1967).

III   Articles

Baras, Victor, 'Beria's fall and Ulbricht's survival', *Soviet Studies*, vol. 27, no. 3 (July 1975), pp. 381–95.

Barker, Elizabeth, 'The Berlin crisis: 1958–1962', *International Affairs* (London), vol. 34, no. 1 (January 1963), pp. 59–73.

'The discussions on E. Varga's book on capitalist war economy', *Soviet Studies*, vol. 1, no. 1 (June 1949), pp. 28–40.

Galay, N. 'Berlin: on the eve of dénouement', *Bulletin of the Institute for the Study of the USSR*, vol. 8, no. 10 (October 1961), p. 23.

Galay, N. 'The numerical strength of the Soviet armed forces', *Bulletin of the Institute for the Study of the USSR*, vol. 9, no. 5 (May 1962), pp. 41–3.

Galay, N., 'The burden of Soviet military expenditure', *Bulletin of the Institute for the Study of the USSR*, vol. 8, no. 3 (March 1961), p. 31.

Griffith, William E., 'The November 1960 Moscow meeting: a preliminary reconstruction', *China Quarterly*, no. 11 (July–September 1962).

Hammond, Thomas T., 'Did the United States use atomic diplomacy against Russia in 1945?', in Peter J. Potichnyj and Jane P. Shapiro (eds), *From the Cold War to Detente* (New York: Praeger, 1976).

Lowenthal, Richard, 'The impossible defensive', *Encounter*, vol. 17, no. 98 (November 1961), pp. 20–6.

Marantz, Paul, 'Soviet foreign policy factionalism under Stalin? A case study of the inevitability of war controversy', *Soviet Union*, vol. 3, pt 1 (1976), pp. 91–107.

Merritt, Richard L., 'A transformed crisis: the Berlin Wall', in Roy C. Macridis (ed.), *Modern European Governments* (Englewood Cliffs, NJ: Prentice Hall, 1968), pp. 140–73.

Mitchell, Judson, 'The revised "two camps" doctrine in Soviet foreign policy', *Orbis*, Spring 1972, p. 21.

Murphy, C. J., 'The Berlin airlift', *Fortune*, November 1948, pp. 90–3.

Payne, Samuel B., Jr, 'The Soviet debate on strategic arms limitation: 1968–72', *Soviet Studies*, vol. 27, no. 1 (January 1975), pp. 27–45.

Rosenberg, David Alan, 'American strategy and the hydrogen decisions', *Journal of American History*, vol. 66, no. 1 (June 1979), pp. 62–87.

Rosenberg, J. Philipp, 'The Cheshire ultimatum: Truman's message to Stalin in the 1946 Azerbaidjan crisis', *Journal of Politics*, vol. 41, no. 3 (August 1979), pp. 933–40.

Schilling, Warner R., 'The politics of national defense: fiscal 1950', in Warner R. Schilling, Paul Y. Hammond and Glenn. H. Snyder, *Strategy, Politics and Defense Budgets* (New York and London: Columbia University Press, 1962), pp. 5–266.

Shulman, Marshall D., 'What does security mean today?', *Foreign Affairs*, vol. 49, no. 4 (July 1971), pp. 607–18.

Simes, Dimitri K., 'The Soviet invasion of Czechoslovakia and the limits of Kremlinology', *Studies in Comparative Communism*, vol. 3, nos 1 and 2 (Spring/Summer 1975), pp. 174–80.

Slusser, Robert M., 'America, China and the hydraheaded opposition: the dynamics of Soviet foreign policy', in Peter H. Juviler and Henry W. Morton (eds), *Soviet Policy-Making: Studies of Communism in Transition* (New York: Praeger, 1967), pp. 186–269.

Slusser, Robert M., 'The Presidium meeting of February 1961: a reconstruction', in Alexander and Janet Rabinowitch with Ladis K. D. Kristof (eds), *Revolution and Politics in Russia: Essays in Memory of B. I. Nicolaevsky* (Bloomington, Ill.: Indiana University Press, 1972), pp. 281–92.

Smith, Gaddis, 'The Berlin blockade through the filter of history: visions and revisions of the cold war', *New York Times Magazine*, 29 April 1973.

Thorpe, James A., 'Truman's ultimatum to Stalin of the 1946 Azerbaidjan crisis: the making of a myth', *Journal of Politics*, vol. 40, no. 1 (February 1978), pp. 188–95.

Tigrid, Pavel 'The Prague *coup* of 1948: the elegant take-over', in Thomas T. Hammond (ed.), *The Anatomy of Communist Takeovers* (New Haven, Conn., and London: Yale University Press, 1975), pp. 399–432.

Tucker, Robert C., 'The dictator and totalitarianism', *World Politics*, vol. 17 (July 1965), pp. 555–83.

Valenta, Jiri, 'Soviet decisionmaking and the Czechoslovak crisis of 1968', *Studies in Comparative Communism*, vol. 3, nos 1 and 2 (Spring/Summer 1975), pp. 147–73.

Wohlstetter, Albert, 'Is there a strategic arms race? (II): Rivals but no "race"', *Foreign Policy*, no. 16 (Fall 1974), pp. 48–81.

IV Unpublished Materials

Karber, Phillip A., 'The Central European arms race: 1948–1980', paper prepared for the Conference on Arms Control, Stiftung Wissenschaft und Politik, Ebenhausen (Munich), 11–13 June 1980.

Marantz, Paul, 'The Soviet Union and the Western world: a study in doctrinal change, 1917–1964', PhD dissertation, Harvard University, 1977.

Mitchell, Ralph E., 'Atomic air power and American foreign policy: the period of nuclear monopoly, 1945–1949', PhD dissertation, University of Kentucky, 1965.

Moreton, Norma Edwina, 'The impact of *détente* on relations between the member states of the Warsaw Pact: efforts to resolve the German problem and their implications for East German's role in Eastern Europe, 1967–72', PhD dissertation, University of Glasgow, 1977.

Spencer, Valerie, 'The Iranian crisis of 1945–46', research paper, Royal Military College of Canada, May 1979.

B. INTERNATIONAL RELATIONS THEORY AND SOVIET FOREIGN POLICY

I Books and Monographs

Adomeit, Hannes J., *Soviet Risk-Taking and Crisis Behaviour: From Confrontation to Coexistence?*, Adelphi Paper No. 101 (London: International Institute for Strategic Studies, 1973).

Adomeit, Hannes J., and Boardman, Robert (eds), *Foreign Policy Making in Communist Countries: A Comparative Approach* (Farnborough: Saxon House, 1979).

Allison, Graham T., *Essence of Decision: Explaining the Cuban Missile Crisis* (Boston, Mass.: Little, Brown, 1971).

Aron, Raymond, *Peace and War: A Theory of International Relations* (New York: Knopf, 1966).

Aspaturian, Vernon V., *Process and Power in Soviet Foreign Policy* (Boston: Little, Brown, 1971).

Beard, Edmund, *Developing the ICBM: A Study in Bureaucratic Politics* (New York: Columbia University Press, 1976).

Bell, Coral, *The Conventions of Crisis: A Study in Diplomatic Management* (London: Oxford University Press, 1971).

Bertram, Christoph (ed.), *Prospects of Soviet Power in the 1980s* (London: Macmillan, 1981).

Bialer, Seweryn (ed.), *The Domestic Context of Soviet Foreign Policy*, Studies of the Research Institute on International Change, Columbia University (Boulder, Co, and London: Westview Press/Croom Helm, 1981).

Brzezinski, Zbigniew, and Huntington, Samuel P., *Political Power: USA/USSR* (New York: Viking Press, 1965).

Cohen, John, *Chance, Skill and Luck* (Baltimore, Md.: Penguin, 1960).

Confino, Michael, and Shamir, Shimon (eds), *The USSR and the Middle East* (Jerusalem: Israel University Press, 1973).

Crankshaw, Edward, *Khrushchev: A Career* (New York: Viking Press, 1967).

De Rivera, Joseph, *The Psychological Dimension of Foreign Policy* (Columbus, Ohio: Charles E. Merrill, 1968).

Deutsch, Karl W., *The Analysis of International Relations* (Englewood Cliffs, NJ: Prentice-Hall, 1968).

Edmonds, Robin, *Soviet Foreign Policy 1962–1973: The Paradox of Super Power* (London: Oxford University Press, 1975).

Festinger, Leon, *Cognitive Dissonance* (San Francisco: W. H. Freeman, 1962).

Gallagher, Matthew P. and Spielmann, Jr, Karl F., *Soviet Decision-Making for Defense: A Critique of US Perspectives of the Arms Race* (New York: Praeger, 1972).

George, Alexander L., Hall, David K., and Simons, William R., *The Limits of Coercive Diplomacy: Laos, Cuba, Vietnam* (Boston: Little, Brown, 1971).

Greenwood, Ted, *Making the MRIV: A Study of Defense Decision-Making* (Cambridge, Mass.: Ballinger, 1975).

Halperin, Morton H., with Priscilla Clapp and Arnold Kanter, *Bureaucratic Politics and Foreign Policy* (Washington, DC: Brookings Institution, 1974).

Halperin, Morton H., with Priscilla Clapp and Arnold Kanter, *The Decision to Deploy the ABM: Bureaucratic and Domestic Politics in the Johnson Administration* (Washington, DC: Brookings Institution, 1973).

Hermann, Charles F. (ed.), *International Crises: Insights from Behavioral Research* (London: Collier Macmillan, 1972).

Herz, John H., *International Politics in the Atomic Age* (New York: Columbia University Press, 1959).

Holsti, K. J., *International Politics: A Framework of Analysis* (Englewood Cliffs, NJ: Prentice-Hall, 1967).

Horelick, Arnold L., Johnson, A. Ross, and Steinbruner, John D., *The Study of Soviet Foreign Policy: A Review of Decision-Theory-Related Approaches*, Rand-R-13334, (Santa Monica, Calif.: Rand Corporation, December 1973).

Hough, Jerry F. and Fainsod, Merle, *How the Soviet Union is Governed* (Cambridge, Mass.: Harvard University Press, 1979).

Hyland, William, and Shyrock, Richard W., *The Fall of Khrushchev* (London: Pitman, 1968).

Jervis, Robert, *Perception and Misperception in International Politics* (Princeton, NJ: Princeton University Press, 1976).

Johnson, Lyndon Baines, *The Vantage Point: Perspectives from the Presidency* (London: Weidenfeld & Nicolson, 1971).

Kahn, Herman, *On Escalation: Metaphors and Scenarios* (New York: Praeger, 1965).

Kaplan, Morton A., *System and Process in International Relations* (New York: Wiley, 1957).

Kaufmann, William W., *The Requirements of Deterrence* (Princeton, NJ: Center of International Studies, 1954).

Kennan, George F., *Russia and the West Under Lenin and Stalin* (New York and Toronto: Mentor Books, 1960).

Kennedy, Robert F., *Thirteen Days: The Cuban Missile Crisis* (London: Macmillan and Pan, 1969).

Knorr, Klaus, and Rosenau, James N. (eds), *Contending Approaches to International Politics* (Princeton, NJ: Princeton University Press, 1969).

Kulski, W. W., *The Soviet Union in World Affairs: A Documented Analysis, 1964–1972* (Syracuse, NY: Syracuse University Press, 1973).

Laqueur, Walter, *The Struggle for the Middle East: The Soviet Union in the Mediterranean, 1958–1968* (New York: Macmillan, 1969).

Leites, Nathan, *The Operational Code of the Politburo* (New York: McGraw-Hill, 1951).

Leites, Nathan, *A Study of Bolshevism* (Glencoe, Ill.: The Free Press, 1953).

Leites, Nathan, *Kremlin Moods*, RM-3535-ISA (Santa Monica, Calif.: Rand Corporation, 1964).

Lenin, V. I., *'Left-Wing' Communism, an Infantile Disorder: A Popular Essay in Marxist Strategy and Tactics* (New York: International Publishers, 1969).

Neustadt, Richard E., *Alliance Politics* (New York and London: Columbia University Press, 1970).

Osgood, Robert E., and Tucker, Robert W., *Force, Order and Justice* (Baltimore, Md: Johns Hopkins University Press, 1967).

Paige, Glenn D., *The Korean Decision* (New York: The Free Press, 1968).

Ploss, Sidney I., *Conflict and Decision-Making in Soviet Russia: A Case Study of Agricultural Policy, 1953–1963* (Princeton, NJ: Princeton University Press, 1965).

Ra'anan, Uri, *The USSR Arms in the Third World: Case Studies in Soviet Foreign Policy* (Cambridge, Mass.: MIT, 1969).

Quester, George H., *Deterrence before Hiroshima: The Airpower Background of Modern Strategy* (New York: Wiley, 1966).

Rapoport, Anatol, and McSchammah, Albert, *Prisoner's Dilemma: A Study in Conflict and Cooperation* (Ann Arbor, Mich.: University of Michigan Press, 1965).

Rapoport, Anatol, *Strategy and Conscience* (New York: Harper & Row, 1964).

Schelling, Thomas C., *Arms and Influence* (New Haven, Conn.: Yale University Press, 1966).

Shub, Anatole, *The New Russian Tragedy* (New York: Norton, 1969).

Skilling, Gordon H., and Griffiths, Franklyn (eds), *Interest Groups in Soviet Politics* (Princeton, NJ: Princeton University Press, 1971).

Snyder, Glenn H., *Deterrence and Defense: Toward a Theory of National Security* (Princeton, NJ: Princeton University Press, 1961).

Snyder, Glenn H., and Diesing, Paul, *Conflict among Nations: Bargaining, Decision Making and System Structure in International Crisis* (Princeton, NJ: Princeton University Press, 1977).

Starr, Martin K., *Management: A Modern Approach* (New York: Harcourt Brace Jovanovich, 1971).

Triska, Jan F., and Finley, David D., *Soviet Foreign Policy* (New York and London: Macmillan/Collier Macmillan, 1968).

Williams, Phil, *Crisis Management: Confrontation and Diplomacy in the Nuclear Age* (London: Martin Robertson, 1976).

Willner, Dorothy (ed.), *Decisions Values and Groups*, Vol. I (New York: Pergamon, 1960).

Wolfe, Thomas W., *Soviet Power and Europe: 1945–1970* (Baltimore, Md, and London: Johns Hopkins University Press, 1970).

Young, Oran R., *The Politics of Force: Bargaining during International Crises* (Princeton, NJ: Princeton University Press, 1968).

Zhurkin, V. V., and Primakov, E. M., *Mezhdunarodnye konflikty* (International Conflicts) (Moscow: Izdatel'stvo 'Mezhdunarodnye otnosheniia', 1972).

Zimmerman, William, *Soviet Perspectives on International Relations, 1956–1967* (Princeton, NJ: Princeton University Press, 1969).

II   Articles

Adomeit, Hannes, 'Consensus versus conflict: the dimension of foreign policy', in Seweryn Bialer (ed.), *The Domestic Context of Soviet Foreign Policy* (Boulder, Co, and London: Westview Press/Croom Helm, 1981).

Adomeit, Hannes, 'Ideology in the Soviet view of international affairs', paper delivered at the Twentieth Annual Conference of the International Institute for Strategic Studies (IISS), 7–10 September 1978; repro. in Christoph Bertram (ed.), *Prospects of Soviet Power in the 1980s* (London: Macmillan, 1980).

Allison, Graham T., 'Conceptual models and the Cuban missile crisis', American Political Science Review, vol. 62, no. 3 (September 1969), pp. 689–718.

Allison, Graham T., and Halperin, Morton H., 'Bureaucratic politics: a paradigm and some policy implications', in Raymond Tanter and Richard R. Ullman, *Theory and Practice in International Relations* (Princeton, NJ: Princeton University Press, 1972), pp. 40–79.

Armstrong, John A., 'The domestic roots of Soviet foreign policy', in Erik P. Hoffman and Frederic J. Fleron, Jr (eds), *The Conduct of Soviet Foreign Policy* (Chicago, Ill., and London: Aldine-Atherton/Butterworth, 1971), pp. 50–60; repr. from *International Affairs*, vol. 41, no. 1 (January 1965), pp. 37–47.

Atkinson, John W., 'Motivational determinants of risk-taking behavior', *Psychological Review*, vol. 54 (1957), pp. 359–72.

Bauer, Raymond A., 'Problems of perception and the relations between the United States and the Soviet Union', *Journal of Conflict Resolution*, vol. 5 (1961) pp. 223–9.

Bernouilli, James, 'Exposition of a new theory on the measurement of risk', *Econometrica*, no. 22 (1954), pp. 23–6.

Block, Jock and Peterson, Basil, 'Some personality correlates of confidence, caution, and speed in a decision situation', *Journal of Abnormal Psychology*, vol. 51 (1955), pp. 34–41.

Dallin, Alexander, 'Domestic factors influencing Soviet foreign policy', in Michael Confino and Shimon Shamir (eds), *The USSR and the Middle East* (Jerusalem: Israel University Press, 1973), pp. 31–58.

Dallin, Alexander, 'Soviet foreign policy and domestic politics: a framework for analysis', *Journal of International Affairs*, vol. 23, no. 2 (1969), pp. 250–65.

De Finetti, 'Recent suggestions for the reconciliation for theories of probability', in J. Neyman, *Proceedings of the Second Berkeley Symposium on Mathematical Statistics and Probability* (Berkeley, Calif.: University of California Press, 1951).

Edwards, Ward, 'Probability preferences among bets with differing expected values', *American Journal of Psychology*, vol. 67 (1954), pp. 56–7.

Freedman, Lawrence, 'Logic, politics and foreign policy process: a critique of the bureaucratic politics model', *International Affairs* (London), vol. 52, no. 3 (July 1976), pp. 434–49.

Fukuyama, Francis, 'A new Soviet strategy', *Commentary*, October 1979, pp. 52–9.

George, Alexander L., 'The "operational code": a neglected approach to the study of political leaders and decision-making', in Erik P. Hoffmann and Frederic J. Fleron, Jr (eds), *The Conduct of Soviet Foreign Policy* (Chicago, Ill., and London:

Aldine-Atherton/Butterworth, 1971), pp. 165–90; repr. from *International Studies Quarterly*, vol. 13, no. 2 (June 1969), pp. 190–222.

Golan, Galia, 'Soviet aims and the Middle East War', *Survival*, vol. 16, no. 3 (May/June 1974), pp. 106–14.

Gould, Stephen Jay, 'Darwin's untimely burial', *Natural History*, vol. 85, no. 8 (October 1976).

Gray Colin S., 'What RAND hath wrought', *Foreign Policy*, no. 4 (Fall 1971), pp. 111–29.

Jervis, Robert, 'The costs of quantitative study', in Klaus Knorr and James N. Rosenau (eds), *Contending Approaches to International Politics* (Princeton, NJ: Princeton University Press, 1969), pp. 177–217.

Kaplan, Morton A., 'Traditionalism vs science', in Klaus Knorr and James N. Rosenau (eds), *Contending Approaches to International Politics* (Princeton, NJ: Princeton University Press, 1969), pp. 39–61.

Krasner, Stephen D., 'Are bureaucracies important? (Or Allison Wonderland)', *Foreign Policy*, no. 7 (Summer 1972), pp. 159–79.

Labedz, Leo, 'Ideology and Soviet policies in Europe', paper delivered at the Twentieth Annual Conference of the International Institute for Strategic Studies (IISS), 7–10 September 1978; repr. in Christoph Bertram (ed.), *Prospects of Soviet Power in the 1980s* (London: Macmillan, 1980).

McConnell, James M., and Kelly, Anne M., 'Super-power naval diplomacy: lessons of the Indo-Pakistani crisis 1971, *Survival*, vol. 15, no. 6 (November–December 1973), pp. 289–95.

McConnell, James M., and Dismukes, Bradford, 'Soviet diplomacy of force in the Third World', *Problems of Communism*, vol. 28, no. 1 (January–February 1979), pp. 14–27.

Mackintosh, Malcolm, 'The Soviet military: influence on foreign policy', *Problems of Communism*, vol. 22, no. 5 (September–October 1973), pp. 10–11.

Meyer, Alfred G., 'The functions of ideology in the Soviet political system', *Soviet Studies*, vol. 17, no. 3 (January 1966).

Pierre, Andrew J., 'America down, Russia up: the changing political role of military power', *Foreign Policy*, no. 4 (Fall 1971), pp. 163–87.

Pipes, Richard, 'Some operational principles of Soviet foreign policy', in Michael Confino and Shimon Shamir (eds), *The USSR and the Middle East* (Jerusalem: Israel University Press, 1973), pp. 5–30.

Pipes, Richard, 'Operational principles of Soviet foreign policy', *Survey*, vol. 19, no. 2 (Spring 1973), pp. 41–61.

Ploss, Sidney I., 'Studying the domestic determinants of Soviet foreign policy', in Erik P. Hoffmann and Frederic J. Fleron, Jr (eds), *The Conduct of Soviet Foreign Policy* (Chicago, Ill., and London: Aldine-Atherton/Butterworth, 1971), pp. 76–90. Reprinted from *Canadian Slavic Studies*, vol. 1, no. 1 (Spring 1967), pp. 44–59.

Quandt, William B., *Soviet Policy in the October 1973 War*, R-1864-ISA (Santa Monica, Calif.: Rand Corporation, May 1976).

Schwartz, Joel J., and Keech, William R., 'Group influence and the policy process in the Soviet Union', *American Political Science Review*, vol. 62, no. 3 (1968), pp. 840–51.

Shubik, Martin, 'On gaming and game theory', *Management Science*, vol. 18, no. 5 (January 1972), pp. P-37–P-54.

Shulman, Marshall D., 'What does security mean today?', *Foreign Affairs*, vol. 49, no. 4 (July 1971), pp. 607–18.

Stewart, Philip D., 'Soviet interest groups and the policy process', *World Politics*, vol. 22, no. 1 (1969), pp. 29–50.

Triska, Jan F., 'The Soviet Union: reckless or cautious?', in Jan F. Triska and David D. Finley, *Soviet Foreign Policy* (New York: Macmillan, 1968), pp. 310–49.

Valenta, Jiri, 'Soviet decisionmaking and the Czechoslovak crisis of 1968', *Studies in Comparative Communism*, vol. 8, nos 1 and 2 (Spring/Summer 1975), pp. 147–73.

Verba, Sidney, 'Assumptions of rationality and non-rationality in modesl of the international system', in James N. Rosenau (ed.), *International Politics and Foreign Policy*, rev. edn (New York: The Free Press, 1969).

Wesson, Robert G., 'Soviet ideology: the necessity of Marxism', *Soviet Studies*, vol. 21, no. 1 (July 1969), pp. 64–70.

White, Ralph K., 'Selective inattention', *Psychology Today*, vol. 5, no. 5 (November 1971), pp. 47–86.

White, Stephen L., 'Contradiction and change in state socialism', *Soviet Studies*, vol. 26, no. 1 (January 1974), pp. 41–55.

Williams, Harry B., 'Some functions of communication in crisis behavior', *Human Organization*, vol. 16, no. 2 (Summer 1957), pp. 15–19.

Zimmerman, William, 'Elite perspectives and the explanation of Soviet foreign policy', *Journal of International Affairs*, vol. 15, no. 1 (1970), pp. 84–98.

Zimmerman, William, 'Soviet foreign policy in the 1970s', *Survey*, vol. 19, no. 2 (Spring 1973), pp. 193–4.

III Unpublished materials.

Adomeit, Hannes J., 'Soviet risk taking and crisis behavior: a theoretical and empirical analysis', PhD dissertation, Columbia University, 1977.

Caldwell, Larry Temple, 'Toward a theory on the political uses of strategic military power by the United States and the Soviet Union', PhD dissertation, Tufts-Fletcher School of Law and Diplomacy, 1968.

Ellsberg, Daniel, 'Risk, ambiguity, and decision', PhD dissertation, Harvard University, 1963.

Index

Note: numbers in italics refer to figures and tables

Studies of the Russian Institute, Columbia University

Abram Bergson, *Soviet National Income in 1937* (1953)

Ernest J. Simmons, Jr, ed., *Through the Glass of Soviet Literature: Views of Russian Society* (1953).

Thad Paul Alton, *Polish Postwar Economy* (1954).

David Granick, *Management of the Industrial Firm in the USSR: A Study in Soviet Economic Planning* (1954).

Allen S. Whiting, *Soviet Policies in China, 1917–1924* (1954).

George S. N. Luckyj, *Literary Politics in the Soviet Ukraine, 1917–1934* (1956).

Michael Boro Petrovich, *The Emergence of Russian Panslavism, 1856–1870* (1956).

Thomas Taylor Hammond, *Lenin on Trade Unions and Revolution, 1893–1917* (1956).

David Marshall Lang, *The Last Years of the Georgian Monarchy, 1658–1832* (1957).

James William Morley, *The Japanese Thrust into Siberia, 1918* (1957).

Alexander G. Park, *Bolshevism in Turkestan, 1917–1927* (1957).

Herbert Marcuse, *Soviet Marxism: A Critical Analysis* (1958).

Charles B. McLane, *Soviet Policy and the Chinese Communists, 1931–1946* (1958).

Oliver H. Radkey, *The Agrarian Foes of Bolshevism: Promise and Defeat of the Russian Socialist Revolutionaries, February to October, 1917* (1958).

Ralph Talcott Fisher, Jr, *Pattern for Soviet Youth: A Study of the Congresses of the Komsomol, 1918–1954* (1959).

Alfred Erich Senn, *The Emergence of Modern Lithuania* (1959).

Elliot R. Goodman, *The Soviet Design for a World State* (1960).

John N. Hazard, *Settling Disputes in Soviet Society: The Formative Years of Legal Institutions* (1960).

David Joravsky, *Soviet Marxism and Natural Science, 1917–1932* (1961).

Maurice Friedberg, *Russian Classics in Soviet Jackets* (1962).

Alfred J. Rieber, *Stalin and the French Communist Party, 1941–1947* (1962).

Theodore K. Von Laue, *Sergei Witte and the Industrialization of Russia* (1962).

John A. Armstrong, *Ukrainian Nationalism* (1963).

Oliver H. Radkey, *The Sickle under the Hammer: The Russian Socialist Revolutionaries in the Early Months of Soviet Rule* (1963).

Kermit E. McKenzie, *Comintern and World Revolution, 1928–1943: The Shaping of Doctrine* (1964).

Harvey L. Dyck, *Weimar Germany and Soviet Russia, 1926–1933: A Study in Diplomatic Instability* (1966).

(Above titles published by Columbia University Press.)

Harold J. Noah, *Financing Soviet Schools* (Teachers College, 1966).

John M. Thompson, *Russia, Bolshevism, and the Versailles Peace* (Princeton, 1966).

Paul Avrich, *The Russian Anarchists* (Princeton, 1967).

Loren R. Graham, *The Soviet Academy of Sciences and the Communist Party, 1927–1932* (Princeton, 1967).

Robert A. Maguire, *Red Virgin Soil: Soviet Literature in the 1920's* (Princeton, 1968).

T. H. Rigby, *Communist Party Membership in the U.S.S.R, 1917–1967* (Princeton, 1968).

Richard T. de George, *Soviet Ethics and Morality* (University of Michigan, 1969).

Jonathan Frankel, *Vladimir Akimov on the Dilemmas of Russian Marxism, 1895–1903* (Cambridge, 1969).

William Zimmerman, *Soviet Perspectives on International Relations, 1956–1967* (Princeton, 1969).

Paul Avrich, *Kronstadt, 1921* (Princeton, 1970).

Ezra Mendelsohn, *Class Struggle in the Pale: The Formative Years of the Jewish Workers' Movement in Tsarist Russia* (Cambridge, 1970).

Edward J. Brown, *The Proletarian Episode in Russian Literature* (Columbia, 1971).

Reginald E. Zelnik, *Labor and Society in Tsarist Russia: The Factory Workers of St. Petersburg, 1855–1870* (Stanford, 1971).

Patricia K. Grimsted, *Archives and Manuscript Repositories in the USSR: Moscow and Leningrad* (Princeton, 1972).

Ronald G. Suny, *The Baku Commune, 1917–1918* (Princeton, 1972).

Edward J. Brown, *Mayakovsky: A Poet in the Revolution* (Princeton, 1973).

Milton Ehre, *Oblomov and his Creator: The Life and Art of Ivan Goncharov* (Princeton, 1973).

Henry Krisch, *German Politics under Soviet Occupation* (Columbia, 1974).

Henry W. Morton and Rudolf L. Tökés, eds, *Soviet Politics and Society in the 1970's* (Free Press, 1974).

William G. Rosenberg, *Liberals in the Russian Revolution* (Princeton, 1974).

Richard G. Robbins, Jr, *Famine in Russia, 1891–1892* (Columbia, 1975).

Vera Dunham, *In Stalin's Time: Middleclass Values in Soviet Fiction* (Cambridge, 1976).

Walter Sablinsky, *The Road to Bloody Sunday* (Princeton, 1976).

William Mills Todd III, *The Familiar Letter as a Literary Genre in the Age of Pushkin* (Princeton, 1976).

Elizabeth Valkenier, *Russian Realist Art. The State and Society: The Peredvizhniki and Their Tradition* (Ardis, 1977).

Susan Solomon, *The Soviet Agrarian Debate* (Westview, 1978).

Sheila Fitzpatrick, ed., *Cultural Revolution in Russia, 1928–1931* (Indiana, 1978).

Peter Solomon, *Soviet Criminologists and Criminal Policy: Specialists in Policy-Making* (Columbia, 1978).

Kendall E. Bailes, *Technology and Society under Lenin and Stalin: Origins of the Soviet Technical Intelligentsia, 1917–1941* (Princeton, 1978).

Leopold H. Haimson, ed., *The Politics of Rural Russia, 1905–1914* (Indiana, 1979).

Theodore H. Friedgut, *Political Participation in the USSR* (Princeton, 1979).

Sheila Fitzpatrick, *Education and Social Mobility in the Soviet Union, 1921–1934* (Cambridge, 1979).

Wesley Andrew Fisher, *The Soviet Marriage Market: Mate-Selection in Russia and the USSR* (Praeger, 1980).

Jonathan Frankel, *Prophecy and Politics; Socialism, Nationalism, and the Russian Jews, 1862–1917* (Cambridge, 1981).

Robin Feuer Miller, *Dostoevsky and The Idiot: Author, Narrator, and Reader* (Harvard, 1981).

Diane Koenker, *Moscow Workers and the 1917 Revolution* (Princeton, 1981).

Patricia K. Grimsted, *Archives and Manuscript Repositories in the USSR: Estonia, Latvia, Lithuania, and Belorussia* (Princeton, 1981).